Credit Management

The Institute of Credit Management

The Institute of Credit Management (ICM) is Europe's largest credit management organisation. The trusted leader in expertise for all credit matters, it represents the profession across trade, consumer, and export credit, and all credit-related services. Formed over 70 years ago (in 1939), it is the only such organisation accredited by Ofqual and it offers a comprehensive range of services and bespoke solutions for the credit professional (www.icm.org.uk) as well as services and advice for the wider business community (www.creditmanagement.org.uk).

The services offered by the ICM include:

Professional membership grades | Recruitment agency | Conferences and seminars | Professional Qualifications and unit awards | Bookshop | A network of local branches | Consultancy | Training | Credit Management Helpline | Online services through icmOS | Credit Management magazine and monthly email briefings | Member website forums | Quality in Credit Management accreditation | Member benefits and discounts | Social networking community

Credit Management

Sixth Edition

Edited by
GLEN BULLIVANT

GOWER

Credit Management was published in previous editions as *Credit Management Handbook*.

Published by
Gower Publishing Limited
Wey Court East
Union Road
Farnham
Surrey, GU9 7PT
England

Ashgate Publishing Company
Suite 420
101 Cherry Street
Burlington,
VT 05401-4405
USA

www.gowerpublishing.com

British Library Cataloguing in Publication Data
Credit management. -- 6th ed.
  1. Credit--Management.
  I. Bullivant, Glen. II. Credit management handbook.
  658.8'8-dc22

ISBN: 978-0-566-08842-1 (hbk)
    978-0-566-08843-8 (pbk)
    978-0-7546-9215-7 (ebk)

Library of Congress Cataloging-in-Publication Data
Credit management / [edited] by Glen Bullivant. -- 6th ed.
    p. cm.
  Rev. ed. of: Credit management handbook. 5th ed. c2004.
  Includes index.
  ISBN 978-0-566-08842-1 (hardback) -- ISBN 978-0-566-08843-8 (pbk.) --
  ISBN 978-0-7546-9215-7 (ebook) 1. Credit--Management. I. Bullivant, Glen. II. Title: Credit management handbook.
  HG3751.C728 2010
  658.8'8--dc22

2009052390

Mixed Sources
Product group from well-managed forests and other controlled sources
www.fsc.org Cert no. SA-COC-1565
© 1996 Forest Stewardship Council
FSC

Printed and bound in Great Britain by
MPG Books Group, UK

Contents

---

*   All Chapters up to Part VI have been written by the Editor, Glen Bullivant. The authors of the subsequent chapters are as indicated.

List of Figures

Foreword

This is now the Sixth Edition of Burt Edwards' excellent text covering all aspects of credit management, and I am acutely aware of the honour in following Sir Roger Cork and his father Kenneth in writing the foreword.

Good credit management, and by definition good credit managers, have always been important, but in recent times such importance has taken on new meaning. 'Good' is almost not enough any more; 'Excellence' is what every credit manager should be striving for, and what the Institute of Credit Management looks for its members to attain.

This handbook is a vital text for credit managers, and indeed anyone interested in the subject, looking at all areas of the subject in detail.

Divided into ten distinct 'parts', it explores, for example, the role of credit management in business, looking at the factors affecting credit terms and the different ways of assessing risk. There are specific sections dedicated to the Sales Ledger, cash collections and credit insurance, as well as chapters on exporting and consumer credit.

Every aspect of credit management is covered, including commercial credit law and details of a range of credit services that a credit manager may encounter.

Sir Roger, in his foreword to the fifth edition, described the book as 'practical and comprehensive'. It is indeed both of these things and more. Whether you are a student or a more experienced practitioner, an aspiring credit manager or seasoned professional, *Credit Management* is an essential reference, and I have great pleasure in recommending it.

Philip King
Chief Executive – The Institute of Credit Management

Introduction
Glen Bullivant

When the Institute of Credit Management was first founded in 1939, it perhaps reflected the prejudices (and the actualities) of the time by being known as the Institute of Creditmen. Hardly had the fledgling organisation established itself than the Second World War intervened and matters as obtuse as the attempts to bring professionalism to credit management naturally receded into the background. It was 1946 before the relaunch, and by now, commonsense prevailed and the Institute of Credit Management banished prejudice and pre-war notions for ever.

For many years, the only publications to be found regarding the practice of credit management came from the US, either in the form of academic papers, or more often policy documents or procedures adopted by the large US corporations and imported for use by their subsidiaries. Occasional articles and guides were published in the UK, but nothing of any substantial nature, and nothing that sought to embrace all the areas of expertise which credit managers were expected to have at their fingertips. However, from 1946 onwards, the growing number of credit professionals in the UK helped companies recognise that maximisation of cash flow was the key to business success. Indeed, the whole concept of maximising cash flow, protecting the investment in receivables and growing a successful business through professional risk management had been well established for generations. What was missing was that home-grown textbook of best practice: all you need to know, more or less, in one readable volume.

The first edition of the *Credit Management Handbook* was put together in 1976 by Burt Edwards, one time Credit and Treasury Manager with ITT Europe Inc. and later, Managing Director of the Jardine Mathieson Group, and this handbook was recognised as the first British book on credit management. Burt Edwards had long run his own company, Capital Business Training, providing training and consultancy in credit and finance techniques, particularly in international business. Preparing course notes and material really highlighted to Burt the lack of a definitive textbook, and writing articles on credit became second nature. This inevitably progressed through to no fewer than five editions of the *Credit Management Handbook* over a period of nearly 30 years.

Since those tentative beginnings, the profession of credit management in the UK has made great progress, benefiting from input from all parts of industry and commerce. It has to be said, however, that there remain far too many companies in the UK who are obsessed with winning orders and making 'sales' at any price. The small and medium-sized (SME) sector in particular has a belief almost ingrained that if the sale is made, and the job is done, payment will be forthcoming. No concept of customer identity, customer probity or customer reputation – business is booming when sales are being made. The experience of loss through bad debt, the culture of high interest rates and the realisation that nothing can be what it appears to be, often brings home the message that it is better to treat receivables as an asset to be sensibly managed and protected and not allowed to be some unimportant accounting exercise.

A period of high interest rates can cause CEOs to be sales focused, but the same can equally be said of a period of low interest rates. Money may well be cheap, and sales may well be booming, but the same facts prevail – customer identity, probity and ability remains fundamental to asset management. Furthermore, the very fact that money and finance are both cheap and readily available can itself breed a feeling of false security and less risk – the risk is just as great, but perhaps masked by the good times. Indeed, it is arguably more important to establish sensible routines and policies when times are good so that they are in place and robust when trading circumstances become more difficult. The financial crisis of 2008 and the subsequent world recession which bit deep in 2009 clearly demonstrated that very need, perhaps far more forcibly that any previous crisis – it remains to be seen what lessons will be learned by bankers and financiers. Credit managers learn those lessons every day of their working lives.

The fact is that the 'debtors' asset on the company balance sheet is not only a substantial consumer of borrowed capital, diverting capital required from other aspects of running the business, but also represents, in many cases, the largest single current asset on the balance sheet. As such it demands professional management. Not to grant credit in a controlled and sensible manner is just as damaging as giving credit freely and irresponsibly, but not to give credit at all brings business grinding to a halt in the same tragic and fatal way. Credit is all about risk, and credit management is assessing and managing that risk – high risk calls for special terms but need not prevent business. Ultimately, credit risk is unavoidable, but it is a calculated risk, and under no circumstances should it ever be a mere gamble. Casinos and horse racing are for gambling, accounts receivable are not.

Bad debts can not be avoided altogether – having no bad debts at all is more likely to indicate that the company is not taking any risk, calculated or otherwise. Not to grant credit would restrict business development and growth, and close market opportunities which would otherwise be available. For that reason, credit is an integral part of the sales and marketing operation and is vital to success and profit. However, until payment has been received, the sale has not been *completed* and suppliers are simply adding to their costs, and so reducing any net profit, the longer the sale remains unpaid. Unpaid sales are always dangerous, costly and risky, and the Golden Rule (that is, the longer a sale is unpaid, the greater the chance it will never be paid) is the top priority which guides credit management. Cash is King, and the customer only wears the crown when he can show that he is worthy of so doing.

In many respects, the credit manager is as responsible as the sales director in finding customers who can pay, and as responsible as the finance director in ensuring that the resultant investment in those customers proves profitable and of minimum risk. A combination of human skills and computer support provide the means – if the largest and most successful global corporations see the need and the worth of employing specialist credit staff, then even the smaller 'ordinary' companies should recognise that need and value likewise.

Good credit management is at long last beginning to replace the seat-of-the-pants self-delusion of the past, and this process can only be enhanced by the fall-out from the global financial crisis which began in 2008. Central bank interest rates fell in 2008 and 2009 to record lows, not only in the UK and Europe, but in the world's largest economy, the US, and across the powerhouse economies of what has become known as the Pacific Rim. The rates that banks charge between themselves for lending and borrowing did not follow central rates, however, reflecting the lack of confidence and trust between the banks themselves. The consequence of this was that bank lending to commerce and consumers dried up, putting more pressure than ever before on both business and credit management. Business has *always* relied upon the support of suppliers and related trade credit to maintain operations and employment – unsecured trade credit 'lending' has consistently run at levels of between two and two and a half times that of total bank lending, so trade credit managers are well experienced in that field. It has been argued that trade credit managers are in fact the real bankers in the commercial and industrial world, undertaking loan negotiation, offering support when there are difficulties and being flexible in their approach. The very fact that the bulk of *trade credit* lending is unsecured, whereas the overwhelming majority of *trade bank* lending is secured, does in itself speak volumes about the crucial role played by trade credit suppliers.

This book deals separately with Trade, Consumer and Export credit, but there are obvious overlaps. The Consumer Credit Act decides largely how companies must interface with individuals on credit agreements. Commercial credit between companies, the Business to Business (B2B) sector as it is known, has the freedom of negotiation, subject to the Companies Act and various trade laws and conventions. International trade may well be subject to UK law in respect of contract terms and conditions with the UK seller being the exporter, but has to take account of a world of over 200 countries, all individual with their own cultures, laws and banking procedures.

There are many external support services for all these different forms of credit, from credit information, through methods of financing, to handling collections and litigation. Insolvency itself, once a minefield of complex and detailed procedures, was simplified initially by the Insolvency Act 1986, but complicated again by subsequent amendments and regulations. Legal proceedings themselves have been amended, altered, simplified and complicated by legislative changes in recent years. Indeed, the volume of new legislation following the General Election in 1997 has been almost overwhelming.

On the subject of legislation, it is still believed by many in the SME sector (and elsewhere) that 'the Government' does not do enough to help business with the problem of late payment. It is believed by some that companies should be forced to pay on time by some sort of legislative framework. The incoming UK Government in 1997 did introduce the Late Payment of Commercial Debt (Interest) Act 1998, subsequently incorporated into the European Directive on Late Payment. The law, however, could only ever be 'enabling legislation', allowing companies a statutory right to interest, if they so chose to apply it – it did not, nor could it, actually force the issue. As an attempt at culture change, it has proved to be less than successful and it is ironic that, in 2010, the same voices calling for 'legislation' are again in full cry. The real answer to slow payment is not legislation, but simply better credit management and to this end, the same UK Government, through the then Department of Trade and Industry (DTI), issued thousands of free copies of the *Better Payments Practice Guide*, a package of illustrated procedures designed to help smaller firms. During the boom of the last half of the 1990s and the early years of the twenty-first century, some of the lessons were yet again forgotten – indeed the UK Government even withdrew funding and support for the Better Payment Practice Group! Now that the financial world has been turned upside down and inside out, it comes as no surprise that there are initiatives promoted by BERR (the successor to the DTI and now part of BIS) to promote a better payment culture in another attempt to answer the calls for legislation. It also comes as no surprise that the UK Institute of Credit Management was approached by the Government Minister in charge (Lord Mandelson) to put together a package including free leaflets, websites and other support, including a Better Payment Practice Code to which companies would be encouraged to sign up. The European Union has also issued another Directive – the outcome is hardly likely to be more successful than previous attempts at legislation.

The real key to success in surmounting all the problems posed by late payment, lack of credit access, protecting the investment in receivables and all those issues, lies in well-trained credit professionals. When credit control staff are treated only as juniors chasing overdue debts, they are rarely adequately trained and equipped to deal with all the complications of risk assessment and legal considerations – the consequence is that motivation and confidence is lost in a fog of uncertainty. The Institute of Credit Management is firmly behind the policy of empowering the credit profession to undertake the real job in hand. Burt Edwards' contribution to this effort, by putting together the first real handbook of good practice, is to be applauded.

Putting together a workable, as well as readable, handbook such as this edition has been quite difficult. Much of the foundation laid down by Burt Edwards all those years ago remains as relevant as ever and a great debt of gratitude is owed to him for his vision as well as for all his hard work. Much of what he said back in 1976 is still being said today, and no apology is made for that. This edition includes immense contributions from Peter Coupe and Glyn Powell. They have both had the unenviable task of reviewing, revising and rewriting the chapters relating to Consumer Credit and Export Credit respectively.

Glyn Powell is a leading industry expert on export financing, insurance and reinsurance, having been consulted by leading companies throughout the

UK. He is a Fellow of the Institute of Credit Management (ICM) and a member of the ICM's Technical Committee (TAC). Peter Coupe, also a Fellow of the Institute of Credit Management and a member of the ICM's TAC, is the leading industry expert on all matters relating to Consumer Credit. For litigation and insolvency, Gerard Barron, one of the country's most successful debt litigants, has contributed in his unique style. All three major contributors bring to this edition many years of actual experience at the coalface – and all three have been faced with a morass of new legislation, rules and regulation which have been introduced into trade, consumer and export credit management in recent times. This has been far more than an update of previous editions, but in crucial areas, a complete rewrite.

The purpose of the book remains the same as Burt Edward's first edition back in 1976: to help speed up satisfying the needs of all its users and helping those users become more professional in all their efforts.

PART I
The Credit Management Function

1

Credit Past and Future

Glen Bullivant

• Origins • The role of credit and its importance in the economy • Capital and credit • The development of consumer and export credit • Secured and unsecured credit • Information Technology • External services • Credit management as a profession • Coping with change and the path forward •

Origins

It is easy to imagine that credit is a modern invention, like the DVD player or the mobile phone. The reality is that DVD and the mobile phone are little more than the development of previous methods of display and communication, in the same manner that the motorcar is an advancement on the horse and cart. Credit has been a part of human existence for a very long time – the levels of sophistication and progress in utilising and controlling credit continue to improve. Who would argue that today's family hatchback is not a much more versatile and reliable form of transport than the 1920s 'any colour you want so long as it is black'? From the earliest times, three principal factors became apparent as humans began to populate the planet and form themselves into groups or communities. From the beginning, some people, for whatever reason, would have more than others – today we recognise the word 'surplus' – and others would want some of it, but not have the means to pay. No change there then! If we add to that the seasonal agricultural factor, the roots of today's credit cycle are even more obvious. Plant the seed, grow the crop, sell the crop, plant the seed can be illustrated by a twenty-first century flow chart, but remains as ancient a credit problem as ever – income is derived from selling the crop, but what pays for the seed in the first place? The buyer would want to see the product before paying for it, and if the source of supply was a long way from the source of demand, a period of time elapsed before payment would be made.

We are aware of credit being documented in the ancient civilizations of Egypt, Assyria and Babylon over 3000 years ago, but it is to the Middle Ages and Europe that we look to see real growth in credit trading as we recognise it today. Great trading fairs were held in Europe in the twelfth century, with merchants travelling from fair to fair, buying and selling on an ongoing basis. It became common for a trader in one place to buy out of the proceeds of sale in another place, and it was at this time in Italy that the trade agent came into being. The agent was created to handle all the buying, selling and settlement details on behalf of travelling clients. The 'Cambium Contract' was a powerful document which recorded multi-contracts, including those in different currencies, and instigated the transfer of funds from place to place.

For example, it is recorded that in 1253 a merchant of Genoa purchased English cloth in France from an Italian seller, agreeing to pay four months later with funds to be derived from the sale of his own spices elsewhere. The idea of discount for bulk purchase is not new either, nor is the practice of large discounts for cash in advance. Monasteries in medieval England, dependent on income from sales of wool from their sheep flocks, would give attractive discounts for large purchases by Italian and Flemish merchants for delivery in the next season. The 'Bill of Exchange', much as we know it today, was a product of fourteenth-century Italy on the sound basis then that gold and silver were available at all times to cover acceptance values. The creditworthiness of the issuer later replaced the gold coin as the basis for bill of exchange transactions. It was not until the seventeenth century that it became accepted practice for banks and nation states to issue paper at a greater face value than underlying deposits. Simply stated, receipts began to be issued for gold deposited, and notes were produced with a gold face value which could be exchanged for goods or services. The assumption was, and remained, that not everyone would ask for their gold back at the same time. 'I promise to pay the bearer on demand the sum of…' was an undertaking signed by the Chief Cashier of the Bank of England, appearing on every bank note produced for the Bank. This assumption became the foundation of the banking and fiscal systems, though today bank notes are not actually backed by gold deposits. It was the creation of the Bank of England in 1694 that was itself a catalyst for credit growth – the Bank remained privately owned, and therefore ostensibly independent, until it was nationalised in 1948. Though remaining publicly owned, the Bank's independence of Government was restored in 1997.

The Industrial Revolution, born in the north-west of England at the end of the eighteenth century, gathered pace throughout the nineteenth century and made hitherto unprecedented demands on the credit culture. The UK underwent a momentous transformation in only a few short years from an agricultural economy to one dominated by manufacturing industry. All manner of new products were now being made and sold to new markets and to more and more customers all over the world, increasing risk and unknown exposure. New and varied credit and financing methods were introduced, not least of which was the raising of money via share issues from a greedy, gullible and inexperienced public. Again, nothing really changes! Venture capitalists (as we now know them) are not new. The wealthy and the adventurous have always been called upon to back expeditions and adventures into new and exciting areas. Good Queen Bess and her spirited servants, Drake and Raleigh, had illustrated the practice in the sixteenth century. What was new, however, was the deliberate raising of capital from the public via share issues, with the promise of riches beyond imagination. The scandal of the South Sea Bubble led to the Bubble Act of 1720, which banned the raising of public capital and the use of limited liability by firms, which remained in place until 1862, during which time partners in businesses and anyone investing for profit were personally liable for the debts of the businesses. In spite of limited liability, it is not difficult to see similarities between the gullibility and inexperience of the South Sea Company investors of the eighteenth century, the railway mania of the nineteenth century and the dotcom frenzy of the late twentieth century.

Throughout the Industrial Revolution, trade expansion was assisted by loans from local banks to local businesses, and the growth in diverse products and markets saw an expansion of trade credit as a significant source of financing businesses. Because interest rates were low (typically 2 per cent per annum) bank loans were cheap, and this bred something of a tolerance to late payment. Indeed, because rates above 5 per cent were banned by law until 1832, the cost of late payment was not recognised as having any material impact on profits, and extensive payment terms were both given and taken. It was only when bank loans were renewed after 12 months that firms noticed any cost element associated with customers who had not paid and the interest burden of unpaid bills became apparent. The legacy of extended terms remained, however, and has survived into more recent times. In the printing trade, for example, it was common for the payment chain through publisher, printer, printer supplier and author to be totally dependent on the book being sold to the customer, and extended terms in that trade still linger today. It is something of an irony that the financial meltdown of 2008 and 2009 brought with it a return to near zero interest rates and brought into sharp focus the need to collect accounts when due – the tolerance of delinquent payment habits was severely eroded.

Methods of payment progressed to keep pace with developments. Until around 1875, cheques were a rarity, debts being usually settled about one-third by cash and two-thirds by bill of exchange. The growth of banks with an increasing number of branches – the beginnings of what we now recognise as 'high street' banks – produced rapid expansion in the use of cheques for payment, as it became relatively simple to transfer funds between businesses a long distance apart. Local branches of banks made credit more accessible to all, which lessened the need for extended trade credit and brought about a general reduction in credit terms to what we now accept as normal or monthly terms. The expansion of trade, the proliferation of customers in far-flung places and in a variety of shapes and sizes, brought an appreciation, later rather than sooner, that giving credit was an aspect of the trading activity which required the same degree of management and discipline which applied to other aspects of day-to-day business operations. In other words, allowing time to pay and then getting paid needed some skilled effort to make it worthwhile. That which has been labelled the 'UK disease' of late payment has always been closely linked to the unwillingness of suppliers to ask customers for money. As long ago as 1689, a Lancashire merchant recorded 'it being a year since I began to trade, I have been too forward in trusting and too backward in calling'. In 1780, a bookseller wrote: 'I resolved to give no person whatsoever any credit, having observed that when credit was given, most bills were not paid within six months, some not for a twelve month and some not in two years. The losses sustained of interest in long credits and by those bills not paid at all; the inconvenience of not having ready money to lay out to trade to advantage; together with the great loss of time in keeping accounts and collecting debts… [but] I might as well attempt to rebuild the Tower of Babel as to run a large business without giving credit.'

The Role of Credit and its Importance in the Economy

Credit has been described as the oil of commerce, and it has been an accepted feature, since the early part of the twentieth century, that businesses allow customers time to pay. In normal trading, not to give credit would restrict sales, reduce volumes and increase unit costs. It is not true of every business, at least on the face of it. Many businesses selling direct to consumers do so on a cash basis (usually) – supermarkets, fast food shops, cafés, for example, B2B sales, however, would consider cash trading impracticable, and it would be a barrier to sales growth in most cases.

It is also not sufficient in this modern age to artificially restrict the granting of credit to business customers – only to allow credit to existing well-known and established customers. It is true that, up to the end of the first quarter of the twentieth century, companies with established and protected markets could afford to be particular and only give credit to those that they knew and trusted. The combination of increased competition and the need for business growth pushed businesses beyond the 'tried and trusted' and led them into the hitherto unknown. Vast ongoing volumes of goods and services, which provide employment for millions, became possible only on the basis of 'buy now – pay later'. That growth in business, both domestically and worldwide, made it all the more important for the seller to know about the customer, judge the amount of credit it was feasible to advance, and correctly calculate the length of time it could afford to let that credit period be. Equally, businesses needed to recognise the worth of ensuring that the amount granted was actually paid on time, so collection processes needed to be in place. Credit, therefore, has become very much an essential part of the whole marketing cycle, but it has also to be recognised that there is a cost involved.

Credit has become an integral part of modern industrialised economies. In manufacturing, the more that is made and sold, the less the unit production cost of each item – this is known as economies of scale. Allowing for inflation, the true cost of manufactured goods in general falls year on year as both production techniques improve and markets for the finished product grow, though increasing scarcity of raw materials can have a negative impact on price reductions. The reduction in ultimate selling price is acutely visible in consumer goods and in consumer services, ranging from washing machines to airline tickets – the more you sell, the cheaper they can become. The credit cycle can begin with importing raw materials, through the manufacturing and distribution process, through to the sale of the finished product and ultimate payment. In all stages of the cycle, there is an element of credit granted and taken, and the contribution made by credit is basic to the success of the whole. There are drawbacks, however, to both seller and buyer in the credit environment. For the seller, there is the risk of late or non-payment, which will have a negative impact on both profits and liquidity. There are many examples of companies with full order books finding survival threatened by delinquent customers. The seller also has to set up costly procedures to control credit granting, the administration of which is a constant feature of modern trading. The buyer can face increased prices for credit-related supplies, without the advantages of discounts for full cash purchases. In addition, the buyer has to protect a reputation in respect of payment, which can suffer if payments are delayed, and which can in turn lead to difficulties in obtaining continuity of supplies.

Capital and Credit

The relationship between capital and credit lies at the heart of understanding the growth of, and the need for, credit. Over the millennia of human development, there remains a fundamental truth, which is that some have and some do not have. Put another way, the granting of credit rests in the hands of those who have, and the need for credit and its use is with those who do not have. It is also a fundamental truth that the value of assets will diminish in time, if those assets are not utilised for profit. It may be argued that the fixed asset value of a house will inevitably rise over time (notwithstanding the spectre of an over-heated housing market as experienced in the UK in the 1990s and 2007/8), but it is the exception that proves the rule. A machine for producing plastic toy ducks will only retain any value if it actually makes plastic toy ducks for profit, and to maintain profit margins requires new investment in new machines. New investment comes from earning profits.

Ownership of capital has changed over the centuries. Whatever the political climate, capital ownership has spread more widely in more recent times. Capital was always in the hands of the Crown, State, Church and ruling classes. Governments remain prime sources of capital, and in some regimes, virtually the only source of capital. The Industrial Revolution saw the beginnings of the accumulation of capital by industrialists, and many of the large national and multinational corporations of today have their origins in the nineteenth century. The growth of industry and commerce saw the spread of capital ownership, and the development of that capital itself was encouraged by the use of credit and its wider provision. There is therefore a relationship between those who have capital and those who have not, which is the foundation of sales and credit.

The Development of Consumer and Export Credit

CONSUMER CREDIT

The aim of all production is consumption, and the ultimate beneficiary, and mainstay of the whole credit cycle, is the consumer. In times past, apart from the wealthy few whose buying power allowed them to insist on credit terms from generally poor tradespeople, most of the population had to find cash to buy their needs. Moneylenders and pawnbrokers, rather than banks, were the only source of borrowing for the man in the street, and, with the exception of the 'slate' at the local corner shop, credit was not available.

There was another exception, however. The eighteenth century saw the growth of the 'tallymen', itinerant traders who sold clothing at people's front doors in return for small weekly payments. Their frequent contact with customers, to collect instalments, allowed them access to further sales, and many credit arrangements or 'agreements' became permanent. A form of tally trade still exists, though it is not as extensive as it once was, having been largely replaced by a modern retail environment, offering a wide variety of credit arrangements. The concept of weekly payments remains strong in certain sections of society, however, and yet again the 2008/9 'Credit Crunch' has revived amongst many consumers the advantages of making regular, if small, payments to collectors.

The common man was not recognised by the term 'consumer', a relatively modern label, but consumer credit itself has old origins, even ancient beginnings. What we now recognise as instalment credit, however, and the precursor to hire purchase, came out of the aftermath of the French Revolution. Asset-rich French noblemen who had escaped Madame Guillotine were short of ready cash to furnish their recovered town houses in Paris, and turned to furniture manufacturers and traders, who would provide their goods on hire. Monsieur le Comte could choose to own the furnishings later, and deduct the paid rentals from the final purchase price.

The growth of mass production and the desire of ordinary people to own labour-saving consumer durables led to real retail credit 'agreements' from the nineteenth century onwards. The Singer Sewing Machine Company of the US claims to have invented hire purchase as we now know it, to enable them to flood the world with millions of treadle, later electric, sewing machines. Similarly, the expansion to the west in the US from around the same period introduced the concept of catalogue shopping, with the retailers 'back east' looking to expand their customer base beyond the confines of the location of their stores.

In the 1860s, the idea of specialised companies financing transactions began to flourish, the way being led by the great railway boom. Coalmine owners wanted more and more wagons to transport their coal from mine to factory, and finance was seen as an ideal vehicle for providing the cost-effective solution. The fathers of today's large finance companies hired the railway wagons to the colliers, who ran them on the railway companies' tracks, and were able to buy them later for a nominal sum. It is not a great leap of the imagination to see the application of that idea to consumer goods. Towards the end of the nineteenth century, finance companies were formed to specialise in consumer goods, but the combination of capital shortage and lack of job security through some turbulent times meant that 'buy now – pay later' remained patchy until after the Second World War. Banks resisted unsecured loans (until very recent times), and it was the finance companies and some larger retailers in the early 1950s who adopted the tallyman's principle of credit for people with a steady, albeit low, income.

The real growth burst forth from the 1960s onwards, with lenders recognising the vast source of funds in the hands of private individuals, and the desire of those individuals continually to acquire the trappings of success and modern convenience. Credit lending developed at a phenomenal rate, at one time seemingly out of control, and in the UK, successive governments imposed, or relaxed, rules governing credit transactions in attempts to regulate the economy as a whole. The Consumer Credit Act of 1974 (later amended by the Consumer Credit Act 2006) established sensible controls, and the rights of both lender and borrower. Nevertheless, consumer credit remains readily available, despite its high interest cost, and is viewed by many with concern from time to time as being too conducive to over-commitment, and to be inflationary.

It has been argued that one of the great concerns of the first few years of the twenty-first century, that is, the huge growth in personal finance and debt, was unsustainable, and the crash when it came would be both painful and long running. The real dilemma, however, was always the knowledge that consumer spending fuelled the powerful manufacturing economies, and that consumer spending itself was credit financed. One supported the other, and when that stopped (for whatever reason), so came the worldwide recession and what became known as the 'Global Downturn' or 'Credit Crunch'. In other words, when the consumer starts spending again, global economies will revive.

The promotion of credit offers to the consumer is relatively easy, and there have been a great many sources open to the man on the Clapham omnibus (see Figure 1.1). Managing the risk and the subsequent collection of the accounts is not easy, however, and this is now very much a specialist job, with professional qualifications.

Banks and Building Societies	Finance Companies	Retail shops	Other sources
Overdraft	Hire purchase	Credit account	Mail order – instalment credit
Personal loan	Credit sale	Credit sale	Loans against life insurance policies
Credit card	Personal loan	Budget account	Second mortgage loans
Debit card		Credit card	Check and voucher trading
		Debit card	Moneylenders
			Pawnbrokers
			Credit unions

Figure 1.1   Principal sources of consumer credit

EXPORT CREDIT

A study of human history is a study of economic rises and falls, of dominance and decline, and of shifts in power and influence. Above all it is a study of trade. From the earliest times, it has been necessary to conduct business over wider and wider geographical areas, which ultimately evolved into national and international boundaries, and as we have seen (see 'Origins' above), credit and international trade grew hand in hand.

Empires have come and gone, and the world is full of relics of those great imperial presences, from the ruins at Karnak and Ephesus to Windsor Castle or the Palace of Versailles. English, Spanish and French, languages spoken all round the world, testify to a legacy of great power in bygone days. The European 'Old World' countries with their imperial territories evolved over 300 years to dominate international trade, with the British Empire pre-eminent until around the time of the First World War. That wealth and strength declined in the twentieth century, being overtaken by the 'New World' of North America, whose economic power is best illustrated by the spread of multinational companies throughout the world, and the almost unbreakable link between the US dollar and many national currencies.

Following the Second World War, international boundaries were substantially redrawn, and the balance of economic influence shifted into emerging power blocs. Germany and Japan rose from the ashes of ruin, Germany leading the resurgence in Europe, and Japan igniting frenetic economic activity in what became known as the 'Pacific Rim'. The new 'empires' of the twenty-first century are financial – there is no need for armies to invade and conquer territories, when fast food chains and soft drinks combines create global dominance even more effectively. Add to that the fabulous wealth of the oil-rich Middle East and the seemingly never-ending need for 'black gold' to feed the voracious appetites of the industrialised nations, and it is clear that the world's balance of power has changed out of all recognition in the space of two generations.

Something approaching three-quarters of the world's 200-plus countries remain poor, and are designated 'Third World'. It is interesting to speculate when 'Third World' becomes 'First World' – India, for example, has rapidly developed into an economic power of some considerable influence, driven by the IT industry as well as the call centre culture. As indicators of economic power, it is worth observing that the original 'G8' group of Northern Hemisphere major industrialised nations, whilst still influential, is largely succeeded by the 'G20' worldwide group of industrialised nations. Nevertheless, 'Third World' countries remain – they can be described as technically insolvent, in that they continually import more than they export, and have little or nothing in the way of asset. The prime concern of the developed countries is where the hard currency funds will come from for the 'poor' countries to pay for future imports. The major banks involved in lending to 'sovereign risks' and the credit insurers of every OECD country study the foreign debt situation of each country and its ratio of earnings to cost of servicing debts (the Debt Service Ratio) before making and insuring further large loans. The developed countries, at the end of the twentieth century and beginning of the twenty-first century, came under some pressure to relieve the debt burden of poor countries, principally by writing off huge capital sums, or at the very least cancelling interest, but this may remain only be temporary relief, even when universally applied. Taking Zimbabwe as an horrific example, major political and infrastructure change is as necessary as debt relief in order to alleviate poverty.

Export credit, therefore, relies on all the expertise of credit management in just the same way as domestic trade and consumer credit: assessing the risk; striking the right balance between risk, exposure and payment; and financing and collecting debt. It matters not whether the potential customer is a lorry driver on a housing estate in West Bromwich, a building company in

Weston Super Mare or a clothing retailer in the West Indies – knowing the customer and knowing the risk is a constant.

Secured and Unsecured Credit

Credit is all about trust. The word itself derives from the Latin word *credere*, ,meaning to trust or to believe. The dictionary defines trust in a number of ways, but the main definition is pertinent to credit management: 'reliance on and confidence in the truth, worth, reliability, etc., of a person or thing'. A thesaurus offers a varied but just as meaningful set of alternatives: 'assurance, belief, conviction, certitude, expectation, faith, hope', and so on. To underline the connection, the thesaurus also offers 'credit' as an alternative to 'trust'. There can be no doubt as to the serious nature of credit management when the whole business of granting credit, domestically and internationally, has its roots in trust. The Credit Manager's job is to justify that trust in the customer in granting the required facilities, and to maintain that trust through the cycle of trading.

All this means is that the seller of the goods needs to establish the confidence that the buyer has the intention to pay when due, as well as the ability to pay when due. It is therefore a judgement of both character (the intention) and capacity (the financial ability). Situations are not always straightforward, and there will be circumstances when extra security may be necessary.

Trade suppliers are usually unsecured creditors. Security in the granting of credit is maintaining a legal right to recover money owed in the event of non-payment of the debt by the customer, from the sale of specified assets (or one specified asset) which are owned by the customer. It is often the case that the only way that trust can be demonstrated, all other things being equal, is to allow, or for the supplier to require, a measure of security in the transaction.

Banks usually look for some form of security when making loans to customers, though there have long been anomalies in the attitude of banks to consumer customers and to trade customers. Banks look for personal guarantees from proprietors or directors of small companies to support even modest overdrafts, while at the same time their credit card divisions have allowed unsecured limits of much larger value. When a bank takes security over a customer's property or other asset, this is secured credit. Unsecured credit is exactly as described – credit granted without any form of security or guarantee.

It is perfectly possible, but much less usual, for trade creditors to look for forms of security. This question will be examined in more detail in later chapters.

Information Technology

It is now difficult to imagine how the Credit Manager, or indeed any other manager, coped with the difficulties of running any business without the assistance of computerisation and all its spin-offs. We now take for granted that our PC, modem and phone together give us access to worldwide information via satellite, for example, between offices of a company, sellers and buyers, electronic libraries of financial reports and credit reports, and databases of every word ever printed. Add to that the communication revolution of phone, fax, electronic data interchange (EDI), videophone and email, and what was once a world where it took weeks for messages to be received and answered is now one of instant contact.

There is some justification in the view that each new innovation outshone its predecessor, and took over as the prime mode of contact. The letter was overtaken by the telephone, which in turn lost ground to the fax, and now the email is regarded as the best thing since sliced bread. The telegraph and the telex, not too long ago the wonders of the world, are now consigned to history. Letters, phones and faxes still remain, of course, and later chapters will expand on their merits and uses.

The fax is cheaper than the phone, and in its first few years was certainly regarded as being more effective than either the phone or letters. Faxes are targeted to specific people, and overcome the barrier of people avoiding taking telephone calls. As fax technology has improved, so have quality, speed and variety. Many companies use faxes for what used to be described as telemarketing – instead of people phoning with cold call sales pitches, faxes are sent as marketing shots in batches overnight and during the day. Copy documents, colour faxes, route maps and meeting agenda – all manner of instant copy to the right person, all over the world. However, people can ignore faxes, much as they ignore letters or avoid taking telephone calls – faxes are just as easy to screw up and throw into the wastepaper bin as letters! It is, nevertheless, a fast, cheap and convenient method of transmitting a message and plays a vital role, if used correctly, in the credit management function.

The world is now influenced by cyberspace. Email, with all its scope and variations, is the tool of the day. It is fast and interactive, and both customers and suppliers expect its use. The scope seems limitless – you draft an agreement for account settlement; you email it instantly to the customer; he copies it instantly to relevant colleagues; they add their views and flash it back to you; you agree or not, and confirm; you send key details to your boss, sales colleagues, production people, amd so on. The text can be printed off, though this is not always necessary, and because it is a PC screen display, it is absolutely clear and readable, which is often more than can be said for faxes from Bristol, Berlin or Buenos Aires! Emails can carry attachments, spreadsheets, presentations, pictures, documents and so on and their worth is invaluable in getting information to anywhere in the world, avoiding the vagaries of postal systems, telephone lines and time zones.

The use of emails in the collection process will be discussed fully in Chapter 11, but it is worth noting that there are pitfalls. The instantaneous nature of the transmission demands care – it is all too easy to press 'send' without properly reviewing what you have said. Once 'sent' there can be no going back; except, of course, to send a second email apologising for the tone or error of the first, but by then the damage has been done. In addition, there is 'email fatigue', where the volume of important emails is contaminated by 'spam', or speculative junk mail. US studies have shown a growing frustration with the volumes of email traffic faced by staff, which can lead to emails being ignored, in just the same way as the fax or letter, and deleted from the system with the same effectiveness as throwing the letter or fax into the wastepaper bin.

The mobile phone is as much part of twenty-first century culture as television or DVD. The technology is nearly as mind blowing as email – making instant contact from head office in Leeds with the Export Sales Executive as he rides in a taxi from his hotel to the customer's premises on an industrial estate in outskirts of Mumbai. With the launch of '3G' ('third generation') mobiles in 2003, the mobile became a visual as well as audio communication device, with Internet access and myriad other features.

Videoconferencing has been a feature of business for some years, and in the aftermath of 11 September 2001, increased considerably in use. Many Credit Managers will agree that quite often the best way to resolve complicated issues with customers is by face-to-face meetings. These can be difficult enough to arrange within the UK, but are an even rarer feature of export credit management. The video link, however, enables such a meeting to take place, over vast distances, and not only has the advantage of allowing body language to be read, it also avoids all the hassle and time associated with travel. Many large multinationals now use the facility as a replacement for sales conferences, where travel is a minor issue compared to the expense of hotel accommodation, conference rooms, food and refreshments.

EDI, initially introduced by large companies to speed up and reduce the cost of ordering from their many hundreds of suppliers, is now widely used by many organisations, large and small. After terms have been agreed, all stages of a transaction – order, acknowledgement, amendments, dispatch notes, invoices, credit notes, remittance advices and Banks Automated Clearing System (BACS) instructions – are sent between the computers of buyer and suppliers. Paper is not essential, as the computer file can be accessed when needed. There remains some dispute in certain areas as to the legal validity of paperless contracts, but Courts now recognise computer evidence in given circumstances, and it is inevitable that, sooner rather than later, such paperless contracts will be as universally recognised as any other form of contract. It is interesting to note, however, that purchases of goods or services through the Internet nearly always require the buyer to 'print this page' when the order has been confirmed, and confirmation is often reinforced by a fax! The role of the Credit Manager in the world of EDI contracts is not diminished – on the contrary, the Credit Manager's task is to set up and monitor the account through all its stages, including reconciliation.

External Services

Every credit manager is expected to be their company's expert on the services available to improve the debtors asset. They may not all be relevant, but information should be reassessed from time to time. Examples of highly useful *external services* are:

- credit data;

- credit insurance;

- factoring;

- collection agents;

- risk 'watch' services;

- outsourcing credit staff/shared credit manager.

All credit managers will have seen brochures and handouts from suppliers eager to sell their services, and many will take stands at exhibitions and conferences, as well as sponsoring meetings.

Customer credit reports are supplied online by all the major credit agencies, to enable quick decisions. Prices vary, but it makes commercial sense to apply the 80/20 policy, that is, to receive regular reports with credit recommendations on the 20 per cent of customers who account for 80 per cent of sales and cash.

Automated credit ratings and risk categories can be produced via proprietary software which enables the credit manager to input a customer's financials to a spreadsheet-style worksheet. Weightings can be customised for preferred ratios and these can be applied to the customer's financial capacity to calculate a value of credit which can safely be allowed.

The *credit watch service* of some agencies flashes information to the credit manager if relevant data is picked up – a County Court Judgement, adverse press report, new charge registered by lenders, poor ratios in the latest filed accounts, and so on. It makes sense to buy this service for accounts marked on the ledger as 'high risk', to enable the credit manager to get out before it all goes pear-shaped, but still be selling and making money while the going is good.

Credit insurance, especially for domestic trade, is still underused in the UK. This means that the biggest asset on most balance sheets is largely unprotected. In return for a negotiable premium, some companies will protect sales against a number of reasons for not being paid. Specialist brokers will do the legwork and the analysis to get alternative quotations to suit particular business, and are useful in negotiating annual renewals, getting claims paid and having a good ongoing rapport with the underwriters. Some companies offer *credit-insured credit opinions* on customers, providing credit reports and arranging credit insurance for the recommended credit levels.

There are hundreds of *collection agencies* offering to collect both commercial and consumer debts; in the main those debts that have been through the supplier's own collection process but still remain unpaid. Ideally, two or more should be used to compare performance. They may well be recommended by credit acquaintances in other companies. Fees are negotiable, and passing debts over to an agency leaves the credit manager more time to concentrate on current debts. Most agencies have a good success rate with collections, partly because of the impact of third-party intervention and partly because they have to succeed to earn their fee. No collection means no fee.

Factoring suits those companies growing fast, with a good net margin, who do not yet have resources in-house to do the credit and collection task. Factors do an excellent job, usually collecting the money faster than the client was, but naturally there is a charge for the service. A service fee of anything from 1–4 per cent of sales is a greater cost to the company than a credit department.

Outsourcing and/or *receivables management* has developed from the need to reduce staff costs, whether temporary staff agencies, staff working from home, job sharing, subcontract credit managers or full-blown ledger management by an outside specialist company. Some companies, especially growing SMEs, prefer to use an expert credit manager only as needed. Such a self-employed credit manager may work for five or six companies, receiving occasional requests to calculate credit ratings, sort out payment disputes, collect debts, write credit policies and devise credit/collection procedures and contract wordings affecting payments.

Credit Management as a Profession

In the years which have passed since the first edition of *Credit Management Handbook* in 1976, it could easily be argued that either nothing has really changed or that everything has changed. The essence of credit and its underlying trust has not changed. Allowing customers time to pay for goods or services still carries the risk that payment will be late, or not made at all. The amount and its credit period still depends on risk assessment and all those elements of human nature that have existed since Adam was a lad. However, the credit scene has certainly changed. Think of emails and the Internet, computers and data transfer, global economies and dependencies, the European Union and the euro, and the decline of 'traditional' industries and job skills and the rise of high-tech devices and service industries.

All these various points could be debated *ad nauseam*, but there is a fundamental truth, which is that a credit manager has always had to be something of a jack-of-all-trades, and as near as possible a master of them too. The Institute of Credit Management, in its Education Syllabus, aims to equip the successful MICM(Grad) with a sound footing in all aspects of credit management, from law to insolvency, from risk assessment to debt collection, and thus increase the standing and appreciation of the function at a *professional* level. In that respect, the years since 1976 have seen considerable change.

It is no longer acceptable for the credit function to be seen in isolation, either as a debt collection operation or an order barrier. It is no longer acceptable for credit control to be an afterthought, something that Edna comes in on Fridays to do. Nor is it any longer acceptable for the credit manager to be marginalised in matters relating to profits and company health. The Credit Management Research Centre, at The University of Leeds Business School, has shown repeatedly in its Quarterly Reviews that proactive credit control significantly reduces bad debt losses and contributes positively to bottom-line success.

It is true that credit control is a Cinderella activity in some organisations, and it is also true that there are still very few Credit Directors in UK boardrooms, compared to all the Credit VPs in the USA, but awareness and appreciation are now growing at a faster pace than ever before. In addition, credit management is increasingly being seen also as a customer service and a marketing function, and therefore sits just as easily with sales as it does with finance.

The credit manager needs to have a sound understanding of the basics:

- know the financial ability of customers;

- assess how much credit to allow;

- process orders quickly;

- collect funds on time.

To achieve the best results, the credit manager needs to have those interpersonal skills which complement numeracy and literacy. Leading a successful team and being part of a larger successful team requires training and effort, and all the more so if *professional* credit management incorporates:

- integrating with sales colleagues;

- cultivating/meeting customers;

- automated risk assessment integrated with order processing;

- collection techniques including email, fax and videophone;

- electronic transfer of funds;

- external services: credit reports (online),insolvency warnings, credit insurance, factoring, collection agents, temporary staff, outsourcing, shared service centres, call centres, query resolution and analysis;

- international cross-border trade, using EDI documents and payments;

- computer literacy.

Credit training needs to concentrate on all these as well as focusing on the impact of any actions on customer relationships and the needs of the business.

There are many aspects of changes in legislation which require the credit manager not only to keep up to date with what is going on, but also be in a position to advise sales and marketing, production, transport and distribution – in other words, be very much part of the eyes and ears of the company.

Coping with Change and the Path Forward

Nothing stands still, and change is an inevitable part of progress. For most people, change can be stressful, even if they do not realise it, though the pace of modern life would suggest that more and more people are suffering from stress-related illnesses and it can only be a matter of conjecture as to how much of that can be put down to change. Sometimes it can be difficult to accept change as progress. Many SMEs, for example, no longer enjoy the kind of relationship with their bank that existed some years ago. Trying to phone the manager of a Bank Business

Centre one may go via a call centre in some far-flung place, a tedious 'security verification' process, and an interrogation as to whom one wants to speak to and why, only to discover that the required manager, after only a few months, has moved on to bigger and better things. So the whole task of building a relationship has to start all over again. Little wonder, then, that a customer finds it easier to delay payment to a supplier than to try to get extra financing from his own bank!

Since the early 1970s, perhaps the biggest change that has taken place is that in employment itself and the introduction of different work patterns. Our forefathers may well have had to endure far worse working conditions, longer hours, less pay and very little in the way of added benefits. Not for them employment rights, maternity and paternity benefits, flexible hours and all the other things we now take for granted. What they did enjoy (if that is the right word), however, was a job security which is now rare. They could talk about 'a job for life' and though the apprenticeship may have been long and hard, the employment which followed was secure and virtually guaranteed. Not so today. The mass of failures, mergers and acquisitions which began around 1970 ushered in an era of downsizing and a shift from large traditional industries to smaller, more speculative ones. The consumer has been urged to 'shop around', and supply sources have moved from home bases to cheaper labour areas all over the world.

The UK has not been alone in this change – it has taken place throughout the industrialised west. The European Union, providing a huge single market, has created employment mobility and has thereby given companies the opportunity to choose the right base for their operations. Communication technology has in effect removed the physical miles, so the location for a service industry, for example, or the service division of a manufacturer, need no longer be alongside the market served, but can be virtually anywhere.

Technology means fewer people producing more. Any cost-cutting exercise always begins with the workforce, seen as the most expensive outlay for any business. Downsizing and relocation is the norm, although 2001 research in the US began to question the philosophy – research since has argued that to prune the rose tree too heavily actually kills the plant rather than encouraging vigorous new growth. Technology also means that the credit manager, whilst having instant access to more information than ever before, is under greater pressure to do more with less.

The most startling aspect of change, however, has been its pace over a relatively short period of time. Consider for a moment: mankind has been on the planet for only about 40,000 years, and for 39,800 years change was gradual, and usually barely noticeable. The Industrial Revolution introduced advancements that must have appeared spectacular at the time, but which now seem modest when set against the white-hot technology explosions of the last 75 years. From the Wright brothers to Concorde was little more than two generations, and though we now take for granted live televised reports from anywhere on Earth (and indeed, pictures from the Moon and from Mars), it is again little more than two generations since the first flickering black and white images were beamed from Alexandra Palace to a few startled Londoners. In a very few years, the mobile phone has shrunk from the size of a house brick to that of a matchbox, yet has the computing capacity of a machine which once filled a room! There is no reason to suppose that the pace of change in the twenty-first century will slacken. On the contrary, speed breeds speed, and what is amazing today will be commonplace, even old hat, tomorrow.

Change, and its speed, from job security through downsizing to relocation, has altered the attitude of many employees towards their role and contribution. Credit management is no exception. The Japanese car worker may still have to sing the company song each morning, but few organisations now command or provide the loyalty of the past. Career perceptions have changed – the keyword is now flexibility, with the prospect of having several employers in a working life. Gone are the school-leaver's thoughts of finding a 'safe job' with a blue chip company. The only safe strategy nowadays is to regard that company as a rung on the ladder. For the aspiring credit manager, there is tremendous scope for progressing in seniority in the profession, but probably at the cost of changing firms at intervals. Credit management is most definitely a profession. It certainly matters that the credit manager does a professional job at all times. The complacent company will become uncompetitive and the complacent credit manager will be left behind, squeezed out by successive reorganisations. The message is clear – there is an increasing need for growing firms to employ a properly qualified credit management professional. That individual must be the type to meet changing demands and be ready for new directions and innovations. The contribution of credit management will continue to grow, and credit managers must continually develop and hone their skills. It could well be that within the speciality profession that is credit management there will be further subdivisions into technical areas of specialisms in trade, consumer and export. What is certain, however, is that change will take place, just as it has always done, and the credit manager must always be prepared.

2

The Financial Effects of Credit Management

Glen Bullivant

• The cost of credit • Free credit? • The effect of credit on profits • The effect of credit on liquidity • The financing of credit • Cash flow • Measurement of debtors • Cash targets • Planning and budgeting debtors • Summary •

The Cost of Credit

Money costs money. That principle has to be the foundation upon which all credit transactions are based – that is to say that the granting of credit, though beneficial for business as a whole, is not without cost, either to the supplier or to the buyer, or to both. It follows therefore that the process of granting credit to customers, and the tasks of risk assessment and risk analysis, amount to no more than weighing the benefits of granting credit against the cost to the supplier of doing so. Furthermore, that cost element is not restricted to non-payment, or bad debt losses, but applies to cost of the credit period itself *and* the cost incurred in late payment. It should always be remembered that there is an inevitable time delay between funds being expended by the seller in acquiring raw materials, paying wages and so on for the production and delivery of the goods and the receipt of funds from the buyer in respect of those goods or services. The cost can be passed on in prices or absorbed by the seller, but it can never be ignored.

The fact that money *does* cost money is reflected in interest rates. It is dangerous in times of low, or relatively low, interest rates for companies to play down the cost element of granting credit, or even to ignore it altogether. In the UK, interest rates have seen great variations in relatively short time spans. The near zero rates of 2009, the lowest since the Bank of England was established in 1694, were designed to stimulate the economy in a time of recession and not to be taken by companies as a sign that money was cheap and granting credit was not a cost-bearing activity. On the contrary, those companies to weather the turbulent financial weather better than most were those very companies who took credit management in all its aspects most seriously. One criticism of Government has constantly been that of instability – all businesses prosper better when able to plan and forecast their borrowing costs over longer periods of time. Stability of interest rates allows an element of certainty in forward planning and can dictate strategies on investment, marketing, employment and so on. All governments use interest rate manipulation as a method of regulating the economy as a whole, and that will probably always be true, but the policy has to have some built-in stability element for it to achieve the desired results.

When trying to offer simple illustrations of how credit is a cost to the seller it is better to ignore actual rates (as at the time of writing) or predicted rates, but to seek to demonstrate the cost of credit on a formula basis which can be readily understood. Interest rates in the UK, for example, hit their lowest for a generation in the first quarter of 2003, when a decade earlier rates had never been so high. It should also be remembered that the amount charged for loans or overdrafts will always be several points above base rates. A simple example, therefore, would be to assume a seller's borrowing costs to be 12 per cent per annum, because it is easily converted to 1 per cent of the value of the unpaid invoices or debt for every month that elapses. Some companies allowing 30 days credit to their customers include one month's cost of borrowing in their prices. Others, perhaps more cost-conscious, include not one month's interest but the cost for the average debt payment period for all accounts. This may be seen to 'penalise' the prompt payers, who are in effect paying for the costs of late payment by the slow-paying customers. For that reason, some sellers invoke their right, under their conditions of sale, to charge extra interest for late payment. There are some companies, however, who do not build into their prices *any* element of the interest costs being taken into account. It is precisely because credit managers *know* that money costs money, that they should be able to clearly illustrate this fact to their colleagues in sales as well as finance. When customers ask for 'longer to pay' or when extra credit terms are being negotiated, the seller should always recover the extra credit cost either by openly adding it or by price increases.

In the five examples in Figure 2.1, all the firms have a 5 per cent profit level where nothing is allowed in prices for credit and funds cost 12 per cent per annum. It is easy to see how the cost of credit has a direct impact.

	Firm A Cash only	Firm B Cash 2% Discount	Firm C 30 days net	Firm D 60 days net	Firm E 90 days net
Annual sales	12,000	12,000	12,000	12,000	12,000
Debtors	0	0	1000	2000	3000
Net profit (before credit cost	600	600	600	600	600
Cost of credit	0	(240)	(120)	(240)	(360)
Net profit	600	360	480	360	240
Net profit %	5%	3%	4%	3%	2%

Figure 2.1   Depletion of profit by credit terms

If cost/price inflation were present, its percentage should be added to the cost of money in calculating the true cost of credit. For example, if annual inflation is 6 per cent, each month's delay in a customer's payment makes it worth 0.5 per cent less when received. In such an example a 90-day delay costs the seller 1.5 per cent for inflation, plus 3 per cent for interest, totalling a flat 4.5 per cent off the debt value when received.

Free Credit?

It would be easy for anyone to assume that there *was* such a thing as free credit. The consumer is assailed from all angles with 'tempting' offers – '0 per cent finance', 'three years interest free', and so on – and the advertising hype is at every turn, from cars to hi-fis, fridges to caravans, cruises to carpets. Perhaps this influence spills over into trade credit, where there may linger a perception among some companies, particularly those which are sales driven, that credit can be 'free'. The short answer is that it cannot. As we have seen, there is an effect on profit, which is a direct cost of credit impact. The fact remains that money costs money. Where the element of alleged 'free credit' may have some validity is for the buyer himself – it may be on the surface that the selling price of the car is £10,000, and the total amount to be paid over three or four years by the buyer is £10,000. Free to the buyer, then? Not if the price of £10,000 includes the sum of £1000 to cover credit costs! The real nature of both perceived, and perhaps actual, free credit lies in the inability of companies to recognise and account for the cost of credit. Because trade credit rarely includes the cost of credit as a separately shown item on the invoice, it is easy for the uninitiated to accept that credit is free. As we have seen, this is far from the case. The best thing would be for everyone to be able to accept the definition of credit as being something (money) which is bought from a supplier (bank) at a price, in just the same way as any other goods or services are bought.

The real rub comes in the form of extended credit, not negotiated or agreed with special terms, but taken by buyers in the form of late payment. Unless interest is charged, *and collected*, on such accounts, then the supplier *is* effectively giving free credit, the effects of which hit the bottom line just as surely as bad debt losses.

There is, of course, another cost associated with the granting of credit, which further erodes any notion that may linger of credit being free. The credit grantor has to establish and operate a credit department, which involves all the usual costs associated with any working office department, not least of which will be staff salaries. In real terms, the costs associated with financing a debtors ledger will be saved by employing dedicated credit staff and thus reducing the debtors ledger.

The Effect of Credit on Profits

Unless a seller has built into his selling price additional costs for late payment, or is successful in recovering those costs by way of interest charged, then any overdue account will affect his profit. In some competitive markets, companies can be tempted by the prospects of increased business if additional credit is given, but unless it can be certain that additional profits from increased sales will outweigh the increased costs of credit, or said costs can be recovered through higher prices, then the practice is fraught with danger.

In Figure 2.2, Company A has a 5 per cent profit level where nothing is allowed in prices for credit and funds cost 12 per cent per annum. Under its normal terms of 60 days, it is achieving sales of £12,000,000 per annum, and a net profit of £360,000. In an attempt to increase sales, credit terms are increased to 90 days, and targeted sales to go up by one-third to £16,000,000. It will be noted, however, that net profit would drop to £320,000. Sales in fact only increase by a quarter to £15,000,000, and the net profit achieved is only £300,000, a decrease of £60,000 on increased sales of £3,000,000. In some desperation, the company

Company A	Situation A	Situation B	Situation C	Situation D
Sales	12,000,000	16,000,000	15,000,000	18,000,000
Credit days	60	90	90	120
Debtors	2,000,000	4,000,000	3,750,000	6,000,000
Net profit (before cost of credit)	600,000	800,000	750,000	900,000
Cost of credit	(240,000)	(480,000)	(450,000)	(720,000)
Net profit	360,000	320,000	300,000	180,000

Figure 2.2   The effect of credit on profit

extends credit to 120 days and sales are now 50 per cent higher than originally, at £18,000,000. Net profit, on the other hand, is now *down* 50 per cent at only £180,000.

Putting it the other way round, see what can be achieved by increasing sales and *reducing* debtors. If sales of £12,000,000 with debtors of £3,000,000 (90 days) could be brought down to debtors of £2,000,000 (60 days), then reducing debtors by one month saves £120,000 per annum – more than enough to cover the salary of a good credit manager!

Most companies can readily see losses incurred by bad debts, customers going into liquidation, receivership or bankruptcy. The writing-off of bad debt losses visibly reduces the Profit and Loss Account. The interest cost of late payment is less visible and can go unnoticed as a cost effect. It is infrequently measured separately because it is mixed in with the total bank charges for all activities. The total bank interest is also reduced by the borrowing cost saved by paying bills late. Credit managers can measure this interest cost separately for debtors, and the results can be seen by many as startling because the cost of waiting for payment beyond terms is usually *ten times* the cost of bad debt losses.

Figures 2.3 and 2.4 are in active use by many credit managers to demonstrate the need for the right action at the right time. By preventing a bad debt loss, or at least reducing the loss by the time the customer fails, a credit manager avoids the impact of cancelling out previously booked profits on very large sales values. On the chart for overdues, the intersection of borrowing cost with the net profit margin shows the window of time available for collection before

Bad debt	Pre-tax profit percentage			
£	5%	8%	10%	12%
50	1000	625	500	417
500	10,000	6250	5000	4170
5000	100,000	62,500	50,000	41,700
10,000	200,000	125,000	100,000	83,400
50,000	1,000,000	625,000	500,000	417,000
Value or previous sales on which profit has been lost, or extra sales needed to recoup the bad debt total.				

Figure 2.3   Effect of bad debts on sales

Cost of borrowings	Net profit on sales				
	10%	8%	6%	4%	2%
5%	24.0	19.2	14.4	9.6	4.8
6%	20.0	16.0	12.0	8.0	4.0
8%	15.0	12.0	9.0	6.0	3.0
10%	12.0	9.6	7.2	4.8	2.4
12%	10.0	8.0	6.0	4.0	2.0
15%	8.0	6.4	4.8	3.2	1.6
Number of months overdue after which profit is absorbed by interest cost					

Figure 2.4   The effect of overdues on profits

the sale becomes a waste of time. Clearly, high margins and cheap money allow a soft impact, whereas high interest rates combined with poor margins require very strict collection processes.

Presenting the kind of tabulation shown in Figures 2.3 and 2.4 to senior management sharply demonstrates the value of proactive credit management, from the initial process of opening a customer account to the monitoring of that account on the ledger throughout its existence. It also emphasises, if such emphasis is necessary, the need for the company to have collection policies and procedures which encourage prompt and effective action in the right places at the right time.

The Effect of Credit on Liquidity

Liquidity is cash, or cash is liquidity. From either angle, the answer is the same. Looking at a company's balance sheet can reveal the ability of the company to meet commitments as and when they fall due, or whether all their resources are tied up in fixed items such as land or buildings. A company rich in fixed assets may still be short of cash and therefore have difficulty in meeting current obligations. Imagine owning your own house in the leafy suburbs, but having no income and facing this quarter's electricity bill – the house may well be worth £500,000, but the bank account is empty and the only way the electricity bill can be paid is by selling off some of the family silver. Ownership of valuable fixed assets may have a favourable effect on the creditworthiness of an individual or a company, because if push came to shove, the supplier can take comfort from the fact that assets can be sold off to meet debts. Fixed assets, on the other hand, have little or no impact on credit *ability* – it is the ability of the buyer to pay bills when they are due which can make or break. The cash needed to run a business comes from somewhere, and at its most basic, there are two contributors:

- owners' capital and reserves;

- borrowing.

The first relates to the amount put into the business by its owners – proprietors, shareholders, and so on – and the amount built up in reserves from trading profits from previous years. It makes good business sense to utilise some of the profits to create reserves which can assist survival during more difficult trading conditions. Reserves are basically the amounts retained in the business and not distributed to the business owners. They are usually profits made and not passed on to the owners (also known as retained earnings), and capital reserves where there had been a perceived increase in the valuation of some fixed assets. The second contribution comes in the form of capital and loan financing, usually from the bank, and assists in the purchase of fixed assets such as plant and equipment, as well as contributing to working capital. Most credit managers recognise a third source of finance, which even though it may be unofficial is quite often seen as the most readily available – trade suppliers. It is an indication of inevitability that if the owners have no more funds and the bank will not extend any further facilities then the business will rely upon suppliers to enable it to continue trading. It is for that reason that credit managers focus on working capital as a major contributor to the credit decision.

The Financing of Credit

Buying the daily newspaper at the local newsagents is a simple enough transaction by any definition. Though the purchase itself is for cash, the deal is in fact at the end of a very long line of credit arrangements, some substantial. The newsagent receives supplies daily from the wholesaler (which may or may not involve credit), and the wholesaler receives supplies daily from the newspaper publisher (which almost certainly will involve credit). Looking at the newspaper itself, however, reveals a maze of manufacturers, service providers, wholesalers and distributors, all dealing with each other on credit terms. Many of those suppliers have their own line of credit deals leading up to supplying the newspaper publisher – trees to paper, chemicals to ink, aluminium to printing plate, and so on – each subsequent deal being dependent on satisfactory completion of previous deals. Throughout this credit chain, sellers are supplying buyers, credit terms are negotiated, invoices raised and payment collected.

The payment of each credit transaction between each of the interested parties has an effect on the whole to a greater or lesser extent, and if a link in that chain is weak, or even broken, this impacts on all, even to the extent of the consumer being not able to walk into the newsagent and purchase the finished product.

The chain can be complicated further by the wide variation in credit terms on offer and taken throughout the cycle. The aluminium supplier wants payment in 30 days, the printing plate manufacturer has terms of 60 days, the publisher 10 days and the wholesaler cash! The balance between the need to pay and the receipt of funds is therefore delicate, and it is the gap between buying in the raw materials, making the product, selling the product and getting paid that has to be funded.

Chapter 3 will look in detail at company credit policies, but suffice it to say at this stage that every company supplying goods or services on credit has to know what it can afford, and what it is willing to afford, by way of funding that credit gap. The longer the credit period (the time between supply and receipt of payment) and the larger the value of debtors, the more expensive it is to finance. It follows that companies look to keep debtors to a minimum, as a proportion of sales, and work towards collecting receipts to due date.

Cash Flow

Even in an ideal world, with all customers paying on time (!), granting credit means that there will be a credit period that will require funding. The company's working capital, including as it does owners' capital and reserves and borrowings, is further supplemented by operational cash flow – indeed, as already seen, that cash flow may in effect *be* the company's only real working capital.

Cash flow is defined in different ways but always comes back in the end to its effect on the surplus, or profits, of the business. The dictionary definition of cash flow is quite straightforward, being 'the movement of money into and out of a business'. Accountants define cash flow as net profits before tax plus depreciation added back, since it has not really left the cash coffers; this may well be technically correct but is not as graphic as 'I know it's my round, but I am suffering from cash flow problems, old boy'. Money comes in from paid sales and goes out in expenses to achieve those sales, mainly to creditors for supplies and in salaries and operating costs. If more goes out than comes in, and if the time lapse between in and out needs financing, then the business falls back on its resources or its borrowings to fund that gap. Bank overdrafts are meant to cope with that circumstance, and it is a fact that the two major users of expensive bank overdraft borrowings are unsold stocks and uncollected debtors.

Successful entrepreneurs, on whose every word market commentators hang, will delight in retelling their tales of growing from humble beginnings to mighty commercial empires, and more importantly exactly how they did it. We have all heard the stories about being in the right place at the right time, having a world-beating product, or knowing the market place better than anyone else. By their own admission, however, the real key to their success was, and is, their ability to keep close control over cash flow, avoiding holding excessive stocks and collecting debts on time. Those failed geniuses, in whom observers may point to technical expertise or wonderful inventions in their financial obituaries, often collapsed because they focused on technical matters and forgot about cash flow. When bills could not be paid, the major suppliers and the banks closed the doors. It appears that this message is still lost on the vast array of small businesses and SMEs which in the last 20 years or so have been gradually replacing the larger companies and corporations as the mainstay of many economies including the UK (4.6 million small businesses in the UK are now the largest private sector employers in the country). A major element missing from business plans submitted to banks for funding approval is covering arrangements for invoicing and account collection – small businesses still believe that simply doing a good job and/or supplying a good product is reason enough to be paid on time. It can come as a great shock, if not a fatal blow, to discover that though the world may beat a path to your door for the product, you have to do something positive to ensure timely payment.

At its simplest, the result of the total efforts of a business is its net profit, after deducting interest on borrowings. The way it manages its major asset, debtors, greatly influences that 'bottom line'. Businesses can pay interest rates which are high compared to their low net profit margins. It follows, therefore, that in order to reduce the impact of interest expense, they must concentrate on ensuring well managed debtors (that is, unpaid sales) in proportion to all sales made.

Sales *volume* is not the same thing, and is often confused with financial success. Inadequate sales are of course lethal if they are insufficient to cover costs, but so too are booming sales if they produce massive unpaid debts for long periods. The interest cost of borrowing, while waiting for so much money to come in, can easily cancel out fragile net profits.

Every Profit and Loss Statement shows 'Interest Expense' as the last cost before 'Net Profit Before Tax (NPBT)'. The interest item results from how the net assets have been managed, that is, stock control, credit control on debtors and the credit taken from suppliers. In most companies, interest is less than 10 per cent of profits, but where it gets to 50 per cent or more, the business is usually destined to fail within a year. This is because the assets are so out of control that the cost of financing them can never be recovered in trading profit and the company is producing more profit for the bank than for its shareholders! But even the bank becomes concerned above the 50 per cent level, which is why it then appoints an Administrative Receiver to protect its own interests (see Chapters 5, 6 and 8 on risk analysis and pointers to insolvency).

There are four key items which progressive, and successful, companies insist on being tightly managed:

1.   annual profit growth percentage, to equal or exceed sales growth percentage;

2.   cash flow effectiveness, to minimise exernal debt;

3.   efficient use of assets, that is, as slim as possible to achieve sales;

4.   interest avoidance, since the cost is a drain on profits.

It is not rocket science to suggest that good credit management benefits all four items!

An often quoted formula or ratio to indicate efficiency and effectiveness is ROCE, *Return On Capital Employed*. This is usually calculated as:

$$\frac{\text{Return (NPBT)}}{\substack{\text{Capital employed} \\ \text{(including borrowing)}}} \times 100$$

The more switched-on finance directors, as well as credit managers, know only too well that faster cash collections improve the ROCE on two fronts – by reducing the interest expense, profit is increased, and at the same time borrowings are reduced. Two for the price of one (or buy one get one free) fits in well in the bargain-conscious environment of today!

Measurement of Debtors

Knowing where we want to be and how we want to get there is very much dependent on knowing where we are today. It is not enough to wait until the auditors are in to see that debtors are out of control, or are growing at a faster rate than we expected in relation to sales. Effective credit management looks to be able to respond immediately to demands, but more importantly looks to be able to see what is happening, not just as it happens, but even before it takes hold. The most common measurement of the debtors situation is expressed as *Days Sales Outstanding* or DSO. There are a number of ways of calculating DSO, and these are dealt with in some detail in Chapter 14, but the most usual calculation is by way of the *count back* (sometimes called the *add back*) method. This measures the level of debtors, indicating the speed of cash intake, and an example of a DSO ratio is shown in Figure 2.5.

The calculation is done at month-end, taking total debtors (current, overdue and disputed), and deducting total monthly sales going back in time until all the debtors figure is used up. In the illustration, therefore, June debtors equaled

30.06.2009	Total debtors	£1,200,000	
	June sales	(£650,000)	= 30 days
		£550,000	
	May sales	(£490,000)	= 31 days
		£60,000	
	April sales		
	(Total £600,000)	(£60,000)	= 3 days
			64 days

Figure 2.5   Standard DSO calculation

all the sales for the last 64 days = 64 DSO. This means that sales take an average of 64 days to be paid.

A feature of any meeting of credit managers is a comparison of their DSOs. 'Mine is less than yours' is not necessarily a bad thing, but nor is it necessarily a good thing either! When looking at performance indicators, such as DSO, it is important to benchmark against the same industry standards. DSO as a measurement by itself does not indicate better or worse performance than *everybody* else, but does measure your own receivables performance against both your own credit terms and those of your competitors in the same industry with the same terms. One drawback of being the credit manager of a company which is part of a larger group with diverse business operations is that head office can fall into the trap of comparing your DSO, as a subsidiary in, say, printing and publishing, to that of another subsidiary making high-performance racing car engines! The printing and publishing sector credit manager needs to be compared with other businesses in printing and publishing in order for that comparison to have genuine relevance.

Given the importance to competitiveness of debtors and cash flow, it would be sensible to find out the level of cash inflow being achieved by major rivals. Every company should aim to be better than the DSO average for its own industry.

It is, however, worth remembering that the aim of good credit management is to contribute directly to profitable sales growth, and to be overzealous in collection and account approval could have a negative impact on sales. It has been successfully argued therefore that though a *reduction* in DSO is always desirable, maintaining DSO at its present level while at the same time sales have gone up by 150 per cent over the same period could well be seen as successful credit control – the investment in debtors has remained stable but sales have shot up, so profits should reflect that success.

The DSO can be used to show how an improvement in DSO performance can also give some degree of competitive edge. For example: You sell £14.6 million a year = £40,000 per day on average. Debtors run at about £2.4 million, that is, 60 DSO. Your competitor has similar sales but debtors of 70 DSO. So, you have £400,000 more cash to use (10 days × £40,000) Your competitor must borrow an extra £400,000 at, say, 10 per cent per annum, costing £40,000 off his net profits.

Another example of DSO contribution can be illustrated by the following. A company has sales of £22 million; makes an average profit margin of 4 per cent; and has unpaid sales of 72 DSO. If it collected cash just 10 per cent faster (65 DSO) its Profit and Loss Account and Balance Sheet would show the following improvement (Figure 2.6):

£000	at 72 DSO	at 65 DSO
Sales	22,150	22,150
Profit before interest (7%)	1,542	1,542
Debtors (= borrowings)	4,370	3,945
Interest expense (at 10% p.a.)	437	395
Net profit	1,105	1,147
NPBT as % sales	5.0%	5.2%
Increase in profit	-	42
Reduction in borrowings	-	425

Figure 2.6   10% cash collection improvement

It is relatively easy to collect cash 10 per cent faster, given top-level support, a good review of procedures and resources and a well-planned and directed strategy. To improve more than 10 per cent might well involve radical changes, and in any case, gradual targeted improvements are generally more successful and reduce the potential for negative customer impact.

Cash Targets

Following the DSO principle, it is not difficult to set cash targets to improve the level of debtors over time. DSO-based cash targets are covered in detail in Chapter 11, which concentrates on cash collections, but a simple example here will set the scene. If a company generally allows 30 days credit to customers but has a DSO of 65 days (as in the example shown in Figure 2.5 earlier), it might decide to target a one-day reduction each month for 12 months, to reduce the asset level to 53 days without detriment to sales efforts: June DSO 64 days – add July sales (31 days) giving a total of 95 days. With the new DSO target being 63 days, then the cash required in July equates to 32 days, that is, the cash to be collected in July would be the *equivalent of* 3/30 April sales plus 29/31 of May sales. The setting of a cash target is simply arithmetical, but achieving it needs specific approaches to larger customers. There are added benefits which make the task worthwhile, in that it·normally leads to better payment continuing in the future with less collection effort and better customer relationships.

Offering a discount as an incentive to prompt payment always looks inviting, but can rarely be afforded. Just as many companies have no real grasp of the actual costs involved in the granting and financing of credit, even fewer seem to realise how much they may be giving away by way of cash discounts. It may be, of course, that some element to cover cash discounts has been factored into the price of the goods, but this is rare – many companies have list prices and *trade* discounts, and some of those fall into the trap of offering cash discounts on top!

Just as a customer would be foolish not to take an offered cash discount, a supplier is unwise to offer one. The rate has to be high enough, say 2 per cent, to be attractive to a customer, but it can still be abused by being deducted by late payers. The real annualised cost of a cash discount is usually much higher than the seller's cost of money and as such it would be cheaper to suffer a 90-day overdue account than to give away 2 per cent for payment in 30 days. Better to establish firm net terms with customers and follow them up efficiently.

Discounts for prompt payment have a cost to the seller which can quite easily be calculated, and is best thought of in terms of the per annum, or annualised, rate of interest. There is a simple formula:

$$\frac{\text{Rate of interest}}{\substack{\text{Credit period} \\ \text{less the discount period}}} \times 100$$

By way of an example, terms of payment of 2 per cent discount for payment in 10 days against terms of 30 days net would be expressed as 2 × 360 divided by (30 – 10), which equates to 36 per cent per annum. It is therefore clear that what on the face of it might not have appeared to be unreasonable, has in fact a quite sizeable impact on actual credit costs. Figure 2.7 illustrates this further.

Credit periods								
30 days			60 days			90 days		
Discount rate period			Discount rate period			Discount rate period		
(%)	(days)	% p.a.	(%)	(days)	% p.a.	(%)	(days)	% p.a.
1	10	18	1	10	7.2	1	10	4.5
1	15	24	1	15	8	1	30	6
2	10	36	1	30	12	1	60	12
2	15	48	2	10	14.4	2	10	9
3	10	54	2	15	16	2	30	12
3	15	72	2	30	24	2	60	24
			3	10	21.6	3	10	13.5
			3	15	24	3	30	18
			3	30	36	3	60	36

Figure 2.7   Annual percentage costs of cash discounts

A photograph of Aunt Edna on the beach at Bridlington is the freezing of a moment in time. It gives no explanation as to what brought her to the beach, what she was doing up to that moment, or what she did next. Apart from the smile for the camera, it does not tell us either anything really concrete about

Aunt Edna, her state of mind, or health, or indeed her intentions. It simply records that moment in a very basic form. The debtors' figure on the ledger at any time is exactly the same as the snapshot of Aunt Edna. It provides the basic data of numbers and values, but no more. To say, therefore, that there is an amount owing of £23 million as at 31 March says nothing about how that sum is made up in any detail, and certainly of itself cannot give any guide as to the age and collectability of all the individual debts.

Finance directors will often look at the figure and judge the impact of such a level of debtors on the profitability of the company. They can have some indication of possible speed of cash intake by way of the DSO calculation, but what they cannot see is how much *can* be collected, and how much is tied up in unresolved disputes, awaiting credits or awaiting replacement goods. The total debtors figure does not by itself indicate the age of individual debts, and it is only when the totals start to be broken down by analysis that the true state of cash inflow can be both seen and predicted.

How collectable are the debts on the ledger? Are they new and worthwhile, or very old and mostly uncollectable? It is well known that the older a debt is, the harder it becomes to collect. Many experts in the collection of debts apply percentage probabilities to the age of debt, for example:

Age	Worth %
Current, that is, within terms	100
60 days overdue	80
180 days overdue	50
12 months overdue	10.

Are there a high level of queries and disputed accounts, and are these recent or long-standing? It may well be that the ledger represents a mixture of all these – mostly current debts, but with some old, some very old, some disputed, some with genuine customer queries yet to be resolved. The Aged Debt Analysis is the most useful management tool in this respect, showing at a glance the status of debts within the total. It is an established fact that for lenders, auditors, analysts and those on the acquisition trail, the liquidity of any company can be judged largely by the quality of its debtors.

Whether judging liquidity in general, or simply assessing the collectability of debts in particular, the analyst, the auditor, the lender and the acquisition predator look at the two main elements of the debtors ledger – age and risk. It helps if risks are coded to indicate an opinion as to the solvency of the buyer – for example, A (no risk), B (average risk), C (high risk), and so on – but even in the absence of risk codes, the details held in each customer file should point to degrees of risk. Some debts, already identified by the seller as uncollectable, may have Bad Debt Provisions shown against them, and it may also be that there is a special section of the ledger, headed Bad and Doubtful Debts, into which all those seriously uncollectable debts have been transferred for ease of identity. Such a section of the ledger also serves the useful purpose of clearing some 'dead wood' from the 'live' ledger and enabling uncluttered focus on those debts which are worthwhile.

The Aged Debt Analysis also, of course, by definition shows at a glance all the customer accounts by invoice age – not yet due, current, one month overdue, two months overdue, three months overdue and three months and over. On the balance sheet, debtors are a *current asset* and should be capable of conversion into cash within 12 months, and usually much sooner. There are many reasons for debts to be written off, usually insolvencies, but it is a sad fact that many debts are written off by companies simply because they have not been collected and have become so old as to be more difficult to achieve success. This is apart from the obvious effect of old age, in that any profit to have been derived from that sale has long been eaten up by interest costs and further pursuit has become uneconomic. In such circumstances, the passage of time has made proving the debt in the first place more problematical, staff at buyer and seller have come and gone, invoices or delivery notes have gone missing, and the whole scenario has become untenable.

Time is of the essence, and it is not an option to let debts collect themselves. The whole sequence of delivery, invoice and account collection is a disciplined time-constrained exercise, and the Aged Debt Analysis is the window on liquidity for anyone to peer through.

Many sales personnel are on a basic salary, with commission earned on sales, and each year, or sales period, they can be set targets for the following period. Achieving those sales targets can earn 'extras' over and above commission, which can range from cash bonuses, through a whole variety of gifts and incentives, to top awards of holidays, cars, and so on. In other words, it is an established feature of sales and targets to provide a varied array of incentives to encourage the meeting of those targets and the rewarding of such achievements. The same principle can apply to those whose task it is to turn sales into cash. It is doubtful if such collection activity earns holidays in the Bahamas, but bonuses and gifts are by no means uncommon. There are many ways to set targets for cash collection, according to company cultures and cash needs, but given that there is a clear list of debts becoming due on defined dates, plus other debts past their due dates, it is very simple to determine the expected cash, based upon that date plus the known payment habits of customers and various states of solvency.

Targets have to be achievable, even if difficult, because the surest way to demotivate any staff member is to set impossible aims. Total cash targets should comprise individual customer accounts, rather than simplistic overall percentages, and input into those targets should come from the collectors themselves. They know their customers, both from a payment habit perspective and from a culture and reality standpoint, and have the experience of actual collections to add to an accurate and meaningful collection objective. It will be for more senior management to verify that such targets are acceptable, again based upon culture and cash needs, but once accepted it becomes the collectors' commitment for that month, which can represent a considerable motivation to deliver.

There will be further discussion of cash targets and incentives in Chapter 11, but it is worth noting here that incentives can carry dangers. Just as it would be inefficient business practice to offer incentives to sales staff to bring in orders regardless of risk, and then expect uninvolved credit people to try to collect from customers who have no liquid resources, so too would it be to set cash collection targets that would ride roughshod over good credit management practice. It would be easy to collect from customers if there was no concern about repeat orders or future business – the essence of effective credit management is to educate customers to terms and to promote profitable trading.

Planning and Budgeting Debtors

Most people recognise the need for planning in some form or other, and would regard sudden whims or fancies as at best somewhat risky, and at worst foolhardy. Getting married, buying a house, going on holiday or changing the car usually involve forward planning, with arrangements to be made and eventualities covered. Starting a business and seeking cooperation and assistance from the bank entails a business plan, with all aspects of the proposed business operation from marketing through production to cash generation being part of the plan.

Financial planning in trading companies does in fact vary enormously. At one extreme, there is no advance planning at all, with day-to-day survival as the prime motive, borrowing what is needed at very short notice. At the other end of the scale, many multinational giants employ whole armies of planners and business analysts, who look at every aspect of the company's trading. They look at results, make forecasts based upon an array of 'knowns' and 'variables' (such as raw material costs, production expenses, wages, marketing expenses, and so on) and prepare budgets for the short, medium and long term.

The pressure for planning and forecasting can come from a variety of sources, and reaction to that pressure can have very significant impact upon day-to-day operations. It is well known, for example, that publicly quoted US corporations are required to report results quarterly, and that each quarter's numbers can strongly influence how the company proceeds in the following quarters. On the other hand, some planning has, by its very nature, to be long term. Building a new cruise ship incorporates a mass of planning on different levels, from design and construction through financial borrowing and outlay to actually earning income from fare-paying passengers – it could be many years before the ship actually earns profits for the owners and it may well take the whole lifetime of the ship in service for it to be seen to have paid for itself in total.

Cash planning is a crucial part of the overall process. As debtors are usually the largest company current asset, that asset should be constantly under close scrutiny. Debtors represent cash and cash is the lifeblood of any business – knowing what we have, what we are expecting to have and when will enable us to know what we can spend, and when. Since debtors are a dynamic but risky asset, it makes sound commercial sense to know how debtors are made up and to have a real 'feel' for the collectability of sales. The size and quality of the debtors ledger should be regularly reviewed by the credit manager, the finance director and the main board of directors:

- the credit manager is controlling the ledger directly on a daily basis;

- the finance director has an overview as and when required; and

- the board of directors are kept informed by regular reports for action as needed.

The way in which the size and quality of the debtors asset is reviewed should involve the following measurements:

1.   *Aged debt analysis:* listing all accounts in either alpha/numeric, or, better still, descending value order, with columns for current, one, two, three and over three months overdue, plus other details (these are described in later chapters). This measurement tool is used daily by the credit manager and is available for overview by the finance director.

2.   *Cash target sheet:* listing the debts comprising, say, 80 per cent of the month's cash requirement, however calculated, and showing actions taken, payments arranged and payments received. This would be used by the credit manager, and collectors, and updated daily.

3.   *Cash forecast sheet:* showing total amounts of cash expected, split by type of account, either as single totals or divided into daily or weekly totals for the month ahead. It is useful to show the DSO which would result if the forecast were achieved. This would be prepared by the credit manager and used by the finance director.

4.   *Monthly debtors report:* one page only, on the month just ended, showing total, current, overdue and disputed debtors, all in sections as required, with aged subtotals, and columns for last month and budget or forecast. A few lines of commentary should be included, to explain both exceptionals and ongoing actions. The report would be prepared by the credit manager and issued to the finance director and to the main board.

It may be necessary for the credit manager to also prepare and issue a separate schedule of disputed debts and unresolved customer queries. Although usually incorporated into the monthly debtors report as outlined above, there are circumstances where the level of queries or disputes is such that both the finance director and the main board should be aware of the impact on cash collection and cash inflow. There can be instances of queries appearing to get out of hand because of some change in processes or practices, and lack of response from those whose role should be to ensure customer satisfaction. In such circumstances, senior management should be involved in the task of putting matters right, and restoring the collectability of the debtors asset generally.

Summary

The management of the cash-producing debtors asset should be proactive, and not simply reactive or, worse still, passive. Sales are made to customers who vary in states of solvency and liquidity, and therefore they *must* be risk-assessed in order to be able to decide both credit worth and credit ability. It follows that collections then have to be organised to suit both volumes and levels of difficulty.

Cash inflow can be measured by the DSO method and speeded up gradually, over time, by reducing the ratio of days sales unpaid. Companies should be aware of their industry average DSO and set out to improve their own competitiveness by having faster cash inflow and fewer bad debts than their rivals. All key managers, including sales, should know and understand the meaning of *Net* profit margin, and be fully aware of their own company's net profit margin. They should not confuse 'net' with 'gross' – gross margins of 30 per cent or even 60 per cent still only produce net margins of 3 per cent or 4 per cent in many sectors of business. Understanding their own net margins should lead to an equal understanding of the cost of credit and therefore not be drawn into frittering away the NPBT in 'free' credit concessions. Nor is it usually profitable to 'buy' customers' loyalty by allowing them to defer payments.

Every company that grants credit to customers should have a simple structure of measuring debtors regularly, regardless of their size, and should be in a position to take prompt action to correct problem situations.

INSTITUTE OF CREDIT MANAGEMENT – JANUARY 2008

Introductory Credit Management: Level 3

Question 6: You are the credit controller for a local company. The company finances the trade credit it offers from its internal resources, that is, through operational cash flow.

    a)   Explain the potential problems that may arise from using operational cash flow to fund the credit period.

    b)   Describe three other methods of financing trade credit and in each case, assess the costs and benefits arising from their use.

3

Credit Policy and Organisation

Glen Bullivant

• A credit policy • The key features of a credit policy • Credit risk policy • Credit policy for export sales • The functions of a credit department • The role of the credit manager • Reporting structure and organisation • The qualities of the credit manager • Credit staff and their training •

A Credit Policy

THE BENEFITS OF HAVING A CLEAR CREDIT POLICY

If we accept that it is simply not good enough to sell, issue an invoice, sit back and wait for the payment to come in, then we must also accept that it is equally unwise to conduct any operation without really understanding its whys and wherefores. In a new business start-up, for example, the bank will ask various questions of the applicant for financial support. Looking at the business plan, high on the list will be, 'Will you be granting credit facilities to your customers?' If the answer is 'yes', then the next question will be, 'How do you propose to assess risk and collect accounts?' In other words, 'Have you drawn up a credit policy?'

The very word 'policy' may appear off-putting to some, but in essence all it means is 'this is our preferred way of doing things'. There can be nothing onerous or contentious in that definition, and in many spheres of any business operation, various policies will guide bosses, employees and customers alike. It should go without saying, of course, that any business should conduct its affairs in a lawful manner. There is legislation covering a range of issues, including health and safety, employee rights and benefits, environmental protection and so on. We drive on the left, tyres have a legal minimum tread depth and the movement of aircraft is under strict control. In other words, guidance exists in many spheres, whether as legally enforceable obligations, or as strong recommendations. To enter into any situation without a plan of action or any guidelines to cover problem situations can only lead to inefficiency, loss and possibly ultimate failure.

The goal of every credit manager is to achieve 'the highest level of profitable sales, over the shortest period of time, with the minimum of bad debts'. It always sounds easy when said quickly! That aim is consistent with the aspirations of every business seeking to succeed by exploring every way of maximising profitable sales. Both the business and the credit manager know that, to do this, it is naturally preferred that all customers and potential customers will be solvent, there to provide future business growth, and able to meet financial commitments on time. The reality is that in the modern, highly competitive market place where companies vie with each other for sales growth, it is inevitable that sales will have to go beyond the safer customers into the area of those who are a higher credit risk. That requires good routines for checking credit worth, systems for monitoring accounts and procedures for following up slow payers. It also means everyone involved knowing what we are doing, why we are doing it and the consequences for all if it is not done.

Every company does in fact have a credit policy, even if it does not realise it. It may not be written down anywhere, and may simply be passed through the organisation by word of mouth, continued as an accepted working practice and operated because the Chairman says so. Having no credit policy, either written or assumed, actually operates as a policy in itself because it says that our policy is 'to let staff do as they like'. Not to be recommended! The range of written credit policies is also quite vast, from one-page documents of intent, to lengthy manuals of detailed policy aims and even more detailed procedures and reports.

It is clear, therefore, that in the environment where competitive pressures require sales wherever and whenever they can be made, a clear and understood credit policy is of paramount importance. If all those sales, the more risky as well as the less risky, are to be turned into cash as quickly as possible, then management must support the credit operation directly, not just with policy words, but also with all the necessary resources, both human and technological. At the highest level, every company management, large and small, should say: 'Our company will grant credit to facilitate sales; will collect sales revenue efficiently; will service customer complaints rapidly; and will use the best people and technology to achieve this – all under the direction of the credit manager (financial director, financial controller and so on), who will be responsible to the board for the management of the vital debtors asset.'

If this is the declared intention of the board of directors, then it makes sense for the delegated credit manager or director to produce a brief document of policy and procedures, signed off by the chief executive and issued to all affected functions, and in particular sales, production, quality control and customer service. The very act of producing (or updating) a credit policy forces people to decide on responsibilities and levels of authority. Knowing 'who does what' in given situations removes any uncertainties and avoids people being left to stew in increasingly unpleasant and damaging juices. It also provides an excellent opportunity for credit and sales to get together on all customer and credit-related issues. There is no better way for a credit manager to explain the credit function than by addressing a sales meeting with the credit policy high on the meeting agenda.

ELEMENTS OF A COMPANY POLICY FOR CREDIT MANAGEMENT

'Is our cash inflow planned and reliable, or is it uncertain and handled reactively?' is the question that every company boss should ask at least once a year. To know that income can be relied upon, and that planned sales growth can be accommodated by planned revenue, sets the foundation for financial well-being. The following are usually found in successful companies:

1. *Credit policy:* credit as part of our overall objectives; responsibilities of credit staff and others.

2. *Credit objectives:* (stated criteria and ratios).

3. *Annual budget or plan* for one year ahead: monthly debtors results; monthly credit department expense.

4. *Organisation chart:* for credit staff and related functions.

5. *Procedures:* for credit and collections.

6. *Month-end report:* debtors results (and compared to budget); expenses (and compared to budget).

THE CONCEPT OF DEBTORS REQUIRING MANAGEMENT AS AN ASSET

There will always be factors outside the control of the credit manager, or of the finance director (see Figure 3.1) whose responsibility it is to manage the above structure, but nonetheless it does illustrate a planned and managed approach to a company's investment in the debtors asset. It also shows an understanding of the components that contribute to the make-up of that asset, and where and when intervention is required.

It is worth labouring the point about 'investment' in debtors. All companies can point to their investments in capital equipment, land, buildings, machinery and so on. For example, as a business progresses it may outgrow its existing premises, and hence need somewhere larger. This would involve finding the right premises, at the right price, and commensurate with the planned needs of the business over the following years. Investigations would consider the location, whether to rent or buy, to build or convert. All the financial factors would cover outlay now against expected return, increased overheads against increased sales volume, not to mention the disruption costs associated with any move. In other words, all the pros and cons of buying, renting and moving would be set against all the pros and cons of not moving at all. The company

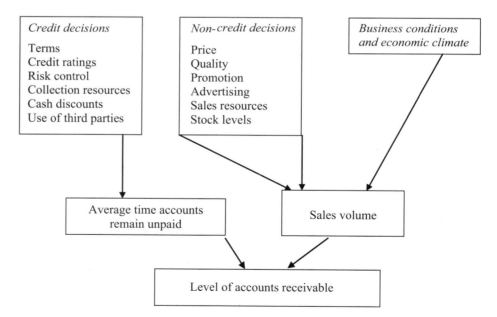

Figure 3.1   Factors affecting the level of investment in debtors

will determine the cost benefits involved, and finally quantify what it can afford to spend – or not, as the case may be.

Similarly, when upgrading plant and machinery, decisions have to be made as to what the company can afford to invest in new equipment and what that investment will bring as a return in the form of improved efficiency, higher productivity, reduced production costs and ultimately increased profitable sales. In other words, before moving premises or buying new equipment, full cost/benefit analysis is undertaken, and the bottom line has to be what the company can afford.

Debtors are no different when viewed as an asset. The company can only support a level of debtors which it can afford – to exceed that level, planned or unplanned, can lead to severe financial problems. Debtors can be planned as a specific investment of a certain amount of borrowed funds, or capital, for a stated period of time, for example, 'We will borrow £5 million to support our debtors asset to cover 60 days sales at any one time.' The total credit possible may be limited by banks imposing limits on borrowings, and the non-credit policy of 'selling all we can and then doing our best to collect the cash' is doomed to fail if the bank puts the brake on subsequent lending. Many a company has failed with a full order book simply because it has not quantified the level of debtors it can sustain and has run out of both funds and time.

Credit has to be on the shortest possible basis, all other factors being considered, because in the context of return on investment, net profit only comes from paid sales. That means that the company only sees the benefit of its investment in debtors when those debts are turned into cash – in the same way that it only sees the benefit of its investment in new plant and machinery when that plant and machinery is up and running efficiently. The time lag between investment and return must therefore be as short as possible.

Another credit investment approach might be that 'debtors should not exceed X per cent of annual sales'. If credit terms were 30 days from invoice and all customers paid on time, borrowing could be arranged for one-twelfth of the planned annual sales value, or 8.33 per cent. In reality, however, not all customers pay on time, sales staff may allow longer terms, some accounts may be in dispute, and so on, and therefore the investment of borrowed funds has to be greater. A more workable ratio would be 16 per cent, or 58 days of sales value. This approach can be more revealing, when debtors clearly exceed planned targets, and it is a useful way to illustrate to both sales and senior management the value of good credit control.

The overall benefits of having a credit policy can be summed up as:

- setting out the company's intentions for the granting of credit;

- removing any uncertainties about the authority levels and responsibilities for the setting of credit amounts, payment terms, risk categories and for accepting orders;

- providing an operating guide for credit staff;

- helping to eliminate 'special' credit deals by unauthorised staff;

- demonstrating a positive business attitude towards customers;

- simplifying the work of auditors and other visitors (and speeding their departure!) recognising, at the highest level in the company, the importance of the role of credit management and its contribution to sales and profits; and thus the need to support it fully.

The Key Features of a Credit Policy

No credit policy should be drawn up in isolation. Many factors contribute to the policy's actual nature and contents, which are discussed below, but the prime concern is to get everyone on board from the outset. Rules are always much easier to understand, and therefore more likely to be followed, if all participants have been involved in their formulation. A policy drawn up by credit *and* sales staff and then endorsed by the board stands a far greater chance of successful implementation than one worked out in an ivory tower and imposed by an unconnected faceless executive.

The credit policy should always take into account prevailing business conditions, both in respect of the company's own market place, and in the general economic climate.

Normal business conditions apply where:

- the seller is in a good financial condition;

- stock is carried at levels which satisfy customer needs;

- good profit margins are generally achieved;

- most customers pay between 30 and 60 days, with relatively few late payers;

- business is expected to continue in the same way.

It is has always been difficult to define 'normal' business conditions and most of those involved in credit management will experience, through the course of their careers, varying degrees of 'abnormal' business conditions. These may be brought about in a variety of ways, with external influences often gaining the upper hand, not to mention wars and pestilence. The Wall Street Crash of 1929, post-war austerity, the Wilson years, the Thatcher years, nationalisation and privatisation, Black Wednesday, the dot-com boom and crash, and the financial meltdown of 2008 – what can be considered 'normal'? They can, on the other hand, be self-inflicted, with unfortunate executive business decisions, the wrong product in the wrong place at the wrong time. Whatever the reasons, business conditions will influence the credit policy.

More generous credit is needed when:

- stock is abnormally high;

- demand is falling;

- the seller is creating a new market for new products;

- profit margins are higher than average;

- high sales expense has been incurred;

- high output is needed to recover overheads or plant costs;

- changes in style may risk surplus stocks or obsolescence;

- seasonal business leaves surpluses to shift;

- a customer is risky, but has a lucrative contract;

- a seller wishes to build up outlets;

- serious competitors must be followed.

On the other hand, *more restrictive credit* is needed when:

- low net profit cannot afford extra interest expense or bad debts;

- stocks are low and demand is high;

- products are tailor-made and cannot be resold elsewhere;

- the production process is very lengthy;

- customers have good cash flow (for example, supermarkets).

All these factors have a common thread – they are not solely the preserve of either the credit or sales functions. It is imperative, therefore, that sales and credit between them know all there is to know about:

- the behaviour of existing customers;

- the financial status of prospective customers;

- the company's future plans in respect of product and market.

Both sales and credit can help each other for the overall good of the business. There will be disagreement on some issues from time to time, but minor friction can be resolved by the senior board member. There should never be any circumstance where some disagreement at a relatively low level is allowed to fester and grow into open warfare. Friction between sales and credit damages the business and only benefits the competition. No company should *ever* allow non-communication between sales and credit, which is little more than a state of war between the departments. It is often the credit manager who has to work the hardest in this scenario, and running fast just to stand still is no real incentive to progress.

At the outset, it is important to remember all the ramifications of allowing goods or services on credit, and how, why, where and when credit is to be granted. It is also equally sensible to know all there is to know about the goods and services, the price structure, the way business is usually (or intended) to be conducted and how marketing is carried out. For example:

- Does the price include the costs associated with granting credit facilities, in particular the interest cost of payment terms and/or the average DSO for all accounts?

- Is it necessary always to grant credit in every sale, or would it be possible for some customers to pay deposits, or pay in full in advance, or on delivery?

- Does competition mean that not only must credit be allowed, but that it may be possible to gain marketing edge by offering longer or cheaper credit than competitors? If that is the case, is it possible to accommodate the cost?

- Must credit offerings to customers be uniform, or will it be possible to negotiate non-standard terms with specific customers? If the latter, what will be the circumstances, the criteria and the control?

- On the basis that 80 per cent of sales revenue usually comes from 20 per cent of customers, will the full financial standing of those major customers be fully investigated?

- Will senior people be designated, perhaps reporting to a senior manager, responsible for planning the overall investment in credit and will the senior manager himself/herself be controlling that plan personally each day?

The credit policy is designed to answer all these questions in full. Drawing it up involves input from finance, sales, marketing and general guidance from the board. All manner of plans and related costs have to be taken into account, as well as the nature of the product (and its shelf life) or the scope of the services provided. If starting from scratch, or if reviewing an existing credit policy with the object of updating it, those involved should set out the criteria by which they will operate:

1. What is the extent of available borrowing, or likely available borrowing? This will indicate the scope for allowing credit.

2. What will be the intended level of debtors? This means, in effect, what is the planned level of sales, and therefore (in connection with (1) above), what level of debtors as a proportion can be supported?

3.   What is the company's market strength? The position of a leader in the market will be far stronger than that of any of the many followers in the market.

4.   What are competitors doing? In a normal competitive environment, to succeed requires not only knowing what others are doing, but also avoiding being markedly out of line.

5.   What are the current and likely business conditions and business prospects? Interest rates and regulations are subject to change, and the prospects for a manufacturer of steam engines in 2010 are not what they were in 1910!

6.   What is the make-up of the customer base, both in the mix and the quality (small, large, blue chip, sole traders, well established, new and so on), and the possible volume of sales and customers to be handled? A limited number of very high-value customers will require disciplines which may well differ from those needed when dealing with vast numbers of small value customers.

7.   What will be the availability of good quality staff and the costs associated?

8.   What will be the process for credit checking? This covers the extent of information required, and the costs of obtaining that information. It should also take into account: customers, countries (for exports), action at order acceptance, action at pre-delivery.

9.   What are the credit objectives?

10.   What will be the required level of collaboration between sales and credit? This will extend beyond the basic 'who does what?' to the more detailed 'who will be responsible for what?'

11.   What will be the targets for customer service, returns, disputes and so on?

12.   What will be the cost of overdues and bad debts, and what will the effect be on net margins? Put another way, what are the bottom line

margins taking *all* costs into account, *including* overdues and bad debts?

13.   Will the credit control function be centralised or decentralised? There may well be a measure of centralised control at a certain level, with regions left with particular responsibilities, or fully controlled from a central location.

14.   What will be the line of command for credit responsibilities?

15.   It will be seen from the sample credit policy in Figure 3.2 that the policy does not have to be extensive or complicated by hard-to-follow equations – all that is required is a straightforward statement of aims and intentions:

•   the company's business and aims;

•   types of customers and business sectors;

•   conditions of sale, as issued to customers;

•   selected conditions of sale, requiring credit management: payment terms, cash discounts, special arrangements, extensions, instalments, and so on, interest charges, reservation of title;

•   bad debt level;

•   DSO objective;

•   system of vetting customers;

•   collection methods and timetable;

•   staff responsible for implementation of policy;

•   responsibility of other departments to help achieve firm's credit objectives.

Thus the policy will explain to all staff and management just how the company does its credit checking and uses the resulting credit ratings and risk

This policy is designed to improve the debtors asset and to meet the company's wish to arrange sound terms for every possible sale. It is the company's aim to gain financial benefit whenever possible from every profitable revenue source.

Assessment of risk Every customer will be given a *credit rating* and a *credit code*, established by the credit manager with the cooperation, where required, of sales personnel. To achieve meaningful ratings and codes, the credit manager will use financial and other data obtained from specialised credit reference agencies (Experian, Dun & Bradstreet and so on), together with trade and bank references when required. The credit rating and codes assigned to each customer will be reviewed annually, or more often if deemed necessary.

Credit rating This is the assessment of the liquidity of the customer. It is the maximum amount a customer can settle within the specified credit terms. If a credit rating is exceeded, the account will in all probability become overdue, which will reduce profitability and may even lead to a loss for the company.

Credit code This is the assessment of the solvency of a customer. Each customer will be coded A, B, C or D, according to its financial strength and perceived risk as follows: *Code A*: Negligible risk. All inter-company and government accounts, and large companies considered extremely unlikely to fail. *Code B*: Average risk. Customers who are not A, C or D. *Code C*: High risk and/or bad payment record. Small companies with little financial stability. New companies with no track record established – up to two years old. *Code D*: Cash only. No credit allowed. (Note: Customers who are coded 'C' are marginal credit risks, possibly with little future, so sales efforts should be focused on B and A customers. Note also that customers can move between codes following review by the credit manager based upon experience of payments, trading history and specific events, such as dishonoured cheques and so on).

New accounts No deliveries can be made on 'open terms' basis until a credit rating has been established. Where the prospective customer has requested immediate delivery, payment in advance is required. A credit application form will be completed by the customer. The credit manager will attempt to establish a line of credit appropriate to the volume of orders expected from the customer. After credit has been approved, a unique account number will be assigned by the credit department and used in all transactions and communications.

'Quick start' limits Intended for use in fast-moving sales operations, such as telephone orders. An immediate rating of £x will be established to enable same day delivery to the customer up to that value. No further orders will be accepted or delivered until the appropriate credit rating has been established and the credit line approved.

Figure 3.2   A sample credit policy document

Existing accounts It is the responsibility of the credit department to persuade all customers to pay their accounts within the specified credit terms. Collection activity will include letters, telephone, text message, fax and email. Customer visits in association with sales will be undertaken as required. With the exception of major accounts, all accounts becoming 30 days overdue will be subject to delivery suspension. Any orders on hand, or subsequently received, will be placed on 'stop list' until the overdue account has been paid. If overdue invoices are known to be in dispute, the credit department will ensure that disputes are resolved within seven working days, by credit notes to the customer if the dispute is genuine, or by payment if not. (Note: ALL sales managers will ensure that sales personnel are aware of the commitment to swift resolution of disputes and will instruct *ALL* sales staff accordingly). Pre-delivery, order values will be added to account balances and compared to the customer's credit rating. Orders for delivery to over-limit accounts will be referred to the credit manager for review.

Order entry All new orders will be added to existing orders plus the account balance for comparison with the credit rating. Orders in excess will be referred to the credit manager, who will urgently seek ways of accepting such orders (part-payment of the account, guarantees and so on). No order acknowledgement will be sent to the customer unless and until that order has been credit approved. In most cases, this process will be automatic, but referral to the credit department may be essential in some instances.

Credit/sales relationship The credit manager will undertake to inform the sales manager of any changes in customers' status which may affect sales to those customers. Monthly meetings will be held between credit and sales staff to exchange recent experience with problem customers, to decide action assignments, to discuss the credit activities of competitors, and to discuss any changes that may be required to credit policies or procedures.

Figure 3.2   *Concluded*

categories, as well as its approach to late payers. There should be no confusion or dispute between departments, in particular sales and credit. Nor should anyone be under any illusion about company policy in respect of use of the stop list, legal action or interest charges (if such charges are included in the policy). The company will send reminder letters, it will make telephone collection calls, it will use ethical collection practices – it says so in the policy.

What will give the credit policy its merit and its authority will be the fact that it has been approved and issued by the board. Senior management have endorsed its contents, and it is now to be effective the length and breadth of the organisation. Dated when issued, showing pre-arranged review dates, the document now has universal recognition – it should be part of any new starter's induction process in the organisation to be made just as aware of the credit policy as they are of any other significant company policy.

If it is remembered that the credit department is *not* the 'stop all orders' department but is the 'try to find a way of accepting all *profitable* orders' department, it follows that some customers carry a higher risk factor than others. Not all customers are 'no problem' or 'not to be touched with the proverbial barge pole'. A large proportion of any customer base is made up of those in the middle range of risk, neither very high nor very low risk. At one end of that middle spread, however, are the risky customers, with whom trading can be profitable over a limited period of time, provided strict controls are in place. By definition, high-risk customers are those still able to place orders today, but likely to fail over the following 12 months as indicated by financial reports, ratios, excuses, broken promises and so on. For such customers, a policy tailored to the risk that they represent is a sound addition to the general credit policy.

Credit Risk Policy

There are two ways of looking at risk policies for all customers:

1. *Maximum sales and no credit checking:* Higher sales, and therefore higher profits, are certainly possible, but so is high interest expense because of more overdues. There is a much greater risk of losses due to bad debts, and it is not difficult to calculate the volume of extra new sales required to recoup the losses from one bad debt, particularly in a low-margin environment. Add to that the expense of employing extra resources to collect ballooning debts on the ledger and dealing with myriad unknown customers with little or no knowledge or previous experience, and it is apparent that such profits as can be obtained from higher sales can soon disappear.

2. *Selective sales and credit checking:* Sales may be lower, but profits from those sales will be much more *reliable*. Fewer bad debt losses will be incurred, there will be more accounts paid to terms and less in the way of interest costs on overdues. Rather than throwing the sales net out as far and wide as possible, targeting of known better customers and reducing sales to bad risks ultimately leads to fewer collection resources and a general reduction in overheads.

To achieve profits from high-risk customers, it is necessary to have strict controls in place, from risk assessment until collection. That much is obvious, but it is just as important to know how much should be at risk as a percentage of total debtors as a maximum. In other words, the total value of high-risk debtors should be kept within known and decided limits. For example, a company may decide that 15 per cent of debtors can be in the high-risk category. If average debtors are £6 million, then the high-risk limit should be £900,000, that is, 15 per cent of £6 million. If credit assessments are accurate, then bad debt losses should only come from accounts in the £900,000 sector, apart from the totally unexpected collapse, which is usually rare. Both credit and sales staff know from this simple formula what efforts are required, both in selling and collecting, as far as high-risk customers are concerned, and the company is working within acceptable high-risk bounds. It would soon become apparent if the limit were exceeded, with drastic remedial action instantly required.

As a further precaution, it would be prudent to accrue additional provisions for bad debts, and to ensure that sufficient resources are allocated to monitor the high-risk accounts. As the purpose of a high-risk strategy is to be able to squeeze extra sales from customers identified as risky, it would be pointless to use up the high-risk limit with delinquent overdues or by extending terms in other areas. It also follows that collection procedures and/or application of the stop list must be firmly and swiftly enforced to ensure minimum exposure.

The credit manager should also study and report on the progress of the strategy, looking for variation or deterioration, with revision when needed. The selling price in the high-risk area *must* be commensurate with the fact that such sales *are* high risk – extra profit is necessary to offset extra losses and higher credit and collection expense. Losing sight of the objective is losing sight of the profit, and if it is not done properly, it is not worth doing at all!

Credit Policy for Export Sales

Chapters 17, 18 and 19 concentrate on credit matters relating to export, but it should be part of the company credit policy in much the same way as the policy and process for home sales. It is even more important to have a properly worked out export credit strategy because the pitfalls in export are additional to those in the home trade. There are differences in banking, currency, documentation, payment terms and credit cultures throughout the world, which all add to both risk and cost.

Successful exporting is a team effort involving sales and credit working in harmony. Support by export sales staff, in terms of account issues, possible terms of payment and collection processes to be employed, is essential. Equally, credit staff should be fully aware of all the difficulties encountered by sales people in overseas markets, and avoid treating foreign customers to UK-style strident collection methods. Much is different in export, not just in language or culture, and an understanding of international business methods is essential to effective professional export credit management. A company usually has good commercial reasons for entering or expanding a particular export market, and the export credit manager should seek profitable ways of supporting those reasons.

The questions that follow obviously apply to a first time exporter, but are also valid for exporters at all stages of experience. They carry an implication of what should be done, and discussing them can be very useful in producing good policy decisions. The right working procedures then become clear.

- Has the figure for working capital needed to support debtors been calculated by multiplying planned sales by the average *Collection* Period? (Note: *Not* the credit terms. The time between shipment and payment is usually much longer than in the home trade.)

- Has one individual been delegated to build up the company's export credit expertise? (Sharing it between functions can seriously fragment the experience needed.)

- Are there written procedures for order approval, credit terms, collections and financing methods, and do all affected departments have a copy of it?

- Who is authorised to visit, telephone, fax, email and write to overseas customers on credit and collection matters?

- Before assessing the credit worth of actual customers, is the ability of the foreign country to remit hard currency checked? In other words, is there a need for secure terms, regardless of the individual customer's own credit rating?

- Has the range of allowable credit terms for each market been specified, and where credit insurance exists, does the policy permit those terms?

- Is pricing quoted and billed in sterling or a specified convertible currency?

- Are payment terms shown on all quotations and acknowledgements?

- How are new customers checked for creditworthiness and is a list of essential credit questions given to the salesperson?

- Is there reliable local representation in each market to obtain credit data and help with accounts collection if required?

- Have credit agencies been signed up to provide rapid credit reports on markets as well as customers?

- Are all customers given credit ratings to avoid risky excesses? Are they reviewed regularly to adjust up or down for latest results?

- Will security or extra controls be required for extra risky accounts?

- Who authorises credit extensions?

- Does the Sales Ledger system show online data plus payments history and are problems and worsening trends reliably exposed?

- Does the system produce accurate invoices which clearly show payment terms and standard international data?

- For bank collections (cash against documents, bills of exchange and letters of credit), can all the essential documentation be gathered rapidly?

- Have good payment methods been arranged with each customer, utilising bank sort codes and account numbers?

- Is an export debtors report reviewed critically each month, leading to action assignments to improve problem situations?

- Are all accounts contacted just before due date (where appropriate according to local culture), just after if needed, and soon after that if promises are not kept?

- Is the policy clear on when to charge interest on overdues, how to use agents and associates, when to protest bills of exchange and how to act on bank advices of dishonour?

- Has the total cost of credit staff, documentation and export finance been budgeted in relation to sales and profits?

- Will the export receivables position be discussed regularly with the bank to ensure that the best possible finance is made available?

- Is factoring a cheaper credit management alternative?

International credit requires expertise to influence all the company activities which affect export payments and to bridge the gap between commercial and financial interests. Skills also have to be developed in the legal, documentation, shipping and banking areas. The export credit manager fulfils this role, as well as running all the daily credit and collection tasks. The role may simply be part of the credit manager's duties generally (many credit managers are responsible for both domestic and export), but particular expertise applies to export. The aims of debtor quality and the maximisation of profitable sales are the same in both home and export, but good export management involves more focused responsibilities for the export credit manager. For example, they should:

- in collaboration with sales management, arrange suitable payment terms for new and existing customers, in line with market risks, the status of the buyer and the cost of the resultant credit;

- maintain up-to-date status files on all active accounts;

- maintain up-to-date information files on all markets into which the company sells or intends to sell;

- set credit ratings for all buyers according to status, in line with the terms of payment and the level of sales, and review them at least once a year;

- check orders and shipments against credit ratings and take action in the event of excesses;

- monitor the payment performance of all buyers, with prompt contact to collect where needed;

- arrange transfer of foreign funds to ensure that cash inflow is as fast as possible;

- be thoroughly conversant with credit insurance facilities;

- have knowledge of the types of export finance to be able to advise sales and take part in negotiations if required;

- have knowledge of foreign currency to be able to advise sales on the use of currencies and to protect against exchange losses;

- maintain contact with overseas agents and representatives, to obtain credit status information and follow up outstanding accounts;

- prepare reports on the level and quality of export debtors as required;

- review, at regular intervals, debts needing Bad Debt Provisions;

- ensure that staff receive good training in topical export credit developments.

The Functions of a Credit Department

For many years, credit control or credit management was regarded in many businesses as simply the process of collecting debts. The less well informed may still hold this view, but in recent years the role of credit management has become significantly more extensively understood and appreciated. Although collection of funds remains one of the most important parts of the credit function, it is only a part.

The aim of good credit management is the maximisation of profitable sales over the shortest acceptable period and with the minimum of bad debt losses. To put it another way, the basic objective is to protect the company's investment in receivables or, in yet other words, to provide the best possible return for the company from the funds invested in accounts receivable (the debtors ledger).

The five main areas of operation cover:

1. *Assessment of credit risk:* trying to find ways of accepting and controlling all business, including high-risk opportunities.

2.   *Establishment of credit terms and limits:* taking into account the risk involved and liaising closely with sales.

3.   *Monitoring and control of debt:* ensuring that agreed terms are adhered to, all high-risk customers are kept under control, and action is taken promptly to resolve any queries or disputes.

4.   *Maintenance of the Sales Ledger:* ensuring that the customer master file is up to date and accurate, and that payments and other adjustments have been applied promptly and accurately.

5.   *Collection of payment:* in a manner which creates the optimum cash inflow while at the same time ensuring continuity of business.

It will be seen that, while item 5 (collection of payment) remains a prime credit task, close attention to items 1 to 4 greatly improves collection prospects. It is usually seen in successful firms that the greater the attention at the 'front end' (1 and 2), the less activity is needed at the 'back end' (5).

To achieve optimum results, the duties of the credit department are many and varied:

- risk assessment;

- credit ratings;

- credit risk categories;

- opening new customer accounts;

- maintaining and updating the customer data file;

- over-limit situations;

- order referrals;

- credit insurance;

- bad debts and insolvencies;

- legal action;

- customer meetings;

- support for marketing information;

- cash collection;

- cash allocation;

- planning levels of debtors;

- planning departmental expense;

- reporting, departmental and corporate.

The Role of the Credit Manager

Below the level of the board of directors, somebody has to be responsible for running the credit function on a day-to-day basis. Although that task requires someone with full management responsibility, the reality in some organisations is that there is no one who fits the bill, so the finance director – the board member nearest to the 'action' – has to take on the role. 'The credit manager's job is one of the few jobs in a company where the responsibility exceeds the authority' – so said Dennis Williams, one-time Credit and Treasury Manager for Texas Instruments, and a very experienced authority on credit-related matters. Not a flippant remark, since it is true that a credit manager has the responsibility for an asset (debtors) worth, possibly, many millions, but does not always have the actual authority to do what is expected. The difference between responsibility and authority is therefore a 'gap' which has to be filled by a talent for persuading other managers to do the right things all the time.

This can be illustrated by listing the company's expectations of the credit manager:

- contribute to increasing profit;

- contribute to obtaining sales;

- speed up cash flow;

- reduce borrowings;

- improve customer relations;

- use cost-effective systems;

- develop motivated staff.

The list shows that the expectations encompass every aspect of credit management in its most professional sense. Not all people can have these abilities (see 'The qualities of the credit manager' below). There has long been confusion over job titles and related responsibilities, often brought about by employers not appreciating what they were actually expecting their credit people to do, and by some credit people themselves attaching some status, mythical or otherwise, to what is merely a job title.

It is now generally accepted that 'credit controller' is usually a job which is subordinate to a credit manager or credit control manager. For example, a credit manager may have six credit controllers, each handling a different section of the ledger and each with specific authority and responsibility limits. The credit manager is in overall control of the credit function, though in smaller organisations it may be the finance director who is responsible for credit management and has credit controllers to undertake the ledger work. There are group credit managers, running regional credit functions up and down the land, each regional office having its own credit manager and credit controllers. There are many other variations, such as: credit sales manager; manager, credit and collections; and general credit manager. Some customer service managers have credit as an integral part of their duties and responsibilities. Credit management is increasingly being seen by many as a fundamental customer service function, so whereas customer service managers may have had credit as part of their duties, it would perhaps now be more accurate to say that credit managers now have customer service as part of their function.

It is not difficult to see why this should be so. For many years, professional credit managers argued that a satisfied customer, all other things being equal, was far more likely to pay than a customer who had been let down in some way. That being so, it was therefore in everybody's interest, not least the credit manager because he or she was the person entrusted with the cash collection role, to see that the customer was satisfied with the goods or service.

It is also true to say that credit staff became customer service staff by accident over the years – if a collector called a customer, was told a tale of woe and grief by that customer and henceforth proceeded to sort it out then sure enough, the next time that customer had a query of any kind, who was the first point of contact? The collector who had sorted him out before!

Whatever the job title, the duties of the person in charge of the credit function are:

- running the credit department;

- analysing credit risks and obtaining security when needed;

- collecting accounts;

- dealing with collection problems beyond routine stages: devising special letters to customers, discussing debts with sales offices, using third parties such as collection agencies, handling compromise settlements, processing insolvency cases, recommending write-offs;

- applying payments to accounts, approving cash discounts, banking cheques, maintaining cash book records (in larger companies, such activities may be undertaken by different departments – the credit manager still needs to be confident of accuracy – and in SMEs almost certainly the credit manager is responsible for the function);

- maintaining customer data files, including credit ratings and payment trends;

- checking customer creditworthiness to establish suitable credit ratings and risk codes, and country status reports for exports;

- fixing payment terms for export customers;

- supervising credit activities of branches and depots;

- coordinating credit activities with other departments;

- developing good relations with banks, credit organisations and so on;

- training staff as required;

- keeping top management fully informed via reports and analysis;

- setting cash targets to meet company plans;

- contributing to sales conditions;

- contributing to company business planning;

- achieving targeted DSO and aged debt plans;

- contributing to debtors budgets and forecasts;

- measuring and reporting debtors results;

- budgeting and controlling annual departmental expense;

- recruitment, training and motivation of staff;

- arranging a job succession plan.

Duties are aimed at achieving objectives and those objectives for the credit manager can be more easily broken down into:

- the assessment of the creditworthiness of customers;

- helping sales staff to obtain maximum business within acceptable limits of risk;

- protecting the investment in debtors via daily credit and collection controls;

- achieving the planned intake of cash by competitive methods to attain cash targets;

- keeping within an acceptable level of bad debts by closely monitoring risky sales;

- improving the return on assets by reducing the debtors ratio to sales over agreed timescales; and

- increasing customer loyalty via personal contacts and constructive attitudes.

A truly motivational objective for the credit manager would be: 'Achieve planned debtors/sales ratios – at the planned cost of doing so.' This can then be applied firmly to separate targets, including specified reductions in:

- DSO;

- values overdue totals;

- overdue percentage;

- credit terms;

and improved:

- payment methods (for example, more direct debit accounts);

- security for the more risky accounts;

- age analysis quality.

Reporting Structure and Organisation

The reporting lines for credit management have been the subject of heated debate amongst credit managers for many years. As a function which on the face of it handles money, it has long been held that credit management sits more comfortably within finance or accounting. There are some who argue that promoting profitable sales places it squarely in the sales area, and that reporting to the sales director is more natural. Others see it as important that reporting lines are separate from both sales and finance, and thus go directly to the managing director or chief executive. Another view is that asset control is a treasury function, especially if a large proportion of receivables is generated from export sales.

A further aspect involves customer service, as referred to above. It could be said that the customer service focus may be more sales-oriented than finance, but the reality is more that credit control is very much part of the overall customer service sphere of operation.

Because of different company cultures, it is not possible to be definitive over the best 'home' for credit management, though undoubtedly the credit manager is the bridge between finance and sales. As such, he or she has a degree of comfort under either umbrella, but as credit is regarded by most as a financial function, it should report to the finance director, financial controller, chief accountant and so on.

Some of the more obvious pros and cons may be:

Responsible to:	Advantages	Disadvantages
Sales	Credit becomes sales-minded	Credit sense may give more aware of company goals way to higher sales
Accounting	Can influence cost and profit	May not receive adequate priorities sales data or cooperation
Treasury/Finance	Close identity of interests	Isolation from daily sales and finance activities

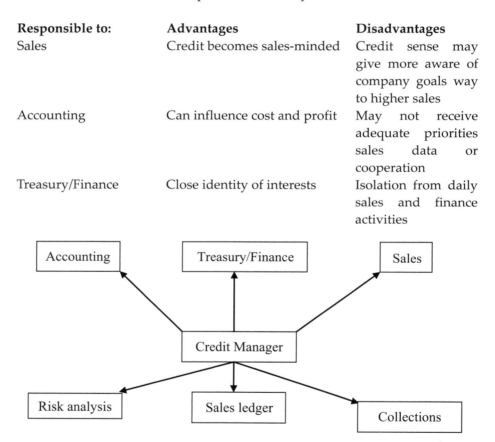

Figure 3.3   Example of credit department reporting structure

The number of people to be employed in the credit department and how they are organised will depend on the number of customer accounts and what tasks are required. Many companies expect each credit person to perform a variety of roles, while others will have specific staff for specific duties. In general, the department will:

- maintain the customer data file;

- operate the Sales Ledger;

- allocate the cash received;

- analyse risk;

- approve orders and dispatches for credit;

- operate the credit insurance policy;

- undertake collection activity.

If the Sales Ledger is divided up, say, alphabetically, then some companies would put credit controllers in charge of each section of the ledger and would expect them to be responsible for all aspects of their section. A typical controller's day in such an environment would begin with cash matching and allocation, updates to the customer file from correspondence received, including amendments to names and addresses, followed by opening new accounts in their section and notifying all concerned. When all the 'housekeeping' was complete, collection activity would be undertaken. This scenario is by no means unusual, even in large companies, and is quite the usual process in the SME sector.

It is quite normal for the activities of Sales Ledger management (housekeeping) and risk analysis to be split, with specialist staff to carry out the risk assessment tasks without any involvement in other duties.

In other words, credit staff could be 'generalists' or 'specialists'. Generalists do everything on their accounts, while specialists do only the credit checking, or the collections, or the Sales Ledger work.

On average, generalists cannot adequately cope with more than 600 trade credit accounts without results suffering, and to attempt more in most circumstances would be a false economy. In today's climate of 'downsizing', companies find it almost irresistible to expect more out of less, but to overload the generalist and then expect the same accuracy, attention to detail and high level of customer service and involvement would be unrealistic. Quality will inevitably suffer. It is also easy to forget that in trade credit (there are different criteria for both consumer and export credit) a trained telephone collector can usually only effectively handle about 20 to 30 calls per day. This assumes that about 50 per cent of all calls made require a call back (messages left, follow-up on promises and so on). With an average 20 working days in a month, this equates to about 400–600 accounts per month. Organisation and staffing levels are therefore very closely allied to numbers (and quality) of customer accounts.

The credit manager must also establish where the authority and responsibility lie for resolving customer disputes and queries. Some disputes may be quite simple – errors in delivery, for example, or pricing – but resolution finally comes with the production of the credit note to correct the errors. Speed is vital, because collectors can only collect that which is collectable. Unresolved queries cost money directly (financing the debtors ledger) and indirectly (customer satisfaction). Once resolved, who raises the credit note? If not agreed, who tells the customer? The whole subject of queries and resolution will be covered in Chapter 9, but what becomes increasingly clear is the question of 'ownership' – if the credit manager is responsible for cash collection and for protection of the investment in receivables, it follows as naturally as night follows day that the credit manager owns the query resolution process. In other words, yet again we see that the credit manager is the customer service manager, if not in name, certainly in fact. A final note on the reporting line for the credit manager and his/her place in the total organisation structure. Reference has already been made to those circumstances where, for example, the task of cash allocation is separated from that of risk assessment or collections. It is growing business practice, chiefly in large national or international companies, to operate centralised 'shared service' functions, where the cash matching and posting is undertaken for a variety of member companies, separate from any risk assessment or collection operation. Whilst not in itself a bad thing, there is a danger that the credit manager loses sight of some aspects of what had hitherto been regarded as their own responsibility. It is important, therefore, for the credit manager to have absolute confidence in any shared service and ideally have a direct reporting connection with the head of that individual function.

The Qualities of the Credit Manager

The credit manager must:

- be able to influence others;

- have good communication skills;

- have top-level support;

- perform consistently;

- be experienced in successful credit techniques.

Not everyone will make a good credit manager, just as not everyone can be an airline pilot or a brain surgeon. There is more to success in any role than knowledge, or experience, more than just technical competence or even personal drive. Traditionally, the credit manager has been seen by many as 'a Jack of all trades, and a master of most of them'! That may be something of an exaggeration, but it is true that some of the roles expected of the credit manager require a level of commercial expertise and understanding which goes beyond the boundaries of some more specialised professions, such as the tax accountant or the matrimonial lawyer. Risk assessment involves balance sheet analysis, as well as interpretation of factors such as market position and trade experience. Collection activity requires both interpersonal skills and commercial awareness. When the managing director hears that customer X has 'gone bust' it is almost certain that they will turn to the credit manager to find out what to do next, so knowledge of insolvency is required. Issuing a Court claim or a writ means knowing not just a good solicitor, but also the ramifications of taking one action as opposed to another.

A good place to start would be to look at personal qualities, because much of the credit manager's daily role will be dominated by matters of personality. Tact – knowing when and when not to, how and why. Diplomacy – being right, being sure of the facts and convincing others who disagree at the outset, for whatever reason – requires careful persuasion and also patience and understanding. The authors of reminder letters to be sent to customers know they must be 'firm, but fair' – so too must the credit manager – and be seen to be so by his or her staff.

Good organising skills are essential, as is the ability to handle people. No credit manager will want to do every job in the department (even though they should be able to), but they must know and encourage the different capabilities of staff, to get the best out of each of them in each task they perform. Good judgement of people does not stop with staff. It is a prerequisite for believing the customer or not when they promise to pay, or makes a complaint. Persistence and tenacity, accounting ability and a good telephone manner are in there somewhere together with a pleasant personality and, above all, integrity. It goes without saying that the credit manager should know all the techniques, ancient and modern, of credit management itself and not be afraid to make judgements and take those risks which calculation and analysis have shown to be worth taking. Not every one will be a winner, but the good credit manager is usually right far more often than wrong. When all is said and done, credit granting is all about calculating the risk, making the judgement and going with the decision. For anyone connected with export, some linguistic talent is an advantage because, in spite of popular opinion, not everyone in the world speaks English. Even though English may be regarded as the universal language of business, the impression gained by the customer when spoken to in their own language is one of a supplier who cares about customers. That can deliver an important PR advantage.

The credit manager needs to motivate staff. The prerequisite for this is to determine what drives each and every member of staff and find ways of encouraging each one according to those individual needs. To get the best out of people requires *knowing* them – not all respond to the same stimulus, and not all will be capable of doing every task. A prime example is in collection activity – he is nervous and uncomfortable using the phone, but his ledger work and letter writing is flawless; she cannot cope with ledgers and columns of figures, but has a telephone manner that wins every time. Who does what is no contest, then, except that if training is required, it is clear who needs what.

A team is made up of people with different abilities and motivations – those who can or cannot use the phone effectively, those who can or cannot readily reconcile accounts – and the aim of each is to succeed in whatever it is that they are doing. Mix the group, and the team benefits from the success of each. The team has an objective, for example, a collection target set by the credit manager. It should be a tough but achievable target; and achieving that goal brings rewards to the team, the efforts of each participant being recognised for the value of their contribution.

The manager must have the ability to support as well as motivate. In fact, strong support from the leader is itself a motivating factor for each member of the team. Staff want to believe that the manager can resolve those problems that lie within his or her domain, and would also respond to a manager who has earned the support of senior management. Managing staff is never easy, and there are as many textbooks on people management as there are football club managers who survive a season with the same club.

Fundamentally, however, it is a matter of personality, observation, motivation and awareness of anything that might act as a stumbling block or a source of encouragement. The credit manager should be able to lead from the front, push from behind and scrum down in the middle. But mainly, to lead.

Credit Staff and Their Training

Staff numbers depend upon volumes but also upon systems in operation and the support that can be expected from today's computerised environment. Sadly, not all credit managers are properly consulted when new systems are installed, which may explain why some are reluctant to become involved in specifying their requirements when such consultation does take place. Chapter 10 looks at computer systems for credit management in some detail, so we shall confine ourselves here to examining computer support in so far as it concerns staff.

Computer systems serve to remove all the deadly chores from the day-to-day operation of a credit department. The computer is a great help in risk assessment, payment history, records of promises kept and broken, production of invoices, statements and reminder letters, cash allocation and other features of the daily grind. Whatever is done by the computer, it represents something that was previously done by a person, thus freeing that person's time for something more expert. Long gone are the days when it took weeks to open a new account and set up the ledger details. Long gone, too, should be the days when cash was updated weekly, or even overnight. Now, with real-time cash allocation, if the screen display says that the account has not been paid then it has *not* been paid.

What is needed are people who are computer literate, able to find their way round keyboards and systems, as well as having the personal communication skills for collection activity, customer contact and interdepartmental cooperation.

Implicit in all staff management is staff development – enhancing those skills which exist, introducing those that do not, and developing those that may become necessary through changes in work patterns or even company ownership. Training is the key to all success, and the pity is that many companies do not see investing in their staff in the same light as investing in new equipment or new processes. Staff represent an expensive outlay, but they are also the company's greatest asset. As such, they have to be worth at least the same measure of care and attention as that lavished on the new lathe or the new R&D facility. The returns will far outweigh the investment.

External training is available from a variety of sources, with foundation courses run by commercial organisations such as Dun & Bradstreet or the Institute of Credit Management (ICM). The ICM itself now provides Level 2 to Level 5 diplomas in credit management, delivered through colleges, in-house on company premises and online, as well as in-house training in specific areas such as telephone collection techniques, negotiation skills and so on.

Many organisations hold seminars on many credit management topics throughout the country (the ICM alone runs over 150 such seminars and one-day courses each year). The topics range right across the credit perspective, with a wide selection of speakers and presenters, many of them practicing credit managers with many years' experience in consumer, home trade and export. Details of some of the courses available can be found in the Appendix.

The ultimate aim for any credit professional has to be membership of the ICM, the only professional institute for credit managers in the UK, with membership in the region of 9000. The ICM has 26 branches throughout the UK and Northern Ireland, each one holding its own series of meetings, and some (notably Merseyside and North Wales, Wessex, and East Midlands) additionally holding Annual Conferences. The various Scottish branches of the ICM hold an Annual Conference to focus on particularly Scottish aspects of credit management, of which there have been a number since devolution.

Perhaps the most thorough training in credit management available today is the personal study necessary for the ICM examinations to qualify as a Graduate Member of the Institute (MICM(Grad)). Tuition is available through a number of local colleges, as well as by distance learning, together with the growing availability of web-based support.

'On-the-job' training also has great value, provided that it is part of an overall training programme. A sustained period of on-the-job training in credit assessment and balance sheet analysis is useful, since these skills are not acquired quickly or by theory. Some credit functions can only be learned by experience, but are learned faster if the credit manager is on hand to give support and encouragement, evaluate and advise. No new recruit should ever be sat alongside a busy member of staff and simply left to get on with it, just as a learner driver should be taught by a driving school – a parent can provide practise but should not be passing on bad habits!

When the credit manager identifies specific needs, then relevant training can be arranged – telephone collection techniques, effective letter writing, interpretation of balance sheets, the dos and don'ts of emails, and so on. Companies and organisations that run credit seminars in hotels, conference centres and in-company (on site) can be asked to tailor their sessions to individual client needs. Where several staff are available for training, in-company sessions can be much cheaper than external courses and benefit from being tailored to specific company requirements. However, external courses and seminars expose staff to people from other companies and can open eyes to better ways of doing things.

A mixture of internal and external training is ideal, but whichever methods are used, the credit manager should hold a debriefing session with the delegate(s) and generate action assignments to use the knowledge gained. A manager is well defined as a person who achieves the required results through other people. A credit manager, therefore, is only as good as his or her team and it is a sensible manager who ensures that the team is thoroughly trained and equipped.

INSTITUTE OF CREDIT MANAGEMENT – JANUARY 2009

Advanced Credit Management: Level 5

Case study: Trade Credit

Toygam Ltd., a manufacturer of toys and games, with sales of £95m, 40 per cent of which is to the export market, is in the process of relocating its entire operations from the South East of England to Doncaster in Yorkshire. As this is a major project it has naturally been decided to carry out the move in a number of stages. For now the manufacturing operation will remain in the South East until the sales and admin functions have been completed and are fully functional.

Although offered a generous relocation package, the existing credit manager has declined the offer and you have been recruited to replace her. At the selection process, it was your people management skills that impressed the interview panel and secured you the job. These skills will be put to early use, as one of your first tasks is to recruit a team, which will form the new credit management department. Only two of the existing staff decided to relocate, so you will require eight staff, two of whom will be at supervisory level.

Together with your boss, the finance director, you will decide the organisation's structure and staff training requirements. While all of this is going on, you will also be required to coordinate the department's move, which, in the early stages, will involve you in travelling quite extensively between the two sites.

Task:

- Prepare a suggested organisation structure in chart form with a brief description of the responsibilities of each role.

- Draw up a person specification for the non-supervisory roles.

- Explain how you would: identify a training programme that meets the needs for staff; assess the benefits of training for both the company and the individual.

- Bearing in mind your other responsibilities, suggest how you might handle the coordination aspect of the move, ensuring that you maintain the status quo in terms of performance.

PART II
Credit Terms and Conditions of Sale

4

Credit Terms and Conditions of Sale

Glen Bullivant

• Credit terms • The factors affecting credit terms • Conditions of sale • Types of credit terms • Other credit terms • Cash discounts • Late payment interest • Progress payments, retentions and consignment accounts • Methods of payment •

Credit Terms

We have already established, in Chapters 1 and 2, that there are both benefits and costs for the seller in granting credit. No doubt, sellers would be tickled pink if all sales were for cash only, if only because, by definition, the sale is only a complete sale when it has been paid for. In reality, however, trade needs credit to stimulate sales growth, and credit enables sales to be made which would not otherwise be possible. Offering time to pay adds value to the relationship between seller and buyer. It promotes customer loyalty and encourages repeat business.

For the professional credit manager, it is difficult to think of anything more important in credit sales than the actual credit terms agreed between seller and buyer. There can be a number of influences on the decision of what/how/when in respect of credit terms, and it is important not just to view credit terms in the context of what is 'normal' or what 'others' do. Contract negotiations involve many factors, from colour and price to delivery and after-sales, and making the sale, getting the best deal, landing the profitable job is the aim of all concerned. The terms of credit on offer are the hub of the contract; they encompass the planned profit, the sellers' need for cash funds and the competitive situation.

Too often, decisions regarding credit terms are not given the careful consideration they deserve – sales may be competed for at any cost – and some firms ultimately pay the price for that lack of care. If the company is in a strong or even dominant position in its particular market place, this lack of concern may only be peripheral. It is unprofessional by any measure, and most businesses operate in a competitive environment, where attention to every aspect of trading is vital to success or even survival. In any event, good businesses always aim for maximum success and this can only be achieved when they are run by professional managers who know what they are doing and who consciously manage all the factors which influence the business. Allowing credit professionally is certainly a prime item among those.

The Factors Affecting Credit Terms

A number of factors can influence the choice of credit terms, which may well be specific to the trade or product. Most businesses have an environment of traditional custom and practice. However, some factors are common to all businesses, and for most sellers, the following points will almost certainly apply:

- the seller's strength in the market;

- the credit terms which the seller gets from its own suppliers;

- the availability of the capital needed to finance sales and if this is to be borrowed, at what cost?;

- the volumes of sales and the range of customers;

- the profit margin;

- any special payment arrangements, including longer terms and/or instalments;

- competitive pressures (restricted facilities may be called for, but where competitors offer more advantageous terms, it may be necessary to match them);

- the character of the market. for example, the shorter the shelf life of the goods, the shorter the credit terms should be; compare broccoli with greenhouses

- the period the buyer will have the goods, for example, if the buyer will resell them at once, payment should be prompt. If the buyer needs time to resell the goods, the credit facilities may also need to be extended;

- the condition of the customer's finances and the risk for allowing time to pay – the amount at risk is not just the monthly total of sales to the customer but the maximum total unpaid at any one time;

- seasonal and incentive factors. Sales may be greater at certain times in the year. Incentives to boost sales may include extra time to pay. The effect of this on the total exposure, its risk and cost must still be acceptable;

- the existence of any form of protection for the exposure, such as a legal charge, third-party guarantee, a Retention of Title clause or credit insurance.

Many businesses, large and small, will add to the above list, according to their own special circumstances. These might involve the time involved in the production of the goods and/or whether the product is customer-specific – making bespoke products for one customer carries its own special risks in respect of non-payment, with or without Retention of Title, for example. If the business has a monopoly, it may want to try to enforce its own terms and conditions, which customers may take or leave, though there could be legal consequences! Other specific factors may embrace the company's marketing policy, possibly involving quality considerations, the repetitive character of sales and whether the products are for luxury or utility purposes. The common thread through all these factors is the decision whether to trade on restrictive or more liberal credit terms.

A bone of contention frequently aired between sales and credit management is the interpretation of the credit terms. In reality, credit terms should not be subject to interpretation – they should be clear and unequivocal by definition. The application of the terms, however, may well be subject to individual action. Thirty days net should mean the same thing to both sales and credit, and equally should be clear to both seller and buyer. The credit terms decided upon, therefore, should be more than just the right ones – they must also be simple to understand and be capable of enforcement. Weekly credit terms, for example, would be meaningless unless the seller and the buyer both agree on what actual day payment is to be made. An example of poor terms is: 'payment 15 days after receipt of invoice'. The date of receipt of the invoice can only be guessed at by the seller and would certainly be difficult to prove. The agreed terms should always have a clear due date, or be capable of arriving at one without disagreement.

Having agreed the credit terms, with a due date which is clear to all concerned, the seller has a responsibility in his own best interests to ensure that the customer keeps to those terms. If a seller consistently fails to enforce the originally negotiated and agreed credit terms, he is condoning late payment. The customer knows that his pattern of late payment has been accepted as satisfactory by the seller, and that a precedent has been established. The outcome is that the seller cannot now enforce the original credit terms because he has endorsed 'new' terms – the only option would be to sit down and start the negotiation process all over again. This scenario is all too common, and the professional credit manager should never allow it to develop.

Conditions of Sale

Everybody knows about small print! The reverse side of order acknowledgements or quotations are favourite loitering grounds for masses of paragraphs and words about shortages, breakages, interest, title to goods, storage or temperature control and a variety of other matters. Conditions of sale may be small in print, but are big in content and importance.

Conditions of sale are the prerogative of the seller as covered by Act of Parliament. Legislation overrides all trading activities via the Sale of Goods Act, the laws of contract, restrictive trade practices, the Consumer Credit Act, the Competition Act and other legislation intended to achieve fair trading for both seller and buyer. They do not just protect the buyer.

Every order, whether written or oral, has all the ingredients of a contract in the eyes of the law. There is an offer to sell on the part of the seller and an acceptance by the buyer. Both parties enjoy a consideration (the goods or service for the buyer and the payment for the seller) and they act voluntarily in the sale, whether it is for cash in advance or on a credit basis. Credit terms are an integral part of the contract terms and every contract must be free from duress (that is, undue pressure to agree) or onerous conditions. A monopoly situation which enables a seller to impose onerous credit terms is always vulnerable to legal pressure.

The seller's conditions of sale for long-term agreements are best established by a written contract, which reflects the commitments of both sides. To be enforceable in law, a seller's conditions *must be known to the buyer at or before the time the contract is made.* This can be done via brochures, catalogues, price lists, written quotations, special letters or orally. An order confirmation, or acknowledgement, is probably the vehicle most widely used for this, and conditions are often restated on delivery notes, invoices and statements subsequently issued by the seller. Delivery notes, invoices and statements are *after* the event, however, and can only be useful as reminders of conditions of sale; they should not be the first indication.

The credit manager and anyone else pursuing a customer for a debt should always be absolutely sure of which documents or witnessed conversations made the conditions of sale known to the customer – *before the goods or service were supplied.*

Types of Credit Terms

As part of the overall marketing mix, there is a fundamental relationship between the credit terms on offer and the sales to be obtained. Ideally, credit periods should be as short as are necessary to obtain the sale, and should also be stated as straightforwardly as possible to ease the sale process. Apart from the great mass of transactions in retailing on a cash or credit card basis, most sales between companies (trade credit) are on 'open account' terms. Open account represents the simplest basis of supply by the seller, but must always state a period of credit. An invoice is sent for each transaction, and the seller waits until the due date for payment. Some transactions can be less 'open', with various degrees of security being sought, and in export it is quite usual to sell on the basis of sight drafts, promissory notes or letters of credit. These are instruments of payment, which, together with the more usual cheques and direct debits, are used for open account credit terms.

The normal range of terms associated with open account are related to delivery or time. Note: the term 'cash' usually means cash or cheques, though in certain circumstances cash can mean coin of the realm or bank draft – in other words, cheques are acceptable unless circumstances, such as a cheque being dishonoured, dictate otherwise.

Payment related to delivery:

- *CWO:* cash with order;

- *CIA:* cash in advance;

- *CBS:* cash before shipment;

- *COD:* cash on delivery;

- *Net:* payment due on delivery (a weak term – should be avoided);

- *CND:* cash next delivery;

- *PF:* pro forma, that is, cash before shipment.

Payment related to time:

- *Net 7:* Payment seven days after delivery.

- *Net 10:* Payment 10 days after delivery (terms which involve time from 'delivery' will require evidence to establish the delivery date and therefore the calculated due date).

- *Weekly credit:* Payment of all supplies Monday to Sunday (or as otherwise defined) by a specified day in the next week.

- *Half-monthly credit:* Payment of all supplies made from the 1st to the 15th of the month by a specified date in the second half of that month; payment of the 16th to month-end by a second date in the first half of the next month.

- *10th and 25th:* International terminology having the same meaning as half-monthly credit but specifying payment by the 10th of the month covering supplies from the 16th to month-end and 25th of the month covering supplies made in the first half of the month.

- *(Net) monthly account:* Payment of all invoices dated in one month by the end of the following month, for example, all February invoices to be paid by the end of March. (Note: This is often a disputed matter between sales and credit staff! Net Monthly Account means payment *by* the end of the following month, not *at* the end.)

- *Net 7 prox:* International terminology, having the same meaning as monthly credit but meaning payment by the 7th of the following month.

- *Two-monthly credit:* As for monthly account but with one extra calendar month. Three-monthly or longer is indicated by the appropriate figure.

- *30 (or 60 or 90) days:* Payment due by the 30th (or 60th or 90th) day calculated from the date of invoice.

It is worth looking again at *net monthly account* and *30 days* in the light of common UK trade practice and that which may be considered best practice. Much debate surrounds the interpretation of monthly account, by both sellers and buyers. Monthly account is much abused. Most buyers time their payments to be sent on or just after the end of the month so that in fact funds are not with the seller until well into the following month. The terms are quite specific in that funds for the February invoices should be in the seller's bank by 31 March, and that those funds are 'cleared' by 31 March. To ensure cleared funds by 31 March the cheque needs to be received and banked three working days before. Because most buyers see 31 March as the time when they should initiate a payment, it is important for the seller to find ways of making clear the true nature of the term.

On the other hand, 30 days from invoice date gives a precise due date. It could be argued that customers who receive 20 deliveries and 20 invoices every month are hardly likely to send 20 cheques or make 20 BACS transfers. Tolerant sellers may well allow customers to bulk a month's invoices into a single month-end payment, but every chance should be taken to stress to the customers that this is a concession and that the contractual terms of 30 days from invoice date give the seller the *right* to demand each payment 30 days after each invoice if they wish. This is an important *right* for the seller, especially if the customer gets into financial difficulty, because the seller has the legal advantage of being able to demand payment sooner than the seller who only has monthly account terms.

Other credit terms

- *Journey terms:* Where payment is made to the representative or van salesperson.

- *Contra terms:* Where payment is effected by offsetting the value of supplies against purchases from the same firm. Periodic reconciliation and settlements are necessary, and these terms should *always* be agreed in writing. In the event of insolvency of the buyer, a Receiver or Liquidator is entitled to claim payment of sums due to his failed company, regardless of any offset which has been made *informally* – therefore official prior agreement in writing to such offset is essential, to be shown to a Receiver or Liquidator if needed.

- *Stage payments:* Specified amounts or percentages, normally instalments, to be paid at defined stages of a contract.

When deciding credit terms, it is worth remembering that funds should always be regarded as 'cleared' funds. Banks continue to aim for speedier clearance, and there have been many claims in recent years that cheque clearance periods have moved from two or three days to 24 hours. It is certainly not unreasonable to assume that with all the technology at their disposal, banks should be able to guarantee 24-hour clearance of cheques. They remain under pressure from both consumer and business alike to achieve that clearance rate – in 2009 some undertakings were given to move in that direction. In practice, however, two to three days should still be allowed for clearance. Many former building societies, now banks, run business accounts for customers, and cheque clearance for those banks can still take much longer than the well-known 'high street' banks.

Cash Discounts

The cost impact of cash discounts were examined in Chapter 2. To be worthwhile, cash discounts should offer a benefit to both seller and buyer. The main considerations for cash discounts can be simply stated. They are:

- the seller's cost of waiting versus the annualised cost of the discount;

- the seller's need for payment due to cash flow considerations;

- the cost of the discount taken by some customers who pay on time anyway.

An example of cash discount would be '2 per cent/10 or Net 30'. This means 2 per cent discount may be deducted by the buyer for settling within 10 days, or alternatively, the full amount is due at 30 days. Where a seller can afford them, early payment discounts should be announced at the same time as a price increase, this being a way for the buyer to offset increased cost. In any other circumstances, the seller should consider spending the extra expense on improving collection procedures and activities, which would give a much better return. Most customers who pay late (and who therefore might be interested in a discount for paying earlier), take up to two months' extra credit. For simple comparison, if a seller borrows at 12 per cent per annum, then giving customers a 2 per cent discount costs as much as waiting 60 days for late payment.

Fewer companies now offer cash discounts because it is simply not economic. If offered, a seller will take the discount for the same reason (in their favour) – the discount, less the cost of borrowing the cash to settle, provides a net surplus, or effectively a price reduction.

The real problem lies with those who pay late *and* still take the discount. The ledger becomes clogged up with unauthorised deductions. Marketing and policy decisions have to be made as to the worth of chasing the balances, and it becomes necessary to operate a determined and potentially costly follow-up procedure to disallow and collect unauthorised discounts.

Late Payment Interest

There are two views about charges for late payment. The first is that it may be construed as an authority to pay late and simply pay extra for the extended credit. Where credit risks are high, this could be the opposite of the seller's wishes. The other view is that the cost of unauthorised late payments should be recovered from the customers concerned, rather than passing on the cost in future prices to all customers.

Businesses have always been able to charge interest in respect of late payment, providing that the clause detailing the rate and the amount was clearly included in their terms and conditions. Whether they implemented that clause or not was up to them. In the late 1980s and early 1990s a debate began in the UK around the so-called UK 'disease' of late payment, prompted on the one hand by representatives of the small business sector and supported on the other largely by collection and reference agencies. The argument was always that small business was suffering at the hands of large companies – 'the 'bully boys' who deliberately paid late and used their market strength to dictate terms. While recognising that some companies may have taken that dominant stance, in general credit professionals recognised that late payment legislation could interfere with the right to freedom of contract and as such any legislation would lack enforcement teeth.

To some extent, the debate was overtaken by events, and legislation was introduced enabling companies to charge interest on late payment if they so choose. The Late Payment of Commercial Debt (Interest) Act 1998, which first came into force on 1 November 1998, was intended by the Government to reverse what had been seen as the bad practice of deliberate late payment. The Act was to be introduced over a period of six years:

- 1 November 1998 to 31 October 2000 – small businesses (under 50 employees) were enabled to claim interest from large businesses and the public sector on debts incurred on contracts agreed after that date.

- 1 November 2000 to 31 October 2002 – small businesses were enabled to claim interest from other small businesses for debts on contracts agreed after that date.

- 1 November 2002 onwards – all businesses and the public sector were enabled to claim interest from all businesses and the public sector on debts incurred on contracts agreed after that date.

The rate of interest stipulated under the Act is the Bank of England Base Rate (otherwise known as the official dealing rate) plus 8 per cent. If the base rate were 2 per cent, for example, then interest could be charged at the rate of 10 per cent.

The final phase, for all businesses, was actually brought into force on 1 August 2002, the timetable having been brought forward to bring the Act into line with the European Union Directive on Combating Late Payments in

Commercial Transactions, which had been passed by the European Parliament on 15 June 2000. This Directive also allowed for reasonable recovery costs to be claimed, and the UK legislation was also amended to include recoverable costs such as:

- debts up to £999.99 – recoverable costs £40;

- debts £1,000.00 to £9,999.99 – recoverable costs £70;

- debts over £10,000.00 – recoverable costs £100.

It is important to note that the late payment legislation does not *oblige* businesses to charge interest, but simply enables such action if required. Equally, the legislation does not replace any existing clause which a company may have in its terms and conditions in respect of the right to charge interest on late payment. Businesses can negotiate contracts freely between themselves, and are quite entitled *not* to take advantage of the late payment legislation.

The decision to charge penalty interest, whether under terms and conditions or under the legislation, remains a matter for management judgement, and there could be commercial considerations which decide against. If it is the intention to charge interest under the company's conditions of sale, then it is a requirement that the intention *is* actually stated in the terms and conditions and is made known to the buyer at the contract negotiation stage. It is also helpful to include some notation on the invoice as a reminder.

The rate of interest to be charged should be enough to be a deterrent against late payment, but not a rate which would be regarded by the Courts as excessive or usurious. It should also be decided when that interest should be charged – either at intervals, while the debt is unpaid, or as a single calculation retrospectively once the debt has been paid. The former is recommended.

It is quite possible, of course, for interest to be negotiated after the contract stage, even if not in the terms and conditions in circumstances where, in effect, the buyer and the seller are renegotiating. For example, a buyer has got into genuine difficulties, the supplier is willing to support through a restructuring and the debt is being rescheduled. The new payment plan is acceptable to both sides, and a charge is made to cover the late payment and the new payment period. Any such arrangement should be confirmed in writing so as to avoid any dispute which may arise later, especially in the event of changes in personnel.

Progress Payments, Retentions and Consignment Accounts

Stage (or progress) payments are relevant where there is considerable capital outlay coupled with an extended period before delivery or completion. Large projects, such as building bridges or dams, cruise liners or aircraft carriers, nearly always require payments at certain stages during the course of the contract. At the agreed stages of the contract, independent certification justifies payment claims, the number of stage payments having been negotiated at the outset.

Retentions are usually associated with capital intensive industry, where a percentage of the purchase price is held back for a period, for example, 10 per cent payable 12 months after commissioning. The purpose is to tie the supplier into accepting a continuing responsibility for the building, ship or machinery supplied. This equates to a warranty period, not dissimilar to the kind of guarantee that would be expected by a consumer when buying a washing machine. The period can run from delivery, or from commissioning, and the percentages to be retained and the time period of the retention are invariably laid down by the buyer, and part of the negotiation of the contract.

Where possible, it is better for the seller to avoid having his ledgers cluttered with retention balances. This can be done by offering a 'retention bond', issued by a bank or insurance company, in return for full payment. If the buyer then suffers problems and costs during the agreed retention period, he can claim against the bond instead of having to pursue the supplier for recompense. Having paid for the bond, the supplier has a 'clean', fully paid ledger.

Consignment account is a variation of 'sale or return' and is more common in export where lines of supply are very long and the need for delivery certainty is critical. Title passes to the end customer only when payment is made, or via the invoice when credit terms apply. The seller records the consignment stock as unsold stocks rather than as debtors for goods sold. The term covers the physical transfer of supplies where the consignee acts as the seller's agent. There may be special conditions which require the seller to keep ample stocks with the buyer, rather than supplying to individual orders as they are received.

The consignment stock system also provides a way of improving security when the customer's finances are particularly weak. There is a benefit to both parties, as consignment stocks enable the customer to continue trading and make profits; and the seller to recover unsold stock in the event of customer difficulties.

One variation is the *'depletion contract'*, which enables the seller to keep the customer topped up to an agreed level of supplies, while the customer pays only for the amounts used. For example, a printer in California orders printing plates from the supplier in the UK and negotiates consignment stock of 1000. The supplier ships 1000, which are held as supplier's stock but in the buyer's California warehouse. If the lead time for the product from order to delivery is 10 weeks, and the buyer uses 100 plates per week, he has 10 weeks' stock at the outset, and therefore has confidence in stock availability for his needs. As he draws 100 from stock, the supplier is notified, raises an invoice for 100, and arranges to ship 100 to keep the consignment stock level at 1000.

Another variation is the *'stock maintenance contract'*. In this case, the supplier maintains an agreed level of stock at the customer's location, based upon a single 'blanket' order. Each new consignment is invoiced at the time and payment is due on the credit terms agreed. It is important to be clear about when title passes from the seller to the buyer.

Methods of Payment

There are a number of ways in which customers can make payment for supplies. Technological advances, coupled with changes in working practices, have dictated much of the progression over the years from one form of payment to another, but what remains is the fundamental purpose of transferring funds from buyer to seller.

- *Cash:* Although convenient as a quick method of payment, especially when small sums are involved, cash is cumbersome and has the great disadvantage that, once it has changed hands, it is unrecognisable against the debt to which it refers. Serial numbers on bank notes are seldom recorded and large sums of cash should be regarded with the greatest caution – the legislation now in force in most industrialised countries in respect of money laundering is quite rightly extremely severe. In any event, large sums of cash also bring problems of security, insurance and safe handling. Generally speaking, credit managers require accounts to be settled by ways other than cash.

- *Cheque:* A cheque is a bill of exchange, ordering a bank to pay a specific sum to a named party, or to that party's order. It must be presented within six months, and it is one of the most common forms of account settlement. Cheques, however, have drawbacks. After being deposited in the creditor's bank, they take two to five days to clear, that is, to be paid from the drawer's bank account. Banks have been under pressure to reduce this 'clearance' time to 24 hours, and there is no doubt that this is technically feasible. Progress is being made, but many of the former building societies, now banks, are still not tied in to the 'high street' banks' system, so clearance remains two to five days in general. Also, cheques can be invalidated by errors such as the words and figures differing, the cheque being undated, post-dated, unsigned or signed by an unauthorised person. There may be insufficient funds from which to make payment. On this latter point, there is growing pressure to introduce legislation in the UK which would make it an offence to issue a cheque knowing that there are insufficient funds in the account to pay. This is already the position in France, for example, and the European Commission has been reviewing the situation across the EU. Despite these risks, cheques are a convenient and flexible method of payment, and millions of commercial cheques are cleared every day through the banking system. Security was improved by adding the words 'Account Payee Only' to cheques, so that payment of these cheques can only be made to the named payee's bank account.

- *Debit cards:* Based on EFTPOS (Electronic Funds Transfer at Point of Sale), debit cards are a form of electronic cheque, most widely known as 'Switch/Maestro' or 'Delta'. When a sale is made, the card is inserted into an electronic reader at the seller's till, the buyer entering a 'PIN' number. The buyer's bank account is debited and the seller's bank account is credited. Debit cards are increasingly popular with both buyers and sellers – buyers need not carry cash, and sellers do not need to get involved in cumbersome cash handling. Transactions are quickly completed at the point of sale with minimum clearance delay through the bank computer system and offer a safer and quicker alternative to cash and cheques at retail outlets.

- *Banker's draft:* Instead of sending his own cheque, a risky customer may be persuaded to arrange for his bank to provide its own cheque which should have the words 'Bank (or Banker's) Draft' printed across the top. The payee shown on the bank cheque is the supplier to be paid. The full financial standing of the bank replaces that of the customer.

- *Traveller's cheque:* Issued by banks in sterling or foreign currency, usually in standard denominations of 10, 20, 50 or 100 (pounds, Euros or US dollars). Holders of traveller's cheques may exchange them overseas for cash in local currency at banks, hotels, various trade premises and exchange bureaus. If unused, they will be bought back by the issuing bank. The risk is limited to the face value of the cheque, but loss or theft is a constant problem, and great care should be exercised by the holding traveller, who should always make a note of the serial numbers.

- *Eurocheque:* Identified by their EU logo, these can be bought from clearing banks, and are honoured in many countries with advantages compared to traveller's cheques, as they are drawn in local currency and can be used to pay for purchases or to obtain cash. Holders of these cheques look for the EU logo in banks, shop windows, hotels, garages and so on. Clearance through banking systems can take from six days to six weeks before the debit arrives on the holder's bank account, and large fees can be deducted by some banks.

- *Postal order:* These can be particularly useful for sending money through the post when individuals do not have a bank account. They are obtainable from Post Offices and should be 'crossed' in the same way as cheques. They are only suitable for small transactions, however, and are increasingly rare in commercial trading situations.

- *Bank standing order:* The customer instructs his bank to make a series of fixed amount payments to the seller's bank account, usually at monthly intervals. The customer, on providing the written instruction to the bank to do this, advises the sum to be transferred, the date of transfer and the recipient's bank account details. Bank standing orders are particularly suitable for the regular payment of insurance premiums, rents and other similar fixed sums.

- *Direct debit:* This operates in the reverse way to the standing order. The debtor gives his supplier a written authority to make future charges, on normal due dates, to his bank account. The amounts can be fixed in sum or variable, and are increasingly popular with both suppliers and customers. In the case of variable direct debits, the supplier is required to give notice each month of the amount to be collected, ensuring that at least 14 days elapse between the date of the last invoice to be collected and the date of the collection. Charges are then made through BACS (Banker's Automated Clearing System).

  Just as standing orders gained acceptance through consumers in the first instance, so too direct debits gained acceptability through consumers paying utility bills, council tax, TV licences and the like. The process is still largely underused in trade transactions, however, and many organisations offer their customers one-off incentives to persuade them to change to direct debits.

  There are many advantages to direct debit, such as: payment is made accurately on due date; account queries are brought to light earlier as customers do not want to be debited for disputed items; customers are relieved of the task and costs of making payments; customers have no 'hassle' from suppliers chasing overdue accounts; there is no risk of stopped deliveries due to late payment from all the above; customer/supplier relationships are improved.

  All customers who sign a direct debit authority receive a bank indemnity that should any error be made (for example, too much deducted or too early), it will be corrected immediately with no penalty to the customer. If an honourable customer intends to pay the supplier on time, there is absolutely no reason why he should not pay by direct debit.

- *Bank transfer:* If the supplier gives the customer details of his bank account, the customer can arrange to make payment via BACS. The supplier should establish the bank transfer date to be used by the customer, to match the agreed credit terms. The supplier should also request a remittance advice from the customer, so that the supplier knows how much is being sent, and which invoices are covered by the payment. Bank transfers are increasingly replacing cheques as a preferred method of B2B payment, and unlike cheques they cannot be lost in the post and are cleared funds on arrival. However, unlike direct debits, timing of payment is in the control of the customer, not the supplier, and BACS payments can be delayed, and are not received by the supplier on the same day as they are released by the customer.

- *Bank telegraphic transfer (TT):* Designed for transfers in excess of £5000, the main advantages of TTs are that they are very rapid and are cleared funds on receipt. The customer completes a bank form instructing his bank to transfer payment to his supplier, advising details and amount to be transferred. Internationally, the system can be further speeded through the banking SWIFT system (Society for Worldwide Interbank Financial Telecommunications), which combines bank computer systems and the electronic messaging method.

- *Credit card:* Worldwide there are many hundreds of organisations issuing credit cards, predominantly for use by individuals, though many companies have 'corporate' credit cards for employees to use for authorised purchases and for travel expenses, for example. The main issuers in the UK were the big banks in the early days, but many organisations now issue cards. In addition, charge cards are issued to approved customers by department stores, retailers, garages and so on. Sellers paid by credit card obtain rapid reimbursement but pay the credit card companies a percentage of the sales value. (See Chapter 25, which is devoted entirely to credit cards.)

- *Postal collection (COD):* Companies that sell directly to the public should be aware of the Royal Mail's 'Postal Collection' service by which suppliers may send goods and packages through the post on a 'cash on delivery' basis. Postal staff will take small packages requiring cash payment in their house-to-house delivery service. For items of high value, the postal worker delivers an advice, notifying the addressee to collect them from the sorting office. If the recipient pays cash at that time, he may take the goods. If he pays by cheque (above the cheque card guarantee value), he must wait seven days before collection of the goods. The charges for this service are modest.

- *Bill of exchange:* This is defined by the Bills of Exchange Act 1882 as 'an unconditional order in writing addressed by one person to another, signed by the person giving it, requiring the person to whom it is addressed to pay on demand or at a fixed or determinable future time, a sum certain in money to or to the order of a specified person or to bearer'. There are therefore three parties to a bill: the 'drawer', the 'drawee' and the 'payee'. The drawer (normally the creditor) draws up and delivers the bill to the drawee (the debtor). If the drawee is a bank acting for a debtor, the bill is called a bank bill. The drawee is ordered to pay the sum stated to the payee. Bills are negotiable and may be transferred from one payee to another by endorsement. They can be made payable at sight or any future date, and are thus very appropriate for long credit arrangements. Inland bills are those drawn and payable in the UK, and foreign bills are those drawn on drawees abroad. A bill payable at a future date requires 'acceptance' by the drawee, who writes 'accepted' across the face of the bill and adds his signature. Only after acceptance does the term bill have value. It may be 'discounted' at a bank which provides the funds, deducting an interest charge for the credit period. Otherwise, the payee can await the maturity date for payment in full. A cheque is also a bill of exchange but is drawn by the debtor (the drawer, in this case) ordering his bank (drawee) to pay the amount shown to the payee (the supplier), immediately on presentation.

- *Promissory note:* This is described by the Bills of Exchange Act 1882 as 'an unconditional promise in writing made by one person to another, signed by the maker, engaging to pay, on demand or at a fixed or determinable future time, a sum certain in money, to, or to the order of a specified person or to bearer'. It is therefore not a *true* bill of exchange. The best known examples of promissory notes are bank notes, which contain the words 'I promise to pay the bearer on demand the sum of X pounds'. Commercial promissory notes are mainly used in relation to loan instalments. There is no required format and they may be written on plain paper. There are only two parties involved: the maker and the payee, and the main difference between it and a bill of exchange is that it is a *promise* to pay and not an *order* to do so. Whereas a bill is drawn by a creditor, a promissory note is made by the debtor, and, unlike a bill, it does not have to be 'accepted'. Promissory notes are similar to post-dated cheques, which have no standing in law until their date of payment, but notes are a promise of payment and establish that the sum involved is indeed due to be paid. Depending on the standing of the issuer they have a high degree of negotiability, and in the case of bank promissory notes, they can change hands many times. They can be supported by security, in which case they are usually known as 'collateral notes'.

- *Letter of credit (LC):* Used principally, though not exclusively, in foreign trading, letters of credit are arranged by a buyer with his bank to open a credit payable usually through a bank in the country of the seller. The bank accepts responsibility for payment by standing in the place of the buyer, substantially improving the security of the transaction. Payment is passed to the seller's bank on the date of maturity following presentation by the seller of the relevant shipping documents called for in the LC wording. When the seller has been notified of the arranged credit, it becomes irrevocable and the buyer's bank cannot withdraw from its commitment to pay. 'Confirmed' letters of credit are those which are further guaranteed by a bank outside the country of risk. Letters of credit normally cover transactions to be paid in 30 to 180 days, but can be for any length of time, or at sight. Inland letters of credit can be arranged for UK home trade business and there are special kinds which can provide funds in advance of delivery performance. Banks make very high charges for all types of LC transactions, from opening through to final payment (and for any amendments necessary in between). The contract should make the buyer liable for all charges, but in reality they are often shared between the parties.

- *Sight draft:* This is a bill of exchange payable as soon as it arrives – that is to say, when the buyer has sight of it. It enables a seller to obtain payment from a buyer, usually overseas, before releasing control of the goods. This is done by the seller attaching the shipping documents and an instruction form to the seller's bank. These are forwarded by the seller's bank to the buyer's bank for payment. When payment is made, the documents are passed over to the purchaser to obtain physical possession of the goods.

- *Peppercorn:* The dried berry of the pepper vine has given its name as an object of minute value to be accepted in rent and lease agreements which require only a nominal payment. It is worth so little that the beneficiary in the contract does not need to collect it. Nevertheless, the term 'peppercorn rent' serves its purpose as the essential consideration in a contract.

- *Novel payments:* When agreed by both sides as a fair consideration, novel payments are acceptable in law. For example, an arrangement whereby a philanthropist hands over a plot of land to a local council in exchange for one pint of ale each Michaelmas for the next 10 years, could be legal and binding if properly agreed between the parties.

- *Barter:* Probably one of mankind's oldest forms of trading, the bartering of goods and other commodities remains in widespread use today, particularly between less developed nations. One government, for example, may exchange oil for machinery. At the commercial level, barter is also practical if both products can be precisely regulated in quantity to match the sales value of each other. For example, a farmer may pay for livestock with wheat. Instead of straight 'goods for goods' agreements, there is now a proliferation of 'countertrade' methods whereby separate contracts requiring actual payment are made for both products, linked by an agreement. These are described in some detail in Chapter 17 on export collections.

From the bartering of ancient times to the electronic transfer of funds today, payment methods have developed and matured. A key role of the credit manager today is to be fully conversant with all the methods now available and being developed in the future. The main aim is to secure swift payment, and not act as either a bank or a philanthropic institution.

INSTITUTE OF CREDIT MANAGEMENT – JANUARY 2008

Introductory Credit Management: Certificate Level 3

Question 7: As well as establishing credit terms with customers, it is important for the credit department to agree with their customers the most suitable and cost effective way for payment of invoices. You have been asked by your credit manager to encourage customers to pay by bank transfer instead of by cheque.

Explain to customers how a payment is made by bank transfer or BACS. Compare the advantages and disadvantages of payment by bank transfer or BACS with payment by cheque. Direct debit is the most common method of payment for most forms of consumer credit and its use in trade credit is growing rapidly. Explain the benefits to both your company and customers of payment by direct debit.

PART III
Assessing Credit Risk

5

Assessing Risks in Trade Credit

Glen Bullivant

• Credit assessment overview • Marketing and risk assessment • Customer identity – types of customer • Trade credit information and its sources • Interpretation of accounts • Summary •

Credit Assessment Overview

The credit manager is often seen as something of a cynic, never believing anything he is told unless, and until, it can be verified. The embossed notepaper, the fashionable address and the imposing façade do not impress, by and large – established facts and actual experience account for much more. The cynic tag can apply simply because the credit manager is trained not to accept everything at face value, not to judge solely on appearances and certainly not to enter into the risk environment without having first weighed up all the factors. Who is to say that had the same level of 'cynicism' been imbued into the psyche of senior bank executives in the run up to 2007, we would not have entered the financial turmoil of 2008?

Hundreds of businesses close down every day in the UK, more often than not due to insolvency, and usually leaving suppliers and others unpaid. Suppliers are often in a state of denial about the possibilities of their customers failing, and can be quite surprised when it happens. A few, the well-organised ones, have seen the end coming and, depending on the speed of the collapse, have reduced their supply and collected most of the outstanding debt, before the doors are locked for good. The credit manager in such well-organised supplier companies has not been gazing into a crystal ball, but has simply kept in touch with all his or her bigger customers, had regular reviews of the accounts with up-to-date filed information and with credit reports. He or she has, therefore, been able to assess risk ongoing, and be in a position to act promptly when circumstances with customers have taken a turn for the worse.

So why do many firms send their wealth off to customers, regardless of their ability to pay? Principally because they are as keen as mustard to sell as much volume as possible without regard to actual *net* profit and an almost indefatigable belief that 'the customer is always right'. Meeting customer demands and ensuring customer satisfaction takes preference over cost. The fact remains, however, that the customer is *not* always right, and not all customers are worthy of the same credit facilities. Customers are always important, of course, and the assessment process is there to sort the wheat from the chaff – some customers will not be as profitable as others if they pay late, and nobody makes a profit if they do not pay at all!

However keen the supplier may be to sell, the ultimate aim of any business is to make a profit and to that end the astute supplier will always keep his eye on the ball – the ball being net profit, that is, that tiny percentage of sales value that is left when the customer has paid. Until payment has been received and are cleared funds in the bank, the sale has not been completed and the supplier is simply adding to his costs (by the interest costs of waiting), so reducing any net profit the longer the sale remains unpaid. Unpaid sales are always dangerous, costly and risky, and the Golden Rule (that is, the longer a sale is unpaid, the greater the chance it will never be paid) is the top priority which guides credit management. Cash is King, and the customer only wears the crown when he can show that he is worthy of so doing. To be truly cynical, the easiest way to increase sales volume would be to advertise: 'buy from us and don't bother to pay' – hardly a strategy for success!

Successful companies know the value of cash inflow, and they also know that keeping an eye on customers' ability to pay does not of itself hinder sales growth. Good risk assessment methods not only increase profits by avoiding the costs of waiting and bad debts, but also increase sales opportunities by directing competitive selling efforts away from failing customers to those who are good, growing prospects. The simple fact is that, knowing that a customer was going to close next week, would it make any sense at all to supply goods today, payable at the end of next month? The answer is obvious, of course (no, that is, for those of you who have not been paying attention!), but the trick is to *know* that the customer is going broke next week. The real skill is in knowing the customer's ability to pay on time, and to recognise the signs and the trends which indicate growth, or decline and failure.

With the best will in the world, there will always be business failures and the economics of the modern world point to peaks and troughs in business activities, with global effects and consequences. In a recession (and there have been regular recessions both in the UK and globally since the end of the Second World War) record numbers of businesses fail, leaving creditors with bad debt losses. Slow payment is a worldwide phenomenon with even the one-time boom economies of Japan and Germany experiencing increasing problems at the beginning of the twenty-first century, and as a result the squeeze on profits has intensified. By the same token, the pressure to sell and grow market share intensifies, and with it all the risks associated with the granting of credit.

To sell at any cost is bad practice, and both credit and sales should not only always sing from the same hymn sheet, but should always cooperate at every level to ensure *good* business. This means that both credit and sales recognise that no business stands still – it can grow larger or smaller, be more cash rich or less, borrow more or borrow less, and so on. For profit reasons (the effect of delays or losses) or for sales reasons (the ability of customers to buy), someone has to assess the credit ability of customers, and though this is usually the specialist task of the credit manager, the sales manager needs to know all about it as well.

To put all this into a bite size chunk for all to understand, sales should remember:

- not all customers are entitled to credit;

- volume does not take care of minor losses;

- not all customers will pay in the end;

- late payment is hugely costly;

- the customer is always potentially important, but not always right.

If that can be accepted, the next simple fundamental for everybody, from the chief executive downwards, is to remember that credit means *trust*. Trust has to be based on *knowledge* for it to have any real value or meaning. Knowledge covers everything you need to possess to make the informed decision, simply broken down into three basic credit questions:

1. is the customer about to fail? (the *solvency* risk);

2. can the customer pay our account on time? (the *liquidity* risk);

3.   is the customer growing or declining? (the *volume* risk).

Risk assessment is not haphazard, nor should it be anything other than structured and logical. For a business relationship to grow from a sound base, a well-defined sequence of events should be established at the outset, which can be followed by both credit and sales personnel in order to define, from the earliest point in the relationship with the customer, the manner in which such a relationship will be conducted. A simple but reliable sequence consists of:

- *Credit Application Form*: This is the customer's request to borrow our money. If the bank wants to know something about us before lending to us, so we should want to know more about our prospective customer.

- *Check on creditworthiness*: Thorough or brief, according to order value or projected volumes.

- *Credit rating (limit) and/or risk category*: The application form and the credit report have provided information upon which to make a quantified decision as to how much we can allow, and what the perceived level of risk is likely to be.

- *Credit terms*: Standard or special, according to the buyer's status.

- *Allocation of account number*: No deliveries until this is done. The allocation of an account number is the confirmation to all that the seller is prepared to allow credit.

- *'Welcome letter' to customer (to their payment person)*: The important first contact with the person responsible for payment.

- *Special ledger section for three months*: This allows close monitoring of the new account by the supplier, and to make extra contact in the initial stages to try to help the customer avoid bad payment habits.

Some of the above actions would be equally applicable to existing customers, both as regular review and as ongoing monitoring – it is just as important to keep accounts under scrutinised control as it is to set them up correctly in the first place.

In addition to an obvious logical sequence, there should be an equally obvious line of responsibility for risk assessment and credit decisions.

Many a credit manager has the motto 'a sale is not a sale until it is paid for' engraved on a plaque on the desk as well as on the heart. That could be seen as negative – better would be 'a sale is only a cost to us until it is paid for'. Perhaps the two mean the same thing, the latter, however, has more of a positive ring to it which sales managers could understand. The really positive motto for all professional credit managers should be 'my job is to look for a way to take every possible order'.

This brings us back to our old friend – the true role of the credit manager is to seek the highest volume of *profitable* sales over the shortest period of time with the minimum of bad debt.

The correct credit structure in any business is to have the three basic credit functions – risk assessment, Sales Ledger and cash collection – under the control of the credit manager. They are essentially related, along with the integrated computer systems, to support all the procedures involved. Many companies separate out the three basic functions in respect of personnel involved – that is to say someone handling risk assessment does not deal with cash postings. There are sound auditing reasons for an approach such as this, but companies should not make the mistake of removing the overall authority and responsibility of the credit manager from all or any of these tasks. In other words, if, for example, the credit manager directly controls risk assessment, he should also have an overview of Sales Ledger maintenance and cash collection, even if not under his direct control. It is easy to understand the mistakes and expense incurred when the functions are completely separated, and when responsibility is equally segregated. Orders can be taken from customers who are being sued for non-payment of previous supplies, or cash postings are two weeks behind because of other accounting priorities, or collection requests are ignored by regional sales offices and depots. The credit manager's role is to protect the company's investment in accounts receivable, and by definition that has to mean the risk, the invoiced sale, the collection of cash and the correct and prompt allocation of that cash. If the credit manager only has control, or responsibility for one of the three basic areas, then any staff weakness or inefficiency in either of the other two can seriously impair performance, and in effect there is nothing directly that the credit manager can do about it. By any definition, this must be totally unacceptable.

Credit management, therefore, is as much concerned with identifying good sales prospects and cultivating strong relationships as it is with standard collection actions and ledger-keeping. The credit manager should be seen by other staff as responsible for the credit policy being carried out, applying commercial sense to resolving customer problems. Risk control does not mean saying 'no' to poor risks, just because the policy allows this. It means looking for ways of saying 'yes' – in other words a constructive attitude coupled with sufficient seniority to be able to make agreements with customers. This may include variations on a theme, such as part deliveries, special credit terms, instalments, discounts, deposits and so on.

If a company is large enough to have a sales manager and a credit manager, both should be at the same middle-management level. Both are then able to argue their respective cases in a constructive and healthy manner, with any serious disagreement being referred (and resolved) at sales director and finance director level. It makes no sense for the company's credit policy to be operated at too junior a level, when the real manager of credit is the credit manager's boss. It is more than likely that the boss will not have the time for daily hands-on control, and certainly not have the depth of knowledge and accumulated experience of the credit manager himself. In smaller companies, the credit controller is often the person responsible for day-to-day running of the Sales Ledger, and his or her boss is in effect the credit manager, with the time and the skills necessary to set credit levels, monitor them against debts and take prompt action to resolve high-risk problems. Where resources allow, it pays for the larger operations to have a credit risk specialist, reporting directly to the credit manager, who again will have overall responsibility for all aspects of the credit function.

Where accounts are both home and export, the credit checking task should either have separate people, or at the very least, separate time allocated for home and export. It takes time to build experience in overseas trade and spreading the job between several people can seriously hinder that experience building process.

Marketing and Risk Assessment

Marketing is defined as the commercial activity prior to selling, that is, identifying markets for products, finding the substantial customers for those products, advertising and promotion plans, seeing how the competition operates, including their credit terms, and early discussions with prospective customers. Selling is best defined as persuading customers to buy products and the whole process of taking and servicing orders.

At various early stages, well-organised companies assess the viability of prospective customers, as well as deciding what investment will be needed for the possible volume of sales and their credit periods. For example, planned sales of £100,000 per month to customers enjoying 60 days' credit will mean an investment in unpaid sales of £20,000 plus, for an element of overdues and disputes of say 20 per cent, a further £4000, making a total of £24,000. If any contracts need special, or non-standard terms, the investments will alter.

It pays, therefore, to identify prospective customers for, say, 80 per cent of planned sales and have them credit-checked:

1. *Early warning*: As possible prospects are identified by sales or marketing staff, their names are passed to the credit manager to assess for credit. The expense and effort may be wasted if orders do not materialise, but delays are avoided when they do. In addition, the company feels better equipped for strong sales when it knows the good, average and poor risk accounts up front. It is also less likely that the poor risk accounts will place orders anyway.

2. *Sales planning meetings*: The credit manager attends when names of prospective customers are being discussed. He may already know them, and in any event is in a position to move quickly to check them. This involvement can help direct sales plans to the right customers.

3. *Visiting prospective customers*: A joint visit with the sales or marketing person, before the business becomes firm, provides a good opportunity of assessing the people and the premises. This can help in two ways: it adds depth to the written credit reports; and it is the chance to start building strong personal contacts for future collections.

It is of the utmost importance for customers to see sales and credit as a united and money-conscious team, and it is equally important for personnel throughout the selling company to recognise that too. When this team approach is not promoted, the wrong kind of customer can easily play one function against the other in future negotiations, for example, alleging concessions and old agreements.

Opening new accounts invariably begins with the requirement for new customers to complete an 'application for credit' (see Figure 5.1 and accompanying notes). Apart from providing more accurate details than those given orally, or on orders, the customer is reminded of the terms of payment and his commitment to paying them. The form should also provide the name of a contact for payments. If the business is deemed to be too fast-moving to wait for form-filling, a first order can be taken up to an agreed maximum – that is to say a value that, if lost, would not be too painful for the seller, say £1000. The credit application form should then be completed before a second order is taken.

The decision to open the account should be communicated with enthusiasm to the customer's financial contact by a credit person. This is a good opportunity to firm up the relationship and restate the payment terms. As a control for this step, it is beneficial if only the credit department is authorised to allocate new account numbers, without which the business cannot go ahead.

Newly opened accounts should be placed in a special section of the Sales Ledger for a period of three months or so. Then, regardless of value or the standard collection system, every new customer should be telephoned and followed up personally for that period in order to try to ensure that no bad habits develop.

It is extremely valuable to make immediate contact with the customer's payment person by sending a *new account letter*, a friendly version of which is illustrated in Figure 5.2. The letter should always be signed personally, and should of course look like an individually prepared letter for that customer only, rather than what appears to be a standard computer produced print-off. The follow-up call a few days later is vital, since the reaction of the customer may indicate what kind of account behaviour can be expected.

Notes on credit application form, Figure 5.1:

- *Name of applicant:* This defines the type of customer (person, sole trader, partnership, limited company or non-standard), which is essential to decide the risk, the type of collection approach and to capture the precise name and style for possible need.

- *Address for invoices and statements*: Sometimes the payment address is different from that for deliveries. Invoices sent to the delivery address may suffer delays before they are passed to the payment office.

Name and address of applicant

State FULL name of proprietors/partners

State FULL trading style, if any: and home addresses

_____

_____

Postcode_____

Address for invoices/statements Ltd

Company Registration No

if different from above: Registered Office address:

_____

_____

Postcode_____

How long business established: _____

Name of payment contact: _____

Phone number and extension: _____

E-mail address: _____

(Please attach a copy of your letter heading)

Credit references:

1 Bank Name _____ Sort Code_____

Address: _____

2 Trade Ref.* Name: _____

Address: _____

3 Trade Ref.* Name: _____

Address: _____

4 Trade Ref.* Name: _____

Address: _____

* Not to be completed by customer – names to be supplied by salesperson

[Seller company name] will make a search with a credit reference agency, which will keep a record of that search and will share that information with other businesses. In some instances we may also make a search on the personal credit file of principal directors. Should it become necessary to review the account, then again a credit reference may be sought and a record kept. We will monitor and record information relating to your trade performance and such records will be made available to credit reference agencies who will share that information with other businesses when assessing applications for credit and fraud prevention.

I/we agree that this information may be used to support a request for credit facilities with [seller company name], and associated companies (a list is available upon request) in accordance with their credit vetting procedures.

Customer signature_____ Position_____

Estimated purchases £_____ per month. Credit rating required £_____ (i.e. 2 x monthly purchases).

We note your Standard Conditions of Sale, and agree to all clauses and will pay for any goods/services supplied by you on the stated terms, i.e. ALL invoices are payable 30 days from invoice date. In addition, our attention has been drawn to the clause relating to Retention of Title, which we have duly noted.

Customer signature_____ Position_____

Figure 5.1   Application form to open a credit account

- *Full name(s) of proprietor or partner(s) and home address*: The customer should know that anything less than limited liability means personal liability of owners or partners for debts. There is every reason to contact home addresses if no satisfaction is achieved at the place of business. In credit checking, the home premises may well represent wealth for future recovery if needed. With partnerships, unless limited by deed between the partners, or by limited liability statute, there is joint and several (that is, separate) liability on all partners.

- *Limited company registration number and office:* This is needed for legal action, where writs and claims are required to be served on the official address. Registered numbers are unique and useful when requesting credit reports, to avoid similar but different firms.

- *Length of time established*: Firms less than two years old have a high failure rate – possibly in excess of 50 per cent of businesses fail within the first two years. Good policy is to restrict credit until a relationship has matured somewhat, or obtain third-party guarantees for higher credit. Longer-established firms have track records which can be checked.

- *Name of payments contact*: This is extremely useful for future collection efforts, but may not be obvious at this early stage involving salesperson and buyer.

- *Letterheading request*: This is a useful check on the name, address and style data given earlier. Even customers themselves can be inaccurate when completing forms, and sales personnel are well known for their shorthand!

- *Credit references*: Bank details and trade references are much questioned these days as to value, but as a quick and cheap (relatively) source can help to establish basic details. Data Protection legislation now makes it imperative to be clear as to what will, or will not be done in respect of credit enquiries, and sellers should ensure that their intentions are both clear to the customer, and accepted by the customer.

- *Estimated purchases*: This must be the customer's estimate, not the salesperson's, which may be optimistically higher and frustrate the real credit rating needed.

- *Credit rating requested*: This must be a multiple of monthly sales, since the second month will be delivered before the first month is paid.

- *Acceptance*: It is important to give the customer sight of the conditions of sale (even on the reverse of this form), and get agreement to them here – in particular the credit terms, but also any specific special terms which it will be the seller's intention to enforce.

On receipt of the credit application form, the credit manager should organise the required credit checks, according to policy and, if acceptable, allocate an account number.

For the attention of Mr/Mrs xxxx (name of payment contacts person given on credit XYZ LTD application form)
etc
etc.

New Account Number _____

Dear Mr/Mrs xxxx,

I am very pleased to tell you that we have opened a credit account for your company with the above account number.

A credit rating of £_____ has been applied to your account. Please let me know if this will be sufficient for your needs – I will be happy to discuss it with you.

Our credit terms of ____ days from invoice date were agreed by your authorised person on the Credit Application Form, and I look forward to your payments to these terms. Prompt settlement of accounts will be much appreciated and to our mutual benefit, and will avoid any difficulties with supplies.

We strive for accuracy in our invoices and statements. Please do not hesitate to let me know at once of any errors or queries. As the person looking after your account, I will undertake to give any such matters my prompt attention.

I shall telephone you in a few days to make sure that you are quite happy with the credit arrangements and look forward to talking to you.

Yours sincerely,

Credit Controller
Direct Phone/Ext.
Email:

Figure 5.2   Example – new account letter

Customer Identity – Types of Customer

Almost every Sales Ledger that the author has ever seen has contained errors of name, address, postcode or some other combination. Sometimes these errors are of comparatively minor importance, perhaps a postcode not complete or some spelling mistake in the address. It is easy, after all is said and done, to confuse 'row' with 'roe' or 'plane' with 'plain', especially with oral orders, and as such these errors may not have a significant bearing initially on day-to-day dealings with the customer. Having said that, accuracy is indicative of efficiency and professionalism, and customer data should be correct from the outset.

What is unforgiveable, however, is inaccuracy in customer name. Not only does it display an approach to detail which is at best haphazard, it has a more than significant impact on collection and litigation activity. Many organisations have computer systems which integrate throughout the order, sale, delivery, invoice, statement and ledger process, so that the wrong name at the front end of the operation is repeated throughout. Some organisations even have systems which put a constraint on name and address fields, for example, so that in order to accommodate long names and addresses, some degree of 'editing' is required. If possible, such systems should be replaced at the earliest opportunity! In any event, the customer name is sacrosanct and should never be 'amended' to suit computer needs. It should be less of a problem to us in the twenty-first century than it was to our Victorian forebears – we like short, snappy company names these days, whereas the Victorians would try to encompass in the name the activities of the company as well as its title. It may well have been known as the Red Funnel Line, but for very many years, the company operating one of the Isle of Wight ferries was 'The Southampton, Isle of Wight, Royal Mail Steam Packet Co Ltd'. It is possible of course that even today a company may have a long name, in full, but is best known by its initials, such as the now defunct GNER (Great North Eastern Railway Ltd). Therein, however, lies the heart of the problem of name, and therefore customer identity.

Establishing customer identity is in fact establishing the legal status of the customer. It is therefore important to capture *exactly* the correct legal identity, because the seller should always know precisely who is responsible for the debt incurred. The difference between Smiths on the High Street, John Smith, John Smith & Sons, and John Smith & Sons Ltd is acute. Customers may well be known by everybody as Smiths, but is that a trading name used by Bubblesqueak Ltd or John Smith & Sons or is it in fact just Smiths?

The sole trader, or proprietor, is an individual and is a legal entity in his or her own right. As such, the sole trader is personally liable for all debts incurred up the full extent of his/her personal wealth. In other words, there is no screen to hide behind, and in the event of business failure, personal insolvency means bankruptcy. Sole traders are not obliged to lodge annual accounts or any details of the business for public scrutiny, though they are required to make tax returns and, if registered, VAT returns. These are not publicly available. It can be argued that the sole trader has much to lose in the event of business failure, and for that reason has every incentive to pay debts as and when they fall due. It is also argued, with justification, that it is not possible to distinguish between business debt and personal debt as by definition for the sole trader they are the same, and therefore the personal lifestyle of the sole trader is as significant as the business itself. For credit checking purposes, the sole trader is as much a consumer as any other – his or her home address is perfectly suitable for debt recovery, as are his or her personal assets.

The partnership is, unless otherwise stipulated, a partnership of proprietors or sole traders, each liable for the debts of the business up to the full extent of their personal wealth. Each individual in the partnership is equally liable, jointly and severally (separately) as described, and it is for each partner to be aware of the activities of their colleagues. They cannot avoid liability simply by saying they personally did not order the goods, or they personally did not know what was going on.

To cater for those large partnerships, such as the big accountancy and solicitors practices, as well as others, there is a Limited Liability Partnership (LLP), which restricts personal liability in the event of failure. LLPs are more common where partnerships encompass a wide scale of operation, both geographically and physically, and where it would be deemed unreasonable to hold each individual personally liable.

The limited liability company is a legal entity in its own right, just as a person, able to own property, sign contracts and engage in trade. The concept of limited liability was designed to restrict the liability of the owners of the company, the shareholders, to the extent of their shareholding. As such, creditors have no claim on them as individuals (unless it can be shown that they acted fraudulently). The Public Limited Company (PLC) is owned by shareholders and shares can be bought by the public. Liability is limited in the same way as the private limited company, that is, limited to the extent of the shareholding. Public companies have the advantage of being able to raise capital quickly by the sale of shares. Limited liability, therefore offers a degree of protection to its shareholders, be it private or public, and restricts creditors to pursuing only the legal entity itself, and not its shareholders, for recovery of sums due.

It can therefore be appreciated that having the exact customer name is of the utmost importance, and that exact customer name should exist on all of the seller's documentation throughout his computer system. Distorting a name to fit a computer field radically alters the whole picture – in the event of litigation, it would be disastrous, not to say costly to issue a writ against John Smith & Sons Ltd when the real customer was Bubblesqueak Ltd, trading as John Smith & Sons.

Apart from the above principal business entities, there are many other types of customer, where again it is important to correctly identify names and organisations. Friendly societies, clubs and institutes, and increasingly in the late 1990s to date, those organisations, ostensibly in the public sector, but self-funding and expected to operate in much the same way from a financial control standpoint as businesses – schools, hospitals, universities and so on. They bring their own special problems for both the credit manager and the collector, not withstanding the still present bureaucratic style of management. It is as vital as ever to establish where the responsibility for payment lies, and certainly not to assume they are risk-free

Shakepeare's Juliet may well have asked: 'What's in a name?' The modern answer in business is: 'Everything!'

Trade Credit Information and its Sources

It is worth reiterating that credit is always a risk, but should never be a gamble. Risk is determined by calculating the likelihood of prompt, slow or non-payment from as much information as it is both possible and feasible to obtain. In any walk of life, if knowledge is king, then information is the throne. The level of potential risk exposure will dictate the extent to which information is sought, but a wide range of information is available if only we knew where to look, ranging from free(ish) to quite expensive:

COMPANY SALES FORCE

Sales staff may not always be appreciated by some in the credit function, but they should be the good credit manager's first insight into the potential customer, and indeed also a source of information about the existing customers. They talk to, and visit, customers regularly, are aware of industry developments, and keep their ears to the ground for information which could be useful to them in the competitive environment, but also useful to the credit manager. Naturally, they prefer not to waste their time with declining customers, or those going into liquidation – but do they know who these are? Sales are constantly learning about their customers and it is this which helps them to sell successfully. Their input of data to the credit area must be reliably organised, and the credit manager should look for sales personnel to contribute in the following areas:

- *Outward impressions*: What is it like to deal with the customer? Are they well organised? Do they reply promptly to phone calls, letters and emails? Are the premises and plant in good order? Does it feel like a hive of activity, or are people standing about looking aimless? Do staff look cheerful or morose? Bad impressions can be a warning sign.

- *Customer's product*: Is it attractive? What is the quality? Does it use latest technology? Is it in demand? The fortunes of a customer depend on their product range.

- *Product demand*: Is the market expanding or contracting? Is it seasonal? These factors help show how easily the customer can earn his own money.

- *Market competition*: How is the customer placed versus his own competitors? The strength of the competition is a prime factor in company survival. Where demand is limited, only the strongest survive.

- *End customers*: Is your customer's product aimed at the best companies or is it budget quality for the bottom (and riskiest) end of the market?

- *Management ability*: Is their management experienced and of good repute? Or is there an autocrat in charge? Does every large payment have to be referred to the board, perhaps because a shortage of cash has forced tight controls? Are the directors' parking spaces occupied by expensive cars when the business would not appear to warrant opulence?

The sales force should be involved in gathering customer intelligence because the more they do, the more they will be able to understand those factors which precede slow payments and insolvency. Sales information is free – no bad thing in a cost conscious environment.

ACCOUNT EXPERIENCE

Monitoring the payment performance of existing customers reveals trends and gives early warning of trouble ahead. Payments getting later every month, calls not answered or the named contact becoming increasingly more difficult to actually contact are all signs of a deteriorating situation. The ledger shows valuable trends in payment performance, sales value and disputes, both getting worse and getting better.

If payments are made later as sales increase, this may indicate stretched resources. Customers who begin to raise an undue proportion of disputes and queries may be trying to delay payment – assuming, that is, that all remains efficient and organised in the seller company. If there is no reason for a high level of dispute from an existing customer as far as the seller is concerned, the obvious answer lies with the customer and his need for more time.

INDUSTRY CREDIT CIRCLES

Industry credit circles often form part of trade associations and can be extremely useful grapevines. Many credit managers find it productive to join the relevant credit circle for their industry, but the approach and use must be professional. The benefits depend upon input; and it should be treated as an opportunity to exchange accurate customer information and keep up to date with industry practice. Legislation covering both data protection and competition has made some companies wary about allowing their credit managers to join credit circles in recent times, but there is nothing illegal about credit circles. They are in fact no more than a form of personal trade reference, providing discussion is restricted to past facts and there is no collaboration, intended or implied, to restrict future trade. It is recommended that credit application forms include an acceptance section for completion by customers relating to shared information, as illustrated in Figure 5.1.

PRESS REPORTS

Press reports disclose useful interim company results of publicly quoted companies, and reports of resignations and appointments of key people. The financial pages of the quality broadsheets, and in particular the *Financial Times*, should be standard reading for all involved in credit management, together with those industry magazines and journals relevant to their own particular market sector. The great benefit of the press is that information is highly topical, and 'local' press may be even more topical in respect of plant closures or 'downsizing'. Sales staff will no doubt also read the trade publications, as well as local and national press, and they should be encouraged to pass on any pertinent data on existing or prospective customers to the credit department.

CUSTOMER VISITS

For many credit managers, customer visits are more common after problems have occurred (and are often seen as collection visits), but it is extremely valuable to visit large accounts on a planned and regular basis. An on-site customer meeting is a very effective way to evaluate creditworthiness, with the credit manager looking out for all those signs as discussed above in *Company sales force*. A visit to sort out payment problems may be a good way in, and can lead on to more detailed financial matters. Quite often, the customer is keen to show the credit manager around the whole operation to encourage confidence and to facilitate a satisfactory outcome from his standpoint. No credit manager should ever turn down such an opportunity. It can set his mind at rest or confirm his worst fears – either way, some of the uncertainty will have been dispelled. The first visit may be with the salesperson, to ease introductions and allow him to find out more about his customer, but out of both courtesy and professional integrity credit should always both inform sales of the intention to visit and give sales the opportunity to accompany or not.

CREDIT AGENCY REPORTS

Credit agency reports are the most comprehensive form of data. Either the stated credit ratings can be taken, or the data used by the credit manager to calculate his own ratings. Reports vary in form and content, ranging from a brief summary of main details to a full-blown financial analysis of the customer and industry, with a recommended credit limit. Agency reports are still available by post, phone or fax, but most are now delivered online direct to the credit manager's desktop PC, and as such information on prospective customers can be delivered in seconds rather than days. (Note: details of some agencies' products and services can be found in the Appendix.)

Typical sections of agency reports are:

- *Full name and address*: Including trading names and styles.

- *Legal status of the business*: Sole trader, partnership, limited company. It should be noted that information on sole traders and partnerships may well be less available than in respect of limited companies, who are required to file accounts at Companies House (within 10 months of the financial year end for private companies, and within 7 months of the financial year end for public companies).

- *Ownership of the business*: The names of the shareholders and the extent of their shareholding may be significant. Limited companies are subsidiaries when the parent company holds over 50 per cent of the shares, and a parent company is not obliged to pay the debts of a subsidiary. In practice few parent companies are willing to give guarantees in respect of their subsidiaries. Often the only connection is in a group overdraft facility, which may have a cross-guarantee to the bank from all the members of the group.

- *Time in business*: This is also significant, and a good report will show the customer's previous trading activities, perhaps as a proprietor or partnership, or as a company with different owners. If there is a year in the company title, for example, XYZ (2004) Ltd, this may indicate the revival of a previously failed business, often with the same owners or directors.

- *Activities and industrial sector*: The company's financing will differ according to its activity, as manufacturer, distributor (wholesale or retail), services or a mixture of all three. The customer's industrial sector affects the credit risk. Some are highly competitive (engineering), have high failure rates (construction, motor trade), many new and small companies (computer software, electronics), or must be in good high street positions, such as department stores and retailers generally. Some industry sectors have tiny profit margins (commercial vehicle makers), while others need very high margins (fashion retailers). It is useful to know also if the customer exports to risky markets, which may indicate sluggish cash inflow.

- *Financial information*: Good reports provide three years of balance sheet and profit and loss information, allowing simple comparisons and trends to be seen. Some reports provide ratios already calculated and explained, and some compare them with industry norms.

- *Background information*: Number of employees, size and ownership of premises, trade marks and product names, associated companies and directors other directorships can be useful.

- *Legal action and collection information*: Many agencies have their own collection divisions, so are aware of accounts passed by client to them on the subject of enquiry. Any County Court Judgments show that other suppliers have had to sue to obtain payment. There may also be comments on major Court cases, such as product liability claims in process or pending.

- *Payment experience*: Some reports give calculations of the payment times experienced by suppliers to the subject company, with an average of the delay for all payments.

BANK REFERENCES

Bank references have been around for a long time. In the dim and distant past, requests for bank references were usually for people, rather than companies, and banks were far more outspoken.

Given by the Bank of Liverpool in 1831:

> *'Thou may'st trust them.'*

Given by Smith, Payne and Smith in 1777:

> *'His connections are not very considerable, nor his fortune, but he is represented to me as an industrious, careful man, and worthy of any reasonable credit. As to his religion, I can learn nothing.' (This was an enquiry as to whether a Liverpool merchant was a person of good moral character and suitable to pay 'his addresses' to a young lady with a large fortune.)*

Royal Bank of Liverpool in 1844:

> *'The party named in your favour of yesterday has only recently compromised with his creditors, and I must leave you to draw your own inferences.'*

Bedfordshire Leighton Buzzard Bank in 1854:

'They are shady. No reliance should be placed upon their name.'

Cumberland Union Banking Company in 1857:

'One of the most dangerous men you can have to deal with, utterly unscrupulous and extremely plausible. The creditor will get a dose he little expects, and richly deserves it for associating himself with such a notorious gambler.'

In the twentieth century, bank references matured into brief and cryptic replies to status enquiries, usually open to a degree of interpretation, dependant upon the actual words themselves or the context in which they were delivered. Up until 1994, it was common practice to obtain bank details from the proposed new customer and for the supplier to approach his own bank to request a reference, usually in the simplest of formats:

'Bubblesqueak Ltd, £10,000 monthly on 30 days terms.
(Customer) Bank – Sort Code xx-xx-xx Bank reference please.'

It was even possible to approach the customer bank direct, but either way, back would come some form of reply, for example: 'B Ltd considered good for your figures and purpose.' There may not even have been any bank fee (depending on the supplier and his bank), but any fee would be small in any event, and debited directly to the enquirer's account.

This method of credit checking was used for many years, and indeed for many suppliers was often the only form of credit check undertaken. The view was that they were quick, were standard business practice and were inexpensive, though it has to be said that their usefulness and reliability was for those same many years the subject of lively argument between credit managers, ranging from 'wouldn't move without them' to 'waste of time'. They were confidential, of course, between the supplier and the banks and no authority was required from the customer himself to undertake such an enquiry.

There was a major overhaul by the banks of the whole reference process, which came into effect in 1994, as follows:

- Express written consent must be obtained from the subject of the enquiry. This must be signed by an authorised signatory under the customer's bank mandate.

- Normally, the authority of the customer is specific to a particular enquiry, known as 'specific authority'. However, the customer could also give his bank 'blanket authority', which is his consent for his bank to reply to each and every enquiry, from whatever source, without further reference by the bank back to the customer.

- The customer can also give his bank 'continuing specific authority'. This is where the relationship between supplier and customer is likely to be ongoing, and the supplier may require further bank references on that same customer as business develops and grows and where credit reviews are carried out regularly as part of the monitoring process. The bank is able to reply under this authority without further reference back to the customer.

- If so desired, the subject of the bank enquiry can receive a copy of the reference supplied by his bank.

- The request for a bank reference is sent to the supplier account holding bank on a standard form supplied by his bank and recognised by all clearing banks. The bank receiving the enquiry will reply directly to the enquirer.

- The fee (which varies from bank to bank and includes VAT at the standard rate) should accompany the request for the reference, and the replying bank should issue a VAT receipt with the reference.

- If the subject of the enquiry refuses to consent to his bank supplying a reference, the fee is returned to the enquirer, together with a note of explanation. (It will be for the enquiring credit manager to form his own opinion as to the significance of such a refusal.)

Some concessions followed the introduction of these new procedures in 1994, including allowing the use of credit cards to pay for references. It was long held that banks did not actually like providing references, the new rules being seen as a way of deterring reference requests, and certainly the decline in bank references since 1994 proved to be nothing short of dramatic. As bank references were never popular with many credit managers in the first place, the end result may not seem to have much importance to the business community. However, for many, bank references still remain a positive credit check action and it is useful to understand bank responses and their meaning:

- *'Undoubted'* – highly unusual, and means that the company is an excellent risk for the amount.

- *'Good for your figures and purpose'* – means 'probably good'. The bank has not said undoubted.

- *'Would not enter into a commitment they could not see their way clear to fulfil'* – this probably means that the amount enquired about is high.

- *'Unable to speak for your figure'* – this means the figure *is* too high, and should be taken very much as a warning.

- *'Resources appear fully committed'* – about as bad as you can get, implying that there is an inability to meet obligations and the bank would not lend them any more.

The bank may also report 'There is a charge/debenture registered', which is an additional comment to show that the bank have a first claim on assets, as registered at Companies House.

Often, in the past, experienced credit managers could add interpretation to bank replies by noting what the bank did not say, or by the actual words used, and different variations (such as 'would', 'should' and 'could') may well have altered the meaning to a degree. Late in 1998, banks appeared to change wording further (an example was the use of 'likely' in references where hitherto it had been 'would' or 'should'), using the argument that they were trying to 'modernise' the language used in references. Some confusion abounded, compounded by the fact that individual banks appeared to be making up their own form of wording, but some degree of commonality did return over the ensuing years.

Whatever the arguments and debates surrounding bank references, past and present, it should always be remembered that such a reference is only an opinion. That opinion is based solely on the account-holding bank's knowledge of the subject of enquiry using its own records as the basis for that knowledge. The subject may well have substantial funds elsewhere, about which the bank knows nothing, and it is not unusual in these days of high bank charges for customers to maintain in their current accounts only that which is needed to fund day-to-day trading activities, with funds not immediately needed deposited elsewhere earning interest.

TRADE REFERENCES

Trade references were once as common as bank references, and again thought by many to be inexpensive and often quick, using telephone or fax. Like bank references, however, they have long been considered to be of limited use, and not recommended if supplied by the customer himself – it is hard to imagine a customer providing names of dissatisfied suppliers. There is also a great danger of 'cultivated' suppliers always being quoted for trade reference purposes – those suppliers which the customer pays well at the expense of the majority of his other suppliers.

Referees are busy and have no obligation to an enquirer, but most credit managers act professionally and respond to each other. It can also be a useful way of making contact with others in the industry where, for example, there is no established credit circle. It can save time and avoid inaccuracy if the enquirer makes it easy for the referee to respond by having boxes for ticking, as shown in Figure 5.3 (page 134). Enquiry by telephone may produce more information, on a confidential basis.

FINANCIAL STATEMENTS

Balance sheets on all limited companies registered in England and Wales are required by law to be filed at Companies House, Cardiff and are available for public scrutiny. The balance sheet is the company's financial statement and can be obtained from Companies House, credit reference agencies or directly from the customer. In the case of non-limited company businesses, the likelihood is that accounts have been prepared (for tax and VAT purposes), so it is possible to ask the customer directly for copies so that credit terms and amounts can be assessed.

The set of financial statements is a very readable picture of the health of a company, giving the credit manager the opportunity to calculate credit

---

Enquiry for a credit reference
(please tick appropriate box and return to us in the prepaid envelope – we will be happy to reciprocate at any time)

Subject of enquiry...

How long known?

Only recently...

Less than one year...

Several years...

What credit terms?

30 days..

Longer (details?)..

How much sold per month?

Up to £1000...

£1000 - £5000...

More than £5000...

Payment experience

Prompt..

Up to 60 days slow...

More than 60 days slow...

Name of collection contact:..

Other useful information:..

Figure 5.3   Credit reference enquiry form

levels by the use of ratios. However, a balance sheet is a historical snapshot of a company at a moment in time now past. They are therefore out of date before they are issued, can be subject to a degree of 'window dressing' and can carry auditors' 'qualification'. Nevertheless, the vast majority of accounts are straightforward, and analysts can develop experience in studying their customers' accounts, spotting inconsistencies or identifying misleading parts. Except when the actual page called the 'balance sheet' is being discussed, the term 'balance sheet' covers the complete set of financial statements as required by the Companies Act 1985 to be filed annually at Companies House (within 10 months of the financial year end for private companies, and within seven months of the financial year end for public companies).

The statutory set of documents is submitted in a wide variety of style and quality, from glossy publications with photographs from the large corporations wishing to impress the market and investors, down to basic typed pages from accountants representing small companies. Whatever the style and presentation, the content still consists of the key documents listed below:

1.   Cover page (showing name of company and date of balance sheet).

2.   List of directors, registered office, auditors and bankers.

3.   Report of the directors to the shareholders.

4.   Auditor's report to the shareholders.

5.   Profit and Loss account, for the year (usually) up to the balance sheet date.

6.   Balance sheet, as at the date shown.

7.   Cash flow statement.

8.   Notes to the accounts.

Before going on to look at ratios, and their use in interpretation of accounts, there are useful points for credit managers to look at when assessing potential credit:

- *Report of the directors*: This presents the accounts to the shareholders and shows the principal activities and a review of the year (often just by referring to the later accounts). It also states the export content of the turnover, says whether dividends are being paid or not, shows directors' interests as shareholders and in any holding company, shows the dates of appointment and resignation of any directors, gives a table of fixed assets (or refers to its being in the notes to the accounts), and names the auditors and whether or not they are to be reappointed. Analysts should note the tone of the report for any optimism. It is reasonable to pay dividends to reward shareholders, but not if large losses have been sustained, or if the company is less than three years old, when profits are better retained to strengthen the new business. Resignation of directors may be significant – they may have advance knowledge of bad news which only becomes public later. Auditors normally continue, so not reappointing them may indicate a serious disagreement over the true results, or simply over audit fees. In the wake of the Enron scandal, and the involvement of Arthur Andersen, the question of auditors, their relationship with the client company, and their reappointment or otherwise remains the subject of ongoing debate and review. Directors' connections with other companies may be interesting.

- *Auditor's report*: This should simply state that the figures add up and are legal ('give a fair and true view' and 'comply with the Companies Act'). Sometimes, there is a qualification, where the auditors are not totally happy (for example, 'where complete figures were not available to us, we have accepted the assurances of the directors'). A more serious qualification would be 'the company has not complied with the Companies Act, Section XXX'. Where auditors say that the 'going concern basis depends upon continuing finance from Anybank Ltd' or that 'new finance is being sought', this is a distinct warning of credit risk and deserves clarification.

- *Notes to the accounts*: These refer to numbered items in the accounts and items of particular interest to credit managers are details of the parent company and 'contingent liabilities' which show possible debts which may hit the company later. For example, cross-guarantees may bring down the subject company if the bank calls on all group members to repay a loan to one of the group's companies in trouble.

- *The profit and loss account*: Sales less costs equal the profit for a stated period up to the date of the accounts, normally the financial year end. Four different stages of profit are shown: *gross profit, operating profit, net profit before tax* and *net profit after tax*.

  - *Gross profit* is the difference between total sales and the cost of raw materials, wages and overheads in producing the sales. (Sales less cost of sales = Gross profit.)

  - *Operating profit* is what is left from gross profit after operational expenses, such as office costs, sales commission and so on. (Gross profit less operating expense = Operating profit.)

  - *Profit before tax* includes items after the operating profit level, for example, interest paid on loans or received on deposits, non-standard profits or losses such as sale of investments or fixed assets. (Operating profit less non-operating expenses = NPBT.)

– *Net profit after tax:* Tax must be paid on final profits, reducing the total available for dividends or to be retained in the business. (NPBT less income tax = Net profit after tax.)

- A further calculation normally shows the retained profits from previous periods, plus the net profit after tax for the year, less any dividends payable. The balance is the new retained profit figure carried forward on the balance sheet (included in shareholders' funds in the net worth section).

- *The balance sheet*: This is a statement of the assets and liabilities of a business at a certain date, usually the financial year end. Larger companies produce yearly, half-yearly or quarterly (often monthly for internal purposes). Assets are owned by the business: liabilities are what the business owes. The total assets must always equal the total liabilities (hence 'balance'). The liabilities indicate the money made available to the business and not repaid at the date shown, for example, bank overdraft and trade creditors. The assets show how the business has used the money made available to it, for example, in debtors and stocks. (See Figure 5.4 for a table of assets.)

- *Group accounts*: A company with subsidiaries (that is, owning more than half their share capital) is required to produce accounts covering the whole of the group, usually comprising a consolidated Profit and Loss account and balance sheet. Associated companies are usually those in which the investing company holds 20 per cent or more (up to 50 per cent) of the shares in a company which is not a subsidiary.

- *Types of liabilities*: There are three groups of liabilities: current liabilities; long-term liabilities; and shareholders' funds (or equity). Shareholders own the business, so their funds are listed separately from 'outsiders', such as banks and creditors. Current and fixed liabilities are referred to as 'outside' or 'external'. Long-term liabilities represent long-term finance and normally carry interest charges. Current liabilities represent short-term finance, repayable within 12 months, for example, bank overdrafts, short-term loans and accounts payable (or trade creditors).

- *Shareholders' funds (equity)*: When a company is formed, part of its funding is provided by investors who buy shares. In return, the shareholders expect to receive dividends each year from the profits made. The balance sheet also shows profits retained in the business and not paid out as dividends. Every limited company is authorised to issue a stated amount of shares, called the authorised capital. Until it requires it all, it only invites shareholders to subscribe to the amount needed. Thus, the issued capital cannot exceed the authorised capital. Many companies are formed with £100 authorised capital and operate for years with only £2 issued capital. The company itself has a liability to shareholders for the capital subscribed, only repaid when a company is wound up, and only then if there are sufficient funds when all other debts have been paid. As both the investment by shareholders and the retained profits are owed by the business to the shareholders, they are known together as shareholders' funds, or equity. Profits earned and kept in the business are called retained earnings, or earned surplus. Increased value from revaluing assets is capital surplus. Earned surplus and capital surplus on the balance sheet are cumulative totals built up over the past years up to the balance sheet date.

- *Net worth*: The worth of a business is said to be the stated value of its assets (short term or current plus long term or fixed) minus all external liabilities (short and long term). The result is the total shown for shareholders' funds. In other words, the net worth of a business is the amount owed to its internal lenders, that is, shareholders. It should be noted, however, that in a break-up situation, such as insolvency or acquisition, assets are rarely found to be worth their balance sheet figure, whereas liabilities always are!

- *Cash flow statement*: This summarises the cash flows into and out of the business during the financial period showing purchase of stock not used during the period under review (the financial year), payments to creditors, purchase of fixed assets, payment of dividend and payment for redemption of shares, receipts from customers, receipts from any sale of fixed assets, loans received and receipts from any share issue. The purpose is to show how the cash flows (which could be negative as well as positive) over the year, all the major financing activities and also how any reported profits differ from related cash flows. In other words, a record of sources and uses of cash:

– Sources include cash from sales, injections of capital, long term borrowing, disposal of fixed assets and bank interest received.

– Uses include trading expenses, payments to suppliers and services, new fixed assets, long term loan repayment, interest paid, tax paid and withdrawal of capital by the business owners.

With cash and liquidity being vital for business survival, the cash flow statement focuses the attention of creditors more purposefully than the Profit and Loss account in so far as it more clearly illustrates the ability of the business to repay debts and is therefore of more concern than profitability. Profit can be generated on paper, but cash is far more objective from the perspective of the supplier or potential supplier.

As previously stated, private and public limited companies are required to file statutory documents at Companies House. At one time, there were few exemptions granted to companies, however small or large, but in recent years exemptions have been granted by UK governments to small and medium-sized companies. These are currently as below:

	Small companies	**Medium-sized companies**
Balance sheet	Abbreviated content	No concession
P&L account	Not required	Can start with gross profit
Notes to accounts	Very limited requirement	No need to show turnover/ profit by activities or markets
Directors' report	Not required	No concession

The definition of small and medium-sized companies and therefore the qualification for exemption is any two of the following three factors (from 6 April 2008):

	Small companies	Medium-sized companies
Turnover not exceeding	£6.5m	£25.9m
Balance sheet total not exceeding	£3.26m	£12.9m
Average employees not exceeding	50	250

The most important of these provisions for the credit manager is the absence of a profit and loss account for a small company. If the assessment is important enough, it is worth approaching the customer directly to request the missing data in order to decide on the credit level.

The above definitions are an increase on previous qualifications for exemption and there are currently proposals to increase these further from 2010. The ICM has consistently opposed exemptions on the grounds that limited liability is a privilege, protecting directors and shareholders in a way not accorded to sole traders and proprietors. The ICM has also vigorously contended that exemptions equate to restrictions available to creditors of information necessary to reach sensible credit decisions. It is stated that the latest proposals are to keep the UK in line with EU law, but the opposition, led by the ICM, has strongly argued that a turnover of £6.5m and a balance sheet total of £3.26 is hardly 'small' by any reasonable definition – constant increases have a negative impact on the whole credit granting process, and hence on business generally.

An exemption for the requirement for a company to have a statutory audit was first introduced by the UK government in 1994, at which time the turnover threshold was £90,000. Over the following years, the threshold has been raised at regular intervals, reaching a turnover not exceeding £5.6m (and gross assets not exceeding £2.8m). Combined with actual account filing exemptions, the result is far less 'accurate', and 'audited', figures being available to assist credit managers in making sensible balanced credit decisions. This cannot make commercial sense by any measure and since the banking fiasco of 2008, it has fallen more and more upon trade creditors to support businesses ongoing by granting credit facilities – it is utter nonsense on the part of the authorities therefore to constantly reduce and dilute the information available and necessary for credit managers to make the right decisions. What is more ridiculous is the contention that such exemptions 'reduce red tape' and 'encourage entrepreneurs' – companies still have to prepare accounts for their bankers and for the tax authorities, and full audited accounts remain the best weapon in their armoury in the battle for funding support from whatever source. The credit management profession, through the ICM in the UK and throughout Europe will continue to lead the fight against constant erosion of information quality.

Asset	How valued
Quick assets (most liquid)	
Cash at bank	actual
Cash in hand	actual
Marketable investments	at lower cost or market value
Other current assets	
Deposits paid	at cost
Pre-paid expenses (e.g. rent)	at cost
Accounts receivable	at full value less doubtful debt provision
Employee accounts	at full value less doubtful debt provision
Other debts	at full value less doubtful debt provision
Stocks (inventory), i.e.	
Finished goods	at lower of cost or current value less depreciation
Work in progress	at lower of cost or current value less depreciation
Raw materials	at lower of cost or current value less depreciation.
Fixed assets (least liquid), i.e.	
Land	at cost or valuation
Buildings	at cost less depreciation
Plant	at cost less depreciation
Machinery	at cost less depreciation
Fixtures and fittings	at cost less depreciation
Motor vehicles	at cost less depreciation

Figure 5.4   Table of assets (and their valuation method)

Interpretation of Accounts

It is worth deciding a 'pain' level, that is, an amount which would really hurt if it were lost and then organise an ongoing view of the financial status of all debtors above this level, using an analysis of key balance sheet items. Even when analysis is not made in depth, most credit managers would at least check the basic solvency and liquidity of customers with significant exposures. Much time and expense can then be saved by not giving as much deep analysis to small value (that is, not too painful if lost) accounts.

SOLVENCY

Solvency is calculated as a percentage or a number of 'times'. It indicates the proportion of shareholders' funds in the total liabilities and is sometimes called the *creditors' protection ratio*. The higher the proportion of shareholders' funds, compared to external debts, the more comfort is provided for creditors.

The expression *gearing* has different definitions and can be misleading. For credit analysis, it is best used to show assets financed by shareholders' funds versus interest-bearing borrowed funds. A high solvency ratio (high proportion of shareholders' funds) represents low gearing, low risk and the customer's capacity for borrowing more external finance, or credit. A low solvency ratio indicates high gearing, high risk and less scope for further borrowing in the event of credit difficulties.

LIQUIDITY

Current ratio = current assets divided by current liabilities.
Quick ratio = current assets less stock divided by current liabilities.

There should be sufficient current assets to turn into cash with which to settle current debts. A current ratio below 1 indicates a credit risk because of insufficient cash-producing assets, depending on the due dates of liabilities. A very high ratio, over say 3, although comfortable for creditors, indicates inefficient use of assets.

The quick ratio, also called the *acid test*, measures the more immediate liquidity, to meet current liabilities (that is, cash and debtors). A quick ratio of 1 or above is good, although many companies these days survive with a quick ratio of about 0.8.

SALES COMPARISON

This is sales for the current year compared to previous years. A reduction leads the analyst to see how other ratios have been managed in a decline.

PROFIT COMPARISON

This is the profit for the current year compared to previous years. The percentage should match or exceed the percentage of sales growth or decline. Lower growth in profits than sales indicates lack of management control and should be investigated further.

SALES COMPARED TO NET ASSETS

This refers to the use of assets to produce sales. Increased ratio year on year is desirable as long as profit growth keep pace.

SALES COMPARED TO WORKING CAPITAL (THAT IS, NET CURRENT ASSETS)

This shows the efficiency in use of working capital to produce sales. An excessively high ratio, or sudden increase, may indicate overtrading, where profits are not retained in the business. Where sales race ahead of liquidity, the company may have to delay payment to suppliers.

The following ratios are also widely used in credit analysis:

Net profit before tax as a percentage of sales

Shows overall efficiency and control of costs. It is difficult when sales decline to reduce costs in the same proportion, and serious trouble can follow.

Net profit before tax as a percentage of net assets (current and long term)

Shows the efficiency in using assets to produce profits.

Sales compared to stocks

Shows how long stocks take to be sold, for example, a ratio of three times means that it takes four months to achieve sales. A higher than average ratio for the particular industry indicates competitive success. Slow moving stocks can be a major reason for slow payments.

Stocks compared to working capital (net current assets)

Shows how much of the working capital is tied up by raw material, work in progress and finished goods. It should be steady in relation to sales growth, subject to seasonal trade. An increasing level may indicate obsolete stocks or weak stock control.

Current liabilities compared to net worth

If short-term debts are well covered by net worth, there is a good chance of creditors being paid. Secured creditors are paid before unsecured creditors receive any payment at all; so information is needed on the proportion of the debtor's outstanding debt that is secured.

Sales compared to trade debtors

Shows the average time taken by the company to collect debts from customers. A ratio of 3:1 indicates one-third of a year's sales unpaid, or 120 days. If terms are 30 days, this is excessive and indicates a lack of credit control and a shortage of liquidity to pay creditors.

Current assets cover for current liabilities

Shows the assets available to produce cash to meet current debts. A ratio of 2:1 may be regarded as comfortable, but it has to be said that in recent years a ratio of 1:1 has been seen and regarded as not abnormal. Some current assets are not very liquid and a high stock figure can mean excessive stocks, whether raw materials, slow-moving finished goods; or work in progress which is blocked for technical or customer reasons. Current liabilities differ also in their urgency. Most trade creditors expect to be paid within 60 days but a bank overdraft, although repayable on demand, may be allowed to run on without pressure to repay or reduce it.

QUICK ASSETS COVER FOR CURRENT LIABILITIES

Known as the 'acid test', this is the most useful guide to the customer's ability to pay its way in the short term. It excludes stocks from current assets and assumes that the customer's own trade debtors will become cash soon.

The following is a recommended set of ratios for risk assessment:

1.   *Current ratio*: Current assets cover for current liabilities. This shows the ability to meet debts from assets becoming cash in the short term.

2.   *Acid test*: The more available cover for debts after excluding stocks. A company should be able to meet most of its debts without selling more stocks.

3. *Stock turnover*: Stocks x 360 days divided by annual sales gives the rate at which stocks are sold. This is especially useful when added to DSO to show how long the purchase-to-cash process takes.

4. *DSO (days sales outstanding or Collection Period)*: Debtors x 360 divided by sales, to show how long sales are unpaid.

5. *External debt/net worth*: Either all debt, current and long term, divided by net assets, or just the current liabilities. This shows how reliant the customer is on lenders (trade and bank) compared to its own investment.

6. *Interest cover*: Interest payable as a proportion of profit before tax and interest. Obviously, interest expense should not exceed profit. Even 50 per cent is a warning sign. When a bank sees its income (that is, interest) not being covered by earnings, it tends to begin to contemplate receivership.

7. *Profit on sales*: NPBT as a percentage of total sales. This shows how much is left from sales after total costs, and is thus available to pay out as dividends or retain in the business; 5 per cent is typical for many industry sectors, with firms varying within them.

It should be remembered that ratios alone can be misleading. It is always better to compare any one ratio with the same ratio for the previous year, or better, two years. Three successive years of financial ratios are a reliable indicator of the progress of a company.

To this end, it is worth devising a standard worksheet to record a customer's ratios and trends. The worksheet is then available at a glance, instead of having to remember the basis for previous credit decisions. Key ratios for a simple credit assessment worksheet follows:

LIQUIDITY
1. Current ratio (times) = Current assets ÷ Current liabilities
2. Quick ratio 'Acid test' (times) = Current assets less stocks
     ÷ Current liabilities
3. Stock turnover (days) = Stock × 365 ÷ Sales
4. Collection period – DSO (days) = Debtors × 365 ÷ Sales

DEBT

5. Creditor protection ratio (%) = Net worth × 100 ÷ Current liabilities
6. Interest cover ratio (%) = Interest expense × 100 ÷ Profit before tax + interest
7. Net margin (%) = Profit before tax × 100

SALES

8. Net worth growth (%) = Net worth current year less previous year × 100 ÷ Net worth previous year
9. Sales growth (%) = Sales current year less previous year × 100 ÷ Sales previous year
10. Profit growth (%) = NPBT current year less previous year × 100 ÷ NPBT previous year

A pro forma worksheet with these ratios is given in Figure 5.5

RATIO ANALYSIS – WORKSHEET

CUSTOMER :			Date:	
	Latest year	Previous year	Year before	Comments
LIQUIDITY				
1 Current ratio (times)				
2 Quick ratio (times)				
3 Stock ratio (days)				
4 Collection period (days)				
DEBT				
5 Creditor protection ratio (%)				
6 Interest cover ratio (%)				
PROFIT AND GROWTH				
7 Net margin (%)				
8 Net worth growth (%)				
9 Sales growth (%)				
10 Profit growth (%)				
OVERALL OPINION (including credit rating if needed)				

Figure 5.5   Blank worksheet for risk assessment

BUBBLESQUEAK LIMITED

FINANCIAL STATEMENTS

YEAR ENDED 31 MAY 2008

Figure 5.6   Sample set of financial accounts: Bubblesqueak Ltd

BUBBLESQUEAK LIMITED

DIRECTORS, SECRETARY AND ADVISERS

DIRECTORS: (Chairman)
                                                                 (Managing Director)
                                                                 (Finance Director)

SECRETARY:

REGISTERED OFFICE:

AUDITORS: & Co
                                               Chartered Accountants

BANKERS: Bank Plc

Figure 5.6   *Continued*

BUBBLESQUEAK LIMITED

REPORT OF THE DIRECTORS

The directors present their report with the accounts of the company for the year ended 31st May 2008

PRINCIPAL ACTIVITY

The principal activity of the company in the year under review was the manufacture and provision of PVC doors and windows.

REVIEW OF BUSINESS

A summary of the results for the year's trading is given on page 5 of the accounts.

DIVIDENDS

The directors do not propose any payment of a dividend for the year.

DIRECTORS' INTERESTS

The directors in office during the year held no interests in the issued ordinary share capital of the company.
The directors' interests in the company's holding company are shown in the accounts of that company.

FIXED ASSETS

Acquisitions and disposals of the tangible fixed assets in the year are shown under Note 8 in the notes to the accounts.

AUDITORS

The auditors, Messrs.   & Company will be proposed for re-appointment in accordance with Section 384 of the Companies Act 1985.

BY ORDER OF THE BOARD

SECRETARY

DATED:

Figure 5.6   *Continued*

REPORT OF THE AUDITORS TO THE MEMBERS OF
BUBBLESQUEAK LIMITED

We have audited the accounts set out on pages 5 – 12 in accordance with approved
auditing standards.

In our opinion the accounts, which have been prepared under the historical cost
convention, give a true and fair view of the state of the company's affairs as at 31 May
2008 and of the profit cash flow satement for the year ended on that date and comply
with the Companies Act 1985.

                                   & COMPANY
CHARTERED ACCOUNTANTS

DATED:

Figure 5.6   *Continued*

BUBBLESQUEAK LTD
PROFIT AND LOSS ACCOUNT
FOR THE YEAR ENDED 31st MAY 2008

	Note	£	2008 £	£	2007 £
TURNOVER	2		3,361,275		2,784,760
Cost of sales			2,031,824		1,610,520
GROSS PROFIT			1,329,451		1,174,240
Distribution Expenses		82,715		56,103	
Administrative Expenses		355,214		329,363	
Other Operating Charges		780,283		679,784	
			1,218,212		1,065,250
			111,239		108,990
OTHER INCOME					
Commissions Received		29,535		32,939	
Discounts Received		38,414		3,440	
Regional Development Grant		1,270		1,500	
Interest Received		1,048		1,091	
			70,267		38,970
OPERATING PROFIT	3		181,506		147,960
INTEREST PAYABLE	6		6,085		7,880
PROFIT on ordinary activities before taxation			175,421		140,080
TAXATION	7		48,023		46,330
PROFIT on ordinary activities after taxation			127,398		93,750
RETAINED PROFIT at 1st June 2007			93,750		-
RETAINED PROFIT at 31st May 2008			221,148		93,750

Figure 5.6   *Continued*

BUBBLESQUEAK LTD
BALANCE SHEET
FOR THE YEAR ENDED 31st MAY 2008

	Note	2008 £	£	2007 £	£
FIXED ASSETS					
Tangible assets	8		113,333		142,352
CURRENT ASSETS					
Stocks	9	150,072		154,772	
Debtors	10	343,934		333,384	
Cash at bank and in hand		128,177		97,754	
		622,183		585,910	
CREDITORS: Amounts falling Due Within One Year	11	511,664		626,339	
NET CURRENT ASSETS (LIABILITIES)			110,519		(40,429)
TOTAL ASSETS LESS CURRENT LIABILITIES			223,852		101,923
CREDITORS: Amounts Falling Due After More Than One Year	12		2,702		8,171
NET ASSETS			221,150		93,752
CAPITAL AND RESERVES					
Called up Share Capital	13		2		2
Profit and Loss Account			221,148		93,750
			221,150		93,752

DIRECTOR:

DIRECTOR:

THESE ACCOUNTS WERE APPROVED BY THE BOARD ON:

Figure 5.6   *Continued*

BUBBLESQUEAK LTD
STATEMENT OF CASH FLOW
FOR THE YEAR ENDED 31st MAY 2008

	2008 £	2007 £
Operating profit from continuing operations	175,421	140,088
Depreciation	36,894	36,025
Amortisation of intangible fixed assets	73	(2,857)
	212,388	173,256
Changes in working capital		
Increase/Decrease in Debtors	10,550	333,384
Increase/Decrease in Creditors	114,675	(580,002)
Increase/Decrease in Stock	(4,070)	154,772
	121,155	(91,846)
Cash generated by operations	333,543	81,410
Income taxes paid	- 48,023	-
Net cash from operating activities	381,566	81,410
Purchases of fixed assets	26,070	254,667
Proceeds from sale of assets	12,722	79,146
Commission received	29,535	32,939
Interest received	1,048	1,091
Interest paid	(6,085)	(7,880)
Cash and cash equivalent	30,350	527
Increase	73	97,225
	30,423	97,752

Figure 5.6 *Continued*

BUBBLESQUEAK LTD

NOTES TO THE ACCOUNTS
FOR THE YEAR ENDED 31st MAY 2008

1. **ACCOUNTING POLICIES**
    a) Basis of Accounting:
       The Accounts have been prepared under The Historical Cost Convention.

    b) Turnover:
       Turnover represents net invoiced sales of goods, excluding value added tax.

    c) Tangible Fixed Assets:
       Depreciation is provided at the following annual rates in order to write off each asset over its
       estimated useful life:-

Plant and Machinery	10% on cost
Fixtures and Fittings	12.5% on cost
Motor Vehicles	25% on cost

    d) Stocks:
       Stock and work in progress are valued at the lower of cost and net realisable value, cost
       includes all direct expenditure and a proportion of factory and other overheads.

    e) Deferred Taxation:
       Deferred taxation is provided wherever a liability is expected to arise in the foreseeable
       future.

2. **TURNOVER**
    The turnover and Profit before taxation is attributed to the one principal activity of the company.

3. **OPERATING PROFIT**

	2008 £	2007 £
is stated after charging:		
Depreciation of Tangible Fixed Assets	36,894	36,025
Hire of Plant and Equipment	16,355	22,014
Directors Remuneration (Notes 4 & 5)	37,384	46.136
Staff Costs (Note 5)	273,622	213,256
Auditors Remuneration	5,000	5,000
and crediting other operating income		
Commissions Received	29,535	32,939
Discounts Received	38,414	3,440
Grant	1,270	1,500
Interest Received	1,048	1,097

Figure 5.6   *Continued*

BUBBLESQUEAK LTD

NOTES TO THE ACCOUNTS (continued)
FOR THE YEAR ENDED 31st MAY 2008

	2008 £	2007 £
4. DIRECTORS EMOLUMENTS		
Directors emoluments disclosed in accordance schedule 5 of the Companies Act 1985 and excluding Pension contributions are:		
a) Emoluments of the Chairman	_	11,666
b) Emoluments of the highest paid director	37,384	34,470
5. STAFF COSTS		
Directors remuneration	37,384	46,136
Wages and Salaries	188,592	192,503
Social Security Costs	20,665	20,753
Pension Contributions	1,014	20,000
	247,655	279,392

The average weekly number of employees during the year was as follows:

	Number	Number
Office and Management	16	16
Production , Distribution and Sales	10	10
	26	26

6. INTEREST PAYABLE	£	£
Pension fund loan	2,299	3,161
Hire Purchase	3,786	4,607
Taxation	-	111
	6,085	7,879

7. TAXATION		
Corporation tax on the adjusted results of the year	-	46,337
Group Relief Payment	48,023	=
	48,023	46,337

Figure 5.6   *Continued*

BUBBLESQUEAK LTD

NOTES TO THE ACCOUNTS (continued)
FOR THE YEAR ENDED 31st MAY 2008

	Leasehold Properties (Short Lease) £	Plant Fixtures and Fittings £	Motor Vehicles £	Total £
8. TANGIBLE ASSETS				
AT COST				
At 1 June 2007	20,252	112,202	82,530	214,984
Group Transfer	-	-	4,750	4,750
Additions	-	8,773	8,830	17,603
Disposals	-	-	(28,545)	(28,545)
At 31 May 2008	20,252	120,975	67,565	208,792
DEPRECIATION				
At 1 June 2007	-	45,988	26,343	72,161
Group Transfer	-	-	1,683	1,683
Charge for the year	-	11,687	25,207	36,894
Eliminated on disposals	-	-	(15,750)	(15,750)
At 31 May 2008	-	57,675	37,783	95,458
WRITTEN DOWN VALUES				
At 31 May 2008	20,252	63,300	29,782	113,334
At 31 May 2007	20,252	66,214	55,887	142,353

9. **STOCKS**

	2008 £	2007 £
Raw materials	76,408	92,607
Work-in-progress	14,960	4,000
Finished Goods	58,704	58,165
	150,072	154,772

Figure 5.6   *Continued*

BUBBLESQUEAK LTD

NOTES TO THE ACCOUNTS (continued)

FOR THE YEAR ENDED 31st MAY 2008

10. DEBTORS	2008	2007
	£	£
Accounts receivable within one year –		
Trade Debtors	178,811	264,416
Other Debtors	-	9,502
Prepayments	65,123	59,466
	343,934	333,384

11. *CREDITORS: AMOUNTS FALLING DUE*
    WITHIN ONE YEAR

	2008	2007
Trade Creditors	222,614	197,599
Customers Deposits	75,823	103,475
Hire Purchase	8,861	17,288
Social Security and Other Taxes	52,983	58,445
Other Creditors	-	16,403
Accruals	82,366	78,025
Amounts owed to Group Companies	22,680	82,422
Pension Fund Loan Account	-	26,345
Corporation Tax	46,337	46,337
	511,664	626,399

12. **CREDITORS: AMOUNTS FALLING DUE**
    AFTER MORE THAN ONE YEAR

	2008	2007
Hire Purchase	2,702	8,171

Figure 5.6   *Continued*

BUBBLESQUEAK LTD

NOTES TO THE ACCOUNTS (continued)

FOR THE YEAR ENDED 31st MAY 2008

		2008	2007
13.	**CALLED UP SHARE CAPITAL**	£	£
	Authorised:		
	10000 Ordinary Shares of £1 each	10,000	10,000
	Allotted, issued and fully paid:		
	2 Ordinary Shares of £1 each	2	2

14. **HOLDING COMPANY**

The company's ultimate holding company is Squeakbubble Group Ltd, a company incorporated in Great Britain and registered in England. The proportion of the company's issued ordinary capital held by the holding company is 100%.

15. **CONTINGENT LIABILITIES**

There is a contingent liability in respect of cross guarantees given to   Bank plc on behalf of Squeakbubble Group Ltd and all of its subsidiaries in the normal course of business amounting to £440,718 at 31st May 2008 (2007: £NIL).

Figure 5.6   *Concluded*

There are computer-assisted methods available for risk assessment, which include self-designed PC spreadsheet programs, using balance sheet data loaded by the user to produce ratios as defined in-house, which may also produce credit ratings and risk codes. It is possible to purchase proprietory PC programs, the user specifying the data to be loaded, with some leeway for weighting preferred ratios. Solvency model programs enable the user to load specific data, obtain ratios and scores, and compare them to average industry performance, sometimes with predictions of insolvency risk, based upon scores for past failures.

Using the example financial accounts of Bubblesqueak Ltd (Figure 5.6) and the blank worksheet for risk assessment (Figure 5.5), what follows is a completed Ratio Analysis Worksheet (Figure 5.7):

RATIO ANALYSIS – WORKSHEET				
CUSTOMER: Bubblesqueak Ltd			Date: 22.10.08	
	Latest year	Previous year	Year before	Comments
LIQUIDITY				
1 Current ratio (times)	1.2	0.9		Improved
2 Quick ratio (times)	0.9	0.7		Improved
3 Stock ratio (days)	16.3	20.3		faster sales
4 Collection period (days)	37.3	43.6		faster cash
DEBT				
5 Creditor protection ratio (%)	43%	15%		better cover
6 Interest burden ratio (%)	3%	5%		negligible
PROFIT AND GROWTH				
7 Net margin (%)	5.2%	5.0%		more profitable
8 Net worth growth (%)	135%	n/avail		excellent
9 Sales growth (%)	21%	n/avail		very good
10 Profit growth (%)	25%	n/avail		better than sales %
OVERALL OPINION (including credit rating if needed) Only two years available – subject to this, progress has been very good. Noted big contingent liability in notes to the accounts. Subject to satisfaction on investigation of this, propose a credit rating of £22,000 – based on lower of 10% net worth or 20% working capital. Risk category = 'B' (average).				

Figure 5.7   Completed worksheet – Bubblesqueak Ltd

Summary

Credit managers should not become obsessed with balance sheets – many factors point to credit *ability* as well as credit *worth*, but not to utilise every piece of financial data available would be like driving an expensive car with the handbrake still on. It is easy in this era of Internet access to download bucketfuls of data on to PCs, and complete worksheets such as illustrated in Figures 5.5 and 5.7 with comparative ease.

Proper risk assessment must be carried out on major accounts, say, those making up 80 per cent of the debtors total, both at the outset and at reasonable intervals. Conversely, there is no need to do a lot of work on small accounts, for which brief references will suffice – subsequent ledger experience and growth prospects may justify fuller reviews.

Remember, credit worth can either be calculated from data, or purchased via credit reference agency reports. An agreed policy is needed to decide how much time and effort it is worth expending to match sales values and the amounts of possible losses

Good risk assessment means: *no expensive shocks.*

INSTITUTE OF CREDIT MANAGEMENT – JANUARY 2008

Introductory Credit Management: Certificate Level 3

A credit manager needs to be aware of the risks involved in granting credit to different types of customer.

Identify the characteristics of the following most common type of business organisations in the UK, and for each assess the factors a credit manager would take into consideration when granting unsecured credit.

Sole traders

Partnerships

Limited companies.

6

Credit Ratings and Risk Categories

Glen Bullivant

• Why have credit ratings • Calculating credit ratings • Risk categories • Identifying and dealing with high-risk accounts • Bad debt reserves • Effective credit management •

Why Have Credit Ratings?

Life is never easy, nor it would seem was it ever meant to be. In any profession or workplace, there will always be the need to find more efficient, as well as more reliable, ways of doing things. For employers, there are cost implications and for employees, the sometimes seemingly impossible goal of job satisfaction. Perhaps in some circumstances, it is desirable for the credit manager to see and approve every single customer order that is received – in the vast majority of trades and industries, this is, of course, time consuming and totally unnecessary. Indeed, the credit manager should only *need* to see the exceptions, or those orders where customers do not fit previously judged and established criteria. The principle is to decide beforehand what a customer is worth, what level of exposure would be considered acceptable and what would be the likelihood of that customer meeting obligations on time. These criteria can easily be computerised, enabling orders to go whistling through without interruption on the provision that those criteria are met.

Many companies talk of 'credit limits' or 'credit lines'. 'Credit limit' is perhaps the most widely used expression as far as customers are concerned, but it does have a restrictive ring to it, and 'credit line' sounds more positive, as well as more appropriate, especially to sales staff and customers. However, 'credit rating' is in common usage when describing countries (the USA has a higher rating than Argentina, for example), and the term is now increasingly understood by consumers. It follows that most sales and marketing staff, as well as customers and those not directly involved, would better appreciate 'credit rating' as a measure against which decisions can be taken quickly and easily.

Not all companies bother with specific credit ratings for customers. Some operate quite happily by running checks on customers, deciding they are a good or bad credit risk, then allowing credit accordingly, without recording any figures or codes. This approach is often decided in the sales area and usually done when an account is opened. Fortunately, in recent years this practice has declined in popularity as more and more companies recognise that this informal approach is inherently weak, since:

- decision making is subjective, with little method or explanation;

- customers' fortunes change, requiring updated reviews, when little evidence is on file for the previous credit decision;

- there is no strong belief in the credit decision, put to the test when and if subsequent disagreements arise;

- junior staff remain untrained in company credit decision making.

Calculating and recording credit ratings on the other hand carry benefits:

- the policy decision to allow a customer time to pay is quantified into a maximum that can be owed to a seller, based on information;

- the decision-making process can be operated consistently;

- the mass of data examined can be condensed into a credit figure;

- there is little need to keep re-examining paperwork;

- the credit rating is easily shown on computer files and screens, for example, Sales Ledger, order processing systems, customer lists and so on;

- staff respect the credit ratings and operate to them with confidence;

- credit ratings are easily justified to customers and help in negotiations;

- the whole process is transparent, and objective.

Calculating Credit Ratings

Credit managers will all have individual ideas about how best to calculate credit ratings, and in essence there is no standard, agreed method. The bottom line, however, must always be the answer to the question, 'How much are we happy to be owed by this customer?' A variety of data input will be used by most, if not all, from financial analysis of balance sheet numbers, payment references and local knowledge through to full blown risk analysis carried out by specialists.

A seller can purchase an opinion from a credit reference agency, obtain a decision from a credit insurer, or simply undertake his own calculation and assessment. For those who undertake the risk assessment role themselves, and decide upon their own credit rating to apply, there are two main approaches, either:

1. if the financials look good enough for our proposed sales, then our monthly figure (or two or three times this) shall be the credit rating; or

2. regardless of our intended sales, we shall set a maximum level we believe to be safe and are willing to be owed.

The first method may be considered adequate, but it is in reality a rather lazy approach, and certainly not forward looking. For one thing it requires constant revision. All too often accounts are opened with a credit limit which may appear adequate at the time, but which soon become out of date as business grows and needs to be revised upwards. It can also appear restrictive, in that the message sent by credit control looks as if the figure opened as the credit rating is a 'limit' and there is no encouragement for sales to seek additional business. It can actually put sales people off, in that they know that increased business will trigger the whole credit assessment process off again, and may be perceived by them to be another hurdle to jump, placed there by credit control. It is true to say, of course, that a rating based upon current anticipated levels of business will act as a trigger to review payments and risk if sales do increase.

Where the *maximum* debt level is used, as in the second method, a typical approach is to take a proportion of the customer's known financial worth, such as the lesser of 10 per cent of net worth or 20 per cent of working capital, with an overriding maximum of say 20 per cent of total creditors (never wise to become too prominent a creditor – eggs in baskets and so on!). The great benefit of this second method is that it encourages sales staff to sell up to the published figure without the need for prior credit approval. If the *rating* is the *limit*, as perceived by sales, it is far better for that limit to be seen as both realistic and non-restrictive.

A more refined way of using a percentage of net worth or working capital is to allow a smaller or larger percentage according to risk code, namely:

Risk category	Net worth %	Working capital %
High risk ('C')	5	10
Average ('B')	10	20
Low risk ('A')	15	30

Using the Bubblesqueak Ltd example given in Chapter 5, a 'C' category may be justified because of the contingent liability. In that case, their credit rating would become £11,000, not £22,000.

The concept of 'Working Worth' invented by John Coleshaw in his book *Credit Analysis* (1989), averages working capital and net worth. As such, working worth is a good description of the capital available for further credit.

The 'proportion of worth' approach is enhanced in many companies by PC-based scoring systems. The credit analyst loads items from the balance sheet and profit and loss account for the last two or three years, and using preset parameters, the data produces a score. This score can then be applied to the net worth or working capital figure. Again using the Bubblesqueak Ltd accounts from Chapter 5, this approach is well illustrated in Figure 6.1. It can be done

---

BUBBLESQUEAK LTD

Current Assets/Current Liablities   1.2

Quick Assets/Current Liabilities   0.9

Net Worth/Current Liabilities   0.4

Net Worth/Total Liabilities   0.4

Score   <u>2.9</u>

Working Worth = (£110,519 + £221,151) /2 = £165,835

Scale to produce percentage of working worth

- 4.5 or worse	=	0% of Working Worth
- 3.2 to –4.5	=	5% " "
-1.8 to –3.2	=	10% " "
-0.4 to –1.8	=	15% " "
+0.3 to –0.4	=	17.5% " "
<u>+0.3 or better</u>	=	<u>20%</u> " <u>"</u> = £33,000 Credit Rating

---

Figure 6.1   Credit rating using scoring from four ratios

manually, provided it is kept simple, but as most credit managers are now deemed to be PC literate, it is reasonable to assume that the trusty desktop or laptop will take whatever strain there is.

Another simple way of 'scoring' is to use a combination of latest year and year-on-year figures. The case for this is that relatively poor ratios that have improved over the last two years are better than currently satisfactory ratios that are deteriorating.

Many companies, organisations and individual credit managers have developed their own approaches to the calculation of credit ratings. A typical example would be that used for some years by a building trade association, which checked prospective members for technical performance and financial capability. Once admitted, a member was entitled to use its qualification to take deposits from the public so it was clearly important that the prospective member was seen to be able to complete orders without risk of loss by consumers of their deposits.

The list of parameters in Figure 6.2 was developed after analysis of 100 randomly selected companies in the building industry sector, who were trading three years previously. Twenty two had since ceased trading. There was a clear distinction in the listed ratios between failed companies and survivors. The '100 company' sampling exercise, retested every two years, confirmed the pattern. Statistical experts agree that 100 companies existing three years ago, selected at random, are a sound basis for sampling trends of success and failure.

Trade Association Risk Assessment: Bubblesqueak Builders Ltd (score = *)		
NPBT % (average 3 years)	over 8% 5–8% 2–5% below 2%	0 1 2 3*
NPBT Trend	increases years 2 & 3 mixed decreases years 2 & 3	0 2* 3
Interest to NPBT % (latest year)	below 50% 50–90% over 90%	0* 1 3
Creditors to net worth % (latest year)	below 75% 75–100% over 100%	0 1 3*
Current ratio % (average 3 years)	over 150% 100 – 150% 85–100% below 85%	0 1 2* 3
Current ratio trend	increases years 2 & 3 mixed decreases years 2 & 3	0 1* 3
Liquidity ratio % (latest year)	over 100% 75–100% below 75%	0 1 3*

Figure 6.2   Credit scoring for risk assessment

Trade Association Risk Assessment: Bubblesqueak Builders Ltd (score = *)		
Collection period (days–latest year)	below 40 days 41–90 over 90	0* 1 3
Stock turnover (days–latest year)	below 60 days 60–110 over 110	0* 2 3
Stock trend	reduction years 2 & 3 mixed increase years 2 & 3	0 1* 2
Personal assessment (from overall scan of data)	excellent status good status slight concern serious concern	0 1 2* 3
Possible score range 0–32 * Applicant score 17 = Fail (Company invited to reapply the following year if results are better, or to supply financial guarantee of third party who pass this test)		
Basis for acceptance: score 16 or less to 'pass')		

Figure 6.2   *Concluded*

Risk Categories

Alongside the credit rating, which is a guide to the liquidity of a customer, there should ideally be a risk category, or risk code. This is an indication as to the solvency of the customer and is more to do with the likely survival of the company in the short, medium and longer term. Levels of solvency vary between companies (and can vary considerably between industries) and though it may be appropriate in principle to view all customers as being of equal importance and value from a customer service standpoint, it is not appropriate to treat all customers as being equally valuable when the likelihood of survival of some is less than that of others. In other words, why spend marketing efforts and budgets on failing customers at the expense of those much more likely to survive and prove profitable to the seller?

Credit ratings (limits) and risk categories (codes) sit together as a real guide to assist credit managers in the smooth flow of order process and account management. Some companies use only risk categories, not bothering with credit value ratings. This is in the belief that risk categories alone decide priorities for pricing, delivery and after-sales service, and that strong collection action will take care of any overdues. The contrary argument of those in favour of credit ratings is that problems and costs are avoided without friction at an early stage by selling only up to calculated limits. Combining both categories and ratings draws from the best of both – the seller can be confident in value *and* in ability, so that sales effort and collection effort are both concentrated where they are needed.

A basic system of 'A' = no risk; 'B' = average risk; and 'C' = high risk indicates the likelihood of a bad debt. It is possible to have a larger number of categories, representing several other shades of definition, but too many codes are counter-productive. If the category system becomes too complex, explaining the more subtle differences between a customer in category 'B1' or 'D2' becomes almost impossible for the average managing director or sales manager to understand. On the other hand even non credit people can clearly see the distinction between 'high risk' and 'no risk'.

Code 'A' can be allocated to government departments, official bodies and the major 'blue chip' companies extremely unlikely to fail leaving bad debts. It is unlikely that there will be many of these! Code 'C' should be applied to persistent slow payers, customers admitting cash flow problems and those with recent Court judgments. Also in category 'C' will be those companies with declining solvency ratios and increasing interest burdens – it is quite likely that their lending bank will not remain patient for ever, and their prime responsibility is to protect their own interests. The rest, those who do not readily qualify for 'A' or 'C' will naturally fall into category 'B', and for most companies the majority of their customer base will be in this section.

In the majority of instances, assuming that the customer base has been correctly coded, no future insolvency should come as a surprise on the grounds that insolvencies should be 'C' code accounts. This knowledge gives a useful focus for risk control steps.

It is important to remember that none of the customers and their codes are set in concrete. It is quite likely that customers will move between codes from time to time, up or down. Regular credit reviews, payment experience and other events can move a previously 'no risk' into 'average risk', and it is not unknown for customers who had initially been identified as 'high risk' to actually survive and prosper, thus elevating themselves from 'C' to 'B'. It is also important to be aware of the fact that the sellers' own collection experience will influence the coding in so far as customer X, though coded 'A' might well be financially sound and unlikely to fail, but customer X is a persistently slow payer and requires more than usual collection activity than most 'A' customers. Hence, code 'B' might be more appropriate for customer X.

Why should a company even bother to sell to 'C' types if they are highly risky? Probably, and quite likely, because they need the volume, and profits can be made as long as those customers survive. It is difficult to get all orders from 'A' and 'B' customers, and by identifying the 'C'-types action can be taken to secure the risk or reduce it. Further, the sales force can try to get more orders from 'A' and 'B' customers and give less priority to 'C' accounts, who may not even be in business in a year's time.

Instead of defining 'no-risk' and 'high-risk' accounts as described above, some companies use actual ratio analysis to determine codes. On the basis that limited companies file accounts at Companies House, which are available for public scrutiny, it is possible to use those accounts in a way which can identify potential risk. The following example has been used successfully by at least one major corporation and seen to be useful for commercial staff as well as being deemed reliable by credit management personnel:

	'C'	'B'	'A'	'U'
	High risk	*Average*	*Low risk*	*Undoubted*
Current ratio	< 1.25	1.26–2.00	> 2.00	'A' ratios plus net worth over £10m
Quick ratio	< 0.50	0.50–1.00	> 1.00	
Current debt/ net worth	> 1.25	1.24–0.75	< 0.75	
Total debt/ net worth	> 2.00	1.99–1.25	< 1.25	

- 'C' risk is where *any* of the four ratios is achieved.

- 'B' risk is where there are *no* ratios in the high-risk bracket.

- 'A' risk needs all four ratios to be achieved.

From these results, the credit manager also calculates credit ratings, as:

- 'A' are rated at 5 per cent of working worth.

- 'B' are rated at 15 per cent of working worth.

- 'A' are rated at 20 per cent of working worth.

- 'U' can have unlimited credit.

Risk categories are of great assistance to both sales and credit, being that they are visible, reliable and understandable. For sales:

- 'A' customers: more sales time spent with theses than 'B' or 'C':

  - priority for phone calls and correspondence;

  - priority for delivery dates;

  - best prices and discounts (subject to volumes and so on);

  - priority after-sales service;

  - fast action on claims and disputes.

- 'B' customers – standard performance levels.

- 'C' customers – minimal sales resource:

  - no advance expense;

  - no special production/procurement actions;

  - observe 'stop list' action by credit departments;

- low priority on service, claims, and so on (that is, after As and Bs)

- list prices and minimal, if any, discounts;

- inform credit staff urgently of any adverse input.

Credit staff benefit from the use of risk categories:

- 'A' customers – unlimited, or extra-generous credit ratings:

    - never put on stop list (that is, collection may well be needed but is little risk of failure);

    - always personal contact for collections – no standard letters;

    - priority action on claims and disputes;

    - maximum support for sales efforts.

- 'B' customers – standard credit and collection actions:

    - stop supplies if accounts are x days overdue.

- 'C' customers – marked as high risk on listings:

    - absolute control of debts to keep within credit ratings;

    - stop supplies as soon as overdues occur;

    - special actions to control risks (for example, guarantees and so on).

The fact that all customers are different is best illustrated by the continued update and use of credit risk codes. Risk categories in effect bring the customer profile to life, and it becomes clear to both credit and sales that the differing viabilities that live within the customer base can be used objectively by the seller. All customers are important while alive, but a seller's expense and future planning should vary with their prospects for survival and growth.

It may be a laborious task to risk assess every single customer and potential customer in any organisation, and it is not always necessary if it is seen that losses or risk up to a certain level are acceptable, even if not entirely desirable. There are therefore ways in which the risk assessment workload can be reduced:

1. Decide a quickstart limit value – very small – which can be allowed to any account for initial business, to get it started, with no checking. The quickstart limit should be a painless figure, which will vary from company to company, but could be, say, £500 or £1000. The figure will be one which, if lost, would not cause undue damage to the seller. It should be made clear that this applies to one-off, first orders only and that any further orders would be subject to the normal credit checking procedures. This approach is popular with sales (no delays, perceived or otherwise), and is good for the credit area – they can get on with more important matters – and allows time for credit checks if, and when, business develops and they become necessary.

2. Use the 80/20 ratio to identify the few accounts which buy 80 per cent of total sales, and so provide 80 per cent of cash. Identification is easy – list the debtors in descending order of value, drawing a line where the cumulative balance reaches 80 per cent of the total debtors figure (even fewer for 50 per cent!). There will usually be a large number of accounts buying only 20 per cent of sales. A full credit check should be done on the few large accounts and the lesser value customers looked at as time permits. Below a certain value, some accounts may never be checked at all. Never start a credit checking system in alphabetical or account number order. Select the customers by size, hence value and importance, and so avoid being guilty of having had insufficient time to deal with large exposure that has gone down the tubes on you!

3. Use the risk codes to decide priorities. Since 'A' and 'B' are the most creditworthy organisations, checks can be related to payment experience and sales reports

Any *large* 'C' category accounts justify extra credit effort, such as:

- monthly review of account payment experience;

- semi-annual update of agency reports and references;

- regular review of opinions with sales staff;

- discussions with the customers themselves.

It is worth repeating that customers can, and do, move between codes. It is more likely that a previous 'B' will move to 'C' or that it will be possible to promote a 'C' to 'B'. Experience shows that it is much rarer for an 'A' account to become 'C' (though it does happen) and even rarer for a 'C' to be promoted to the 'A' category. Such movements *can* take place on a temporary basis, however, if, for example, a cheque bounces, or acquisitions or mergers throw some doubt on a customer's status, or, indeed, improve a customer's status.

For those credit managers who have hitherto not used risk codes, or who would like to validate their existing process, a retrospective test can be undertaken. Make the time to go back into your records for the last ten accounts which went into Administration, Administrative Receivership or Voluntary Liquidation. Pull out whatever credit reports you previously held, plus your own account experience up to the failure. Decide, objectively, if they should have been 'A', 'B' or 'C' risk categories, if you had such a system. Almost certainly, they will all have been 'C' types. If you had had a risk code system, or if your current system is correct, they would all have been in the high-risk group and subject to special controls. The question then would be, 'How much sales and credit effort and bad debt cost could have been saved?'

Identifying and Dealing with High-risk Accounts

If credit management is restricted to working to fixed procedures, related to what are perceived as acceptable levels of risk, the likelihood is that supplies are stopped to late payers and accounts are dealt with in chronological order. That in itself may be enough for some to warrant the description of credit control, but it is in fact not enough to be described as effective credit management. Orders may well be rejected from those accounts judged to be risky, but bad debts and overdues will be suffered in any case, simply because of the lack of priorities.

Good credit management encompasses a commercial approach, which not only earns the respect, and hence more cooperation, from sales colleagues, but also generates extra income for the company. The commercial approach embodies 'risk awareness'. It recognises varying levels of risk and is saying to sales: 'We'll get information on customers, identify the risky ones and tell you (sales) who they are. You can sell up to the limits we indicate, and in return, you will support the controls we have to exercise, because of the chances we are taking.' Credit management is calculating the risk, not gambling, and sales are encouraged to see the end result as being in everyone's best interest.

It also means that in identifying high-risk accounts, orders from all other customers can flow through quickly, uninterrupted by unnecessary controls. This 'marginal risk policy' actually demonstrates the extra sales and profit that can be obtained, and does not label credit control as being the 'order prevention' department.

Credit information should answer the three key credit questions concerning solvency, liquidity and growth:

1. *Solvency* – is the company highly likely to survive?

2. *Liquidity* – can the company pay its proposed commitments on time?

3. *Growth* – is the customer likely to buy more from us in future?

Negative answers will mean a high-risk probability, and if risk categories are in use, such customers will be 'C' accounts. Defining 'C' as marginal or high risk does not confine them to cash only, or payment before dispatch, because it will be possible to control such accounts by:

- *pre-delivery controls* – these include the referral of all incoming orders to compare values and dates to the existing balance and credit rating, and also updating credit data at defined intervals;

- *collection actions* – these depend on size of account, but will require telephone contact at intervals to judge customer situations and attitudes. After a first reminder, supplies should be held until the account is straight again. Payments in advance, the larger the better, should be encouraged;

- *risk reduction measures* – there are a number of measures that can be taken to reduce the risk of non-payment or loss.

Some risk reduction methods are more effective than others, and their use will depend upon the severity of the risk envisaged. Not all are of themselves either definitive, or indeed easy to obtain, but each is worthy of consideration and application, according to circumstances:

Guarantees from acceptable third parties – a guarantee is a written promise by a third party to pay a debt if the actual debtor cannot or will not settle. Figure 6.3 gives an example. Guarantees are, however, only as good as the businesses giving them, so the creditworthiness of the guarantor must be checked.

It is sensible only to accept company guarantees of trade debts, since it is nigh on impossible to adequately check the ability of an individual to honour a guarantee or to establish how many other guarantees that person has given. Directors' guarantees for the debts of their own companies fall into that category, though some comfort can be derived from the fact that a director may be willing to give such a guarantee, perhaps an indication in his/her own faith in the future of the company. This may, however, be misplaced! The essential elements of the guarantee are a consideration, for example, the seller's willingness to supply, an obligation to honour the guarantee on first demand, that is, not after a prescribed delay or set of actions, and no limitation as to expiry date or amount.

In practice, a guarantor may insist on a time limit, for example, one year, or a limit of liability. If these elements are acceptable, the guarantee can still be worthwhile.

It should be noted that 'a letter of comfort', that is, a letter from a parent company reassuring the supplier that the customer is reliable, is not enforceable in law and as such may simply be some encouragement to trade, but no real guarantee of payment. Comfort letters are sometimes offered in place of a proper guarantee of payment. Experienced credit managers know not only that parent companies are *not* responsible for the debts of their (limited company) subsidiaries, but also that the rock solid reputation of a group of companies does not guarantee that a particular member company will be a good credit risk.

Credit insurance – this is covered in great detail in Chapters 15 and 16. Suffice to say at this stage that credit insurance will of itself only really be available at reasonable cost to the less risky customers, and for those in the highest risk sector, insurance may well not be a viable option.

Special short payment terms – for example, seven days' credit, allows the customer to receive the goods and turn them into profit, but keeps the risk horizon for the seller very short.

Cash discounts – these are only a good incentive if the seller's margin is high. 2 per cent is more than likely the *minimum* attractive rate for early settlement, and for sellers on low margins, even that minimum can turn profit into loss very quickly.

Offsetting payables – high-risk accounts should always be matched against payables, even for other group companies, so that no money is paid out while debts are still owed to the seller.

Retention of title – included in a seller's conditions of sale should always be a clause reserving title to the goods, if the goods indeed lend themselves to intact recovery (which usually means identifiable). Obviously services do not apply – a service provided is not recognisable as a recoverable item. The general rule under the Sale of Goods Act is that property passes *when the parties intend it to pass*, for example, at the time of contract, irrespective of the time of delivery or payment. The parties are free to agree that, although the buyer is entitled to possession of the goods, ownership does not pass until the price is paid. Section 19 of the Sale of Goods Act 1979 provides legal power to effect retention, and the precedent was effectively set in *Aluminium Industry* v. *Industrie Vassen Romalpa Aluminium Ltd (1976)*, known usually as the Romalpa case which gave its name to what has become known as the Romalpa Clause in terms and conditions of sale. It was followed by other cases, but the principle remains much the same, in that the court established that the seller had the right to recover his property in the event of non-payment.

Insolvency legislation has placed, and continues to place, limitations on the operation of Romalpa clauses. No Administrative Receiver, whose task is to obtain the best recovery, is keen to see the potential asset base of the company in receivership diminished by certain creditors being able to remove their property and so reduce the prospects of the best possible return on sale of assets or disposal of the business as a going concern. Administration Orders and Company Voluntary arrangements provide further limitations, for example, section 15 of the Insolvency Act allows an Administrator, with leave of the court, to dispose of goods which are subject to retention clauses, but maintains the priority of those particular creditors.

Dear Sirs,

In consideration of your readiness to supply goods or services to:

(hereinafter referred to as 'the Buyer'), we hereby guarantee the due payment of all sums which are now or may hereafter become owing to you by the Buyer.

Our liability shall not in any way be diminished or affected by your giving time or indulgence to the Buyer, nor by any release, agreement not to sue, composition or arrangement of any description granted or entered into by you to or with the Buyer and we shall be liable to you in respect of any obligation accrued hereunder as if we were principal and not surety.

This guarantee shall be a continuing guarantee, subject to our right to give notice of revocation thereof. Any such notice shall be in writing and become effective upon its actual receipt by you at (address..........) but no revocation shall in any way diminish or affect our liability to you in respect of any indebtedness of the Buyer incurred under contract or obligation entered into between you and the Buyer prior to your receipt of such notice.

Yours faithfully,

Witness to the signature of...

(Signed)..

Address...

 Date...

Figure 6.3   Third-party guarantee

A retention clause has, therefore, to be carefully worded to suit the particular seller's business and the practical lessons learned from experience with Receivers and Liquidators who are reluctant to release goods from their stock, are that:

1. the goods being recovered must be easily identifiable, for example, with a serial number;

2. the goods being recovered must be the actual goods which are the subject of the unpaid invoice(s). It is not unusual for repeat deliveries to have taken place over a period of time, and the customer has not 'rotated' stock correctly. In other words, the goods may be on the shelf, but they are the subject of an invoice which *has* been paid, and that the goods referred to in the unpaid invoice no longer exist; and

3. there must be evidence that the seller's Retention Of Title clause was known to the buyer before the insolvency, for example, via contractual conditions of sale. A good way to ensure this is to have a separate signature box on the original credit application documentation which the customer can sign to indicate he has read and understood the clause.

ACTION PLAN FOR HIGH-RISK ACCOUNTS

1. Identify your risky customers.

2. Get information on them.

3. Sell to the risky ones – with extra controls.

4. Monitor and get involved where needed.

5. Get out before it all goes pear shaped!

Bad Debt Reserves

One sensible outcome of identifying high-risk accounts is having some prior anticipation, knowledge or perception of debts likely to turn bad. Bad debts have a direct impact on profits, and every attempt is made to avoid them, but some bad debts are inevitable, and seeing them coming not only gives the opportunity to reduce the ultimate exposure, but also to forecast the likely level of bad debt to be experienced. Having made that forecast, the correct procedure is to make a bad debt provision, that is, noting a reduction of booked profits.

Bad debt provisions are expensive, and deplete current profits, because making such provisions come out of profits, but they are necessary. The Companies Act clearly defines debtors as a current asset, that is, capable of being liquidated within 12 months and as auditors in the UK expect any doubtful debts to be fully provided for, the net balance sheet figure should reflect debtors as collectable and less than 12 months old. There is some confusion surrounding provisions, both general and specific (more on this below), not least because many credit managers in the UK work for the UK division or the UK subsidiary of a multi-national corporation. The parent corporation may well operate in a different bad debt provision environment and expect their UK businesses to operate in the same way. For example, it is common practice for some US corporations to 'take the hit' as soon as a bad debt occurs, and not make any specific provision as a yearly or half-yearly exercise. The hit comes straight off the bottom line, and not taken against any provision, which in some cases does not actually exist.

Common accounting practice in the UK is to make provision on an ongoing basis for bad debts, both as those actually quite likely to happen (specific) and a figure to cover the unexpected (general). Often, in the year end rush, accountants will make provisions based on history, or as a simple percentage of total debtors. It is the credit manager, however, who has the greater knowledge as to the collectability of debts and, having identified high-risk accounts, it seems not unreasonable to base the bad debt provision on these only.

As stated, the provision is a charge against profit, and it is not unusual for credit managers to look at the bad debt provision from two standpoints. If the company is likely to be making a very healthy profit, and may be seeking to reduce its tax liability (or dividend distribution), it may well ask the credit manager to do a 'belt and braces' job on the provision. In other words, provide for all known doubtfuls, all borderline possibilities, and any other accounts which might have been particularly troublesome with payments and in the extreme could, maybe, possibly, perhaps be considered likely to fail soon! On the other hand, profits may be thin and the company is looking to restrict charges against the profit base to an absolute minimum. In this scenario, the credit manager is required to justify in detail each customer provision, and the slightest chance of recovery may lead to that customer not being provided for. Credit managers will readily recognise either situation, but the commonsense approach is always to be realistic – there is always the danger that unnecessarily providing for a not particularly doubtful customer will deflect normal collection activity with that customer and actually precipitate a circumstance which might otherwise not have taken place.

Old or disputed debts should not be cleared out by writing them off against the bad debt reserve, if those customers are still trading. That should be done by sales credit. Real bad debt write-offs are a measurement of the effectiveness of the company's risk assessment and credit controls and should not be distorted by other kinds of write-off.

Typical, bad debt reserve policies include:

1.   *100 per cent with reversal*: Each month, the *total* value of all 'C' category accounts is reserved, that is, a transfer is made from profit and loss to bad debt reserve. As accounts are paid, the value is reversed, that is, transferred back to profit and loss. In practice, all that is needed is to keep a separate bad debt reserve for the total of high-risk accounts and adjust it each month to agree with the new total balance. Whilst this may seen by some as not good accounting practice, it is regarded by prudent financial controllers as keeping a close look on potential bad debt losses.

2.   *Reserve according to age*: This method recognises that risk increases with the age of 'C' risk accounts. Therefore, a reserve is made as a per cent of the age analysis of 'C' accounts, for example, 25 per cent of balances one month overdue, 50 per cent two months overdue, 75 per cent three months overdue and 100 per cent at four months. The percentages are the company's experience of the collectability of its marginal accounts. To avoid a heavy depletion of profit, this method provides an extra incentive to collect overdue 'C' accounts.

3.   *Annual write-off experience*: This method recognises a company's bad debt experience each year. It may have a policy of reserving 1 per cent of *all* sales, but finds that its *actual* bad debts occur only in the 'C' category accounts. For sales to 'C' customers, the bad debt losses may be 5 per cent. So the company gradually builds a reserve

through the year of 5 per cent of sales value to 'C' accounts. This can considerably reduce the profit reduction caused by excessive bad debt reserves.

4.   *General and Specific*: Something of a combination of the above methods whereby a sum is transferred each month to the bad debt reserve, based upon either a small percentage of total sales, or a larger percentage of 'C' sales (as above), *plus* accounts specifically recognised by the credit manager as being potentially doubtful. The likelihood is that these will be 'C' accounts, but losses in 'B' and even 'A' can be experienced, and their transfer to 'C' may well follow.

Many credit managers hold a 'Bad and Doubtful' section on the live Sales Ledger, transferring accounts to that section when liquidation or receivership occurs, or any other event leading to loss. The total value of that ledger section is provided against (it could be reduced by dividend payments, VAT bad debt relief and so on) and the account only actually written off against the provision when the insolvency process has been completed or when the insolvency practitioner has confirmed that there are no prospects of any further dividend, or indeed any dividend at all.

Where credit insurance cover is held, it is normal to reduce the bad debt reserve expense, so that only the *uninsured* portion of 'C' accounts is reserved. This is an obvious benefit which offsets the premium cost of the insurance.

Effective Credit Management

Controls can only be effective if the credit manager has the authority to approve or reject orders, within the support of a proper credit policy. With that power comes the responsibility to reject the bare minimum, and accept the profitable majority, or find ways of accepting the majority which will earn profit. That power also requires the ability to communicate reasons fluently to the affected sales area when the bare minimum has been rejected and to do everything to arrange terms to be able to accept orders.

In computerised systems, orders can flow uninterrupted into the order processing drills if they meet set parameters, for example, credit rating less existing balance plus this order. Orders that fail this test or those from customers on a 'stop list' *must* be extracted for expert action. By assessing credit risks in good time for prospective customers and by keeping assessments updated for larger active accounts, almost all orders each day should flow quickly into the order-processing system.

The stop list is always regarded as a contentious document or process. Orders should not be rejected lightly, without good reason, genuinely explained, and no account should be stopped simply because an item is overdue. It is the nature of that overdue (one invoice, value £32.36 on an account in category 'A' worth £200,000 per annum!!) which should be investigated *before* the stop list is produced. Only those accounts genuinely over their correctly calculated credit limits, or genuinely overdue as a matter of late payment fact should be stopped. There is nothing more likely to demolish any trust and respect built up between sales and credit than inappropriate, indiscriminate and ill-prepared stop lists.

Building the stop list into the sales order processing system emphasises this need for diligence even more, because in effect the 'system' has taken over and the remoteness of the decision-making process can be thus exaggerated. In essence there are two kinds of stop list: the *refer* type, where the credit manager is alerted to incoming orders from listed customers because every movement on an account needs appraisal; and the *actual stop list*, where credit has been withdrawn because of a serious debt situation. Held orders may be a good lever to obtain payment if the customer is desperate for more product. There should be a daily review of any orders held, to identify what can be done to release them.

Cash received daily should also update the stop list – those accounts temporarily held pending payment should be cleared just as soon as payment is received and stop list amendments should be available, online and in print for sales and order staff.

It follows that if a stop list is produced, so should a 'go' list. This can be supplied by the credit staff to the sales department, showing customers who are good credit risks and pay their accounts well, where further business would be welcomed as a means to faster cash.

Effective credit management, that is, controls at order entry stage, the stop list, accurate and regular risk analysis and attention to changing patterns, are the main weapons in the fight against what has long been known as Long Firm Fraud. This commercial evil involves the purchasing of substantial amounts of goods on credit with the purposeful intention of disappearing or deliberately going bust without paying for them. Large sums of money can be invested by the architects of this kind if fraud, although the creditors who supply the goods end up as the main source of finance. Success for the fraudster depends upon immediate acceptance of their orders, and quick disposal of the goods, which tend to be fast-moving consumer goods, rather than industrial materials. The closing down of the fraudulent firm is often marked by an 'event' such as an alleged burglary or fire, which helps to justify a stock deficiency, or, better yet, the destruction of all records. The fraudsters themselves, those behind the scam, rarely appear on the premises themselves, but may be directors of the company. If that is the case, it is quite common for them to resign some time before the final fraud, later claiming that the business was run properly while they were in charge.

Pre-planned frauds in the Long Firm variety fall into two types:

1.   formation of a new business intended to last six months or less;

2.   purchase of an existing legitimate business.

In the first case, the fraudsters obtain substantial credit straight away, by offering attractive orders to greedy salespeople; or, if actually asked for references, by offering phoney ones. If the company already exists, it will have a good credit rating, bank facilities and regular suppliers. The new owners delay filing accounts at Companies House and make their quick killing before the authorities can take action.

Good credit control can restrict the losses with Long Firms, as vigilance coupled with decisive action reaps dividends. There are warning signs:

- very large orders immediately from a newly formed firm;

- very large orders following satisfactory trading for a month or two at modest levels;

- unusual increase in credit requested by an existing customer with new owners;

- large orders placed at trade fairs;

- large orders placed for 'out-of-season' goods;

- orders placed with reps too easily, with price not an issue;

- bank references showing account recently opened where trade references say that the account has been running for years;

- trade references received from different firms with identical wordings.

It is often the case that the first clue can come via a credit report from a credit reporting agency – Long Firms often seek credit from several suppliers at the same time, so producing a spate of credit enquiries. Good credit management practice, applying the standard caution to newly formed firms and changes in ownership will keep losses to a minimum.

The risk of slow payment remains the credit management priority, followed by the risk of bad debt. Even in times of low interest rates, borrowings will always remain expensive compared to the net margins which most businesses are able to achieve, and strong and effective credit management will continue to be seen as the only real safeguard against loss and ultimate failure. The future will see a growing need for a positive sales/credit relationship, and the growing demands on everyone in any organisation brought about by the ever rapid expansion of technology will require all companies to take a positive view on asset protection and enhancement.

The mobile phone, email and e-commerce mean that ordinary human beings will have less and less time in which to carry out specific tasks, with more reliance being placed upon comprehensive systems and trust in the ability and the integrity of those whose function requires instant and accurate decision making.

Well-organised companies should have:

- top management support for credit and collection procedures;

- data on all key customers (type of firm, financial status, contact names and so on);

- good procedures for opening accounts, for example, the credit application form online, providing key data and the essential customer commitment to the payment terms;

- new account letters (email preferred) to make immediate contact with the payments person – followed by a friendly call for more personal contact;

- specific cultivation of key customers, to ensure priority payment treatment;

- reliable data sources for fast access to credit information – online;

- computerised methods of deciding credit ratings and risk categories;

- automated credit approvals and rapid processing of 'OK' transactions.

The future of credit management is closely tied to rapid improvements in communication technology, and is now undoubtedly true that the email address on the credit application form is just as important as all the other more traditional fields which require customer completion. Most credit managers now have Internet access for credit information, and instant credit decisions are now the rule rather than the exception.

The use of emails will continue to grow, and there can be little doubt that this revolution in communication technology will continue to play an increasingly important role. There is, however, something of a backlash, already experienced in the US and the UK, whereby the effectiveness of email as an actual tool is being brought more and more into question. The subject of emails is discussed more fully in Chapter 11 – suffice it to say here that any method of communication still requires the skill and the commonsense of the user to be effective.

The key to effective credit management remains, and will continue to be, support from top management. The ICM has witnessed remarkable growth since 1996 in the number of employees now looking for 'trained and qualified' credit managers, and the parallel growth of employers willing to invest in their employees by way of training and staff development. No organisation in the future will be able to operate both effectively and profitably without company-wide agreed and implemented policies, including credit.

Credit management is about protecting the company's biggest asset and turning sales into cash as fast as commercially possible. It always has been so, but now, and in the future, it will be seen more in the context of marketing, and less in the backroom of financial services.

INSTITUTE OF CREDIT MANAGEMENT – JANUARY 2008

Introductory Credit Management: Certificate Level 3

A risk category system is a valuable tool for credit managers. It enables the credit department to assess different types of customer against set criteria to indicate their perceived level of risk. From the trade point of view:

- recommend and explain **four** appropriate risk categories that a credit manager may use;

- evaluate the merits of applying a risk category system.

7

Predicting Corporate Insolvency by Computer

Glen Bullivant

• Background • Developing and using a solvency model • Credit management applications •

Background

It has often been said that credit management is an art, not a science. It is true that in consumer credit, much of the decision-making process, and the predictability of accounts being good or bad, has been increasingly performed in the last 40 years by a range of scorecard products and services. It is not difficult to see that statistical probability, the basis of consumer credit scoring, is comparatively accurate founded as it is on definitive criteria such as age, employment, marital status and so on – evidence of stability, in other words. It is also not difficult to see (though not always easy for us individual humans to accept) that we consumers can be 'categorised'. Men of a certain age in a certain social group are more likely to 'x', while women of the same age in the same group will most probably 'y'. Car drivers over 45 are safer than car drivers under 25, and so on. The accuracy of predictions regarding the consumer comes from the millions of items of data that can be processed, researched, analysed and experienced, and that science is now well established.

Scoring techniques in respect of corporate entities are less well established, not least because there has always been comparatively less data available, both in volume and in reliability. It has always been recognised that there are many more variables in the corporate sector, and that certainty is dependent upon known facts, not unknown variables. Nevertheless, there are constants in the financial structure of limited companies which are capable of analysis and comparison. Features of those constants can, and do, indicate degrees of growth and solvency, slow down and failure. Relationships between the constants also bear witness to inevitable consequences, bad or good.

Developing and Using a Solvency Model

There are a number of acknowledged financial ratios (20 or so), which can be used, in various groupings, to identify strengths and weaknesses which in turn make up the financial health of a company. Taken individually, no single one could be used in correctly judging the overall financial strength of the company, but each variable, when grouped together in part or in total, is part of a relationship of variables which do in fact reflect the general financial well-being of the company.

For many years, many people recognised that financial ratios were speaking quite loudly about something, but harnessing what they were saying into a way of predicting failure proved to be somewhat elusive. At first, it was held that comparing Net Working Capital to Total Assets represented the best ratio for scrutiny with a view to failure spotting. Later, Return on Net Worth and Net Worth to Total Debt were identified as being more specific and more reliable. Other ratios came into the picture, notably Current Ratio, Net Worth to Total Debt, Times Interest Earned and Net Profit to Sales. All had merit, and all contributed to some forecasting possibilities.

Dr. Edward I. Altman, Professor of Finance, New York University School of Business devised the Z-Score Insolvency Predictor in 1968, publishing those most pertinent variables that statistical analysis had shown were present in insolvency. Experience showed that the Altman Z-Score, which was originally developed from sampling drawn from manufacturing companies, also worked well in the non-manufacturing sector. Those using Altman's Z-Score have consistently reported a 95 per cent accuracy of insolvency prediction up to two years prior to failure in non-manufacturing businesses, which is on a par with the failure prediction rate in the manufacturing sector. Continually updated since 1968, the Altman Z-Score remains the foundation of corporate scoring principles. Altman defined the variables for both private and publicly quoted companies as being:

- Current Assets (CA)

- Total Assets (TA)

- Net Sales (SL)

- Interest (IN)

- Current Liabilities (CL)

- Market Value of Equity (VE)

- Earnings Before Taxes (ET)

- Retained Earnings (RE).

Using the above variables, Altman devised five major components for the Z-Score formula:

1. *X1* Working Capital/Total Assets (or CA-CL divided by TA). Perhaps not the most significant of factors, as a measure of the net liquid assets of a company in relation to its total assets, it does indicate the direction in which a company is going in respect of working capital. A company repeatedly experiencing operating losses will generally suffer a reduction in working capital relative to its total assets.

2. *X2* Retained Earnings/Total Assets (or RE divided by TA). This component provides information on the extent to which a company has been able to reinvest its earnings in itself. It is a measure of profitability over time, but has the weakness of being able to be manipulated to an extent. Older, more established companies could have had much more time to accumulate earnings, so there could be a bias towards older companies. On the other hand, deterioration in amounts retained speaks for itself.

3. *X3* Earnings Before Tax + Interest/Total Assets (or ET + IN divided by TA). Probably the most important factor, being that profit is the principal objective of any commercial enterprise, and as such is the driving force that ultimately determines the viability of the company. The ratio in effect adjusts the earnings of the company

for income tax factors which vary, and similarly adjust for varying borrowing levels. This allows a more effective measurement of the way in which the company utilises its assets.

4.   *X4* Market Value of Equity/Total Liabilities (or VE divided by TL). This gives an indication of how much the assets of a company can decline in value before debts may exceed assets. For publicly quoted companies, equity is deemed to be the market value of all outstanding common and preference stock. For private companies, assuming the company records its assets at market value, then the book value of assets is used in this ratio.

5.   *X5* Net Sales/Total Assets (or SL divided by TA). Another most important component, in that this measures the ability of the company's assets to generate sales. Some analysts omit this ratio in the Z-Score of a private company.

The Z-Score calculation in effect combines the above ratio factors, with each ratio assigned a different weighting, and calculates a score, which itself then is the indicator of likely failure or continued success. The formula devised by Altman is:

$$Z = 1.2\ X1 + 1.4\ X2 + 3.3\ X3 + 0.6\ X4 + 1.0\ X5 \qquad \text{(Publicly quoted companies)}$$

$$Z = 6.56\ X1 + 3.26\ X2 + 6.72\ X3 + 1.05\ X4 \qquad \text{(Private company)}$$

Interpretations vary between analysts, and there can be influencing factors in differing industries, but broadly speaking, the following can be deduced from final scores:

- *3.0 or more* – the most likely to survive;

- *2.7 to 3.0* – should survive, but bordering on a grey area, and certainly below the line for more definite chances of survival;

- *1.8 to 2.7* – could well be heading for insolvency within two years. If the total 'doubtful' area is taken as 1.8 to 3.0, then this is more doubtful in order to be sure of survival a company with this score may well have to take serious action;

- *Below 1.8* – most likely to founder. A company with this score is rarely expected to recover in time.

These are generalisations, of course, and being based upon financial data, they do not take account of other influences. For example, a 3.0+ may be defined as healthy, but is then the victim of fraud, mismanagement, recession, floods and any number of mishaps which turn a statistical success into an actual failure. By the same token, prompt and efficient action by 'turned on' management brings a 1.8–2.7 into the safer haven of 2.7–3.0.

The important point about the Z-Score technique, however, is that because it is drawn from suitably weighted financial ratios, measured against known factors, and can be analysed automatically, the whole process lends itself to computerisation. All the data is loaded into the program, written for the purpose, and out pops the score. By updating with new figures as they become available, the system can constantly review the score.

There are a great many insolvency prediction models commercially available, and there is no let up in the development of ever more sophisticated programs. The Credit Management Research Centre at the Leeds University Business School has been studying neural networks for some years. These networks work on the principle that every factor in every situation has a connection with one or more other factors – none are in splendid isolation. Therefore, some change in one has a cause and effect in another. Computer models run for hours, days and even months, linking every item to every item, up and down, across and sideways in a never ending spider's web of interlocking causes and effects. No doubt the ultimate answer will be an all consuming process which can identify not just major ratios which lead to doom within two years, but the more trivial which if left unattended will eventually bring the edifice crashing to the ground. The main beneficiaries will be corporate recovery specialists, company doctors, bankers and financiers, as well as credit managers.

What is important about any research, however, is that the ultimate outcome or formula has to be capable of simple understanding and explanation to all those affected by its use. If it is not practicable and understandable, it will be of little use.

The basic Z-Score, and the various modifications and enhancements which have followed, can itself be supplemented by additions, such as Performance Analysis. This permits a company's relative performance to be followed through time, and produces a Performance Analysis score (or PAS-score). By reading the trend in a PAS-score, both below and above the risk threshold, the momentum of the decline, or indeed recovery, of the company can be seen at a glance. Early warning is evident, and even before the Z-Score really signals imminent doom, action can have been taken to rectify, or to protect interests according to the score user.

In simple terms, the PAS-score is the relative ranking of a company based on its Z-Score in a particular year in percentage terms on a scale of 1 to 100. For example, a PAS-score of 50 would suggest that the performance of the company in the year is average. On the other hand, a PAS-score of 10 says that only 10 per cent of companies are performing less well on this overall basis, which is clearly an unsatisfactory position. Having computed a Z-Score for a company, it becomes possible to transform what is an absolute measure of financial health into a relative measure of financial performance. Put another way, the Z-Score tells the credit manager that the company is, or is not, at risk, and the PAS-score puts the historic trend and current performance in perspective. The PAS-score can show the risk attached in a particular company to those who have not had financial training in a way which is clearly understandable – if only 10 per cent of companies are performing worse than customer W, then customer W is at the lower end of the safe ladder. Combined with the Z-Score, credit limits and risk categories, everyone can be aware of the need to take appropriate action.

It is useful to pick up on the point of limits and categories, because the Z-Score and its descendants and colleagues, can of itself be one of the factors in determining limits and codes from the risk perspective. Indeed, it is possible to utilise Z-Score techniques to rate companies according to risk, and to apply this 'risk rating' to customers over and above any previous limit or risk category in place. The risk rating can be statistically determined and calculated only when the company has a negative Z-Score. It is based upon the Z-Score trend, the size of the negative Z-Score and the number of years the company has been at risk. By using a 5 point scale, with 1 indicating 'at risk but with low probability of immediate distress' and 5 meaning 'usually beyond saving in its present form', the credit manager is provided with a ready means for assessing the overall balance of risk in the customer base. The financial modelminded among the more technically adept credit managers can develop this further by determining the actual failure probability associated with each risk rating value depending on the state of the economy. Even in a boom economy, it is unlikely for company W to survive, and when the recession bites, many more companies can be seen to be vulnerable.

Credit Management Applications

Developing sophisticated techniques to forecast likely outcomes would only ever be academic exercises unless they had both practical and understandable applications for the likes of credit managers. Happily, Z-Scores drop comfortably into the credit manager's array of usable information. By producing an objective and reliable measure of a company's risk of financial distress, the Z-Score approach provides the credit manager with a sound basis for decision making. The fact that only a small percentage of the company population, depending on the health of the economy, will have an 'at risk' profile, means that the credit manager has access to a reliable screening mechanism, directing attention to those customers or prospective customers requiring more in-depth analysis, with the risk rating helping determine the actual degree of risk. In addition, by periodically building up the data on file relating to a customer, the system provides a ready means of monitoring a company's performance over time on an ongoing basis. Whether this is done by using annual, interim or even forecasting accounting data will depend upon factors relevant to particular credit managers, but most credit managers would agree that there is very rarely such a thing as 'too much information' – the cry is more often 'too little'.

The system's facility for sorting and tabulating data means that the credit manager can obtain an overview of the PAS-score spread in the debtors' ledger and the presence of customers with different levels of risk rating. This is particularly useful where the credit manager is in a position to take a strategic approach to the risk management of receivables.

It also gives marketing a powerful aid. The system is linked to a large database of corporate accounting information, and builds up a large database in its own right. This gives marketing insight into the highs and lows of risk in their own industry and market place, and can point marketing efforts in more profitable directions as and when required.

The Z-Score approach to assessing company solvency continues to be increasingly used by credit managers in the UK. Using a number of items from a company's financial statements, the computer system automatically enters these into a formula, so producing the Z-Score for that particular company. This Z-Score will then reveal whether the company is at risk or not and the degree of risk, and can then be further transformed into a PAS-score which will highlight that company's relative performance in its industry and compared to others. This analytical approach is a practical tool for assessing the risk attached to a debtors' ledger. When armed with such knowledge, the professional credit manager knows when to vary terms of trade, avoid or manage high risk business, apply restrictions or ease previously applied restraints. The credit manager is equally better equipped to point sales towards the more healthy companies (those which can provide profit to the seller), and can prioritise collection and related credit activities within the department.

It is not the be all and end all. Nothing ever is – but it is yet another string to the credit manager's bow of useful expertise. The more we know, the better able we are to make the right decision.

INSTITUTE OF CREDIT MANAGEMENT

Though there is no exam question relating directly to Z-Scores in the current ICM Education Syllabus, learners are recommended to consider the possibility of analysis of customer accounts as they exist on ledgers under their control at present. The exercise should assist in understanding related factors which make up customer risk.

8

Insolvency Warning Signs

Glen Bullivant

• Background • Attitude • The three phases of failure • Can it be avoided? • Conclusion •

Background

No one can doubt that the Great Pyramid in Egypt is an impressive structure, not just in its stature, but also in the fact that it has stood for thousands of years. How it was built intrigues many, and how or why it has lasted for so long intrigues many more. It is its longevity which can in fact impress us today just as much as its technical merit, simply because we live in a society where nothing actually lasts long. Manufactured goods have a built in obsolescence, if not in quality then definitely in design. Products and brands, familiar to our parents and grandparents, are less familiar to us, and we are no more likely to bequeath our products and brands to our own children and grandchildren.

There are exceptions, of course, but they are comparatively rare. Mergers and acquisitions constantly replace once well-known names, and corporate imaging and rebranding has been a feature of commerce for a good many years. A stroll down any high street will reveal names not known 10 or 15 years ago, and fewer names (with notable exceptions) which can be traced back two, three or four generations. Even among the notable exceptions, the ravages of a recession can be the end – in January 2009, Woolworths closed its final door in its final store after being a feature of practically every UK high street for nigh on 100 years. Mergers and acquisitions, corporate rebranding and commercial ambitions account for some of the change – business failure accounts for much of it. It is a fact that in the UK, for example, less than one-third of all family businesses survive beyond the first generation of the family, and only about 14 per cent ever make it to the third generation.

The overwhelming majority of limited companies currently on file at Companies House, England and Wales, were registered *after* 1995 (approximately 70 per cent) – in other words, most of the companies trading today in England and Wales are under 15 years old. The general consensus is that failure is most likely to occur within the first two to three years, that five years is a milestone and that to make it to 10 years is something of an achievement! With that in mind, the likelihood of insolvency in any customer base, almost regardless of trade or industry, is extremely high.

The credit management task is often described as protecting the company's major current asset, namely debtors, and the vulnerability of that asset is therefore obvious. Proper risk assessment, as described in Chapters 4 and 5, provides the basis for conscious decisions to allow credit or not and/or to decide how much to allow and over what period. From then on, the protection is evident from the lack of credit shocks and losses. Failure amongst the debtors is inevitable, but at least if risky accounts are identified and monitored, such failures should not come as a complete surprise. In other words, good front-end credit management means:

1.   conscious credit decisions, not credit for all;

2.   no surprise bad debts.

The Insolvency Act 1986 defines insolvency on the following two bases under Section 123:

The *cash flow test* whereby a company is deemed unable to pay its debts if:

- a creditor to whom the company is indebted in a sum exceeding £750 then due has served a statutory demand on the company and the company has for three weeks thereafter neglected to pay the sum or secure the debt to the reasonable satisfaction of the creditor; or

- execution is returned unsatisfied; or

- it is proved to the satisfaction of the Court that the company is unable to pay its debts as they fall due.

The *balance sheet test* whereby a company is also deemed unable to pay its debts if it is proved to the satisfaction of the Court that the value of the company's assets is less than the amount of its liabilities, taking into account its contingent and prospective liabilities.

(Note: the third bullet point of the cash flow test and the balance sheet test do not apply to individuals.)

In other words, the law of the land expects companies to organise adequate funds to pay their bills whenever the various due dates come along, for orders they have placed on credit terms. This is equitable and protects the credit terms in the many thousands of contracts being made every day in the UK. However, legal contracts are being broken every day by companies paying later than agreed terms. That is just as much a breach of contract as the supplier charging a higher price or sending different goods than agreed. It is both morally and legally wrong for customers to demand perfect performance by a supplier and then choose to pay when it suits them.

The UK has had a not very good company payment performance record, compared to some European partners, but the problem of late payment is not just a so-called British disease and the downturn of the economies in Germany and France through 2000–2003, for example, saw a sharp decline in the payment performance in those countries. Attempts have been made to improve the payment culture, both within the UK and across the EU. In the UK, the Late Payment of Commercial Debts (Interest) Act, 1998 came into force on 1 November 1998, followed by the European Directive on Combating Late Payment in Commercial Transactions, passed by the European Parliament in June 2000, and introduced into domestic legislation in each member state in August 2002.

The Better Payment Practice Group (BPPG) was formed in 1997 to create a partnership between the public and private sectors with the aim of improving the payment culture of the UK business community, and a number of public and private sector organisations signed up to the BPPG code of payment practice. It is a matter of some regret that the UK Government lost interest in the BPPG through the boom years leading up to 2007, but interest was revived following the crash of 2008. The Government looked to the ICM for assistance in promoting a Prompt Payment Code and used ICM expertise in producing both handouts and web access to publicise and encourage.

Nevertheless, payment performance remains poor, in the main, and it is the rather peculiar tolerance of late payment that is deemed by many observers to be a major reason for the high level of insolvencies experienced in the UK in recent years. In other words, the creation of laws to encourage prompt payment is not enough – sellers must also exercise good management of the time they allow customers to pay.

In good times, tolerance of late payment is at its worst – in bad times, the weak go to the wall. While a supplier waits, usually from a misplaced fear of upsetting a valued customer by asking for payment, the debtor company runs out of liquidity. The bank says 'not a penny more', demands repayment of its overdraft and in no time at all, hey presto, in pops the Administrative Receiver.

Insolvency lurks amongst all the overdue accounts on the Sales Ledger. They do not come out of thin air, but out of businesses currently trading and placing orders. The slide occurs over a period of time, far more often than not, and the signs are *always* there for those who care to look or listen. Sadly, even when a supplier *does* see signs of impending doom, he is often not willing to act until it is too late.

Attitude

It is sometimes difficult for a creditor to know what is going on, unless either the customer tells him, or someone else does. That 'someone else' could be another creditor, or an up-to-date credit agency report, or a credit agency alert report – any of those could be a sign of something amiss. The problem with the customer himself is quite often he will not face up to the reality of his situation until it is too late, often because he is too lenient in collecting his own sales revenue – either that or he will deliberately ignore problems in the foolish hope that they will go away. In the latter, he may have some cause for hope, because commercial pressures are such that suppliers will do almost anything to hang on to existing customers rather than risk losing them altogether. This means that the benefit of the doubt rests frequently with the customer, to the ultimate detriment of the seller. Many creditors are put in an impossible situation by customers, who will not respond to requests for payment or requests for information and the creditor is left with no alternative but to fear the worst and act accordingly. This is a reaction to a negative, and the creditor should really be trying to read the signs and be proactive in advance of the really bad news.

Customer attitude is all important. There are two main types of attitudes displayed by customers when an inability to settle debts comes along.

Type 1 says (or thinks): 'It's your problem, not ours. If we can't pay you, you will just have to wait.' This totally disregards the legal obligation to have the funds organised *at the agreed date,* disregards the fact that *the seller's price includes the cost of credit only for the proper credit term,* and makes the assumption that payment *sometime* will be acceptable. There are sub-attitudes such as, 'Obviously, we can't pay you until we are paid by our customers, can we?', which assumes that the supplier is willing to be a bank in the business of lending money. At some point, the supplier's real bank, or another big creditor, insists on settlement to the point of having the business closed down, leaving the mass of 'tolerant' suppliers unpaid for ever.

Type 1 companies are frequently those where management have believed in maximum sales as the answer to any cash problems. They have paid little attention to managing their own stocks and debtors, and indeed are frequently seen to be positively opposed to 'managing' their own debtors on the grounds that they would upset *their* customers if they asked them to pay. Equally guilty in this scenario, however, are the suppliers who have continued to deliver goods or services in spite of slower and slower payments and broken payment promises. Frequently, at meetings of creditors, the comment is heard: 'I'm surprised that they went bust. I've known the owner for years and I didn't think that he would let me down.' In other words, in the mass of failed companies, there is a disregard, whether callous or naïve, or both, for collecting their own bills on time and settling debts to suppliers on time, as per the terms of legal contracts, however simple or complex, verbal or written.

Then there is customer Type 2. He says: 'We're good at what we do, we're not accountants', with sub-comments such as, 'We're so busy, working all hours, that we didn't have time to worry about accounts. We expected the bank to be more understanding and our auditors said nothing about cash difficulties. Technically, our product was among the best.' This type also falls into the trap of self-reward for hard work. The two working directors in a graphics company put in 16 and 17 hour days at the benches, secured good contracts and made money – instead of either a) ensuring that suppliers were kept up to date and b) putting something aside for next year, they felt the need to congratulate themselves with a Porsche apiece – the rest, as they say, is history.

Even in very large companies that have failed (and the bombshells at the end of the twentieth and beginning of the twenty-first centuries are testament to this), all the senior jobs were in sales, engineering and technical functions, with scant regard to cash management, and the resource needed in that area. An unbalanced focusing on technical merit is often the main defect in this kind of company.

The conclusion has to be that the credit manager has to be alive to customer attitudes, which are just as vital to assess and judge, as much as financial ratios and credit references. If proof of this is necessary to convince the sceptical, take the time to look at the last six bad debts you wrote off. Look at your files and records, and talk to the relevant commercial people about each customer. Jot down comments made on customer attitudes to payment requests – what excuses were given; what impressions did your collection staff get when they telephoned or visited the failed firm when they were still placing orders? It is more than likely that you will find that four or five were Type 1, and that one or two were Type 2. Then, to make the research more worthwhile, discuss your risky or slow-paying *live* accounts with sales people and see if the same signs exist. Following that little exercise, act jointly with sales staff to improve payment commitments from senior people, or, if unsuccessful, reduce your exposure before it is too late.

The positive approach *has* to be the seller's attitude. The seller is naturally looking for profitable sales all the time, and profit comes from managed debtors, not from a free for all. Credit management is about positive action in assessment, judgement, cooperation, collection and protection It is not about being a soft touch, or about being hard nosed or overzealous. Above all it is about watching for the signs and using common sense.

How much of the following would sound familiar? A plastics company was owed £35,000, up to three months overdue, by a medium-sized manufacturer of builders' hardware. When asking for payment, the collector was told, 'You'll just have to wait until we get a big cheque in from (famous name).' The collector asked the salesman to speak to his buying contact. The salesman's reply: 'I'm pushing for a big order from them to make my month-end target. By the way, I thought their offices were very scruffy the last time I was there and the buyer was really fed up. And, orders are taking longer to get authorised. I'll try to have a word with the buyer next time I visit. But *don't* upset them at this stage. If they are going down, I want to get this big order first.' The next event was a letter from a Receiver, acting for the customer's bank. There was no recovery for unsecured creditors when the firm was later liquidated. The £35,000 had to be written off and the plastics company, crippled by that bad debt and others, became an easy victim for a takeover.

Who was guilty of anything? The customer for not paying on time? The too-tolerant collector? The order-greedy salesman? In this particular case, the supplier's managing director held a post-mortem session, and when all the facts were spelled out, the dangers were obvious to all. All the danger signs had been there, but not acted upon. It is perhaps forgivable in the daily hurly-burly of business for some people, especially those not directly connected with credit, to be too busy to notice the obvious. It is, however, the role of the credit manager to notice both the glaringly obvious and the less transparent signs, and have the authority or influence with colleagues to take the required action in time.

There are three essentials for avoiding harmful debts:

1.   frequent personal contact by visit or phone;

2.   easy communication between sales and credit staff;

3.   corporate willingness to act immediately failure is expected.

It may be that lessons sometimes have to be learned the hard way, and those signs which lead the credit manager to believe that danger is looming are less apparent to sales. An excellent lesson for sales is for the sales manager to attend a creditors meeting along with the credit manager. When the sales manager can see not only the result, but also in retrospect the events leading up to the end, degrees of appreciation and understanding go up in leaps and bounds. Some years ago, a sales manager attended the meeting of creditors of a large book printer in the south east, along with the credit manager. He sat, jaw dropping through the whole proceedings, and afterwards was asked one simple question by the credit manager: 'Would you have taken an order from that company yesterday?' The answer was a further dropping of the jaw and a very slow, guilty nodding of the head. From that day, the sales manager was as committed to acting upon information received as the credit manger.

The signs are always there for those who bother to look, ranging from the obvious, through less obvious to too late:

Obvious

•   payments getting slower with increasingly poor excuses;

•   reports from other suppliers of severe problems in collecting;

- comments made by customer staff to sales or credit people;

- worsening atmosphere and morale in customer's premises;

- adverse press comments (profit dives, reorganisations, lay-offs, short time, resignations, and so on);

- County Court Judgments recorded recently;

- inputs from credit agency 'watch' services;

- announced payment moratoria;

- refinancing discussions with the bank;

- 'refer to drawer' cheques or 'bounced' direct debits.

Less obvious

- very late lodging of accounts at Companies House;

- serious qualification of the accounts by auditors;

- bad ratios in the latest accounts, especially interest cost versus profits;

- severe downward trend in key ratios.

Too late!

- appointment of Administrative Receiver (usually by the bank);

- meeting of creditors;

- petition for winding up (company) or bankruptcy (individual);

- Corporate Voluntary Arrangement (CVA).

All credit managers can add their own experiences and come up with additions to any such list, but some signs that can happen at any time are well worth taking careful note of, especially if the account has always been regarded as high risk. For example:

- sudden or rapid closing down of premises;

- rationalising activities into fewer locations (often described initially as an exercise in cost control and efficient use of resource, but frequently the precursor to the downward slide, already there but not yet public knowledge);

- changing banks (*always* worth asking why!);

- frequent changes of suppliers;

- change of ownership (who is now responsible for existing previous debts?).

Many a credit manager will recognise less 'official' signs as being important indicators of impending doom nonetheless. The bad paying customer, who has come up with excuse after excuse every month, made part payments and missed promises (all bad signs in themselves, of course) can add the icing to the cake by telling the supplier's credit manager 'everything will be alright from now on – we are factoring our debts'. With apologies to the factoring houses, at this stage in a company's decline, most credit managers would agree that we are talking 'kiss of death'! Companies should not start factoring their sales when they are in deep trouble.

As long ago as 1985, a then leading insolvency expert, William Mackey, drew up a list of defects he had observed when he went in to liquidate failed businesses. His list totalled 14, and though he had never seen all 14 in one company, he certainly reckoned to be able to say that five or more indicated an irrecoverable slide into the abyss. Even though his list is some 25 years old, and both fashions and habits have changed, there is resonance today (for credit managers, too, there is a degree of 'been there, seen it, done that' – not a lot changes in the broad scope of things):

1. *Rolls-Royce out front with personalised number plates.* Today, it may well be a directors' car park with top of the range Mercedes or BMWs, all with personalised plates. Remember the two Porsche above? Who is rewarding whom with whose money?

2.   *Fish tank, fountain or atrium in the reception area.* No change there, then. It is one thing being smart and presentable, looking efficient and pleasant to work in, but quite another to engage in frivolous corporate 'showing off'.

3.   *Flag pole.* Indeed, the more the merrier! Three or four flagpoles outside a corporate headquarters? Enron? WorldCom?

4.   *Three or more knighted directors.* How about peers of the realm? How close would they really be to the action? Back to Enron again!

5.   *Chairman honoured for services to industry.* Reputation and ability do not always go together.

6.   *Recently moved to super-modern offices.* As true today as ever. The even more cynical would point at super-modern offices (or factory) having been officially opened by a dignitary, or worse yet, a member of the Royal family.

7.   *Chief accountant elderly or unqualified.* It is often the case that second generation family companies have loyal retainers who have been with the firm from the beginning, and who are unqualified, holding senior positions through length of service and experience. They may well be experienced in the nature of the business, but have not kept pace with modern requirements in law, taxation, computerisation and so on.

8.   *Products are market leaders.* Being the best there is breeds complacency and the feeling that 'we are the best and will always be here'. The more successful a product, the more it is exposed to new competition all the time.

9.   *Recently announced change of bank.* Changing banks has always been something of a nightmare for most, however easy competitive banks claim they make it. To change banks is a major exercise, and rarely done 'willingly'.

10. *Audit partner went to school with managing director.* Post Enron and so on, there were serious moves to separate entirely the audit function and/or any other relationships between client and

auditor. It remains a major bone of contention, however, that appointment of auditors is more a rubber stamp exercise in many companies, based upon who knows whom, and/or its easier not to change. The tender process is a long way from being the accepted approach.

11.   *Chairman well-known for political work.* Back to Enron, again!

12.   *Recently announced huge export order from Mozambique.* Or anywhere, really, let alone a risky market. Orders and the ability to carry them out, collect the cash <u>and</u> make a profit are not necessarily connected. A badly managed company can go to the wall whatever the size and shape of its order book. Better to get it properly funded before any commitment.

13.   *Recently announced a technological breakthrough.* As above, plus turning an innovation into a profitable product takes clued-up management. One should also question the motive behind the announcement – bolster share price?

14.   *Salesmen (only) rewarded with annual 'jolly' to an exotic place.* It is still the case that any company which has sales at any cost as its driving force (and these are the companies who see Singapore or Fiji as a good reward for its top sales people) is bound to encounter turbulent times later, if not sooner. Such incentives to maximise sales are rarely matched by good credit control – volume at any price brings more bad debt.

All of the above may be regarded as perhaps somewhat tongue-in-cheek by some, but many credit practitioners will recognise the basic reality of this list in their own experience. Taken singly, perhaps none of the above would bring about the collapse of the edifice, but taken in multiples, experience shows that disaster is not far away.

The Three Phases of Failure

From time to time, there are catastrophic events that can have an impact which perhaps could not have been either foreseen or planned for. Many would place September 11 in this category. Others would say that post-September 11, there should be no reason to not plan for worse case scenarios in any walk of life, or business activity. Sometimes, it is not appreciated that one event, say the Hatfield rail crash, can have consequences not on the face of it directly connected. Taxi drivers in Doncaster and York lost thousands of pounds of business in the months following Hatfield. London trains still ran, and still made their usual stops – the problem was they were not carrying anybody. Nobody used the railway in the same numbers for a long time. None of that was 'planned for' and many failures followed.

For the most part, however, the failure of companies is gradual, comparatively, painful and in the end, inevitable. Company failure is seen to have three distinct stages:

- poor management structure;

- bad operating decisions; and

- the final few weeks or months.

Ultimate failure inevitably begins with a poor management structure, or with a change in the management structure or management role which deflects from doing the correct thing:

- *Autocratic boss*: He often has spectacular success initially, particularly if in the wake of some invention or niche market penetration. Soon, however, his overbearing style loses good people and those that remain fail to do the right things in fear of his wrath. The outward sign is of functional heads being constantly overridden instead of being allowed to do what they are employed (and paid) for. In some very large publicly quoted organisations, this symptom is often misleadingly encouraged by the financial media, who like 'characters', but is fortunately tempered by shareholders looking to safeguard their investment.

- *Chairman is also chief executive* (especially if also an autocrat!): Ideally, a company chairman should be the elder statesman who keeps an eye on the whole set-up, especially on the actions of the chief executive, and advises the board accordingly. When the chief executive lacks a separate chairman, the company can lack direction in a crisis.

- *Weak directors*: Directors are employed to run a company for the shareholders and their duties are laid down in law. The function is defined by the Companies Act, and other Acts of Parliament, and their actions must always comply. In addition to satisfying shareholders and producing results which will satisfy both owners and lenders, there is a requirement under the Insolvency Act which in effect gives each director the joint and several responsibility of running the company. It used to be that a sales director, production director or similar non-financial officer could plead a certain amount of ignorance about the financial health of the company. They left 'all that sort of thing to the finance man'. Any director, of any limited company, whatever his or her actual technical or specific role within the company has, by virtue of a seat on the board, a joint responsibility for the successful running of the company. The real problem with inadequate or 'figurehead' directors, notwithstanding their legal obligations, is that they may not apply skill, forward planning or the clout needed at the right times to achieve the right results. They are outwardly visible as reacting to crises rather than proactively avoiding them.

- *Unbalanced board of directors*: A balanced board has directors with executive authority for each major function, for example, sales, production, technical and finance. Over time, some companies promote a surfeit of one kind, such as engineering experts in a technical company, at the expense of other skills needed on the board. Not surprisingly, the boards of failed companies often exhibit a complete absence of any financial skill. This is notwithstanding the comments above in respect of the *responsible duties* of all company directors, whatever their particular role.

- *Management gaps*: There may be a lack of senior supervision between director level and working staff, resulting in a severe communication gap in both directions and, usually, poor morale at the working level.

- *No cash planning or business strategy*: Some companies have no annual budget process to plan operations or expense levels; no structure for reporting monthly results and no analysis of variances to enable corrective action to be taken in good time; no cash flow planning or day-to-day control of it. Indeed far too many companies have no perception of the cost of credit and the effect of late payment on profits, and those companies usually do not see any problem accruing from overdues. An unbalanced board (see above) is often heard to observe that future volume will take care of past losses.

- *Inability to change*: Older companies, or those using old technology, often find it difficult to modernise, whether intellectually or finding the necessary investment. They lack the ability to keep pace with market trends (as well as with manufacturing, production and distribution techniques), and soon lose market share and go into decline. This inability to change is often very closely associated with an autocratic boss, weak directors and management gaps.

None of the above are mutually exclusive, indeed as pointed out in the last bullet point, there is very frequently a combination of some or all of these features in the first stage of company failure.

The second stage, and very much the end of the beginning and the beginning of the end, broadly comes under the heading of bad operating decisions:

- *Over-borrowing*: Through lack of management, some companies borrow more and more until the cost of servicing loans exceeds any profits being made. When the bank becomes worried (as banks do), they will insist on a reduction of their loan. When that happens, companies in this situation find that there is no way to raise money or to cut spending quickly enough; nor is there any external confidence in further investment.

- *Over-extended contracts*: In an attempt to put things right, some companies take on very large deals which turn out to be beyond their scope to perform properly.

- *Too-fast expansion*: Another way that companies in trouble try to get things right is to expand sales significantly by discounting prices to get the volumes needed. This cannot produce either the cash flow or the profit soon enough to keep the now larger creditors paid or to service short-term loans. In any case, if margins are already tight, taking on significant extra work on an excessive cost and expense base is hardly going to lead into improved profits.

- *Borrowing short term to finance long-term loans*: Fixed assets are there to produce sales over many years and should always be financed over similar periods. A company soon gets into trouble when it has to borrow new money at short notice to pay instalments falling due. The period of repayment of loans should always be less or equal to the time that assets produce income.

The third distinct phase in the downhill slide towards failure manifests itself in the more obvious and recognisable symptoms of a very sick company. Some of these symptoms can in fact be displayed by companies not necessarily on the brink of failure, but taken together, and following stages one and two, there can be little doubt that the end is nigh:

- *Excuses for late payment*: Payment promises not kept and increasingly poor excuses given. Very obvious avoidance of taking phone calls, and/or not answering letters, faxes and emails.

- *Signs of poverty*: Premise and equipment become poorly maintained for lack of funds; staff morale becomes low due to cut-backs, pay problems and worry about the future of their jobs.

- *Image problems*: These are soon evident in complaints about quality and delays in customer service, resulting in lower order levels from major buyers who soon find more reliable sources. Quality complaints themselves can arise due to the failing company sourcing inferior materials from wherever it can get them, as usual suppliers exercise stop list options.

- *Creative accounting*: This is seen only when there is access to financial accounts, revealing profits boosted by questionable treatment of stock values, low depreciation compared to previous practice, invoicing in advance of completed contracts, and many other dubious entries. Creative accounting was taken to new heights in the Enron scandal, followed by many other company revelations of 'black holes' in their accounts. This alone is enough to bring even the mightiest edifice crashing down. It is a matter of opinion as to whether the 'toxic assets' issue which came to light in 2008 and 2009 would come under the heading of creative accounting or not – what is certain is that gross overvaluation of doubtful assets brought down not just one bank, but very nearly the worldwide financial structure.

- *Bad ratios*: Balance sheet analysis shows severe deterioration in main ratios since the previous period, often quarterly or half yearly, especially lower net worth and a poor quick ratio or acid test.

- *Legal action by creditors*: This is publicly evident in County Court Judgments and High Court writs. In trade circles, there may be news of joint action with Statutory Demands, often leading to winding-up orders.

- *Resignation of key people*: This may be actual or rumoured, especially of directors who can say later that they were not directors when failure occurred.

It is not difficult for even the less experienced credit managers to be able to see the stages in the decline – the order may be somewhat disjointed, some features will be missing, and some more prominent and important than others. But the end result is the same – failure.

Can it be Avoided?

There are two very short answers to this question – yes and no! Yes, companies can avoid failure themselves by taking all the action that is necessary to ensure a profitable and healthy enterprise. Yes, suppliers can avoid losses by taking all the risk assessment precautions in the first place, closely monitoring the account and taking prompt action when required. But – no, it is the nature of free enterprise that some will succeed and others will fail, sometimes with the best will in the world. And, no – losses cannot be totally eliminated, though they can be substantially reduced.

It is for the supplier to take the steps to keep losses as low and painless as possible. If a stubborn debtor ignores every request for payment, exhibits any of the above signs of trouble, the seller should seriously consider the legal process to recover a large debt before it is too late to do so. It is pointless waiting to see if others sue – the likelihood is that you are not the only supplier in this position, and however reluctant you may be (competitive pressures, market position, and so on), it is almost certain that some other supplier is not willing to wait a day longer. The sensible decision, once the failing status is clear, is to collect through the Courts while there are still some funds to be had. Small debts may not be worth the expense of legal action, though collection agencies may be able to assist (see Chapter 13), but they are not too painful and can be written off against a provision especially made to allow for such debts.

The way to move quickly to recover a debt before insolvency is made official, is to send the debtor a *final letter before action*, and follow without protracted delay with a County Court Summons, which the creditor can issue, or a High Court writ, issued through solicitors. The *Statutory Demand* is a well-used process, and can have some effect, because the serious threat of closing a business down or making a person bankrupt often produces payment from somewhere. If they are really able to pay, closing down is an option few debtors would willingly choose. It is likely, of course that any commercial relationship would be damaged beyond repair by such action, but the fact of the matter is that by this stage, self-inflicted damage by the debtor themselves has destroyed effectively any such relationship, and the end of the road is in sight. Chapters 22 and 23 extensively cover the legal collection process and insolvency, the point being made here being simply that of taking the right decision in time. Proceedings will always be viewed by creditors as a last resort, but having been through the collection process without result, it would be less than sensible just to let the debt sit there until it was too late. Some recovery of VAT is possible, and it may be that creditors can arrange a joint petition to help spread the costs.

It is also important for any supplier, in any industry, to avoid falling into the trap of being seen as a 'soft touch' by debtors. Legal action, even in cases where the prospects of recovery are very small, sends a message to all in the trade that the supplier is not prepared to tolerate serious default, and that action will be taken. It is also worth remembering that if the seller/creditor has evidence of *wrongful trading*, this information should be given to any subsequent Liquidator. Wrongful trading is when a company continues to trade, obtaining supplies on credit, when the directors knew *or ought to have known* that the company would not be able to settle its bills when they fell due. Directors can face penalties of up to 15 years disqualification from being a company director, and under some circumstances can be ordered to pay the debts of the company out of their own pockets. Fifteen years is still unusual (only the most serious cases, and especially those involving distress to members of the public), but disqualification orders themselves are now quite frequently made, and it is up to creditors to assist by passing on all relevant information.

Conclusion

There is no doubt that computer predictions of insolvency, as discussed in Chapter 7, continue to become more reliable and accurate. It is always going to be virtually impossible to say exactly *when* a company will fail, but combining predictive tools with personal observation and experience will bring some certainty to an uncertain science.

More often than not, the debtor's responses to requests for payment are the best indication of the real slide taking place, which taken together with the computer predictions and other signs should spur the taking of the required action. If the risk category approach, as outlined in Chapter 6, was already in place, the likely level of risk with the customer had *already* been identified. The creditor knows not only what might happen, but how to act when it does. The signs are always there, and the instances of totally unexpected failure are very rare indeed.

Sales may have the opportunity to turn a blind eye to the obvious – credit managers know that 'see all, hear all, say (do) nothing' is not a profitable option.

INSTITUTE OF CREDIT MANAGEMENT

Though there is no exam question relating directly to insolvency warning signs during the lifetime of the current ICM Education Syllabus, in Advanced Credit Management questions and case studies frequently require some imaginative thinking by candidates. That is to say, for example, that a case study involving the interpretation of ratios in a subject company, calls for both the ability to calculate the ratios and identify the significance of trends year on year. Implicit in such a task is to identify potential weaknesses which would lead to serious consequences, not least of which would be failure. Equally implicit, are those questions where candidates are asked to respond to customers' excuse and/or reasons for late payment.

It would be useful for candidates to take time to study their own receivables ledgers, and identify 'suitable cases for treatment'.

PART IV
Sales Ledger

9

Sales Ledger Administration

Glen Bullivant

• Administration and format • Statements • Customer service – disputes and queries • Order vetting and the sales ledger • Cash matching • Collection aids • Controls •

Administration and Format

Any reader who has been studying this publication in the time-honoured fashion of starting at the beginning can hardly have failed to notice that great emphasis is constantly being put on the fact that debtors, or accounts receivable, is an asset. Not only that, but the asset may well be one of the most significant on the company's balance sheet, representing as it does up to 35/40 per cent of the total asset value. Furthermore, like stocks, it is both a current and adjustable asset – that is to say, it can increase and decrease in value according to a number of actions, and the impact of such movements can be considerable on the health and wealth of the company.

The Sales Ledger is a complete record of all sales transactions made by the company, incorporating as it does:

- sales – invoices sent to customers;

- receipts – payments made by customers;

- credit notes for goods returned, or allowances (such as goodwill gestures and so on);

- write-offs;

- write-ons;

- adjustments and transfers.

All these entries must be traced so that the final summary is an accurate record of all sales, and the total figure of gross debtors can be posted to the balance sheet. At any given moment, the difference between what has been invoiced to customers and what has been paid by them is the balance owing. That owed balance is the amount at risk of not being paid, and is the centre of attention for credit managers and their teams. The Sales Ledger therefore represents the source of evidence in the pursuit of cash, the analysis of outstandings and the identity of income sources. Apart from the paramount need for a company to know its daily, weekly or monthly sales data, the analysis of the debts can be used for many purposes:

- setting collection targets;

- forecasting cash receipts;

- identification of priority follow-up activities.

The Sales Ledger is therefore far more than a mere audit statistic, to be recorded, filed and forgotten about.

Because the Sales Ledger is a chronological record of sales to and payments from customers, it provides a wealth of statistical information. Just as examples, analysis by region, by representative or by branch, the highlighting of products or services, and so on can indicate where the greatest sales volumes (and possibly profits) take place. Such an analysis can be of value to marketing departments when researching sales trends, and can lead to greater or lesser efforts in certain products, areas, or even customers where circumstances demand. Plotting this kind of sales data, together with payment history and patterns of customer behaviour, can also help the credit department reassess customers, amend credit limits and risk categories, and negotiate improved credit terms. The ledger is used to monitor delayed payments and overtrading and can highlight activity by customers which may indicate financial difficulties.

Whether the system is computerised or manual, the essential requirements of a Sales Ledger accounting process are promptness and accuracy. It represents the source of most of the data used in day-to-day credit control – it follows that being up to date and accurate is fundamental to the success of the credit control activity in the company. In collection work, for example, the collector needs to be absolutely certain that the information displayed on the screen, or held in the file, is correct. Asking for payment for something that has already been paid or already notified as being under query is at worst unprofessional and at best an indication of lack of customer care and inefficiency. More than that, it can be extremely damaging to the credibility of the collector, and undermine his or her confidence in making the next collection call to the same customer.

The Sales Ledger, as a prime record of all transactions, is very much at the heart of the monitoring of credit risk to identify potential failure. Many of the insolvency warning signs discussed in Chapter 8 are there for all to see in the ledger, if only they will look. In the excitement of gaining an order, it is easy to overlook the routine of assessment and monitoring an account – change of name, change of bank, delays in payment becoming longer, dishonoured cheques, failed standing orders or direct debits. The size and frequency of orders and changes in buying habits are reflected in the Sales Ledger, and the daily routine in the Sales Ledger department should always include *daily* monitoring. The signs should be acted upon as soon as they are evident, and not left until the month-end, or next time a review is undertaken or only when time permits.

For centuries, books of account and therefore the Sales Ledger were all recorded manually and only the advent of the more primitive accounting machines brought about some attempt at early mechanisation. Computerisation, and later the development of the PC and the laptop, the work station and the network brought about a transformation in the accounting process in only a comparatively short period of time. As a result, manual book keeping has all but disappeared – even the one-man business can operate a PC-based system, buying off-the-shelf ledger packages and programs. When these are combined with inexpensive, modern printers, it is now possible for *every* business to produce neat, informative, business-like invoices and statements – and produce them promptly.

It is usual for companies to send out statements, which is a customer version of the Sales Ledger record. The information on the statement is the same as that on the ledger, so the collector and the customer can both be looking at the same thing when talking on the phone. The printed statement of account can be viewed as a collection document in its own right, as well as a summary of transactions to date. Generally, statements fell into two broad types: brought-forward and open item.

- *Brought-forward statements* have fortunately been disappearing over the years, and it is not hard to see why. It starts with the previous month-end's total, then lists each transaction for the current month, as illustrated in Figure 9.1. The drawback is obvious – details of the previous month's total have gone, and to obtain a breakdown of that total, the previous month's statement will have to be retrieved. Unpaid or disputed invoices from the previous month's invoices are lumped together and lost to view. It is easy to see why brought-forward was popular in the manual system days, and equally to understand how computerisation made it all but redundant.

STATEMENT OF ACCOUNT WITH XYZ LTD
ABC Ltd
High Street
Anywhere
Somewhere
ZZ99 9ZZ

ACCOUNT NO: 1234567			STATEMENT DATE 28 FEB XXXX	
ITEM DATE	**ITEM REF**	**DESCRIPTION**	**AMOUNT**	**BALANCE**
31 JAN XX		B/FWD		297.00 **
09 FEB XX	043567	INVOICE O/no 9017	71.69	368.69
20 FEB XX	045934	INVOICE O/no 9163	62.96	431.65
20 FEB XX	045935	INVOICE O/no 9164	174.70	606.35
** OVERDUE	**297.00**	**PLEASE REMIT**		

TERMS – NETT CASH PAYABLE BY 20TH OF MONTH FOLLOWING DATE OF INVOICE
NOTE – PAYMENT MADE BUT NOT SHOWN ABOVE SHOULD APPEAR ON NEXT STATEMENT
TOTAL NOW DUE £606.35

Figure 9.1   Statement with brought-forward balance

- *Open-item statements* were always the best option, and rocketed in popularity once computerisation had taken hold. They are by far now the norm in B2B trade credit and Figure 9.2 opposite clearly shows why. All unpaid items are still listed in detail and are not lost to view.

Statements

The above illustrations are designed simply to differentiate between the open-item and the brought-forward types of statement – in reality a statement should show considerably more information. As well as clear figures, the statement

STATEMENT OF ACCOUNT WITH XYZ LTD
ABC Ltd
High Street
Anywhere
Somewhere
ZZ99 9ZZ

ACCOUNT NO: 1234567   **STATEMENT DATE 28 FEB XXXX**

ITEM DATE	ITEM REF	DESCRIPTION	AMOUNT	BALANCE
20 DEC XX	033641	INVOICE O/no 8736	58.75	58.75**
11 JAN XX	035341	INVOICE O/no 8814	171.07	229.82**
27 JAN XX	040425	INVOICE O/no 8910	67.18	297.00**
09 FEB XX	043567	INVOICE O/no 9017	71.69	368.69
20 FEB XX	045934	INVOICE O/no 9163	62.96	431.65
20 FEB XX	045935	INVOICE O/no 9164	174.70	606.35
** OVERDUE	**297.00**	**PLEASE REMIT**		

TERMS – NETT CASH PAYABLE BY 20TH OF MONTH FOLLOWING DATE OF INVOICE
NOTE – PAYMENT MADE BUT NOT SHOWN ABOVE SHOULD APPEAR ON NEXT STATEMENT
TOTAL NOW DUE £606.35

Figure 9.2   Open-item statement

should also contain enough information to assist the customer in making the right payment to the right location (at the right time!). In other words, if the customer is used to dealing with a branch or depot, and the statement is issued by a central accounts office or head office, then the payment address should be prominent, together with due dates, bank name, address, sort code and account number for those paying by BACS.

Many companies include an analysis of the ages of the unpaid items – current, 30 days, 60 days, and so on. It is also common practice to incorporate a tear-off remittance advice which can be sent with the cheque, or sent direct, without a cheque, if payment has been made by credit transfer. In the same way that it is important that an invoice should be clear and free from unnecessary clutter, so to with a statement, clarity is important. It is not encouraging to pay, or making plain the purpose and contents of a statement by making non-relevant additions, such as new marketing initiatives, new products or promotions. Besides, the statement is aimed at accounts payable staff, who may have no interest in the latest sales promotion data, but do need to see a clear statement of their suppliers' account.

The whole question of sending out statements has long been the matter of debate in credit management circles, it often being argued that many customers do not need them on the basis that they work with suppliers' actual invoices. In that respect, they argue that producing and dispatching a statement is a fruitless exercise, and what is more a needless expense. On the other hand, many customers in fact use the supplier's statement to reconcile their own purchase ledgers. Receipt of the statement with the full listings of invoices rendered enables the customer to match against their own record of purchase invoices, identify any missing items and request copies if required. The expense of production and postage of statements is minimal when set against the cost of the collection process as a whole, and because it is little more than a copy of the seller's own Sales Ledger, it is in fact being produced anyway. Why not let the customer have his copy?

There are two other strong reasons for producing and sending statements. Firstly, if we agree that the invoice is not just 'the bill' itself for the work done or the goods supplied, but is also in reality the first request for payment, then the statement can readily be viewed as the *second* request for payment. On that basis, without reminder letters, telephone calls, faxes or emails, the customer on receiving the statement has now been asked twice for payment. Secondly, it is a feature of the legal process and the consequence of the arguments in respect of consumer over indebtedness and the subsequent bank-led financial meltdown, that creditors have to show that they have taken all reasonable steps to obtain payment and given the debtor all reasonable opportunity to pay. Though this 'Pre-Action Protocol', as it is known, is clearly aimed at the consumer industry, business-to-business also has to follow the protocol to the extent that they are dealing with sole traders and partnerships, who, in all major respects, are consumers. In any event, better in the event of any subsequent litigation to be able to show all the steps taken in the recovery process, the statement being but one step. On balance, more customers use statements than throw them away, and for the seller, it remains a useful collection document.

Cash received can be displayed on a total 'credit' item, cross-referenced against the invoices cleared, and either removed when the account is updated online or remain on screen until the next open-item statement is issued.

The Sales Ledger can be subdivided by customer type, alphabetically or otherwise, and can group customers by region, sales representative, sales volume, importance and level of risk. The golden rule for any method of organising the Sales Ledger is that it must be easy to find an invoice, credit note, debit note, journal or cash entry instantly from the records.

Prompt postings to the ledger, and a firm cut-off date at the month/period ends, allows for the rapid issue of statements and, in turn, the equally rapid follow-up of overdues. The statement of account is a perfect opportunity to show a bold message requesting payment of any overdues. For ease of customer reconciliation, and cash matching, it is sensible to display cumulative invoice totals, with a grand total. If sellers have high volumes of invoices per account (for example, daily delivery and invoicing), then there should be monthly subtotals.

Customer Service – Disputes and Queries

From whichever direction it is approached, there is no going away from the fact that the credit function is the 'front line' of any business operation. Sales and marketing may claim that distinction, and to some extent they have some justification. However, when it come to customer contact, customer interface, customer liaison or whatever label it may be given, there is no question that the credit function is the real 'front line'. Perhaps when the account was first cultivated, there was some sales interplay, but since the account was established just look at what happens:

- An order is placed (letter, phone, fax, email) – if for any reason the order cannot be immediately accepted (overdue account, over credit limit and so on), who informs the customer?

- The order is processed, and acknowledged (letter, phone, fax, email) – if for any reason the order is going to be a problem (out of stock, wrong size, colour and so on), who informs the customer?

- The order is picked and dispatched.

- The order is invoiced – who contacts the customer?

- The invoice is rejected – who contacts the customer?

- The query is resolved – who contacts the customer?

It is not difficult to see who is actually the main point of contact in the seller's company. As will be shown in Chapters 11 and 12, collection is more than just recovery of sums due – it is about education to terms and about *keeping* the account. Indeed, we need today's invoice paying, and a new order, please! That requires a real customer service ethic throughout the seller company, not just from credit control but right the way through from chief executive to gatehouse one security night-watchman, receptionist to lathe operator. Those at the front, however, have to face the customer with the answer, explanation, apology, redress, correction or replacement on the one hand, or rejection of complaint, explanation or firm request to settle on the other.

Credit control staff have a vested interest in seeing that the customer is satisfied and has no complaint. Every disputed invoice is an unpaid invoice, and it is only ever possible to collect what it is in fact possible to collect. Until the dispute is resolved, it represents an item not possible to collect!

Most computerised systems will allow disputed items to be flagged. If necessary, these can be excluded from due or past due totals (the collectability issue as above), but they certainly should not be excluded from the statement or the statement total balance. Debts may be disputed, but they remain unpaid, and therefore a cost to the business, and require resolution by credit note or by payment. If the system does not allow disputed items to be flagged, the statement should carry a message to show the total amount under query – the customer can see that his queries have been noted (and can assume that they are being acted upon), and the collector can see that such invoices still require attention. In an online system, the screen display replicates the last statement sent to the customer, subsequent items being added daily.

Customer dissatisfaction, shown in disputing invoices and raising queries, is expensive for any seller, in terms of both unpaid accounts and reduced sales. All the more reason for the sales manager *not* to delay approving the credit note – 'I don't want it to come off this months figures' should be banned outright in any organisation. If it does not come off this month's, it will come off next! There is no good time perhaps from a sales perspective to approve a credit, but if the credit is agreed, now is the very best time from the company perspective. The sooner the uncollectable becomes collectable, then the sooner the revenue from cash inwards offsets the cost of maintaining the debt on the ledger. It really is a 'no brainer', and it is unforgivable that any sales manager be allowed to delay a genuine customer credit for internal, selfish and totally unprofitable reasons.

Every successful seller knows that it is important to deliver the right goods, at the right price, to the right place, in the right quantity, at the right time, and with the right documentation. It is then so much easier to demand payment. Get any of the rights wrong, and the right to be paid is in jeopardy. It would also be wrong to assume that every customer query was merely a delaying tactic. Some are, but all must be taken seriously until and unless proved wrong or unfounded. If the customer is right in a disputed debt, the sooner the credit is issued, the sooner the rest of the account can be collected, and *the sooner a potentially dissatisfied customer is pacified to smooth the way for further business* – sales and marketing, please note!!!

Queries are often first notified soon after the statement is issued, or when payment is made. The customer may deduct a debit note, or merely comment on the remittance advice that a particular invoice is being withheld for such and such a reason. Apart from the larger organisations like supermarkets, for example, debit notes are in fact becoming rarer. Customers raise debit notes so that the undisputed part of the invoice or debt can be paid – far more popular now is to grab the complaint as a reason for non-payment, and hold on to all the money until the dispute has been resolved. It may be 'immoral' in the eyes of some to hold up payment of a £10,000 invoice because of an error on a wrongly priced £100 item, but it certainly should focus the mind of the seller to get this £100 error rectified without delay – far more 'imperative' to solve £100 to release £9900 than simply to solve a £100 debit note, with the £9900 already in the bank. Morality works both ways.

Except in the smaller organisations, it is unlikely that the seller's person who is responsible for cash allocation will also be responsible for account queries, or even chasing overdues. The query may well have surfaced through some other route, such as sales or marketing. However and wherever it arose, it will be down to credit control to instigate the resolution process. Whatever the seller's system for processing sales disputes, it is essential that they are not allowed to accumulate. If not dealt with promptly, they can (and most certainly, do) cause interruption of payment, interruption of purchases, create ill-will and give an overall impression, not just of inefficiency, but also of scant regard for customer care.

What is required, therefore, is a query system whereby every dispute or complaint is reported, logged and acted upon, and *all* affected company staff are alerted. The best way to achieve this is to establish a Query Register, with basic easy to understand and to follow rules to progress disputes. It is important to identify the root cause (which may be an individual, a department, a process, a particular product and so on), and have rapid follow-up procedures for resolution. Query analysis is vital to identify the source of poor performance *within* the seller's organisation. An example would be a high level of price queries in a particular sales region, which could point to a rogue sales representative negotiating special prices and not informing the invoicing department so that products are billed at the standard prices already held on the system. Constant short deliveries or wrong size/colour could be due to people or system problems in the warehouse or dispatch areas. Account disputes have a wider importance than just in the Sales Ledger operation and in companies with good resolution procedures there is a strong involvement of senior people in all affected departments.

All queries should be logged by date, customer name, invoice number(s), nature of dispute, to whom it will be passed for resolution, with a prescribed timescale for action, and the date and the nature of the outcome. Timescale is important, and it should be clear that if x does not resolve by such and such a date, the matter will be escalated to manager y – and so on. The dispute itself can be broken down into appropriate categories:

- price

- discount

- shortage

- damage

- model

- size

- colour

- early delivery

- late delivery

- credit terms

- credit limit

- wrong delivery

- special deal agreed with sales

- wrong rate of VAT

- errors in extension

- wrong address

- wrong description, or misleading description

- insufficient details

- customer order number

- unable to match to order

- unable to match to quotation.

Depending on the type and nature of business, there could of course be others. For example, performance may be an important issue – there can be many disputes from customers claiming that the product did not 'do' what the salesperson said it would do. The important point is that by breaking down disputes into recognisable categories, and by allocating responsibility for resolution and a timescale for that resolution, no query should go unnoticed, and no query should be allowed to become old and grey. In the final analysis, the credit department have undertaken a massive customer service operation, and the company should continually strive towards dispute free sales and service.

Order Vetting and the Sales Ledger

If there is to be a true credit control system, and not just a simple cash collection operation in the Sales Ledger, vetting of incoming orders against credit limits, risk categories and past due accounts is essential. Where the product being sold has a lengthy lead time, order vetting can be carried out both on receipt of the order itself, and again when the order is actually ready for dispatch.

The subject of stopping supplies is a very emotive one, and the cause of more 'friction' between sales and credit than perhaps any other credit activity. It is vital to have some real-time method of flagging queries so that customers are not placed on stop for unpaid items which are subject to a genuine unresolved query. Company policy should not be so rigid as to place all customers immediately on stop the every moment an account becomes overdue. It is better to produce a 'refer' list, or list of potential stopped accounts which can be discussed between sales and credit before the 'live' stop list is produced.

There are literally thousands of accounting software systems on the market, many hundreds of which include specific integrated credit management features. Development of Sales Ledger systems was once just one of the tasks of an in-house computer department, but rising costs and the falling price of 'off-the-shelf' solutions, have meant that it is now usual for even the largest corporations to buy ready-made systems and contract the necessary support from the supplier. Most of the purchased systems will require some degree of bespoke work to make them fit particular company needs, but the overall credit management requirements are in general well covered.

The main problem for client companies is to decide exactly what their Sales Ledger requirements are, and it is important for the credit control department to be closely involved in this area of decision making. Most companies now enjoy real-time (or online) functionality, so that immediately cash is posted to the ledger, or an invoice or credit note is raised, the customer account is updated. A collector can therefore look at a customer's account on a screen display, and know that all the information displayed is 'now', and not waiting for a batch run or for an overnight update.

Such a system is of immeasurable value (and often simply taken for granted), both for order vetting purposes and for collection activity. Because it enhances the credit department's efficiency and knowledge, it also enables them to create a better customer relationship. It is both embarrassing and inefficient for a collector, chasing with incomplete information, to be told by a customer that he holds a credit note which clears the outstanding balance.

Cash Matching

To guarantee that the quality of the Sales Ledger is maintained, it is imperative to ensure the prompt allocation and accurate reconciliation of incoming cash payments. Cash should be allocated to customer accounts to clear unpaid invoices immediately it comes in. If the customer does not supply sufficient information, then the customer should be contacted to obtain full details. In extreme cases, where the payment just cannot be identified, it can be posted to a suspense account, but action should be taken urgently to trace and identify these payments. Audit costs rise considerably when hours are spent trying to reconcile old unallocated cash, and collection credibility is endangered when chasing a customer for a payment which has already been made. In many large corporations, there can be vast amounts 'unallocated' on a daily basis, and rather like an old debt, the older the entry becomes, the harder it is to trace back and reconcile. It is simply not good enough to 'allocate' and balance each day, when at the end of the accounting period, the suspense account contains dozens of entries amounting to millions of pounds.

Controls should be implemented to ensure that the cash allocated equals the cash received, and this check should be made per account. The total amount received from the customers equals all the individual amounts paid, which in turn equals the amount allocated to the customer accounts on the ledger. All the customer totals add up to all the cash received, and everything balances. It is a fundamental of cash posting that this process is conducted vigorously – it is simply not acceptable that the ledger does not balance on a daily basis. However, it is equally unacceptable to 'make' it balance, by writing off without proper reason and authorisation, or by misallocating. We are talking here of customers' own funds, and what they say they are paying is what they are actually paying. One of the traps that credit staff can fall into, especially when under time pressures, is to decide for themselves which items the customer is paying. For example, some accountants and finance directors insist that, where the detail is not clear, the oldest invoices should be taken out first, making the Aged Debt Report look better, even though the customer may in fact be paying later invoices. There may well be a good reason for the customer leaving older items, such as disputes or queries, and to remove those items could mean that the query never gets resolved. It also means, in the event of subsequent administration or liquidation, that the Administrator or Liquidator cannot agree the creditor's claim.

For the same reasons, care should be taken in removing the actual numbered invoices as stated by the customer – it is not uncommon for invoices of the same value to be confused, and when chasing for payment of alleged unpaid items, even though the value may be correct, the customer can justifiably argue that the invoice has in fact been paid.

Batch controls should be maintained, even when using real-time systems. This is even more important when more than one person is involved in the allocation of cash.

Computer programs are readily available which perform automatic cash matching. This entails the operator posting only the customer's account number or other specific identification, and the total payment received. The computer will then allocate the cash using a number of preset algorithms, the most common of which are payments against:

- total account balance;

- total overdue balance;

- overdue balance less debit notes;

- overdue balance less unallocated cash;

- single item;

- any cumulative balance on the statement.

Such programs will vary according to user requirements, and there can be a number of different algorithms. If a perfect match is found, the computer automatically clears the items. Otherwise the cash will be posted 'on account' and an exception report will be issued to enable staff to reconcile the payment and complete the allocation.

Without doubt, this system is of the utmost benefit to those companies with a high volume of straightforward accounts, in so far as such accounts can be easily incorporated into an automatic system. This releases the clerical staff to clear the more complex receipts speedily and efficiently. Great care is still needed, however, in respect of multiple same-value invoices. As previously stated, it is important for the system to clear only those invoices identified by the customer as being those covered by the payment.

Where debit notes are raised by customers, it is fundamental that when the cash allocation is undertaken and the debit put back on the ledger, it is not simply left. The credit department should begin the full query resolution process, notifying the relevant department and personnel – an unpaid portion of an invoice is clearly an indication of a dispute of some kind, and requires all concerned to resolve within the laid down query resolution timescale. To ensure complete accuracy, any computer system should include the facility to create debit entries to agree with the customer's own debit note reference, which will give them very easy identification on the statement. For ageing purposes, it is better to be able to flag such disputes so that they can be omitted from stop or referral lists, or from direct collection activity, and be readily identifiable for the purposes of analysing dispute totals. This confers even greater importance for systems which have automatic credit sanctions according to age and value of debts.

Collection Aids

The Sales Ledger, and its derivative the 'Aged Debt Analysis', is the prime tool used by the collector. From the input created during the course of an accounting period, usually one month, a statement of account is produced showing the individual balance on each account. Although different companies may choose from a variety of formats, the basic needs are always the same:

- How much is outstanding?

- How is the outstanding balance made up?

- How much of the outstanding balance is overdue?

- By how long is it overdue?

- What are the payment terms on the account?

- When and how should an aged analysis of the ledger be produced?

The Aged Debt Analysis (often referred to as the Aged Debt Report or Aged Receivables Analysis) is the prime source of information used for collection activity. An example is illustrated by Figure 9.3.

The analysis can show a single line balance for each account, aged in days or months. If the ledger is divided into more than one working section (area, representative, customer size, product type and so on), each division should be

AGED DEBT ANALYSIS			MONTH-END: 31 MAY XX				PAGE 42		
Account No Name Credit Data	Total Current	Overdue Debt	Total	1-30	31-60	61-90	91+	Under query	Over limit
MC3564 Main Trader Ltd C/L £5000 Code C Terms 30	4805	1960	2845	2810	35	0	0	0	0
MC3581 Bubbles Ltd C/L £1000 Code C Terms 30	1300	150	790	220	310	245	15	360	300
MC3666 Squeak Ltd C/L £2000 Code A Terms 45	21215	12240	7885	7700	10	0	62	1090	1215

Figure 9.3   Aged debt analysis

subtotalled for ease of reference. For the purposes of cash collection, the analysis brings into highlight those oldest items which require attention, and can be used very efficiently as a chasing document to record payments promised and received. With query flagging, it also identifies those items which are both collectable, and those which at the time of chasing are not collectable, cash collection targets should be set using *collectable* invoices – it is self-defeating in terms of meeting targets to include those amounts which are known to be under dispute. They only become collectable when resolved and only then should be brought into the target setting process. A running total of cash collected against the preset target shows clearly how much more needs to be collected, daily and weekly.

When the open-item ledger system deletes paid items, it makes sense to transfer the information to a 'history' file, with a defined layout which can be used with customers to improve payment performance or discuss new terms or credit ratings. The customer history analysis, showing a rolling 12-month history, can be both a screen display and a hard copy, and is in effect simply a month by month repeat of the Aged Debt Analysis with the addition of a days sales outstanding (DSO average credit taken) figure.

The Aged Debt Analysis highlights the collectable balances in a convenient way, but usually it is the statement of account which details the make-up of

CUSTOMER ACCOUNT HISTORY AS AT 31.05.XX										
Account No Name	Month	Total debt	Current	Overdue 1-30	31-60	61-90	90+	Disp	Sales YTD	DSO
MC3564	06.XX	4616	1649	1846	1050	71	0	0	1649	96
Main	07.XX	5636	1810	1649	1846	260	40	31	3459	98
Trader	08.XX	5331	1805	1810	1649	36	0	31	5264	95
	09.XX	5160	1545	1805	1810	0	0	0	6809	92
	10.XX	5267	1917	1545	1805	0	0	0	8726	92
	11.XX	4196	1816	1917	463	0	0	0	10542	71
	12.XX	2445	0	1816	629	0	0	0	10542	71
	01.XY	1347	135	0	1212	0	0	0	10677	81
	02.XY	2297	2162	135	0	0	0	0	12839	61
	03.XY	4972	2810	2162	0	0	0	0	15649	62
	04.XY	4805	1960	2810	35	0	0	0	17609	60
MC3581	05.XY	3542	1162	1960	420	0	0	0	18771	64
Bubbles	Etc.	Etc.	Etc.	Etc.	Etc.	Etc.	Etc	Etc.	Etc.	Etc.

Figure 9.4   **Revolving 12 month customer history analysis**

those balances. Even in the hi-tech environment of today, there are a good many collection staff (especially in the SME sector) who still prefer to work from documentation. An additional aid for such staff would be the availability of a printed version of the screen display. It is equally important to be able to look at an invoice or statement, especially in the exact format of that received by the customer – in the event of a customer query or simply when in discussion with a customer. It is of immense value for both the collector and the customer to be looking at exactly the same information. Further details or other information may well be available in other files or displayed on other screens.

Copies must therefore be easy to produce and reproduce, and if stored, done so in a secure environment or medium. The constant cry from customers ('copy, please') means that they need to be retrievable without delay, and preferably in original format. Copies are not just required for those customers who seem to make a habit of losing them, but frequently invoices have to be supplied in multiples, such as in export. There is also the statutory requirement for holding copies of all financial transactions for six years. The importance of easy retrieval and access cannot be overstated, nor can the desire to ensure that both the copy and the original are exactly the same in every way. Electronic filing of all documentation on datafile, CD, Internet, access, filing and so on is commonplace – the common requirement will always remain to be ease of retrieval.

The Aged Debt Analysis, the statement and the invoice remain the prime data source for all collection activity.

Controls

Every customer has a unique identity allocated at the time of opening the account, being the customer account number or code. To have two accounts with the same code would cause endless confusion, not just in the Sales Ledger department but in many other areas of the seller's company. The customer should retain this unique allocation even if subject to a change of name, merger or acquisition. Similarly, it is important to ensure that every invoice and credit note produced is numbered or coded in such a manner as to distinguish every separate individual transaction. Many systems produce a potential invoice number when the order is first processed, being a works order number, the actual invoice being produced on completion or delivery.

In an ideal scenario, when an order is received and processed into the system, it is given a transaction number which will appear on all documentation prior to invoicing, including: order acknowledgements, advice and packing notes, and any subsequent order amendments. The invoice is created on completion, dispatch or delivery – if the invoice contains both a unique invoice number and the original transaction number, these references give ease of identification for both the buyer as well as the seller. Computer systems automatically generate invoice numbers in the preset order, whereas manual systems require some control to ensure that no numbers are duplicated, that control being ideally within the credit department.

Computer systems are also programmed in such a way that invoice number duplication cannot occur, and missed numbers (void, cancelled, raised in error) are accounted for and listed. Manual allocation of invoice numbers call for a great deal of care, but the principle remains the same. The purpose is to ensure that one transaction can readily be identified, wherever and whenever it took place, and both the seller and the buyer can be certain that the invoice refers to the goods supplied, and that the money owed refers to the invoice in question.

It is extremely important that all cash receipts, whether cash, cheques or credit transfers, are actioned immediately. Cheques should be banked on the day of receipt, preferably before 3 p.m. – there is no purpose to be served in hanging on to cheques to bank them 'when convenient'. The cheque has been sent now, so 'now' is when the sender should expect the cheque to be banked and cashed – there may not be sufficient funds in a week's time! Ideally, cheques should be handled by a cashier, operating separately from the credit department, and cheques and remittance advices totalled separately to ensure they agree. A cash sheet, manual or computer produced, lists the customer by name and by the amounts paid.

The cash sheet, dated and numbered, goes to cash allocation, together with the relevant customer remittance advice, the totals having been entered into the cash book by the cashier. Once all the cash has been allocated against the correct customer accounts, total allocation is matched against total received to agree value, and the Sales Ledger account controls agree to the cash value posted.

Cash sheets can be produced separately for cash, cheques and credit transfers, each going through the same control and allocation process. Many companies access their bank accounts daily by password-protected processes to check receipts.

Once all the entries have been posted, it is useful for all cash allocation totals, receipt listings, bank paying-in book and bank statements to be checked and initialled by the credit manager or the cashier to double check that all the balances agree.

The entries which are all posted to the Sales Ledger are also posted independently to the nominal (or general) ledger. With a completely integrated computer system, there will be an interface which performs this task automatically, coding the entries appropriately as predetermined in the system. Whether this is the case, or whether the items are posted manually, a complete reconciliation of the sales and Nominal Ledgers must take place at the end of the accounting period. Any differences should be investigated and corrected immediately. The Nominal Ledger is the basis for the company's profit and loss account and balance sheet and must be maintained with scrupulous accuracy (the Sales Ledger section of the Nominal Ledger shows on the balance sheet as 'debtors').

The purpose behind all these processes is to ensure that there is an audit trail of all transactions which have taken place, from the raising of a sales invoice to the correct banking and cash matching of all cash received. Each year, the books of the company are audited to ensure their accuracy, and as part of their duties, auditors are required to be satisfied that invoicing is taking place correctly. This also encompasses the correct authorisation and raising of credit notes, the accurate posting of cash and the determination of correct balancing. They also plot the sequence of events through from the placement of the order to the eventual payment receipt ('order-to-cash'), the whole process constituting the audit trail. When any Sales Ledger system is changed, or related computer processes updated, or replaced, one of the prime considerations has to be the provision of an adequate audit trail. The auditors will be quick to report any deficiencies, which should be rectified without delay, and it is by no means a bad thing in fact to satisfy auditors before any change or installation of a new system – it can save both expense and embarrassment. All reputable software companies provide Auditor's Packages which are compatible with the client company's computer ledger system, allowing auditors to simply log in and run the required check programs. In any event, any computer software package worth buying will already have audit trail approval.

Good administration of the Sales Ledger requires several areas of control:

- processing of documents;

- knowledge of staff;

- training of new staff;

- communicating new systems or changes;

- observance of company policies;

- meeting financial controls;

- liaison with other functions, especially sales;

- output of effective reports.

Whatever the size of the business, it is worth producing a manual for the guidance of all concerned. This provides the opportunity in a single publication to set out general policies as well as detailed procedures, with sample forms and documents. It minimises misunderstandings, either in the credit department or any other company area which works closely with credit, and forms one of the basic documents in the induction and training process for new staff.

The Sales Ledger is an essential source of information for any well-managed company. Aside from the legal requirement to record accurately the company's sales transactions and their subsequent payment, credit, adjustment or write-off, the Sales Ledger is the 'nerve centre' of the business. It is capable of supplying highly usable information for credit and collection purposes, for sales and marketing uses, and for a variety of management reports.

Every business should aim to have the best computerised Sales Ledger affordable and relevant to the needs of the particular business, automating all the more mundane chores as much as possible. If well-planned invoices, statements and analyses are specified, more time can be created for credit staff to actually use the Sales Ledger to its full potential, rather than spend all their efforts merely maintaining the ledger.

INSTITUTE OF CREDIT MANAGEMENT

Diploma: Level 3

The design of a statement and the purposes of the fields contained is a regular and popular question in the Level 3 Module. It appears in a variety of forms of wording, but in essence it seeks to test candidates as to their understanding of the purpose and the use to which statements issued by companies in business to business dealings are used.

10

Computer Systems for Credit Management

Glen Bullivant

• System requirements • The sales ledger and customer file • Invoice input • Cash • General ledger • Reporting • Computerspeak •

System Requirements

We live in an age where the computer is an integral part of our daily lives, and has been for a good many years. We talk of 'the computer' often in terms of endearment, often in terms of derision, but whatever we do, say or think, there can be no escape from the extent to which every aspect of our very existence is now subject to the all embracing warm glow of the computer microchip. The invasion of the office began decades ago, followed latterly by the take over of home life by the PC and the Internet. As the older generation still struggle to set the video recorder in an attempt not to miss a favourite programme, grandchildren send each other pictures by phone, surf cyperspace for exam revision hints and download tomorrow's newest smash hits yesterday.

A boon or a blight? Any progress will always be dogged as much by detractors as it will be hailed by supporters, but the real answer lies in perspective. Although we can marvel at being able, for example, to put a piece of plastic in a wall machine 12,000 miles from home, and within seconds draw out money to enable us to buy a cup of coffee in downtown Auckland, or book a flight to Barcelona without leaving the living room, it should always be remembered that the computer is little more than an adding machine. Very sophisticated, true, but only really capable of performing the task it was designed to undertake if the right information has been put into it in the first place. 'Garbage in, garbage out' is as true today as it was when the phrase was first coined. In other words, we can blame computers for getting things wrong, but if they do, it is principally because we have got it wrong to start with.

As individuals, citizens, consumers or whatever, we can be deemed to exist if we are recorded somewhere. Not to be on some file and not to exist in the eyes of officialdom, the bank, the finance company and so on, brings with it a host of problems, ultimately only really resolved when somebody creates a file for us! That, then, is the nature of the developed, sophisticated society in which we all live, and the computer is as important as the clothes we wear, the food we eat or the relationships we enjoy.

Computerisation, therefore, is necessary for all – it takes the drudgery out of the monotonous or the laborious, undertaking those repetitive tasks which are both difficult to endure and even more difficult to manually maintain the same high standard throughout. They free us up to carry out those tasks that require more of our time and expertise and they promote consistency. The downside can be seen in the actual fall in the levels of expertise in some areas of a company's operation – too many companies see computerisation not as an enhancement, or improvement, but more as a direct replacement. They pay lip service to staff training, working on the basis that the system will run the operation, and only one or two less technical people will be required to deal with that most difficult of animals, the customer, It will be enough to tell the customer what the computer says, they maintain, forgetting that knowledge, experience and above all the ability to interpret output is as vital as the output itself. It is also all too easy to assume that the computer actually runs the business, and the downfall of many is the belief that it does just that. Nothing is further from the truth, which is that the computer is there to *support* the running of the business – an entirely different proposition altogether.

No credit manager can afford to be left behind with the pace of developments in computerisation as it affects the credit department and the Sales Ledger function, and though it is not the intention here to delve in detail into the wires and microchips of computer systems, it is important to be aware of the areas which can be utilised through computerisation to the benefit of the credit function. There will always be pressure to improve collection performance, better cash flow and reduced DSO, and the more a system can be developed and enhanced to assist, the better the chance of objectives being achievable. It would be just as counterproductive to not allow a member of staff a new biro, as it would to try to reach targets set now on systems that have been in operation for 20 years and never upgraded. 'Give us the tools, and we will do the job' sounds familiar.

The credit manager should be part of any team set up to review, replace, enhance or upgrade the credit computer systems, and any such review should begin with a fundamental list of basic requirements. The computer system for credit control centres around the Sales Ledger and customer file, but is much more than that, and a shopping list of credit needs is the starting point:

Basic functions include:

- the Sales Ledger;

- the customer file;

- full data screen, with all customer information;

- history of past collection activity;

- efficient cash collection;

- payment history;

- turnover, year to date;

- diary system to produce full work lists;

- notepad facility to show full history of customer contact;

- ability to monitor, log and report on disputed invoices;

- ability to identify and classify customers with indicator flags or markers;

- immediate update of all input;

- full and detailed exception reporting, regular standard reports and 'one off' special reports;

- adaptability for enhancements such as predictive dialing;

- links to order input;

- stop list and referrals;

- credit limits.

The list could be added to, no doubt, but the point is simply to emphasise the fact that the credit manager and the credit/collection team need more than just a ledger – they need a process which leads to better cash flow and all the advantages that brings to the profit bottom line. They need a process which adds value to what they do, that meets the business need and which offers good customer service. An additional downside with computerisation can best be illustrated by those corporations, usually big and perhaps multi-national, who lose sight of the needs of the customer in the drive to 'improve' internal processes and procedures. It has been said that every company has two kinds of employee, *including directors*: those who stand at the factory gate looking *inwards* and those who stand at the factory gate looking *outwards*! Commerce is littered with the corpses of those companies who took their eye off the customer and put all their efforts into 'internal cost saving initiatives' for their own sake.

The Sales Ledger and Customer File

An automated Sales Ledger comes top of the list of all trade credit departments as the principal system requirement. At the very least, it provides the means to hold and update customer information, post all billing transactions (invoices, credit notes and debit notes) on to the ledger, apply incoming cash and generate the appropriate General Ledger accounting entries. Online and in real time is the ideal, but more than that the system needs to be able to give the credit manager those facilities which lift the system from being simply Sales Ledger to one which is designed to support credit management activity. In other words, it needs:

1. Cash/collection aids, to help reduce periods of unauthorised extended credit.

2. Credit exposure monitoring, to consolidate exposure across a group of accounts, for example; to reflect in base currency (sterling, for UK-based companies) the debts of customers trading in foreign

currencies; and to help monitor outstanding debts against payment trends.

3.   Flexible screen-driven reporting, to retrieve information, in whatever format required, without the need to have the specialist IT department do it on behalf of credit. In other words, the ability to write one's own reports.

It is true to say that the early days of computer Sales Ledger systems were largely designed by technical experts in computerisation, but lacking in credit control knowledge or experience, and for a long time, credit managers have had to beaver away with systems which were less than adequate in meeting their needs. This has been recognised by the better software companies, and today's market place has a good many systems available which combine a comprehensive mixture of efficient Sales Ledger features with effective aids to credit control.

If nothing else, a credit manager needs information, and a good system provides comprehensive, up-to-date and easily accessible information. This basic requirement is best provided online in real time, so that postings of cash, invoices, changes of name, changes of address and all the myriads of data bits which make up the ledger file can be processed instantly, and hence instantly available.

There are six main ingredients:

1.   billing;

2.   collection aids;

3.   cash allocation;

4.   customer reconciliation;

5.   General Ledger postings; and

6.   customer information.

All feed into the Accounts Receivable System, the Sales Ledger, and it is the management information and the reporting capabilities which determine how good the system is from an overall credit management perspective. Each component is important in its own right, though the improved efficiency and flexibility of cash allocation often produces the greatest time-saving benefit in the receivables department. However, the whole process begins with the customer.

CUSTOMER INFORMATION

One of the most vital aspects of the good system is the ability to maintain up-to-date, comprehensive customer account records. Even the most basic Sales Ledger system should contain two levels of customer information: summary and background data; and detailed, open-item information. Typically, these would be spread over at least two information screens.

The summary screen would contain the more basic customer data, together with as much other useful information as is both practical and desirable to include:

- customer name;

- address (statement, invoice, delivery);

- telephone number:

- contact name;

- fax number;

- email address;

- total amount owing, broken down by ageing category (weeks, months, 30-day breaks, and so on);

- the number of open items on the account;

- credit limit;

- credit rating;

- one or more account classification codes;

- account status;

- Sales Ledger clerk responsible for the account;

- salesman and/or sales territory;

- amount of last payment and payment method (cheque, BACS, direct debit);

- date of last payment;

- year-to-date and period-to-date sales.

All these account-level indicators, including some of the financial details, should be capable of being maintained real time, so there is no reason for the information not to be up to date.

Full details of all outstanding items for any given account will usually be available on supplementary screens, and it is these that are probably referred to when telephoning, emailing or writing to the customer. For open-item accounts, the basic information would of course be the invoice number, date, value and customer order number. The latter is often missed from Sales Ledger systems and any collector knows that if a customer asks for nothing else, he will certainly require his order number to be quoted in any contact or correspondence. It is also extremely useful to be able to show invoice due dates, even more so when there is the possibility that the same customer can have several invoices, not all with the same terms. Special promotions or deals can result in a normal 30-day customer enjoying, say, 60 days on purchases of obsolete stock or a new line, and such items should be clearly separated from the normal when it comes to collection activity. In the case of export customers, it is important to be able to see the amount of each invoice in both the base currency (sterling) and the currency in which the invoice was raised.

Item status indicators to distinguish between normal invoices and those in query or dispute are a key requirement – queries have to be resolved before collection can proceed, and the system needs to be able to show at a glance those items, if any, which need resolution. Another useful feature would be the ability to resequence, whenever required, the items on the customer account. They may be held in chronological or due date sequence most of the time, but perhaps need to be reordered into, say, purchase order number for reconciling with the customer over the phone. Reageing, or changing due dates may also be required, in the event of special arrangements.

Periodically, it will be necessary to trawl the whole Sales Ledger for reports on activity, or inactivity, and it is quite useful to allow a system to remove accounts automatically if there has been no activity for a specified period of time. All data takes up space, and if a ledger file is full of 'one-off' sales type customers over many years, any search of the ledger for customer account numbers, for example, will take that bit longer than necessary, simply because the system is having to go through a lot of data. Twenty-four months is often the criterion in many companies, so no activity for two years initiates removal from the system. It may be preferable for this to be preceded by an alert report, so that the credit manager can decide if a particular account should remain open.

This basic information is common in most systems, even those now somewhat long in the tooth, and may be considered enough for credit control activity to be productive in the normal course of events. Credit managers usually require a greater level of sophisticated help from a computer system, so that a number of manual records and procedures are themselves part of the computer process. A good system, therefore, should offer more customer information screens and functions. Customer notes, for example, and a diary feature. The credit/collection clerk can key in any relevant information into a free-format text area which is held against a particular customer and can be viewed and updated at any time. Customers can have multiple pages of notes attached to their accounts, and the online 'memo pad' (which is what it is) makes redundant record cards and account status files which have hitherto cluttered up filing cabinets. Anything you need to know about the customer, what happened last and what should happen next is displayed on the customer information screen. The diary prompts action on specified dates – when the collector switches on in the morning, the 'to do' list is produced, online and/or printed out as a report. Many credit managers use this facility to allocate and prioritise work activity in departments.

One of the most powerful credit management innovations, certainly from the point of view of credit monitoring aids, is the provision of the online sales and payment trends screen. This function comes in many forms, but the principle remains the same: the credit manager can see at a glance the actual, recent sales and payment track record of any given customer. The typical screen shows, for each of several time periods, comprehensive sales, payment and deduction statistics, and these are automatically updated whenever new invoices are posted or cash applied. This facility has two great pluses: it quantifies the actual payment habits of each customer, giving the credit manager the facts and figures with which to tackle the customer, or perhaps his sales people; it also highlights trends, such as decreasing sales and worsening payment performance, which could make the difference between a collected account and a bad debt. No computer system is going to automatically prevent bad debts, but the good one can certainly help the credit manager to be wise before the event.

The more sophisticated a system, the more there is a danger of it becoming difficult to use. 'User friendly' is a much vaunted phrase, usually promoted by software salesmen and designers in an attempt to convince users that the whole thing is as easy as riding a bike. To the well trained, this may prove to be the case, but the majority of system users in the majority of companies are not well trained to the extent of complete familiarity with systems, and have become familiar through experience and use. Such experience with a particular system can disappear when the old is replaced with the new, so training *does* become a prime requirement. The real problem with sophistication is often, however, that so much is built into it, only extensive training will ever reveal its full potential.

There is a trend amongst software designers and suppliers to make certain assumptions, clearly illustrated in the home computer market. If Joe Public ventures into the store and purchases a PC, ready installed with ProgramX, Version II, there is an in-built assumption in the designers of Version II that everyone by now must be familiar with Version I, and, therefore, the instructions and help notes accompanying Version II are less an A to Z guide on how to operate, but more an update on the enhancements now featured. What is often forgotten, of course, is that nobody is born computer literate, and every day someone somewhere starts for the very first time.

The truth is that no system is easy to use – training and familiarisation is a must – but designers can help by clear displays, pop-up panels, pull-down menus, action bars and 'hot' keys, all of which go a long way towards making systems more straightforward to use. It is also an advantage to purchase systems which have been designed in module form – it may well be that there can be additional, more advanced modules which can easily be linked at a later stage in the development of total systems. It is often better to approach in bite-sized chunks. If the air is cleared of all jargon, and all sales assertions about their system being 'user friendly', there are real yardsticks by which to measure ease of use:

1. A good system must offer flexibility in enabling the user to assess customer information, that is, there should be multiple access keys to find a given customer. In other words, to find a customer on a good system, it will not just, or only, be the account number which is the route. It should be possible to locate an account by invoice number, customer name (or part of a customer name, often known as a short code), parent account identifier, postcode, telephone number, customer order number and so on.

2. It should be possible to jump from any screen in the system to any other directly, without having to go through hosts of intermediate menus. Although many systems are still menu-driven (which makes them easy to learn and understand), they need not be menu *dependent*. The menus still exist, but are not necessary for quick screen jumps, once the user has gained some experience and knows what to look for. There is no doubt that it can be both frustrating and time consuming to have to go through three or four unnecessary screens just to change functions or to look at a different piece of information.

3. There should be a clear HELP facility. For the novice user, or person who is unfamiliar with a particular system, it is extremely valuable to have help available at the touch of a button. Field level HELP, that is, help at any particular point, or field, in any particular stage or process, is without doubt the best sort of HELP available. The system can provide, for example, a drop-down list of valid entries or options for that field, allowing the user to select one from the list and insert into the field.

Invoice Input

There must clearly be a robust and reliable link between a company's invoicing system and its Sales Ledger. This usually takes the form of an automatic interface which feeds details onto the ledger, often nightly. A good system also allows manual input of invoice information directly via the user's screen, which can be extremely useful when there are sundry debts, such as a freight charge, to be manually posted to the ledger.

The manner by which invoices appear on the ledger is often of little importance to the credit manager as such; what is important is that the invoice information is comprehensive enough for the assisting in the collection of the debt on time. Over and above the basics of invoice number, date and amount, the summary level detail that should be visible against each invoice is customer order number, category of goods or services involved and perhaps the relevant sales person or sales region.

In the case of export customers, invoices can be posted in the appropriate currencies, and the open-item listing shows invoice values in both foreign and base currencies. It is usual to input exchange rates into the system (daily, weekly, monthly – some less aware companies only input annually!), so that the system automatically calculates and reports, by transactions, the gains and losses arising from exchange rate variances between invoicing and payment dates. It can also report unrealised gains and losses if a revaluation of debts is requested, perhaps because of a currency devaluation.

Some systems are designed such that, if a credit is issued which completely cancels a specific unpaid invoice, and the credit is cross-referenced to that invoice, the system drops the two items automatically, with full subsequent reporting. Credit managers can have different requirements – some like this idea but others do not. It is often the case that even if an invoice is cancelled in full by a credit note, the customer pays the invoice and takes the credit in separate accounting transactions, and some credit managers therefore like to see items remain until they are removable due to customer action, rather than internal housekeeping.

CASH COLLECTION AIDS

As discussed in Chapter 9, the Sales Ledger and the Aged Debt Analysis remain the prime collection aids for most credit managers, whether in screen display or hard copy. A mandatory requirement for any system, therefore, has to be the ability to produce statements. The content of the statement is open to debate – it has always been possible to produce statements on even the most basic of systems, but what has not always been possible is the right amount of control and flexibility. For many users, the statement is not only a formal confirmation of debt, but is the base collection tool. As such it should be possible to vary the content of the statement and have the ability to add messages of different types – overdue, please remit and so on. Statements which have the debt aged (current, due, one month, two months and so on) are favoured by some – others argue that to show debts aged in such a way to the customer indicates a tolerance of overdues and in effect merely invites the customer to pay the oldest, rather than everything which is overdue! That argument has raged amongst credit managers for many years, and still continues today. The important issue here, however, is to have a system which can produce what is actually required by the user, and not just an automatic provision of what there is.

The other prime collection tool is the reminder letter. The value (or otherwise) of collection letters is discussed more fully in Chapter 11, and there is little doubt that credit managers have different views on their use. What is true, however, is that if the system is capable of producing reminder letters, then at least the option is available if so required. In other words, the system needs to have the same flexibility attributes for letters as it does for statements – at least then the credit manager is able to take advantage of varying contents of letters as well as varying contents of statements. The credit manager must be able to dictate what each of the varying letters says, and the parameters which will govern its production. It is worth emphasising that the quality of any computer-produced letter, in terms of appearance, is a direct function of the quality of the paper and the printer on which it is produced – the more a letter looks like an individually produced document the better.

In addition to the basics of Sales Ledger, aged debt, statement and reminder letter, there are many screen-based management tools which have been developed over the years, continue to be developed further and are now in daily use. These all revolve around the use of online action lists and online diaries and prompts. In addition to standard enquiry screens, the system can be interrogated to provide specific information, such as priority accounts, follow-up lists and 'to do'. For example, a collector can request a list of all accounts that are his responsibility with a due balance in excess of £10,000, or balances of £5000 over 30 days overdue, or any combination desired. The collections supervisor or credit manager can similarly request listings, or schedules for each staff member and allocate work accordingly. The collector then works the listing, making diary or notepad comments on the system as to what was said, by whom, the amount promised, when and where, and what follow-up action will be required and at what date. The system relies on the flexibility of online report writing, and generates less paperwork (if any), and allows time at the work station to be spent on actual collection activity.

The diary facility was a later additional function, now developed to a high degree of sophistication. A collector contacts a particular customer in respect of the account on the 17th, and a cheque is promised for the full amount first-class post that evening. The collector keys into the notepad the message, and also keys in the prompt for the 18th/19th to follow up in the event of the cheque not being received. The advantage is that the system prompts the collector at the right time. If the collector is away (vacation, illness and so on) the prompt remains on the system, along with all the other prompts, for attention on his return, or for attention by another collector who is filling in for the absentee. The collector could, of course, enter more dates going forward – each date prompt will be on screen at the correct time.

Systems such as these have the benefit of being able to reveal to supervisors what stage has been reached in the collection process with the stated accounts and allows other people to pick up where the previous collector left off.

Cash

CASH ALLOCATION

It is one of the most debated issues within credit management – the allocation of cash. Many large organisations now have centralised shared service centres where dedicated teams undertake the cash function for various members of the group, often over national geographical boundaries. In such scenarios, it is not uncommon for that area of operation not to be within the sphere of the credit manager, who is then totally reliant upon another department to carry out work, the accuracy and speed of which is vital to successful, and credible, credit management. The majority of companies still retain cash allocation as the responsibility of the credit manager, but in either situation it is true to say that in non-automated or partly automated systems, the process is time consuming. Indeed, it can represent one of the most time-consuming operations in the whole credit management function.

For the credit department to be able to make sound order approval decisions and chase debts efficiently, it is vital that accounts be updated rapidly. The good real-time system is designed to be enable all incoming payments to be quickly reconciled and allocated, and for the accounts to reflect their new positions as soon as possible after the receipt of cash. Brought-forward systems have now all but disappeared in trade credit, so most systems will cater principally for open-item ledgers.

In essence, incoming cash from customers goes through three stages:

1. *The account is identified.* Knowing who the cash is from, identifying the correct account on the ledger, is a prerequisite. There should be multiple ways of establishing the account number (identifying the account). Most good systems offer a minimum of three: account number, customer name (or short code), and item number. A useful additional key is the customer bank details. This comes into its own when those odd customers send cheques with no remittance advice at all, nothing written on the back of the cheque or attached, and where the name on the cheque bears no resemblance to the name in the ledger. The system uses a look-up table to match bank details, and cross refers customer bank details to customer accounts. Regrettably, many credit departments no longer actually see cheques, and shared service centres, or finance centres, often do not see any significant benefit in taking details from cheques for notation.

2. *Payment allocation.* Flexibility is key here, with a number of options open to the cash applier. It is in this area that many systems fall short, due to the lack of flexible options being available. The cash applier should be able to:

    •   remove individual items or item ranges by 'tagging';

    •   remove items in a date range (or full month);

    •   remove items by reference number;

    •   make partial payment of single or multiple invoice(s);

    •   place payment on-account; and/or split cash allocation.

    Not all of these will be necessary in all cases, but some will cover most, and a few will be required from time to time. The real error of many systems, working on a 'cost benefit' basis is to say that because 75 per cent of all transactions are date range, then that will be the only option available. This may well then work quite satisfactorily for the 75 per cent of payments received, but the remaining 25 per cent are then by definition more difficult to allocate and therefore much more labour intensive. Equally silly would be to limit cash allocation to the one item tag system, which is fine if an account has only one or two invoices to deal with but hair raising if there are 30 or 40 pages of invoices to remove on the account!. The split cash facility is now much more common than in the past – in these days of mergers and acquisitions it is quite common for one head office company cheque or transfer to pay for invoices on more than one account. In these circumstances the parent company code, or major group account code, comes into its own.

3.   *The handling of discrepancies.* Discounts, overpayments and underpayments should all be capable of being handled in the allocation process. The system should check discount deductions for validity, and to be able to place unauthorised deductions back on to the customer account, either against the invoice reference to which they refer, customer debit note number or other specified item. If the original invoice is not taken out in full, the deduction is aged as per the invoice – this can be an issue, of course, for if the deduction is in respect of a dispute, the balance is not due, let alone overdue, unless and until the dispute is resolved. It will be for individual credit managers and their companies to decide exactly how such items should be treated, but the point to make is that the system has to have the flexibility to cope with these oddities.

Some systems have an automatic cash tolerance facility which enables very small discrepancies, within defined parameters, to be automatically written off. It is a common feature of today's purchase and Sales Ledger systems for there to be different decimal points being utilised – the seller works to two decimal points and the buyer to three, which can lead to being pennies out between invoice and payment – these are not worth pursuing by any yardstick, and to write off automatically is a great boon.

Other possibilities in real-time cash allocation are the automatic generation of 'invalid deduction' letters, and 'request for payment details' letters. Everything should be designed to enhance the overall operation of the allocation process to ensure that it is versatile, fast and easy to use, and of course that the system audits and balances each allocation to ensure full control is maintained.

Automatic cash allocation continues to grow in popularity, and is certainly a facility which is worthy of consideration. It allows the user to feed in the amounts paid by each customer, with the system automatically attempting to match the remittance amounts with the outstanding items on the customers' accounts. In order to achieve this, it uses a predefined set of comparisons, known as algorithms or payment rules, to match each payment amount to an invoice or combination of invoices. Payments can be compared to:

- an obvious single invoice;

- each open item until a match is found;

- a complete month's total of invoices;

- the total outstanding balance;

- any single ageing category as it appeared on the last statement;

- cumulative ageing categories beginning with the oldest;

- the total due less one open item;

- cumulative open items until a match is made, starting with the oldest;

- all possible pairs of items;

- any or all combinations of 10 items or fewer (unless the account has more than 10 items);

- any of the above, less a later credit note;

- any of the above, less a flagged disputed amount.

The success rate is usually quite high, certainly 70 to 80 per cent accurate matching is not uncommon, and it does prove effective for many types of accounts. When setting the algorithms, the process can be thoroughly tested for suitability and accuracy, and items such as settlement discount can be catered for. If necessary, it is possible to exempt a customer, if so desired, from algorithm testing – all that will happen will be that any cash received from that customer will be automatically posted to his account as unapplied cash, and will have to be manually sorted after the event.

Further sophisticated enhancements include the matching of BACS remittance advices with BACS bank entries against customers accounts in the same way – the system reads the bank statement and allocates the cash to the customer account.

There are pitfalls, as one might expect. In practice, automatic allocation tends to work better with small accounts – those with only a few invoices per month or accounting period. The likelihood of multiple invoices of the same date and value is much less, and therefore the likelihood of the system identifying and matching exactly is therefore much greater. It is less successful where in large accounts there are many invoices of the same value on one account.

If automatic allocation is switched on for an account, but the system cannot find a match for a given payment, the cash is always unallocated on to the account, so that the actual account balance is at least up to date, even if an operator has then to manually online allocate the amount(s). Unallocated cash should always be kept to a minimum, and reconciled and allocated as soon as possible. Some systems have a specific unallocated cash screen which shows all accounts with unapplied cash sitting on them, and usually a screen which shows any cash entered into the system but not yet even applied to an account. This system gives supervisory management the ability to check periodically that all operators are actually attempting to allocate cash, and not just 'filing' the more difficult entries somewhere convenient.

This is often seen as the other downside to automatic allocation – the system takes care of the majority, but the minority need skill and expertise, as well as discipline, to follow through. In this respect, too many companies see the introduction of automatic cash allocation as replacing rather than enhancing. Auditors often point to ledgers of unapplied cash in their interim reports, and customer accounts become clogged with 'unidentified' items, which in turn become labour intensive to resolve. It is easy to see how in very large organisations, vast sums of money can be involved – although the overall debtors balance may be truly reflected by cash received, individual customer accounts may well show inaccurate past due balances. This can lead to unhelpful problems with supplies, and cause considerable damage to customer relations.

CUSTOMER RECONCILIATION

It may well be that a better subheading would be *Good Housekeeping*. Everything to do with the customer and the customer file, from name and address, through invoice and credit note to cash and allocation revolves around the concept of good housekeeping. In order to keep everything where it should be, systems are required that enable the user to undertake a variety of varying tasks and be able to interrogate the database for a answers to a wide range of questions. For example:

- When was the account opened?

- When was the name/address/telephone number amended?

- When was the last payment?

- How much was the last payment?

- What invoices did the last payment clear?

- How often has the account been stopped?

- When was the last credit limit/category reviewed?

- What is the balance outstanding?

- What is the amount overdue?

The number and variety of features under the catch-all heading of customer reconciliation should be as extensive as required by users, with the principle of ease of access and retrieval being paramount. It embraces all those features necessary to keep the account in good order, and is additionally useful in the area of customer queries. It is also advantageous to be able to identify, and rectify mis-postings. For example, if an invoice or credit note has been posted to the wrong customer account, or if cash has been applied incorrectly, it should be possible to move the entry to the correct destination, restoring the account to its original position, that is, before the error posting took place. Restoring to the original position also means correct updating of all related analyses both for the incorrect account and subsequently the correct account.

'Playing' with an account in such a way does carry with it, of course, certain dangers. It should go without saying that certain controls are required to avoid or misuse. The facility should be restricted, by password controls and other authorisation processes, to certain individuals who are empowered to carry out such adjustments. There would also be an authorisation procedure, duly logged, and a clear audit trail to verify the course of action taken.

Accounts receivable systems benefit greatly from the perspective of the user by having payment enquiry facilities. An uncleared item on the ledger is described as 'open', those invoices and credit notes which have been settled being described as 'closed'. It is understandable that a facility to view 'open' items is universally recognised as a fundamental feature, but less well appreciated has hitherto been the need to view 'closed' items. The closed-item enquiry facility gives access to details of past payments and invoices no longer outstanding. Flexibility is important, so that the user can go into a closed-item enquiry facility by different routes. For example, a customer may need to know what invoices were cleared by his last cheque – the user may enter the system by customer name or account number, by cheque value or date range, and the system responds by giving a list of all appropriate remittances and details of how each was allocated. Possibly, the user simply enters an invoice number, cheque or payment number, the system identifies the payment in question and again details the allocation. Full details of each allocation should be available. This means not simply the value of the appropriate payment and invoices cleared, but details of who applied the cash, and details of any adjustments (overpayments, underpayments, discounts, write-offs, bank charges and so on) that were made during the allocation. The advantages to ledger clerks, auditors and supervisors are obvious.

It should always be remembered, however, that even in these days of everything micro, there are practical limits (usually dictated by cost) on the amount of information which will be stored online. Storing data takes space on any computer system, costs money, and can slow down access and retrieval. Data can be archived, and year to date, or better, a rolling 12 months online is usually quite adequate. Many companies carry out archive procedures following the completion of annual audits, so that year to date is currently online at least. Working on the basis that most queries raise their heads fairly quickly, this is usually adequate. In any event, stored data should be comparatively easy to retrieve, at least in report format.

General Ledger

Management accountants are more interested in the workings of the General (or Nominal) Ledger than credit managers or credit controllers, but it is important for credit managers to know the links, and to be able to understand the relationship between entries on both the Sales and General Ledgers. In accounting terms, when invoices are raised they must be posted to both the accounts receivable account in the subledger and the double entry made to the General Ledger. Similarly, every time cash is received, it has to be posted to the customer's account in the receivables system, with the appropriate entries again being made to the General Ledger. This is the more traditional method of double entry account ledger maintenance which requires reconciliation between receivables and general at month end (or on a daily basis).

Most systems now cater for automatic postings, where the Accounts Receivable System itself automatically creates the necessary double entry bookkeeping postings for the General Ledger. This happens whenever entries are made to the Sales Ledger (invoices, credit notes, cash and so on) and because the Accounts Receivable System is the single source, everything is automatically kept in balance. It is all a matter of adequate interface between ledgers, and upkeep of all automatic links when new systems or add-ons are introduced. The extent of automatic postings can be dictated by the number of subcodes or subsystems required – for example, not only does the cash posting to the Sales Ledger make the appropriate entry to the General Ledger, but any amount written off to say, currency loss or bank charge, is automatically posted to the correct code on the General Ledger.

The good interface system should therefore be seen as an old-fashioned railway marshalling yard. Each entry to the Sales Ledger is a freight wagon, sourced at a single point and then marshalled into the correct siding in the General Ledger freight yard. It is not rocket science, and the only confusion that can arise is the age old debits by the door, credits by the window! Many a credit controller, when writing off bank charges has to be reminded of the credit Sales Ledger, debit General Ledger bank charge code – it is sometimes easier to try to imagine the General Ledger as a mirror. The only problem there is knowing what is being looked at when looking in the mirror!

Reporting

All systems should be able to provide extensive and flexible reporting options. Reports are usually divided into two main categories, hard copy and online, and then subdivided between management reports and control reports.

Control reports are mandatory, and because of their nature and purpose are normally fixed with the minimum of flexibility. They exist primarily to provide a full and comprehensive audit trail through the system, enabling every transaction to be tracked. They also enable both the transactions and the system itself to be verified. Any anomaly which shows up can be identified, researched and checked against the set parameters, and errors can be identified both at transaction and at system level. Typically, most of these reports will be provided daily on a period-to-date basis for ease of reference.

Management reports should be available on a periodic basis, and on request at any time, and should be easily changeable if required. Examples would include:

- the Aged Debt Analysis, both in detail and summary;

- credit limit exceeded;

- overdue accounts;

- stopped accounts;

- orders against stopped accounts;

- and general account status printouts.

It should always be possible to produce cash forecast and reports, obtained by looking at all outstanding debts, recent payment performance for each customer and the prediction as to when every amount is likely to be paid. The figures are accumulated and the report predicts daily cash flow over the next specified time period, say 30 days. No forecast can ever be totally accurate, but payment performance to date is a very good indicator of likely payments in the immediate future. Credit managers can find this a very good tool for setting cash targets and work priorities.

The emphasis is normally now with the user undertaking the specification, design and requesting of such management reports direct through their own screens, or as print-outs, with less and less involvement directly from the technical staff in computer departments. Many 'off-the-shelf' packages come equipped with reporting tools already installed, leaving the user to produce such individual reports as may be pertinent to his particular company or industry. The underlying concept in every reporting system has to be the fact that if the information is sitting there in the computer system, then it must be possible both to extract it, and to extract in a format which adds value to the data. In other words, whatever it may say on the restaurant menu as standard fayre, if chef has the ingredients, what is wanted can be made. The difference now is that every credit manager should be his or her own chef, and not have need to constantly call on the kitchen for provision of what is required.

It is now common for all or at least the majority of reported information to be available online. This enables work to be centred around the terminal or work-station, rather than working from hard copy reports. There will always be the need for some basic hard copy, of course, and most credit managers will utilise both functions in order to achieve success in their operations. The point is that, with the exception of principal month end runs, for example, the vast majority of all reports will be initiated by the user at his terminal and on request. It will simply be for the user to decide whether it is more convenient under some circumstances to print out on his own printer, or to work from a screen display.

Computerspeak

We live in an age of jargon, with new words or abbreviations appearing with remarkable regularity as systems and hardware advance and progress. People 'in the know' can baffle ordinary mortals by speaking a language incomprehensible to the uninitiated, and it is a fact that many computer personnel guard their expertise simply by their own use of buzz words, acronyms, initials and system concepts. It would not be possible for everyone to keep pace at all times, but as more and more credit managers are involved in the design and production of their own reports, it is important that they keep up as much as they can with what is happening around them. Indeed, it is always strongly recommended that no Accounts Receivable System be installed in any company without the credit manager having specified requirements, and being a member of the project team. To that extent, at least, the credit manager should know something about what everyone else is talking about! In any event, the growth of home computers, use of the Internet and familiarity with servers, search engines, emails, file attachments, spreadsheets and databases must mean that in order to survive and prosper, the language should be learned.

REAL TIME

Real time is the instantaneous processing of information, as opposed to batch or offline processing where the updating is performed 'en masse' sometime later.

In Sales Ledger terms, the nightly invoice run can be a batch process, as can a number of month-end processes. On the other hand, input of cash in a good system should be real time, with the ledger updated as soon as the cash allocation transaction has been completed (this process also includes validation and balancing). Although it is deemed advantageous to have everything in real time, it is neither always necessary nor even desirable. Computing time is expensive and to operate systems with the capacity for total real-time operating can be disproportionately costly – many operations, such as production of invoices or statements lend themselves admirably to batch processing, and the process can take place overnight or at weekends when there are no other demands on computer time. Whatever the computer marketing people may say, there is no point in trying to have far too sophisticated a system than is actually needed.

RECOVERY

If a system crashes, or a transaction fails for some reason, the operator must be able to:

- bring the system back up;

- go back to the point just before the failure without loss of any prior transactions;

- still guarantee the data integrity of the system.

It could well be that computer staff may be needed to resolve some hardware or software problems and therefore be responsible for instigating the recovery procedure. A good system will enable the actual user, however, to effect recovery himself in many cases.

It is worth mentioning computer staff at this point. Many companies have computer departments with different names – MIS (Management Information Systems), ISD (Information Systems Department), IT (Information Technology) and so on – but all have one thing in common. They are there as providers of a customer service, the user being the customer, and as such should be able to respond quickly to calls for help, and to *explain in plain English* where it is evident that the system is working correctly, but the user has simply miskeyed or undertaken an illegal action. Much is said about systems being 'user friendly' when what is really meant is user understood. Computer anoraks often like to keep things to themselves in the mistaken belief that their indispensability is thus guaranteed. The reality is that the more that the user can dictate his own agenda in respect of uses and processes, the more time and resource is applicable for development and enhancement.

INTEGRATION

Computer systems were initially developed as discrete units, each supporting its appropriate business function. This approach brought with it difficulties, particularly in the medium to long term for both service provider and user. Interfaces had to be written, joining systems up together and trying to establish and maintain compatibility. Data was duplicated quite often, there were differences in both design and functionality, and worse still, users had to learn and master more than one system at a time. To overcome this problem, the concept of integration was born – true integration is a philosophy which embraces every aspect of multi-system operation, with efficient data flows, common disciplines, hardware integration and cross-system information retrieval. It implies a strategic design and development approach leading to interdependent systems that are fully compatible and truly work together in the most efficient manner. A typical example of integration would be an online order processing system linked to accounts receivable, reading credit limits and risk codes, as well as stop lists. Entering the customer order, the system reads all the connected data files in real time, checking the order value against the existing balance outstanding and the credit limit, reading the stop list or referral files, overdues and so on, and will take into account orders already in the system for that customer and not yet invoiced. Only then will the order be processed, or the credit management team alerted in the event of one or more criteria not being satisfactorily met.

THE PC, THE MICRO-MAINFRAME LINK, AND INTELLIGENT WORK STATIONS

During the 1980s the personal computer, or PC, emerged as an effective business tool. Originally used in free-standing mode, by managers and executives as an accounting aid (or even an executive 'toy'!), it soon became apparent that much of the information held on company mainframe computers could be transposed to the desktop PC and used by operators to formulate individual reports and use that data in many new and innovative ways. The good idea became something of a problem when inaccuracies surfaced, the problem being solved by what became the micro-mainframe link. This allows the operator to use the PC as either a dumb terminal or to be linked directly to the mainframe and to download the data to the PC. With the proliferation of more and more powerful PCs, the term 'intelligent work stations' was coined to describe them.

This in turn led to what we now describe as networking, where a number of intelligent work stations are linked together on a network, itself linked directly to the mainframe (see below).

In some ways, these advances have returned the computer user to days prior to integration in so far as there are now many processes and tasks that can be undertaken at an intelligent work station which need raw data from a central source (the mainframe) but then stand entirely alone. This has meant the for security reasons each PC is password protected and many of the functions and programs used by the operator are themselves password protected. Not only does the typical user now have a complicated log in process to go through each working day, with different passwords for different programs, but the passwords themselves change regularly – anything from weekly to monthly, with only the very basic program having a password of any real duration. Many systems also lock the user out completely if the correct password is not used within, say, three attempts – security is paramount, but stress levels can be high!

CLIENT/SERVER

The advent of the PC brought many advantages, not least of which was the ability to give the credit manager and the credit team tremendous computing power at their desks. That power is harnessed very easily by the graphical user interface (GUI), literally point and click. However, the PC alone does not provide the traditional strengths of the mainframe or mid-range systems, namely corporate-wide integration of applications and data, effective control of all business processes, data integrity, ease of maintenance and security.

The computer industry talks of 'client' and 'server', or more properly 'client/server'. This describes the ideal model combining the relative strengths of the decentralised PC-based system with the host-centric mainframe or mid-range environment. Client/server systems are characterised by users having the PCs (the clients) networked to each other and to a larger host machine (the server), with some of the system's logic and processing taking place on the PC and some (perhaps the majority) on the server.

Many companies hold different main functions on different servers – for example, the growth in email traffic has led to servers for that purpose only, and it is quite common for the email server to be maintained in a different physical environment to other computer servers. It is also a separate housekeeping exercise to monitor email server capacity and to instruct users on a regular basis to tidy up their email folders, getting rid of unwanted, out-of-date, messages.

While the potential gains in flexibility and productivity are compelling, implementing fully functional client/server systems is still a challenge, and industry standards have been developed, known as configurable network computer (CNC) with the objective of providing a technically cohesive, adaptable and predictable environment. Many a home computer user will have seen the difference between many Internet sites, and their respective servers, and there is still some way to go for client/server to reach its full potential.

Any professional needs the right tools to do the job, and for the credit manager, this has to be a good real-time computer system, with intelligent work stations and full network capability. Ease of access, ease of use, and up-to-date information are prerequisites for effective cash collection, efficient Sales Ledger management and good customer relations. It should therefore be part of every credit manager's brief to maximise and protect the quality of the information available to the credit management function. That means keeping up to speed with the latest developments and innovations, and constantly examining in a critical manner the system, processes and procedures currently in use. A good system helps, a bad system clearly hinders, and if staff are spending all their time maintaining a ledger in a quill pen fashion, they are not collecting cash and contributing to profit. It is comparatively easy to cost justify enhancements, improvements or even full-blown replacement. Change needs justification, of course, not change for its own sake or the need simply to have the very latest gadgets and twiddly bits.

As said many times before, the credit manager and the credit team need the best available and affordable in order to fully achieve their potential – never let the computer people tell you what you can have. You have to tell them what you NEED.

INSTITUTE OF CREDIT MANAGEMENT – June 2008

Introductory Credit Management: Level 3 Diploma

The company you work for has decided to upgrade its computer system. As credit manager, you have been asked to specify your requirements for the new system from a credit management point of view.

1.   Identify *key* features that should be included in a computerised credit control system and explain the benefit of each feature to the credit department.

2. The computerised master file will contain both static and variable data. Using appropriate examples, explain the difference between the two types of data.

PART V
Cash Collection

11

Collection of Trade Debts

Glen Bullivant

• The front end • Collection attitudes • Days sales outstanding and cash targets •
Incentives • Computer aids to collection • Methods • The future •

The Front End

It has often been said that cash does not collect itself. Equally, old hands will
talk of that golden age, when Sir Nigel Gresley's 'Flying Scotsman' dominated
the East Coast Main Line, all trains ran on time and everybody paid their bills
when due. Rose-tinted spectacles may have convinced some of the reliability of
the London & North Eastern Railway, but the truth about bills being paid when
due is a little more murky. What is true, however, is that the perception was
always one of the vast majority of customers toeing the credit terms line, and
running a Sales Ledger meant little more than keeping everything tidy, sending
a few discreet letters from time to time and making sure that at the end of the
month the cash was all posted and the figures balanced.

Whatever the fond memories of days gone may be, there is no doubt that
the market place is a jungle, and payment habits, whatever they may have been
perceived to be in the past, are certainly today not conducive to 'invoice and
let's see what happens'. The changing role of banks in the last quarter century
are said by many to have contributed to a late payment culture, and there is
little doubt that the role of the local bank manager, who knew his customers,
was replaced by career business managers, working to head office targets and
parameters, and with little or no local knowledge. The whole banking edifice
imploded in 2008, and despite billions of dollars, pounds, yen and euros
being poured into the system by central banks and governments (that is, you
and me, the taxpayers!), it would prove to be a long time before banks began
lending to business again. In any event, trade suppliers have *always* been the

principal providers of the majority of funds in business to business trading – it has been true that even in the golden age of banks (whenever that was) when the customer runs out of bank funds, he starts living on yours! Whatever the reasons, late payment became a fact of life, and now customers can be summed up by four distinct types:

1.   those who pay when they should;

2.   those who only pay when reminded;

3.   those who only pay when threatened;

4.   those who go bust before they pay.

It should come as no surprise that most companies, if they care to check, will find that the majority of their customers are number 2. Most customers pay when reminded, and if they are not reminded, they will pay when it best suits them, not the seller. The sooner you ask, and the better you ask, the sooner you will get paid.

No trade or industry is immune, and no individual company is either. At any given moment in time, companies are issuing thousands of invoices, customers are receiving thousands of invoices, and all these go into a system which will grind at a pace dictated by policy, circumstances or poverty. However special our invoice is to us, to the customer it is just one of many – somehow or other it is up to us to make our invoice *special* in every sense of the word in the customer's eyes.

What we need to do is make sure we get paid, regardless of whatever happens to everybody else. Not only does that mean proactive collections, it means positive collections; it means recognising the weak as well as the strong; it means being alert to everything that is happening, both in the industry or market place, but also in the customers themselves. It means, first and foremost, know the customer and get it right first time.

Chapter 2 tried to explain in some detail the effect of overdues and bad debts on profit and the true cost of giving credit. Whichever way it is looked at, cash is the vital force in any business. Profit margins vary from industry to industry, but in effect all this means is that positive cash flow is even more critical for some than it is for others. It does not detract, however, from the fundamental fact that cash is important to every business – it is certainly no exaggeration to talk of 'life blood'. It is quite astonishing that even today, many companies still believe that making the sale is the be all and end all and that actually getting paid, that is, receiving the cash, is of secondary importance. It is simply not true, and no company can possibly survive without cash. Equally, it is simply not true that getting paid late is of little consequence – being paid in time to pay your own bills is a fact of life, for consumers earning a wage just as much as for companies trying to make profits.

The real point is that the profit of any company always has to be enough to more than cover the borrowing costs. This is true in good times as well as bad – recession and high interest rates only make matters worse for companies who do not control their cash. Bad habits die hard, so companies must look to have efficient cash collection programmes at all times.

Collection begins way back is a fundamental reminder to companies that they should not just sell, then expect accounts staff to collect whatever comes up on the ledger. The collectability of a sale starts with the selection of customers, that is, identifying their ability to pay. It continues with the way credit terms are explained to the customer; with the promptness of invoices and statements; and with the time created for personal contact of key people.

The sooner you ask, the sooner you are paid is an equally fundamental reminder to those misguided managements who believe that customers are upset by being asked to pay overdue bills. On the contrary, it is company policy in many organisations is to hold on to cheques until actually asked for payment.

A sale is not a sale until it is paid for reminds everyone that sales are just notional book entries, a catalogue of costs, until payment is received. To the smart salesman who declares to credit control that they would not have a job were it not for him, the response is full agreement – sales and credit are now on the same side!

Effective collection of trade debts, therefore, really does begin at the front end of the whole credit management process. Nobody is insulated from bad debt losses, because they will occur in the best regulated environment. However, for each insolvency, there are many more companies in difficulty and these are the ones that cause the serious overdue accounts. It has been labelled the 'iceberg risk' – actual insolvencies are the tip of the iceberg, but the most dangerous part causing damage to sellers is the mass below the surface. It follows quite logically that the chances of payment for credit sales is dependent upon the financial quality of customers.

The decision to allow credit to a customer has to be a conscious one, not an accident of selling, and not a gamble. Neither customers nor salesmen should take it for granted that all sales qualify for credit terms. They don't. If you know that a company is going bust tomorrow, would you deliver goods today on 30 days credit terms? Of course, you would not. If all the credit reports and references indicate that the customer takes months to pay other suppliers, it would be naïve in the extreme to assume that you, and you alone, will be paid promptly. In other words, not all customers are equal in terms of viability, and therefore should not be treated equally.

Sales should never be lost through risk controls. Remedial action can ensure that payment can be received before disaster strikes. It is well argued by professional credit managers that sales are actually increased through positive credit vetting, because good growing customers are identified as well as failing ones. Sales efforts can thus be directed to those areas where the return is more likely, and therefore more profitable. There are two strong reasons for managing credit risk in a professional and competent manner – the commercial advantage of a good base of customers, with sales effort in the more productive areas; and the financial advantage of increased profit through fewer bad debt losses and lower interest expense while waiting to be paid.

So, to make the whole collection activity effective and rewarding, let's be professional and positive about creating the customer account to begin with. The vital act of adding a new credit to the debtors asset should be centralised and consistent, encapsulating as it does:

- a valuable new customer outlet;

- the start of a profitable relationship;

- the result of a conscious decision on credit worth;

- a package of accurate customer information;

- the first positive financial contact;

- the opportunity to get the customer paying properly from the start.

This is the process which requires special attention – those companies who sell, credit check or not, with the first invoice creating an account number, are in effect putting the cart before the horse. All that is achieved is a new account, with no detail of who to contact in the event of payment not being forthcoming, and no idea as to what to do next. Putting some effort into this vital stage pays dividends – after all this is, or should be, the beginning of a fruitful relationship, and all relationships require working at. The key word is *relationship*, a human activity, not just a credit and debit ledger record.

Chapters 5 and 6 lay out in detail the account opening procedure. Just to remind ourselves, there are five basic and controllable events which significantly firm up the prospects of payment:

1. *The credit application form.* This should be completed by the customer, and not by sales. It should capture all the data needed for invoicing, follow-up and serious collection (for example, legal action). Data should also include the name of the financial contact person for payments, as well as clearly stating the seller's payment terms. The customer should indicate how payment will be made (cheque, credit transfer, direct debit and so on, with direct debit being offered as a preference by the seller), and bank account details provided. The form should be signed by a duly authorised signatory, acknowledging that payments will be made promptly to the seller's terms. If the customer is not prepared to sign to this effect, then the first warning bells have been rung, and now is the right time to sort this out, not later. If the seller intends to particularly enforce clauses such as Retention of Title, it is also beneficial to obtain the customer's signature now to the effect that he has read and understood the clause.

2. *The account is credit checked.* Whatever methods are used, from bank references to credit agency reports, they should be as comprehensive as the potential value of the account dictates.

3. *New account number.* The control on unauthorised new accounts is that the computer system for booking revenue, raising invoices and so on should refuse to operate unless an account number has been allocated. The authorisation for account numbers should logically only be made by the credit manager. If a new order is too urgent, for any reason, to wait for the standard checking procedure to be

completed, the credit manager should take a calculated decision, based upon whatever information is already to hand, to open a new account. Before the second dispatch, the application form and credit checking process should be completed.

4.   *New account, or welcome, letter.* When the formalities have been completed, it is good practice to send every new customer a 'welcome' letter to establish the relationship between financial staff and to remind the new customer of the payment arrangements. The customer will have supplied a financial contact name on the application form, and this letter, personally addressed and signed, now supplies that contact with the seller's payment contact for payment matters. An example is given in Chapter 5.

5.   *Special ledger section.* Newly opened accounts should be held in a separate section of the Sales Ledger for three months, or so, giving the account special personal attention. This helps to prevent bad payment habits developing, having been spotted quickly and dealt with. Even if the account value is below that normally stipulated for telephone contact, early intervention in the event of slow payment being identified can prevent problems later as the account grows in value and importance. It is also a reinforcement of the relationship between the financial contacts of buyer and seller and reminds the customer of the commitment he made when he signed the application form.

6.   New customers should be aware from the outset what the payment terms are – it was part of the sales dialogue, on the application form, in the welcome letter, on the invoice and on the statement. It is vital not to let a new account become just another ordinary overdue account, and getting it right at the front end eases the pain later.

Collection Attitudes

OK, so now we have accounts on the ledger, some are paying to terms and some (perhaps most) are going to need some form of reminder. One thing is certain, everyone has to be positive about cash collection. There are some unfortunate attitudes which still linger in many organisations, not least of which is the idea that collecting cash is a little distasteful and damaging to customer relations.

It cannot be distasteful to ask for what is rightfully ours, and as for damaging relationships, nothing can be further from the truth. So often, people seem to think that asking for money will upset a customer. There are two things to say about this:

1.   *It is almost impossible to upset a major customer, that is, a big account.* Big customers are big companies, and collection staff deal with payables staff. It is not their money, and they follow procedures laid down in their organisations. Some middle-sized companies may *pretend* to be upset, but as often as not this is merely a tactic for getting rid of a collection attempt. The idea of 'upsetting' XYZ plc is little short of preposterous – far easier to upset one man band Joe Soap sole trader where in effect you are trying to get his own money out of his own pocket!

2.   *The customer knows that the account is overdue.* The awkwardness of the situation, if any, is with him, not with the seller. He knows that the seller has supplied what he ordered, and he has had the benefit of the goods or services – he is legally bound to pay for it and at the agreed time. All the collector is doing is asking for what is rightfully his.

There are other damaging attitudes, which need to be got rid of at the outset:

1.   *The customer is always right.* Utter balderdash! Many companies go down the tubes because they believe so strongly that they cannot ask a customer for money (it would not be right/we've known them for years/don't upset them), to the extent that they forget that customer cash is their lifeblood. The customer is always *important*, true, but often wrong, and never more so when he does not pay his debts on time. If the seller has satisfied the order correctly, and the customer has had the benefit of the goods or services, he is legally bound to pay on time. Not when he feels like it – but on time! So let's kick that one out straight away!

2.   *We can only do our best.* Just what is 'our best'? It is beyond doubt, and has been proved time and time again that collection productivity is raised higher than people thought possible by the use of targets, controls, incentives, visual aids and staff motivation.

Slogans abound in credit control departments up and down the land, and many a credit manager will point to the plaque on the wall or the plastic sign on the desk as his or her driving philosophy. Some are useful, some are more subtle than others, and though taken in isolation, some could be seen in a negative light by sales, they are all nonetheless true:

- A sale is not complete until the cash is in our hands.

- Every penny the company earns comes in through us.

- Profit is reduced more by slow payers than by bad debts.

- Collection of cash is highly competitive.

- The sooner we ask, the sooner we are paid.

- It's our money – the customer has only borrowed it.

- Payment is a key part of the deal – just like the price and goods.

- Customers are never genuinely upset by being asked to pay.

- Customers respect suppliers with a professional approach.

- We believe in first-class service to customers and we expect first-class payment in return.

- We can't pay salaries or suppliers with sales – we need cash.

At one time, somebody once said that there were but two kinds of creditor when it came to collecting their cash – Type 'A' and Type 'B'.

Type 'A' had a bookkeeping approach and tidy accounts:

- worked through the ledger from A–Z each month, but rarely got all the way to the end;

- decreed that staff must allocate cash to the ledger first, before chasing overdues;

- if there was enough time, the next letter in a long series was sent to the customer;

- *'did our best'* and waited to see what happened.

Type 'B' had a competitive approach to cash:

- targeted cash required each month, using DSO ratio;

- analysed accounts by value, to ensure 80 per cent of cash sources were identified;

- allocated staff to cash entry or collection (or cash entry during early morning, mid-day and late evening; collection only during the productive part of the day);

- allocated collection staff to priority accounts, and diarised follow-ups;

- visited and/or telephoned large accounts, letters only for small ones;

- exhausted standard approaches within a fixed timescale, say four weeks;

- had a clear policy on the continuation of supply to slow payers or not;

- measured results monthly and decided action points for the next month.

It is not difficult to judge which of these two competing types had faster collections, fewer bad debts and lower interest charges, and which could therefore carry more stocks, improve quality, reduce prices, increase R&D or do other things to increase market share and beat the competition out of sight.

Types 'A' and 'B' still dominate. It is a salutary fact that at any given moment in time, there is not enough cash in industry to pay all bills on time, and as a result, the cash collection job is highly competitive. Cash collectors need training,

motivation and rewarding, just like sales people. Collection needs special
people with a committed attitude to succeed in spite of all the obstacles, but do it
politely – an iron fist in a velvet glove has been one suggestion! They have to be
outgoing persuaders, not introverted methodical people who prefer accounting
work. Collectors are the *only* financial people working in the commercial
area, interfacing with customers to complete a process which started with the
sales people. Indeed the qualities of persuasion, personality, commitment and
determination are not a million miles from those qualities required by good
sales people – that is no coincidence. Even though collectors invariably come
from an accounts background, the similarity with sales is genuine:

- *polite but firm* – never guilty of rudeness;

- *good communicators* – find a way of getting the message over;

- *outgoing, but not over talkative* – establish a brisk rapport;

- *persuasive* – usually succeed at the first attempt;

- *persistent* – not distracted, do not give up on obstacles;

- *target-oriented* – find ways to collect the totals required;

- *keen to beat deadlines* – arrange time effectively;

- *good listeners and problem solvers* – work to help customers;

- *confident* – know they have right on their side;

- *authoritative* – rarely have to refer to others for decisions;

- *well-trained* – knowledgeable on all the key areas required.

   The job does not suit most people, yet many employers casually expect
any spare person to 'chase a few debts'. Good collectors are worth cherishing
and rewarding, and to get the best from all staff, training is the most positive
investment any company can make. Well-trained, motivated and rewarded
collection staff have a dramatic effect on the company's profit performance. It
almost beggars belief that many companies still will not look beyond the ends
of their noses!

Days Sales Outstanding and Cash Targets

The Sales Ledger is a record of all customer transactions – when a sale is made, the debit is recorded, and when cash is received the appropriate credit is applied to the ledger. At any given time, therefore, the ledger represents the sum total of all that remains to be paid – in other words, *a fund of cash waiting to be collected* from customers.

It is good thinking to be able to restate the month-end ledger debtors total, or fund of cash, into an index which relates the debts to all the sales made. This will show how much credit is being taken by customers, and will include everything: current, overdue, awaiting credit, disputed – the whole shooting match. Such an index reveals the credit being taken by all customers, on average, and can be compared to the intended credit period allowed by the seller. Many companies call their credit index DSO, or Days Sales Outstanding.

The DSO index allows the ideal level of cash to be collected to be targeted, comparisons of improvements month by month, and is the perfect tool for calculating specifically just how much cash needs to be collected during the current accounting period in order to be able to achieve a stipulated DSO result.

DSO indicates:

- the total Collection Period;

- the average time taken to pay, regardless of supposed terms;

- the total debtors expressed in proportion to sales made.

(A not untypical DSO in a manufacturing company may be 58 days, where all sales are made on 30 days credit terms. Thus the mix of customers, large and small, cash rich or struggling, take about twice as long to pay as the seller intends. Of course, some customers pay exactly on time while others delay for several weeks, and others have raised disputes to be resolved before they will pay. But the total of unpaid invoices equate to all the sales made to all customers for the previous 58 days in this example.)

The ratio between sales and debtors, also known as the Collection Period, can be expressed in days (say, 58), weeks (say, 8.3) or months (say, 1.9), and is not affected by sales volume – more sales produce more debtors, less sales produce less debtors. It is affected, however, by the credit period allowed to customers and by the efficiency of the cash collection process. There is no better indicator of collection performance.

The usual method of calculating DSO is by a method designated '*add back*', taking total debtors at month-end, and deducting total monthly sales going back in time until the debtors figure is used up:

DSO EXAMPLE – DEBTORS AT 31 AUGUST

	£000	
Total debtors 31.8	1200	
Sales August	(650)	31 days
	550	
Sales July	(490)	31 days
Sales June (600)	(60)	3 days
		65 days

August debtors standing at £1,200,000 are equivalent to all sales for the last 65 days = 65 DSO. This means that cash takes an average of 65 days to arrive after invoicing.

The DSO should be used proactively to calculate the money needed to be collected in order to finish the month with a planned level of debtors. That activity should also include targeting positive quality improvements, such as clearing old overdues, resolving disputes and special exercises on certain accounts. The alternative in going simply for a cash total at the expense of everything else could mean that difficult accounts are left (and worsen), dependency increases on current cash and even getting special payments from friendly customers. It may well be possible to achieve cash targets which on the face of it look acceptable, but at the expense of an Aged Debt Analysis which reveals growing past due accounts and unresolved queries. Quality collection activity combines cash totals with overdue reduction to some kind of plan.

Calculating the cash needed to achieve a planned DSO level is straightforward. (Note: the calculation may be easy, but actually collecting the cash will be much more difficult!). As an example (using the 65 days as above) it is assumed that the target DSO at next month-end is 63 days. The cash required is calculated as follows:

This month (August) debtors ended at 65 DSO:

August 31 days sales value	£650,000
July 31 days sales value	£490,000
June 3 days	£ 60,000 (part of £600,000)
65 days	£1,200,000 Total debtors

By the end of September, a further 30 days will be added to the existing 65 days, making 95 days if no cash came in at all. So, to finish September with the required 63 days, it is necessary to collect the equivalent of the oldest 32 days (95-63=32), which are:

June	3 days	£60,000
July	29/31 days	£458,000
Total cash required	=	£518,000

Collecting £518,000 in September *guarantees* a 63 DSO finish; more than £518,000 will produce better than 63 days, and not achieving the target of £518,000 will leave more of the July sales equivalent unpaid, that is, a greater total than 63 days.

Secondary targets, to keep difficult debts in good order, might be:

- all debts over £x more than 60 days overdue;

- final review of pre-write-off accounts;

- one meeting with a major account to resolve old items.

Credit managers often use charts or graphs to illustrate both monthly cash targets and daily progress towards achieving those targets. These can be displayed prominently in the cash collection office, often on a wipe board with daily intake added, totals adjusted and amounts still needed highlighted. The charts can be for total department, section or individual collector, and can also be used to timetable specific actions and review dates. There is no doubt that charts invariably motivate staff to put in that little extra effort needed (and think of useful steps) before the month-end deadline arrives.

It is also useful to produce special listings for each collector, not just showing monetary values, but specific customers in descending value order, to illustrate the larger accounts to be collected that month. There will be a cut-off value, below which smaller accounts are grouped into one line values, with comments columns for cash promised and cash received. As the month progresses, collectors can focus on the gaps, for example, at mid-month where no promises have yet been received; and at nearly month-end for promised payment which have not yet arrived. By concentrating on this progress sheet for large accounts, 80 per cent of the target amount can be secured, at the same time as many small payments are coming in anyway from routine collection efforts.

Successful credit managers are an imaginative bunch, and graphs, charts, displays and the like come in a wide variety of formats.

Incentives

Incentives for sales staff are well known, and well established as a motivational practice. Commission is an obvious incentive, and often the cause of some friction between sales and credit, especially if that commission is only payable when customer accounts are actually settled! It is also well established in the sales environment to reward high flyers with special goodies, such as exotic holidays or large cash bonuses – incentives not only drive the salesman to achieve and exceed his own target, but create a competitive culture which binds the team as a whole and drives the whole process forward.

Motivating staff in the cash collection area is less well established, but nowadays many companies are drawing in cash faster by rewarding staff with incentives of cash, or kind, or simply recognition. Cash collection targets are ideal for incentivising, just as sales targets. Some companies set collectors against each other, or regions against each other, looking for the 'best performer' award but retaining a team approach. In many ways the team approach is better as an incentive for the department as a whole, where success results in everyone sharing in the rewards, and divisive rifts do not develop.

Typical targets are:

- total cash this month to exceed £X (this to achieve a specific DSO reduction);

- overdues older than 60 days to be reduced to £X;

- DSO to be x days lower than last quarter, or last year-end, or this month last year (especially where seasonal businesses are concerned);

- overdues percentage of total debtors to be lower than last quarter, and so on.

Typical rewards would include:

- a personal 'thank you' from the managing director or finance director;

- an article and photo in the company magazine, and/or an announcement on the company notice boards;

- email announcement to all staff;

- framed certificate, for example, 'collector of the month';

- silver cup for office display (often seen in inter-company competition).

These rewards would be come under the heading of *recognition*. Often that is simply enough to motivate staff – it is a sad fact in the downsized, dog eat dog environment which is the business world of today, that not enough managers say 'thank you', 'good work' or 'well done' to their staff. It is often assumed that incentives *have* to be cash or kind in order to achieve any beneficial results. That may now be true to a degree, but 'thank you' goes a long, long way.

Cash or kind rewards include:

- bonus added to payslip;

- a night out (at the best restaurant in town, or a show especially for a team effort);

- company product (though that would naturally depend upon what the company made or sold!);

- use of company flat in London, villa overseas for a holiday, and so on;

- holiday voucher, store voucher, hampers, and so on.

Any incentive scheme must be easy to measure, visibly fair and include relevant support staff. The targets should be difficult, but must be achievable – there is nothing more actually *demotivating* than setting targets that nobody can ever hope to achieve.

Many managing directors (and even finance directors) do not really understand DSOs, the wonderful benefits from their reduction, and what is required in DSO reduction in real cash terms or realistic timescales – macho management does not achieve the right results in the long term, and certainly does not achieve sustainable improvement. Credit managers should always be ready to explain the calculation and the results of the DSO performance to their senior management people. It is well said that the loudest squeak gets the oil!

It is often easier to set up occasional unexpected schemes than run continuous monthly ones, and any ongoing schemes should be varied and not allowed to be taken for granted. Nor should the measurement make it easier for certain staff always to win, so that others are demotivated by the impossibility of winning. For example, the split of the ledger between collectors should always be equitable in terms of customer type and collectability, so that any performance measurement is both fair, and seen to be fair.

The benefit to the company in interest saved on borrowings is always vastly in excess of the cost of prizes or gifts. Incentive schemes, however, should not be used merely to bring poor performance up to scratch – collection staff should be performing to certain standards anyway. Good management to motivate staff is needed to achieve at least the average DSO level for the industry. Incentives are to help to achieve cash results which are *better* than industry competitors.

Computer Aids to Collection

There is no doubt that the computer, as described in Chapter 10, has major benefits for the credit management function, not least in the area of accounts collection. The flexibility of both computer packages and PC-based functions has added a dimension in recent years that is beyond the imagination of credit managers of old. In transferring as much traditional chore work, such as listings and analyses from the desk to the computer, far more valuable human time and resource can be focused on actual customer contact. The credit management and collection 'add-on' packages now available offer a wide range of functions, aids and tools for the collector, but the real benefits can be listed as:

- *easy access enquiry screens* available via several criteria, not just the account number;

- *online generation of reports*, with the ability to ask for any listing from stated criteria, such as all accounts with more than £x and/or more than X days overdue;

- *online notes and diary dates*, with the ability to record details of phone calls plus review dates, with accounts for action automatically brought up on the prescribed dates;

- *automatic statement production* on preset dates with different formats for types of accounts, optional messages for overdues and the ability to produce statements at any time;

- *automatic production of copy invoices* on request and any other copy documentation such as order acknowledgements or delivery notes;

- *automatic reminder letters* with variable wordings to suit different customers and situations, plus variable appearance to increase impact;

- *automatic invalid deduction letters* triggered when cash is allocated to accounts paid too late to qualify for cash discount;

- *automatic part payment letters* triggered when cash is allocated to the ledger for less than the value of the invoice(s);

- *detailed Aged Debt Analysis* sequenced as invoice within customer within ledger section with each invoice in its age slot, or in any format specified by the user;

- *summary Aged Debt Analysis* (the 'prime tool'), with one line per customer, representing total aged debt for each account, by region, by salesman, by product or again in any format specified by the user;

- *consolidated credit exposure for national accounts* or major group accounts, with aged details of each branch account, or subsidiary account, with a total group exposure and ageings to show different branch or subsidiary performances;

- *cash forecast (by day and by month)* with automated projected inflow based on outstanding invoices and payment times/habits of each customer;

- *customer status report* for accounts meeting certain criteria, such as amounts overdue or exceeding credit limits;

- *disputed items report* with listings per collector of disputed invoices not yet resolved, with codes for the type of dispute, and action timetables and status;

- *exception reports* for any of the above, but on a 'flash' basis for certain serious criteria;

- *stopped accounts* by collector, region, sales, or any specified format of accounts on hold where certain action is required by both collector and other departments;

- *summary of reminder letters* to assess which kind of letters (wording and/or timing) work best.

The size of a company's customer base, both in customer numbers and sales values, will be just one of the many decision criteria which will decide the level of investment in computer aids to collection, and some functions will undoubtedly be more appropriate than others. The one common theme, however, has to be the release of time for the collector to get on with actual collection.

Methods

Before looking at actual methods (letters, phone calls and so on) it is well worth considering the benefits of knowing who your customers are and cultivating those accounts which will have a major impact on collection performance and actual cash totals. The primary objective of cultivating key accounts is to obtain consistently reliable payments as a 'most favoured' supplier. In most businesses where the 80/20 principle applies, and only 20 per cent of customers account for 80 per cent of cash, the reality is that cash targets can only ever be achieved if the really large accounts pay reliably each month on time. These accounts should be well known to the credit manager in just the same way as they are courted by the sales manager and well known to him. There should be a credit/payables relationship to match the relationship that undoubtedly will exist between sales and the customer's buyer. It would be less than helpful, to say the least, if there was a close relationship between sales and customer and at the same time the relative accounts departments were at loggerheads.

It could well be beneficial to understand why the customer is large to you. They are buying quantities of your product because they want to, and because it is preferred to the competition's product. That should put you in a stronger position and give confidence in the collection process – the customer is not going to buy elsewhere just because they are asked to pay the account when it is properly due. The customer is important to you, and the volume of purchases illustrates that you are important to the customer. Any indication of difficulty or off-handedness should be met with a polite reminder to the customer of the agreed terms, and if difficulty persists, involve sales and their buyer contacts to help bring the account back to its correct position.

Customer contact at all levels is vitally important, and visits by the customer to sales or technical staff in your company should be taken as an opportunity for the credit manager and key credit people to also meet the visiting customer. It may not be the actual payables people making the visit, but a brief, friendly chat can unlock doors later, and it also elevates the function of credit management in the minds of key people within your own organisation as well as the customer's.

Credit staff have the advantage of plenty of telephone contact with major customers and should be taken as a two-fold opportunity to build a friendly relationship and obtain a thorough inside knowledge of the chain of command for payments. Credit staff should be able to fully understand the customer's payables process and how to get priority treatment when it is needed. Any such useful details should be recorded on the customer master file.

Visits by credit to customers are not necessarily collection visits or dispute resolution visits – credit are just as capable of meaningful PR as anybody else, and frequently customers are pleased to 'show off' their operations to financial staff. Not infrequent friendly meetings can pay dividends in the long run, and being top of the customer's accounts payable pile is the object of the exercise. Much can be learned from the salesperson dealing with that account, and as soon as the chance arises for a personal visit, the credit manager should jump at the chance. Whatever the stated purpose of the visit, it should be preceded by a well thought out action plan. For example:

- confirm the appointment and include an estimate of how long the visit will take;

- confirm the location and journey time to ensure prompt arrival;

- take a slimmed down file of only the essential papers (if any), with a top sheet of key data. *Don't* look overloaded and disorganised, even if you really are;

- do lunch (you pay!), or at least a coffee and sandwich, if it has been possible to arrange the meeting near to lunchtime;

- spend a few minutes on friendly introductions and personal stuff; *don't* rush straight into the business bit;

- make sure you feel that both of you know about each other's companies;

- try to meet at least two other people for possible future contact;

- find out their payables process – and how your invoices get through it;

- agree a short list of action points – information, credit notes, copies, and so on;

- close with a clear summary of who will do what – *don't* leave in a flurry of goodwill and vague, half-remembered commitments;

- always leave a pleasant atmosphere, even if this means compromising on round one;

- when back in your own office, *always* phone, fax or email to 'keep it warm';

- build credibility and respect in your career – *do what you said you would!*

It is always both courteous and good practice to not only inform sales before a visit, but also to invite them along if they want to go. After the visit, the same courtesy and good practice is to report to sales as to the outcome and any general observations. Sales will appreciate your input, just as much as you appreciate theirs.

In future dealings with the payables person, refer to the meeting warmly. Don't waste the opportunity, but build on it. Try to visit all the key accounts at least twice a year, more often if necessary and especially if a visit can be seen as the opportunity to nip a crisis in the bud. Visits take some organising – that is what diaries or personal organisers are for, so use them!

The test of successful cultivation is that your payables contact comes readily to the phone – and does not try to avoid you – *and has a smile in his or her voice* – not hostility, off-handedness, or anonymity. The cultivation exercise becomes more immediate and self-evident now that both mobile phones with text and picture facilities as well as vidphones and vidconference calls are becoming more commonplace.

Collection is all about timing – the sooner you ask for money, the sooner you get paid. There is no getting away from that fact – indeed the opposite is self-evident. Doing the work, or supplying the goods, not issuing an invoice until accounts have time to do it, leaving statements on one side, and hoping that the customer will pay anyway is an invitation to a disaster party, and one which should be readily rejected! The customer wanted the goods or the work doing when *he* wanted it, and you had to pull out some stops to comply. Now you want paying when *you* want it – what is wrong with that?

Reliably, therefore, and without fail:

- send the *invoice* the same day as the goods;

- send a *statement* immediately following month-end;

- send a *simple reminder* seven days after due date;

- send a *final reminder* no more than 14 days later;

- *do not churn out* printed reminders three, four, five, six and so on;

- complete all *routine* reminders within four weeks from due date.

Special action is needed by then if the customer has not responded – there is no point whatsoever in carrying on a routine reminder process. Timing should be varied occasionally so that customers do not become over familiar with your routines and take advantage. There is nothing to be gained, and certainly no profit to be made, in continuing to supply customers who obviously cannot pay for past supplies.

In essence, the real collection process has begun even before the invoice has been issued. That is to say that before the goods are supplied or the work undertaken, the task of educating the customer to the supplier's terms is well in train. The customer's order has been confirmed, presumably, that confirmation clearly stating the supplier's payment terms (sales conditions supersede buyer's conditions, or they should do!). The customer should be told his payment obligation at least *five times* before payment is due. Think about it:

- told by the salesperson, (or brochure, catalogue and so on);

- informed by the contents of the initial account application form;

- reminded on the order confirmation;

- shown on the invoice;

- and shown again on the statement.

If those 'reminders' succeed in producing payment, expensive follow-up methods will not be needed. What is certain is that that customer cannot say that he was not made aware of your credit terms.

INVOICES

The invoice is the first request for payment and its sole purpose is to make that claim. The customer may have all sorts of reasons for wanting an invoice, and many varied processes through which that invoice will go, but first and foremost it is the seller's document of claim. It is difficult to think of any other piece of paper in the whole operation which has more importance attached to it.

Invoices come in all shapes, sizes and colours. Credit managers should have input into design, layout and content – it is sadly true that many credit managers often have to cope with what they are given. A simple exercise is to go into your own accounts payable department and have a look at invoices coming in to your company from suppliers. Pick a random sample of, say, 10 and sort them out, left to right, from the most effective to the least effective. Then ask yourself, why did you decide that some were better, more effective, than others? Colour? Layout? Clarity? Apply your reasons to your own invoices – yours should be as good as any others you have seen, or better. So:

- make sure your company has a simple, effective invoice document;

- show the customer's order number – *make sure of this;*

- show clearly the date, reference and total;

- have a good layout for description of the goods or services – goods *need* to be described and not just a series of reference or code numbers which might be meaningful to your computer system but are a mystery to the customer;

- show the method of dispatch;

- cut out all unnecessary data, which only obscures the important bits;

- most of all, *show clearly the payment terms* and ideally show the payment due date as well;

- *do not* include advertising clutter, for example, special promotions;

- *do not* include technical product information – invoices go to a payables person to match with orders and obtain authorisations to pay. Promotional and technical data belong to other documents aimed at different people.

Nothing happens in respect of payment unless and until the seller's invoice is actually in the buyer's accounts payable department. It is important to critically review invoicing procedures regularly. It is good to remember all those complaints that you have had about invoices – wrong prices, late receipt, unclear data, lack of order numbers and so on. Be certain, therefore, to ensure that these defects are eliminated from your invoices. Confidence in your own invoicing accuracy adds credibility to the collection process and ensures that your invoices are not in any way the cause of late payment.

STATEMENTS

Statements are argued about in credit management circles. Many claim that customers don't want or use them, only paying on invoice. Nevertheless even if customers say they do not need them, it is often more economic to send them out than to extract a certain few (unless the computer system can be amended to print only those required). Many customers do use them, however, often as a reconciliation aid identifying any items not received, as well as using them for payment purposes. Whatever the opinion, the statement remains a valuable summary of transactions (both to the supplier and the buyer), it aids the customer's bought ledger, and for the seller *it is a vehicle for the first reminder to pay overdues*. Open-item statements are better than carry forward ones, showing all uncleared debits and credits in chronological order. The statement should be reviewed and designed just as critically as the invoice, for all the same reasons and to ensure that it is as good as it can be.

The statement should be issued as quickly as possible after month-end closing. Address it clearly to a named contact in the accounts payable department, with any overdue items highlighted. It is good practice to print the first collection message on the statement. As invoices contain the customer order number, it is simple for the computer to repeat it on statements. Remember, if statements work first time, without creating queries or delays, then time has been saved for more difficult accounts. So, to make statements more effective:

- achieve eye-catching appearance (colour and layout);

- make it easy for customers to identify and match data;

- highlight overdue items prominently;

- print variable messages about overdue items;

- encourage customers to return the statement, or a tear-off section, with their payment, to make cash matching and posting that much easier.

TELEPHONE CALLS AND LETTERS

The debate about statements is repeated just as vigorously about the two traditional methods of collecting accounts – letters and telephone calls. Comparisons of the *effectiveness* of phone calls versus letters have shown conclusively that phone calls win, but that does not mean that there is no place in the collection process for reminder letters. On the contrary, they can be often the *only* cost effective method of collection. Lack of time precludes phoning every account, so letters need to be sent, and in addition, many accounts are so small that they do not carry enough profit to justify telephone calls. Remember, too, that sending reminder letters guarantees that *every* account on the ledger that needs reminding has in fact been contacted.

A simple approach might be:

- *Where there are few accounts, but large* phone them all. If a call is unsuccessful, send a stiff final letter to a top person.

- *Where there are masses of small debts* have a good letter programme. Where they do not work, follow up by telephone, starting with the largest overdues.

- *Where there is a mix of large and small debts* separate the ledger into major and non-major accounts. Reliably always phone the majors (it is not good practice to send major accounts the standard stereotyped letters, especially if there are friendly contacts). Have a good letter programme for non-majors, phoning to follow up when time permits.

It is frequent practice also to replace standard letters in many instances with standard faxes, and emails. Both often carry the same wording as the letter would have done, but are deemed to carry a degree more urgency.

TELEPHONE CALLS

This is covered in more detail in Chapter 12, but it as well to cover just the main points here. It is generally accepted that the most effective way to collect cash is by telephone. The phone has the advantage over the letter of making contact, hopefully instantly, not only with an actual person, but also the person actually wanted. Speaking to a human being directly means that he or she has to give some sort of answer – the letter can be thrown into the waste paper bin, but people have to speak to each other once contact has been made. The main disadvantage, of course, is that time is at a premium, and the constraints of time mean that fewer customers can be contacted by this method.

Collecting by phone is like selling by phone – both require specialist training, and it would be entirely wrong to assume or presume that anybody can do it. The key elements of telephone collection are:

- preparation, so you do not have to call back;

- control of the conversation; the caller being in charge, and not to be deflected;

- closing the call with a reliable promise – in other words, a result.

The aim should always be to succeed in one call. This means being ready with information on whatever might crop up, and practice in overcoming excuses and objections. It should always be remembered that in agreeing that telephone collection is the most effective, it is not cheap, and to be *cost* effective, the right balance has to be struck – type of account and time of day. If smaller accounts do not warrant an expensive phone call, don't phone just for the sake of telephone call targets – send them a letter, instead – and certainly do not clog the telephone time available with non-value-added calls at the expense of those with worthwhile returns. Cost effectiveness also means telephoning customers at the times most likely to make good contact and bring results. In other words, contact customers when they can be contacted, not when it is 'convenient' to you, or because your boss says 'all calls after 3.00!' When telephoning is mixed with other departmental duties, make sure that prime time is given to the telephone activity and 'dead' times are for other things. Many companies have varying policies on making (and receiving – 'Accounts Payable takes calls p.m.'), but in general contact with the right person is more likely in the morning between 9.30 and 12.30 and in the afternoon between 2.30 and 4.30. The secret, of course, is to get to know your customer, and get to know the best time to contact the right person – that information should always be noted on the customer file.

The three key stages in telephone collection should be recognised as being separate, that is:

1. *Before you pick up the phone* – have all the available information ready for any eventuality; you do not want to have to call back. Separate

'static' data (name, phone number, last actions and so on) from 'live' data (the account details and the order file).

2. *Making the call* – you are persuading and negotiating. Keep control. Be ready with standard, well-rehearsed responses to excuses. Smile! It really does help. Use the other person's name when needed, but don't overdo it – three or four times is usually enough in the average collection call.

3. *Closing successfully* – every good collector knows a promise is more reliable if the customer repeats back what has been agreed, how much, when and by what method. *Do not say it for him!*

Keep sequential records of phone follow-ups for each account, and *don't* just jot down on the ledger or Aged Debt Analysis hard copy – they will only have to be transferred at month-end. Better, use the diary notepad system on the computer and have it prompt the next move.

LETTERS

Accepting that reminder letters are weak (have they even arrived?; have they been read by anyone?; how long should we wait before we decide that they are not going to answer?) – and more so with those debtors determined to avoid paying until absolutely necessary – they do have a place in the collection cycle. There may not be enough time to telephone every customer, values may not warrant expensive telephone time, and in any event, reminder letters are the seller's evidence of the reminder process having been equally and fairly applied to all. Letters are an integral collection feature, therefore, and are worth trying to make as effective as possible. Be polite, of course, but be firm – it is your money, after all. Do not plead – it has been said before, but will constantly be repeated: *it is your money, the customer has only borrowed it, and you are entitled to be repaid.* Word the letter carefully, with not just the objective of getting paid, but also with the longer term in mind.

Key points for collection letters are:

- address it to a named individual, otherwise to a job title;

- sign it personally;

- show a job title with authority;

- show a phone extension and email address (if you have one) to encourage a response;

- make sure that it is accurate, to avoid time-wasting queries;

- keep the words simple and direct, none exceeding three syllables;

- no collection letter should ever exceed one page in length;

- the amount being claimed should be given prominence at the top of the letter and not buried somewhere in the text;

- always show how the debt is made up, and if it is in any way complicated, then add a copy statement;

- avoid reference to the passage of time, for example, 'within seven days'. Either state the expiry date, for example, 'payment by 15th December', or, better still, require overdue amounts *by return*. Note that even if you do allow seven days for the customer to respond, the last thing you should do is tell him that!;

- there can, by definition, be only one final letter (think about it!). Do not follow a final request with a final reminder followed by a final demand!;

- remember to include the debtor's buyer in any collection difficulties. He can be influential in ordering payment;

- there is no reason not to keep sales informed of the collection letter scenario – they too can bring some self-interest muscle to bear if so inclined!

Unless you have some specific information to the contrary, it would be wrong to assume the worst at the beginning. There may be a good reason for non-payment, something that you have not yet been told about. The first letter should therefore be polite and simple. Ask the customer to pay the overdue account or tell you why he cannot. Remember, the purpose of the letter is to extract a response – if it does raise a query or a dispute, contact has been made and you can deal with the problem. Reminder letters do not have to be masterpieces of brilliant prose, worthy of performance at the Old Vic! Aim the letter at an individual, preferably by name, and sign it as a person with authority. A direct line, extension number and email address shown on the letter are invitations to respond.

Never, never send letters that end with an unintelligible signature, or simply 'Accounts Department', or 'Credit Control Department'. To get attention, name and title have the greatest external effect, for example, Jack Jones, Regional Credit Controller. The letter should never be seen as merely part of a longer routine – it is to be hoped that there are no more companies out there who number reminder letters to customers 'No 3 of 6'! Reminder letters should look as if they have been individually produced for that customer, and definitely not pre-printed computer produced paper complete with sprocket holes!

The overdue debt continues to cost you dearly the longer it remains unpaid. You are entitled, therefore, to be unhappy with the customer who has not only withheld payment unlawfully but has also failed to respond to a polite reminder. The *final reminder letter* thus requires to be strongly worded. It should certainly refer to the lack of response to previous reminders, ask for the overdue debt and end with the threat of some special action, such as:

- collection, with costs, by a third-party agency;

- referral to solicitors, for possible Court action;

- where vital further supplies, or spares, are needed, a hold on that supply.

Never threaten anything that you do not intend, or are not prepared to undertake. The debtor will soon discover your bluff, and your position is weaker than before.

If a partial payment is received, do not restart the letter sequence, but acknowledge the part payment, and insist on the remainder by return. The only justifiable reason for halting the letter series is if the customer does respond with a query or complaint, either by letter or by telephone. The response has to be dealt with, and there can be little more damaging to customer relations than reminder letters of any kind, without any acknowledgement or indication that their complaint is being dealt with.

A number of sample reminder letters follow. They are not intended to be exhaustive, or even the only ones acceptable, but are intended to give a flavour of simple, polite and direct wording and format. Many innovative collectors have produced letters over the years which at first glance do not look like reminder letters – they have to be read first before the proverbial penny drops. It should also be noticed that 'Final Notice', 'Notice Before Proceedings' or 'Intention To Proceed' can be seen by some as imitating Court documentation. To pretend to be a Court document is, of course, illegal – care should be exercised in the grey area between effective attention grabbing documentation and breaking the law. You have been warned!

Samples – first reminder letters

Dear Mr Paine

£1,645.39

Our last statement showed in detail the amount of £1,645.39 which is overdue for payment to us.

We again attach details of this amount. Will you please pay this sum to us immediately, or alternatively let me know your reason for non-payment.

Yours sincerely

D. Marks

Regional Credit Controller

Direct Line ....

Email ....

---

or

We have not yet received your payment for the August account of £652.00 which became overdue two weeks ago.

This consists of:

15.7.XX – Invoice 1234 Order 651 £300.00

22.7.XX - Invoice 1341 Order 660 £352.00

Please pay this to us without delay or let us know if there is any problem affecting payment.

---

or

> It may be useful to remind you that our contracted credit terms are net 30 days from invoice date.
>
> On this basis your account shows £689.26 overdue and we look forward to your payment by return of post.
>
> A copy of the unpaid invoice is attached.
>
> We enclose a pre-paid envelope for your reply.

Samples of second reminder letters (only if a series of three is used)

> Dear Mr Paine
>
>   £1,645.39
>
> We wrote to you two weeks ago about your overdue account of £1,645.39. Details appear on the last statement sent to you.
>
> So far, we cannot trace your payment, nor any reply. If we do not hear from you by return, we shall transfer collection to
>
> (name the solicitors, collection agency, or whatever).
>
> We look forward to your response.
>
> Yours sincerely
>
> D Marks
>
> Regional Credit Controller
>
> Direct Line.....................
>
> Email...........................

or

> We have now sent you a detailed statement of overdues, and a polite request for payment,
>
> yet we have not received the courtesy of a reply.
>
> Can we please have your payment of £652.00 by return, in order to avoid passing the account to
>
> a third party for collection, with possible extra cost.

or

> As there has been regular business between us for a long time, we are concerned that you have not responded
>
> to our previous request for overdues to be paid. They now total £689.26.
>
> Please send us your remittance for this sum.
>
> If we do not hear from you, we shall hand the matter to a specialised agency to resolve.

Samples: *final reminders*

For the attention of The Chief Accountant

Dear Sir

Re: OVERDUE ACCOUNT: £1,645.39

We regret to note that you have not responded to our previous reminders about the above debt.

Details appear on our last statement and were repeated in our previous requests.

As we mentioned to you in our last letter your account has now been transferred to ....

for collection, with allowable additional costs charged to you.

Receipt of your payment in full can stop this action.

Yours faithfully

A. Benson

National Credit Manager

Direct Line...................

Email........................

---

or

For the attention of the Finance Director

Dear Sirs

Re: Final Demand: £652.00

Our last statement detailed the overdue debt shown above, representing goods dispatched to your order.

We are not aware of any dispute on the debt, but have received no reply to the payment requests sent to

your bought ledger department.

Our next step is third party collection action without further referral to you.

Your immediate payment of £652.00 will prevent this action which may involve extra costs for your account.

Yours faithfully

A. Benson

National Credit Manager

Direct Line................

Email.......................

As previously stated, none of these examples is either definitive or exclusive. The purpose is to illustrate tone, simple content and clarity. Readers will no doubt be able to formulate many interesting and concise variations.

Having received payment for less than the required total of overdues, and with no accompanying explanation or request for further time or assistance, it is important to notify the customer immediately of the discrepancy. The deficit should not simply be rolled into the next reminder letter. A part payment, particularly a round sum, may be the first warning of cash flow problems, where the customer sends everyone a small amount to get a breathing space.

There are other possible reasons for short payment, and it would be wrong, in the absence of information to the contrary, just to assume that the customer is short of cash. Other reasons could be:

- deduction of a disputed amount, not explained;

- an instalment, agreed with other staff;

- a payment to suit his own systems;

- (most frequently) invoices not yet cleared.

If time allows, and there are not too many cases, it is better to telephone for the reasons, and this is frequently done by the credit controller who has the dual role of allocating cash as well as chasing payment. In such circumstances, this can be done as the cash is actually being posted. Alternatively, there can be a letter system to pick up on part payments:

Dear Mr Hudson

We thank you for the payment of £356.00 received today in respect of your account with us.

As notified to you on recent reminders, the amount actually overdue totalled £1,577.00 and your payment is

therefore short by £1,221.00.

We would appreciate your remittance for this amount by return, or the reason for the short payment, and enclose

a pre-paid envelope to assist your fast reply.

Yours sincerely

M. Baker

Credit Supervisor

Direct Line................

Email......................

When the short-payment problem has been settled, remaining arrears should be followed up with the next appropriate stage of letter, so that the debtor does not successfully sidestep the procedure by making part settlement.

In some collection situations, non-standard letters may be deemed to be more appropriate than the usual standard letters regularly in use. It may well be that something requires to be acknowledged, information being given in response to a customer request, or indeed information actually being sought. It is also worth taking some time to actually think about who is being written to (as well as why), and how best to get through to him and to get the message across.

The target reader may be busy – we are all busy, so it should be simple enough to understand that busy people need special attention. He (or she, of course) may even be hostile, or at least uninterested. They may be 'protected' by a secretary or assistant, so any letter targeted at that reader has to be worded in such a way that the minder feels it necessary to pass on to the boss. Easy enough, especially if it is a follow-up on some previously agreed point or action – 'as we discussed last week and you asked me for written confirmation'.

If we have got through to the intended reader, and we know he is busy, uninterested or even hostile, we must be even more sure that he reads what we have written. The letter, therefore must start clearly with a reference to the purpose, make its point with precision and clarity, escalate from polite to firm, and close with a precise request. Decide upon a follow-up period (it may be days or weeks, depending on the purpose) and then follow up by referring to that letter by date and reference. If in doubt, telephone.

Letter writing will always be regarded as something of an art by many, but collection letters, both in standard and non-standard format should adhere to the same basic rules:

- polite, no matter how wrong the customer may be;

- clear, not rambling or over-elegant language;

- factual, not chatty or anecdotal;

- never more than one page;

- never more than 25 words in a sentence;

- a separate paragraph for each topic.

Letters have been part of the collection process for centuries, the telephone for generations. Later developments and techniques have added to the collectors portfolio, with varying degrees of impact and success.

FAX

The fax, when it first came on the scene, was initially seen by many as replacing the letter and the phone, mainly on the basis that it did in effect combine the two disciplines. Certainly faxes to senior people can have some shake up effect on slow or lazy payables staff, especially when supplies are under threat. It used to be argued that faxes conveyed more urgency than letters, and that fewer ignored faxes than ignored letters. As time has gone on, however, and the fax become part of any normal office routine, the fax is simply now seen as another collection method, with little or no discernible advantage over other methods. It is true that the same thought which should go into letters should be equally applied to faxes – indeed letter wordings put on to faxes are more effective. The fax is also useful in involving buyers and often overcome barriers when letters *are* being ignored and telephone calls not returned.

EMAIL

Emails exploded on to the collection scene in the 1980s, and became as commonly used as any other method of communication. They are undoubtedly useful in getting immediate access to the right person, with full details of the debt, and any related data direct on to the recipients screen. Messages can be deleted and ignored, of course, but at least the sender can be certain that the message has been delivered. Emails will be discussed later in this chapter, because there are pitfalls, and abuses, and the future of emails as an effective collection method may not be all that was initially promised.

PERSONAL VISITS

Personal visits form part of the collection armoury. It is not unusual for a large percentage of sales to be made up from a small percentage of customers. These are the key, or major, accounts and each one should be visited at intervals to strengthen the relationship. Visits are expensive and time consuming, so they should not be used just to collect cheques or resolve issues, but also to generate discussions on why payments may be slow – indeed they are also quite simply valuable public relations exercises.

Visits need to be arranged, and should never be on a 'cold call' basis. Make an appointment with a suitably ranked person. A well-planned visit, a thorough discussion and plenty of clarification about how both companies work can all help to speed up future payments. It is certainly courteous and usually effective to confirm in writing the main points discussed as soon as you get back to your office. It is also equally courteous to invite and/or inform sales of your intended visit and purpose – they may want to come along, and in any case it will prevent any feeling of 'poaching' on what they may see as their territory.

Some companies employ accounts 'representatives' to call regularly on large customers, to collect payments and resolve problems. Where customers are large corporations with slow-moving bureaucracy and even slower-moving, or system-bound, computers, such reps soon cost-justify their existence by obtaining very large amounts sooner than would have been paid out by the standard ponderous process of such customers.

USE OF SALES STAFF

There are good arguments both for and against allowing sales personnel to handle debt collection. Much will depend upon the relationship between credit and sales and also the basis upon which sales personnel are paid. For example, a good working relationship, built upon mutual trust and understanding will see customer service, including account collection, as a joint undertaking. Equally, if commission is based upon paid accounts rather than just sales, then it is evident that there is an advantage to sales personnel in helping to ensure that all accounts are indeed paid. There are often many more sales people than credit or collection staff, so they can cover more ground. Not only that but sales can use their numerous company contacts and can exert product leverage. Often, however, there is not that close relationship, and sales do not have the time, or the inclination, to do the collecting job properly or see it through to the end. There is also the split loyalty to avoid alienating an order prospect.

It is courteous to include sales in credit personnel visits, and it may often be necessary to actually use sales people and their contacts as the best way to obtain access. Many companies do in fact have a policy which binds credit and sales together. The important point to bear in mind at all times, for all personnel, is that no one employee, sales or credit, 'owns' the customer. The customer is a customer of the company, and both sales and credit in fact work for the same company – a fact often forgotten by those who see individual customers as their own property!

If company policy specifically requires sales to be involved in collection activity, then it will be for the finance director, through the credit manager, to ensure that all accounting timetables, cash targets and deadlines are adhered to, and that feedback is maintained at the required level. The real problem in a highly competitive environment is that sales will inevitably have a high degree of focus on meeting sales targets, with little time for other activities.

TRANSPORT STAFF

In many industries, even though delivery drivers may not be expected to actually handle cash, for security and insurance reasons, they are often required to be part of the collection process by picking up cheques when making deliveries. This often follows where accounts have been on hold, pending payment, and the next delivery is only on the basis that the last delivery will be paid for when the drop takes place. In addition, 'switched on' delivery drivers are often a good source of information for the credit department – returning after a delivery round with tales of confused goods inwards, staff standing about doing nothing, gates locked, stock not booked in, and so on.

It is a matter of some regret for many credit managers that fewer and fewer companies employ directly their own transport, with deliveries being outsourced to contractors – there is a resulting loss in the availability of using transport staff to assist credit control.

DIRECT DEBITS

Direct debit, common in consumer collections, is becoming much more widely spread in the trade environment. Variable direct debits have made it possible for different amounts to be collected each month, and for those customers who want to pay their bills on time, it is a valuable boon to the seller. Many sellers offer incentives to get customers on to direct debits, such as keener trade discounts and prices, or one-off inducements such as an extension to facilities in the initial phase. Direct debits can bounce, of course, just like cheques – if there are insufficient funds in the account on the day the debit hits, then it will be returned unpaid. So they are not a guarantee of payment, but with good customers, they are a foreseeable sum of money at a particular time, so cash forecasting is made easier and more accurate. Of course, suppliers must give the banks indemnity against errors – the banks will only follow instructions and if the seller is wrong, it has to be his fault, not that of the bank. The banking system in turn gives its indemnity to the customer in the event that the supplier cannot refund an amount taken in error. This is obviously important to customers signing up to the system, but it means that the banks will only allow suppliers into the scheme if they consider them creditworthy – that is, highly unlikely to be unable to correct an erroneous debit.

CASH DISCOUNTS

Cash discounts are a bone of contention, even though many believe that they encourage prompt payment. Perhaps in some cases they do, but the reality is that only companies with large net margins can actually afford to give cash discounts. Offering cash discounts can have the advantage of earlier payments – the downside, of course, is customers paying outside agreed terms, and not being therefore entitled to discount, often take the discount anyway. This leads to deduction debits on the ledger, and recovery action needed to clear. The real question for suppliers to ask themselves, however, is why give discounts to customers who pay usually to terms? Cash discounts in fact often mask price increases – it is logical for suppliers not already giving cash discounts to only be able to afford to give away cash when their goods carry a price sufficient to cover. Money costs money – there is little point in lending customers even more than they manage to borrow from suppliers already!

SETTLEMENT REBATES

The same is true of settlement rebate schemes. It is not uncommon for volume customers to negotiate further price discounts based upon target purchase levels, often measured half-yearly or annually. Although the scheme has attractions, not least of which are the purchase incentives for the customer and the continuity of supply for the seller, the need is again to ensure that it is only available on the condition of payment to terms. If slow-paying customers can be seen to cost the seller money in interest and collection, then however big and important the customer may seem to be, there is no point in eroding margins even more by offering further price discounts. Any invoices paid late should be deducted from those sales qualifying for rebate. Many companies successfully negotiate the prompt payment requirement with purchasing staff who are themselves rewarded for getting price reductions. The result is much faster cash inflow with relatively simple controls to achieve it.

EXTERNAL COLLECTION SERVICES

There are several cost-effective reasons for collection to be put into the hands of external services, usually collection agencies and/or solicitors. More can be found in Chapters 13 and 22 on collection agencies and the use of the courts. All that need be said here in the matter of collection of trade debts is that credit managers should never close their minds to the idea of outside help. If third parties can deal with those difficult debts before they become write-offs, the credit manager can spend more time on those more worthwhile accounts, maximising cash inflow.

INTEREST ON LATE PAYMENTS

Most companies have the right to charge interest on late payment enshrined in their terms and conditions. As unplanned interest expense will be incurred on overdue debts up to the date of eventual payment, it is logical to pass the cost on to the actual late-paying customers, rather than absorbing it and charging it on to all customers in future prices. That is the theory, at least, and to have the right included as a standard sales condition, strengthens the hand of the seller, *if it chooses to exercise that right.* Thereby hangs the tale of modern business in the UK. The culture makes it actually commercially difficult to enforce that right, and many companies see charging interest as the least attractive of options in a highly competitive market place where there is a daily struggle for sales and market share.

There is legislation. The UK Government introduced the Late Payment of Commercial Debts (Interest) Act 1998, which first came into force on 1 November 1998. This gives business the statutory right to charge interest on late payment, and was introduced in three stages:

1. 1 November 1998 to 31 October 2000 – small business (under 50 employees) able to claim interest from large businesses and the public sector on debts incurred under contracts agreed after that date.

2. 1 November 2000 to 31 October 2002 – small businesses able to claim interest from other small businesses on debts incurred under contracts agreed after that date.

3.　　1 November 2002 onwards – all businesses and the public sector able to claim interest from all businesses and the public sector on debts incurred under contracts agreed after that date.

The timetable was actually brought forward, the final phase C actually coming into force on 1 August 2002. This followed the requirement to bring the UK legislation into line with the European Directive on Late Payment. The rate of interest is set at 8 per cent above the Bank of England Base Rate. Research from the Credit Management Research Centre at the University of Leeds Business School has consistently indicated that though there is widespread awareness of the legislation, actual take-up under the Act remains at around the same level as at introduction of the legislation, around 5 per cent. The point is that both the Act and the Directive are *enabling* legislation – companies can charge interest if they want to, but it is not compulsory. As a consequence, the commercial questions remain.

A typical approach among companies that *do* charge selective interest is:

- do not book interest as income until it is paid;

- cancel unpaid interest once the main debt is paid;

- do not spend money pursuing unpaid interest only.

Court action does allow statutory interest to be added to the debt, of course, and it is usual practice to include this in litigation – details of actions through the courts are covered in Chapter 22.

SUSPENSION OF SUPPLIES

Continuity of supply is of prime importance to most buyers, especially if they depend on a supplier's particular product, or if the price and service satisfactorily suits their requirements. Under these circumstances, the suspension of supplies to slow payers is a major collection tool. If a customer cannot pay for a past delivery, why make a further one? A well-defined credit policy needs to deal with how much tolerance to show to slow payers before supplies are discontinued, and it is vital that it is understood by all staff, particularly in the sales area. If it is the intention to hold orders, the collection cycle must include notifying the customer's buyer, that is, the one who actually wants the goods or services. A fax or email to that person *before* the stop is actually implemented can, and often does, produce the required payment, allowing the order to go forward. Notification of the intention to stop supplies serves two purposes – it alerts both buyer and seller to the potential for a difficult collection situation (if the buyer ignores the warning), and it is better to give notice (and be paid) than actually having to disrupt business by cessation of supply.

Stop procedures can be tailored to suit almost any business environment and computer system. They can also vary from rigid enforcement at all times to selective application as circumstances dictate. For example, if risk categories are in use, and category A customers are deemed blue chip and without risk, even overdues would not trigger a stop. At the other end of the scale, the high-risk category accounts would be subject to automatic stop when an overdue situation arose, usually regardless of value. The stop scenario applies to credit limits as well as overdues, though it should be remembered that stopping due to exceeding the credit limit is tied very closely to having the right credit limit in the first place, *and* ensuring that credit limits are constantly and regularly reviewed.

A sensible approach to stopping supplies is to produce a 'pre-stop' list. The system provides the accounts which are overdue (or becoming overdue) in a listing for both credit and sales to preview and edit. Accounts can be deleted, added, values amended and so on, and completion of that exercise prompts the issue of the 'live' stop list. The disadvantage is that this can be labour-intensive, but the advantage lies in the cooperation and collaboration between credit and sales, early involvement in the collection process and the reduction in the likelihood of inappropriate stopped accounts.

The stop list is updated daily to take account of cash received, and must be capable of being added to in the event of something happening, which is neither excess of credit limit nor overdue. Notices of meetings of creditors, or appointment of Administrators or Administrative Receivers are usually predictable, but they can come out of the blue, and clearly in such circumstances, the account should be immediately frozen. Equally, a dishonoured cheque should set off alarm bells, with the account stopped until the matter is resolved.

'BOUNCED' CHEQUES

When cheques are returned by the bank marked 'R/D' or 'Refer to Drawer', there is always the chance of a bad debt. Even though some may have an innocent reason, dishonoured cheques require the *immediate* attention of the credit manager. An R/D cheque should *never* be sent back to a customer, as it is valuable evidence of debt in the event of any subsequent litigation, as well as evidence of an insolvent act. In any case, it is useful as an interim tool for collecting the debt.

There is often an additional comment on the returned cheque, such as 'please re-present' or 'insufficient funds'. When the bank writes 'please re-present', they are indicating that the account is subject to variable cash inflows, and although at first presentation there was not enough to cover, there is a likelihood that in a day or so funds will be available to meet the cheque. If the bank comment is 'insufficient funds', or indeed if there is no bank comment at all, it is the bank's way of saying that they do not believe that further funds will be available and there would be no point in trying to present the cheque again. Many companies have a policy which allows only one presentation, and if the cheque is not met first time it should be returned immediately to the supplier for the appropriate action to be taken.

Any returned cheque should be scrutinised for the reason for return. The 'innocent' reasons include not signed, wrong date, not signed in accordance with the bank mandate, words and figures differ or cheque mutilated in the post. Interpretation of 'innocent' will of course depend upon previous history, but whatever the reason, the prime action is customer contact without delay:

- photocopy the dishonoured cheque; send the copy with a letter, recorded delivery, to the finance director or owner, or scan and email;

- say that the cheque is being put into Court action without further notice, but that the action can be halted by immediate cash, bank draft or acceptable third-party cheque;

- phone the customer to say that the letter is on the way, seeking resolution there and then; if there is no satisfactory response, proceed with litigation;

- sue on the dishonoured cheque, not the unpaid sale itself. There is no real legal defence (except perhaps 'cheque issued under duress'), and the debtor knows that the seller will *always* obtain judgment.

It would be wrong to assume that dishonoured cheques are a common occurrence these days, and therefore a normal business hazard. They are undoubtedly more common than they should be, but becoming complacent about it is not an option. Each dishonoured cheque should elicit the same urgent and determined action. It is an offence for a company to issue a cheque *knowing that there are not enough funds in the account to meet it, and where a deliberate attempt to defraud can be proved.* A one-off happening may not warrant the police being informed and action being taken, but if the supplier knows that the same customer has been issuing worthless cheques several times recently, the local fraud authorities may well be interested. It could fit a pattern and justify the intervention of the authorities.

The Future

Methods of recording and storing information, retrieval and availability of data, the transfer of funds and the way that customers can be contacted have been developed over a number of years. That process of modernisation and improvement is bound to continue, though the principle of supply and right to be paid will remain as true tomorrow as it ever was. The credit manager can expect improvements in computer support, funds transfer, the use of credit and debit cards, laptops and mobile phones, videocam and vidphones, power dialling, emails and better customer contact.

BETTER COMPUTER SUPPORT

Chapter 10 emphasised the need for credit managers to be involved in computer installations in their department, and detailed some of the functions and features which are now an everyday part of the credit manager's working life. The point to stress going forward is to ensure that, when the time comes for any existing system to be replaced or enhanced, the credit manager should be looking for more than just a faster version of what exists already. In other words, use the development and consultation time in a constructive way:

- build a 'wish list' of the good credit management features that others appear to enjoy and you wish you had.

- talk to other companies who have gone through the system changes and updating pains, so that you do not have to reinvent the wheel and waste many months. Most suppliers of systems will supply reference sites, and they are usually more than happy for you to visit see for yourself. An invaluable source of information for members of the ICM is the member's Bulletin Board (see Appendix), an online message board full of questions and answers, experiences and advice,

- above all, the credit manager should seek formal agreement from the board that he will be consulted, and not just given a system that some computer boffin thinks he ought to have.

New systems are designed to last for some years (at least a payback period – systems are not cheap), and should therefore be able to cope with foreseeable improvements and developments. Desirable features would be access to the credit and collection systems, all relevant data, use of terminals and remote PCs and laptops, mobile phone connections, printouts anywhere, anytime, on demand and so on. The list is neither exhaustive nor prescriptive. The point is to think ahead, plan and implement, and then do it all over again.

FUNDS TRANSFERS

The advance of technology remains a great and continuing opportunity to change the payment culture in the UK. The 300-year-old anachronism known as the cheque is a perfect vehicle for controlling, and thus delaying, payment. It is only, after all, a written instruction to a bank to pay an account to somebody. It may well have been viewed as a marvellous breakthrough in the 1600s (as indeed it was – a few notes in a folder was far more convenient than a saddlebag full of gold) when it was introduced as a method of transferring funds, but by the methods of today, antiquated is the word that springs to mind. With the debit card and EFTPOS (Electronic Funds Transfer at Point Of Sale) terminals in daily use in shops and supermarkets, the consumer is now comfortable with the habit of paying for the week's shopping at the supermarket with his account debited immediately, and the supermarket credited a very short time later. If only trade debtors and creditors could grasp the same concept! Well, actually they can – it is just that while the consumer is happy and the supermarket no longer accepts consumer cheques, in trade credit, the debtor still wants to exercise independent control of outgoings, so the cheque still retains a large slice of the funds transfer business. It is not unusual now for companies with one-off transactions for comparatively small amounts with their trade customers to insist on payment by debit or credit cards and direct debit, in both domestic and international trade transactions, continue to gather apace.

It should be remembered that the multi-nationals and major corporations embrace funds transfer technology far more readily than small business, and though the demise of the cheque was foretold some years ago (and prophets of cheque doom still say the end is nigh), the nature of business make-up in the UK and across Europe has changed dramatically in the last 15 years. The mighty corporations are now the exception – there are over 4.6 million small businesses in the UK (small in this context defined as under 50 employees) and they now represent the largest private sector employers in the kingdom. Those SMEs are the ones who continue to prolong the life of the cheque as a key method of funds transfer – they control how much and when, in other words.

The banks themselves have improved the way in which funds are transferred between accounts. In the UK the consumer is familiar with paying for the car, the mortgage, council tax and so on, without having to remember payment dates and without having to write and post cheques. The funds can be instantly transferred on the required date, with same-day cleared funds being the norm. Internationally, as well as in the domestic market, electronic transfers take place through SWIFT (Society for World Wide Interbank Financial Telecommunications), which is the banking sytem's computer messaging process.

Electronic Data Interchange (EDI) systems allow paperless messaging of orders, delivery and invoicing material, commonplace between supermarkets and their thousands of suppliers. Indeed, supermarkets will provide and install the required equipment and systems in their suppliers' premises if required, and provide the necessary staff training and support – it could well be a condition of supply, in addition to price, quality and delivery of the goods or produce on offer. Supermarkets also led the way in insisting on at least a BACS transfer in payments as a vital step in the process, and increasingly that is being replaced by direct debit. This trend is bound to continue, led by the supermarket groups and large corporations, and it has to be assumed that the rest will follow in time. The pace of change, however, will no doubt be dictated by considerations other than efficiency.

LAPTOP PCS AND MOBILE PHONES

The laptop and the mobile phone, well established in their own right, are formidable collection tools. Combined, the mind can well boggle at the possibilities for the 'switched on' credit manager to get to grips with any situation at any time and in any place. Text messaging, both in marketing and accounts collection are commonplace, though great care is needed in finding and using the correct wording. Companies jumped at the advantages to be gained from providing employees with the mobility and flexibility of mobiles and laptops, from credit to sales, transport and distribution. Wireless operation, access to mainframe data via phone or laptop, email by phone, the list goes on. It is easy to take it all for granted and not appreciate the enormous investment and development that went on, and goes on, in the 'back office'. Faxes, emails, messages, online credit reports, websites, route maps, location planning, whatever is required – all there at the push of the tiniest of buttons. From the car park, the park bench, the café, the back of the taxi in downtown Buenos Aires, or at 36,000ft over the Atlantic Ocean – the combinations are awesome and the trend is for more power in a smaller unit. There is a 'but' – there is always a but. Being contactable when on holiday on the beach in The Canaries is all very well, but making a decision when toasting nicely and on the third cervesa of the afternoon? Take care!

WEBCAMS/VIDPHONES

The concept of videophone or vidphone has been around for some years, being first commercially available in 1992. The take up was always slow, with problems of quality and resolution in the early days. It has always been seen by credit managers that the advantages of 'face-to-face' meetings lay in the area of character judgement – eye contact, body language, attitude and so on – and the debtor (or customer) could not hide behind faceless anonymity. Multi-national companies have long utilised videoconferencing facilities, saving both the time and expense involved in travel.

In the aftermath of September 11, this option was pursued further and the global downturn of 2008 added to the cutback on travel, hence the increase in videoconferencing. It is, however, the laptop and the webcam which has made the most giant of leaps – the kids chat to each other all the time and mums and dads chat for free to their grown up families now living in New Zealand or Fiji. It is the confidence of the young, and the great strides in technology, that makes this medium the fastest growing of its type, and companies are being quick to grasp the opportunities. There will always be some who resist – not everyone likes to be seen, and the labyrinth of privacy laws may well preclude any form of automatic visual connection unless previously agreed. The technology is there nevertheless, and it unlikely to be uninvented!

POWER DIALLING

Power dialling interfaces accounts lists with the telephone so that customers are dialled automatically in the right sequence, as the telephone becomes free. Commonplace in consumer collection environments, the system lends itself perfectly well to large trade organisations having extensive customer bases. Various systems can redial engaged numbers, leaving specially prepared messages on answering machines if required, ranging from initial contact to stronger collection content. Result codes can be added to the customer data, so that the screen display for the operator at any time gives a complete picture of the story so far. Much is made in the consumer environment about the time allocated to each call, with maximums set in the system – such timings are not necessarily appropriate in the trade environment, where calls have to be put through to various departments and hold while accounts are looked up on systems and enquiries made. That aside, the facility is both available and technically feasible for appropriate organisations.

EMAIL

The email has overtaken the fax, and for many, even the telephone, as the preferred method of instant direct person-to-person communication. Attachment of statements, scanned images of invoices and delivery notes can be sent from one to another in an instant, worldwide, and both marketing and debt collection have moved very close to making the email their prime method of contact.

There are many pitfalls, however, and in some way the advantages of the speed and ease of contact can actually be outweighed by such dangers. The explosion of emails around the business and private world has begun to run into trouble. A syndrome known as *email stress*, first recognised and diagnosed in the USA, has inevitably spread around the developed world – each morning the employee logs into his or her system to be met by a screen full of new messages, some important, some less important and some junk and even some not really intended for them ('just thought I'd copy you in'). Email stress causes both apathy and carelessness, and in sending an email, the only thing that the sender can be sure of is that it has been delivered. There is no guarantee that it will be open or read, or still less acted upon – indeed the more the number of messages, the less likely that they will be effective. The delete button, trash bin or trash folder soon fills up as quickly as the older wicker waste basket in the corner of the office.

There is another real problem – may people use emails as an excuse not to talk. This had been labelled *email cowardice*. Instead of going to the office next door, or downstairs, and actually talking to the sales manager to discuss the issue, they send an email. The thinking behind this is often the misguided belief that it will avoid confrontation, whereas the reality is quite often the opposite. Confrontation can be made inevitable by a badly worded email, and avoided by face-to-face discussion, even on a contentious matter. Emails can be typed out in a mood of anger, sometimes not even spell checked, and sent. Pressing 'send' is the point of no return for most, and the mind of the reader can seriously misjudge both the mind and the mood of the sender. Emails carry no voice inflection, no facial expression, no pause or moment for reflection – in short, no human emotion. They can also be much abused by those seeking to earn 'brownie' points by including in the circulation those *they* think should know, those *they* would *like* to know, and those *they* would like to impress. By its very nature, that can cause ill feeling and mistrust, escalating an already delicate situation into something totally out of proportion with the seriousness or otherwise of the original subject matter.

Combining the email with the mobile phone is also breeding in many people, especially more senior executives who should know better, a feeling of being indispensable. Laptops and mobiles are taken on holiday, as well as on business trips so that 'I can keep in touch'. Delegation of authority and responsibility is thus watered down in the process – there is less need to pass on responsibilities to subordinates whilst out of the office, and as a consequence less opportunity for those subordinates to learn, either by their mistakes or by their successes. Who knows what Jones is capable of, if Jones is never allowed to run the shop properly when the boss is away? This in turn breeds a far less capable second tier of command than would otherwise be the case and the feeling of being indispensable is strengthened accordingly. It may well be *technically* feasible to contact the managing director as he sits in business class on an Airbus 380 two hours out of Singapore, but the real question to be asked – is he really in such a situation in a position to make rational decisions based on all the facts and relevant data?

Emails between companies, chasing accounts or acknowledging orders, or whatever, are business letters, no more and no less. As such they deserve exactly the same care and attention to content, spelling, grammar and tone as would be contained in a traditional printed and posted communication. The only difference is that the information contained in the letter is transmitted in a different way. What they are most certainly NOT are invitations to Nicola's party, or a catch up on the goings on in the stationery stores.

The future of emails is secure and assured – what will continue to be developed over the coming years, however, is an increasingly busy training industry in their correct use. Technology can be said to be outstripping our ability to cope with it professionally and effectively. Misuse of emails can seriously damage your wealth!

BETTER CUSTOMER CONTACT

The future of collections lies in effective and meaningful customer contact. Modern technology, correctly used, will enable this to continually improve, but above all else, training in all the relevant skills will assume ever-increasing importance. Improvement in techniques and disciplines increases the prospects of successful collections, combined with keeping the customer happy and ready to order again.

Training and experience go hand in hand, and it is an interesting phenomenon of today that the decline in the strength of company and public pension schemes is forcing employees to plan for later retirement rather than early retirement. This in turn has led employers to rediscover the value of experience, and the value to be gained from keeping on the old hands with a view to them passing on all they know to those who will follow. If the future lies in training to acquire the right skills, it most certainly also lies in trainers with those skills being both allowed and able to pass them on.

INSTITUTE OF CREDIT MANAGEMENT

Introductory Credit Management: Diploma Level 3

Recurring themes in Level 3 examinations have always been around the two topics of invoice design and statement design, with candidates expected to be able to define the importance of content and clarity – what fields should be on an invoice and why? What is the purpose of the statement and how should it be designed for greater effectiveness?

12

Telephone Collection

Glen Bullivant

• The telephone • Staff • Making the call • Customer excuses • Win-win • Conclusion •

The Telephone

Over many years, successive inventions and innovations have contributed to the changing face of credit management. The principle of money owed and money due to be paid is as old as the hills, and the need to remind buyers of their obligations is likewise not new. What has also not changed is the constant search to find better and more productive ways of communicating with customers. However, the *method* of communication keeps on evolving. Economic climates vary from time to time, cycles of boom and bust being a common feature of industrialised economies throughout the twentieth century, and the crash of 2008, though not quite the same as the hitherto cyclical boom and bust, was nevertheless in essence the same, but bigger and global. Those cycles themselves have led to the search for more effective means of getting through to customers to obtain due funds.

The telephone has long been recognised as having a substantial role to play in the improvement of cash flow, simply because it is an immediate method of contact. It is hard to think of a better way of getting the message across than actually talking to the person who can pay the bills, and extracting a payment or a firm promise there and then. There is no risk of letters going unanswered or getting lost in the post, faxes unread, or emails ignored. We have the advantage of talking to the customer now, right this minute. The telephone can bypass or link up with a normal collection process which produces a pattern of reminder letters, and as such offers an unscheduled, spontaneous and persistent method of cash collection. The instrument itself continues to develop into sophisticated and high-tech areas of design and capability, and now also allows visibility between the caller and the called. Deregulation in the provision of telephone services created fierce price competition between service providers, which in turn has had a dramatic effect on prices – making the telephone way of collecting cash even more cost-effective.

The main pitfalls lie in the hands of the untrained or the unwilling. Even in the twenty-first century, there are people who are uncomfortable with the phone. Some feel the need to shout if calling long distance, and some do not like talking to a person they do not know, cannot put a face to or cannot shake by the hand. In the same way that the most respectable of people can become aggressive and intolerant the moment they get behind the car steering wheel, so some can act on the phone in a manner that they would never adopt in a face-to-face meeting. It may well be that the growth of the visual impact of videophones and webcam will go some way to converting what would otherwise be a telephone call into that actual face-to-face meeting, but progress on that front is slow – and, in any event, it is the actual anonymity of the telephone which will deter many from going down the videophone route.

The telephone of itself will not influence the hardened slow payers, certainly not on its own, but as part of the comprehensive collection armoury of letters, faxes, emails and personal visits, and in the right hands, it will continue to be the best way of persuading somebody to part with what they think is their cash, but which is actually our cash!

The question of when and how to use the phone in the collection process is fundamental. Because there is no guarantee that a reminder letter ever reaches the right desk of the right person, the sender has to decide when it is that no response will be forthcoming. The phone at least demands a reply, even if that reply is unhelpful, or even downright abusive. At worst it tells the collector something about the customer. In turn, that helps the decision about the next appropriate collection action. What cannot be tolerated is the attitude of 'wait and see'. The invoice should be paid to terms, and the longer the wait, the greater the expense and the smaller the profit. Sooner rather than later should be the watchword. And what better way can there be to explain the situation and develop personal contacts than by telephoning?

Staff

Just because everyone uses the phone in their private lives, it would be entirely wrong to assume that anyone can collect funds by phone, and that all that is needed is a telephone, a telephone number and an amount from the ledger. The task does not suit everybody, so to sort out who is suitable and to get the best out of them it is necessary to look closely at:

- the way staff are selected and controlled;

- the way staff are trained and supported;

- the development of techniques for collecting and overcoming objections.

SELECTION AND CONTROL

These days, practically everybody has a telephone at home, and/or carries a mobile phone wherever they go, but this certainly does not mean that everyone knows how to use a phone persuasively and effectively, such as for selling or collecting debts. On the contrary, it takes a certain kind of person to be able to use the phone to its full potential – no sales director would employ telesales staff without ensuring that they have had the right experience or are being given the right training. No less important is getting the right people for the collection role. Outgoing and persuasive staff must be selected who can cultivate and maintain a high level of cash intake month after month, and who have the ability to communicate with any required level of management. Staff need to be trained in the techniques of collection as an activity needing specific communication skills, not just handled by any person in the office with spare time!

Techniques are needed to ensure that every call objective is met, customer barriers are overcome and collection is successful. It is not a matter of simply learning a few lines from a script. Every call is potentially different, and a script will be of no use except in the most straightforward situations – and in collections, very few situations prove to be straightforward! At one time, call centres and call centre staff were coached in keeping to a script, but more and more companies have recognised that the listener can not only detect a script when it is being repeated parrot fashion, but can also easily deflect the caller by calling the bluff of the script. That not only in effect terminates the call, but also severely reduces the credibility of both the caller and the organisation he or she represents.

Staff selection begins with a clear job specification and a personality profile. Both indicate the kind of person needed to fulfil the role. Some questions to consider:

- To whom is he/she responsible?

- What daily volume of telephone work is expected?

- Is it a solo or a team task?

- What level of responsibility would he/she have?

- Does the job title describe the authority needed in the role?

- Is there sufficient cash collection activity to utilise all working hours?

- What training is needed, and by whom?

- Is there a meaningful method of control and motivation?

- What is the likely/possible career path?

Some form of control is necessary to ensure the success of any telephone collection activity. This may be a simple brief daily activity sheet, but thought should be given to the purpose, not just the record. The best control methods are seen to guide personal development, and not just time-wasting forms filled in and never seen again. The telephone collector's ability should be judged on the number of payment commitments obtained each day, and the proportion of those commitments which actually turn into cash received. Therefore, the control should:

- stimulate constant interest to achieve the workload;

- motivate to produce more than the previous best;

- develop confidence, pride and responsibility;

- keep a constant record of names/dates/times and results of telephone contacts;

- increase liaison with management;

- ensure the collector keeps a regular note of conversion rates;

- give an easy visible check on the amounts promised/collected;

- achieve ongoing job satisfaction.

The controls should be visible to the collector, and not held in secret by management. If the collector knows that the control sheets are being analysed, then he/she can be aware that results are being judged. The data can also form the basis for discussion points during personal training, with strengths recognised, weaknesses identified and the appropriate development undertaken.

TRAINING AND SUPPORT

No salesperson would be sent out into the field on their first day without training and support, so why should any collector be expected to pick up the phone and dial? It is intolerable that so many companies pay such scant regard to this aspect of collection work, and no surprise that so many fail because they have neglected the right level of investment in such a fundamentally important area. To take the salesperson/cash collector comparison further, it is certain that in any given working day, the collector will contact many more customers than the salesperson. No salesperson would consider meeting a client without planning the visit, and checking on names, previous correspondence and problems. Armed with the same, the collector can confidently begin negotiation, and the skills then used will ultimately decide success or failure.

The call may take a few minutes, but the collector has only a few seconds in which to stimulate sufficient interest to hold the attention of the listener. For that reason, any slap-happy 'dial and try' type of approach is doomed before it begins. Telephone collection is all about training – induction training, ongoing on-the-job training and team motivational training.

Company induction training is becoming more widespread. Any new employee should go through some sort of induction process in most organisations, to introduce them to the company, its products, its culture, its policies on health and safety, fire drill, its position in the market place, and so on. Equally, induction also involves introduction to work colleagues, both in the immediate context of actual department and in a wider sphere. When the new collector is first introduced to colleagues, a good induction programme will ensure more rapid understanding of the job and the importance placed by the company on the cash collection process. Particular emphasis should be given to overcoming customer excuses and the vital role of cash to the company. It is beneficial for the collector to be able to go out and visit customers with the field sales force. This gives the collector the chance to develop mental pictures of customer types when negotiating with them on the phone at a later date, and it also provides an opportunity to be introduced to the customer as the person who will be looking after their account. Visual contact usually results in better returns and is an effective method of maintaining a high level of goodwill.

Briefing on the type of customer is useful as it affects the approach needed for collections. For example, is the contact a sole trader handling their own money, or an employee in the accounts payable department of a large multi-national? Does he or she work unsocial hours and is the timing of the call crucial in order to catch them?

Once the collector begins work, training must be personalised to identify and rectify any working weaknesses. This should be done early before any bad habits take hold. This individual training *must* be handled personally by the credit manager or section supervisor with the appropriate experience and *not* by another collector with a few more months' experience. During the first few weeks, worries concerning the job may develop and it is *only* the credit manager who can really deal with them. Each collector should have an individual training file containing the appraisal form, reliably updated after each training session. The appraisal contains constructive suggestions for improvement together with objectives to be achieved before the next training session.

The appraisal and observation process cannot be undertaken by simply sitting next to the collector and listening to what he or she is saying – one half of any telephone conversation is misleading at best, and likely to be completely misjudged at worst. It is technically feasible to listen in to both sides of the conversation with the right equipment. This is common practice in modern call centres, for example, and indeed it is also common practice for telephone conversations to be recorded for training purposes. If this is the practice, both participants should be informed, that is, both the caller and the recipient of the call.

The essence of training is the collector's motivation in knowing that he or she will regularly have the undivided attention of the manager. During these sessions, the activity control sheets or record can be examined and discussed.

It should also be recognised by management that any telephone work can become repetitive, as well as stressful, and variety should be available both in content and timetable. New stimuli should be introduced at intervals, with wall graphs or similar displays showing time and intervals spent with individuals.

These act as a good control for the manager and can be seen by staff as part of their regular development.

Arranging training for the telephone collection group is an integral part of the credit manager's responsibilities. If the team of collectors consists of more than a certain number (four is usually seen as the benchmark), the most experienced should have daily control, with the line of responsibility being clearly defined for any new member joining the group.

A good way of building team spirit as well as individual confidence is to hold regular group meetings to discuss recent successes, the latest customer excuses and ways that others have used to overcome them. Each member of the group should feel able to contribute to the discussion, encouraged to make a small presentation if so desired, and made not to feel in any way inhibited. As well as increasing their confidence and adding substantially to the group's body of knowledge, it has the added bonus of allowing the credit manager to identify the movers and shakers, leaders and followers.

DEVELOPMENT AND TECHNIQUES

The importance of techniques and the development of those techniques in collection staff cannot be overstated. This is gone into in some detail later in this chapter, but at this stage recognition has to be given to the importance of such development. No business ever stands still, and motivation plays a major role in all working lives. Motivational aids can be of great value but must be seen to be fair in that all members of the team have a chance of doing well. Financial incentives can be useful, but should be varied – once they become accepted as standard as far as pay is concerned, they lose their incentive effect. There is also the competitive element to consider, and 'fair' means a level playing field for all collectors – a similar spread of 'easy' and 'tough' accounts. If, however, aids to motivation encourage best practice in achieving success, then they are of value. Best practice has to be the aim of all employees, and the target is to have a department of collectors, each motivated, each trained and each capable of moving forward.

Training and motivation requires support, and not just from immediate line management. The board, in agreeing the credit policy, are implying commitment and active backing for that policy. This does not just mean spending money on fancy computer systems or office water coolers – it means recognising that training is an investment, just as necessary as expenditure on a new lathe or production facility. It also means the education of all involved in the sales process to ensure that not only do they themselves understand the company's terms and conditions of sale, including payment terms, but that sales personnel in particular are trained to explain that in detail to customers at the time of making sales. The right information in the customer's hands at the beginning, and the collector knowing that it is, makes the collection process easier, which means a better cash intake. A sale is only completed when that circle has been squared!

Making the Call

PREPARATION

Golden rule number one is always going to be about preparation. The decorator will invariably achieve a better result if the surface is prepared before the paint is applied, and no collection call should be undertaken before certain processes have been gone through:

- clearly define the objectives of the call, primary and secondary;

- know who is the decision maker, who can actually make the payment;

- prepare for likely non-payment excuses;

- be in the right frame of mind to suit the objectives;

- plan the best time to ring (by knowing the customer and/or their business or trade);

- have the correct telephone number;

- have the name, extension number, job title or position of the customer contact;

- be prepared for an alternative contact;

- be away from all noise and distractions;

- have to hand details of the outstanding account, including the items which are due or becoming due, as well as any items which are overdue;

- have to hand invoice numbers and values, together with customer order numbers;

- know the customer credit limit and risk category;

- have details of the last payment received, date, value and items cleared;

- know the details of the last telephone contact, including any undertakings given;

- also be aware of any queries raised and resolved, together with dates;

- do not chew gum (or anything else);

- smile.

It is important for the collector to be completely clear about his or her company's payment terms as well as the customer's credit history. What efforts have been made so far to obtain settlement? Is the contact at branch or head office level? Does the customer have a prompt payment list (note: it *will* have, whatever they say!) and how does one get on to it?

There are other issues that the collector should be familiar with as part of preparation and knowing the customer. Everyone is familiar with computers these days, but is there any compatibility between the buyer's system and the seller's? Comparison of accounting cut-off dates can be interesting – if the seller cuts off at, say, 20th of the month, and the buyer works to calendar month accounting, the collector needs to be clear about invoices which are due, overdue and not yet due – the two systems may well age in a different way, and with the best will in the world the buyer is not going to accept an item as overdue if his system shows it as only just due. Be sure that the customer knows how and where to pay (just as important as when, but often overlooked). Above all, remember that the objective of the call is to get the customer's commitment to pay the account in full.

Let's just repeat that:

The call objective is to get the customer's commitment.

Confidence is a key element in telephone collection, and preparation includes company support for the activity itself. It is obvious that full and accurate, up-to-date debt information is essential, but just as important is the knowledge that immediate superiors will support the collector's decisions and/or threats of subsequent action. The collector should know his or her own lines of authority and discretionary behaviour – the parameters for negotiating with customers should be quite clear. Sales can also support, by ensuring that the collectors are aware at all times of any 'special' deals which have been arranged for individual customers, or if any customers are the subject of any current special treatment.

Full preparation leads to the next stage, that of actually reaching the decision maker. The fact that he or she *is* the decision maker has already been established, and now the purpose is to make effective contact. The collector should be clear as to how to approach the contact – surname, title and first name – and the collector should also be sure that this is the right person to speak to. It is not uncommon, in family businesses, for father and son, say, to share the same names, and if the desired intention is to establish a dialogue and ongoing relationship (which it should be), then getting the right person at the beginning is obviously important. Remember, too, that there may well be someone other than the actual decision maker who could be worth cultivating, and may be of assistance in the commitment to pay process – secretaries, personal assistants, wives/husbands, colleagues, superiors, fellow supporters of the same football team and so on.

You only get one chance to make a first impression!

The first impression at the start of the call will set the scene – first impressions always count, whether meeting face-to-face or speaking on the phone. A business can be judged (often unfairly) by the telephone manner of the switchboard operator, the salesperson, the distribution manager. There is growing unease nowadays about both call centres and the 'press 1 for sales, 2 for service' syndrome which seeks to remove the human being as much as possible from the customer-supplier interface. That in itself is defeating the object of one-to-one service, and certainly has no place in the collection process – the collector, however, may well have to negotiate this automated quagmire in order to reach the desired contact, and any frustrations experienced in the battle against technology must not be carried forward into the actual conversation. All the more reason (going back to preparation) to have direct line or extension numbers already known – mobile phones are often used as the best way for some to make contact.

The 'body language' of the telephone is the tone of voice, and that tone should be displaying the firmness needed to gain commitment of the overdue debt. Voice projection, tone and emphasis must be correct, reflecting the company's image and attitude towards the debt. It does not impress, nor does it convey any degree of either professionalism or impact, to use slang words or phrases – you can say 'hiya' to mates at the disco if you like, but not when making a professional collection call. Friendliness is in the voice, not in the casual jargon. Equally, the caller is *not* reading from a set script – the curse of the age has to be the uninformed, uninterested and downright bored speaking to others in dull monotones, and intent on getting through the strictly laid down dialogue before being interrupted or pausing for breath.

The call should be timed to catch the customer at his most vulnerable. An early morning call at the start of the working day shows how seriously the account situation is being taken by the supplier, and gives the customer all day to arrange payment or sort out the query which has caused its delay.

Full preparation means that the collector will have everything to hand when making the call, so there should be no reason to leave the listener hanging on while something is looked up. It is *very bad* practice (as well as inefficient) to leave the customer 'alone' on the phone – the contact has time then to think up further excuses, or just simply hang up.

THE CALL

When through to the right contact, it is for the caller/collector to control the conversation and develop the dialogue. Mention the exact amount of the debt at the start of the call, again during the call and yet again at the end of the call when confirming the amount promised.

The key to controlling the conversation lies in asking 'open' questions, not 'closed' ones. Open-ended questions are used to elicit information, for example, '*Where* did you say you sent the cheque, Mr Brown?'; '*Which* branch was handling your query, Mrs Green?; '*When* will you be sending us the cheque, Miss White?'

Where, when, which, how and so on require an answer which is more than 'yes' or 'no'. Yes and no are the standard answers to 'closed' questions – 'Have you sent us the cheque?'; 'Did you send payment first class?'; 'Has our invoice been passed for payment?' Yes and no are easy answers for an uninterested customer to give. Furthermore, *never answer your own questions!* Use silence at the end of each question to add strength to the point being made.

Once the information is complete, then 'yes' questions can be used to lead the customer logically to where he will find it difficult to refuse to settle the amount in question, for example, 'Can I confirm that you did receive the goods from us during July?' (Yes); 'Do you agree that there is an outstanding balance of £650 now due for payment?' (Yes). Questions should be well-timed – developing the dialogue with well-timed questions implies strength, builds good customer rapport and draws out those problems, if any, that need to be resolved. As a consequence, any further delays in settlement of the account can be avoided. Some customers rely on excuses to avoid payment now, and the professional collector must be ready to handle these smoothly and confidently. Avoid, though, the impression of arrogance or instant dismissal of anything the customer says – he may not always be right, but he may not always be wrong, either! To handle an objection, query or excuse: *Listen* carefully to judge the customer's mood to establish the *real* reason for non-payment. There is a difference between 'listening' and 'hearing' – ask any parent of a teenager who has been asked to tidy up the bedroom! Many customers will exaggerate their problems (as part of any delaying tactic), and the collector should make notes as the 'excuse' is being related and plan how to tackle it as the conversation goes along.

Acknowledge the problem in a way that remains neutral. Any argument at this stage would simply be counter-productive – the customer *may* be right, but even if not, and the collector *knows* not, any sensible dialogue will be instantly ruined by an argumentative approach or response.

Apologise if it transpires that some promised action has not been carried out (for example, goods damaged have not yet been replaced and so on) and give an undertaking that such remedial action will be taken. Build integrity by keeping your word. Many collectors, and through them the credit management function, become the focal point for query resolution, and successful outcomes enhance the collection activity considerably. Customers know when somebody cares!

Develop questions to establish that the facts are correct, to involve the customer and keep control of the call.

Collectors should strive to be consistent in controlling the call throughout, retaining a calm but firm attitude. Being helpful in overcoming any problems that the customer has either experienced or perceived adds to the credibility of the collector.

CLOSING THE CALL

Once a positive dialogue has taken place, move quickly to conclude the call. The customer is already costing the supplier money because the account has not yet been paid; it is important that the collection call should be effective and as brief as possible to avoid larger telephone bills adding to the costs. It is, however, useful to recap at intervals during the call on the amounts and the timescales being mentioned. What is required is precisely the exact amount, when it is being sent and where. In other words, the collector needs to establish the exact facts, and not a vague 'a cheque is coming out this week' or 'the invoice has now been passed for payment' – what is required is: 'The cheque for £655.36 clearing all the August invoices will be posted first class tomorrow, the 23rd, and sent to your head office address in Manchester.' If it is needed, the customer can be reminded that payment now will save any further phone calls, no problems with supply and so on.

At the end of the call, the collector should get the customer to repeat the amounts, dates and destination of the promised payment. This greatly increases the customer's sense of commitment. Confirm that a further telephone call *will* be made if payment does not arrive when expected – though not always possible because of time constraints, many companies have found great benefit in their collectors actually calling to say 'thank you' when payment has been received. It certainly enhances goodwill.

Collectors (and managing directors and sales directors!) should *always* have uppermost in their minds the fact that it is their own money which is being asked for. The goods were properly ordered and properly delivered, and there is no reason at all why payment cannot be requested. Being defensive or apologetic about asking only shows weakness, and weakness allows the customer to take control of the conversation. The collector should also remember that making the call interrupts the customer's work. He may be very busy. So he should certainly not be antagonised by aggression or rudeness – how would the collector feel if he himself were interrupted on a busy day by some uncaring brute! Speak as you would be spoken to – most human beings are in fact nice people.

So:

1.   Get the customer's attention with your opening statement.

2.   Be positive rather than critical.

3.   Let the customer 'save face' whenever possible.

4.   Admit mistakes frankly if you or your company are in the wrong.

5.   Overcome objections and gain a firm commitment to pay.

Customer Excuses

The variety of excuses from customers in respect of non-payment is immense, and even those credit managers who believe they have seen and heard it all will readily admit that today they heard a new one. Excuses, however, can usually be grouped into a few categories, for which responses can be practised. Time constraints dictate that the aim is to keep control of the call, gain commitment to pay and resolve problems as they arise – the last thing any collector should have to do is fall at the first call with 'I will have to look into it and get back to you'. That response is more often than not due to lack of preparation before making that first call, but equally common is collectors' inexperience in instant, winning responses to excuses.

It is good practice for telephone collectors and credit managers to have regular meetings and engage in 'brainstorming' sessions as a group. Here they can openly discuss the latest excuses and how they dealt with them, thus setting a benchmark standard going forward for all to pick up on. It is a sad fact that many otherwise decent human beings move into a play-acting mode of pretence and deceit when asked to pay properly due bills. Although the goods or services have been provided at their own request, they appear to regard the agreed credit period as an optional date – on the one hand they insist that suppliers deliver on time, but on the other, they can pay when it best suits them.

Sometimes there is a genuine reason for delaying payment, though usually the collector has to deal with a resistance based upon flimsy or spurious reasoning. There have always been fashions in customer excuses for non-payment. One of the three greatest untruths has always been 'the cheque is in the post' (the other two are 'I am from head office and I am here to help you' and 'I will still love you in the morning!'). Requesting copy invoices became the norm, putting off payment for a while longer. The fax machine supplies an instant copy, and email attachments of scanned documents now deliver precisely what is requested without any delay. The 'we have cash flow problems' became popular in recent years as a reason for delaying payment, customers believing that such a plea would fall on sympathetic ears. The Insolvency Act 1986 precludes companies by law from having 'cash flow problems' – not being able to meet commitments as and when they fall due means that the company is insolvent, and therefore should not be trading and obtaining supplies on credit.

The problem really lies with the tolerant suppliers who seem content to be free bankers to their customers. The experienced collector, however, can assertively sort out the excuse, obtain payment and maintain the good commercial relationship.

Although the following is by no means a definitive list, the excuses, background and responses are aimed at guiding collectors along a successful collection route. The aim will always be to collect the cash, *and ensure future orders*. The reader will no doubt be able to add to the list with his or her own experiences – collecting will always be a learning curve.

Excuse 1: 'The cheque is in the post' or 'payment has already been made'. This could be true. If so, the customer will be satisfied to go through the questioning. If not true, he will recognise the thoroughness of the collector and think twice about using the excuse again. If it was only sent two days ago, it may still be wandering through the post. If apparently sent several days ago, either it has gone astray or was never actually sent. Ask for it to be stopped and another sent, or better still try to get commitment to direct debit methods. In any event the collector will state that a further call will be made in two days if not received. So:

Response 1: 'Thank you. To be sure that it has not gone astray and so that I can progress it at this end, could I ask you to tell me the date it was sent, the amount, the cheque number, where you sent it to, and was it sent first class?'

Excuse 2: 'Our payment terms are xxx days' or 'we always pay at xx days'. It will be necessary for the collector to explain the supplier's terms, and indeed explain in more detail the fact that the supplier's terms supersede those of the buyer. It may be also necessary for the credit manager to write or speak to the customer at a higher level, or get the salesperson to sort it out with his buying contact. The important point is that this wrong attitude to terms *must* be put right immediately. So:

Response 2: 'You know that sales are made on conditions of sale and you signed your agreement to our terms of 30 days on the credit application form. Our sales to you have always been on 30-day terms. May I confirm that the amount owing is now £xxx and is now xx days overdue?'

Excuse 3: 'Our books are with our auditors (or accountants).' The whereabouts of the books do not affect the customer's legal liability or their obligation to pay accounts when due. The collector should test the excuse with sensible questions to see just how robust the excuse is. This will throw up a different route to gain settlement. The more cynical may question how wages are being paid, and how business is being conducted from day to day. So:

Response 3: 'I can see how that gives you a problem. Can I confirm with you the amount owing to us is £xxx and is xx days overdue? May we have the name and phone number of your auditors as our discussion with them may affect what they are doing? Meanwhile, could you let us have a cheque on account for £xxx?' (a round sum a little less than the full debt).

Excuse 4: 'We are going into liquidation.' The collector needs to be absolutely certain that this is true. It can be said as a throwaway line, just to put creditors off, or it may be actually happening. The collector needs more information, and if still unclear, should speak to a director or owner. The real point is to push hard for payment now, while there may still be time. So:

Response 4: 'I appreciate that this must be a difficult time for you. Can we just go through the details on the statement and perhaps sort out the best way of making sure our claim is recognised by the Liquidator? Can you give me the name of the Liquidator and his telephone number?'

Excuse 5: 'We are waiting for our customers to pay us.' A very common excuse, and one often used by small companies when being asked for payment by big companies ('It's all right for you, you can demand your money, but I can't'). Collectors should not fall into the trap of feeling sorry for the customer, as trading terms were agreed and the customer is responsible for finding the funds on time. The customer should not just expect the supplier to wait and the collector may have to escalate to someone more senior as well as threatening to suspend deliveries. Many large companies, however, through their own professional credit departments, can offer advice and even assistance by utilising their own staff resource to help collect customers' debts. If this can be seen to ensure the customer's survival and secure ongoing business, it may have real possibilities. So:

Response 5: 'I can appreciate that cash flow is very important (particularly as you are a small company), and that it can be very annoying if customers don't settle invoices promptly. We are in the same situation and I'm sure that you don't expect us to act as your bankers. I just want to confirm with you that our credit terms are 30 days. This £xxx is now overdue by xx days and we are looking for complete settlement now.'

Excuse 6: 'We need a copy invoice (or proof of delivery).' Check, explore and clarify. 'Copy invoice, please' is a very successful delaying tactic used by many firms as standard on the first request for payment. The collector should always ask for the rest of the account to be paid anyway. Faxing copies of invoices (or proof of delivery) has been fundamental to the success of demolishing this obstacle in many instances, as email and scanned attachments have also proved to be. A note of caution, however. Part of preparation is knowing the customer's system. Some large organisations do not *register* incoming invoices on receipt, but only when the relevant department or person has authorised them for payment. Accounts payable staff in such companies may genuinely not know where the invoice actually is until it returns to them duly authorised. Therefore, when receiving a call from the collector, asking for a copy invoice is their way of trying to be helpful, not evasive – all they are asking for is an identification of the goods or services so that they can pin down where in their own organisation the offending document might be. If the collector knows that the customer operates this system, the request for copies will be routine, and not seen as a delaying tactic. So:

Response 6: 'Fine, I can fax that to you but as we are talking, can you just confirm that the overdue debt is for £xxx and that it is xx days overdue. Now, is this request for copies a one-off or are we sending our invoices to the wrong address? You'll get my faxed copy in the next few minutes. Can you confirm now that you can then let me have your payment in full? We have supplied you correctly and you have had the full credit period. If you can't pay today, I need to speak to someone who can authorise it. A manual cheque will do fine.'

Excuse 7: 'We are having a reorganisation here (or being merged or taken over).' This is probably just an excuse because companies in upheaval normally continue paying suppliers or announce beforehand alternative arrangements to suppliers. The collector should be willing to speak to a more senior person, showing that the supplier is determined to be paid – that willingness also pushes the excuse credibility to the limit. So:

Response 7: 'Yes, it can certainly be disruptive being reorganised (or taken over). May we just confirm that you have received our goods as per our account for £xxx which is now overdue for payment by xx days? To keep to the agreed payment terms, you should let us have your cheque straightaway. In your present state of upheaval, do you have to speak to a more senior person to get it authorised? I will, if it would help. A manual cheque will be fine.'

Excuse 8: 'Who is supposed to have signed the so-called agreement to your terms (or this order)?' This excuse could be actually genuine – it is not uncommon for accounts payable staff to automatically allocate payment terms to accounts as standard if no one has told them differently. On the other hand it may just be that person's ignorance of the terms agreement. The collector will need to stress that the terms are correct, the debt is fully payable, and be prepared to speak to someone more senior. So:

Response 8: 'There seems to be some confusion in your company about this. We would like to get it sorted out as much as you would. I can fax the original agreement to you after this call. I can assure you that it will show our standard terms but I appreciate that you will need to know who signed it. While we are talking, can you confirm the account shows £xxx overdue to us by xx days? As soon as you get my fax copy, can you release a cheque for the full amount?'

Excuse 9: 'The goods were damaged (or defective, a shortage, wrong price, too early and so on).' Defects should have been notified before the time was due for the account to be paid, and certainly before it fell overdue. Late disputes are often a delaying tactic, but can be bolted on to a genuine dispute, even if the query has been raised late. It is not unusual either for the customer to have already notified the supplier, perhaps the salesperson, pricing department or dispatch and they have failed to notify credit control. The collector needs to concede 'without liability' to get the balance paid, and commit to getting the matter resolved. So:

Response 9: 'I can well understand that you would not be willing to pay for an unsatisfactory delivery. Can you just let me know how much of the total balance is affected by the error? Have you notified us already of the error, because our conditions of sale do require you to notify defects and errors within 14 days? May I suggest you deduct the wrong items from the total and let me have a cheque today for the balance which is not under query?'

Excuse 10: 'There's nobody here to sign the cheque.' No company can afford to leave itself 'unmanaged' for more than a couple of days – it is far too risky, and the bank, not to mention shareholders, would not be happy at all. If they are really absent (and this should be checked most carefully), then they will almost certainly have left authority with others to sign, or even left a number of signed cheques with the accountant to meet special needs. The collector should regard his account as a special need – it is to him – and insist on somebody releasing the payment. Remember too, that we live in an age of mobile phones and emails. They exist to make contact possible anywhere. So:

Response 10: 'How long is he/they away? How are you making essential payments in the meantime?' (It is certain that they are – staff don't work without wages, for example.) 'Can we agree that the amount that should be paid to us is £xxx and that it is overdue by xx days. Who else can I speak to in Mr Brown's absence? Do you know what other names are on the bank mandate?'

Excuse 11: 'There is no order number on the invoice.' It is reasonable for customers to expect their order number be shown on suppliers' invoices for matching to orders. It may be possible to argue that what has been supplied was what was ordered, and that this justifies payment, but the reality is that the order more than likely required the number to be shown on all subsequent documentation, including the invoice, and the supplier has therefore failed to complete his part of the agreement. The collector should have picked this up in preparation for the call, and in the event of no order number having been given, tried to find out from sales any names of relevant people within the customer's organisation. In any event, the right information should be faxed as soon as possible. So:

Response 11: 'We do normally make sure that customers' order numbers are shown, but we appear to have slipped up in this case (or, no order number was quoted, but your order was from Mr Green). If you actually need the number to make payment, I will fax it to you in a few minutes. While we are talking, do you agree that the amount due to us is £xxx and that it is xx days overdue?'

Excuse 12: 'Your sales rep agreed that we could take another month to pay.' The collector may have to lose this particular battle in order to win the war. The matter should be escalated within the supplier organisation most strongly – sales are undermining the cash flow by extending unauthorised credit, and are seriously damaging the collector's credibility in the process. Any special deals should be at the correct level, and credit informed so that inappropriate collection activity does not take place. On the other hand, if the statement turns out to be untrue, the collector should get back on the phone to the customer immediately and clearly point out the customer error. So:

Response 12: 'Well, that is a problem because our sales staff are strictly forbidden to extend credit terms without the authorisation of the credit manager. This has not been authorised, so I must ask you to settle on the terms shown on the invoices. Was our rep Mr Dozy? I will speak to him or his manager about this.'

Excuse 13: 'We are changing our bank/don't have any cheques at present.' This can be a traumatic experience for any company, large or small, and impacts on both customers and suppliers. Banks are not the efficient organisations they once were, and the process of change is never as smooth as national advertising would have anyone believe. Nevertheless, no company should be in a situation where they have no access to their funds, nor the ability to operate a temporary cheque book. The collector faced with this scenario should show interest and acknowledge the situation (changing banks should be noted on the customer file), but not accept this as a reason for non-payment. The customer can always issue a temporary cheque, or request his new bank to make specific payments. So:

Response 13: 'I know that changing banks can mess things up for a while but I am sure you have an emergency cheque book or a few cheques to use in the meantime. Otherwise you will have all sorts of problems, besides our account. For my records, what is the name and address of your new bank? Do you agree that the amount overdue to us is £xxx and that it is xx days overdue? When can we expect your cheque?'

Excuse 14: 'There is a postal strike here.' It is good practice to rehearse various alternative transit methods for situations like postal strikes, transport disruption, or even critical time periods such as month-end deadlines. It impresses on the customer that the supplier is looking for ways all the time of getting properly due sums paid and in the bank quickly. Postal strikes are not alone these days in causing delays! So:

Response 14: 'Strikes are very disruptive, aren't they? Luckily, there are other ways of getting your payment to us. Would you be willing to contact your bank today and arrange a bank transfer to our account? I'll give you our bank sort code and account number, though it is shown on our invoices and statements. You may find this a more convenient method for the future, and you can always fax your remittance advice to me. If not, I can arrange for a courier/salesperson/ local branch/member of staff to pick up the cheque from you. While we are talking, do you agree that there is £xxx overdue to us by xx days?'

Excuse 15: 'The computer is down/it's in the computer, and so on' There can be little doubt that as each year goes by, the dependence upon computers increases. This means that more and more companies appear to be working in a culture which is completely governed by the computer, in spite of contractual obligations – any failure, shutdown or blip throws even the largest business into disarray. Thus it takes hard assertiveness to extract a non-computer payment, but the collector will always have right on his side – the customer is in the wrong because he still has to meet his obligations, whatever his system problems may be. Every single company, including the world's largest, can issue a non-computer payment if it really wants to – the method is called a cheque book and pen! So:

Response 15: 'Yes, I know we all depend on the computer, but you've had the benefit of the goods you ordered and the credit period as well. Do you agree that the overdue debt is £xxx? Can you arrange a manual cheque? Or does somebody else have to authorise that? Would it be easier for you if I speak to that person?'

Excuse 16: 'We can't pay. We have no money.' Well, at least he is being honest. Or is he? The liberal use of 'we have cash flow problems' as an excuse these days is troubling, in that many people now use the phrase without really knowing what they are saying. Are they genuinely having cash flow problems? As a limited company, that means real trouble. If it is just a throwaway line, do they really understand the seriousness if what they are saying is taken at face value? The collector has to throw the problem back at the customer to really get at the heart of it. The problem is theirs and suppliers should not readily accept the cash flow excuse without real information to substantiate it. Depending on their proposal, it may be possible to negotiate payment by instalments, keeping the end date short, of course. If a limited company, cash flow means real trouble, insolvency and wrongful trading perhaps, and the collector should speak to a director – the possibility of personal liability in the event of wrongful trading can have a very sobering effect. So:

Response 16: 'I'm sorry to hear that. You have always paid fairly promptly before. Can you tell me what has gone wrong? Do you agree that £xxx is overdue to us? What do you propose to do about this problem?'

On the subject of non-payment excuses of all kinds, the collector should always remember that he is the seller and, provided he has supplied as ordered, he has legal and moral right on his side. The customer must pay on the agreed terms. Not doing so is just as much a breach of contract, and illegal, as the supplier delivering different goods or charging a different price from that contracted. The due date can only be changed by the supplier, and because the supplier knows the real cost of credit, it is for him to decide what he can and cannot afford to do.

Subject to being a good listener and having a friendly tone of voice, the collector's attitude should always be 'sorry to hear that, but what are *you* going to do about it? We need your payment now, because we've done our bit and we are neither a bank nor a charity.' These words are not spoken, of course, but telephone collection must be approached with that in mind.

Win-Win

Not everyone is suited to collecting debts, yet many are expected to. Some are so timid that they prefer to send letters rather than have to speak to people about debts. The purpose of business is to make money, and collecting money on time is as much a part of making money as having the right product at the right price in the first place. It should be company culture from the top down – making money is what we are all about, producing profits for shareholders and salaries for ourselves.

Successful entrepreneurs have always kept one eye on cash flow, controlling stock and debtor levels, and utilising bank finance for expansion and growth, rather than just to keep the business running. Successful credit managers never have any hesitation in asking for money owed, it is part of their job after all, and the best actually enjoy the cut and thrust and the sense of achievement. Their positive attitude is founded upon a sense of justice, and their unwillingness to let debtors take advantage of their trust. Good payers should not have to subsidise poor payers, and no one knows this better than the successful credit manager. All this translates into: 'We've done what the customer asked. Now the customer must do his part. I'll ask him. Now!'

A collection is a negotiation, in every sense, usually straightforward, but sometimes more difficult. There are two parties, and in a contest between two parties one can be a winner, and one a loser. Or it can be a draw. It is much better if both win – if the real winner leaves the other person feeling good.

I lose – you lose is the worst possible outcome. This is where the poor attitude of the collector, whether aggressive or timid, gets no result and leaves the customer feeling dissatisfied about the conversation.

I lose – you win is the usual outcome with a *timid* collector, who is always apologetic, vague and good at backing down to avoid conflict. Even being actually refused payment is seen as being 'well, I tried' by this person, who should not be employed as a collector in the first place.

I win – you lose arises from an *aggressive* approach which may succeed with one collection this time, but does absolutely nothing for ongoing trading relationships and future payments. Indeed, it can be extremely damaging, and knowing that this collector is on the phone will mean that the contact person will inevitably avoid the call and go into a meeting. This approach is the best way in life to make enemies.

I win – you win is the sensible outcome of the collection call and one which does not damage the relationship. Taking somebody to court or stopping supplies is easy – anyone can do it – but it should only be done after all else has failed. Lateral thinking says that we don't head quickly towards threats of dire action, and at the start it should be assumed that they are not even available or possible, in order to encourage other solutions. Depending on what the other party is saying, the good collector is going for something now, the rest soon; or a special meeting to clear the air for the future; or taking the customer's proposal (just this once – it buys goodwill!). The collector uses assertive skills, not aggressive, and will listen, question, get clarification and speak confidently. The collector has right on his side, but there is no need to actually flaunt it. If the chat is expanded, and the debtor does most of the talking, then it is quite likely that a good solution will come out of the chat.

A modern approach to staff selection has been psychometric testing where attempts are made to identify those who are leaders, team players, thinkers, doers, plodders and so on. People are often classified as assertive, aggressive or timid. Collectors should be assertive, similar to good salespeople, and if it does not come altogether naturally to them, then to succeed they must practise dialogues to achieve the right effect.

Assertive: This means standing up for your own rights in a way that does not violate the other person's. The assertive person is *honest, direct* and shows *understanding*: 'As I see it...'; 'What are your thoughts on...?'; 'How do you think this will work?'; 'How does this affect you?'; 'How can we get round that?'; 'What can you do about this problem?' All these approaches come from sensible mindsets and are not either disruptive or destructive.

Aggressive: This means treading on the rights of the other person, believing that your opinions are more important than theirs. (Some readers may well recognise this as what many US companies call 'macho management'.) The aggressive person *blames, shows contempt for, attacks* or *patronises* others. 'Rubbish!'; 'Do it or else'; 'You cannot be serious'; 'It's your fault'; 'I suppose you can't help it'; 'If you know what's good for you'; 'I'm surrounded by idiots, and so on.' Sound familiar?

Timid: This means failing to stand up for your rights so that the other person easily disregards them. The timid or submissive person is *apologetic, cautious* and *self-effacing*. Timidity manifests itself in 'Sorry!'; 'I'm hopeless at this'; 'Leave it'; 'It doesn't matter'; 'Er, I'm not sure'.

THE VIDEOPHONE

The one thing that could change telephone collection activity more than anything else would probably be the wider use of the videophone. Here, the caller and the called would be virtually face-to-face, so that the effective collection techniques developed for the ordinary telephone would be enhanced by visual benefits. Because the telephone collector would now see, and be seen by, the customer, all that pre-call preparation would come into its own. Not least would be the right frame of mind and the right attitude.

People are generally more agreeable when meeting face to face, rather than hiding behind the anonymity of the phone. Body language, facial expressions, the smile, the eyes, all would lead to improved judgement as to truth and lies, honesty or evasion. In effect every videophone call would be a customer visit, and the same rules apply. Perhaps because of this very personal contact, the videophone and its webcam brothers would be highly unlikely to be welcome in accounts payable departments!

The technology has been with us for some years, and back in the 1990s it was thought that the whole use of videophones would catch on in a big way. It did not, and now looks increasingly likely to remain more a managerial toy for the foreseeable future than an actual practical collection tool. The jury is still out on this one – wait and see.

Conclusion

Be prepared: plan your call carefully; have the paperwork ready. *Be persistent:* don't be deflected; return to asking for payment. *Be prompt:* ring when you intend to; when you said you would. *Be urgent:* make the customer feel he must pay today. *Be courteous:* build goodwill and enhance your company's image. *Be tactful:* acknowledge comments; be polite even if the customer is not. *Be businesslike:* be friendly but always firm, not frivolous. *Be cooperative:* show you want to help in order to get paid. *Be repetitive:* keep mentioning the amount required.

Remember: Collection may be the end of one sale but it should also be the start of another!

INSTITUTE OF CREDIT MANAGEMENT

Introductory Credit Management: Level 3 Diploma

Questions regarding the use of the telephone as a collection tool, and/or the comparisons to be drawn between the telephone and letters as effective collection methods are one of the most popular recurring themes throughout the ICM Level 3 examinations in recent years. They take many forms, sometimes drawing on particular aspects of call making but a good general question would be:

What are the benefits of using the telephone as a method of cash collection? What preparation should be made prior to telephoning a customer? Identify those telephone techniques that will help in reaching a successful outcome.

13

Using Collection Agencies
Glen Bullivant

• The collection agency • The right agency? • Choosing the agency • The Credit Services Association •

The Collection Agency

It is almost inevitable in any trading entity that a proportion of debts will remain unpaid in spite of the best efforts of the collection staff. This need not be taken as a criticism of either staff or procedures in those businesses. Equally, it is not because of ineffective phone calls or reminder letters, lack of training or management support. It is simply to recognise that some debtors will not pay until they really have to, despite contractual terms.

Also at this stage of the collection process, the supplier has to weigh up the expense of staff resources, time and effort in pursuing the delinquent debtor, perhaps to the detriment of devoting time to other, more substantial debts, against the cost of using third-party assistance. In considering the next move, the supplier will take account of the value and volume of past dues, his need for speedy and efficient settlement and, perhaps just as important, their value as future customers.

It is by no means inevitable that the next move requires the use of legal action. Litigation may ultimately be the only remaining course of action, but it should always be regarded as absolutely the last resort. Indeed, in recent years the Ministry of Justice (MoJ) in England and Wales has made it quite clear, under the direction of UK Government policy, that it does not approve of the use of the courts for 'debt collection'. The courts exist, according to the MoJ, to settle 'disputes', such as breach of contract. We may well argue that non-payment of the account to terms is in fact a breach of contract – nonetheless, it has become a much more time consuming, not to say expensive, exercise to settle debt breaches of contract. So much more, in fact, that use of litigation really has to be the very, very last resort for any unpaid supplier. It is difficult to justify allowing further credit to a customer who only pays when sued, whereas a collection agency can be regarded as an operating part of the seller's collection team, so that trading may continue when a debt problem has been resolved.

Independent collection agencies are without doubt the most accessible and economically effective third-party debt collection assistance available. Their popularity with suppliers can be best illustrated by the fact that members of the CSA (see below) were instructed by clients in 2008 to collect some 20 million debts worth around £15 billion, a tidy sum by any measurement and a not insignificant contribution to the economic welfare of UK plc. Members also undertook 9 million traces in 2008 – that is a lot of people on the move! Use of an agency to collect a debt is in itself an indication to the defaulting customer that the situation has gone beyond merely being late and tells him that the supplier intends to pursue for recovery. The introduction of a third party into the supplier/customer relationship could well lead to difficulties in obtaining credit facilities elsewhere, a fact of which many experienced defaulters are well aware. It follows therefore that third-party intervention is usually enough to secure payment and litigation becomes unnecessary.

In many trades and industries, where the market is highly competitive and sales staff have to work hard for every scrap of business, credit managers are well aware of the need for preserving the customer base and goodwill, balanced against the obvious requirement of being paid for goods supplied or services rendered. In this situation, the professional collection agency acts as an extension of the credit department with the aim of securing prompt recovery and ensuring that the client benefits from continuing to trade with the customer, if that is what the supplier wants.

In a large company, the bought ledger manager or payments clerk has no personal connection with the cheque being sought for payment of the outstanding account and it does not affect his or her own financial affairs. Payment from an individual, sole trader or proprietor, however, is very much their own concern, and the question of continuing relationships can be more critical.

Litigation, on the other hand, is usually terminal in terms of supplier/ customer relations – it would be difficult to describe the High Court or the

County Court as an extension of the credit department! Indeed, reforms to court procedures in recent years (see Chapter 22) have laid great emphasis on the fact that the courts are not for debt recovery as such, but are intended for dispute resolution as indicated above. We can repeat the supplier's argument that the dispute he has with the customer is that the customer has not paid his account, and the only way to resolve that dispute is by use of the court. A dispute defined as non-payment, however, can well be resolved by a collection agency.

The Right Agency?

Some collection agencies specialise in either consumer or commercial debts, and some deal in both, including export. Clearly, there are different techniques required and the agencies' services are structured accordingly. Although there is a common thread of basic services which runs through all good agencies' operations, the credit manager must ensure that the agency selected is suitable for his or her needs.

The agency should offer to collect by a rapid and short-lasting series of letters, phone calls, faxes, emails or personal visits, or a planned combination of these. It should also be flexible about the way in which payments from debtors are passed on to the client – whether directly or via the agency – and when this should happen – either immediately, usually for single or very large amounts, or at agreed intervals when the volume is greater, such as consumer instalments. In any event, there should be a minimum of delay in the client receiving debtors' payments.

The agency should be able to respond immediately to telephone enquiries from clients and to operate an efficient system for keeping clients up to date with the status of accounts passed to it for collection. In return, the agency is entitled to be kept informed without delay of any payments received or arrangements made between client and debtor.

Many agencies use their own solicitors, so should be able to offer a good litigation service to clients should that be required – the advantage to the client of the agency having a good solicitor practice at hand (or even 'in-house') is that the relationship between the agency and the dedicated solicitor offers experience and dedication, as well as acting as a 'one-stop shop' for all collection matters. The professional agency offers an effective and close relationship to its clients to achieve the highest possible results in collections, resolution of queries or complaints as they arise and prompt processing of all monies collected.

Many agencies are empowered by clients to negotiate on their behalf to reschedule payment plans and arrange instalments with debtors. The relationship extends to the agency being able to advise the client on the most appropriate steps in particular cases, where legal action may or may not be recommended, based on the debtor's current position and quite possibly the agency's own experience with that debtor on behalf of other clients.

Choosing the Agency

Debt collecting by a third party is as old as the practice of credit – trusting customers to pay later for value received today. The image of the bully with the wooden club is also out of date and has no place in the professionalism of the activities of modern collection agencies. On the contrary, it is that professionalism rather than thuggery which explains the success of the collection agency industry. Any illegal or unethical actions taken by a disreputable debt collector reflect just as adversely on the instructing client as they do on the thug himself. Turning a blind eye to unacceptable third-party practices may seriously damage the client's business health.

In the nineteenth century, there was a growth of mutual societies formed to operate on a non-profit basis for the benefit of subscribing members. This was a time of 'high' interest rates (4 per cent was considered excessive in the 1830s and 1840s!) and many business failures, including banks. These trade protection societies, as they were known, flourished throughout the UK, collecting debts and collating information on debtors for members. The most notable of these was the West Riding Trade Protection Association (WRTPA), established in the city of Leeds in 1848. Mutual societies, such as the WRTPA, worked on behalf of their members, so the relationship between member and society is different from that of commercial collection agencies. Only subscribing members were entitled to use the societies' services. By the end of the twentieth century, nearly all had been absorbed into larger commercial agencies.

As far as commercial agencies are concerned, the seller is not tied to that agency for specified periods of time and is free to use the agency as frequently or infrequently as required. Most agencies work on the basis of 'No collection – No fee' and only charge a negotiated and agreed rate of commission on actual recoveries. In other words, it is possible that an unsuccessful collection attempt costs nothing (up to the litigation stage) – yet for no fee at all, the seller has discovered that the debtor has gone away or has no assets worth pursuing in court, thus saving substantial court costs and further delays.

Commission rates are usually subject to negotiation and depend on a number of factors, such as the number of accounts to be passed for collection on an ongoing basis, their average value and extent of being overdue. The older a debt, the harder it is to collect, and as much effort can be involved in collecting £100 as £100,000. Many agencies therefore offer a sliding scale of commission, with minimum and maximum charges. As a doorstep collection service for consumer debts is clearly labour-intensive, this service is normally more expensive, albeit very effective for certain debts.

As commission rates are usually negotiable, clients should always be aware that they will get what they pay for and the lowest commission rate does not necessarily mean the best service. Indeed, the highly professional agencies invest heavily in skilled staff and the latest technological developments, so that cut-throat commission rates are as damaging to the industry as are disreputable operators, which is ultimately to the detriment of services available to clients. At the other end of the spectrum, requests for large lump-sum fees up front should be refused and a 'no questions asked' service is a sure sign of dubious methods, and to be avoided.

Credit managers should choose an agency which is licensed to collect debts by the Office of Fair Trading (under the Consumer Credit Act 1974 and 2006) and one which has professional indemnity insurance with directors, partners and staff fully bonded. The agency should operate an audited trust account for banking money collected on behalf of clients and should itself be well established and financially sound. Prospective clients should take out credit checks as they would on a potential customer and ask for sight of the agency's accounts. A visit to the agency's premises is of great value, to assess the methods and the technology used, the professionalism of the management and staff, and whether their collection attitude matches the expectations of the client. The prospective client should also be enabled to contact one or two other clients of the agency to obtain background data and references. There is no substitute for a personal recommendation of an agency from a respected source.

An agency may offer additional services of benefit to the credit manager, such as credit reference and tracing facilities, and, as already stated above, its own solicitors specialising in debt work. As the agency should always complement the credit manager's own department, it is essential that the agency's efforts tie in with action already taken by the seller.

The Credit Services Association

The collection agency should be a member of the Credit Services Association (CSA), the body which monitors the activities of its members to ensure compliance with a strict Code of Practice, recognised by the Office of Fair Trading. Prospective members are vetted for ethics, financial stability and operating methods. The Association outlaws all dubious practices and is committed to the skill and professionalism of all members and their staff in the performance, including its own education and training courses, of their collection and other activities. To this end, the CSA has close working relationships with several other organisations and professional bodies, including international organisations. Some reputable agencies, for their own reasons, are not members of the CSA, but membership should be regarded by prospective clients as highly desirable, if not a prerequisite.

Members of the CSA offer a wide range of credit-related services, including credit investigation and status enquiries, company searches, tracing, bailiff work, debt collection, debt purchase and debt outsourcing, credit insurance, and many aspects of credit control, training and support.

Details can be obtained by contacting the Executive Director, Credit Services Association Ltd, Wingrove House, 2nd Floor East, Ponteland Road, Newcastle-Upon- Tyne, NE5 3AJ. Telephone: 0191 286 5656; Fax: 0191 286 0900; Website: www.csa-uk.com.

Using an agency as an early line of attack on book debts makes sound commercial sense. Chosen wisely, this not only assists in improving cash flow, but also in keeping valued customers intact, wiser than before and probably less likely to default in the future!

INSTITUTE OF CREDIT MANAGEMENT

Though there have been no recent examination questions relating specifically to collection agencies and their use (this is a small part of the ICM Level 3 syllabus), the Distance Learning Notes contain self-test questions for those studying: What factors should a credit manager take into account when choosing a debt collection agency?

14

Planning, Measuring and Reporting Debtors

Glen Bullivant[1]

• The need to plan debtors and report the results • The days sales outstanding ratio •
Budgets and reports • Measurable items •

The Need to Plan Debtors and Report the Results

This chapter was originally introduced by Burt Edwards with the following
quote: 'By achieving the planned debtors level, month after month, the Credit
Manager is contributing greatly to profit by *guaranteeing* the intended cash
inflow – a very powerful aid to any company.'

Debtors are at the heart of any company, trading on credit terms. They are a
large asset but also vulnerable, being a rich vein of unborrowed cash with built
in susceptibility to loss due to failure and slow payment; the link between sales
and profit but subject to the payment whims of customers.

Debtors – that is, unpaid sales – should always be a priority for the constant
attention of senior management, to be monitored and supervised as any other
valuable company asset. Debtors, called Receivables or Accounts Receivable
in many companies, say so much about the way the business is managed
and controlled to any analyst, consultant or bank manager – it beggars belief
therefore that some companies do not bother to measure or analyse their
debtors at each month-end, let alone plan those month-end results in advance.
All they look at is just the total of the Sales Ledger to make up their monthly
balance sheet.

---

1   From the original by Burt Edwards.

The better managed, which should include the larger organisations, go to great lengths to prepare for the debtors volumes they want, so that they can plan the borrowings and interest expense needed to support that level of credit sales. They analyse the month-end Sales Ledger into types of debts, their age, the ratio to sales made, and make comparisons with previous periods, budgets and forecasts. Various explanatory commentaries are written to be acted upon by the appropriate people.

To explain the difference in approach from the worst to the best-managed companies, it is probably true to say that the more analytical companies have evolved over the years and experienced enough bad debt panics and cash flow crises to teach them to keep a close eye on their big cash asset. This suggests that companies that do not bother will suffer those panics and crises at some point – and clearly in many cases, cash flow/borrowings crises prove fatal.

To put it into the simplest terms possible, so that even the most naïve senior management can understand, it is just irresponsible *not* to monitor the company's largest current asset.

There are two powerful measurement tools:

1.   the DSO, or Collection Period, shows the speed of converting sales into cash;

2.   the Aged Debt Analysis shows the quality of the asset (that is, older = profit leakage).

In principle, a company's debtors asset is worthy of senior management attention, to keep it as slim and current as is commercially possible. In companies that can afford specialist staff, the duty is that of the credit manager, reporting to a director and fully supported in daily control matters.

A company has to decide what it would like to see as the ideal shape and size in future months. Whereas the overall requirement is the fastest possible cash inflow, which is demonstrated by the ratio of days of sales unpaid, or DSO, debtors can also be planned ahead in terms of their age groupings.

Good credit management from the beginning means planning future debtors, taking the management control task right up to the end. That is to say reporting the actual debtors results and commenting on them. This approach provides a sound basis for improvements to procedures, rather than general neglect interspersed with panic collection blitzes on the Sales Ledger.

Most financial planning commences with a sales budget, usually for 12 months ahead. Planned costs are then input to arrive at net income. Two of the key costs are Interest on Bank Borrowings and Provisions for Bad Debts (that is, totally uncollectable sales). The interest item is an overall figure for all the company's net working capital, but is largely caused by waiting for sales to be paid (the Collection Period for debtors).

Planning cash inflow and outflow, leading to how much is needed in bank borrowings, essentially requires a budget for debtors. The credit manager is the best qualified person to produce the debtors budget because of his or her detailed knowledge of the collectability of sales and of the payment habits of customers for projected sales.

The Days Sales Outstanding Ratio

The ratio between sales and debtors is decided by credit terms and collection performance, which combine to give the time it takes to turn sales into cash, expressed as a number of days, weeks or months.

That DSO ratio is the prime tool to measure efficiency in managing debtors. The existing level can be applied to the sales budget to produce a reasonably accurate debtors budget, as well as interim forecasts.

The most common way of calculating the DSO is to take the month-end debtors figure and deduct the latest month's *total* sales, then the previous month's *total* sales and so on back in time until the debtors are used up. If all sales are being made on 30-day terms, then allowing for a level of overdues and disputed items, the debtors should equate to all the sales for the previous, say, 40 to 50 days. However, a mixture of longer terms and a few large accounts that pay very late can easily push the ratio up to 70 or 80 days.

The average for all UK companies has remained around the 70 DSO mark for a good many years, regardless of boom/bust, recessions, government initiatives, UK and European legislation. Most progressive companies know their own DSO and also the average DSO for the industry they are in, that is, for competitors selling roughly the same kind of products to the same range of customers. It follows that any company should aim at having a DSO which is better than the average for its industry – turning its sales into cash faster than the rival companies do.

Once the debtors budget has been accepted, the credit manager has an official yardstick by which to be measured and motivated. Staff and resources can then be organised to achieve budgeted levels each month.

Budgets and Reports

By achieving the planned debtors level, month after month, the credit manager is contributing to profit assurance by *guaranteeing* the intended cash inflow. This is a very strong contribution to the successful management of any business.

Since a seller is competing with other suppliers for the current cash of customers, actual results may be better or worse than the budget. It is important to know why, and monthly reporting should pick up the reasons for this. In turn, the monthly report should encourage action to be taken with delinquent customers, perhaps with Sales or Technical involvement.

The sequence for good budgeting and reporting should be:

1. Obtain the sales budget, by class of debtor (especially separate exports) and by month.

2. Apply the Collection Period (DSO), plus or minus expected changes.

3. Produce the budget for debtors by monthly total, DSO and percentage of overdues.

4. Report monthly actual results and compare them with the budget.

5. Explain any variances.

6. Identify actions to cure weaknesses.

Measurable Items

Performance can only be judged by those things that can be measured – it is objective, looking at numbers and from those numbers, the success or otherwise of any undertaking can be assessed. In terms of the company's debtors, the following are measurable:

- debtors expressed as a number of days of sales (DSO);

- overdue percentage of total debtors;

- aged analysis within total overdues;

- disputed debts as DSO and percentage of total debtors;

- debtors as percentage of sales;

- cash collected as percentage of cash collectable;

- bad debts and provisions for doubtful accounts, as percentage of sales;

- any of these by class of customers.

DAYS SALES OUTSTANDING (DSO)

Sometimes called the 'Collection Period', DSO expresses debtors as being equivalent to a number of days of sales. It is not affected by sales volume (more or less sales simply produce more or less debtors, not the ratio), but is certainly affected by the credit period allowed to customers and by the efficiency of collecting.

1. *Countback method* (see Figure 14.1): Since debtors relate mostly to the latest sales, the ratio is best calculated using latest sales rather than annualised or average figures. This is the calculation most commonly used in the UK and USA.

2. *Quarterly averaging method:* This is a way of calculating DSO if monthly sales are not available or not accurate.

$$\frac{\text{Debtors}}{\text{Sales last three months}} \times 92 = \text{DSO (68 in example)}$$

DSO	Bubblesqueak Ltd				August 20XX
A: Debtors total (£)					1,200,000
Equivalent to:					
Sales (£)			Days		
August	650,000		31		650,000
		Balance			550,000
July	430,000		31		430,000
		Balance			120,000
June	600,000		6/30		120,000
		Balance			0
	Total days sales outstanding		68		
B: Average sales per day £1 200 000/68 = £17 647 Overdues £230 000/£17 647 = 13.0 days sales Therefore current = 55.0 days					
Part A: Can be made as soon as the ledger closes. It shows that debtors are equivalent to 68 days of sales, despite payment terms of net 30 days. This means that tomorrow's sale will be paid on, average, 68 days later. Part B: Can be added when the overdue total is known. Expressing overdues as days of sales is more accurate than as a percentage of debtors. Current days of 55 indicate that some sales are on longer than 30-days terms, or that overdues are understated, or the books were closed late.					

Figure 14.1   DSO – the countback method

This averages the sales per day for the most likely period relating to debts and is slightly less accurate than Method 1 because it levels out peaks and troughs in sales.

The following shows an example of this (same figures used):

$$\frac{£1,200,000}{£1,680,000} \times 92 = 65.7 \text{ DSO}$$

3. *Annual averaging method:* This is a further way to calculate DSO when only year-end figures are known:

$$\frac{\text{Year end debtors}}{\text{Annual sales}} \times 365 = \text{DSO}$$

It compounds the weakness of averaging, as in the equation:

$$\frac{£1,200,000}{£6,165,000} \times 365 = 71.0 \text{ DSO}$$

4.   *Aged debt category method:* This method is preferred by some credit managers because it combines the total credit taken by customers with the ages of debts. The total debtors used in this method are made up of the residues of each month in which the sales were made. For example:

£000							
	August	**July**	**June**	**May**	**April**	**March+**	**Total**
Total Sales	650	430	600	550	510	620+	
Sales/day	21	14	20	18	17	20	
Unpaid	630	310	120	85	30	25	1200
Debt days	30.0	22.1	6.0	4.7	1.7	1.3	65.8

Total debtors £1,200,000 = 65.8 DSO

OVERDUE PERCENTAGE OF TOTAL DEBTORS

This is a not uncommon measurement of debtors, but in reality is somewhat meaningless. A typical remark is: 'Our overdues are only 12 per cent of debtors, whereas they were 15 per cent a few months ago.' It is meaningless because the ratio has variables. For example:

Total debtors   £1,200,000
Overdues   £120,000
Overdues per cent =   10 per cent.

But if current sales were £750,000 and not £650,000, the table would read:

Total debtors   £1,300,000,
Overdues   £120,000
Overdues per cent =   9.2 per cent.

An apparent improvement, down from 10 per cent to 9.2 per cent. Yet the overdue debts have not changed at all – the total debtors have increased because of extra new sales. The overdue percentage is dangerously misleading to use alone.

ANALYSIS OF OVERDUES AGEING WITHIN TOTAL OVERDUES

This is one of the most useful tools for improving overdues. Taking the total of all overdue debts, establish the amounts overdue in monthly groups, for example, 1–30 days, 31–60 days, 61–90 days, 91–120 days, 121 days and over. Then, express each age group as *a percentage of the total overdue*, as illustrated:

Total Overdue	Overdue Ageing				
	1–30	31–60	61–90	91–120	121+
£120,000	83 000	21 000	12 000	1 000	3 000
100%	69.2%	17.5%	10%	0.8%	2.5%

Ideally, any overdues should be *only just* overdue, that is, 100 per cent 1–30 days. Real life is different, of course, so monthly collection activity should concentrate on increasing the left-hand percentages at the expense of the right. Some credit managers budget certain percentages for each age category.

Golden rule: The percentages of overdues should always reduce to the right!

DISPUTED DEBTS

Most businesses suffer a continuing level of debts unpaid because of claims against sales or disputed account balances. Although claims are resolved sooner or later, a distortion of total debtor balances continues because of the inflow of fresh claims. It is important for budgets to take account of the running level of uncollectable cash due to unresolved disputes. The effect can be stated either as a percentage of debtors or as a number of days of sales, for example:

Total debtors	£1,200,000 or 68 DSO
Disputes	£48,000 or 2.7 DSO (or 4 per cent)

In other words, the company's borrowings could be reduced by 2.7 days of total sales value, if disputes were resolved straightaway. For internal action purposes, it is useful to age disputes in the same way as overdues, so that the oldest problems get priority, as they represent the most serious drain on profits, as well as the customers dissatisfied the longest.

To express disputed debts in either DSO or percentage terms is one of the most effective ways of bringing the problem of unresolved customer queries to the attention of senior management. Where companies have a high level of customer disputes, and a sales management reluctant to authorise credits ('don't want to reduce my sales figures this month') the DSO is higher than it needs to be. Time and time again, credit managers are judged on DSO and overdues – time and time again, those numbers are severely distorted by what is in effect uncollectable cash due to dispute. In other words, Mr Chief Executive, if we got it right first time we would have much improved cash inflow.

DEBTORS AS A PERCENTAGE OF SALES

For balance sheet comment and end-of-period reports, some companies express debtors as a percentage of annual sales, for example:

Annual Sales	£6 165 000
Debtors	£1 200 000
Percentage	19.5%

It is possible to divide the debtors into the sales figure and express the answer as the 'account turnover period' (see Figure 14.2).

If debtors equal 19.5% of annual sales, then,

100/19.5 = 5.13 times per year

or

£6,165,000/£1,200,000 = 5.13 times per year.

Figure 14.2   Account turnover period

This illustration shows that sales are turned into cash received, on average, 5.13 times a year. Although both measurements are valid for comparable periods, they are too loose to be of value in the credit department where more precision is needed from month to month. It is more motivational to express debtors as a number of days credit taken. However, it may be useful for finance directors to plan borrowings as a percentage of budgeted sales.

CASH COLLECTED AS A PERCENTAGE OF CASH COLLECTABLE

This ratio is valuable as long as the data can be assembled without disproportionate effort. If collectable cash can be calculated in advance, that is, debts becoming due in the month plus debts already overdue, it is useful, for subsequent forecasts, to record the actual collections made as a percentage of the collectable figure.

The resulting deficit (for example, 92 per cent collections = 8 per cent deficit) becomes fresh overdue debt for the following period. This procedure can be refined as an accurate forecasting tool, as illustrated:

Record the collected proportion of each month's sales, for example, August:

Collected in August: 5 per cent, leaving unpaid 95 per cent.

Collected in September: 20 per cent, leaving unpaid 75 per cent.

Collected in October: 65 per cent, leaving unpaid 10 per cent.

Collected in November: 10 per cent, leaving unpaid 0 per cent.

% unpaid	J	F	M	A	M	J	J	A	S	O	N	D	J	F	M	A	M	J
same month	98	98	97	93	95	93	95	95	95	91	92	89	97	98	96	93	94	93
previous month	80	77	78	75	72	73	71	73	75	68	66	67	81	78	79	74	71	72
2 months previous	16	14	12	10	9	10	11	10	12	10	9	8	15	15	13	11	10	11

Figure 14.3   Seasonal effects for cash forecasts

From the illustration, we can see that collections were heavy in the last quarter, October to December, but fairly poor in the early part of the year.

Payment of any one month's balance can be tracked by the left-to-right diagonal pattern, for example, November balances remained 92 per cent unpaid by the end of November, 67 per cent by December and still 15 per cent by January.

BAD DEBTS AND PROVISIONS FOR DOUBTFUL ACCOUNTS

Losses through bad debt are inevitable in any trading operation where the granting of credit is fundamental to profitable sales. What that means is that some of the 'planned income' (that is, income from sales) will be lost. By definition, bad debts are those sales which prove, for whatever reason, (usually insolvency) are uncollectible – difficult, well overdue accounts are not 'bad' unless and until they become uncollectable.

All sorts of company policies exist for making provision out of current income against future losses. In the total task of planning debtors, the credit manager should take account of possible losses and the reduction of net balances caused by deducting reserves or provisions.

There are two internal and two external influences on the amount of bad debt provision. From the company's viewpoint, there is the amount of profit the company can afford to deduct; and company policy may dictate a certain level of provisions, for example, 1 per cent of balances. Externally, the auditors will insist on adequate provisions, defined as leaving the remaining balances fully collectable; while the tax inspector will only allow provisions for specific bad debts against tax.

Some different approaches to Bad Debt Provisions are set out in Chapter 6.

DEBTORS RATIOS BY CLASS OF CUSTOMER

It helps to separate the different classes of debtors for budgets, forecasts and reporting results. This might be geographical, by product (or sales division) or by risk category.

For example, a company may sell to industrial, export and government customers, and also to associated and subsidiary companies in UK and abroad. The company in the example shown operates credit categories for the UK trade accounts only. The sales/credit analysis for August reads as shown in Figure 14.4.

	Sales £000 as % of			Debtors	
	August	**YTD**	**Total**	**£000**	**DSO**
Home					
North	160	1702	11.9	532	72
South	230	2554	18.0	670	65
London	390	4256	30.0	1170	68
Total	780	8512	59.9	2372	66
Export					
East	94	521	3.7	182	86
West	101	1609	11.3	644	98
Total	195	2130	15.0	826	96
Government	130	1406	10.0	334	56
Associates	191	2140	15.1	501	60
Total	£1296	£14,188	100%	£4033	68

Figure 14.4   Sales/credit analysis

The home trade sales in that chart are analysed by credit risk, as in Figure 14.5.

Area	Sales August	£000 YTD	as % of total	£000	Debtors DSO
North A	16	170	9.9	45	65
North B	95	982	57.7	258	65
North C	49	550	32.4	229	86
Sub Total	160	1702	19.8	532	72
South A	74	744	29.1	190	61
South B	116	1300	50.9	358	66
South C	40	510	20.0	122	76
Subtotal	230	2554	30.1	670	65
London A	80	860	20.2	215	62
London B	210	2228	52.3	590	68
London C	100	1168	27.5	365	77
Subtotal	390	4256	50.0	1170	68
Total A	170	1774	20.8	450	62
Total B	421	4510	53.0	1206	65
Total C	189	2228	26.2	716	78
Total	780	8512	100	2372	66
Notes					

1. This shows, true to form, that C accounts pay more slowly than B, who pay more slowly than A
2. There are regional differences, which warrant further investigation
3. The spread of business between categories shows North has too few 'blue chip' customers and too many risky one, requiring greater financial resources. South and London have better spreads. In all cases, the trend from period to period will show if the drift is towards better or worse risk customers.

Figure 14.5   Sales/credit analysis by risk category

BUDGETS FOR DEBTORS

A budget for intended debtors for the months ahead can easily be constructed from a sales budget for the same period. To that sales budget, the credit manager can apply historical payment trends plus his own foresight, market knowledge and opinions of sales management.

STEPS IN MAKING A DEBTORS BUDGET

List assumptions for the budget period (for example, DSO approach, overdues, market oddities and so on). Assess the DSO level for each month in the year ahead. Apply the DSO to the sales estimates for the preceding number of days, to arrive at the total debtors figure for each month.

Then, for further refinement (selecting as appropriate):

- Assess the level of overdues for each month – use average sales per day to calculate overdues value and percentage of total debtors.

- Split the first three bullet points between classes of customer and/or regionally or between business divisions.

- Assess disputed debts by DSO value and percentage for each month.

- Calculate cash figure for each month, as a result of subtracting debtors total from previous month's plus this month's sales.

- Assess transfers out to bad debt suspense and budget reserve against gross debtors to produce net debtors.

- Trim debtor budget where necessary to meet financial planning requirements.

SUGGESTIONS FOR DEBTORS BUDGETS

There are a number of ways in which the credit manager can budget debtors going forward, and many alternatives dependent upon the nature of the business, product, market place, customer base and so on. Whatever format is used, common to all debtors budgets would be the kind of assumptions it would be usual for credit managers to make. For example:

- DSO for home trade to be 10 per cent worse than last year, due to longer terms being granted and difficult trading conditions (then some detail to justify).

- Export payments to remain roughly the same.

- Government DSO will benefit from new paperwork system – 25 per cent faster payments.

- Major customers to buy less.

- Sales to marginal risks up by 20 per cent – effect of these on DSO to be calculated after discussing with sales staff.

- Transfer of staff functions to new computer system in mid-year could slow up collections for one to three months until teething over. Allow for this in June to September.

The credit manager would discuss these assumptions with the sales manager, seeking his input. That input might be, for example:

- Agrees that home trade will be worse in terms of DSO.

- Sales have more detailed estimates now available.

- Less business in USA and France, but increases in Scandinavia and Japan.

- Sales hope that the new paperwork system does benefit Government DSO.

- Sales do not agree definition of marginal risk customers. To discuss further.

- Sales to clear disputes faster. Plan closer collaboration with credit staff. (Collaboration then follows to agree on final assumptions to be built into budget.)

Given that credit and sales work together to forecast the debtors budget and DSO outcomes, the credit manager can budget in more detail, looking at the different classes of customers within the sales regions and consolidate into a final budget forecast.

CREDIT DEPARTMENT EXPENSE BUDGET

Whether the credit function is a separate department or part of a general accounts function, it is well worth identifying and controlling the cost of managing credit separately. Forms used for such department budgets would follow the style of the company for all departments. The subjects which can usefully be planned and measured on a month-by-month basis are:

- number of staff, part or full time (show as supervisory or not);

- salary costs – and related costs;

- computer and related equipment charges (these may be allocated centrally);

- telephone and post charges;

- travel and entertainment costs;

- credit insurance premium, if any;

- bad debt reserves;

- training costs.

The total costs for credit administration should then be related, on some standard form, to sales and debtors to provide measurements of efficiency from one period to the next, for example:

- sales made per credit person;

- debtors value per credit person;

- cost of department as a percentage of sales;

- cost of department as a percentage of debtors.

CREDIT OPERATING REPORTS

These are: accurate records of results means of reporting to top management action tools for the credit manager.

Where good budgets are in operation, reports should include variances from budgets and explanations of the variances. Computer outputs should be designed to match reports and reduce the time and expense of editing results, for example, due to date differences or different customer groupings.

Figure 14.6 illustrates a simple report layout showing various debtors results and comparing them with budget, the previous month and the previous year. (Note: in a business with seasonal peaks and troughs, comparisons with the same month last year may be more useful than comparisons with the month before.)

Bubblesqueak Ltd								
Item	Reference	Actual	Budget	Fav/ Unfav	Last month	Fav/ Unfav	Last year	Fav/ Unfav
1	Trade-current £							
2	Trade-o'due £							
3	Trade-total £							
4	Retentions £							
5	Non-trade £							
6	Suspense £							
7	B/D Reserve £							
8	Discounted £							
9	DSO Current							
10	DSO Overdue							
11	DSO Total							
12	Overdue %							

Figure 14.6   Debtor report

Reports for record purposes should be as detailed as possible, in a layout which will quickly produce the data needed for future research. Reports for action purposes should normally highlight only exceptional items needing attention, which some companies call 'red flag' items. Reporting upwards should show selected items of interest to top management. This should be *minimal key data* (not obscured by masses of detail); highlighted variances from budget and previous periods; and brief reasons for these. It makes sense to add a few lines of actions under way, to show the firm control of the asset and especially to mention any major customers giving severe payment problems or credit risk worries, so that the board is forewarned of possible shocks and may be able to contribute useful advice.

AGED DEBT ANALYSIS

This should have just one line per customer and debts aged horizontally, typically:

1. account number;

2. name (plus short form address if room);

3. payment terms;

4. sales code;

5. total debt;

6. current total;

7. overdue total;

8. overdue 1–30 days;

9. overdue 31–60 days;

10. overdue 61–90 days;

11. overdue 91–120 days;

12. overdue over 121 days;

13. credit rating;

14. credit risk category;

15. excess of debt over credit rating;

16. DSO for account.

The Aged Debt may be difficult if all 16 items are in strict columns – it is usual for the amounts (totals, due, 1–30 and so on) to be in columns and the additional items such as risk category, credit limit and so on to be extra lines under the customer name. Formats of aged debts reports vary enormously, but they should have ALL the above included. The reports are grouped to suit the business, for example, by sales office, geographical area, type of ledger and so on, with a final grand total.

AGED TRIAL BALANCE ANALYSIS

A one-page, clear display can easily be produced monthly from the Aged Debt Analysis. An example is given in Figure 14.7:

Bubblesqueak Ltd			Analysis of debtors			Dated:					
Item	Accounts	Balance	Current Reg Spec		Disp	O'due	1-30	31-60	61-90	91-120	120+
	1	2	3	4	5	6	7	8	9	10	11
	Trade Debtors										
1	Key										
2	Minor										
3	Govt										
4	Export										
5	Subtotal										
6	Non-trade										
7	Assoc. co										
8	Total gross										
9	Less; discounted										
10	B/D reserve										
11	Total net										
Remarks											

Figure 14.7   Aged trial balance analysis

DEBTORS REPORT

This report should compare the main debtor items with the budget and previous periods (see Figures 14.6 and 14.14).

The variance analysis detailed in Figure 14.8 shows that the over-budget debtors of £200,000 were due to sales exceeding budget by £300,000, but this excess investment is reduced (that is, improved) by achieving an actual DSO of 84 days against the budgeted 90 days, so generating an additional £100,000.

	£		
Actual debtors	1 400 000		
Budget debtors	1 200 000		
Excess investment	200 000	(poor credit control?)	
	BUT		£
Actual sales at budget DSO (90 days)			1 500 000
Less budget sales at budget DSO			1 200 000
Sales volume variance			300 000
Add: Debtors at actual DSO	1 400 000		
(say, 84 days)			
Less: Debtors at budget DSO	1 500 000		
		Credit efficiency variance	100 000
		Net variance (over-investment)	200 000

Figure 14.8   Variance analysis of debtors exceeding budget

DAYS SALES OUTSTANDING REPORT

As shown earlier, there are many ways of calculating the speed of collections, or days of sales unpaid. Figure 14.1 gave a sample form layout. Points to remember:

The resultant number of days is the equivalent of *all* sales for that preceding number of days, not the *unpaid* sales. The DSO is the time it takes to turn sales into cash. Despite the actual payment terms on a transaction, the average time it will take to be paid is the DSO figure for all debts. Discounted debtors and bills receivable not yet paid by customers should be added back to the net debtors to obtain a meaningful DSO, since they represent credit granted to customers, with a recourse risk.

ANALYSIS OF DISPUTED DEBTS

The purpose of the analysis of disputed debts is to expedite settlement of disputes. It can be produced either as a complete list or an extract of disputes above a certain value or age, as frequently as the user needs. For maximum effect, it should be circulated to Sales, Quality Control, the board and so on. See Figure 14.9.

Bubblesqueak Ltd		Disputed Debts	Date:	
Above £1000 A/C Customer	Reason for dispute – Action taken	Person responsible for clearance	Expected settlement date	Value
Subtotal				
Subtotal of sundries below £1000				
Total disputes				

Figure 14.9   Analysis of disputed debts

ANALYSIS OF RETENTIONS

Where a business has to agree retentions as part of contract conditions, it is essential to record them accurately in order to achieve payment when due. *Do not* treat them as mere underpayments to be chased up in future when time permits. A system of formal advice to the customer setting out the retention details and requesting payment in line with agreed dates needs a strict ongoing action report. Retention data can be tabulated in a monthly report to accompany the credit manager's debtors reports

SUSPENSE ACCOUNT REPORT

A suspense account is a halfway house for bad and doubtful debts, prior to writing them off. It is very useful for moving uncollectable debts out of the Sales Ledger, to achieve maximum focus for any further action and for making proper reserves. The actual write-offs are made from the suspense account against the bad debt reserves/provisions.

The timing of this report can be made to fit the company's actions on bad debts – quarterly, for instance, and can accompany the debtors reports as appropriate.

An alternative is to have an actual bad and doubtful division on the Sales Ledger itself, items on which remain in being until actually written off. The suspense account report can then be the bad and doubtful extract from the Sales Ledger.

RECONCILIATION OF DEBTORS TO THE GENERAL (NOMINAL) LEDGER

There are many styles of producing this to suit company needs and audit requirements. No special format is suggested here, but the principles of reconciliation are:

- do it at the end of each trading period, for example, monthly;

- do not proceed to next month's input until the previous month is reconciled;

- keep a running control record of input data.

In theory, reconciliations are simple: during the month, batches or sequences of invoices, cash and adjustments are posted to individual customer accounts, with the batch totals put to the General Ledger. At the month-end, the total of customer accounts should equal the debtors account in the General Ledger. In practice, minor discrepancies in postings occur so that some fault-finding is required. In particular, adjustments and transfers from one customer account to another may be misposted.

DEBIT NOTE ANALYSIS

In any business subject to an ongoing rate of returned goods, quality problems or price changes, there is usually some delay and difficulty in coping with debit notes raised by customers. Some customers deduct the value from payments (very common practice with the large supermarket buyers, for example), while others are more trusting and pay the full account, expecting a prompt credit note. A delay in responding to claims tends to complicate customers' accounts, delay collections and give an impression of poor customer service.

Any standard report should include an ageing of uncleared claims and show the reasons. Copy the report to all interested parties, especially in Sales and Quality Control. A sample report is shown in Figure 14.10.

Bubblesqueak Ltd Debit Note Analysis Date: 31.08.XX								
Date	Returned goods	Price error	Short delivery	Wrong goods	Repair charge	Other reason	Total	%
	£	£	£	£	£	£	£	
20XX	674	-	26	-	7110	269	8079	9.9
Jan	-	-	152	-	1234	-	1386	1.7
Feb	1210	-	-	-	191	-	1401	1.7
Mar	265	-	-	161	-	156	582	0.7
Apr	1480	629	-	-	263	-	2372	2.9
May	764	1818	1296	-	-	-	3878	4.8
Jun	12136	1990	-	5002	2501	-	21629	26.8
Jul	18919	4163	623	-	1362	-	25067	30.9
Aug	12123	2012	42	-	1761	763	16701	20.6
Total	47571	10612	2139	5163	14422	1188	81095	100.0
%	58.7%	13.1%	2.6%	6.3%	17.8%	1.5%	100%	

Figure 14.10   Debit note analysis

CASH ANALYSIS BY CUSTOMER/INTERNAL INTEREST CHARGES

The purpose of this report is to show where the month's and the year's cash has come from. This is not necessarily in the same proportions as sales, due to longer or shorter payment terms – for example, between home and export sales – or due to better or worse collections by regional offices or divisions. It expresses the varying DSO figures in terms of cash. It is ideal back-up for charging interest to the various divisions or offices, based on their debtors values in excess of budgeted or agreed levels. See Figure 14.11.

Bubblesqueak Ltd	Cash analysis by customer class/Date: Interest charge to sales divisions					
Class	Month's cash	%	YTD cash	%	Overdues £	Interest @ 12% £
Home: North South London						
Subtotal						
Export: East West						
Government Associated Co.						
TOTAL		100%		100%		

Figure 14.11   Cash analysis/internal interest charged

CREDIT MANAGER'S MONTHLY REPORT ON DEBTORS

Finally, the prime report on the topical status of the debtors asset is that issued monthly by the credit manager to his or her boss. It should show selected main features of interest to top management; but also be copied to credit staff and used every month for a detailed discussion on working priorities. A one-page report can show the speed of turning sales into cash, the quality of the unpaid sales in terms of age, and a few other key items.

It should always incorporate the four main measurements, namely:

- DSO overdues as a percentage of debtors;

- aged overdues within total disputed debts.

Comparisons should be made with the budget, if any, and with relevant previous periods. A few lines should *always* be added about, say, the top six problem accounts and show that actions have *already* been assigned to deal with them. That demonstrates the credit manager's control of the asset.

Every credit manager should give careful thought to how to report on all that is going on with the debtors asset. Even if the boss does not call for a report (they should, of course), it should be produced for self-management and, in due course, ways found to distribute it.

The credit manager's monthly report is the perfect vehicle for demonstrating the massive contribution of the credit department to corporate progress and profits. It should be easy to read and understand (senior management tends to have a short attention span), and draw out any unusual or one-off factors which may have contributed to this month's results.

Figure 14.12 is a sample of a brief but clear monthly report.

Bubblesqueak Ltd					OCTOBER	
DEBTORS REPORT						
ITEM	ACTUAL		LAST MONTH		BUDGET	
		£		£		£
1 Total Debtors	64 DSO	4 351 257	65 DSO	4 612 134	60 DSO	4 000 000
2 Overdues	11.2%	487 342	12.3%	567 292	10%	400 000
3 Age of overdues						
1-30	73%	355 760	69%	391 433	75%	300 000
31-60	18%	87 721	19%	107 785	20%	80 000
61-90	6%	29 241	7%	39 710	4%	16 000
91+	3%	14 620	5%	28 364	1%	4 000
Total	100%	487 342	100%	567 292	100%	400 000
4 Disputes	0.6 DSO	39 460	1.2 DSO	85 147	0.5 DSO	33 333
5 Debtors/sales %	17.5%	-	17.8%	-	16.7%	-
		YTD				
6 Bad debts	234	14 480	-	14 226	2 000	20 000
7 Debtors by class						
Home trade	66 DSO	2 894 729	67 DSO	3 302 274	62 DSO	2 600 000
Government	41 DSO	936 428	41 DSO	888 464	40 DSO	900 000
Export	98 DSO	520 110	98 DSO	421 396	95 DSO	500 000
TOTAL	64 DSO	4 351 257	65 DSO	4 612 134	60 DSO	4 000 000

Comments:
Improved on last month, particularly in olde st overdues and disputes but still not on budget
Government and export accounts paying well but slowness being met in Home Trade

Actions for next month:
Special campaign on 60+ overdues
3 meetings arranged with key home trade customers
New targets set for DSO and Overdue %

Figure 14.12   Credit manager's monthly report

PART VI
Credit Insurance

15

Domestic Market Credit Insurance

T Glyndwr Powell

• Introduction • Features of credit insurance policies • When does cover commence? •
Benefits of credit insurance • Importance of brokers • Captives and mutual insurers •
Domestic credit insurers • Further reading • Useful addresses •

Introduction

Credit insurance is not a panacea for poor credit management or a hunting licence for sharp sales staff to sell and forget! As with all insurances, it is to cover an unforeseen event: you must plan to get paid. A sale is not a sale until it's paid for!

The essence of an insurance contract is to indemnify the insured against the financial consequences of a defined loss. In the case of credit insurance, that loss is the non-payment of a valid trade debt, usually for reasons of insolvency. In addition, the credit insurance contract may offer the credit manager added-value services within the whole package. The insurance primarily protects the balance sheet against the loss of a trade receivable, and in certain circumstances may also protect against adverse cash flow resulting from delayed payment. Over the last century, credit insurance has developed to protect suppliers of goods and services against unexpected bad debt losses, and through the provision of credit limit underwriting, manage the exposure to the risk of bad debts from its trade debtors.

Properly used, credit insurance can increase the total receivables value an organisation is able to carry, effectively increasing the total credit sales it can afford to take. It does this by limiting the effect of any potential bad debt.

This chapter is designed to provide the credit manager with an overview of the issues, features and benefits of credit insurance, without reviewing the specific products of each insurer. If the issues are understood, selecting the most appropriate product becomes easier.

Features of Credit Insurance Policies

WHAT DEBTS ARE COVERED?

The first main difference between credit insurance policies is the way that risks are covered, namely:

- whole turnover

- single buyer

- top buyers

- excess of loss

- catastrophe.

WHOLE TURNOVER

Whole turnover is just that: the whole of the organisation's turnover on credit terms to third-party customers, except cash-before-delivery sales and any pre-agreed exclusion. The organisation cannot pick and choose what is covered; it must be all or none within the spread of risks selected. This type of policy is normally provided by four of the larger credit insurers, who are: AIG, Atradius, Coface and Euler Hermes .

Whole turnover policies usually include added services such as credit limit underwriting, provision of information on companies and collection of defaulted debts. A percentage of the debt up to the agreed credit limit is covered, usually 90 per cent. Most whole turnover policies cover sellers against the insolvency of the buyer, by whatever form, and protracted default. Protracted default is the non-payment by the debtor within an agreed period after due date, as long as no contract dispute exists.

SINGLE BUYER/SINGLE RISK

This is the opposite of the whole turnover policy in that specific buyers or single contracts can be underwritten. As the risk is more concentrated for the insurer, premiums tend to be higher than for whole turnover and underwriters tend to be circumspect about the risks they will cover. Certain Lloyd's and London Market underwriters will insure single risks. Cover is normally limited to insolvency.

(WHOLE TURNER OVER) EXCESS OF LOSS

This covers the seller for a slice of its bad debts. It is usually used to protect against higher than normal bad debt losses within one year. For example, a seller may be willing to lose the first £50,000 of bad debts in any one year, but is uncomfortable about losses above this. Therefore it arranges excess of loss cover which covers it for losses in excess of £50,000 up to, say, £250,000. Any losses above the agreed excess are then covered in the same way as they are by a whole turnover policy. Excess of loss policies can pay up to 100 per cent of the loss in the portion covered. As the seller absorbs the most likely losses, the premium should be cheaper than other policies as the likelihood of loss for the insurer is more remote.

CATASTROPHE COVER

This covers against a high proportion of all of a company's debts going bad in a single period, that is, a catastrophic loss. It is designed for companies who can afford their normal level of losses, but who have substantial receivables concentrated in a few key buyers. One format is the 'Top 10 Buyers' policy that covers the seller against the failure of any one of those clients. Given that most companies' largest customers tend to be bigger and more stable organisations, the premium costs may reflect that better risk. In many ways, a catastrophe cover policy is not that much different from a high-level excess of loss policy.

When Does Cover Commence?

The second consideration in insurance cover is at what point the debt is covered. There are two kinds of cover, namely:

1.   risks attaching;

2.   losses arising.

RISKS ATTACHING

In a 'risks attaching' policy, cover attaches from the date of the invoice, typically on shipment. It does not cover debts in existence before the policy commences, but it does cover debts until they are paid, even if that is after the end of the policy period. In an annual policy period, the policy would cover all invoices raised during the whole 12-month policy period . The credit manager has the certainty that if the goods have been delivered and invoiced within the policy period, cover is in place.

LOSSES ARISING

This differs from the risks attaching policy in that it covers all losses occurring in the policy period. It covers insured debts only if the buyer becomes insolvent or protracted default occurs during the policy period. If the policy is not renewed, goods invoiced within the policy period, but not due for payment until after the policy period expires, become potentially uninsured. This is not such a problem with insolvency, as most policies cover insolvency from the day it occurs, but it does have impact on the so-called protracted default, where the due date and end of wait period may occur after the end of the policy. However, this is balanced by the fact that existing debts, incurred before the start of the policy period, are covered. Renewal, therefore, is a major consideration in these types of policy: If a customer's financials have deteriorated during the policy, the insurer may choose to renew but exclude that customer – thus the invoices fall over of cover.

OTHER CONSIDERATIONS

There are other considerations within the policy affecting what is covered which need to be understood:

- first loss;

- non-qualifying loss;

- policy excess;

- indemnity level;

- maximum limit of liability;

- credit limits;

- credit process underwriting;

- commercial risk;

- political risk;

- insolvency cover;

- protracted default;

- legal indebtedness;

- averaging;

- recoveries;

- loss payee;

- wait period;

- credit rating of the insurer.

FIRST LOSS

The first loss is the value of any claim that is borne by the insured before the insurer pays anything. This can be the total of all losses in the policy period (an aggregated first loss or AFL) or, in others, applies to each and every claim. This can be a significant value if it is on each and every claim and there are a series of claims in a policy period. If it is on an aggregated first loss basis, once that has been incurred, claims are paid in full, to the maximum level of indemnity, thereafter.

NON-QUALIFYING LOSS

A loss of less than this value will not become a claim or contribute to any aggregate deduction, although the premium is still payable on these small debts.

If the non-qualifying loss value is exceeded, the entire loss is included in the calculation. For example, on a policy with a £500 non-qualifying loss, anything below that value would not be covered in any event, but if the loss were £501, the whole £501 would be claimable. This can be advantageous to a seller who frequently has small minor deductions on payments received, which although not contractually allowed, are cheaper to write off than pursue, for example, small exchange losses, bank charges and errors in payment. If there is an NQL, not only does the seller write off these amounts under its own authority, but also it has no obligation to inform the insurer of a payment default. In many cases, companies do not wish to claim on small amounts as they affect the numbers of claims made when looking for renewed cover and incur administrative cost and time in processing.

POLICY EXCESS

This is to all intents and purposes the same as the first loss. It is very important to read the wording, since in some policies the term 'excess' may be used in respect of every loss. In others, it will be an aggregate retention for the policy period.

INDEMNITY LEVEL

This is the value of the debt insured. It is normally expressed as a percentage, typically 90 per cent, but on many 'excess of loss' policies can be 100 per cent above the excess layer. Some insurers have different levels of indemnity for political and commercial risks.

MAXIMUM LIMIT OF LIABILITY

This is the maximum cash amount the insurer will pay out on the insured debts within any policy period. The policy is capped at a value written into the policy, ideally based on a percentage of the highest debtor balance of the largest two or three customers. Thus even whole turnover policies have an effective maximum limit. In an average year, however, it is highly unlikely that any insured would reach this value unless it had some highly concentrated large buyers (and for example, if long credit terms were allowed to the top customers). In this case, another policy type might be more appropriate, or a separate negotiation regarding limits for those specific buyers. Some insurers impose a maximum limit of liability, of between 20 and 40 times the expected premium to be paid.

CREDIT LIMITS AND 'WITH LIMITS' POLICIES

This is one of the key issues for any credit insurance policy. When not insured, a seller sets a credit limit in its own way, for example based on the expected level of sales, the credit and delivery periods, any security held and the financial standing of the buyer based on accounts and trading history.

Traditional whole turnover insurers, (such as Atradius, Euler Hermes, AIG, Coface and QBE) provide credit limits for the insured's buyers, which limit any claim. These insurers may grant authority to the insured to write credit limits for low values against third-party credit information and trading experience, which are referred to as 'discretionary' limits.

An underwriter offering a credit limit service also assesses this same information but the limit it may grant may not be that which the insured may desire, even for a 'good' risk. It has an additional criterion: its aggregated level of exposure to that buyer for all the credit insurance policies it has underwritten. If that value is already high, the underwriter may not be in a position to write the required level of credit limit. For example, a company needs a limit of £100,000 on a particular buyer based on long-established trading history, but the underwriter may only have £50,000 available, as it is already covering other clients selling to the same buyer. In these circumstances, a good broker will be able to arrange additional capacity but reaching the full limit may prove impossible.

Alternatively, the insurer may contact existing clients who have limits for that buyer with a view to reducing their limits where possible and using the reduction for the client with a current need.

A major advantage of the credit limit service provided by the main whole turnover insurers is that it is outsourced, thus saving the seller the cost and overhead of its credit management function. The credit insurer has access to considerable credit information including from credit reference agencies, all the reporting agencies, publicly filed information and its own historic data on payment performance. It can often make informed decisions quicker than the seller can itself and have early warning of possible default.

This access to information can also be a further added benefit to the seller as many underwriters or brokers can make their credit information available free or for a small charge, thus reducing the seller's need to subscribe to external credit information.

See Coface's website www.cofacerating.com and AIG's www.aigevents. com/limitsmanager or www.limitmanager.com for further details.

CREDIT PROCESS UNDERWRITING (FOR POLICIES WITHOUT A CREDIT LIMIT SERVICE)

These policies are also normally whole turnover, but apply where the insurer does not underwrite specific limits on agreed buyers, but instead relies on the credit management expertise of the insured to do it for them. Effectively the underwriter is covering the insured's credit policy and credit process, which, provided it is followed, makes claims valid. This is particularly useful for large sophisticated credit departments where credit insurance is procured to enable the company to increase the amount of risk it is prepared to take on its own book, rather than the smaller company who needs the advantage of a third party who can set realistic credit limits for it.

AIG and ACE are typical credit process underwriters, albeit that both review the largest limits set by the insured. If the seller set limits appear imprudent or excessive, or the insurer is aware of other information outside of the seller's knowledge, it may advise the seller of its concern or even refuse to continue cover for that buyer, at that level.

COMMERCIAL RISK

Commercial risk is the risk of insolvency or default (typically defined as non-payment within six months of due date); non-performance, delay, contract repudiation or fraud by the debtor are also commercial risks but are not covered under the credit insurance policy unless they result in a valid insolvency or default claim.

POLITICAL RISK

Political risk includes the risk of contract frustration due to government actions, including the inability of a government buyer to pay; and for contracts with private sector companies, the non-transfer of hard currency, or a change in the foreign exchange transfer rules, changes in the law making the contract illegal, war, cancellation of the contracts by government bodies or loss of export or import licenses. Political risks are only generally insurable in the case of export contracts. It is not normally possible for a company to insure itself against the actions of its own government, although it is possible to protect against the actions of foreign governments.

INSOLVENCY COVER

This covers the seller in the event of the insolvency of the buyer, whether that is by way of liquidation, administration or receivership, or their foreign equivalents such as Chapters 11 and 7 of the US Bankruptcy Code. It does not cover delayed payment or contract non-performance. Should the debt be disputed and not admitted in the liquidation, the claim will not succeed until the debt is proven. Most insurers pay claims for insolvency virtually immediately, typically within one month of proof of debt and formal insolvency.

PROTRACTED DEFAULT

'Protracted default' is insurance language for slow-payment. In policies where this cover is included, the insured may claim after a set waiting period. The insurer will pay the claim provided there is no contractual dispute. Where there is a dispute, legal action may be required to obtain judgement before a claim can be substantiated. The wait period in domestic policies is typically between 90 and 180 days, but in export policies, the wait period for non-OECD buyers can be considerably longer. The big advantage of protracted default cover is that it protects cash flow against non-payment, when formal insolvency cannot be proven or it is not possible or not economic to take legal action to wind up the buyer.

LEGAL INDEBTEDNESS

'Legal indebtedness' is the term used in credit insurance for a valid, due and payable debt. No claim can be admitted and paid if this situation does not exist. The insurer needs to be able to enforce recovery if required and may wish to take legal title to the debt. If a debt is disputed, a court judgement or arbitration award may be necessary for such legal indebtedness to be proven.

While the costs for the enforcement of the debt are generally shared between seller and insurer, the legal costs for establishing indebtedness are the responsibility of the seller.

AVERAGING

Where a seller has traded over the agreed credit limit, the insurer normally pays a maximum claim of the insured percentage of the credit limit. The insurer may retain the right to apply 'average' but it is only likely to use it if premium is payable on insured credit limits. Average is similar in all types of insurance. If, at some point during the policy year, the total amount outstanding from that buyer exceeded the credit insurer's credit limit, any subsequent claim may be 'averaged' in the same proportion. Most whole turnover policies involve premium being applied to turnover, so this will not apply.

RECOVERIES/SALVAGE

These are amounts realised after payment of a claim – for example, dividends from an insolvent estate or the result of enforcement action through the courts. In a normal case, recoveries are apportioned between insurer and insured seller in proportion to the percentage indemnity applied. Where the insured has traded over its agreed limit, the whole debt is split between the insured value and the self-insured portion, then a percentage insured is recalculated. It is done this way to stop sellers taking 100 per cent of recoveries and to divide recoveries on a fair and equitable basis.

For example, XYZ Widgets has sold goods to Hopeless Case Ltd totalling £100,000. The insurer, Coveritall plc, has agreed a 90 per cent indemnity on £50,000 in the event of the insolvency of Hopeless Case Ltd. The insurer would pay a claim for £45,000 being 90 per cent of £50,000, as normal. Recoveries would be split as follows:

Total loss:	100,000
Insurer's credit limit	50,000
Claim paid:	45,000 Indemnity level × Credit limit = 90% × £50,000)
Co insured level:	55,000 (Total Loss less claim paid = 100,000 – 45,000)
Recovery share:	55% seller/45% insurer (Claim paid/Total loss = £45,000/ £100,000)

LOSS PAYEE AND JOINT INSURED

Many companies use credit insurance to enhance their debtors on the balance sheet, and thus raise cheaper finance because of the greater security in the debtor asset and the associated credit insurance. The banks tend to take the view that insurance companies are a better credit risk than either the seller or the buyer, so as banks price their lending according to risk, the rate should be lower, or the facility larger, than the uninsured seller might otherwise obtain. To protect the bank in the event of a claim, it is often named in the policy as the loss payee. This means the insurer must pay the proceeds of any claim to the bank, not the seller, thus repaying the finance facility.

Sometimes the bank may wish to be joint insured, which allows it to make payment of premium to the insurer, submit the period returns and make claims in its own name, to protect against the debt being uninsured due to the failure of the seller to pay premium due, provide the required information or make claim. This can be particularly useful where the insured becomes insolvent and there is no one left around to administer the policy.

WAIT PERIOD

Wait period is the period of time the insured must wait before the insurer pays a valid claim. The intention is that the policy holder works to collect the debt and avoid a claim. (There is a risk of premium increase next year if a claim is submitted.) Within this period, the insured must lodge the claim with any required documentation, to prove its loss. In the event of legal insolvency, the wait period may be very short or even immediate upon proving the claim in the buyer's insolvency. In the case of protracted default, where there is no evidence of legal insolvency, it is longer. 180 days is a typical wait period in domestic policies and for the developed countries, but in the more difficult export markets 270 days or even longer are not uncommon. It is not an unreasonable process to specify in a policy, as it allows the insured seller a further time period to collect the debt before a claim is paid. Many potential claims are settled within this wait period, which has the benefit that the seller does not have to declare it as a loss when negotiating a renewal of the policy. A late payment is a far less contentious matter for the underwriter.

CREDIT RATING OF THE INSURER

This is an important consideration for the seller, since the credit manager must have confidence in the ability of the insurance company to pay out in the event of a valid insured loss.

Benefits of Credit Insurance

There are several benefits to the seller holding insurance of its receivables, which amount to a considerable help in growing its business profitably.

PROTECTS BALANCE SHEET BOOK DEBTS

The largest current asset on most companies' balance sheets is the trade debtors, typically 40 per cent of total current assets. The peace of mind provided by those debtors being protected by insurance helps the management, the owners and banks lending them money to sleep more easily at night. Any loss is reduced to the uninsured element. Credit insurance is also part of good corporate governance – like any other insurance, it involves the protection and better management of the company's assets.

PROTECTS PROFITS AGAINST EROSION

As the premium is paid or accrued as the sales are made, the seller knows its cost of bad debt risk. Any future loss is therefore less likely to seriously impact the profit and loss account. In companies where the gross profit is greater than the uninsured percentage, the insurance has the effect of locking in the profit at the level between the company's cost and the level insured. In more risky transactions, this is a valuable benefit.

LOWER BAD DEBT PROVISION

As the bulk of the receivables are covered by the policy, the level of bad debt provision required by a company can be reduced.

For example, a company with debtors of £1,000,000 has a credit insurance policy covering all its sales at 90 per cent indemnity, with a £10,000 aggregate first loss. It can assume that the 90 per cent insured portion less the first loss is 'safe' and would only need to provide for the £99,000 uninsured element (£1,000,000 less £10,000 = £990,000 x 10%) plus the £10,000 first loss at whatever percentage the company deemed prudent.

The only other items which may vary this calculation would be a provision against any accounts where the seller traded above the agreed credit limit or those accounts not covered by the policy, and write-offs of small items such as bank charges and disputed items.

One additional benefit of this is a windfall profit a previously uninsured seller may receive after its debtor ledger has fallen within the scope of the insurance. Having previously maintained a substantial bad provision account, once the vast majority of the debts are covered by the insurance, the company may release the excess provision to the profit and loss account.

CHEAPER FINANCE

Banks price their lending according to risk and a feature of business life is that most companies are worse credit risks than insurers. Particularly in the case of smaller sellers, the cost of the overdraft may be reduced by disclosing the existence of the credit insurance policy to the bank and determining if a lower interest rate would be available if it were assigned to the bank, and the bank named as 'loss payee'.

HIGHER BORROWING POTENTIAL

In a similar way to the option of cheaper finance, the borrowing potential of organisations with credit insurance is greater. When assessing the level of funds it will advance, the bank will value the borrower's business on the basis of its break-up value, that is, what the company would be worth in the event of liquidation. The most important assets, trade debtors and work in progress, are enhanced by the knowledge that credit insurance is in place, the more so if that bank is the beneficiary of any claim. Typically, without credit insurance, banks value debtors at around 50 per cent of book value, but with credit insurance, this valuation may be increased to 60–80 per cent. This can be the difference between having sufficient working capital or not, particularly for small businesses.

Many corporate managers in banks have found that often the first time the bank discovers there is a credit insurance policy is after the company fails, but if they had known earlier of a policy, they could have been more supportive. In some cases, they may not even have appointed a Receiver.

COMPANY INFORMATION

Sellers should know who their customers are – not just the name and address, but their legal format, ownership and worth. Credit insurance companies subscribe to a number of information providers, including the credit information companies, the news services and the public record registries for legal information. Many credit insurance brokers do so as well. It is often possible to obtain credit data directly from the broker or insurance company, either to complement existing resources or as a replacement. There is usually a charge for this information but, as the brokers or insurers are bulk purchasers, the cost may be more attractive than through the company's own sources.

CREDIT LIMIT SERVICE

'With limits' insurers set credit limits for the buyers individually. The seller's credit function still needs to establish who its customers really are, but no longer needs to do analysis for assessing creditworthiness and setting limits, unless the seller is consistently trading above the insurer's limits or with customers who cannot be covered. For the smaller company, this is an invaluable benefit, especially where it does not have the capacity in-house for risk assessment.

ONLINE SERVICES

'With limits' credit insurers provide their credit limit decisions online. Most are also developing their own reporting facility, which allows the insured seller to make credit limit applications, declarations of turnover, notification of overdue debts and to track the progress of claims. The logical extension is to use the same service to get company and country information. Online policy administration reduces staff costs and paperwork, giving the possibility of lower premium rates.

COMPETITIVE ADVANTAGE

The ability to grant credit to customers, where a competitor cannot, gives the seller an advantage, and thus a chance of increased sales and market share.

ABILITY TO TAKE A HIGHER LEVEL OF DEBTOR RISK

There is a limit to the amount of risk that any organisation is able or willing to take on its own books. This is why prudent companies set credit limits, whether insured or not. Where a set limit is exceeded, the seller may lose business if it is unable to allow further credit except on secured or cash terms. By credit insuring the debtors in whole or part, the seller can increase the level of credit sales by adding the insured portion to the company's own internal limit.

An example of this occurred when a UK manufacturer, exporting to North Africa, wished to increase its sales there. To do so it would need to continue offering open account credit and 90-day documentary term drafts to governmental entities and state-owned companies. The seller's own management was comfortable with a maximum exposure of £1 million on its balance sheet, but no more. Insurance was arranged for £1.5 million, meaning in aggregate the company could advance £2.5 million on credit sales, including some limited extended credit up to 540 days. This enabled the company to grow its sales from around £2.5 million annually to nearly £8 million within some three years.

ABILITY TO TRADE WITH NEW ACCOUNTS MORE EASILY

One of the big problems facing a credit manager when the sales rep walks in with a new account is the lack of any trading history with the potential new buyer or any knowledge of what they are really like. Bank references are rarely enlightening unless the potential customer is seriously overexposed to that bank. Many companies offer a couple of trade referees with whom they maintain an exemplary record to ensure they can give at least two 'good' references to potential suppliers. Meaningful statutory accounts are only filed by larger companies and these are often up to two years old and the latest accounts are often already nine months old even when filed on time at Companies House.

A 'with limits' credit insurer will compile not only the financial history, with trend analysis, of all their clients' accounts, but also the payment history from other policy holders' ledgers. The difference between a credit insurer's limit and the recommendation of a credit reference agency is that the credit insurer will suffer a loss if it is too generous. It is rare for a credit insurer not to know a new buyer already and it can thus provide a credit decision quickly. If the insurer declines the cover, the credit manager has an immediate signal that the potential customer needs to be carefully vetted before being allowed credit facilities. In the absence of good data, the seller may wish to take some security in the form of guarantees or cash deposits.

DISCRETIONARY LIMITS

To enable speedy processing of small value orders for new clients, most insurers allow a discretionary limit, so that the seller can make limited credit sales to a new buyer whilst a full credit approval is processed. Normally such limits are automatic provided the seller has made a search of a credit reference agency and that report has no adverse information or alternatively the seller has sold to the buyer successfully on credit within the last 12 months. Some high-level excess of loss policies operate entirely on this basis, that is, the policyholder sets his own limits and the insurer simply signs off the final decision to cover it.

COLLECTION AND DEBT COLLECTION SERVICE

As credit insurers need to collect the debts they have paid claims for, they have developed fairly efficient in-house collection departments. These have the ability to collect through normal friendly routes including letters and telephone methods, and when these methods do not work, they have capable legal expertise to pursue the debt through the courts if necessary.

Credit insurers realised long ago that debt collection was a highly saleable service to policyholders and even to third parties, especially as most insurers have a local presence in many countries and can collect with local expertise which the seller lacks.

Importance of Brokers

Many companies feel that they can negotiate credit insurance policies themselves without the use of brokers, having the expertise and buying power to so do. However, the advantage of using a specialist broker is that he or she is an independent adviser and can help the credit manager to evaluate the options.

Each credit insurer has particular strengths and weaknesses and it is useful to have an objective view of the alternatives before committing the company to spend possibly 0.25 per cent or more of turnover on protecting receivables.

Brokers also have considerable experience in deciding with the credit manager what level of cover is appropriate and what type of first loss will produce the best return compared to the cost of cover. The broker will also ensure that the correct wording is produced for any complicated type of cover, since not only premium rates but also policy wordings are negotiable with underwriters.

For larger companies – for instance, those with more than one operating site – the broker can be the emissary of the central management, helping local offices to cope with new processes that include credit insurance and possibly finance as set out in an overall plan.

Few credit managers know the market as well as a broker or are aware of all the pitfalls hidden in the small print of a policy wording. Some insurers, including the excess of loss providers and credit and political risk underwriters at Lloyd's, for example, will only work through a broker. Excess of loss insurers need the broker to perform much of the administration function so that the costs of the insurance product are kept low. Lloyd's underwriters rely on the broker not only to collect the premium but also to write the policy wording and arrange syndication (the sharing of risk with other underwriters) where appropriate.

The broker is paid a commission by the insurer or a fee by the insured, but it remains the agent of the insured, not the insurer. It must act at all times in the best interests of the insured, even if it arranges a policy which brings it less commission.

The key benefits of using brokers are:

- Market knowledge – the appropriate price for the policy, based on experience from other clients.

- Product knowledge – which is the best kind of policy for the cover required and who is the best provider of that cover.

- Knowing which onerous clauses can be avoided or, if they are unavoidable, ensuring that the seller knows what is covered and what is not, and what not to do to invalidate cover. This is often called 'policy wording advice'.

- Claims negotiation – making sure the insurer pays out on a valid claim and assisting the insured in providing the right information to get paid quickly.

- Credit limit negotiation – advocating the seller's case for a higher limit than currently granted. In a difficult economic climate, where insurers are reluctant to write adequate credit limits, this is a very important part of the broker's job.

- Setting cover at the right level – ensuring the insured seller does not over-buy or under-buy protection. On deals involving banks providing finance, ensuring the structure and policy wording works for both the insured seller and the bank.

Names of and information concerning credit insurance brokers can be obtained from the British Insurance Brokers Association.

Captives and Mutuals

Some organisations, particularly the large multi-nationals, have sophisticated risk management departments which mitigate the risk exposure of the group (in many cases without buying insurance from third parties) and arrange any legally mandated insurance cover such as employee liability and public liability. There are significant tax and cash flow advantages available to an organisation which has the resources to cover a substantial portion of such risk itself on a self-insuring basis, but who would want protection against the unforeseen disaster.

These organisations establish their own insurance subsidiaries, known as 'captive' insurers, to underwrite these risks on an arm's length basis, taking advantage of these tax and cash flow benefits. As the captive is established as a fully competent insurance company with the necessary authority to trade and underwrite policies, it can provide the required cover. The first loss is usually carried on the captive's own books, and reinsurance arranged with an insurance company for the next tranche.

In the case of credit insurance, a company may use its captive subsidiary to take the first layer of insurance in the same way as other insurance with the captive paying the smaller claims and arranging reinsurance for the larger losses.

The structure often takes the form of the group subsidiaries paying a premium to the captive equivalent to the old bad debt provision, and the captive manages any claims. The subsidiary is paid for any losses and the captive only claims on the reinsurance where the claim exceeds its pre-agreed parameters. As the premium paid to an insurer is fully tax deductible as an expense, the group effectively gets the benefit of a fully deductible general bad debt provision. Further, where it is good at maintaining its bad debt claims effectively, it participates in the profit associated previously in writing back over- provided bad debt provision.

If a portfolio of receivables includes significant political risk, the captive manager may decide that the use of the captive is not appropriate, because the nature of political risk makes it difficult to evaluate and when losses occur they are often 100 per cent, with few recoveries in the short term.

A mutual is similar to a captive in that it is owned by the policyholder, but differs in that it is a group of companies who get together to share the cost and risks of establishing the insurance company. Instead of being a wholly-owned subsidiary, it is mutually owned by a number of participants. Exporters Insurance Company is one example.

Domestic Credit Insurers

There are number of players in the UK/EU domestic credit insurance market, including the following:

- Ace Europe American Insurance Group (AIG)

- Amlin Credit

- Atradius

- CIFS (Novae at Lloyd's of London)

- Coface UK Limited

- Credit Shield (HCC International Insurance Co plc)

- Euler Hermes Exporters Insurance Company

- QBE Zurich

- various Lloyd's syndicates (these are separate legal entities in the same way that Coface and Euler are).

In addition, some of the banks and factoring companies offer credit protection, which has a similar effect.

Further Reading

Paul Barreau, *Credit Insurance*, 2nd Edition, International Credit Insurance Association.

Briggs and Edwards, *Credit Insurance*, Woodhead Faulkner (Publishing) Limited.

Credit Management Magazine, various articles and supplements since the Credit Insurance Supplement April 2001, ICM.

Houlder Commercial Services Ltd, *The Do's and Don'ts of Credit Insurance*, available from Houlder Commercial Services Ltd.

In addition, a wealth of information is available from current booklets and website information issued by the organisations below.

Useful Addresses

ACE Europe 100 Leadenhall Street, London, EC3A 3BP.
Website: www.aceeurope.com

American Insurance Group (AIG) 58 Fenchurch Street, London, EC3M 4AB.
Website: www.aigeurope.co.uk

Amlin Credit 1 St Helens Undershaft, London, EC3A 8ND.
Website: www.creditinsure.com

Coface UK Limited 15 Appold Street, London, EC2A 2DL.
Website: www.cofaceuk.com

Credit Shield The Grange Rearsby, Leicester, LE7 4FY.
Website: www.creditshield.co.uk

Exporters Insurance Company Limited (TUA) 37–39 Lime Street, London, EC3M 7AY.
Website: www.exportersinsurance.com

Euler Trade Indemnity 1 Canada Square, London, E14 5DX.
Website: www.eulerhermes.com/eti/home.cfm

Atradius 3 Harbour Drive, Capital Waterside, Cardiff, CF1 6TZ.
Website: www.atradius.co.uk

UK Credit Insurance Brokers' Committee British Insurance Brokers' Association, BIIBA House, 14 Bevis Marks, London, EC3A 7NT.
Website: www.biba.org.uk

International Credit Insurance & Surety Association 1–2 Castle Lane, London, SW1E 6DR.
Website: www.icisa.org

QBE, Plantation Place, 30 Fencurch Street, London, EC3M 3BD.
Website: www.qbeeurope.com

Zurich London Underwriting Centre Zurich London, 3 Minster Court, Mincing Lane, London, EC3R 7DD.
Website: www.zurich.co.uk

Acknowledgements

Thanks are owed to Susan Ross and Melanie Wartenberg of Aon Trade Credit for their invaluable help on current offerings from credit insurers in a moving market and for acting as a sounding board.

16

Export Credit Insurance

T Glyndwr Powell

• Introduction • Differences between domestic and export credit insurance • Country (political) risks • Commercial (customer) risks • Pre-shipment cover: suitable for companies making specialist goods to order and not easily resold elsewhere • Level of indemnity • Credit insurance compared to confirmed letters of credit • Sources of export cover • The UK's Government-supported export credit agency – ECGD – and medium-term credit • Further reading • Useful addresses •

Introduction

The considerations a credit manager needs to weigh up in export credit are more complex due to the distances involved and the differences in local law and customs. Political considerations have greater impact on managing payment risk and the involvement of banks in the process is much greater. For these reasons, many companies credit insure their export sales where they are happy to cover their domestic sales on their own account. This probably suits the credit insurers, whose export credit insurance underwriting is regularly more profitable than that for UK, EC and North American trade. This is partly because they can charge more for covering export risks whereas the domestic market is very competitive; but the main reason is that the frequency of insolvency and the size of companies becoming insolvent is growing in the developed world. Further, with increased merger activity, the insurers have larger concentrations of risks on these corporate companies.

For much of the last century, export credit insurance was dominated by state-owned organisations, such as ECGD (the Export Credits Guarantee Department), established to promote the export of their own countries' goods and services.

The market for export credit insurance has grown since 1972 when certain Lloyd's syndicates started underwriting political risks and again when, in 1991, the short-term arm of ECGD was privatised and sold to NCM of the Netherlands. Nowadays, many domestic credit insurers also cover both political (country) and commercial (customer) risks for exports.

Since some 95 per cent of all UK exports are on terms of 180 days or less, most of this chapter is devoted to short-term insurance cover. The role of ECGD in providing insurance for the export of capital goods, usually on terms in excess of two years, is covered at the end. Alternative methods of covering such sales are also reviewed in Chapter 26.

Differences Between Domestic and Export Credit Insurance

The key difference in payment risk between the home and export markets is the impact of political events affecting the ability of the buyer to pay and the seller to complete the contract. Political risks include the risk of the imposition or cancellation of controls and licences, economic events and the unpredictability of government buyers. A major difference from the home trade is that a perfectly solvent and profitable buyer may be prevented from settling his debts because of the economic or political situation in his country.

In exporting, payment terms may need to be lengthened to accommodate longer transportation times; there may be language difficulties regarding payment arrangements; it may be necessary to contract in the buyer's currency or a neutral one; and goods may have to be modified to suit local customs and regulations.

Country (Political) Risks

In exporting, the country or market risks may stop a willing buyer from paying due to changes in, or the imposition of, local regulations or shortage of foreign exchange. These risks are:

- Delays or moratoria in transferring hard currency from the buyer's country.

- Any action of the government of the buyer's country which wholly or partly prevents performance of the contract, including the cancellation of import licences where required.

- Political events or economic, legislative or administrative measures occurring outside the UK which prevent or delay transfer or payment.

- War, civil war or the like outside the UK preventing performance of the contract.

- Cancellation or non-renewal of an export licence or new restrictions on export after signature of the contract.

- Where the buyer is a public buyer (government agency or state-owned company), any act which the buyer fails or refuses to perform under its contract obligations.

The first point is referred to as transfer risk, the others political risks. In addition, unfair calling of performance bonds by foreign governments is also covered in many political risk policies, particularly those involved in projects and construction.

Commercial (Customer) Risks

Export credit insurance policies can also cover the following commercial risks:

- Insolvency of the buyer.

- Failure of the buyer to pay within an agreed period, normally around 180 days, often referred to as protracted default.

- The buyer's failure or refusal to take up goods which comply with the contract.

The second point, protracted default, is far more important in exports than domestic trade, as the remedies to enforce collection are often more limited and harder to action than at home. The potential for delayed payment is greater and the costs of potential legal action also. It is not quite as easy to use the local court to recover small claims.

Another key difference between home and export cover is the greater willingness of both seller and insurer to cover specific or limited spreads or risks. For example, a global company's UK office may be responsible for sales in Europe, Middle East and Africa; and the company will be able to negotiate a policy for this section of the world. The policy will be quite separate from arrangements made in the USA for the Americas and in Asia for Asia-Pacific sales. In addition, the Lloyd's political risk market regularly covers specific contracts, as do a number of credit insurers. Premium rates reflect the risk underwritten.

Other forms of political risk that companies consider covering include protection against seizure and confiscation of the seller's goods and assets abroad, business interruption arising from this and protection against the nationalisation of their local investments, including loss of licences to operate. This kind of protection is useful for companies who want to source production in a low-cost overseas location without taking undue political risks to their balance sheet, or whose business plan for a territory is dependent on continuation of a licence, for example, for mining or for a telephone service.

Pre-shipment Cover: Suitable for Companies Making Specialist Goods to Order and Not Easily Resold Elsewhere

This form of protection covers risks of loss before shipment is made. Sellers can incur considerable costs producing goods or preparing services for a signed contract, which they cannot easily recover by reselling the goods or services to an alternate buyer. The seller is covered for losses if the buyer repudiates or is stopped from performing the contract or if it becomes insolvent prior to delivery.

This is a specialised form of cover and not available from all providers.

Level of Indemnity

Typically, the percentage of losses covered is the same as in the domestic market – 90 per cent for commercial risks. For country risks the cover is 90 per cent from many insurers, but may be as high as 100 per cent, particularly on those contracts with high first losses. In very difficult markets it is not unusual for the insurer to cover lower percentages, (75 per cent or 50 per cent even,) especially where otherwise no cover may be available

Credit Insurance Compared to Confirmed Letters of Credit

Frequently credit managers face a situation where a confirmation of a LC is available at the same time as credit insurance, and they must decide which to take. Both cost money and normally confirmed letters of credit are excluded from declarations under the policy. The seller should not pay twice for protection. There is a balance to be struck as to which offers the best value for money.

Country risk premium rates and bank country confirmation fees tend to follow each other, and are, to say the least, driven by supply and demand. Both require correct documents if they are to be effective guarantees. But, whereas for a credit insurance claim it is necessary to have sufficient paperwork to demonstrate the loss, with a LC you will only be able to draw payment if you provide the exact documents by the dates and in the format specified. The features of credit insurance and bank confirmations which need to be compared, when assessing which is better, are:

- What is the seller's profit margin? Lower-margined business needs a higher certainty of payment to be safe. If the seller has a 10 per cent or lower gross margin, given normal indemnity cover of 90 per cent, virtually any claim situation will result in an economic loss to the seller. In these circumstances, unless the risk of non-payment is known to be extremely low, a confirmation may well be a better solution.

- How long is the wait period on the insurance policy? It requires funding. A confirming bank pays immediately. What is the level of the insurance indemnity? The uninsured element is a cost. Bank confirmations cover 100 per cent.

- Related to the above, what is the perceived risk of loss, high or low? Arguably, the bank confirmation is the preferred solution for a high-risk irrevocable letter of credit (ILC). For a confirmed ILC to be secure, the exporter needs to pay for a commitment fee to guarantee cover when the ILC is actually issued. If the ILC is to remain open for some time, sometimes six months or more in the case of manufactured goods, the commitment fees may make the bank option more expensive than credit insurance, as the fee will be payable quarterly for the period the bank is exposed. For example:

  - If the wait period is 180 days and the indemnity is 90 per cent, given interest rates of around 5 per cent per annum, a credit insurance claim is worth, in cash terms, 87.5 per cent of the invoice value less the insurance premium. If the insurance premium including country risk premium is 1 per cent, giving a total paid of 86.5 per cent in the event of a claim.

– If the bank confirmation charge is 1.5 per cent per quarter, and two quarters elapse, that totals 3 per cent, giving a total cash payout of 97 per cent.

Where there is no claim made, the insurance would cost 1 per cent and the confirmation would cost 3 per cent, effectively three times higher.

Sources of Export Cover

There are several sources for insuring export sales against the risks of non-payment, whether from commercial or political causes of loss.

ATRADIUS

Atradius is the current name for NCM, the insurer that acquired the short-term credit insurance division from ECGD in 1991. Atradius offers a wide range of cover. The Company is now in the same ownership as CYC, the Spanish credit insurer.

The basic export policy Atradius offers is the Modula policy, which is designed for all types of exporters, large or small. It is whole turnover and covers both commercial and political risks. Cover normally commences on shipment, but Atradius is willing to include pre-shipment cover for a small premium. This is of particular use to manufacturers making specialist goods to order or where there are considerable pre-shipment costs, such as procuring machinery and vehicles for a construction contract.

Buyer and country risks covered are all those listed above. Cover is normally 90 per cent for commercial risks and 95 per cent for political risks.

Other policies can protect against non-payment of services, royalties on licensing and franchises, sales through an overseas subsidiary and goods sold from stock held locally overseas.

For European, North American and Australasian losses, claims are paid normally:

- immediately on proof of insolvency;

- six months after protracted default;

- six months after due date for political loss;

- extended claims wait periods are specified for riskier markets.

Premium is calculated on annual turnover covered by the policy plus an additional premium for higher-risk export markets (referred to as Market Rate Addition or MRA). A minimum annual premium is chargeable plus any additional premium based on the actual level of export sales declared and a change per credit limit decision.

Cover is normally for goods sold on terms up to 180 days from shipment. One very useful endorsement to the policy available from Atradius is the Extended Risk Endorsement, which extends cover for sales on terms up to two years or where the manufacturing period exceeds 12 months.

AIG UK LIMITED

AIG is a US-owned insurer, which offers the exporter a similar broad range of cover to that of Atradius with a full credit limit service, but also can offer a high level of discretion where there is a large deductible. This excess of loss policy relies on the credit management and credit assessment skills of the seller, effectively underwriting the seller's credit policy and process. AIG can offer excess of loss policies for both political and commercial risks as well as specialist policies for large single contracts and barter, counter-trade and for confiscation of investments.

One key feature of AIG cover is that once a limit has been agreed with the underwriter, cover for that buyer may not be cancelled by the insurer until the policy expires; cover therefore continues unless the exporter becomes aware that the buyer is in financial difficulty. Other insurers offer this as 'binding contracts cover', whereby the company continues to be covered where he has binding contracts, even if the insurer cancels a credit limit – but always subject to his not becoming aware of adverse information about a deteriorating situation. As many sellers are in contract with a buyer and may be sued for damages for non-delivery, AIG's permanent limits are a valuable feature.

AIG's excess of loss policies are really designed for the larger, more sophisticated company with strong credit skills and are not normally appropriate for insured turnovers below £15 million for the commercial risk coverage. Political risks cover only may be appropriate for lower values.

LLOYD'S OF LONDON

Lloyd's is not a single source for cover but a group of individual syndicates, each of which writes on its own account, albeit that they are all regulated by a single body and guaranteed by a central fund. For many years Lloyd's was not allowed to cover commercial credit risks but it became a very important provider of political risk cover. In the mid-1990s their ban on commercial credit risk insurance was lifted. However, only a few syndicates offer this facility, and mostly for insolvency only.

Lloyd's real strength is in the political risk market where over many centuries it has developed a number of products which protect sellers against a variety of government-initiated causes of non-payment. Transfer risks, embargoes, war and default by government buyers are available, as is protection against loss of investment and expropriation. Cover is usually around 90 per cent but it can be higher, especially for excess of loss policies.

Lloyd's syndicates will not deal directly with the insured, insisting that a registered Lloyd's broker must be used. However, as the type of cover required and the policy wordings are individually created, requiring careful negotiation to ensure the correct cover is obtained, this is more an advantage than a disadvantage.

A number of the major credit insurers also participate in syndications with Lloyd's. In these, one underwriter, known as the lead underwriter, acts as the main insurer, agreeing to cover a certain percentage of the risk, and then others, known as following underwriters, join the policy. The broker will seek sufficient capacity on the 'slip', as it is known, to achieve the level of cover required by the seller.

EULER HERMES

Euler Hermes is part of the large Allianz insurance group, and was created from the merger of Trade Indemnity plus SFAC of France and and the German Hermes credit insurance companies. In addition to the Euler Hermes KreditversicherungsAG (German ECA) supported covers, Euler has been writing a book of political risk cover since 1985. It is a whole turnover 'with limits' insurer, providing cover for a similar range of political and commercial credit risks to Atradius, including both insolvency and protracted default. Euler will consider a reasonable spread of risks where whole turnover cover is not required. Maximum terms are usually 180 days but extended terms may be possible. Indemnity is typically 90 per cent.

Euler has traditionally been a very flexible commercial and political risk insurer and its underwriting decisions take into account the credit management expertise of the seller and its experience in any given market.

COFACE UK LTD

Coface is the French national export credit agency, and is now owned by the French banking group Natexis. It was established in the UK in 1993 when it took over the business of London Bridge Finance. Whilst its usual policies are based on whole turnover, it will consider more limited risks in certain circumstances.

A key feature of the Coface pricing model is a blended policy premium rate across the world and inclusions of all policy costs – credit limit fees, collection fees – in the premium rate. Based on the spread of markets declared when the policy is negotiated, Coface fixes a rate for the whole turnover covering both the commercial and political risks for all buyers. It also offers debt collection services through its in-house collections department, which is also available to uninsured parties, and finance of receivables through its invoice discounting arm.

Coface has two valuable networks: its information alliance spans most of the world's countries and is the backbone of its '@rating' service through which it is possible to obtain ratings (of the likelihood of insolvency) of companies and also economic reports on countries.

Coface's other network is its alliance with other credit insurers around the world – the Globalliance. Through this alliance, a multi-national company can negotiate protection for each of its local operations, with a single worldwide policy wording. This suits companies with sales offices worldwide that sell mostly to the local market.

Coface has developed a factoring solution whereby a company can sell its receivables without recourse to Coface, or a second facility where the finance is not drawn unless there is a loss, in which case the claim is advanced immediately, thus doing away with the waiting period.

Coface has a specialised political risk underwriter previously known as Unistrat, which has a reputation for covering good risks in difficult political markets. It places great weight on the skill and expertise of the exporter, and on the reasoning behind the structure of particular contracts and projects.

ACE EUROPE

This large Bermuda-owned insurer provides cover on an excess of loss basis, with up to 100 per cent indemnity and an aggregate deductible. Credit limits are provided, for the top 20 per cent of exposures. Cover can be for both political and commercial risks.

EXPORTERS INSURANCE COMPANY

'Exporters' is a group captive credit insurer that offers credit and political risk cover. It offers both whole turnover policies and specific single buyer cover. It is unusual in being able to offer medium-term insurance, similar in scope to the export credit agencies, but without their condition for goods to be produced in their own country, although this requirement is becoming less important to UK exporters now that ECGD will cover contracts where the UK content is as low as 20 per cent including profit.

DUCROIRE DELCREDERE

This commercial arm of the Belgian ECA offers whole turnover policies to EU companies and has a preference for non-OECD risks.

The Uk's Government-supported Export Credit Agency – ECGD – and Medium-term Credit

The UK Government established the ECGD after the First World War in 1919 to support the sale of UK goods to foreign markets by protecting sellers against non-payment due to commercial and political events. In 1991 the short-term arm was sold to NCM, leaving the government-owned agency to cover medium-term credit sales of high-value capital goods to foreign markets.

ECGD offers a number of different products, which in many ways do not seem to the exporter to be insurance. This is because the cover is usually granted to the exporter's bank, as a buyer credit from which the exporter draws down funds at shipment and the bank collects payment from the foreign buyer or its bank.

ECGD also supports various forms of Supplier Credit, that is, where the exporter in the supply contract offers the credit. In both cases, for ECGD to insure the credit, the credit period must be appropriate for the goods or services supplied; a portion of the product must be supplied from the UK (which may include profit and services); and the payment period must usually be two years or longer. ECGD prefers to insure risks where there is a quality government sponsor or a bank guarantee of payment.

In addition to these facilities, which are discussed in Chapter 26, ECGD also provides cover against risks such as:

- pre-shipment cover;

- tender-to-contract cover: forward exchange cover overseas investment insurance.

Pre-shipment cover is effected through the EXIP. *Bond risk cover* is for the unfair calling of bonds. As with most political risk insurers, ECGD will include non-performance for reasons of force majeure. However, cover is only available where ECGD had provided basic cover for the financing element. Cover is usually 100 per cent of the bond value. Beneficial interest in the cover can normally be assigned to banks providing the bonds, with ECGD's approval. ECGD does not cover tender bonders or off-set performance bonds.

Overseas investment insurance is available to protect UK companies' long-term (typically 15 years) equity and loan investments overseas. It covers expropriation, war and restriction on remittances. As it protects the UK investment, UK goods do not need to be part of the investment.

Further Reading

Briggs and Edwards, *Credit Insurance*, Woodhead Faulkener (Publishing) Limited (useful facts and procedures, but sources now out of date).

Credit Management Magazine (Credit Insurance Supplement April 2001 and subsequent articles). *Institute of Credit Management BExA Guide to Export Credit Insurance* (October 2007). Available from the British Exporters Association or online from its website www.bexa.co.uk.

In addition, a wealth of information is available from current booklets and website information issued by the credit insurers noted above.

Useful Addresses

ACE Europe 100 Leadenhall Street, London, EC3A 3BP.
Website: www.aceeurope.com

American Insurance Group (AIG) 58 Fenchurch Street, London, EC3M 4AB.
Website: www.aigeurope.co.uk

Coface UK Limited 15 Appold Street, London, EC2A 2DL.
Website: www.cofaceuk.com or www.cofacerating.com

Exporters Insurance Company Limited (TUA) 37–39 Lime Street, London, EC3M 7AY.
Website: www.exportersinsurance.com

Euler Hermes 1 Canada Square, London, E14 5DX.
Website: www.eulerhermes.com

Atradius 3 Harbour Drive, Capital Waterside, Cardiff, CF1 6TZ.
Website: www.atradius.co.uk

UK Credit Insurance Brokers' Committee, British Insurance Brokers' Association
BIIBA House, 14 Bevis Marks, London, EC3A 7NT.
Website: www.biba.org.uk

International Credit Insurance & Surety Association 1–2 Castle Lane, London,
SW1E 6DR.
Website: www.icisa.org

Export Credits Guarantee Department PO Box 2200, 2 Exchange Tower, Harbour
Exchange Square, London, E14 9GS.
Website: www.ecgd.gov.uk

Aon Trade Credit 8 Devonshire Square, Cutlers Gardens, London, EC2M 4PL.
Website: www.aon.com

Acknowledgements

Thanks to Susan Ross of Aon Trade Credit for her invaluable help on facilities
on offer from credit insurers.

INSTITUTE OF CREDIT MANAGEMENT – JANUARY 2008

Advanced Credit Management: Diploma Level 5

Riskisales Co sells most of its $50m annual turnover to foreign buyers. Some
large contracts have been insured independently in the past, but there have
been significant losses through bad debts in other uninsured cases, making it
worthwhile now, to take out a whole turnover policy. As the credit manager,
you have been asked to explain to your staff the change in arrangements and
how it will affect their jobs.

- Explain what risks would be covered by whole turnover policy and
  the limitation of the cover.

- Discuss the *advantages* and *disadvantages* of a whole turnover
  policy.

- Analyse which responsibilities in the credit department might be
  more important and which may be less important.

PART VII
Export Credit and Finance

17

Export Credit and Collections

T Glyndwr Powell[1]

• Exporting is expensive – so manage the expense! • Time and cost in export payments • Effective conditions of sale • Agents, distributors and subsidiaries • Export documents • Payment terms • Countertrade • Tender and performance bonds • Getting funds transferred from abroad • Checking the risk of payment delays • Information on country (political) risks • Information on customer risks • Evaluating customer risks • Codifying information • Collecting overdues – an overview • A systematic approach • A word about foreign currency • Checklist: to speed export cash • The future for export collections • Think international • Further reading • Useful addresses •

Exporting is Expensive – So Manage the Expense!

Payment terms in overseas markets are often longer than the traditional UK net monthly terms and given the distances and involvement of banks, the collection cycle is similarly extended. Furthermore, many countries have limited hard currency to pay for imports, further extending the time taken to receive settlement. Matters have improved over the last few years with foreign exchange controls being liberalised.

It is not always possible for exporters to increase price to compensate for the delays, due to competitive pressures. Thus, whilst extra working capital is needed to finance the longer cash cycle, profitability is reduced by additional interest cost of the associated borrowings. The main consequences of slow cash receipts for export sales are:

- the need for additional working capital, usually through additional borrowing; and

---

1   With acknowledgement to Burt Edwards.

- increased risk of shortfalls and non-payment because of the longer time horizons.

Some exporters simply cannot borrow much more from their banks. The risk of bad debt loss is increased – the longer any debt is unpaid, the greater the chance of it never being paid. The total annual interest expense on late-paid export debts can amount to many times more than actual bad debt write-offs and thus make the entire export activity unprofitable.

Apart from the financial effects, there are important commercial ones. It takes time and money to develop foreign customers and markets. Exports cannot be made on a shoestring, because of all the funding needed for the various upfront costs. Exporters need strong, growing customers in countries where sales can be increased. Resources are wasted when applied blindly to product design and marketing for weak customers or for countries where imports are, or will be, restricted.

Good credit management can be of great help in both the financial and commercial areas of exporting. Primarily, the task of getting paid faster needs several actions:

- negotiating the payment terms to match the perceived risk;

- agreeing reliable payment arrangements with each and every customer;

- checking the ability of customers and countries to pay;

- ensuring absolute accuracy of export documents, to get goods in and funds out;

- using local agents or representation more effectively;

- giving correct instructions to the banks at both ends;

- deciding on the best currency to use;

- getting letters of credit to work as intended;

- collecting overdue debts in a systematic way using external credit services where appropriate.

It takes time to build up experience of the right techniques for various markets. The learning curve can be speeded up if particular staff specialise in export credit duties, rather than fragmenting the duties over several people or mixing them in randomly with domestic sales.

Time and Cost in Export Payments

There are only four basic credit situations for customers and markets.

A = Strong customer in strong market.
B = Strong customer in weak market.
C = Weak customer in strong market.
D = Weak customer in weak market.

For example, a sale on 60 days credit; to somewhere taking 2 weeks to arrive.

Time element	Number of days			
Market Category	A	B	C	D
Delivery	14	14	14	14
Credit period	60	60	60	60
Late payment	0	0	30	30
Currency delay	0	90	0	90
Bank transfer	14	14	14	14
Total time taken	**88**	**178**	**118**	**208**
Cost of credit at effective interest rate of 12%	3%	6%	4%	7%

This shows that the intended 60 days credit soon becomes 90 days or more, depending on delays; and that the cost of waiting soon erodes the net profit margin (typically 4 per cent).

Much longer payment delays, which frequently occur, can totally wipe out the profit.

The total payment period can be reduced if all the above stages are managed better. For example, the credit period should run from date of shipment, not delivery, to eliminate 14 days. The 60 days credit period may be negotiable downwards. Late payments by customers can be reduced by more specific payment arrangements and better collection efforts. The delay in hard currency from poor countries (which may be a lot longer than 90 days) can be found out well before shipment, from UK bank reports or credit insurers – so that prepayment or LC may be arranged. The bank transfer time can easily be overcome by specifying a Telegraphic Transfer (TT), which should be same day value. A SWIFT payment will take 3 days. If payment is by euros, you can request payment by EUROCHAPS which is immediate same day value, but you may require a euro bank account in the UK. Improvements are possible, but somebody in the exporting company has to make the time to make the arrangements.

Effective Conditions of Sale

It is wise, both legally and commercially, for exporting firms to have a well-drafted set of conditions of sale. These are useful for everyday disciplines as well as providing clarity before disagreements become really serious and loss-making.

The conditions of sale, to be legally enforceable in a serious dispute, must be made known to the customer before the contract is made. That is good practice anyway, particularly if the customer has already issued his own conditions of purchase. Printing the conditions on the invoice is too late to be legally binding if it is the first time the customer has been made aware of them. It is enough for the customer to be aware of the terms; it is not necessary to obtain signed agreement to them, though always desirable.

Quotations and sales literature should always show the conditions. That enables the customer to challenge anything not acceptable instead of withholding payment later as recompense.

Exporters should scrutinise incoming customer orders to identify unacceptable purchase conditions and negotiate them out. Take an example: the exporter's payment terms are 60 days from shipment date yet the customer's order states 'payment will be made six months after satisfactory testing of the goods at our works'. It would be dangerous to go ahead with the order without challenging and changing such an unacceptable term.

Orders should always be acknowledged in writing, ideally via a formal order confirmation. Export conditions of sale should:

- clearly show that they are subject to English (or Scottish or Northern Irish) law and allow for arbitration of disputes by, for example, the International Chamber of Commerce;

- state that they supersede any conditions of purchase from the buyer.

The conditions should include:

- terms of payment, including the credit period and method of remittance cost escalation, if applicable (the right to increase prices if certain costs increase);

- interest for late payment (the discretionary right to charge interest if payment is overdue);

- Retention of Title (to show when ownership passes);

- currency clause (specifying the buyer's responsibility for shortfalls);

- Incoterms (the delivery term).

APPLICABLE LAW AND SETTLEMENT OF DISPUTES

Although UK exporters may make their sales contracts subject to English law, there is still a cost and delay in enforcement of UK High Court judgments abroad, albeit now under various EU treaties and Commonwealth reciprocal arrangements, UK judgments are automatically enforceable in some 60 countries.

Unlike the UK, where credit managers are used to managing County Court litigation themselves, most foreign jurisdictions do not allow companies to act in person and it is almost invariably necessary to employ local lawyers. This applies to issue and enforcement, with subsequent delays for hearings. It is often quicker to settle any major dispute by arbitration, as provided for in the contract conditions. It is important to specify place of arbitration, method of appointing the arbitrator and preferably the rules, such as UNCITRAL or ICC. Normally, firms appoint a specialised institution such as the Court of Arbitration of the International Chamber of Commerce (the ICC), which follows internationally trusted procedures. A major advantage of an arbitration award is that it automatically enforceable in the courts of many countries, including the USA and Russia, which do not automatically recognise UK judgments otherwise.

One point to note however is that if the matter is a purely debt collection matter and unlikely to be defended, such as a dishonoured cheque or draft, it is better to explore any summary judgment process available through the local courts, as enforcement may be more effective.

COST ESCALATION CLAUSE

Prices may suffer from inflation or sudden changes of commodity costs between quotation and final delivery. It may be uncompetitive to include all possible contingencies in the price but the buyer may agree a cost escalation clause, allowing price increases in specified materials, based on a trusted international index. During a long period of low inflation, these clauses became less common, but escalating oil and commodity prices, and volatility in exchange rates reinforces the need for such, especially in contracts with long durations.

INTEREST CLAUSE FOR LATE PAYMENT

Since a contract specifies terms of payment, it is logical to have the right to charge extra if payment is not made by the due date. Some exporters show an interest rate which equates to their own cost of borrowing, but that could be very attractive to defaulters in countries with very high interest rates. The rate should be a deterrent, such as 2 per cent for each month beyond the agreed due date. Even that is attractive in countries where it might cost the buyer 60 per cent p.a. to borrow the funds to pay a debt. For this reason, some exporters flex the rate according to the cost of money in each country to which they sell. Some jurisdictions, particularly in the Middle East, either do not allow or severely restrict the charging of interest. However, even there, the law recognises the additional administrative cost of delayed payments and lost profit.

In other countries, although interest may be charged, it may not be remitted to the UK because of local exchange controls. This is not the problem it may have been 20 years ago. Elsewhere, a withholding tax may be levied on the interest element of a remittance.

The exporter should use the deterrent purpose of a penalty interest clause by showing the right to charge it in all key collection documents and conversations.

Where the payment is requested through the buyer's bank, such as on cash against documents, it is always worth adding an interest claim to the collection, with the instruction the interest cannot be waived. This often results in the interest being paid. It is particularly valuable where a bill of lading or duty preference certificate are part of the documents submitted, as without paying the charge the goods cannot be obtained or a higher duty incurred.

EXCHANGE CLAUSE

As any contract assumes the stated price will be paid, a protective clause is essential where the customer's currency is different from the invoiced currency. Sterling is not a popular currency in most importing countries and there is often a delay between the customer's payment in local currency and the eventual hard currency remittance by their bank. When the time comes for the remittance, the local currency paid some time earlier may have become too little for their bank to send the full sterling amount, because of its worsening exchange rate.

The customer may feel that they have met their obligation by paying in their own currency on time, but it can only be their responsibility to make up the shortfall with a further payment. A suitable clause might read: 'It is the customer's responsibility to provide sufficient local currency to remit the invoiced currency amount at the date of the remittance.'

RETENTION OF TITLE (RESERVATION OF PROPERTY)

Ownership of goods passes to a buyer when the parties agree that it will. (Note: Possession is not ownership!) Ownership can be agreed to pass at manufacture, inspection, delivery, payment or whenever. For clearly risky customers, or for sales to countries where ownership is routinely retained by the seller until payment, such as The Netherlands and Germany, the seller may specify that goods belong to the buyer only when paid for.

A simple clause might read: 'the goods remain our property until paid for' but the wording really needs legal advice in case of problems when goods are sold on or mixed with others. The possibility of physical recovery is also a consideration for some suppliers.

INCOTERMS

This is a set of internationally agreed rules to codify the obligations of exporters and importers in a sale. The latest version was published in 2000 by the ICC publication reference number 560. The rules have been around since the 1930s so are well tried and tested, being updated every 10 years or so to take account of new modes of transport. The ICC is currently reviewing the rules with a view to issuing a new version of Incoterms in 2009 or 2010. It is therefore important to specify which set of rules are being used as the same initials can have slightly different meanings or obligations under different issued forms. Some terms are changed completely or disappear!

Obviously, it helps to avoid expensive errors and disputes if it is clear what the export price covers. In exporting, the key price factor is the physical point at which the buyer takes over responsibility for costs and risks. For example, a price of just '£100' does not tell if this covers the goods only, or their conveyance to the docks, or whether they are insured, or who pays for port loading and customs duties, or transportation at the other end, and so on. Even when these aspects have been agreed between the parties, they may not be known to shippers or foreign authorities who levy charges. The Incoterms code, applied alongside the price, makes the responsibilities clear to all parties along the way. The terms are shown in Figure 17.1.

Although the Incoterms price basis is primarily a matter for the sales department, the credit manager should be familiar with the meanings of the different Incoterms, to deal with disputes when accounts come to be paid. For example, on CFR, CIF, CPT and CIP terms, although the exporter arranges transport and pays the carrier, the risk of loss or damage to the goods after loading is that of the buyer. Therefore any claim for credit should be addressed by the buyer to its own insurer, not the seller. if the credit manager is not aware of how risk passes in Incoterms, unjustified credit claims may be entertained.

At the very least, exporting firms should ensure that their invoices state one of the standard Incoterms, such as FOB or CIF, alongside the price. They should also check that the Incoterms basis in the buyer's order or correspondence is either followed or renegotiated.

EXW	Ex Works (...named place)
FCA	Free Carrier (...named place)
FAS	Free Alongside Ship (...named port of shipment)
FOB	Free On Board (...named port of shipment)
CFR	Cost and Freight (...named port of destination)
CIF	Cost, Insurance and Freight (...named port of destination)
CPT	Carriage Paid To (...named place of destination)
CIP	Carriage and Insurance Paid To (...named place of destination)
DAF	Delivered At Frontier (...named place)
DES	Delivered Ex Ship (...named port of destination)
DEQ	Delivered Ex Quay (...named port of destination)
DDU	Delivered Duty Unpaid (...named place of destination)
DDP	Delivered Duty Paid (...named place of destination)

Figure 17.1   Incoterms 2000

Agents, Distributors and Subsidiaries

It always helps to have local representation to:

- obtain information about customers and on payment regulations;

- follow up overdues and disputes on the spot;

- collaborate with a local collecting bank;

- respond instantly to any need of the faraway exporter.

Agents are different from distributors. An agent cannot owe the exporter money unless he has bought on his own account. He is appointed to act on behalf of the exporter – the agent *is* the exporter. He normally promotes the exporter's products and obtains orders, for which he gets a commission. If he buys on his own account, he becomes the customer for that order, not the agent.

It is vital, therefore, that the exporter knows exactly the actual customers from whom the agent has obtained orders, even if they pay through the agent. They, not the agent, are legally responsible to the exporter for payment. An agent's commission should be accrued and accounted for to the agent at the invoice stage, but never actually paid out until the underlying debt has been paid. Many exporting firms in recent years have rewritten agency agreements to include financial duties as well as sales generation.

Del credere agents are responsible for the debts on orders they obtain. Although they receive a higher commission rate for this greater responsibility, they are rare these days because of the increase in slow payers and bad debts.

Distributors are not agents. They are independent of the exporter. They are customers in the full sense of being responsible to the exporter for payment of the goods sold to them. However, distributors do receive special support from the exporter to promote products in a defined territory. Since they replace the need to have numbers of direct customers in that territory, they may be allowed longer credit terms and a larger credit rating. Their creditworthiness for this form of financial support may present difficulties for the credit manager, and close monitoring is needed.

Subsidiaries, which may be wholly or majority-owned by the exporter, should be required to act locally to obtain credit information and help with difficult collections. While some groups require their subsidiaries to carry out this responsibility, others operate at arm's length, where subsidiaries have to be persuaded or paid to act for other group companies. Many organisations are not very good at collecting inter-company debts from subsidiaries and associated companies. They think that as they are inter-company debts, they are not as important as external debts. This can be a very dangerous attitude, especially in difficult markets, as political risks and transfer problems can make even inter-company obligations bad debts. Moreover, paying intra-group debts on time ensures good cash flow for the supplying division and better cash management in the obligor.

Export Documents

Unlike home trade sales, exporting involves many different documents stipulated in the contract and required by foreign authorities and the banking system, as well as by the customer. They are used to evidence compliance of contract performance, expedite custom clearance and expedite payment.

Accuracy is paramount, it is not optional. Inaccurate, incomplete or incorrect documents are a major cause of payment delays and can hinder importation, incur additional costs or even cause the goods to be impounded. To get the goods safely to the customer and to get payment out of the other country, exporters must take care to know which documents are needed for each particular market. The recognised authority is *Croner's Reference Book For Exporters*.

INVOICES

The several types of invoice include:

Commercial invoice: More complex than a home invoice, a commercial invoice shows the price base (EXW, FOB and so on) and may have to be in a foreign language or currency. As well as the usual detail of buyer, goods and value, it is normally required to show weights, packing details and a declaration for customs purposes. Obviously, the payment terms must be clearly shown, together with the exporter's bank details, typically the SWIFT code and IBAN number. For sales within the EU the buyer's VAT number is required, thus zero rating the supply. Many countries require the invoice to be signed by the exporter.

Certified invoice: A commercial invoice which is certified as correct by an independent body, usually a Chamber of Commerce. In many cases, the signature of the exporter is sufficient.

Pro forma invoice: An invoice sent in advance of the goods, either at the buyer's request, to obtain permission from his authorities to arrange an import licence or to have foreign currency allocated; or at the exporter's request, to demand cash in advance. The pro forma version of an invoice should show all the detail that will appear on the eventual commercial invoice. Indeed, it is vital that the final actual invoice does not differ in essentials from the pro forma. In many circumstances, the pro forma invoice acts as the quotation, so it is vital that it is correct.

Consular invoice: Required by some countries on forms issued by their own embassies or consulates in exporters' countries for statistical and customs purposes.

Legalised invoice: Similar to a consular invoice. Some countries require commercial invoices to be stamped and recorded by their embassy or consulate in the country of the exporter.

Transport Documents

- *By sea:* Bill of Lading.

- *By air:* Airway Bill (or Air Waybill).

- *By road:* Road Consignment Note (or CMR note).

- *By post:* Parcel Post Receipt (or certificate of posting).

Bill of Lading (B/L): For centuries, this remarkable document has served exporters all over the world very well. It meets three purposes:

- a receipt for the goods from the carrier;

- evidence of the contract of carriage;

- document of title to the goods.

It is the only transport document which gives title (ownership, not possession) to the goods. The consignee cannot get hold of the goods until he is able to present the original B/L to the carrier. Because of this unique quality of the B/L, the credit manager is able to control release of the goods to the customer against full payment or an obligation for a future date.

A B/L can be marked 'Received For Shipment' by the shipping company, or as 'Shipped' by them. A 'Through Bill of Lading' covers all the stages in a shipment to an inland destination. A 'Combined Transport Bill of Lading' is produced when more than one form of transport is needed in a shipment. A 'House Bill of Lading' (often not acceptable to customers and banks) is simply one issued by a freight forwarder in advance of getting the shipping company's actual B/L. A 'Groupage Bill of Lading' shows that the goods have been consolidated with others, usually in a container. 'Short-form' bills are abbreviated versions which show that the full conditions are available at the carrier's offices.

A B/L should be 'clean', meaning that it bears no clauses about defects, such as 'rusty metal' or 'two cartons damaged'. Such comments make the B/L 'dirty' or 'claused'. 'Stale' bills are those issued too late for a particular contract, which may be a LC with a deadline, (normally within 21 days of shipment, in most LCs).

B/Ls are usually issued in sets of three signed originals plus any number of non-negotiable copies. It is important not to let any of the signed originals fall into the wrong hands, since they can then claim ownership of the goods. For example, sending one original to the actual customer, just to be helpful to them, would forfeit the security provided by the B/L.

Airway Bills are issued by airline carriers. They are evidence of receiving the goods and also the contract of carriage but are specifically not documents of title. The stated consignee can take possession of the goods on arrival without even holding the actual airway bill.

Documents or goods sent by courier also have an airway bill as evidence of receipt and for tracking purposes.

Road or Rail Consignment Notes are issued by a road transport company or railway company as receipts and contracts of carriage but, like airway bills, are not documents of title to the goods.

Parcel Post Receipts are issued by the Royal Mail as receipts for accepting goods for delivery abroad. There is no guarantee of delivery, which depends on the foreign postal system. Note: In many countries, post has to be collected or deliveries are spasmodic, and COD is not usually possible for exports.

INSURANCE DOCUMENTS

The terms of delivery define whether the exporter or the buyer is responsible for insuring the cargo. For example, an FOB price makes the exporter responsible only up to the ship's rail, so the buyer has to insure the shipment stage. But with a CIF price, the exporter is responsible up to the ship's rail under its own risk, but is responsible for arranging insurance in the buyer's name thereafter. There are many expensive payment disputes where FOB goods are lost or damaged in transit, yet in law, the buyer should pay to terms and claim under their insurance for the cargo. It is not the exporter's responsibility.

The buyer, their bank or import authorities may need to see evidence of the insurance if it has been arranged by the exporter. Most exporters have a blanket policy with their insurance company for all their shipments, allowing them or their brokers to write individual *insurance certificates* per shipment. Occasionally, the buyer or their government insists on a separate *insurance policy* for a shipment. For valid cover, the policy or certificate must be dated at shipment date or earlier. Normally, LCs do not accept *brokers' cover notes* as evidence of insurance.

Export certificates: Many different certificates may be specified by customers or their authorities, for example:

- *Certificate of Origin (C of O):* While it may be enough to state the origin of goods on the invoice, a separate document may be called for, issued by a Chamber of Commerce. For some markets, the C of O may be combined with a Certificate of Value, for customs purposes. The certificate does not prove origin; it purely certifies the signature is one from an authorised officer of the seller.

- *Inspection Certificate (or Certificate of Clean Findings):* This evidences that the goods conform to the quantity and quality stated, and in some cases, are of the correct commercial value. Due to exchange controls and to avoid fraud and capital flight, certain countries use an independent inspection company, operating in their suppliers' countries, to check that what is being shipped is what was ordered and paid for. The prevalence of this process as a government requirement has reduced dramatically over the last decade as import controls and foreign exchange controls have liberalised, but it remains a commercial requirement where verification of quality and quantity is required to trigger payment, under an L/C for example. Whilst it is a tedious process to arrange, it does offer the seller the security that the goods have been verified by an independent trusted third party for quality and quantity, thereby reducing the ability of a less scrupulous buyer to dispute what was actually sent.

- *Blacklist Certificate:* An exporter may have to certify that he is not blacklisted by the buying country. There are many situations of conflict between nations, causing ordinary companies to be penalised for doing business with certain markets.

- *Weight/Analysis/Health and so on Certificates*: These are called for to prove that the standards in the buying country have been met, or that a particular term of the contract has been adhered to. Weight certificates are also used in insurance claims as many international conventions specify the carrier's maximum liability based on a rate per kilo.

BILL OF EXCHANGE

The bill of exchange is widely used in international business for collecting payment through the banking system. The Bill of Exchange Act of 1882 defines it as: 'An unconditional order in writing, addressed by one person (the drawer) to another (the drawee), signed by the person giving it, requiring the person to whom it is addressed to pay on demand or at a fixed or determinable future time, a sum certain in money to, or to the order of, a specified person (the payee), or to bearer.' That definition has stood the test of time and is recognised and copied internationally.

An example of a bill of exchange is given in Figure 17.2.

A *sight draft* is payable on demand – at the sight of it, by the drawee. A *term draft* shows either a specific future due date or is due at, say, 90 days after sight, or after a particular event which can be dated, such as shipment. Whereas a sight draft has to be paid immediately, a term draft has to be accepted, by the drawee signing across its face, as an obligation to pay it at the future due date.

The exporter prepares the draft and sends it to the customer, via a bank, for payment or acceptance. A standard *instruction form* is used to give the bank all the information necessary to handle the collection to the exporter's satisfaction (for example, who pays the charges, how to remit the proceeds, the name of a local contact if needed). A sample instruction form is shown in Figure 17.3.

Most international banks subscribe to the ICC's Uniform Rules for Collections (URC), publication number 522 (2000 Revision), which sets out the responsibilities of all parties for collections. Under the rules, for example, the collecting bank must advise the exporter 'promptly' of the fate of a collection, including the customer's reason for not accepting or not paying it.

Bills can be *clean* or *documentary*. A documentary bill has the documents attached that the customer needs, so the exporter can control the release of the

EXCHANGE FOR STG£57111.00   BIRMINGHAM 19 May 19

At 120 days after sight _pay_this first **Bill of Exchange to the Order of**

second of this same tenor and date unpaid

G. GREENLIGHT LTD. THE SUM OF STERLING POUNDS FIFTYSEVEN THOUSAND ONE HUNDRED
AND ELEVEN, ONLY. VALUE RECEIVED.

                                             G. GREENLIGHT LTD

AMANI DEVELOPMENT CORPORATION
HARBOUR ROAD
JEDDAH, SAUDI ARABIA.

To   (signature)

                                             (also endorsement on reverse)

Misc. No. 9
* * * * * 5069049
The Solicitors' Law Stationery Society Ltd.,
Pavilion House, 8 Shepherdess Walk, London N1 7LB   10.89 BM
Oyez

Figure 17.2 Sample bill of exchange

UK BANK PLC   **COLLECTION INSTRUCTION**

Please complete this form in BLOCK CAPITALS and in black ink_____

To: Bank abroad name and address

-    **From**
-    UKB, Collections Centre, PO Box 1
-    ANYWHERE, ZZ99 9ZZ
-    Tel: 020 xxx xxxx Fax: 020 xxx xxxx
                                     SWIFT Code UKBKGB1W

                                     DATE :ddmmyy

                     UKB
                     Reference: U- - - - - - - - - -
                Please quote full reference when corresponding

---

Buyer/Drawee

-    **Principal/Drawer reference:**
-    -
- -
-                **Currency:** - - - - -
-    **Amount of Collection:**
                                   -- -

Seller/Drawer

-    **Tenor :**- - - - - - - - - - - - - - - - -
- -
-    Please deal with the enclosed
-    remittance in accordance with the
-    following instructions:
                                     Deliver documents against
                                     Acceptance _ _ **or** Payment _ _

---

1. Documents

Bill of Exchange _ _   Comm'l invoice _ _   Cert/Cons inv _ _   Ins pol/cert _ _

Cert of origin   _ _   Bill of lading   _ _   Parcel post rec't _ _ Air waybill _ _

Comb trans   _ _   **Other:**   _ _   _ _   _ _

---

2. Charges

Collect all charges including ours of ££££.pp   Collect all of your charges, stamps _ _

Charges may be waived   Yes _ _   No _ _

Figure 17.3   Sample instruction form for bill of exchange

3. Non –acceptance/Non-payment

Acceptance/payment may be deferred until goods arrive   Yes _ _   No _ _

If unaccepted   Protest _ _   Do not protest _ _

If unpaid   Protest _ _   Do not protest _ _

Advise reasons for refusal to us and confirm case of need , where given, has been advised

If documents are not taken up on arrival of goods please advise us, stating reason, and

Warehouse goods _ _   Do not warehouse _ _

Insurance covered by buyer/drawee _ _   Insure against fire _ _

Do not insure   _ _

(All charges accrued on the goods are for the principals account)

4. Special instructions:

----

5. Settlement instructions:

----

6. In case of need refer to:
--- For guidance   _ _

--- Accept their instructions _ _

If necessary accept a deposit in local currency together with buyer/drawee's written

Undertaking to take all possible action to ensure remittance of sterling/dollars/euros and

to make good any exchange loss.

Advise date paid in local currency _ _

Figure 17.3   *Continued*

7. Authorisation

Signature   **For Collections Centre use only**

- -

-      Apply forward contract number

- -

Name _ _ _ _ _ _ _ _ _ _ _ _ _ _ _   Bill already accepted   _ _

Date _ _ _ _ _ _ _ _ _

---

1. General Instructions

The following instructions are given by the Bank to the collecting Bank and are applicable except in so far as they may be modified or contradicted by any special instructions from the customer.

1.1. Acknowledge receipt, quoting both your and our reference numbers.
1.2. If documents are not taken up on arrival of goods please advise us, stating reason (all charges accrued on the goods are for the principals account).
1.3. Advise reasons for refusal to us and confirm case of need, where given, has been advised.
1.4. Advise acceptance and due date.
1.5. Send all advices by **SWIFT** unless instructed otherwise
1.6. Term bills not already accepted should be presented on receipt and after acceptance, should be held for payment at maturity.
1.7. When collections cover consignments addressed to yourselves by parcel and/or airfreight, the relative packages should be released in accordance with the instructions given for the release of documents.
1.8. If documents of title are attached and are not taken up on arrival of the consignment or any difficulty arises, please advise us, stating the reason.

Meanwhile, please ensure that the goods are properly protected but do not insure them.
All charges accrued on the goods are for the drawee's account.
Failure on your part to comply with all the instructions given will be at your sole responsibility
Subject to Uniform Rules for Collection URC522, ICC Publication
It must be understood that we assume **NO** responsibility for the correctness, validity, or genuineness of any of the drafts or documents handed to us referring to the goods, the subject of bills of collection or the description, quality, quantity or delivery of the goods which the documents may purport to represent.

Figure 17.3   *Concluded*

goods to a customer by the release instructions given to his bank. A clean bill travels alone and is only an instrument of payment to use where the customer is trusted, that is, for the bank to collect an otherwise 'open account' debt. Bills can carry clauses, for example to charge interest, and can be discounted for cash during the credit period.

Payment Terms

These reflect the *time, security* and *method* of payment. They depend on:

- the exporter's view of the customer risks (commercial risk);

- any existing or expected delays in the transfer of hard currency (transfer or political risk);

- what terms are usual in the market what competitors are offering.

They should not be simply what the customer demands.

Time, or the credit period, can range up to 180 days for ordinary trade (consumer goods, raw materials, components); up to two years for certain semi-capital machinery and manufacturing equipment; and up to seven years, or sometimes longer, for capital goods and projects. There is no international law on these credit 'norms', merely a long-established understanding amongst trading nations.

Security ranges from total risk, by sending the goods and waiting to be paid, to the other extreme of zero risk, where payment is required before the goods are released. However, there is always a trade off between security and cost. Figure 17.5 maps the relationship between the two, and the clear correlation that the greater the security, generally the greater cost and administrative burden attached.

Methods of payment vary from direct remittances from customers to bank transfers and LCs. Figure 17.4 shows a list of 16 different payment terms conveying the above points. Although terminology differs in some countries, the terms shown in the list are widely used by commercial firms and banks.

HIGH RISK	OPEN ACCOUNT
	No terms of payment stated at all!
	x days
	x days from arrival of goods
	x days from date of invoice
	x days from date of shipment
	DOCUMENTARY COLLECTION (via a bank)
	Draft at x days after sight (D/A)
	Draft at x days after arrival of goods (D/A)
	Draft at x days after invoice date (D/A)
	Draft at x days after shipment (D/A)
	Sight draft (D/P)
	Cash against documents (CAD)
	DOCUMENTARY LETTER OF CREDIT
	Revocable letter of credit (RLC)
	Irrevocable LC, by issuing bank in country at risk (ILC)
	Confirmed Irrevocable LC, confirmed by bank outside the country at risk (CILC)
	Confirmed Irrevocable LC, confirmed by UK bank (CILC)
LOW RISK	Payment in Advance

Figure 17.4   Payment terms in order of risk

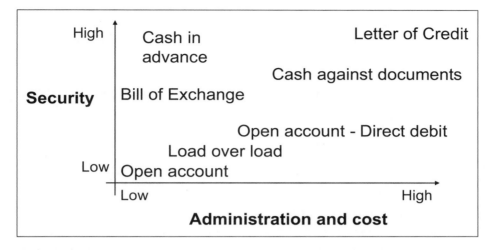

Figure 17.5   Payment terms – security versus cost

No payment terms at all: Difficult to believe, but it happens. In law, this may be a free gift and depends on the goodwill of the customer for payment. Under English law now if credit terms are not agreed or stated, they are assumed to be 30 days, and interest runs from then. Not recommended!

Open account terms should only be used for trusted customers in hard currency markets, since the goods and essential documents are sent directly to the customer as in a normal domestic transaction. He can thus obtain the goods and never pay; nor has the exporter any bank acting for him in the control of release of goods. Where agreed with the customer, the exporter may send a clean, or non-documentary, bill of exchange through the banking system, to strengthen the collection process.

The due date of an open account transaction is important. 'X days from arrival of the goods' is weak, since the exporter cannot be sure when the goods arrive. 'X days from invoice date' is acceptable if the customer trusts the exporter not to pre-date an invoice. The best approach is to date the credit period from shipment, since that is shown on the neutral shipping document and is evident to both parties.

Documentary collections through a bank involve the use of two banks acting for the exporter under strict obligations – the ICC URC. The exporter's bank sends the draft and essential documents to a nominated bank in the buyer's town, to hand them to the customer in exchange for payment if a Sight Draft – hence

'D/P' or Documents Against Payment; or for a promise to pay in the future if a 'term draft', for example, payable at 90 days from the date of shipment.

The promise to pay takes the form of an 'acceptance' written across the face of the bill of exchange – hence 'D/A' or Documents against Acceptance. The bank normally retains the accepted bill and presents it for payment at the due date. The rules for the period of credit on a term draft are the same as those above for open account, that is to say, the date of shipment is recommended.

Cash against documents (CAD) are simply D/P collections through the banking system without the use of a bill of exchange. Bills are sometimes avoided because they can attract stamp duty and are thus unpopular with customers. The expressions *draft* and *bill* are loosely interchanged. In law, the item drawn up by the exporter is a draft. Once accepted by the drawee, it is known as an acceptance, or accepted bill of exchange.

Bills used in exports are known as Foreign Bills and, in order to be easily pursued in the local courts if needed, they must be *protested* for non-acceptance or non-payment. This requires the exporter to give advance instructions to the collecting bank, via the instruction form, to protest the bill in the event of dishonour, by calling in a local lawyer to *note* the default and formally *protest* it, by stamping and signing the bill. The act of protest is powerful in some countries. It is recorded and published in the local business newspaper and can lead to a run on confidence. Exporters with credit insurance cover are required to protest dishonoured bills, to protect the insurer's interests in the event of its collection attempt after a claim has been paid.

Documentary letters of credit have become enormously in demand as a means of getting paid from countries short of hard currency. They represent a strong guarantee of payment from a bank on behalf of the customer but are potentially expensive and administratively onerous, so thus not suitable for small value deals.

A LC is simply a written undertaking by a bank, issued at the request of their client, to pay up a *stated amount* against *stipulated documents* within *a prescribed time limit*. The three main types are *Revocable (RLC)*, *Unconfirmed Irrevocable (ILC)* and *Confirmed Irrevocable (CILC)*.

A *RLC*, as the name implies, can be amended or cancelled by the buyer or his bank at any time up to shipment, thus diminishing its security. An RLC is rare these days and used mainly with traditional markets merely as a means of payment. The latest inter-bank rules for L/Cs, UCP 600, no longer recognise revocable credits, as they are too risky for the banks to administer.

The *Irrevocable LC* is by far the most common type in use. The customer's bank (the 'opening' or 'issuing' bank) gives the exporter its undertaking to pay, provided the conditions of the credit are met. Thus there is no longer any customer credit risk, the risk being that the foreign bank will not be able to pay when the time comes. The ILC is *advised* to the exporter by a bank in the UK, usually in London, and payment is made by that bank in due course, but only if it has the funds from the other end by then. The issuing bank is in the risky country that caused the exporter to ask for the LC in the first place. Its remittance of hard currency to the UK may be prevented or severely delayed by its government. Exporters should be wary of ILCs from countries with a known currency transfer delay.

The *CILC* is more expensive but removes the above country risk, since another bank in the UK (or another hard currency country) adds its commitment to the LC payment. Thus, with a CILC opened by a bank in Bangladesh and advised *and* confirmed by Barclays Bank in London, the exporter can be confident of payment regardless of the customer and the country risk.

Exporters should ensure that LCs they receive show that they are issued under the ICC Uniform Customs and Practice for Documentary Credits, known as UCP 600, which govern the obligations of all the parties and are accepted by banks and courts in almost every country of the world.

However, a major risk remains with LCs, regardless of the bank involved – that of the exporter shooting himself in the foot by not complying with the LC's conditions. Having gone to all the trouble and expense of getting a bank's undertaking to guarantee payment, there is a 70 per cent chance (the international average) that, because of lateness or errors in documents, the exporter will not be paid by the advising bank on first presentation. Banks paying under LCs operate to a *doctrine of strict compliance* and, regardless of common sense or previous practice, an exporter must make sure that he presents to the bank exactly what the LC describes – each and every time.

SITPRO, a government-funded body in London to help exporters, has an excellent set of checklists for LCs. They recommend three stages of control to achieve smooth payments and avoid customer upsets, namely:

- when requesting the LC to be opened;

- on receipt of the LC;

- when presenting documents for payment.

CHECK-STAGE ONE: REQUESTING THE LETTER OF CREDIT

When notifying a customer on a quotation or order confirmation that an LC is required, the exporter should send a standard advice of what he expects the LC to show, especially:

- description of goods weights and prices;

- delivery terms (Incoterms basis);

- port of shipment documents to be presented for that market;

- whether part shipments and/or transhipments will be allowed;

- final date allowed for shipment;

- who pays what bank charges.

All these points should simply reflect the sales order anyway but the customer will find them useful to give to his opening bank.

CHECK-STAGE TWO: ON RECEIPT OF THE LETTER OF CREDIT

LCs arrive in different shapes and sizes from different banks selected by customers, not the exporter, addressed to different people – the managing director, a salesperson, a technical contact, shipping, cashier and so on. The exporter should appoint a single person to whom all LCs should be delivered and that individual should immediately:

- cross-refer the LC to the order then scan it and email it to all departments who will be involved in the export fulfillment process (including sales, customer administration, logistics, warehouse freight forwarder, the people who will produce the documents:

shipping, insurance, invoices, technical certificates, sales items and accounts).

• require a response from the addressees within 24 hours of any changes required, including inconsistencies between the pro forma/ quote and the LC, conditions which cannot be complied with, and the recipients confirmation it meets all their requirements.

For any errors, unworkable documents or impossible dates, the customer can be contacted to arrange a single amendment. If, instead, this is done in several separate requests over the weeks, the customer may justifiably complain and there is a danger of not enough time to alter the LC. Finally, the LC controller should diarise the LC for about two weeks prior to expiry date to allow time to get remaining actions done and avoid the danger of lateness.

CHECK-STAGE THREE: PRESENTING THE DOCUMENTS

A single person, either the original checker, or a credit person, should be responsible for accumulating the specified documents from their various sources in good time to claim payment before the stated expiry date, or the date for presentation if sooner. The final check should be that documents are exactly as called for in the LC; that there is consistency between the documents; and that the presentation to the bank meets the bank's original instructions in its covering letter.

In summary, an ILC, and particularly when confirmed, is an excellent guarantee of payment but the exporter should remember that the London bank acts as a broker between the parties. They will pay the exporter quickly and safely; but they protect the foreign customer by ensuring the exporter has done *exactly* what the buyer has specified.

For all exporters, the SITPRO Checklists for Letters of Credit are highly recommended.

Countertrade

This is a generic term for a variety of ways to exchange goods and services to minimise the need for valuable foreign exchange.

With the liberalisation of international markets and increase in availability of hard currency, even in developing markets, countertrade has reduced in preference to cash transactions over the last 10 to 15 years. Certainly, the fall of the Iron Curtain and the integration of the central European countries into the EU has dramatically reduced its need. However, it is still used in mega-sized governmental contracts, especially in the defence arena, where offset rather than foreign exchange generation is the desired result for the buying country.

Barter is the exchange of goods for goods where no money changes hands. It is usually very difficult to match the timing required for the exchange of goods, so not many such deals are eventually put together.

Counter-purchase involves passing goods or services in both directions, with linked contracts of sale. Hard currency is paid by both parties to each other, with normally the weaker country being paid first. Sometimes a bank is employed to hold the funds in escrow until the other party has performed.

Offset involves one government agreeing to buy from another, on condition that the product contains its own components or labour to an agreed percentage.

Buy-back occurs where a company supplies plant or know-how to a poorer country and agrees to buy back some of the resulting manufacture.

The advantages of countertrade lie in keeping a market open in times of exchange shortage. The disadvantage for the exporter is having to dispose of possibly poor quality goods with little or no after-sales service.

The general advice to exporters is to take customers' countertrade proposals seriously because it may be the only way that an import licence will be issued. The negotiations may later fall away and normal payment be procured, but if they do make progress, there are many experienced agencies to organise disposal of the unwanted foreign product.

Tender and Performance Bonds

A small proportion of international trade depends on processes of tendering and, for the successful bidders, proper performance of the contracts awarded. To protect buyers from frivolous tendering and unsatisfactory performance of contracts, suppliers are usually asked to give guarantees that buyers will be recompensed in those cases.

The guarantees are issued on the exporters' behalf by banks (bonds payable on demand) or surety companies (conditional bonds). Although most buyers insist on 'on demand' bonds, they are disliked by exporters because of the risk that they can be cashed at any time without checking, even after the exporter has performed properly. This problem is known as 'unfair calling', for which credit insurance cover is available where the client is a government or state-owned entity. It is harder to obtain where the buyer is a commercial enterprise.

Tender or bid bonds evidence that the bidder has the financial strength to undertake the contract, and guarantee that the bidder will not walk away if his bid is accepted without penalty. They are typically for between 2 per cent and 5 per cent of the bid price, but can be for as much as 10 per cent.

Performance bonds guarantee that the exporter will perform the contract and are usually between 5 and 10 per cent of contract value but can be a lot higher.

Maintenance bonds apply where a contract calls for maintenance services after start-up and the buyer fears the exporter may not perform these satisfactorily.

Advance payment bonds ensure that any advance payment to the exporter can be recovered by the buyer if the supplier does not carry out the terms of the contract.

Retention bonds are useful to the exporter where a contract allows the buyer to retain a percentage until satisfactory commissioning or for a number of months after completion. The retention bond allows the exporter to be paid in full and the buyer to recover the agreed percentage if a defect occurs.

It is easy to be seduced into accepting advance payments and early payment of retentions against the provision of a bank guarantee, as the cash is in the bank and the debt is off the Aged Debtors Report. The DSO looks great! However, management visibility of the obligation is lost.

But, and it's a big BUT, most banks provide guarantees against a prearranged facility limit, typically as part of an overdraft limit. In essence, if the bank gives the bond, it reduces the overdraft limit accordingly, pound for pound. Not very good for working capital planning in most businesses, as the overdraft is required to fund the work in progress. Taking the advance payment may look good, but in effect the bank will take the cash and put it on deposit, as security for the guarantee. Net effect, zero cash. The bank pays interest on the receipt at a deposit rate, and charges a fee, typically 1 to 2 per cent per annum for priding the bond. Adding the differential between the deposit and overdraft rates of between 2 and 5 per cent, gives a potential real cost to the company of between 3 and 7 per cent. This does not account for any overseas bank's charges and the burden of getting the bond cancelled when it should be, (which it rarely ever is.) To be worth accepting, the fees must be significantly less than cost of the overdraft.

All the major banks offer useful booklets and advice on bonds and guarantees.

Getting Funds Transferred from Abroad

Experienced credit managers know that the job is not yet done when the customer pays. Billions of pounds, dollars and other major currencies are swilling around in the banking system of the world for several days or weeks after the local payment by the importer and before the eventual credit to the exporter's bank account.

Exporters need to: tell customers precisely how the money should be sent understand how funds are remitted by *each* customer apply pressure and skills to speeding up the receipt.

CUSTOMER'S CHEQUE

This may be in sterling, the buyer's own currency or a third currency such as US dollars. Do not encourage payment by cheque unless drawn on a UK clearing account. Otherwise it has to go all the way back to be cleared by the bank on which it is drawn before value can be safely credited to the exporter. There will be delays in clearance, bank charges at both ends and a risk of exchange shortfall. Being a cheque it can also bounce.

Whilst most of the UK banks now offer a good service for negotiating foreign cheques, there will be a delay before the funds are treated as cleared and a charge for the service.

These days it is often cheaper for both buyer and seller to make payment by electronic transfer methods.

BANKER'S DRAFT

A banker's draft is better than a customer's cheque. Their bank, however remote, will issue its cheque in favour of the exporter but drawn on a bank in the UK with which it has a clearing arrangement. The exporter can get the usual UK clearance in the three-day standard period.

MAIL TRANSFER (AIRMAIL)

This is now an unusual method of being paid as most banks work internationally through the SWIFT system. The customer instructs his bank to transfer money to the bank of the exporter who receives payment quite some time later, less bank charges, unless he has persuaded his customer to bear the charges.

CABLE, OR TELEGRAPHIC TRANSFER

TTs are sent by coded inter-bank computer messages. There is no disadvantage for the customer who is debited at the same time as on a SWIFT. If the customer will not pay the extra charge, it is cheaper for the exporter to do so than to wait extra days for the slower SWIFT Transfer.

Most international banks belong to the SWIFT system (see next), which saves them time and labour in sending cross-border payments by electronic computer methods. Precise instructions should be given for TTs. The transfer time can be improved if the exporter asks his customer to give precise instructions to his local bank, such as: 'Pay by telegraphic transfer £xxxx sterling to Lloyds Bank plc, 25 High Street, Ourtown, Midshire, England, sort code 20-01-99, account 12345678, for credit to XYZ Exports Ltd under advice to the beneficiary.'

Most banks in the SWIFT system now use the IBAN which is easier to use in conjunction with a SWIFT or BIC code.

A correct transfer should be credited same day value if properly executed.

Ask customers to pay by TT, and give them full bank account details, especially sort code and account number. If TTs are delayed, check bank advices to identify the blockage, ask your customer to confirm the date they were debited and discuss improvements with the bank concerned. When very large payments are delayed, interest may be claimed from the bank responsible.

SWIFT (SOCIETY FOR WORLDWIDE INTERBANK FINANCIAL TELECOMMUNICATIONS)

The SWIFT system was begun in 1977 by the major banks as an electronic computerised payment method between banks. It achieves an enormous saving in paperwork and human error but is limited to banks that belong, so is only as strong as its weakest link, for example, a non-SWIFT bank in the chain can delay the entire payment.

Ask customers to use SWIFT payments. The charges are usually less than a TT, and these days same day value SWIFT payments may be arranged.

EUROCHAPS

For payments within the euro zone, including the UK for euro payments, one can use the EUROCHAPS system. This makes same day value payments similar to CHAPS payments in the UK. All that is required is the IBAN number and BIC code. It is an extremely effective method of payment.

Checking the Risk of Payment Delays

The four key questions for managing export credit risks are: Will the customer go bust before we are paid? Can he pay our value on our terms? If he can – can his country find the invoiced hard currency? Are he and his country worth marketing for the future?

From experience of real-life claims from exporters, credit insurers have had to amplify these risks into the list below. With or without credit insurance cover, credit managers should examine their list of customers and countries to make sure they are armed with information to avoid the following loss events:

Buyer:

- insolvency;

- default at due date;

- refusal to take up the goods.

Buyer's government:

- cancellation of existing import licence;

- imposition of import licence;

- non-transfer of sterling/other hard currency;

- moratorium on external debts;

- law preventing contract performance;

- war or civil disorder;

- contract non-ratification;

- expropriation/damage to plant/property;

- unfair calling of bonds.

Exporter's government:

- cancellation or imposition of export licence;

- prevention of contract performance.

Any other government:

- actions preventing contract performance (especially important with US dollar payments which may be stopped in the USA if for an embargoed country).

Information on Country (Political) Risks

COMMERCIAL AGENCIES

There are several agencies selling topical information on country risks. The most concise and easily read is Dun & Bradstreet's *International Risk and*

Payment Review, which gives a short monthly digest on key features in over 100 countries. For example, it shows the usual payment terms of other exporters for each market; and the length of transfer delays, if any.

Coface produces its own rating system for countries free of charge know as '@rating' which can be accessed at www.trading-safely.com.

International Trade and Finance newsletter also provides information on country and trade related matters and is available online on Informa Professional, a division of Informa UK Ltd at www.informa.com.

BANK REVIEWS

All the major banks issue free country reports which show, very briefly, if any significant delays are being met in collections for exporters. Some, NatWest Bank for example, publish statistics on the indebtedness of countries, indicating their ability to pay for imports.

CREDIT INSURERS

ECGD, which covers medium-term credit, issues the OECD Consensus list of countries in three categories of wealth, a fair indication of political risk. Eximbank, the US Government insurer, also has an online schedule of what countries it is on cover for, detailing political and commercial risks (www.eximbank.gov).

Attradius, as the main short-term insurer, issues special restrictions of cover for many countries, another useful opinion of risk. By using a specialist credit insurance broker, an exporter has access to a wide range of country risk information.

AGENTS

Local representatives in foreign markets should be required to provide official data to the exporter, particularly on import restrictions and priorities for foreign currency allocations. Agents should also be expected to clarify press reports on governmental actions and perceived risks in their countries.

CREDIT GROUPS

Many industries organise regular meetings of credit and financial staff to compare views on terms, delays and risks for countries their companies are involved in. Local branch meetings of the ICM also enable members to exchange information. There is no collaboration of suppliers against customers or countries, but simply an exchange of established past experience.

FCIB (Finance and Credit in International Business) is a major information body for credit and treasury professionals which organises gatherings in European centres. Members meet to discuss topical questions on country risks and export credit techniques (see Appendix for more detailed information on credit groups and information sources).

Figure 17.6 shows an example of an exporter's approach to controlling the risks in the markets to which he sells, or plans to sell.

LIST the countries to which your company sells (or plans to). COLLECT economic data on each in a country file. ALLOCATE a risk grade to each country, e.g. I = negligible, II = average, III = high. Grade I = hard currency countries Grade III = countries with difficulty to fund imports; oil-dependent with small export earnings; single-crop exporters; dependent on Western aid; military governments; rapid changes of administration, etc. Grade II = all others. USE categories as follows: I = any terms agreed; good for market development II = keep terms as short as possible; good for short-term marketing III = CILC or guaranteed payment only; no marketing expense but take opportunity contracts. AMEND a category when data justifies it. REVIEW categories at intervals.

Figure 17.6   A suggested plan for controlling political risks

Information on Customer Risks

CREDIT AGENCIES

Several UK companies offer a worldwide service and it is also worth looking at the service level and cost of using local agencies in Europe and North America. The data available depend on the sophistication of the market's financial reporting and also the legal form of the company. Principal features to look for in a report are:

- the age of the data;

- a summary of key financial results;

- the company's operations, history and reputation;

- associations and links with other companies;

- payment record to other companies;

- details of security given, charges or legal actions;

- name and address of main bankers;

- credit rating;

- ownership;

- the officers.

Modern communications allow subscribers direct Internet access to data files. Exporters should be careful to use agencies with a substantial database on foreign companies, to avoid any delay in getting data for the purpose.

BANK REPORTS

These are generally more informative than UK bank reports but still protective of their clients and unlikely to relate bad news. Banks in USA and Canada give really extensive reports whereas European trends are for less disclosure. The usefulness of a bank report is in ratifying other data. No major credit granting should be based on a bank report alone. When asking a customer's bank for an opinion, always give an amount and credit period, to create a risk picture for the bank.

Importantly, most countries' regulating authorities require banks to disclose any security it holds on the company reported on. Many give details of lending facilities which can give a good idea of the company's real credit standing.

AGENTS

When obtaining orders, overseas agents should be expected to supply topical data on the customer/prospect; and at other times on demand. Requirements should be formalised in the agency agreement and a standard format used, with a brief fax about turnover, local payment reputation, a credit rating and a comment on premises, equipment and so on.

SALES VISIT REPORTS

A form should be used by travelling staff to record the latest basic financial data on customers and prospects. This helps sales staff to develop financial awareness and put some reliability on the scope of business being discussed.

FINANCIAL ACCOUNTS

Exporters should 'know all about' major customers, for example, those providing 80 per cent of sales and cash. They should be routinely asked to provide their latest balance sheets for appraisal, and refusal can be taken as a warning sign. The attitude to giving suppliers access to company numbers varies from country to country, but unless the latest data is available, exporters are selling blind to their major outlets. Accounts can be obtained from the equivalent of Companies House in most developed countries; but the need to register and file accounts depends on the legal form and size of the business.

For example, in the USA the need to disclose any financial data publicly is very limited unless the buyer is listed on the stock market. Similarly, in many EU countries, as many medium-sized businesses are often not limited companies, but partnerships or sole traders, there may be little public information available.

EMBASSIES AND CONSULATES

These will not usually supply credit opinions but can be very useful for data on local reputations and capability of local companies; and for introductions to other sources of help, particularly business clubs and Chambers of Commerce.

CREDIT INSURANCE COMPANIES

Policyholders get credit opinions on buyers when applying for credit limits or indications for future credit needs. The insurers have vast banks of customer data and there is a high probability that an exporter's new buyer is already known to other policyholders. If not, they make rapid enquiries through their local networks. As with country information, the use of specialist credit insurance brokers can be valuable.

CREDIT GROUPS

As explained earlier for country information, trade groups, professional institutes and organisations such as FCIB provide excellent forums for exchanging topical credit opinions on buyers, as well as credit terms in use and experience of payment problems and solutions.

Evaluating Customer Risks

Remember the requirements: Is he about to go bust? Can he pay our value on time? Is he worth marketing for the future?

The choice is to accept ready-made credit ratings or to make assessments using the sources recommended above. If you gather the opinions of others, build a picture using several information sources. For example, a Dunn & Bradstreet report might speak for £10,000 credit on 60-day terms; the sales visit report and local agent might recommend £100,000 on maximum terms; the comments of a trade group might be that accounts are paid promptly below £15,000 but generally very late for larger amounts. This tells you that the sales input is rather optimistic – the customer may well buy in larger values but cannot generate the funds promptly to pay for larger values.

Your need is to know all about the few customers who buy most of your exports (on the 80/20 basis). By getting closer to the customer, through credit discussions, you may even get preferential treatment, where your ratings exceed those recommended by others. But care must be taken not to overtrade and not to become more than, say, 25 per cent of your customer's total payables ('if a customer owes you £1000 he is your slave – if he owes you £1 million you will be his slave!' – as a wise man once said).

Do not hide behind insurance cover. You still need to know the payment ability of major customers. Making your own assessment means obtaining financial data and doing some analysis of size, sales, profit, net worth, liquidity, debt to equity and interest burdens. Make comparisons with the previous two years to establish trends.

There is no exact science in calculating credit ratings. Typical approaches are:

1. any amount, as long as there are no serious overdues;

2. 20 per cent of working capital;

3. 10 per cent of net worth.

Method 1 is dangerous. Even if it is low (for example, £10,000 when the customer is good for £10 million), it requires extra work to increase it at intervals, when it could have been set much higher in the first place.

Methods 2 and 3 assume it is prudent to risk credit for a proportion of the customer's known financial strength.

Some credit managers use a mixture of these. Imagine a sales requirement on terms which give a regular exposure of £150,000. Analysis might show that the customer is solvent, liquid, not overstretched on interest-bearing debt and has capital and reserves (net worth) of £1 million. A credit rating of £100,000 might be set, with orders put into manufacture up to three times that figure, that is, £300,000. Deliveries and terms can be adjusted to the satisfaction of both sides.

Extracting figures and ratios from foreign balance sheets requires a knowledge of local accounting treatment, for example, allowable reserves for stocks, debtors and so on. The task can be much easier with the help of local agents or international auditors.

Codifying Information

Information on major customers and markets can either be filed for scanning when needed or, much better, coded into credit ratings and risk categories. It is essential that credit opinions are visible to all interested parties, particularly sales staff. Codings are the easiest way to standardise a moving mass of data.

CUSTOMER RISK CATEGORIES

These show, at a glance, the security and care needed with payment terms, for example:

A = No risk; any reasonable terms; review annually.
B = Average risk; care with terms; review quarterly.
C = High risk; secure terms only.

COUNTRY RISK CATEGORIES

These indicate the availability of hard currency; and also the scope for marketing growth.

I = Strong market; any terms; good for marketing expense.

II = Average market; care with terms; short-term marketing only.

III = Weak market; secure terms only; no marketing expense; opportunities only.

DISPLAYING CREDIT RATINGS AND RISK CATEGORIES

Printouts and computer screens should show codings alongside customer names and account numbers, so that there is little need to refer to hard copy files. Examples:

Customer	Country risk	Client risk	Credit limit	Terms
Customer X:	II	B	£10 000	60 days draft
Customer Y:	III	A	£0	Confirmed Irrevocable Letter of Credit

Note: Customer X is an average risk in an average country; although customer Y is 'no-risk', he is in a 'high risk, secure terms only' country, so CILC has to apply.

USING CREDIT RATINGS AND RISK CATEGORIES

Having allocated codes to all accounts, the exporter can systemise them for everyday use, for example:

- incoming orders;

- outgoing shipments.

This permits the system (or a human) check that the value, when added to existing debts, does not exceed the stated limit of exposure. If it does, the order need not be refused, nor a shipment cancelled – it just needs urgent action to secure payment. In this way, the management can relax in the knowledge that all business is within agreed guidelines of exposure – or else that an expert is dealing with specific excesses.

INFORMATION SUPPLIED TO TRAVELLING SALES STAFF.

The codes can be easily built into computer systems at sales order points which include inputs from, and outputs to, travelling staff. Equally, the payment terms, risks and values should be easily accessible to them for assessing the worth of sales and marketing effort with particular customers and countries.

Collecting Overdues – An Overview

Export late payments are significantly minimised if:

- payment terms are arranged to fit the risk situations; and

- payment arrangements are organised with the financial staff in each and every customer.

The 3 Golden Rules for chasing up overdue foreign revenues are:

- *Immediacy:* Phone, fax, email or visit; not letters, which are far too slow. However, some countries require a written demand to make debt payable, if that is so, build it into system.

- *Local contact:* By agents, local offices or travelling sales staff.

- *Systematic attention:* Be organised; act early; be proactive.

ACCOUNT RECORDS

Have an online, updated Sales Ledger with good visibility of unpaid sales grouped by customer, within countries (to detect inconsistencies) and showing all due dates, past and upcoming.

Sales Process Stage	Customer Type	
Enquiry Quotation Sales visit prospects		Early opportunity for credit check ditto ditto
Order	New customer	Assess credit rating Assess risk category Decide payment terms
Order	Approved customer	Check ledger for overdue items Check stop/referral list Compare to e.g. (3 x credit rating less balance)
Shipment	Approved customer	Check ledger for overdues Check stop/referral list Compare to e.g. (credit rating less balance)

Figure 17.7   Typical credit checking system for exports

STAFF RESOURCES

Allocate enough skilled credit staff resource to do the right things on time. Decide how others (sales, shipping, technical and so on) should help.

DECIDE WHOM TO CHASE – AGENT, CUSTOMER OR BANK?

Agents should be paid commission only when sales are paid. They are in the ideal local position to contact customers and sort out problems.

Customers should always know they will hear from you immediately if they miss a payment. Slow payers generally pay those who remind at the expense of those who don't bother. *Always* phone or email a named contact.

Banks are responsible under ICC URC for acting promptly to collect bills of exchange and CAD items and should always be reminded of this and pressed for rapid answers.

Third parties: Pressure may be needed for serious cases. Use local collection agencies rather than lawyers, who may be slow and expensive. Consider court action only as a last resort and only for very large values. In many countries it is unproductive to sue for import debts and legal fees may have to be paid in advance.

A Systematic Approach

Have a monitoring system which follows every transaction through from invoicing to receipt of payment. Also allow the staff time to ensure that customers are asked to pay debts as soon as they become overdue; and that large debts are requested as they approach due dates.

Largest debts should be tackled first. The famous 80/20 ratio means that 20 per cent of customers owe 80 per cent of debts, so rather than working alphabetically, it is far better to have debts listed in order of size.

Use the customer's language if possible, especially if it is French. Use the sales or technical person for messaging if they speak the customer's language and you don't. Or get the agent or rep to do it. When discussing a debt problem with a customer who is using limited English, avoid asking questions which can be answered 'Yes'. Some foreigners will 'yes' just to be polite, without necessarily agreeing with you. To test this, instead of asking: 'Have you paid our invoice for £10,000?', ask: '*When* did you pay our invoice for £10,000?' (The reply 'yes' will be revealing.)

One week after due date is long enough to allow for a foreign payment to come through the banking system. For large debts, ask agents or customers before due dates about the banks to be used. It is an excellent yet polite way of reminding customers to pay upcoming debts.

If initial approaches fail, press more strongly and bring in other available help, for example, the agent, sales rep, local subsidiary and, of course, the banking service.

Redirect your efforts away from the person ignoring you and make good contact with somebody more senior, who should care about the deteriorating commercial relationship.

Consider also:

A local debt collecting agency, on a 'no collect – no fee' basis: A suitable one can usually be arranged through your UK collection agency.

Visiting to collect personally: For large, worrying debts, this can be extremely productive and far cheaper than waiting for other methods to work. Collection visits can be linked to other purposes, such as gathering information, joint 'get-to-know-you' visits with sales people, and sorting out severe account problems, needing compromise and credit notes. Always take the time to get fully briefed on the other country, the customer firm's background, debt details, commercial and account disputes and unshipped orders.

Don't forget to take a full file with you! There is nothing worse than having paid the cost of the visit, to not have all the information with you to resolve the queries. Copy invoices is a good example. Having one with you means the customer may action payment immediately, whereas waiting for you to return to the UK to get the copy sent, loses time and the urgency and commitment you have won by being there!

The apparent glamour of a foreign visit is a myth. Foreign debt collection can be extremely hard work in uncomfortable conditions. However, a successful collection visit can be a 'triple-whammy' in that: funds are collected much faster; a better relationship is built for future contact by phone or email; and the credit person develops a more rounded business confidence.

Legal action: It can be very expensive and drag on for years, with the cost exceeding the debt value. When cases go into foreign courts, debts may be frozen in the local currency at the rate on that day. The exchange value some time later can be very disappointing if that currency has devalued over time.

However, legal action sometimes has to be taken in a trade community to show others that the foreign exporter is not easily deterred. If suing is contemplated, the lawyer to be used should be one recommended by another satisfied UK exporter, or provided by a collection agency which is experienced in that city.

A Word About Foreign Currency

Chapter 19 provides detailed coverage of the foreign exchange market, its terminology and ways for exporters to offset any risk of loss on the exchange rates. The relevance of foreign currency to the collection of debts is the customer's ability to produce the funds at the due date. Sterling is not the currency of any other country and is difficult for the banks to get hold of in many countries. US dollars or euros are far more available than sterling around the world.

Exporters should seriously consider moving to more pricing and billing in the customer's currency, if it is a tradeable one, or to US dollars or euros if it is not. That would both please the customer and help them to remit payment to the UK sooner. The exporter has the advantage of the world's finest foreign exchange market, in London, which, at the end of a phone line, will agree an exchange rate at any time and convert any currency into any other on demand, and can provide foreign currency hedging facilities if required.

Checklist: To Speed Export Cash

Customers and countries checked for payment risks and right terms used? *Payment terms* reviewed? Risks matched? Credit periods negotiated downwards? *Orders* acknowledged? Show terms, bank sort code and account number? Clauses? *Agents* briefed on collection duties? *LCs:* Three checks? – when LC requested: to specify your needs – on receipt of LC: to amend in good time, if needed – at pre-shipment: to correct documents for payment. *Creditworthiness* checked when taking order and at shipment? *Shipping documents* checked for completeness for payment? If *Open Account terms*, invoice copied to local agent? Customer asked to instruct bank to TT funds? If *bill of exchange terms*, bank instructed on release of goods, interest, use of agent, exchange, charges and to TT funds? *Overdue accounts* contacted by phone, email, visit or local agent? *Local pressure* arranged to avoid legal action?

The Future For Export Collections

Many more UK businesses will need to export to achieve enough profit to survive. It is a fact of life that many EU companies are coming to the UK to expand their businesses and acquiring UK firms to service that growth. The EU is now one domestic market, more so in the euro zone. Therefore any company which thinks it can live on its UK business alone is likely to be living on borrowed time.

Unfortunately, companies in other nations have the same need, so the competition is fierce to win orders from the better markets.

There is no such place as the 'export market', unless it just means sales to outside the UK. There are over 200 separate export markets, each with their own laws, payment practices, banking systems and traditional supply sources.

Technology has speeded up bank transfers, and now regulatory action is further reducing delays and the ability of the banks to hang onto your money.

Documentary delays have been shortened by EDI, but many countries still require hard copy documents to actually clear goods.

The biggest single way to improve export cash flow will be to negotiate hard for shorter payment terms, dated from shipment not arrival, and controlling the release of goods.

For all the riskier markets, the demand for LCs will continue. However, the ability of a sophisticated exporter to work on more liberal terms in those markets, due to its better knowledge and capacity to handle bottlenecks, will contribute to reduced cost for both buyer and seller and potentially more business for both.

The ability of a customer in a soft currency market to generate a LC is a good test of the country's official blessing to importing your product. Where a LC is clearly justified but not approved, be warned!

For risky customers, bills of exchange will continue their steady return to use.

Use of Bills in the European market will increase, more so on an electronic basis, to speed cash flow.

The percentage of world trade on open account is increasing as consolidation of the global market means bigger sellers are selling more to bigger buyers.

Integrated supply chain finance is becoming the desired state for major buyers, and the banks are moving to satisfy this requirement.

The global credit crunch increased demand for supplier financing and long terms, whilst greatly increasing the risk. The banks, for example, no longer have the excellent credit ratings they previously enjoyed, and discounting their confirmations and accepted bills is becoming more expensive if at all possible.

THE EUROPEAN UNION

The EU is a today single market of nearly 500 million consumers, in 27 countries, with much loosened national borders. Documents are simplified. Many are members of the euro zone and payments cross-border by EUROCHAPS is fast, simple and inexpensive. The UK's decision not to accede to the euro has left sterling exporters with exchange risk exposures.

Credit periods in each country have evolved over centuries and even neighbouring countries may have very different practices. Terms are short in northern Europe – for example, 30 days in Sweden and Germany – increasing to 60 or 90 days in Austria and France, and stretching to 120 to 150 days in the south – for example, Spain and Italy. No serious seller in the EU can ignore the normal market terms as the customer can just as easily buy on more liberal terms locally.

Payments in France, Spain and Italy tend to be by bill of exchange, through the banking system and widely discounted. In France this is so well established, it is done electronically. Not to take advantage of the system to get paid more quickly and more efficiently loses margin and is not what the customer expects.

THE REST OF THE WORLD

The OECD I, II and III categories will continue as a guide to lending and credit risk.

Division I seems likely to remain as it is: Europe, USA, Canada, the oil-rich Middle Eastern countries, Australia, New Zealand and the six or so rich Far Eastern countries (Japan, Taiwan, Hong Kong, Singapore, Malaysia, South Korea and so on). These are the countries that justify strong marketing effort and normal credit terms. All the others need care in terms and control of marketing expense.

The situation regarding the BRIC (Brazil, Russia, India, China) countries is the challenge. Alone they represent nearly half the world's population and are significantly developing economies. Political risk in the countries is high, the governments having a predisposition to 'meddle.' Russia is taking a much stronger stance on its own national interest and with its dominant position as Europe's principal energy supplier, it can do so with a great deal of impunity.

A great help to exporters in understanding the different credit practices between countries is Dun & Bradstreet's *International Risk and Payment Review*, a monthly digest which keeps its finger on the pulse of world credit risk. It classifies some 120 countries into 'Usual Payment Terms', 'Transfer Risks' and 'Other Risks' and provides an excellent commentary, with statistics, on the progress or otherwise of each country's economy. To support these journalistic opinions, the Review also shows the credit insurance cover available from commercial credit insurers, from ECGD (for medium-term credit) and from Eximbank of the USA.

Letters of credit are now routinely issued by SWIFT. Hard copy LCs are now a rarity.

Whilst much has been done to permit electronic clearance of goods by customs authorities in the developed markets, using documents submitted by EDI, particularly in EU and USA, the rest of the world has lagged behind.

The improved payment of LCs suggested by BOLERO, (the electronic bill of lading), has not materialised, despite many bodies such as the ICC and the banks to have an electronic process accepted.

Cross-border direct debits are generated by the major banks in the UK, France, Germany, USA, Australia and so on, on accounts in each other's countries and this method of transferring funds is expected to expand greatly in the EU. It makes sense, when negotiating payment terms with foreign customers to obtain their mandate for direct debiting at *the agreed due dates*. The technology is in place – it is up to credit managers to make it work.

Letters are too slow for international debt follow-up. Immediacy is achieved by using the phone, despite time zones. Webcam and Skype is slowly increasing in use and will help to improve relationships between financial staff around the world, as well as enabling documents to be displayed instantly in conversations.

Email messaging is ideal for conveying a sense of urgency in wordings.

There has been an increase in shared service centres whereby the global companies establish a single administration, customer service and credit facility to carry out all their operations within a region. In Europe, these are typically covering the EMEA region, Europe, Middle East and Africa. Previously they have been sited in cities with good communications such as London, Paris or Geneva, but now many businesses are taking advantage of the lower operating costs in central Europe or India.

Think International

In summary, one certainty for the credit manager is that international business will grow much faster than in the past, because such business is necessary for most businesses to survive and expand, especially in the single market. Where credit staff have only worked on UK business, export training is essential to avoid years of expensive mistakes while an international attitude is developed. The most useful subject to become expert in is the range of international payment terms, how they work via the banks and how electronic transfers can be arranged.

Shakespeare would have been just as accurate today as he was in 1597 when his Merchant of Venice said: 'Alas, my fortunes are all at sea'!

Further Reading

Credit Management Magazine, Cross Border Collections Supplement April 2001, ICM and subsequent frequent articles. British Exporters Association Guides: Credit Insurance, Letter of Credit, Retention of Title, On demand Contract Bonds, Introduction to Successful Exporting

Available online on www.bexa.co.uk, the guides are written by exporters for exporters.

Useful Addresses

British Exporters Association Broadway House, Tothill Street, London, SW1H 9NQ.
Website: www.bexa.co.uk

Institute of Export Export House, Minerva Business Park, Lynchwood, Peterborough, PE2 6FT.
Website: www.export.org.uk

FCIB NACM 7200 The Quorum, Oxford Business Park, North Carsington Road, Oxford, OX4 2JZ.
Website: www.fcibglobal.com

UKTI – UK Trade and Investment, the government department supporting export and inward investment.
Website: www.uktradeinvest.gov.uk

BERR – the UK's Department for Business Enterprise and Regulatory Reform (now part of BIS).
Website: www.berr.gov.uk/index.html

UKTI Overseas Market Introduction Service (OMIS).
Website: www.uktradeinvest.gov.uk/ukti/fileDownload/omis.pdf?cid=391808

CIA World Factbook.
Website: www.cia.gov/library/publications/the-world-factbook

World Bank Ease of Doing Business.
Website: www.doingbusiness.org/economyrankings

Incoterms 2000.
Website: www.iccwbo.org/incoterms/id3045/index.html

SITPRO.
Website: www.sitpro.org.uk

International Chamber of Commerce – ICC UK – the ICC UK bookshop carries copies of all publications including the rules for letters of credit, documentary collection and other internationally agreed rules.
Website: www.iccuk.net

Freight Forwarding: The British International Freight Association (BIFA) – acts as a trade association for forwarders in the UK and makes available its list of members. It also provides standard contract terms and enforces a Code of Conduct on all members.
Website: www.bifa.org

Chartered Institute of Marketing.
Website: www.cim.co.uk

INSTITUTE OF CREDIT MANAGEMENT – JANUARY 2008

Diploma Level 3

Companies entering the export credit market for the first time need to ensure that the credit department is familiar with the different terms and documentation required for export.

Incoterms are widely used in export.

- Explain the main purpose of Incoterms.

- Describe *three* ways in which Incoterms clarify the position of the buyer and seller.

- Briefly explain the *four* categories of Incoterms, using one example from each.

Bills of Lading:

- Describe how bills of lading operate.

- Explain the value of bills of lading to the seller.

18

Export Finance

T Glyndwr Powell[1]

• The need for special money for exports • Enhanced overdraft • Bill advances and negotiation • Export finance banks • Finance from letters of credit • Export Credit Guarantee Department-backed finance: medium-term credit • The international consensus • Further reading • Useful addresses •

The Need for Special Money for Exports

Earlier chapters have shown how exports remain unpaid for disappointingly long periods; and that the waiting time is not usually costed into prices, resulting in lower than expected profit.

The lengthy unpaid nature of exports creates extra cost and risk, namely:

- cost: the interest on borrowings while waiting for payment; and

- risk: the longer the wait, the more chance of loss events.

In recent years, the major banks have marketed a number of 'export finance products', to offer exporters something better than just using their standard overdraft. Despite the competition between banks to finance the available business, there is still a lack of awareness of the range of funding available amongst smaller exporters. Most firms still use their normal overdraft for paying for their needs until payments come drifting in from foreign customers, despite being up against fixed overdraft limits and paying a high price for that kind of borrowing.

---

1   With acknowledgements to Burt Edwards.

Instead of depending on the main overdraft, it is more sensible to finance exports: without tying up the overdraft in ways that reduce or remove any risk of non-payment receiving the funds at time of shipment at a cost which is economical compared to the cost of waiting, at full risk, for the customer to pay in due course.

How can this be done?

Enhanced Overdraft

Every business maintains a bank overdraft facility to provide funds for their purchases, manufacturing or assembly, credit given to customers, wages and so on. The cost of the overdraft is mitigated by paying in customers' remittances as and when received.

If, despite the alternatives, this is the preferred way of borrowing, it may be possible to increase the overdraft limit by letting the bank know more about the export content of the operations. It is surprising how often a bank does not even know that its client is an exporter of goods or services. It is often possible to increase the overdraft limit by making the bank aware of any security held, such as credit insurance cover. In some cases, banks have slightly reduced the overdraft interest rate because of the security, since some of their charge is to cover their perception of risk. Usually, the bank will want the security to be assigned to itself (that is, the right to claims paid is assigned, rather than the policy itself). Such assignments do not need to be registered at Companies House under the Companies Act, for the world to know about.

Overdrafts are often more expensive than specialised forms of export finance, except when the borrower is a global operation with ample borrowing 'muscle', which gets them the lowest rates and makes them cheaper than other forms of finance, when the cost of administration and documentation is counted in.

It makes sense for smaller exporters to use their everyday overdraft for pre-shipment costs, since most finance schemes operate from date of shipment.

Bill Advances and Negotiation

The use of bills of exchange with export customers has reduced in recent years, yet financing benefits are available if exporters are able to convert some of their open account customers to using bills. Bills of exchange are eminently suitable for getting hold of the funds for transactions at an early stage after shipment.

ADVANCE AGAINST BILLS

A bank processing a clean collection – one without documents attached – will invariably agree to advance an agreed percentage, usually 80 per cent, immediately it receives a bill for collection. The bank then proceeds with the standard collection routine and if the bill is unpaid at maturity, the bank may reclaim the funds from the exporter, although it rarely does this until further attempts have been made to collect through the banking system. Usually, the bank would just continue charging the exporter interest until the funds were in.

This kind of advance carries a similar interest charge to the overdraft but has the advantage of being additional to the overdraft, which may well be fully utilised in everyday operations. Because the bank can reclaim the money if the bill is eventually unpaid, this form of finance is known as 'with recourse'.

NEGOTIATION OF BILLS

Whereas advances against bills are useful for partial funding as and when needed, more reliable and 100 per cent finance is available from a bill negotiation facility. This is a service which must be prearranged with the bank on, usually, an annual basis, for which the exporter must estimate the sales value to be exported using bills of exchange.

The bank then *purchases* the bills sent for collection, credits the exporter's account with the full value and is reimbursed when the bills are paid at maturity. Again, the bank has recourse to the exporter in the event of non-payment. Interest is charged for the period from purchasing the bill until its collection, at rates similar to normal overdraft. Lower rates may apply if credit insurance cover is assigned to the bank. The advantage of negotiation is that financing can be reliably planned long in advance, to assume 100 per cent payment at the dates of future export shipments.

AVALISED BILLS OF EXCHANGE

This is a refinement of the standard bill of exchange whereby the buyer arranges for his bank, or a major and acceptable public body in his country (especially a ministry) to add its guarantee, known as an 'aval', to the bill. This makes the bill highly liquid and the exporter can easily sell the now 'avalised' instrument into the banking market, or hold it until maturity. Because the aval is not added until after shipment, the bill is potentially cheaper to discount than a LC, since with an LC, both buyer and seller pay bank charges from the day it is opened.

FORFAITING (OR BILL DISCOUNTING)

The word is not misspelt. It comes from the French 'forfait', meaning to give up or forfeit something. It is an arrangement whereby a forfaiting house, or the specialised forfaiting department of a bank, buys an avalised bill of exchange and pays the exporter the value less a discount equivalent to the interest for the credit period concerned plus a risk premium for the guaranteeing bank or the country risk.

It is a simple method of generating cash inexpensively for the exporter, as banks tend to understand the credit risk of other banks or public bodies, whereas they may not be so keen on the actual customer for the goods or services. Where the aval is signed by a state bank or ministry, the debt is classed as 'sovereign' or government risk. Banks take up positions in lending to certain countries or parts of the world, and a sovereign risk bill may well be traded between banks after the exporter has been paid.

The interest rate applicable for a first-class western bank is often considerably lower than the exporter's overdraft rate. In some cases, a forfaiting bank may buy a bill accepted by a very strong commercial customer without the need for it to bear a bank's guarantee.

Exporters should always review their upcoming larger value contracts for the possibility of forfaiting the resulting debts. Since the debts are genuinely purchased by the forfaiter, the funds are 'without recourse' and can significantly improve the exporter's balance sheet.

Forfaiting banks normally wish to see deals of £25,000 or more, with no upper limit, on credit terms from 90 days up to seven years or so.

FACTORING

An exporter can make an annual agreement with the factoring branch of his bank to sell his debts to them as export sales are made.

The factoring company will usually pay about 80 per cent of the invoiced value straightaway and the balance of 20 per cent, less charges, when the various customers pay. Because this may be cumbersome if there are many accounts and almost daily invoices, it is usual for the factor to agree an average due date for the balance, usually close to the exporter's previous DSO period.

The factor does the risk assessment task, the management of the Sales Ledger and the all-important collections at due dates, usually with the help of local subsidiaries or associates. Credit ratings are set for each account, and the advances are without recourse for sales within those limits. The exporter is free to exceed the limits, however unwisely, but the factor will reclaim the funds if such debts are unpaid.

Thus the service can replace the exporter's own credit management function and salaries can be saved. However, the factor's charge for the overall service may well be more expensive than the in-house cost savings and the exporter has to weigh up the factor's cost and efficiency against the in-house performance and all-round costs.

The exporter's costs consist of interest on the funds advanced, normally at the same rates as his overdraft with the same bank group, plus a service charge to include the risk assessments, ledger administration and collections. In almost every case, factors collect an exporter's debts faster than the exporter would on their own.

Factoring is very suitable for businesses in certain high-risk trades, where delays could mean insolvency losses, and for firms growing fast, where sales increases are running ahead of adequate credit administration.

CONFIDENTIAL INVOICE DISCOUNTING

This is an alternative service provided by factoring banks. They will advance up to a percentage –usually 80 per cent – of invoice values on a 'with recourse' basis, without providing the full factoring service. It is confidential in that it is not disclosed to customers.

Confidential discounting suits firms who need export funding up front but wish to maintain their own credit management function. Since the service is more risky for the factor, only good quality credit risks are funded and the exporter has to be considered 'creditworthy'.

Chapter 24 describes factoring services in more detail, for both home and export sales.

Export Finance Banks

Most of the major banks have their own, proprietary, versions of export finance without recourse. These schemes normally require:

- assessment of the risks by the bank concerned;

- credit insurance cover for 90 or 95 per cent;

- a fee for the credit period plus a service charge, all calculated as a percentage of the shipment value.

Most of the schemes carry a 'smaller exporter' version, involving less administration and simpler documentation. It is not possible here to define a smaller exporter because the different banks have varying definitions of turnover required, from £250,000 to £2 million.

The Export Finance Banks, or EFBs as they are called, provide UK exporters with cash at time of shipment, against specified shipping documents for each transaction. Most of them offer 100 per cent of the shipment value less the agreed charges.

The banks either use their own credit insurance policy and pass the premium cost to importers, or ensure that the exporters' own insurance cover is applied. Either way, the credit insurance protection enables the banks to offer up to 100 per cent post-shipment money, without recourse for the insured percentage.

Credit managers should arm themselves with their own bank's brochure on export finance, since every scheme has its own individual features.

Finance from Letters of Credit

Exporters should consider using customers' LCs to finance their operations. Various types of LC can also be a useful source of pre-shipment finance.

RED CLAUSE LETTERS OF CREDIT

Known as 'packing credits' in the USA, these provide pre-shipment finance for exporters up to an agreed amount. Exporters ask their own bank to advance up to 75 per cent of the face value of the LCs, enabling their purchase of the specified goods to be made and for them to be shipped to their customers. Once the goods are shipped and documents presented in accordance with the terms of the credit, the paying bank reimburses the bank making the advance.

BACK-TO-BACK LETTERS OF CREDIT

Instead of an advance against a customer's LC, as above, an exporter who has to purchase expensive products may decide to use that LC as collateral with his own bank, to support opening a LC in favour of his supplier.

USANCE, OR TERM LETTERS OF CREDIT

The LC may specify that bills of exchange are to be drawn on the bank for up to 180 days or, for a few countries, up to 360 days. The exporter must ensure the bill is drawn on the bank and not the buyer. Depending on the quality of the bank accepting the bill, it could be discounted if the exporter's bank is prepared to purchase risk in that country.

Export Credits Guarantee Department-backed Finance: Medium-term Credit

Exporters of capital goods such as commercial vehicles, machine tools and contractors' plant usually face requests for credit terms in excess of two years, generally referred to as medium-term credit.

As the mass of UK exports – some 95 per cent – is on short-term credit up to six months, it may be thought that the remaining 5 per cent on medium terms is not too significant. However, not only is the total value important, but also the individual high-value contracts involved are much sought after and competed for internationally. Moreover, if the competition is offering terms which finance the product over its economic life, that is more attractive to the potential buyer, and it is likely to go with the best finance offer, everything else being equal.

Many capital goods contracts are placed by governments and buyers in poorer countries. Thus the risk of non-payment is considerable, the sums involved are very large and the horizon of risk is quite a worrying distance away. For all these reasons, there are not many companies willing and financially able to bid for capital contracts. They benefit from a well-structured system of financing provided by the major banks who are insured against loss by the UK Government's ECGD.

The two broad types of finance for medium-term credit are Supplier Credit, where the UK supplier allows a credit period to the foreign buyer, and Buyer Credit, where a UK bank provides a loan to the foreign country and pays the UK supplier, out of the loan, soon after shipment or at the agreed stages of performance in the contract.

ECGD offers the Supplier Credit Financing facility, or SCF, which is tailor-made for exporters of capital goods on a regular basis. ECGD guarantees directly the bank which provides the exporter with the funds at shipment, usually under a 'master' guarantee. During contract negotiations, the exporter must apply to ECGD to issue a certificate of approval to the bank enabling them to commit 100 per cent of the contract value to be available to the exporter at shipment.

For pre-shipment finance, ECGD offers their Export Insurance Policy (EXIP) as a supplement to the SCF.

FIXED RATE EXPORT FINANCE

This finance for medium-term credit is offered at low rates of interest, as an incentive to help UK exporters to obtain contracts and to help the poorer countries to be able to afford the repayments. The scheme is referred to by banks as the Fixed Rate Export Finance scheme, or FREF. FREF is not available for sales to most other EU states. It is currently available for sterling, US dollar, euro and yen-based contracts.

BUYER CREDITS

For really substantial capital goods contracts, normally in excess of £5 million, ECGD provides insurance and guarantees to enable banks to provide loans directly to foreign buyers, their banks or governments. Called Buyer Credits, the scheme allows the overseas buyer to purchase UK goods or projects with a loan over several years which provides funds to the exporter at the time of shipment or commissioning of the project.

Generally, it is for much longer periods of credit, up to 10 years, at officially supported low interest rates. These rates are known as the 'consensus rates' and are set annually at government level under the umbrella of the OECD.

The international OECD agreement means that maximum credit terms and minimum rates of interest apply to all international competitors, leaving the scope for competition to other features.

LINES OF CREDIT

As well as buyer credits for massive contracts, ECGD also gives the same type of support to banks that provide lines of credit, or general loans to overseas borrowers, normally banks. These are extremely useful sources of ready funding for UK exporters of capital plant and equipment of smaller values.

There are two kinds of line of credit: the specific project type, where a variety of exporters may supply into a particular project; and the general 'shopping basket' type, where the loan is used by the borrowing country to purchase any variety of unrelated goods.

Lines of credit are usually opened on a bank-to-bank basis. They are announced in the business press and details of existing lines of credit are always available from ECGD and the BIS – formery BERR – (but not always from the main banks, who may only publicise their own ones!).

Having knowledge of a line of credit, the exporter directs a potential foreign buyer to the overseas bank involved. The buyer negotiates with that bank, who may or may not agree to allocate funds under the loan. The buyer then safely contracts with the UK exporter and the overseas bank instructs the UK bank to pay the exporter at shipment. (Note: The facility normally requires the buyer to find up to 15 per cent of the contract value on signing it.)

The line of credit is normally established to give the foreign borrower several years to repay. It is open for exporters to use within one or two years and there are stated minimum contract values and sometimes specific intended uses.

However, the lines are frequently underused by the expiry date and sometimes totally unused. For this reason, exporters should always be equipped with details of existing lines of credit to markets they are interested in, to bring into early discussions with potential buyers. At times the loans can be stretched to include related materials that would not qualify as capital goods alone.

The International Consensus

In 1976, the OECD nations established *The International Arrangements on Guidelines for Officially Supported Export Credit*. At semi-annual OECD meetings at ministerial level between governments, the Consensus regulates the export finance granted by member countries. Its purpose is to keep competition for lending within certain bounds, starting with a division of all countries of the world into three categories: Category 1 (relatively rich), Category 2 (intermediate) and Category 3 (relatively poor). This is decided on the basis of per capita income, which tends to relate to the country's ability to pay for imports in hard currency.

Each category defines the longest credit period that may be granted. For Categories 2 and 3, interest rates may be subsidised by the government of the exporter, enabling attractive fixed rates to be offered for the entire credit period.

For Category 1 markets, interest rates must be the same as open market rates, that is, the strong countries do not need cheap money, subsidised by the selling country's government.

The banks providing the low-rate money to UK exporters receive a 'make-up' percentage from the UK Treasury, via ECGD, to cover the difference between the subsidised rate and market rates, plus a small margin for bank profit. Fixed rate low-interest finance requires the exporter to be recourse-worthy and thus only the larger firms qualify.

ECGD are founder members of the Berne Union, an international organisation of the world's leading credit insurance institutions. It was created to regulate the credit granted by member countries, so that credit wars would not develop amongst the richer countries, which would benefit nobody in the longer run.

See Chapter 16 for details of facilities from ECGD and other insurers.

Further Reading

Anders Grath, *International Trade and Finance,* Kogan Page.

Useful Addresses

Export Credits Guarantee Department ECGD PO Box 2200, 2 Exchange Tower, Harbour Exchange Square, London, E14 9GS.
Website: www.ecgd.gov.uk

UKTI – UK Trade and Investment is the UK Government department supporting export and inward investment.
Website: www.uktradeinvest.gov.uk

19

Foreign Exchange

T Glyndwr Powell[1]

• The credit manager and foreign currency • The history of foreign exchange • Present day foreign exchange markets • Dealing operations • Press charts of foreign currency rates • Exchange risks and how to cover them • The euro • The UK and the euro • Summary • Glossary of foreign exchange terms •

The Credit Manager and Foreign Currency

In international business, either the seller or the buyer carries the risk of loss from the conversion of one currency into another – unless both seller and buyer use the same currency. When a UK company issues an invoice in sterling and the foreign customer has to pay it 60 days later, one of them may lose money. The customer planned to find a certain amount of his own currency to buy the sterling to pay the invoice, yet by the due date, if his currency has weakened, his local funds may not be enough to meet the sterling invoice value. He will certainly be unhappy at having to pay more than he originally thought, to make up the sterling amount, thus reducing his planned profit and upsetting his pricing structure. So, between order and payment due date, the customer has an exchange worry. There may be a payment shortfall, or a long delay while he mobilises the extra funds. If, on the other hand, the exporter bills in the customer's currency, say, to please him, or to compete with others, he has the worry that when he receives the invoiced foreign currency, it will not convert to his intended sterling value, because of the passage of time. In any company which has business abroad, the credit manager has an important task to ensure that the best possible arrangements are in place for receiving payments in currencies other than his or her own.

---

1 With acknowledgement to Burt Edwards.

Depending on the company's policy for converting receipts into the home currency, or any other, or holding the currency receipts without converting them, the credit manager needs to know which are the desirable, or 'hard' currencies, and how the international banks operate in sending money across national boundaries.

Billings must be correctly issued to meet the currency arrangements, clear agreements have to be made with customers; and good relationships maintained with the main banks for handling currency receipts in the manner intended.

The first requirement is for the credit manager to overcome any fear of the unknown, and this chapter covers the basic structures, terminology and procedures for handling the company's foreign currency receipts.

UK companies have already seen their customers in most western European countries change from their own currencies to the euro, which has simplified the problem of several currencies fluctuating against sterling by having just the euro's value to contend with.

In the years to come, several other countries will join the euro zone, to reduce the variety of billing currencies even further for UK companies. There is, of course, the much-argued possibility that the UK will make the euro its own currency, which will cause massive social and economic changes for UK companies and citizens, in view of the switch of economic controls, interest rate policy and central planning from the Bank of England to the European Central Bank in Germany.

The obsession with the euro is misleading, since much trading is done outside the euro zone, such as with the USA, Japan, the Middle East and the Far East. The UK has also historically received much US dollar income from North Sea oil and gas sales which are now diminishing, which again increased the dollar total, even though goods may be going to Europe. Finally, the UK is one of the largest beneficiaries in the world of invisible income (banking, services and investments.) These have also had a high proportion of US dollar receipts included. However, since UK exports to the EU now represent some 57 per cent of its trade (Source: NSO June 2008) with 52 per cent going to the euro zone, there is a strong argument for closer involvement with the euro.

Whether the UK stays with the pound sterling or switches to the euro, exchange risks and currency conversions will still have to be managed for sales to all those countries which do not use sterling or the euro.

The key foreign exchange topics for the credit manager to master are:

- to know which are acceptable currencies;

- to be familiar with the press charts showing the rates of exchange as at the previous evening;

- to understand the main, but luckily few, bits of FX jargon (that is the first one: 'FX' means Foreign Exchange!); and

- to know the fairly straightforward ways that a seller can protect and therefore guarantee the intended sterling value of sales.

The History of Foreign Exchange

A passing knowledge of how the present methods of converting other people's currency came about helps the credit manager to operate more confidently. It was only in the twentieth century that dealings in foreign currencies developed into the incredibly efficient market that we now know. It certainly could not function today without the electronic technology providing vital data instantly to all participating banks, in all parts of the world, and which is moving slowly but unstoppably towards paperless contracts and electronic fund transfer systems.

Nevertheless, the basic concept of dealing in a store of value – gold, coin, notes and so on – is a very old one. The profession of money dealer, including changing one country's currency into another's, started in Roman and biblical times (see Chapter 1). Money markets developed in Italy, with the Church an important player, and later, as the New World was opened up, in Spain. Governments had to find ways of raising finance from other countries and bills of exchange became a useful way of pledging funds. Later, the international money centres moved to Antwerp and, in the seventeenth century, to Amsterdam. By then, paper money was coming into use but, as a result of the problems of forgery and physical transport of money, the more flexible bills of exchange became very prominent. Until the twentieth century, most foreign trade was covered by bills of exchange – the clarity of obligations was obvious, and banks all over the world dealt confidently in the paper, discounting it for early payment and developing a set of international banking rules, based on custom and practice.

From ancient times until the latter part of the eighteenth century, money markets remained 'physical'. Notes, coins, gold and pieces of paper actually changed hands. About 1880, more rapid means of communication – faster post, telegrams and then the telephone – allowed a market to develop in 'balances'. A buyer and seller of a currency, situated in different countries, would decide on a rate for the exchange and then rely on each other to deliver the requisite amount from one account to the other on an agreed settlement date.

There was no need for the two parties to meet or even be in the same country. As telecommunications improved, so did the market place, becoming electronic, worldwide, massive and one of the fastest-moving international markets in existence.

However, despite the speed of transactions and the advance of technology, one facet of currency exchange has remained the same since dealings began – that is that some currencies are preferred to others. Traders and banks recognised that, because some countries exported more goods and others imported more than they exported, the supply and demand for currencies differed, thus forming the concept of 'strong' and 'weak' currencies. Countries that consistently import more than they can export inevitably find that their currency is less desirable to others. About 50 of the world's 200 or so countries are net exporters, whereas the other 150 countries struggle to find the hard currency to pay for their essential imports, thanks to their own lack of export earnings.

Since 1979, when UK exchange controls were abolished, UK companies have been free to lend, borrow or invest (such as via subsidiary operations abroad) without official restriction. Before then, the Bank of England kept a close watch on the ins and outs of foreign exchange, by the use of form-filling by importers and exporters. Most other countries still have such controls. Experienced UK exporters know that exchange controls could return at any time by a simple government decree, if a debt crisis arose, although EU regulations would make it difficult to act in isolation, and certainly the use of the euro would defeat such action, since the European Central Bank would take the decision out of any one EU government's hands.

Present Day Foreign Exchange Markets

WORLD MARKETS

Most currency markets consist of organisations linked by international telephone networks but the major dealing operations are now able to deal instantaneously with each other through computerised screen systems which enable people to price, deal and confirm agreements whilst 'conversing' on their monitors.

Hence the markets can function at any time in any place in the world. There is no need for a dealer to be physically located in any particular building or adhere to any particular office hours, although for convenience of staffing, trading tends to follow local business hours. Because of this, world markets are split into zones, primarily those of Europe, the Pacific basin and North America.

European Markets

The main zonal market covers the European area, which coincides at the start of the day with the end of trading in the Pacific basin markets of Singapore, Hong Kong and Australia, covers a good part of the rapidly growing Middle East markets, overlaps the main part of the American Eastern seaboard markets and overlaps for an hour or so the US West Coast market.

With such a massive global coverage and nearly 200 national markets, the European zone has become the biggest and most important of the world markets. Within the area there are major dealing centres in London, Frankfurt and Zurich; also very active are Paris, Brussels, Amsterdam, Copenhagen and Stockholm.

Some countries have several market centres (for example, Switzerland with Zurich, Basle and Geneva; and Germany with Frankfurt, Hamburg, Dusseldorf and Munich), whilst others, such as the UK and France, confine dealing virtually to a single centre.

EUROCURRENCIES

The prefix 'euro' is simply a short way of identifying a banking market (that is, borrowing or lending money) in any currency other than that of the country in which the trading is taking place. The eurocurrency market was started by banks in Europe trading in US dollars, hence 'eurodollars'. Nowadays, trading is worldwide and the Pacific area calls US dollars 'Asian' dollars, yet the currency is still the freely convertible US dollar. It could also be the euro, Swiss franc, Japanese yen, sterling and so on, which are all lent or borrowed to settle trade debts in other markets.

There was a massive increase in eurocurrencies in the late 1950s, for several reasons:

- Communist countries were reluctant to keep their US dollars in America, for fear of sequestration, but as they did not wish to sell them, they sought to lend them outside the USA.

- In the 1957 UK debt crisis, the finance of multilateral trade in sterling was prohibited and the dollar gained in popularity in other countries.

- The US Federal Reserve Regulation 'Q' restricted the rate of interest payable by American banks for deposits, so foreign depositors of dollars sought higher interest rates outside the USA.

- Borrowing dollars from European banks was usually a lot cheaper than domestic funds in the recovering countries of Europe and Asia.

The development of the market in eurocurrencies, principally eurodollars, led many US banks to establish offices in London and other European cities to join in the new scope for lending. There is an inherent danger of massive losses all over the world if ever the US dollar seriously lost its value but the danger has always been contained to date by the general political will to maintain stability.

THE LONDON FOREIGN EXCHANGE MARKET

At one time there was a meeting place for bill traders in the London Royal Exchange, but since this died out in the 1920s the exchange market in London has been entirely telephonic, between dealers in offices all over London. The market rapidly developed after the First World War as sterling became less acceptable as an international currency. No controls existed in those days and brokers, banks, commercial firms and private citizens were all able to engage freely in operations and compete without restriction.

In the mid-1930s, at the instigation of the Bank of England, some order was introduced but now this regulatory function is largely carried out by the Financial Services Authority. Regulatory influence is still exercised by 'the Old Lady of Threadneedle Street' (as the media like to label the Bank of England) in certain areas, but its old regulation of the banks themselves has devolved. Some currency trading is regulated neither by the Bank of England or the FSA, it is regulated by HM Revenue and Customs, under an old arrangement whereby bureaux de change were regulated by the then HM Customs and Excise. Considering the size of bureau such as Travelex, who manage foreign cash transactions for many high street banks, this is a significant portion.

When the end of the Second World War allowed the reopening of foreign exchange markets, dealing was restricted to banks authorised by the Bank of England. The market today comprises hundreds of authorised banks with direct lines to brokers, who supply the banks with a constant stream of buy and sell orders from their clients. For this service, a broker levies a commission or brokerage from each party to each deal.

A DEALING ROOM

A modern dealing room provides its dealers with some of the most up-to-date communication equipment available. Every desk has telephone lines, both general and private, between its customers, brokers and correspondent banks, together with screens supplying the latest rates, news and dealing systems on a worldwide basis. Computers also relay other essential data as well as agreeing orders with correspondent banks and customers alike. The foreign exchange dealer needs every bit of the communication links to operate confidently.

A dealing room can be of any size, employing from one dealer to over 200. In a small room, each dealer is probably involved in every type of business. In a larger room, activities are more specialised, with individuals having responsibilities for particular currencies, but all working as a team under a chief dealer.

Business comes to a dealer from several sources: from customers and correspondents, or from banks acting as principals. A small operation may just seek to cover its customers' requirements, or it may take dealing positions in an attempt to increase its business and profits. A larger operation must always participate fully in the market so that the dealers are conversant with events and can provide a competitive service to customers and correspondents.

Dealing Operations

RATES OF EXCHANGE

A rate of exchange is the price at which one currency can be exchanged for another. It can be expressed as so many units of currency A being worth one of currency B, or conversely as one unit of A being worth so many Bs. For example, the dollar/sterling rate can be expressed either as US$1.5731 equals £1 sterling or as US$1 being £0.6357.

It is always vital to know which way round a rate is being expressed. Mistakes can be costly but fortunately, in the UK, it helps that rates are usually quoted as so many units of the foreign currency to one pound sterling.

A rate of exchange will usually be quoted as a pair of rates, for example, US$1.5731–1.5741 to the pound. The first rate is the selling rate, the rate at which a bank will sell to a client, that is to say, the bank will hand over 1.5731 dollars for each pound. The second figure is the bank's buying rate, that is to say, the bank will require 1.5741 dollars for each pound that it gives. Banks don't charge businesses for buying or selling currency – they make their money from the difference between the buying and selling rates. This is called the 'spread' – in this example, 0.0010 dollars. The spread varies according to the amount being dealt and the state of the market. The basic rate quoted is for marketable amounts on the inter-bank market, say, for about one million dollars or the equivalent. When quoting for a smaller amount, the bank will widen the spread to allow for possible fluctuations before it finalises all its transactions and to cover the inherent cost of making the trade.

SPOT RATES

Spot rates are the exchange rates quoted for immediate delivery of the currency. In reality, custom and practice is for 'spot' to mean delivery two working days from the day on which a deal is transacted. This is to allow time for instructions to be safely exchanged and for the payments themselves to be made. In practice, deals can be completed for any reasonable settlement date, known as the 'value date'. The actual day-to-day exchange rates for spot are decided by supply and demand for the two currencies concerned.

Rates change marginally from minute to minute, although major economic events or political crises can cause larger changes, and the daily press charts show them as at the close of business on the previous day.

Deals can be arranged to switch the delivery value from the spot date to the date required. The margin by which a spot rate is adjusted for delivery on another date is known as a forward margin.

FORWARD RATES

The market for providing rates at future dates is entirely different from the spot market. Forward rates are not predictions or expert estimates of spot rates in the future. They are produced by simple arithmetic, being the difference between the bank interest rates of the two countries, for the period of time between now and the forward value date. The interest rate differential is expressed as a margin. To arrive at the outright exchange rate for a future date, it is necessary to add or subtract the forward margin to or from the present spot rate, as in Figures 19.1 and 19.2. The chance of error is reduced if 'outright' rates are quoted, that is to say, the forward rate after the margin has been added or subtracted.

Sometimes the forward rate is not a simple interest differential, as markets have now become more sophisticated and will price in expected economic changes, such as expected interest rate movements, inflation rate differentials and currency shortages.

A forward margin will be at *a premium* or *a discount* to spot. If the other country has lower interest rates than sterling, its currency is said to be at a premium to sterling. This is because the bank in the other country will pay less interest on the money it borrows to do the deal. The interest differential for the forward period of time produces the premium, which is then deducted from spot to arrive at the forward rate. Conversely, if the other currency's country has higher interest rates than sterling, the difference produces a discount, which has to be added to spot to arrive at the outright forward rate.

It is important to understand that banks look for certainty in financial transactions. Therefore, the golden rule is that transactions are closed, that is, the bank borrows the dollars it will receive at the future date at today's exchange rate plus the interest cost. To guess at the future rate is speculation, and whilst possibly highly profitable is also highly risky and not a few banks have become insolvent due to the massive swings these can generate if the market goes against you.

The example in Figure 19.1 illustrates a forward margin at a premium to sterling, and therefore deducted from the spot rate. When deducted from spot, it gives fewer currency units for the pound, so the foreign currency is more expensive – it is at a premium.

If the US dollar were at a discount, in other words cheaper forward, the margin would be added to the spot rate, giving more dollars to the pound for a future date, as in Figure 19.2.

For simplicity, only one rate is shown in the examples in Figures 19.1 and 19.2. As with spot rates, banks quote forward margins in pairs, for clients buying or selling the currency. An exporter selling goods in US dollars will sell his receipts to the bank for sterling. Thus he would look at the bank's figures for buying dollars (see Figures 19.3 and 19.4).

An example with forward margins at a premium would be thus:

Quotation:	Spot	$1.5731–1.5741
Forward margins:	One month:	0.0035–0.0033 cents premium
Three months:		0.0098–0.0093 cents premium

GOLDEN RULES (WHEN READING PRESS CHARTS)

First figure = bank selling; second figure = bank buying (exporters normally use this).

Deduct premiums from spot; Add discounts to spot.

Spot rate	= $1.5741 = £1 sterling
One month forward margin	= 00.0033 premium
Rate for one month forward	= $1.5708

Figure 19.1   Forward exchange rate: premium deducted from spot rate

If the US dollar were at a discount to sterling, the calculation would be as shown in Figure 19.2.

Spot rate	= $1.5741 = £1 sterling
One month forward margin	= 00.0033 discount
Rate for one month forward	= $1.5774

Figure 19.2   Forward exchange rate: discount added to spot rate

	Bank selling	Bank buying
Spot	1.5731	1.5741
Less one month premium	0.0035	0.0033
Outright rate for one month	1.5696	1.5708
Spot	1.5731	1.5741
Less three months premium	0.0098	0.0093
Outright rate for three months	1.5633	1.5648

Figure 19.3   Outright exchange rates: one and three months premium

	Selling	Buying
Spot	1.5731	1.5741
Add one month discount	0.0035	0.0033
Outright rate for one month	1.5766	1.5774
Spot	1.5731	1.5741
Add three months discount	0.0098	0.0093
Outright rate for three months	1.5829	1.5834

Figure 19.4   Outright exchange rates: one and three months discount

OPTION FORWARD RATES

For exporters, a fixed date for delivering the customer's payment to the bank is not much use if it is not known exactly when the money will arrive. For this reason, some banks offer an 'option forward' contract where the exporter can choose a pair of dates between which to deliver the customer's currency to the bank.

The optional part of the contract relates only to the delivery of the funds to the bank. In all other respects it is exactly the same as the fixed date contracts already described. Because a bank can only cover itself in the market for a fixed date, it has a slight risk in providing option forwards. To compensate for this, it offers the exporter a slightly worse rate than for a fixed date.

CLOSING OUT

This is the term used when an exporter simply does not have the foreign currency to deliver, whether on a fixed or a forward contract, usually due to a delay in an expected payment from a customer.

Because the contract must be fulfilled by the exporter (just as the bank is committed to the exchange rate whatever has happened in the market), he has to purchase the contracted amount of currency at spot rate. This may give the exporter an exchange gain or loss, depending on the currency movement since the deal was made.

So, although there is a well-established procedure for overcoming the problem of a customer's non-payment in time, it is usually recommended that an exporter uses an option forward contract rather than a fixed date one. The strategy of many firms is to sell forward a portion, say, 80 per cent of expected receipts so that there is a smaller risk of not being able to meet a currency delivery date. If, however, there is a reliable arrangement with a foreign customer to get a large currency payment into a specific bank on a specific date, then a fixed forward contract will give the exporter a better exchange rate.

Press Charts of Foreign Currency Rates

The financial sections of daily newspapers and magazines display the rates for the major currencies at the close of trading the previous evening. For UK readers, the rates show how many foreign currency units for one pound sterling. Figure 19.5 illustrates the way the rates would be listed in a UK national daily broadsheet newspaper for, say, 28 August.

Sterling Spot and Forward Rates				
Mkt rates for August 27	Range	Close	1 month	3 month
Copenhagen	10.682 10.749	10.716 10.724	185 76pr	461 270pr
Euro	1.4385 1.4475	1.4432 1.4437	7 10	21 26ds
Montreal	2.1841 2.2104	2.2044 2.2054	18 9pr	48 30ds
New York	1.5664 1.5745	1.5731 1.5741	34.9 32.9	97.5 92.5pr
Oslo	11.968 12.067	12.035 12.040	117pr 10ds	269pr 89pr
Stockholm	13.303 13.403	13.347 13.353	13 2pr	29 13pr
Tokyo	183.86 185.45	185.22 185.32	64 53pr	175 157pr
Zurich	2.2100 2.2218	2.2194 2.2202	70 59pr	194 170pr
Source: AFX				
Premium = pr Discount = ds				

Figure 19.5   Typical press chart of currency rates

This chart shows the range of rates traded during the day of 27 August in the London FX market. The 'Close' rates are for the banks selling and the bank buying when the offices closed on the evening of 27 August, although trading may have continued through the evening and night with exchanges abroad. The '1 month' and '3 month' columns show the forward margins for those periods.

Forward contracts may be made for any short-term period but these are the most usual and others can be assessed from these figures. This chart shows cities and not countries, because these are where trading is concentrated.

The 'bible' for rates is the chart printed in the *Financial Times* on a Monday morning, showing exchange rates in pounds sterling, US dollars and euros for most countries. Many of those countries listed do not have ready markets for the sale of that currency, particularly in developing markets, but the exchange rate is calculated by reference to a second hard currency, typically the US dollar.

This is as most currencies have a US dollar exchange rate readily available, which can be referred to third currency such as pounds sterling or euros by simple arithmetic.

Exchange Risks and How to Cover Them

Whenever an exporter commits himself to receiving payment in a currency other than his own, he incurs an exchange risk. If he does business in sterling, he has no exchange risk but the foreign customer certainly does. To settle a sterling invoice, the customer has to apply formally to his bank to generate a transfer to the UK in an alien currency (sterling) which may require lengthy foreign exchange approval processes.

Where such procedures are required, the customer may have no idea of exactly how much of local currency will be needed at the due date to settle the sterling amount, since the local currency fluctuates every day against sterling, as every currency does.

However, these days most countries have fairly sophisticated banking procedures which will provide the customer a fixed exchange rate at the date of the transaction.

From a marketing point of view, it may make sense to please the customer by selling in his currency, to remove all his worries of exchange risk and workload. The exporter then has the exchange risk but can use the sophisticated London FX market to fix the required forward value of the customer's currency payment.

This strategy only applies where the customer's currency is 'hard', that is, it can be readily converted into sterling in London, or where the company has need of that currency for its own obligations. An alternative in this case is to do business in an acceptable third currency such as the US dollar or the euro in the CFA zone. This is almost certainly more available to the customer's bank than sterling; and there is no problem for the exporter in receiving dollars or euros.

From a cash flow point of view, payment will be faster if the customer only has to find his own currency, or dollars, and not a difficult one for him, such as sterling.

Events in the FX markets show that it is impossible to forecast future trends in rates. Economic factors may well suggest that rates will move in a certain direction but then there are unexpected political events or unilateral changes in interest rates, which immediately swing rates in a different direction. Those who wish to out-guess market trends must remember that any exchange rate is affected by events in both the countries concerned, and often, because of their influence, third countries as well, such as the USA and the euro zone. The game of predicting future spot rates regularly defeats governments, economists, computer programs and 'expert' foreign exchange dealers.

COVERING THE RISKS ('HEDGING')

There are at least five different ways of offsetting exchange risks, or 'hedging' them.

1. *Selling the expected receipts forward:* An exporter can make use of the forward exchange market, by selling the expected payment from the customer at an early stage, thus fixing the sterling value. The early stage can be whatever suits the exporter's operations, such as when invoicing or when reviewing unpaid accounts. It is more sensible, if possible, to 'guarantee' the intended sterling value by making a forward contract when taking the customer's order, or when quoting, or when producing a price list or brochure, or when sending a sales representative on a selling trip.

    In simple terms, if an exporter would like to receive £100 from his German customer who wants to pay in euros, he can quote a euro price today, converted from the planned £100 at spot rate plus the forward margin for the period specified, for example:

    14 days to get the order plus 21 days manufacturing time plus 30 days credit = 65 days ahead.

    On receipt of the customer's euros in 65 days' time, the bank will honour the forward rate agreed today and the exporter should receive his £100.

2. *Borrowing the expected receipts:* Instead of selling forward the future payment, the exporter can borrow today the currency he expects to receive from the customer. The borrowed currency can

be used as such or converted into pounds for normal company purposes. Interest is payable on the loan for the period until the customer's payment arrives, at an interest rate possibly lower than the sterling overdraft. There is no exchange risk because the loan is repaid in the same currency when the customer's payment arrives.

The benefits are in avoiding any exchange exposure and also possibly borrowing more cheaply than in sterling.

3.   *Holding a currency account:* When UK exchange controls were abolished in 1979, it became possible to maintain bank accounts in other currencies in the UK.

The benefit of this is to be able to retain the customer's currency without converting it to sterling, in order to make use of that currency, for example, to settle local commissions or to pay for imports. The loss or gain can thus be limited to the sale of any excess currency in the account.

4.   *Netting accounts between group companies or divisions:* A review of accounts in group companies may show that one company is paying another in a currency, while another company is receiving amounts of the same currency without any use for those funds. Alternatively, companies or divisions may each be managing their own affairs and buying and selling currencies as they need them. It makes sense for an overall policy to notify currency positions to a single point. Then, book entries can be made centrally, with only net differences being actually paid between group companies.

Apart from avoiding exchange risks for the group overall, a good netting procedure also saves much administration for individual companies having to obtain or dispose of currencies.

A more sophisticated use of netting currencies would see the multi-national company seeking to source purchases in those currencies it has excess of and sell more in currencies it is short of. This would lead to an overall balance of the company's exposure to currency movements, albeit that some divisions/subsidiaries may see adverse local movements, but from the global perspective, the corporation was better protected.

5.   *Using currency options:* Foreign currency options were first introduced
      on the Philadelphia Stock Exchange in 1982. They quickly spread to
      all the major exchanges and are now very popular where there are
      very large values of currency exposure.

      An option is an agreement between a bank (the 'writer') and a
      customer (the 'purchaser') that for a fee, the bank gives the customer
      the right to exchange one currency for another at a fixed rate
      throughout an agreed period of time. The bank has the benefit of its
      fee – paid and definite – but also the downside of a potential open-
      ended risk when deciding whether or not to cover the obligation in
      the forward exchange market.

      Conversely, the option purchaser incurs a specific cost – the fee
      – but enjoys unlimited potential benefit in being able to exercise
      the option if the offered rate becomes more favourable or taking no
      action whatsoever if it has moved adversely.

      Thus the exporter (the option buyer) can select an exchange rate
      level for a currency which, when adjusted by the option fee, will
      give a base exchange rate at which his exposure is fully covered,
      with the added benefit of being able to take an exchange 'profit' by
      walking away from the option and dealing independently in the FX
      market (in which case, he loses his option).

The Euro

Businesses prefer stable exchange rates when planning sales, purchases and
capital investments but until 1979 this was not possible because of unpredictable
exchange fluctuations.

In 1979, the first inter-governmental agreement was made to create a 'zone of
stability' in exchange rates between the members of the then European Economic
Community (EEC), envisaging a single currency for a single market of some
350 million people. Using the Exchange Rate Mechanism (the ERM), member
governments agreed to keep their exchange rates within a fixed range of about
2 per cent of each other. To do this meant adjusting interest rates from time to
time, adjusting state spending up or down, and changing tax rates. Occasionally,
genuinely weaker currencies such as the Irish punt and the Italian lira were allowed

a greater divergence, to avoid having to take socially drastic measures. However, the fixed range was clearly artificial, since actual trade performance caused national currencies to be weaker or stronger currencies, as always. The intention was that all the devices needed to prop up the 'stable' ERM rates of exchange would be replaced by genuinely strong economic performance as businesses achieved the envisaged benefits of stability. In due course, the European Currency Unit (the ECU) was devised, as the forerunner of a true single currency.

The ECU was a cocktail of each of the member states' currencies, mixed in proportion to the strength of each country's trading with the others. Later, after much discussion over the best name for it, the euro was born. The word 'euro' was decided by single market bureaucrats as the least offensive to any one member country. 1999 saw the start of various parallel runs between the euro and national currencies, to help the populations of 11 countries to get used to the new money. The 11 were: Austria, Belgium, Finland, France, Germany, the Irish Republic, Italy, Luxembourg, Netherlands, Portugal and Spain. Greece joined in 2001. In 2002, all 12 countries issued euro notes and coins and the single currency became a fact. Denmark, Sweden and the UK chose not to join the single currency for the time being.

Several of the newer entrants to the EU signalled their intention of also adopting the euro as their currency as soon as their economic metrics meet the criteria. For example, Cyprus, Malta and Slovenia are already members, joining on 1st January 2007, and Slovakia joining in 2009. The Czech Republic, Estonia, Hungary, Latvia, Lithuania and Poland have given notice of their intention to join but the target dates have been slipping due to convergence criteria not being met. Some still hope to meet the criteria for entry in 2010 or 2011 but 2012 is looking more likely. Romania has similarly noted its intention to join but it is unlikely to meet convergence criteria before 2014.

In addition to the EU members using the euro as their currency, a number of other countries who have been in currency union with their EU neighbour for many years are also members of the euro area and use the euro. These are Andorra, Monaco, San Marino and the Vatican. Some even issue their own euro coins and bank notes!

The UK and the Euro

For exporters, there will be two broad markets in the future, if or when the UK drops the pound in favour of the euro. One is the countries in the EU and the other is business with the rest of the world. Pricing in the euro will avoid any exchange risk whatsoever for sales to the other EU countries. The hope is that the enlarged and strengthened euro will mean more reliable exchange rates and fewer fluctuations against other major world currencies, such as the US dollar and Japanese yen.

The euro is already in use by most western European countries but has yet to become universally popular with the citizens of those countries, whose criticisms are mainly about the inflationary results of price conversions, even though great advantages are enjoyed by tourists and travellers within the euro area. In the macro field of governments and big business, the euro's problems have centred on the divergent economic situations of its member countries, in view of the need for the richer countries to provide vast amounts of funding to support the poorer member countries (this is analogous to the UK having to redistribute the national wealth-cake, earned in the richer regions of the UK, to the hungrier ones).

Maintaining the future strength of the euro in the midst of all the widely varying economic performances of its member countries will need strong Central Bank economic measures which may be very unpopular, with voters resenting the hardships from increased taxes and interest rates, as well as visible cuts in government spending. The more philosophical man-in-the-street in the richer countries is already having deep thoughts about hard-won lifestyles since the Second World War being worsened by having to share national wealth with the poorer countries.

Euro-critics point to the dangers of having to prop up a single currency with a centrally-directed economy, and cite the eventual collapse of previous empires using a 'bloc currency', such as the USSR and, earlier, the British Empire, because of the wish of the people to break free of faraway central control. Such critics would prefer a 'federation' of nations trading freely with each other on preferential terms, but with their own control of economic policy and their own currencies.

However, there is strong EU Governmental determination to maintain and expand the use of the euro, to compete with the mighty US dollar in the world market place. This means not just using the single currency for cross-border trading, but also as a major currency of aid, with recipient countries around the world being encouraged to spend their aid in euro countries. It is also used for inter-governmental debt settlements, which in itself increases the availability of euros in countries which previously used their own currencies, or gold reserves, or US dollars.

For the UK company, the benefits of the UK adopting the single currency would lie in having no exchange risk for transactions or investments in member countries, and less exchange rate volatility between the euro and the 'outside' currencies, especially the US dollar, than exists between national currencies.

Summary

Sales to other countries have to take account of the future values of the currencies at both ends. UK exporters have the enormous benefit of the London FX market at the end of a telephone line.

Through their bank, exporters can discuss present and future exchange rates and make secure deals to take care of any risk of currency loss. Customers in most foreign countries do not have matching FX facilities, so it makes sense to sell in the customer's currency, if a strong one, and immediately offload the risk. The customer may also pay sooner if he does not have to obtain the approval for, and obtain, the exporter's currency.

Glossary of Foreign Exchange Terms

Currency: Any form of money issued by a government or its central bank and recognised as legal tender and a basis for trade.

Economic and Monetary Union (EMU): The treaty which established the European Community decided the procedures for achieving economic and monetary union in the EU in three stages. Stage One in 1990 was mainly to dismantle international barriers to free movement of capital. Stage Two in 1994 set up new financial institutions for the EU. Stage Three in 1999 began the process of the eurosystem and the euro.

Euro area (aka 'Euroland' or 'Euro zone'): The member states of the European Union who have adopted the single currency and whose monetary policy is under the European Central Bank located in Frankfurt.

Eurocurrency: Any currency lent or borrowed in Europe outside its own country.

Euro symbol (€): The curved E takes the first letter of Europe and the two parallel lines across the middle represent the stability of the currency.

European Central Bank (ECB): Established in 1998 to ensure that the agreed EU monetary policies are implemented either by itself or by the national central banks.

Eurosystem: The ECB and the central banks of the EU member states which combine to maintain economic stability.

European System of Central Banks (ESCB): Consists of the ECB and the national central banks of all 27 EU countries.

Exchange rate: How much each unit of a currency is worth in relation to another.

Forward contract: An agreement with an FX dealer or bank to buy or sell an amount of foreign currency on a given date at a given rate of exchange.

Forward discount: The forward margin between two currencies which is added to the spot rate when the interest rate of the country of the currency being traded is higher than that of the client's country.

Forward margin: The arithmetical difference between interest rates in the two countries concerned in an FX transaction, for the period of the forward contract.

Forward premium: The forward margin between two currencies which is deducted from the spot rate when the interest rate of the country of the currency being traded is lower than that of the client's country.

Forward rate: A rate of exchange for a specific future date, normally calculated by applying a forward margin to the spot rate (see *Option forward rate*).

FX: Foreign exchange.

FX contract: An agreement in writing or by telephone between a client and a bank to buy or sell a specified amount of a named currency at a specified rate of exchange for delivery on an agreed date. It is legally binding and must be completed exactly by due date.

Hedging: Methods of protecting the intended value of a currency against risk of loss during the period between agreement and settlement.

Import cover: The amount of liquid foreign exchange a country has in relation to its average monthly value of imported goods and services.

Option forward rate: A rate of exchange agreed for delivery or take-up of a foreign currency between two future dates.

Spot rate: The rate of exchange between two currencies for an immediate transaction, with value being two days later.

PART VIII
Consumer Credit

20

Retail Credit Management

Peter C Coupe[1]

• Securing finance for the credit operation • Relationship with finance houses • Types of credit available • Credit policy • Controlling the risk • Collection of accounts • Collection letters by computer • Management information and reports •

Securing Finance for the Credit Operation

We are all consumers, and the UK of the twenty-first century is as much governed by retail credit and its availability (or lack of) as by anything else. It is now difficult to imagine not having those consumer goods we want *now* but could only previously have in one, two or three years time when we had saved up enough money to buy them. All major high street retailers offer credit terms, loyalty and incentive schemes, not only to tempt us into their shops, but also to give them the ability, through data collection, to monitor our purchase behaviour. Walking up and down the high street, or wandering around the vast cathedral-like out of town shopping centres, it is apparent that as far as brand, functionality and price are concerned, there is little to differentiate one store from another. The real sell comes in the credit terms on offer, the interest-free credit, the availability 'subject to status' of every possible means of being able to order whatever it is that we have our eyes on.

It is an important aspect of the credit on offer that it is well marketed, and can be promoted by competent well-trained staff. The windows, the newspapers and magazines, the worldwide web and perhaps above all the television remind us that the special once in a lifetime offer must end at 5 p.m. on Sunday, and is not to be repeated. It is, of course, going to be repeated, but now is the time to go and get the sofa – 'now' is all important. The fundamental practice of tying credit in as a product with a product is well established and is

---

1   Update from previous by Glen Bullivant.

designed to increase turnover as more and more customers are attracted to the shops and stores. Sales can be made to customers who could not afford to pay in full there and then, and there is the opportunity, through the availability of credit, to 'upsell' complementary items to the customer – 'we only went in for a sofa, but came out with a three-piece suite'.

Credit promotes sales in more than one way. By offering attractive credit facilities, customers can be tempted by higher-priced goods and stores can offer special promotional discounts on less popular goods, or ends of line, or during quiet periods of trading. Has anyone noticed, for example, how the traditional January sales have been joined by end-of-season sales, summer sales, spring sales, autumn sales, winter bonanzas...? Additionally, the stores themselves can benefit from the increased turnover by negotiating preferential terms with goods manufacturers for bulk purchases.

Although the advantages of credit trading are many and varied, it is of the utmost importance that the business so gained is seen as being in fact additional to cash sales. It is also equally important to see that the person buying the goods has the means and the intention to repay the debt. Credit management, trade or retail – difference? Not a lot!

Not a lot of difference in the principle of credit management, that is. The idea of assessing risk, setting credit limits and categories, controlling the credit and collecting the debt certainly applies across the board of consumer and trade (and export for that matter). What is really different about retail credit is the way in which finance is secured to underpin the credit operation. The provision of monies for this purpose can be achieved in a number of ways. These include:

- funds raised by the business or by bank lending; debentures and share issues;

- credit facilities from external sources such as finance houses;

- a mixture of the two.

Obviously internal finance raised by the lending business is not a million miles from trade credit operations and has a number of advantages:

- the company determines its own credit and risk policies ensuring that profitability, ownership of the debt and risk ratios remain under its control;

- the company itself retains the personal contact with the customer and so again has the final say in the approach that is taken while building a personal relationship and goodwill;

- special one-off promotions can be arranged to promote specific sales campaigns with variable terms and conditions;

- multiple types of credit schemes can be made available, aimed towards particular merchandise types or customer profiles;

- customer spending can be tracked to target future offers to those customers most likely to buy a certain type of product, or respond to particular offers;

All these closely parallel the trade credit operation, but in retail credit only the very large retail organisations can raise sufficient funds, and have the size of customer base, to be able to make this either a cost-effective, or even possible, option. The largest part of retail credit is provided by finance houses and banks.

Relationship With Finance Houses

When approaching finance houses to ascertain the terms under which they are prepared to do business, retailers should expect a detailed study of their accounts prior to credit facilities being made available. The finance company lending the funds will also impose conditions as to who can be offered credit facilities and to what value. Retailers will be required to guarantee agreed levels of profitable new credit business each year.

Commissions paid by finance houses are the norm in high-ticket price items, such as cars, motor homes, caravans and boats, and are not usually linked to lower-ticket price items. Having said that, however, finance for retail credit is a highly competitive market, and individual deals are frequently negotiated between finance houses and retailers. The consumer will see evidence of the retailer/finance house relationship when entering the furniture store or car showroom – he or she will certainly be led to a specific finance house for anything other than a cash purchase.

Finance houses offer retailers the funding and administration facilities to enable them to provide finance to their customers by means of credit sales agreements (which are many and varied but include 'Buy now – Pay later', interest-free periods, deferred interest payment, payment holidays), personal loan agreements, credit card facilities, hire purchase and conditional sale. The retailer will usually perform the role of the intermediary between the customer and the finance house, as evidenced by the signs and leaflets much in view on the retailer's premises.

In order to be competitive and not only gain new customers but also retain existing ones, retailers will demand very flexible terms from their finance house partners. The competitive and ever-changing nature of the finance house business has led finance houses very much towards adopting a flexible approach with retailers to gain and retain business.

Because of the multiple types of credit terms now available, the procedure for granting credit can vary, but the following provides some general guidance to the steps taken in setting up a new credit agreement:

1. The customer responds to an offer to pay for the goods by instalments. The offer may have been advertised in-store, in a television or magazine advert, website and so on – the medium of the offer is not important at this stage. What is important is that the customer has responded. Depending on the value of the goods, the level of risk and the terms of the agreement, a percentage deposit may be required.

2. The credit application form is completed either by the retailer or the customer and signed by the customer (or customers if it is a joint application) and the retailer then supplies the application details to the finance house. This is done in a number of different ways, including directly via a PC in the store connected by secure data link to the finance house, by telephone, by fax or by post.

3. The application will be processed and the details assessed, based upon public information (postal address file, voters roll, County Court Judgments), a credit scoring routine (points allocated based

on application variables), the lenders policy rules (applicants must be aged 18 or over, less than x previous searches in the last 12 months, outstanding debts of £x).

4. If the application is approved, the retailer then in effect sells the goods to the finance house and subsequently sends the VAT invoice with the credit documents which is usually held with a record of the credit enquiry.

5. The finance house then pays the balance of the cash price to the retailer and accepts the agreement. Finally the goods are sold or hired/leased to the customer under the terms of the agreement.

6. The total relationship and financial arrangements between the retailer and the finance house are contained in a master agreement with a detailed service level agreement being put in place.

7. The master agreement will be of a recourse or a non-recourse nature.

A recourse agreement requires the retailer to pay any loss arising from the transactions accepted by the finance house. To safeguard against the loss, the finance company creates a reserve fund by retaining a percentage of the monies due to the retailer. Against this retention fund are charged the balances outstanding on all bad or slow-paying accounts and the agreements are assigned to the retailer who then becomes responsible for any further collection effort. Normally the collection of accounts is undertaken by the finance company and the retailer is advised of potentially bad accounts so that early action by the retailer may prevent write-off.

A non-recourse agreement makes the finance house responsible for such losses, but the charge for credit is usually substantially more. This may not be in the best interests of the retailer (or the finance house) if the customers go in search of better credit terms.

Block discounting is another form of credit sometimes offered to motor traders by some finance companies. Under this procedure, the motor trader enters into an agreement with the customer and collects the instalments as they fall due. These agreements are sold to the finance company in weekly, fortnightly or monthly batches – at a discount. The finance company retains a percentage of the money due to the trader until it has received, in full, the payments due under the terms of the agreement. In other words, the trader receives initially the amount to be paid by instalments, less the retention fund deduction and discount charge. By arrangement with the finance house, the trader may recover the retention over a period by deducting an agreed percentage of the instalments collected before remitting it to the finance company.

Types of Credit Available

The growth of the consumer credit industry saw the formation of the Hire Traders' Protection Association in 1891, which progressed through the Hire Purchase Trade Association to become the Consumer Credit Trade Association (CCTA). The CCTA represents the interests of those businesses involved in the various aspects of instalment credit. These days it is quite normal to find retailers offering several different types of credit facilities to their customers, and the CCTA provides an excellent service to its members by supplying information on all forms of consumer credit. In addition, different credit documents and contracts are designed and printed for purchase by members and a trade magazine is produced. However, perhaps the most important contribution of the CCTA has been to establish a reputation of such integrity and authority that it is able to represent the interests of the instalment credit industry at all levels. The opinion of the CCTA is sought regularly by government departments responsible for consumer credit legislation, or such legislation as may affect the industry, and this opinion extends beyond the UK to consumer credit legislation at the European level.

The following types of consumer credit facilities are generally available:

MONTHLY TRADE ACCOUNT/CHARGE ACCOUNT

The retailer provides goods or services throughout the month, usually up to a pre-agreed credit limit. The customer is obliged to pay the full amount on receipt of a monthly statement. For ease of payment, many lenders offering this product would require that payment is made by direct debit.

BUDGET ACCOUNT

The customer pays a fixed amount each month and is allowed to make purchases up to a fixed limit. This limit is a multiple of the monthly payment and may be as much as 24 or 30 times, although this greatly extends the payment period.

As the balance on the account is reduced by monthly payments, so the customer is allowed to make further purchases up to the credit limit. A charge for credit is calculated as a percentage of the outstanding balance and added to the account each month. This form of credit is popular in the retail trade and is well advertised to attract additional business. It is also a means of building customer loyalty to the retailer offering the credit.

Some identification in the form of a plastic card is usually issued to the customer, bearing a signature, account number, name and date of expiry. The card is used to transcribe the account number and name on to a sales document, which is then signed by the customer and compared by the assistant with information coded into the magnetic strip, or more increasingly now the chip and pin number process. The original of the sales document is given to the customer and the copies are used for amending the account, recording the sale and audit purposes.

As the monthly instalment is a fixed amount, payment is usually required by banker standing order or direct debit. The monthly statement sent by the retailer to the customer shows the brought-forward balance, payment and purchase in the month and the closing balance. The statement is also often used as the vehicle for promoting certain account holder offers or store evenings open to account holders.

OPTION ACCOUNTS

Option accounts are again usually supported by a plastic card. Each month a statement of account is sent to the customer listing the purchases in the previous month. The customer then has the option of paying the balance in full, or of paying part of it (typically £5 or 5 per cent of the outstanding balance, whichever is the greater) and having the balance brought forward.

A charge for credit is generally calculated on a daily basis as a percentage of the balance outstanding and added to the balance monthly, so that any customer not paying the previous monthly instalment has to pay extra interest.

Again, this is a very popular form of credit offered by retailers and department stores attracting additional business and providing in-store credit facilities very similar to those available to credit card users.

BANK-ISSUED CREDIT CARDS

The bank-issued credit card changed the face of credit granting and the use of credit throughout the industrialised world in the second half of the twentieth century. It is probably the best known (though not necessarily the best understood) form of credit in use today. This popular way in which credit terms are now available to customers is by the retailer agreeing to accept credit cards. This can be a third-party agreement whereby the retailer receives payment from the credit card company (bank subsidiary or bank partner) whom the customer repays in instalments or in full. With the introduction of distance selling (mail/telephone/Internet ordering) the bank-issued credit card instantly became the purchase/settlement method of choice.

The retailer must seek approval from the credit card company prior to accepting the transaction. This is done by way of a floor limit – the retailer and the credit card company, in the negotiation of the contract between them, agree an amount which can be accepted without specifically checking with the card company. This amount is dependant upon the type (risk) of business, value of goods or services as an average, and the extent to which credit cards are likely to be used. If, for example, the floor limit is agreed as £75, then any purchase up to that value is guaranteed to the retailer by the credit card company as value given, and can proceed. The floor limit, and the validity of the card, are subject to an automatic validation now that electronic, online terminals are used. (When simple vouchers were being used, it was for the retailer to check the signature and expiry date of the credit card, and also to check that it has not been the subject of a withdrawal notice by the card company as notified at regular intervals.) For transactions above the floor limit, the retailer sought authorisation by telephone or point of sale electronic terminal – the former providing an authorisation code which was written on the voucher, the latter automatically validates and authorises. Vouchers are banked by the retailer as part of his normal banking process, and terminal transactions are credited online to the retailer's account. Much of this process has been replaced increasingly by chip and pin, but the principle of limits and authorisation remains the same.

The retailer benefits by way of additional business (impulse buying or trading up for more expensive goods is a common feature of credit card buying), but a charge for this facility is made by the credit card company through an agreed discount, which is charged directly to the retailer's account. This charge is often referred to as the merchant fee.

A statement is issued by the credit card company to the card holder listing purchases made in the previous month, and the card holder can then pay the balance in full, in which case no credit charge is made. Alternatively, the balance can be paid by instalments, in which event a charge for credit, calculated at a daily basis as a percentage of the balance, is added each month. It should be noted that, if the option is taken to pay by instalments, then interest on the balance is not from the statement date in respect of purchases of goods or services, but as in the case of using credit cards to obtain cash, then interest is charged from the day of the transaction.

HIRE PURCHASE

Hire purchase is a traditional form of credit now mostly used to finance car purchase, although a few companies still offer this facility for some consumer durables. It is the subject of extensive legislation providing a fair measure of protection to trader, lender and customer, enshrined in the Consumer Credit Act 1974. A hire purchase contract is an agreement to hire with an option to purchase. The customer, while having the option to purchase, need not do so and may terminate the agreement and return the goods at any time subject to the terms and conditions of the agreement and the provisions of the Consumer Credit Act.

The purchaser, or hirer, does not get title to the goods, however, until the total credit price, which includes all charges, has been paid. In the event of a default in payment, the owner may commence legal action for the return of the goods and/or claim the amount of the arrears outstanding at the time the agreement was terminated. The deposit, which may include any trade-in allowance, is paid by the customer on signing the agreement. This initial payment is deducted from the cash price of the goods and to the balance is added the charge for credit, which will vary within the period of credit required, and the option to purchase amount. The cash price, less the deposit, plus all charges represents the amount to be repaid by instalments over the length of the agreement. After the creditworthiness of the customer has been established, the agreement will be accepted and signed on behalf of the trader or finance house and the customer given a statutory copy of the agreement with details of how and when payment is to be made.

Payment is typically by direct debit or standing order and rebates for early settlement are available to customers, though these must remain within the terms of the Consumer Credit Act.

CREDIT SALE AGREEMENTS

Credit sale agreements come in many and varied forms and tend to be used for those faster depreciating consumer durable goods where there is little benefit to the retailer to be had in repossession and resale – carpets, furniture, electrical goods such as domestic appliances and so on. Competition in the retail trade has led to an array of marketing initiatives, designed to appeal to consumers, such as:

- buy now – pay later;

- interest-free credit;

- deferred interest products;

- repayment holidays (often around Christmas and the summer school breaks).

A credit sale agreement is a contract of sale in which title in the goods passes immediately to the buyer, so that the retailer or finance house cannot demand the return of the goods in the case of non-payment. The buyer also has the right to sell the goods at any time. Increasingly, retailers are varying the types of credit sale agreements on offer to meet market demands and to remain competitive.

As the terms of the agreement, including any interest charges, are identified at the commencement of the agreement, it is not necessary to send a statement on credit sale agreements. However, many companies choose to send a statement at the time of the penultimate payment to encourage customers to make additional purchases, or to commit to a savings/investments scheme – this is on the basis that the customer is already meeting monthly payments of £x, so to continue at that level would lead to financial benefits for the customer.

CONDITIONAL SALE

A conditional sale agreement is a contract covering the sale of goods in which title does not pass to the buyer until a specified condition has been met – this would be payment of the total purchase price, including the charge for credit. It differs from a hire purchase agreement in so far as the buyer may be committed to payment of the total purchase price, including interest charges, *without* the option for terminating the agreement before the price has been paid. This distinction, however, only applies if the total purchase price exceeds the limitations of the Consumer Credit Act, which was increased in 1998 from £15,000 to £25,000 (note: this upper limit has now been abolished). If the amount was less than £25,000, the transaction was bound by the same rules as would apply to hire purchase agreements.

Credit Policy

Chapter 3 looked in some detail at the need for a credit policy in trade credit and the benefits to be derived from having a clearly defined policy. The market place in retail credit may be different in many ways, but the arguments in favour of a clearly defined and understood credit policy are just as strong. Indeed, as retail credit involves that most vulnerable of beings, the citizen consumer, the arguments have added weight. Public awareness of credit-related issues has increased greatly in the last 20 years, due in no small part to the consumer watchdog type of activities carried out by television and radio programmes and press coverage. Credit reference agencies in the UK have adopted more proactive advertising, consumers are more aware of 'rights' than ever before (oh, that they were equally more aware of responsibilities!) and the role of the consumers themselves in the overall wealth and well-being of the UK economy as a whole has never been more important. It is vital, therefore, that credit facilities are made available in a responsible manner, at the same time communicating clearly and accurately the implications and the responsibility of the borrower.

In setting any credit policy, all areas of the business need to be aware of the types of credit offered, the company's high-level lending and risk policy, and the procedures which are involved throughout the whole process. This should involve sales staff, credit administration, customer service and delivery and installation personnel. Detailed written instructions and procedures are essential, increasingly in the form of computer-based sales aids and training tools. These should include the key roles and responsibilities for all areas involved in the selling and supporting of credit services.

The policy should cover the following:

- what credit and why?;

- the credit application and associated decision making;

- delivery of goods;

- payment and collection.

WHAT CREDIT AND WHY?

While the list of credit and related products continues to grow, the aim of any company should be to offer facilities flexible enough for the market in which they operate. They should also be alert to continually meeting the needs of today's more discerning (some might say, demanding) consumers.

Credit facilities offered will continue to depend upon the type of goods being offered through the retailer. Inflexible 12-month credit terms are unlikely to meet the demands of those customers looking to purchase a car, for example, though would suit a dishwasher purchase admirably. Increasingly, consumers are expecting added-value products such as free insurance, emergency cash, immediate card replacement, and 24-hour customer service facilities. All of these, and others of a more product specific nature, should be taken into account when evaluating which credit terms to offer and the infrastructure required to support them.

THE CREDIT APPLICATION AND ASSOCIATED DECISION MAKING

The way in which applications for credit are handled vary considerably depending on many factors. Initially, this may depend solely on whether or not the applicant is an existing customer with a proven repayment history. However, new technologies and data sources to process applications in a fast and consistent manner have moved companies to look at varied ways of accepting the highest possible number of applications at the same time as aiming for the lowest achievable risk.

Applications for credit are made every minute of every day, in numerous ways and for a variety of lending products. Traditional methods of credit application, where the customer visits the store and is interviewed and asked to complete a written application form still exist. In a retail environment, such as a car showroom, a private area is usually set aside and designated for the application form to be completed by the customer with the assistance of the sales staff, though more often than not the form is completed by the sales staff with the assistance of the customer. In a retail store, where the application is for a store card, for example, the form process may be largely undertaken by the sales staff asking the customer questions and keying the information directly on to the computer system, which links to the decision-making process directly. This will then generate a completed document for the customer to sign (after being directed to read and be happy that the details are correct). The online process can lead to an instant decision – if the lender involved is offering its own in-house facilities and providing the funding itself, the ultimate lending decision is taken by the credit manager responsible for the finance operation. If the retailer is offering finance using the facilities of a bank or finance house, they retain the authority to accept or decline on the basis that it is their money which is being lent.

There are very few types of credit account for which it is not now possible to have either a written application form (traditional) or online application, and it is interesting to see how the more recent types of credit such as credit cards, debit cards and store cards have influenced the more traditional such as personal loans, rental agreements, mortgages, current accounts, savings plans, pension plans, investment plans and secured loans. It is more and more common to make telephone and/or Internet applications for credit facilities, the way having been led by the satellite and cable television companies and mobile phone operators, but the principle throughout whatever method of application is used remains the same – the information provided is used to make the credit decision.

All applications for consumer credit are checked against the databases operated by one of the UK's leading credit reference agencies – Experian, Callcredit or Equifax – who provide information on:

- UK voters roll;

- postal address file;

- bankruptcy/County Court Judgments;

- previous search information (reciprocal);

- credit payment history with other lenders (reciprocal);

- known fraudulent applications.

This is known as raw bureau data, and is used in credit scorecards to predict the likelihood of an applicant defaulting on the credit agreement. What is being sought by the lender, is an answer to five fundamental questions:

- Who is the customer?

- Where do they live?

- What are their credit requirements?

- Do they have any previous credit experience?

- Are they creditworthy?

Additional elements of credit scorecards would be typically length of time at the address, time in employments, time with bank and so on. Policy rules defined by the lender can also be incorporated in the decision-making process, usually reflecting the specific lending practices of the particular company, such as age of applicant (more than 18: less than 70; total unsecured borrowing less than £15,000; previous searches in the last six months less than six).

The purpose of the application form is to gain the maximum amount of information on the customer, to check it for validity and to collate it for marketing purposes. For that latter reason, many applications now ask specific 'lifestyle' questions, or purchasing preferences for future use, enabling retailers to target customers with selective marketing campaigns – this saves costs on producing and delivering information of little or no interest to the customer.

The setting up of an account begins when the prospective customer first decides to apply for credit and goes through the application process – it is the personal information provided in that process which is taken on trust, but is subject to a degree of validation when the credit reference bureau, the raw data, is cross checked: title, forename(s) and surname, present address, previous address if less than three years at the present address, occupation of self and spouse with details of employers and how long in employment, name and address of bank and type(s) of account(s) held, details of existing credit accounts, including credit cards held. Some companies may also require the name and address of a near relative (not living at the same address), the purpose being to provide the creditor with a contact in the event of the customer moving address without notification.

The nature of a consumer credit application requires a large element of trust, but accuracy in the completion of personal details and the subsequent processing of those details through the system is vital so that a correct decision on accept or decline is made in accordance with the company's credit policy. This is the coal face of the company's credit policy, and why there should be a policy in the first place, and in the second, why policies will differ between companies and markets. Comparing the hire purchase of a new car in a prestige showroom, where the sales person depends for commission on good documentation, against that for a television set in the retail store on a busy Saturday afternoon with the salesperson impatient to serve the next customer, reveals two very different circumstances for the origination of application data, their relative value and importance, and the very different markets in which the two 'lenders' operate.

For those applicants who are existing customers and with whom, therefore, there have been previous transactions, an obvious source of information is the historical files of customer accounts. If a customer has been satisfied with previous dealings, it is possible that he or she will return to that source when requiring credit and expect that his/her new application will be speedily processed. The computer system must be capable of searching and reporting promptly the details of previous transactions, usually in abbreviated coded format. The customer may be wanting a new loan for a different purpose, or a higher value, and such cross referencing is vital in ensuring both accuracy in the decision process and customer satisfaction. The existing customer may have accounts still running, so again the cross-reference feature should allow an instant picture of the current level of commitment against future requirements, and projected new total liability.

For those customers who are entirely new to the retailer or finance house, the application form is the basis of the decision-making process as prescribed in the credit policy, and the use of credit reference agencies as outlined should be stipulated in the policy, as well as being advertised to the prospective customer on the application documentation.

DELIVERY OF GOODS

It is sound practice to obtain a signature from, or on behalf of, the customer as proof of delivery when (or if) the goods are in fact delivered. The delivery note should be retained at the store or attached to the credit document for ease of reference in the event of any dispute. Instant credit facilities, especially for those consumer durables which can be carried out of the store, means that delivery as such does not take place, and in those circumstances, the customer proves identity in the normal way – driving licence, bank or credit card, document showing address – with the signatures being compared for authenticity.

PAYMENT AND COLLECTION

The credit policy will establish the methods of payment open to the customer and the responsibility for the collection of the account in the event of default. It is very important that the date from which payments are to commence and the different ways of paying the account are properly explained to the customer at the point of sale and stressed again when the credit documents are sent to the customer.

Increasingly, customers are given a choice as to the way in which the account will be paid, and the remittance slips or monthly statements are usually designed to accommodate various payment methods: direct at the shop or store, by cheque by post to accounts office, at a bank by credit transfer, electronic transfer via direct debit or Internet banking and so on. The majority of formalised period agreements (hire purchase, credit sale and so on) are paid by direct debit or standing order.

Controlling the Risk

Credit scoring and performance scoring are commonly used to assist in the control of credit risk on large customer credit portfolios. While a credit scoring system is an extremely powerful aid to decision making, often other data, not quantified on the scorecard, need to be assessed alongside the credit score before a final decision can be reached. In the case of new applications, for example, a typical situation would be whether or not the applicant is registered on the electoral roll.

A fully automated computer system may be designed to process branch-based credit applications as well as those applications mailed directly to a central point. Such a system would include a data entry facility for capturing the credit application details, the scorecard (that is, the scores allocated for each participating characteristic), links to internal and externally held credit databases, and policy rules. Where large volumes of applications are to be processed, there can be very significant savings in time taken to process an individual application.

In setting up an automated application processing system, care must be taken with regard to the sequence in which the data is actually processed. For example, if an application fails the point scoring system, and will therefore be rejected, there is little point in incurring any additional cost associated with accessing the external credit reference agency's database.

The computer system should be built to deliver a final decision on the majority of applications, but must be able to identify those applications which require the attention of an experienced credit manager. An example of such a requirement would be where the applicant already has a number of credit agreements currently running, or where the credit required on the current application is greater than the value which the credit grantor is prepared to provide under the automated process.

A fully automated system does not stop there. Having made a decision to accept, reject or refer an application it should then automatically perform associated tasks, such as generating customer account numbers, updating the computer master file with new customer details providing an interface for embossing credit cards, generating a welcome letter/pack and producing accurate management information.

Performance scoring systems provide the platform for informed rather than subjective decision making, in the areas of credit limit management, additional credit granting and authorisations on established accounts as well as debt collection. Systems are developed by examining patterns of account purchase and repayment in order to predict future account behaviour. The calculation of performance scores requires the processing of large volumes of historical account data, which would not be economically feasible without the aid of computers.

Performance scoring is dynamic and the scores allocated to individual accounts must be regularly updated to reflect change over time. Use of performance scoring enables credit management to influence behaviour of accounts by timely intervention and so provide a much tighter control on credit risk. At the same time, this improves the service to those customers identified by the score who could qualify for more automatic transaction authorisations, higher credit limits and a more relaxed approach to the issue of collection letters.

Collection of Accounts

The education of the customer in respect of payment should begin at the point of sale. The responsibility for the collection of accounts that have defaulted lies with the credit department of the retail store or finance house – in other words the organisation that has made the loan. The customer should be made clearly aware of how and when payments are to be made, explained in precise detail at the outset and this should be stressed again in the guidance literature sent to the customer with the welcome pack, credit card or monthly statement.

The basis of successful collections is the same with consumer as it is with trade and export – accurate and up-to-date information, beginning with the customer account itself. Accurate accounting is essential to collection activity in any sphere as it endorses the lender's right to collect and ensures the removal of any doubt or concern in the mind of the collector as to the information displayed on his or her screen. All customer payments have to be properly posted to the account before any reminder notices or statements are produced by the credit department or computer centre. The customer is not concerned as to whether the account is maintained by the most sophisticated computer system imaginable or by gangs of book-keepers with ledgers and quill pens – all that matters to him is that any payments made have been recorded and that the account reflects the accurate current position. If it does not, then the customer has every reason to complain, and for the company to put it right before further action is taken.

Nothing destroys confidence in the credit operation as much as sales staff (and others) having to cope with irate customers who may have been sent unnecessary reminder letters or had a store card rejected at the point of sale when in fact the payment has been made. This is even more soul destroying when the shop just happens, at the same time, to be heaving with potential customers. In such a situation, the sales staff may try to get the complaining customer out of earshot quickly, even out of the shop, without investigating the complaint – 'this sort of thing is always happening' or 'it's the computer going wrong again' or 'don't take any notice of the reminder letter, it will be alright'. From that point on, the credit department has a serious problem, because the customer may not take seriously any future collection letters, however accurate and justified they may be – future impact and effectiveness has been destroyed all for the want of accuracy.

The collection effort will deteriorate if slow-paying accounts cannot be followed up with authority because information is not up to date; hence the vital need for the customer accounts to be kept up to scratch with regular determined accuracy. Whether manual or fully computerised, the credit department should have overall responsibility for providing the input and the reconciliation. It is the credit staff who have to answer letters and telephone calls from disgruntled customers and sales managers alike and it therefore has to be in their own interest to keep those complaints to a minimum by ensuring high standards of accuracy in the first place.

It is easy to forgive the more cynical involved in the collection of accounts that the world is full of rogues and vagabonds and that nobody pays their way these days. That is mainly because collection staff deal, by definition, with collections (no surprise, there!) and as a result the majority of customers they actually come into contact with are those customers who have defaulted. The reality is, of course, that the overwhelming majority of consumer customers do actually meet their obligations with prompt payment and that the collectors only deal with the minority. In huge combines, this minority can be a sizeable number, but numbers are relative – 100,000 accounts in default may sound enormous, but set against a customer base of 7 million, it does put it into perspective.

The reasons for default are varied – research has indicated in the past that it is often an event of considerable trauma which sends an account into a downward slide; a death in the family (husband, wife, parent), divorce, redundancy, serious illness. These could be labelled 'understandable' in its broadest sense. The persistent and deliberate defaulter falls into an entirely different category. Missed payments to extend the credit period, over credit limit and fraudulent transactions on blocked accounts are more difficult to collect than the 'understandable' debt, if only because the perpetrator knows the system, knows what he or she is doing, and can play the game. The issue is to recognise default at an early stage, identify the nature of the default and take the appropriate action.

The collections policy adopted by lenders is most likely to take into account previous payment history and payment performance with other lenders. Actions may include the inclusion of an arrears-style statement message, a series of scheduled letters increasing in severity and/or telephone calls from collection staff. The nature of the contract determines whether the goods can be returned with or without the permission of the court, and of course the nature of the goods themselves determine whether or not return is a worthwhile option.

Any series of collection letters sent to overdue customers should begin sufficiently early, and increase in strength, to avoid a serious situation developing by neglect. It has been said many times before, in the context of trade debtors, and it is well worth repeating here in respect of consumer customers – there is nothing difficult in asking customers to pay money that is owed. The methods employed will vary with the type of credit scheme in use, but to be successful, the collection effort has to be consistent and persistent.

Timings will suit particular requirements, but it is usual for the first reminder letters to be sent around 15 days after due date and for the sequence to continue at 15-day intervals. The number of letters will depend on the nature of the transaction, and the amount involved, but for those accounts that miss the first instalment – a first payment default – contact should be made immediately. It may be necessary to make personal contact – the point is that first payment default needs to be nipped in the bud. It should be referred for special attention until the account is brought up to date, or the goods have been repossessed, if appropriate.

It is good collection practice to ask for payment when the customer is most likely to pay, or rather be able to pay. The whole point of a collection letter is to induce payment and should be timed to arrive as soon after pay day as possible – before the wages are spent, not after! It is also good collection practice to ensure that all reminder letters look as if they have been personally produced for that customer – the days of unsigned, unnamed pre-printed 'circular' type letters are long gone.

When overdue accounts have got beyond the routine reminder stage, the attention given by the collection staff must be positive and the collector following up the account should not threaten action unless it is intended to take that action if the account is not paid. The customer will not take collection letters seriously if the collection staff do not mean what they say.

An example of a simple collection routine would be:

1.   *First reminder* – say 10 or more days after instalment due date.

2.   *Second reminder* – produced immediately prior to the next instalment falling due.

At this stage if the customer has not paid the first monthly instalment due under the agreement, further computer reminders should be automatically suspended and the account referred for special attention. A first payment failure form can be issued by the collection department to the sales office, branch or enquiry agent to establish why the account has not been paid. The important point is to act quickly on first default.

4.   *Third reminder* – produced following the second monthly instalment falling due.

5.   *Fourth reminder* – produced immediately prior to the next instalment falling due.

If the account has not been brought back up to date by the next reminder date, it should be automatically included in those accounts requiring special attention by the collection manager. Special attention accounts should be progressed every two weeks, and may involve automatically generated correspondence, specific individual letters, phone calls or visits. The computer system should also be flexible enough to allow credit management and the collection team to be able to suspend and reinstate the letter reminder sequence at any time.

There will always be those debtors who do not respond to written reminders. These debtors may well have to be contacted by telephone, and again the earlier this situation is realised by the collectors as being the most appropriate, the sooner the personal contact should be made. Care must be exercised in respect of the time and place of telephone contact and the collectors need to be certain that they are actually going to be able to speak to the actual debtor. In today's instant communication society, the use of mobile phones, text messaging and email is also now quite widespread. The challenge is to find, and use, the most effective and appropriate method to contact the customer and then get a positive response.

The objective of any collection telephone call is to contact the actual customer, find out why the account or instalments have not been paid and to obtain a promise of payment. Finding out why the account is in arrears is fundamental. It is often believed that large lenders (banks, building societies, finance houses and so on) are totally without any scruples about chasing debtors hard and that they are impervious to unfortunate circumstances. This is not true in most cases – the bad publicity comes from either the minority of less reputable organisations, or from the fact the debtors have not responded to any written communication from the lender. It is a fact that most lenders want to keep existing accounts (marketing experts all agree that obtaining new customers is a more expensive process than retaining existing ones), but they can hardly be expected to be clairvoyant! If debtors do not speak to them, how can they possibly judge as to whether or not they may be able to help? Consumers who ignore debts in the forlorn hope that they will go away are those who will be pursued with vigour – contacting the lender when redundancy, sickness or some other trauma strikes at least gives the lender the opportunity at looking at options, such as reduced instalments and rescheduling. The telephone call, therefore, is primarily an information gathering exercise.

Catching the debtor at home is not always easy – breakfast or early evening are as good as any time – but it is an offence under the Administration of Justice Act 1970 to harass debtors. Harassment is if demands are made for repayment which *'in respect of their frequency or manner or occasion of making any such demand, or of any threat or publicity by which any demand is unaccompanied, are calculated to subject him or members of his family or household to alarm, distress or humiliation'.* Catching the debtor at work may not be easy, either, and in those circumstances, confidentiality is imperative.

The telephone collector in consumer operations will always try to find a way in which the account can be brought back in line, either by payment now of the missing instalment(s) or by negotiating a suitable repayment plan. Encouraging the debtor to talk is important, so that full and frank discussion can take place in respect of present and future financial circumstances. Personal circumstances are often a chief contributor to default, and as much as people don't like talking about personal matters, if the collector can win their confidence, the consumer will see that someone really is interested in trying to help. Lenders are not philanthropic institutions, nor are they a counselling service, but it makes sound commercial sense to listen and discuss – the ultimate settlement and future good performance of the account may well depend upon it.

It is not possible to judge an early settlement rebate as an incentive to customers to pay their accounts, and as the lender makes his profit over the life of the loan, rebate is not designed as an attractive marketable feature of the credit agreement. Furthermore, the customer who wants to settle the account before full term is more than likely to be a prompt-paying customer, and therefore not one who is the subject of much in the way of extra collection activity. However, such rebate is available to customers and some explanation is worthwhile.

Credit cards will normally have interest applied monthly to the outstanding balance, with the amount required for settlement being stated after the application of outstanding purchases, payments and any service charges which may be relevant. There is no rebate, as such, but the credit card holder does have the opportunity to settle the account in full each month and therefore avoid interest charges (except in respect of cash advances). On the other hand, for fixed-term credit and some types of personal loan accounts, the total interest amount is automatically calculated and applied at the initial stage of the agreement. The monthly repayments are thus calculated to include interest charges. If the customer chooses to settle the account early, the rebate regulations under the Consumer Credit Act lay down the minimum rebate that can be given for early settlement of fixed-sum credit.

The regulations provide the formula to ensure correct calculation of the early settlement rebate, taking into consideration the substantial cost incurred in setting up the account. This is known as Rule of 78. There is nothing to prevent the lender allowing more than the Act provides, and a credit policy may well offer higher settlement discounts to obtain a better cash flow and to promote new business. The Consumer Credit (Early Settlement) Regulations 2004 provide the current rules for the calculation of the rebate. In some instances the charge for credit was waived altogether during specific trading periods or if the cash price was paid within a stated time. This was often marketed as 'free credit' but the Office of Fair Trading (OFT) has enforced the advertising regulations to ensure that 'free' meant 'free' and such promotions are seen less and less. It followed that somebody somewhere paid, and inflated cash prices, lower part-exchange allowances and/or manufacturers' subsidies were often the price being paid. Nevertheless retailers can find that this type of scheme attracts additional business and so offer 'free credit', payment holidays or higher settlement rebate as an aid to selling and an encouragement to consumers to pay on time.

Collection Letters by Computer

Any computerised collection system should be flexible enough to deal effectively with all stages of delinquency, from minor to serious. Not all customers will respond to initial letters and the system must, therefore, be capable of producing a series of letters and prompts, with a variety of appropriate wording, leading up to the final demand and the statutory default notice.

To keep administration and other costs to a minimum it is important to decide which categories of delinquency should qualify for letters to be produced automatically by the computer. These will normally be the initial stages and so enable the more serious cases to be dealt with by qualified collection staff and potentially by telephone. It is important, however, that any system should be capable of recognising a genuine first payment default on a newly established account, rather than errors made by the lender in setting up the direct debit or standing order. While such a customer may simply have misunderstood the payment requirement or be dissatisfied with the goods or services, the account may have been opened with the intent to defraud and it is essential that such a condition should be identified as early as possible so that further credit will not be granted.

The collection process should not been seen as being divorced from customer service or the customer relations environment. On the contrary, maintaining good customer relations and positive customer service is the essence of successful consumer collections – the primary aim of the collector is to eliminate delinquency, bringing the account back into good order, and retain the goodwill of the customer for the future. For that reason, the process must be controlled efficiently, and accuracy with the initial setting up of the account of the utmost importance. For example, if the agreement date is incorrect, the account may be assessed for arrears at the wrong time, resulting in an unwarranted letter and a very disgruntled customer. An error in the address can be catastrophic – the letter will not reach the customer and if returned as 'not at this address' fruitless expense may ensue and another customer is lost, all because the address was not accurate at the outset. As an aside, if the address turns out not to be correct, it is important that the account is so flagged in order that further pointless letters are produced and sent.

Typical hire purchase accounts can last three or four years, and some running credit accounts can last many years. A lot can change during the lifespan of an account – people get married and divorced, change jobs, lose jobs, move house and so on – and amendments must be made to the account details as soon as such changes occur, always bearing in mind the need for accurate input. Inaccuracy inevitably leads to customer aggravation, giving the customer grounds for complaint and therefore more reasons not to pay.

We live in an age of high customer demand, and it is not a viable option to hide behind the computer – consumers are as aware as credit managers that it is not the computer that has made up an inaccurate address or other detail.

What is in the computer is what a human being has put into it! Unless errors are recognised and corrected swiftly, customer goodwill flies out of the window along with the company's, and the collector's credibility for the next collection contact. It is good practice to restrict access to the account master file and to use that master to feed other systems, such as delivery or service. By that means only one file needs to be amended at any time, which will reduce the chance of compounding errors.

The debate among collectors in consumer credit in respect of reminder letters is not as polarised as that in trade credit. After all, the only really cost-effective way of contacting many hundreds (perhaps thousands) of customers is by letter. The debate among consumer credit managers focuses on content and format rather than letter versus telephone. When deciding on the wording of consumer collection letters, it should always be remembered that no letter should threaten any action that the sender is not prepared to carry out and that what the letter says will take place, does take place in the event of non-compliance. Idle threats are as effective as chocolate fireguards, and everyone knows it!

The great innovation of the computer, and all the word-processing power it contains, means that there is absolutely no excuse for standard one-size-fits-all letters to go to every customer regardless of the nature of the default, the size and age of the account or the value. Computerised letter production allows letters to be personalised in a manner to suit individual circumstances. Defaulting customers need not, and, indeed, should not be aware that any communication has been issued by a computer. Programs can be written to pick up financial and personal information, which relates solely to the individual to whom the letter is to be addressed. Collation of information carries very little cost in computer processing power, but is an extremely powerful tool in account rehabilitation.

Variable text should be entered into the collection system to be produced automatically by the computer, or driven by an action code if the arrears status is being handled by a collector. Some systems are selected by the collector and merged into the letter production process. Letters should always carry the account reference number and should be signed. This is an area of some discussion, but the consensus of opinion is that a signed letter adds to the individual authenticity of the letter, and adds weight to its importance and effectiveness. The customer will always want someone to talk to if telephoning in response, and if the company really does care about its customers (including those who may default but can be brought back into the fold), it should not subject them to a series of 'on hold' or 'looking for someone who can help you'.

No one is going to sit down and sign 5000 letters, of course, but the computer can laser print the signature, and the name itself. Some lenders use a fictitious name, or a name that is in effect generic to a department, with operators trained to respond when that name is requested. This is no longer a common practice – experience has shown that customers respond to 'real' people, and that much success is achieved when collectors know their customers.

Automated collection systems should make the greatest possible use of parameter settings. For example, a company may operate an in-house litigation department and therefore wish to use different letter headings for advanced stages of delinquency. A parameter can also be set so that a different letter text can be selected for a customer who had recently changed address to that which would be used for a customer where there had been no such file amendment. Such parameters are also linked to the marketing process, so that changes in address, for example, can prompt suitable literature relative to customers who may be looking for further loan facilities following the house move.

In the case of litigation, it should be remembered that an enforcement default or termination notice must be issued to all parties to a joint account and a copy issued to the guarantor, if any. An automated system must therefore be designed accordingly, and the form and content of such notices comply with the relevant Consumer Credit Act regulation.

Parameter settings are also important if any lender is to avoid the pitfall of computers churning out letters regardless of whether or not they are actually sensible. Safety checks should be programmed in to the system to prevent that most annoying of big company habits – the 'ridiculous'. How can the arrears, for example, be more than the balance of the account? Why send a letter to an erstwhile good customer, or any customer come to that, threatening the wrath of the gods for an overdue balance of 45p? The built-in checks using variable parameters should allow for the suspension or suppression of letters in these and similar situations. It is also important that in such circumstances, the computer system should not build up misleading performance information, which could prove detrimental at a later stage. When the credit industry shares information as it does, how damaging it could prove to be if the 45p arrears led to credit difficulties in the future for the unfortunate customer, just because nobody thought to suppress such a trivial and meaningless piece of data.

The timing of the letter process is important. Whatever schedule is established for producing letters, that is, daily, weekly and so on, it should be based on a 'due date'. That is to say the day on which the creditor is entitled to receive the payment. Related to the schedule are two important aspects:

1.   *The receipt and application of cash to customers' accounts.* Payments, even prompt ones, do sometimes become delayed through no fault of the customer. Therefore, before any letter is issued in connection with an arrears condition, it is necessary to allow some interval for any late arriving payments to be applied to the account.

2.   *The amendment of customer details.* The need for accuracy to prevent unnecessary letters being produced has been mentioned earlier and it is obviously important that, before any assessment of arrears takes place, all the known changes, which may affect that assessment, have been made to the customer details.

The timing of collection letters must be established in relation to the calendar schedule. These may differ, depending on whether the payments are weekly, monthly, quarterly and so on., and whether these are due to be paid in advance or in arrears. The following examples of assessment timings for three main types of collection letters are typical of a month in arrears payment cycle:

- First reminder – due date + 10 days, thereby allowing a reasonable time for any postal delay or correction of mis-posting, and to allow for statutory holidays.

- If no response, or insufficient action, second reminder – due date + 20 days.

- Again, if there is no response, or insufficient remedial action, third reminder and probably the final automatic reminder at due date + 35 days.

By now the customer's payment is a month overdue and a second payment will have fallen into arrears. The account should now be referred to a qualified collector to be reviewed at periodic intervals. A good collection system will incorporate a diary facility to enable the collector to override the preset date with an earlier date if appropriate. If and when the account is brought up to date, it should drop out of the collection system automatically.

Collection by letter also embraces the process of letters of congratulation. These may be produced at set times during the life of those agreements where there is an acceptable record of payment. People paying their accounts on time are a valuable asset, and need to be cultivated. For those who are operating fixed-term agreements and have settled early, it is important to issue the congratulatory letter without delay so that they will be encouraged to support that lender with further business before they are tempted to shop elsewhere. For fixed-term agreements that are running their course, it is beneficial to send out congratulatory letters close to the penultimate payment date, just to let the customer know that the lender appreciates the business and is happy to extend further facilities if required. The aim is quite simple – achieve an ongoing relationship with good customers by offering further credit facilities, and in the shared information environment, this is beneficial to the industry as a whole. The letter will not be a guarantee of further facilities, each application being judged on all the criteria pertinent at the time, but it does enhance the relationship and both lender and borrower benefit accordingly.

The final feature concerning reminder letters, which is worthy of careful consideration, relates to the nature of the stationery to be used. Computerisation brings a variety of possible types of stationery, but hopefully no one now produces thin tissue-type paper letters, complete with sprocket holes! Letters should look like letters, not scrap paper, and although it is not necessary here to detail all the various options, certainly some key questions need to be addressed:

1. Is it necessary to have different stationery for certain letters?

2. Is there a need to retain a paper copy of the letter, or does the online system record and store the codes of letters used?

3. Is the volume large enough to justify investment in the appropriate equipment, such as laser printers?

4. Which is better and ultimately more cost-effective – the self-sealing type, cheapest but which most defaulters would instantly recognise as mass produced? Or letter on decent letterhead paper

in a separate envelope, which defaulters would assume has been produced individually for them? The answer lies in the objective of the letters in the first place – improved cash flow.

Printers, folding and inserting machines may have a comparatively high purchase and installation cost, but they are extremely low cost to run, and the overall impression achieved is far more beneficial in terms of effective cash recovery. Envelopes can be printed with a 'return to' address to facilitate early identification of 'gone aways' and pre-sorting by postcode keeps bulk mailing costs down.

There is no point in saving pennies at the cost of low return in customer response. The customer/defaulter/debtor has to be persuaded to open a letter, read it, and respond in the manner intended. To reach that target, a letter to a customer has to actually be *a letter to a customer*.

Management Information and Reports

What is true in trade and export credit, is also true in consumer credit – the credit manager issues regular reports to senior management and provides information. Information has to be presented in such a way that it can be readily absorbed by management so that remedial action can be taken quickly to correct any adverse trends. Like all reports to management, concise and uncluttered is the order of the day – management always like their data in bite size chunks!

Management reports fall into two categories: those that aid management decisions and those that monitor the results of decisions taken. Both should accurately depict the ongoing situation and be as current as allowed by the constraints of the systems in use. Programs should facilitate the issue of management reports at periods that may differ from those accounting reports required for financial accounting purposes – they may coincide, but may also be required more frequently than actual accounting reports. This requires a computer system that is flexible, or has the ability to download from the mainframe to PCs as and when required. Flexibility in data retrieval and interpretation is at the heart of an effective process.

All reports should be readily identifiable – computer-generated reports having a standard heading on each page – with the name of the report, date produced and so on. Subheadings, where appropriate, should be shown, and any relevant notation ('date of last cash posting 31/03/09' or 'arrears equal to or greater than 60 days' and so on) should be clearly indicated. Columns and their headings have to be consistent and recognisable to the reader. It is usual, in fact, for the credit manager to receive all the computer reports him/herself, and then transpose them to PC format for ease of consolidation into readable reports for management.

While management reports should be as brief as possible in giving the required information, they should contain sufficient information and be set out in such a way that management can readily recognise the decision areas. There will also be times when management require the full detail of accounts supporting the summary information contained in the report, so systems and processes have to be flexible enough to be able to provide as much, or as little as required on demand. Flexibility extends to reports from the same basic data source being available at different locations and levels, such as branch or retail store, and formatted to suit particular users, such as geographical split, type of account, arrears and so on. Computers are notorious for churning out reports of rainforest proportions (programmers often believe that if they provide absolutely everything, the user will be able to extract that little bit he actually needs!), and storage on CD, fiche or intranet is commonplace.

We keep coming back to accuracy, but it is as important in reporting management information as it is in contacting customers. Financial values can be critical, and accurate postings to the ledger accounts, from sales and cash received is reflected all the way through the various systems and reports. Each computer-produced report will be subject to control checks, so that the final numbers agree with totals, totals agree with entries and entries agree with input. The audit trail requirements will dictate this necessity and it will enhance confidence in the validity of the data. For those who download to spreadsheets, however, and construct their own reports from the data, great care is needed in maintaining accuracy.

The three main areas of information covered by reports for management are:

1.   new accounts;

2.   cash received;

3.   overdue accounts.

Where companies are using automated scoring and processing techniques to assess applications for creditworthiness, details showing new accounts opened will be a by-product of such a process. The reporting for those companies not using automated systems will require data to be drawn down and analysed, collated and scheduled. Most companies produce periodic targets for new business and the reports of new accounts opened should be produced with the target numbers incorporated – this will provide for immediate performance appraisal. The information, which can be produced at any time frequency required, but is often daily, should be retained so that month-to-date and year-to-date cumulative totals can also be reported. See Figure 20.1.

THIS WEEK				
TYPE OF ACCOUNT	TARGET	NUMBER OF NEW A/CS	CREDIT LIMITS (REVOLVING CREDIT)	GOODS VALUE (FIXED TERM)
OPTION	1500	1656	935,640.00	
BUDGET	900	821	295,560.00	
CREDIT SALES				
AGREEMENTS	3700	3950		
ALL TYPES	6100	6427	1,231,200.00	1,422,134.00

Figure 20.1   New accounts report

This kind of data can be reported in total, or by branch, by store, by region, by sales area or any kind of combination or addition as required. Branches, stores or regions can be compared, and best/worse performers identified. Targets should of course be realistic so that the measure of actual performance against these targets is meaningful and will immediately inform management of branches that have performed exceptionally well and those where some problems may exist. It is important, however, to remind management that chalk should not be compared to cheese – there may be fundamental differences between branches or regions, both in the catchment area for the branch and the make up of the customer base. This should have been taken into account when targets were set, but it is worth a double check.

Cash flow reports monitor the receipt of payments against the amounts due to be paid by customers. The funding of a consumer credit transaction is based on the cost of money with its highly competitive interest rates. At the point when a fixed-term credit facility is granted to the customer, a percentage rate of return (the profit on the transaction) is established. If instalments are received when due, the expected profit is achieved, but those not paid when due increase the administrative costs, thereby reducing the profit. Management must monitor this situation carefully. Such a report plays a less important role in the area of revolving credit where interest, if calculated on a daily basis, will be earned on delayed payments.

As with all reports, this report must be based on flexible parameters to cater for the detail required for any particular level of management. Top management, for example, may only want to see the overall situation, whereas other management levels will want greater detailed information to identify any areas that need remedial action. See Figure 20.2.

CATEGORY	ENTITLEMENT	RECEIVED	SHORT/ OVER	SHORTFALL PERCENTAGE
Current instalments	7,800.00	6,750.00	1,050.00	13.5
Court Orders	100.00	100.00	0.00	0.0
Arrears:				
1 month	3,200.00	1,600.00	1,600.00	50.0
2 months	1,100.00	500.00	600.00	54.6
3+ months	700.00	250.00	450.00	64.3
Legal cases	920.00	45.00	875.00	95.1
Total	13,820.00	9,245.00	4,575.00	33.1
Add: Early instalments	0.00	18.50	18.50+	0.00
Settlements	0.00	200.00	200.00+	0.00
Unidentified	0.00	45.00	45.00+	0.00
TOTAL POSITION	13,820.00	9,508.50	4,311.50	31.2

Figure 20.2 **Cash received analysis (daily by company and branch with weekly, monthly and period-to-date cumulatives where required)**

The second type of report, at monthly intervals, would show the performance of a fixed or rolling period over which the improvement or deterioration of payments can be clearly seen. This report highlights those units, which are regularly not receiving the expected amount of customers' cash thereby posing the question of possible weakness in, or deliberate skirting of, account opening procedures. The example in Figure 20.3 shows a performance for current instalments only but obviously all of the cash received categories, for example, one month arrears, should be reported on as a percentage of payments due. Once any segments have been identified as being problem shortfall areas, then further information would be necessary to show the individual items that have contributed to the problem. It may be only one bad particularly large transaction that has caused the apparent adverse situation in that segment. Management will not want to search for such information so for this level of detail the report should always be based on the 'worst first' principle and produced in descending degree, allowing the user to decide where to draw the decision line for action. The overriding need will be to facilitate the investigation required to pinpoint any deviation from laid down account opening procedures.

CATEGORY	JAN	FEB	MAR	APR
	%	%	%	%
Branch (Month)	90.0	85.1	73.1	93.7
Current instalments (Acc. av.)	90.0	87.6	82.7	85.5

Figure 20.3   Performance of cash entitlement (monthly by company and branch or store)

Overdue reports are concerned with the monitoring of those accounts on which payments are in arrears. Overdue reports highlight the various levels of delinquency for monitoring purposes and link to the procedure discussed above regarding the sending of collection letters to customers when payments are overdue. In an automated collection system, there is no need for reports of individual accounts for follow-up to be produced. The system can be programmed to refer accounts automatically at a certain stage of the delinquency away from the normal collection staff to supervisory levels and ultimately to senior managers. An action code will be entered by the person on whose collection queue the account has been placed and this will initiate the required letter to the customer or other appropriate action.

In non-automated systems, it is normal for a routine report to be run to provide details of accounts, which can then be followed up by the collection staff.

Monitoring reports provide both numbers of accounts and values of arrears and balances, falling in each stage of delinquency, starting from one to 29 days through to a maximum, usually 210+ days. Figure 20.4 shows an example of a delinquency ageing report. Companies will compare reports for the same date in the previous month, the same date the previous year and so on, and this ageing will provide an ideal basis on which to calculate the amount to be reserved against profit for potential bad debt, a percentage being applied to the account balance in each arrears category.

	NUMBER OF ACCOUNTS	PAST DUE AMOUNT	TOTAL BALANCE	% PAST DUE BALANCE TO TOTAL BALANCE
Total X Days	810	12,310.21	296,942.12	7.6
Total 30 Days	205	8,002.50	85,385.16	2.2
Total 60 Days	106	9,284.61	55,162.24	1.4
Total 90 Days	61	7,524.89	39,917.52	1.0
Total 120 Days	39	4,986.48	22,024.55	0.5
Total 150 Days	30	5,021.32	15.698.10	0.4
Total 180 Days	28	5,825.93	14,493.30	0.4
Total 210+Days	205	105,880.10	135,633.48	5.3
Total 30+ Days	674	146,525.83	363,314.35	11.2
TOTAL PAST DUE	1,484	158,836.04	665,256.47	18.8

Figure 20.4   Delinquency ageing report

There is a further simple, but useful report (Figure 20.5) which allows management to monitor the performance of the collection function showing only the number of cases in arrears – it would be equally important to produce a similar report showing the amount of arrears for all categories. A percentage performance represents successful collections of the previous (brought forward) arrears situation. The position is expressed as an improvement or otherwise (carried forward) as compared to the previous situation.

Arrears category	Brought forward	Collected	New overdues	Carried forward	% Perf. of collects	Coll (cases)	Position
1 month	1,000	620	540	920	62.0	-80	8.0
2 months	380	230	380	530	60.5	+150	39.5
3+ months	460	420	150	190	91.3	-270	58.7
Total	1,840	1,270	1,070	1,640	69.0	-200	10.9
Add: Legal	24	11	40	53	45.8	+29	120.8
TOTAL	1,864	1.281	1,110	1.693	68.7	-171	9.2

Figure 20.5   Collection performance analysis (by company, branch or store)

Note: The column headed 'Past due amount' shows the value of arrears at each stage of delinquency. The percentage column shows the percentage of account balances in each stage of delinquency to the total balances outstanding. The values against 210+ days will be dependent on the company's policy for writing off bad debts.

Once again, it is important that reporting should be flexible. In particular, automated collection systems must be capable of reporting on the effectiveness of individual collectors, for example, the amount of arrears collected from best to worst and the performance of any new collector measured against the average of existing collectors. There will also be a need to measure the performance of various segments of the file, for example, arrears recovery in relation to criteria such as age of account on book, or credit score when account was opened, and so on.

Companies will want to be sure that branch and store managers obtain the statistics relevant to their own particular unit for action as necessary. Where it impacts upon them, branch managers must be supplied with information at least equal to that of head office management, and so be in a position to see the same remedial action that may be required.

21

Consumer Credit Law[1]

Peter C Coupe FICM
Proprietor, PCC Management Consultants

• Introduction • Development of consumer credit law • The Consumer Credit Act •
The Data Protection Act 1998 • Other laws • Codes of practice • Conclusion •

Introduction

The granting of credit to consumers is principally (but not solely) regulated by
The Consumer Credit Act 1974 and the Consumer Credit Act 2006. These Acts
contain a large number of separate Sections and Schedules. These, together
with the latest array of Statutory Instruments (that is to say, Regulations and
Orders) made by the Department of Business, Enterprise and Regulatory
Reform (BERR), previously known as the Department for Trade and Industry,
and now Business Innovation and Skills (BIS) under the 2006 Act, are now
mostly in effect. So detailed is the mass of legislation, it can only be described
in outline in this chapter.

Readers should also note that a Proposal, published in September 2002,
entitled Directive of the European Parliament and of the Council Concerning
Credit For Consumers, was formally adopted on 22 May 2008 and is due to be
implemented by Member States by 11 June 2010. Aimed at harmonising the
different consumer credit regulatory cultures across Europe, this Proposal has
provoked fierce debate and negotiation, as it will shape the future legislation
on credit in Europe for years to come.

This chapter also makes brief reference to a number of other Acts that affect
the granting of credit.

---

1   Updated from an original written by P J Patrick.

Development of Consumer Credit Law

The development of consumer credit law in the UK represents, for the most part, two major themes. The first is to ensure that the customer is made fully aware of what commitment he is taking, that is, he is able to make an informed decision, while the second is to provide him with adequate protection against unscrupulous traders and others, once the agreement is made. The law evolved, however, in a fragmented manner, with particular forms of credit being regulated as the need arose.

The first really substantial measure was the Moneylenders Act 1927 which provided a form of licensing, forbade circulars and canvassing and severely restricted advertising. It also set out requirements as to the documents used and included a number of other measures to protect the borrower.

Legislation to control hire purchase and, later, conditional sale and credit sale transactions was first introduced in Scotland in 1932 (the Hire Purchase and Small Debt (Scotland) Act 1932) and was followed in England by the Hire Purchase Act 1938. Under the latter Act, a written agreement form had to contain specified information and the owner under the agreement was made responsible for the quality of the goods supplied. Where an agreement was terminated, the hirer's liability was limited to the arrears plus (where applicable) sufficient to bring the amount paid up to half the total price. Where one-third of the total price had been paid, the owner could not repossess goods without a Court Order, the court being given special powers in connection with actions brought under the Act. The 'one-half' and 'one-third' rules, as they came to be generally referred to, appear with very little change in the Consumer Credit Act.

The next big step was the Hire Purchase Act 1964 which introduced for the first time the following concepts: a 'pause for reflection' where a hirer or buyer signed an agreement at home or away from trade premises and the service of a 'notice of default' by the owner of the goods prior to seeking to recover them. This notice gave the hirer seven days warning in which he could bring his payments up to date. This Act also provided protection for the 'innocent private purchaser' who bought a motor vehicle not knowing it was on hire purchase.

The situation as it stood in 1965 was that hire purchase, credit sale and conditional sale transactions were regulated by one set of Acts while moneylending was regulated by entirely different legislation. Lending by banks and 'near banks', option accounts, budget accounts, cheque trading and some less common forms of credit were not regulated at all. This patchwork form of regulation was replaced by the Consumer Credit Act 1974 which was based on the following principles:

1. Since all forms of credit had a common purpose, there should be one framework of law governing them all, embodying the best features of earlier legislation.

2. There should be fuller disclosure of information in consumer credit transactions, particularly on rates of charge.

3. The Director General of Fair Trading was given the task of licensing credit businesses and overall supervision of the consumer credit industry. Responsibility for local enforcement of the law was given to trading standards officers.

The Consumer Credit Act

The Consumer Credit Act 1974 is, in many respects, an 'enabling Act', permitting the government department responsible to make Regulations setting out the detail. The Consumer Credit Act 2006 amends the 1974 Act and extends the ombudsmen scheme under the Financial Services and Markets Act 2000 to cover licensees under the Consumer Credit Act 1974. It will therefore be necessary when ascertaining the precise requirements in order to comply with the law's requirements, not only to examine both Acts but also to refer in many cases to one (or more) different sets of Regulations.

Much of the complexity of the Acts is due to the rich diversity of consumer credit products to be found in this country.

Part I of the 1974 Act is principally devoted to specifying the responsibilities of the Director General of Fair Trading so far as they affect consumer credit.

TO WHAT AGREEMENTS DOES THE ACT APPLY?

Part II of the 1974 Act defines the contracts to which the Act applies: basically, these are contracts for the provision of credit (whether on a loan, hire purchase, credit sale or any other basis) where the customer or borrower is an 'individual'. The Act also originally specified an upper limit, over which agreements ceased to be regulated. Over the years, this limit has been increased steadily to £25,000. Section 2 of the 2006 Act removes the financial limit altogether – effective 6 April 2008. Residential mortgages are regulated by the Financial Services Authority (FSA) and therefore do not fall within either of the Consumer Credit Acts. However, other mortgages, such as buy to let, have inadvertently been brought within the remit of the Act. The Department for Business, Innovation & Skills is proposing a Legislative Reform Order to provide a specific exemption for buy to let lending. The 2006 Act also allows 'high net worth' or very wealthy individuals to opt out of regulation.

'Individual' means anyone, *except* a body corporate and thus, in the ordinary way, 'individual' means not only consumers as such but also partnerships and sole traders. The Act therefore regulates a considerable number of commercial transactions as well as consumer credit in the true sense. The Government announced in 1995 that it intended to amend the Act to take 'business' lending out of its scope, but it did not commence the consultation process until 2002. This process revealed clear support for maintaining the Act's protection for sole traders, small partnerships and other unincorporated bodies. The Consumer Credit Act 2006 amends the 1974 Act to provide a new definition of 'individual'. Borrowing by partnerships of more than three members is excluded from the Act. Section 4 of the Act provides for exemptions to businesses and excludes credit agreements over £25,000 predominately for the purpose of a business from the regulation.

In addition, the Act applies to contracts of hire (which includes of course, lease and rental) where the hirer is an 'individual' and the amount that has to be paid by the hirer to avoid any breach of contract falls within any upper limit currently in force (if any) and the contract can last for more than three months.

Whilst the applicability of financial limits and 'business' lending for 'individuals' is changing, the Act still provides that certain agreements may be exempted, for example, loans at a very low rate of charge and ordinary trade credit where the whole balance owing on one month's account has to be settled with one payment. Any agreement within any applicable limit or predefined scope is a regulated agreement.

Part II of the 1974 Act also contains a mass of highly technical definitions that cannot easily be summarised and which, for those likely to be involved in these matters, requires detailed study. The Act distinguishes, for example, between debtor-creditor-supplier agreements such as hire purchase or credit sale and in which, of course, the creditor and the supplier may be the same. This category includes loan agreements arranged so that a loan and a purchase of goods are effectively one transaction. Also distinguished within Part II of the Act are debtor-creditor agreements that may be regarded as agreements for an outright loan (the debtor being free to use the money how he likes), fixed-sum credit (for example, a loan for £1000) and running-account credit (for example, a revolving credit card account).

Special provision is made in this Part of the Act (and elsewhere) for 'linked transactions', for example, a maintenance agreement/extended warranty entered into in connection with a TV set on credit.

In almost every case, the definitions are complex and in some they are abstruse. The various explanations given above represent a considerable (and therefore not altogether accurate) simplification.

LICENSING

Virtually anyone who provides consumer credit (or consumer hire) within the meaning of the Act and who provides it more than 'occasionally' will require a licence, issued by the Office of Fair Trading (OFT), to carry on his business. This is by no means all, however, since not only will such people as credit reference agencies, debt collectors, debt adjusters and the like also require a licence but so will 'credit brokers' and this has a very extended meaning.

In general terms, anyone who introduces individuals to a source of finance (or of hire facilities regulated by the Act) is a 'broker' for the purposes of the Act, so that quite apart from the brokers as such, for example, second mortgage brokers, any retailer whose credit business is financed by a finance house is a 'credit broker', as is, for example, a manufacturer who, having a number of unincorporated customers, is in the habit of introducing at least some of them to a finance house from time to time to obtain hire purchase or leasing. In short, the term credit broker includes many people who would not in the ordinary way regard themselves as 'brokers' at all. The 2006 Act has introduced the requirement of people carrying on the business of debt administration and credit information services as now requiring a licence.

Although very detailed provisions indeed are made in respect of licensing as such (Part III of the 1974 Act), only one will be mentioned here. Section 25 of the Act provides that a licensee must be 'fit' to hold a licence and, in deciding whether this is so, the Director General of Fair Trading can take into account whether the applicant *or any associate of his* has committed any offence 'involving fraud… or violence', has contravened the Consumer Credit legislation, has practised 'discrimination' (sex, race, colour, religion and so on) or has 'engaged in business practices appearing to the Director General to be deceitful, oppressive or otherwise unfair or improper (whether unlawful or not)'.

In practice, the Director General has used his powers sparingly. An appreciably greater number of persons have only obtained or retained their licences after giving assurances as to their future conduct and it cannot be doubted that the possibility of licensing action by the OFT is a considerable deterrent against adopting unlawful or even questionable methods of trading. However, the licensing regime in its entirety was reviewed during 2003 and there is now a new, stricter 'fitness' test, a greater role for Trading Standards Departments and more enforcement powers for the OFT together with increases to application and renewal fees, and so on. In determining fitness, the 2006 Act requires the OFT to have regard to the skills, knowledge and experience of the applicant. The OFT is given a new power to impose requirements on licensees.

Failure to get a licence or the actual loss of a licence is potentially disastrous as not only is trading without a licence a criminal offence but it can also result in the trader's credit agreements being unenforceable at law.

Finance houses that take business from dealers or brokers have an additional responsibility put on them by the Act, since agreements made on an introduction by an unlicensed credit broker are also unenforceable at law. A finance house therefore needs to check that any dealer from whom it accepts business has a valid licence as a credit broker.

The 2006 Act additionally extended the jurisdiction of the Financial Ombudsman Service (FOS) to cover businesses holding consumer credit licences from April 2007. Information on this, the licensing system, its jurisdiction and application forms for licences, can be obtained from the FOS and the OFT, respectively.

TRUE RATES OF CHARGE

The 1974 Act requires Regulations to be made to inform customers of the true cost of borrowing. The Consumer Credit (Total Charge for Credit) Regulations 1980 made for this purpose perform two functions. First, they prescribe what ancillary and related charges have to be regarded as performing part of the total charge for credit, for example 'option fees' in hire purchase agreements, compulsory maintenance charges, some types of insurance premiums, charges in respect of providing insurance for a loan and brokerage fees payable by the borrower.

The second function of the Regulations is to provide the basis for calculating the annual percentage rate of the total charge for credit, now universally known simply as the APR. This rate must take into account the amount and timing of all charges forming part of the total charge for credit and must be calculated as an 'effective rate' based on compound interest principles, a rather more complex method than the 'nominal rate' used in the 'truth in lending' legislation used in the USA, but now adopted as the basis of the EC Consumer Credit Directive, which in many respects was modelled on the UK's Consumer Credit Act.

The effect is that a rate of 2 per cent per month, as was common in a department store budget account, gives an APR of rather more than 12 times this amount (in fact 26.8 per cent). For hire purchase or similar transactions the APR is approximately 12 times the 'flat rate' commonly used in the calculation of the charges, sometimes more and sometimes less depending on the rate and period of repayment.

The Regulations also prescribe assumptions to be made in calculating the APR when not all the facts are known and require it to be shown to one place of decimals, further places being disregarded (an exact rate of 21.765 per cent is to be shown as 21.7 per cent). The circumstances where the APR has to be given are prescribed in the Regulations described in the next two parts of this chapter. It is always required to be included in a credit agreement document.

The Consumer Credit (Advertisements) Regulations 2004 and the Consumer Credit (Agreements) (Amendment) Regulations 2004 provide for specific assumptions in the case of APRs for credit cards and other running-account credit.

Tables giving values of the APR for the more common forms of credit transaction are published by HM Stationery Office (the 'Consumer Credit

Tables', Parts 1 to 15). The OFT have also produced a booklet setting out how an APR should be calculated. This is available in downloadable form from the OFT's website, entitled Credit Charges and APR.

The Government have already commenced a consultation exercise with a view to reviewing and simplifying this complex method of calculating the charges applied to credit transactions.

ADVERTISING AND SEEKING BUSINESS

The rules regulating the advertising regime have been modified by The Consumer Credit (Advertisements) Regulations 2004.

The Regulations apply to most advertisements for consumer credit, consumer hire or credit brokerage. They extend to all forms of advertising, including in print (for example, newspapers, circular letters, flyers, catalogues or billboards), on television or radio, on the Internet, on teletext or by way of telephone canvassing. The Regulations aim to ensure that advertisements give a clear and balanced view of the nature and costs of the credit or hire on offer.

In particular, the Regulations require that most credit advertisements must include a typical APR. This is a rate at or below which at least 66 per cent of agreements resulting from the advertisement are expected to be made. The typical APR is required if the advertisement includes:

- any interest rate or APR, or any figures relating to the cost of credit;

- any indication that credit is available to persons who might consider their access to credit restricted;

- any indication that the terms of the credit are more favourable than those available in other cases or from other creditors; or

- any incentive to apply for credit or to enter into an agreement under which credit is provided.

The typical APR must be more prominent than any trigger information, and any other financial information. In the case of advertisements in printed or electronic form, it must be at least 1.5 times the size of financial information including the price of goods offered in the advertisement.

Financial information must be presented together as a whole in the advertisement, and with equal prominence. All information must be easily legible. There are also rules restricting the inclusion of certain expressions, and requiring security statements.

The OFT has produced guidance on the Regulations together with sample advertisements and a flowchart illustrating the requirements.

Section 46 of the 1974 Act prohibits 'false or misleading' advertisements while the Advertisement Regulations themselves ban the use of certain phrases in a misleading way.

Section 56 deals with misrepresentation, that is, untrue statements made by the trader to the customer in relation to the goods before their purchase on credit.

Other Regulations to establish the right of a consumer to obtain a written quotation for a credit transaction were revoked in 1997.

The Act itself restricts 'canvassing off trade premises', in other words visits to homes by salesmen offering credit facilities (although the definition embraces a wider range of activities). Canvassing debtor-creditor agreements, that is, the selling of cash loans door to door is forbidden while the selling of goods or services on credit door to door is only permitted where a trader's licence covers him to do this.

The Act also forbids sending documents, circulars and so on offering credit facilities to minors for financial gain.

Finally, there is a prohibition on sending 'unsolicited credit tokens'. Intended to prevent the mass mailing of credit cards without request, it also affects cheque trading and can impose constraints on some types of credit advertising because of the wide definition of 'credit token'.

ENTRY INTO AGREEMENTS

The rules governing the making of agreements are set out in Part V of the Consumer Credit Act 1974 and in Regulations made under it. Between them, they prescribe the form and content of agreements, the giving of copies to the customer and the customer's right to cancel some types of agreement where he signs otherwise than on trade premises.

The Act itself prescribes that an agreement will not be properly executed (and hence will usually be unenforceable against the debtor) unless a document complying with the Regulations and containing all the prescribed information is signed by the customer and by or on behalf of the creditor or owner. The document must embody all the terms of the contract (or in some cases reference to another document given to the customer is sufficient) and it must be easily legible.

The Regulations specify in considerable detail the information to be contained in agreement documents, much of which has to be set out 'together as a whole'. They prescribe the statutory documents or 'forms' setting out shortly and simply the more important rights given to the customer by the Act. They also require that the customer sign in a 'signature box' with prescribed wording drawing his attention to the nature of the contract he is signing. Separate schedules set out the information to be included in credit agreements, hire agreements and 'modifying agreements' for credit or hire. For all forms of credit agreements this includes the APR. The detail of the Regulations is not appropriate for a work of this nature. Suffice it to say that drafting of regulated agreement forms is a matter for the specialist and that care must be taken to ensure that such forms are fully and correctly completed before the customer signs. Failure to do so can lead to contracts that cannot be enforced against debtors.

The Act specifies the right of the debtor or hirer to receive copies of the agreement that he signs. Where both parties sign on the same occasion the debtor receives one copy, there and then, and the agreement becomes a binding contract right away (except where rights of cancellation apply as described below). When the agreement is signed by the debtor but then has to go to head office or the finance house for consideration, the debtor must receive two copies, one when he signs and one following acceptance and signature by the creditor. The agreement does not become binding on the debtor in this situation until dispatch of the second copy. Failure to observe the rules on copies can also lead to agreements being unenforceable.

The information requirements have been extended by the Consumer Credit Act 2006 and the Consumer Credit (Information Requirements and Duration of Licences and Charges) Regulations 2007. These came into force on 1 October 2008.

The new provisions include:

- annual statements under fixed-sum credit agreements;

- additional information in statements for running-account credit;

- notices of sums in arrears;

- notice of default sums;

- additional information in default notices;

- notices relating to post-judgment interest.

The Government has also announced a consultation process with a view to removing obstacles to the online conclusion of credit agreements. By necessity, whilst maintaining appropriate consumer protection, this will need to address application, agreement and post-agreement issues.

RIGHTS OF CANCELLATION

There are two situations in which the Act allows a customer a 'pause for reflection'. The more commonly found of these applies where the customer signs an agreement at home or otherwise away from trade premises and where there have been face-to-face 'negotiations' before the agreement is made (but not where the agreement is made entirely through the post). In this situation, the customer has a right to cancel the agreement that extends to five days after he receives his second copy of it as described above. Both copies of the agreement have to contain a prominent notice giving details of this right. In the situation where the agreement is executed immediately (signed by both parties on the same occasion) and the debtor only gets one copy only, this must be followed by a separate 'right of cancellation notice'. Any failure to observe the rules about copies of a cancellable agreement will mean that an agreement will not only be improperly executed but will be totally unenforceable against the debtor. This right of cancellation sounds forbidding when set down on paper but in practice problems rarely occur since a customer who genuinely wants what has been sold to him will not want to cancel. The true benefit to the customer is that it discourages undesirable practices by door-to-door salesmen offering credit.

The second situation where the Act provides a pause for reflection is in respect of land mortgages or, as the Act refers to them, agreements secured on land. Not all such agreements are regulated since there are wide exemptions for house purchase mortgages, many of which will also be outside any upper financial limit (if any) of the Act in force or will be regulated by other legislation as is currently being considered by HM Government. Since 31 October 2004, the FSA has regulated those mortgages where at least 40 per cent of the total of the land given as security in a mortgage is used as a dwelling. Variations made on, or after, that date to contracts entered into before that date, are not subject to FSA regulation but may be subject to the Consumer Credit Act 1974. Where, however, they are regulated agreements, as may be the case with 'second mortgages', the borrower must be given a statutory pause for reflection and a special copy of the proposed agreement *before* the agreement is signed and this will apply no matter where the agreement is signed. The reason for providing a pause before rather than after signature is because of problems if a mortgage were to be cancelled after it had been registered.

PROTECTION DURING THE LIFE OF AN AGREEMENT

The nature of hire purchase contracts, together with provisions originally contained in the Hire Purchase Acts means that, where such facilities are arranged through a finance house, the hirer has the right to sue the finance house if the goods are not delivered or are faulty. This was formerly not the case with finance loans arranged by the supplier of goods or payment by a bank credit card. The Consumer Credit Act 1974 allows the debtor to seek redress from the creditor in two ways. First it provides that in all kinds of 'debtor-creditor-supplier' agreements the supplier is to be treated as agent of the creditor when he makes representations about the goods or services to be financed (for example a bank credit card). Second, in the case of point of sale loans, credit cards or similar transactions, section 75 of the Act provides that if there is a misrepresentation or breach of contract by the supplier, the creditor shall be jointly and severally liable with the supplier (but will be able to recover from the supplier sums which have had to be paid to the debtor). This Section does not apply to hire purchase or credit sale through a finance house since the finance house takes on the role of supplier by buying the goods from the dealer and thereby incurs direct liability for their quality and so on.

Part IV of the 1974 Act contains a number of other measures to protect the debtor. He has the right to demand information on the state of his account and where credit is in the form of a running account, he must be sent statements of account at regular intervals. Under the 2006 Act, creditors are required, in regulated fixed-sum agreements, to provide annual statements in a specified format. Failure to give these notices means that the creditor cannot enforce the agreement during the period of non-compliance and the debtor or hirer has no liability to pay interest during this period. Protection is also given under the 1974 Act where, for example, a credit card is stolen or misused through no fault of the debtor. Rules also provide for notice to be given to the debtor if an agreement is to be varied (for example, where a creditor alters the rate of charge on a budget account as such agreements normally permit). Finally, the Act forbids termination of an agreement solely because of the death of a debtor or hirer.

DEFAULT AND TERMINATION

A large part of the 1974 Act's consumer protection is aimed at preventing the creditor from exercising too harshly his remedies against the debtor, where the latter fails to maintain his repayments or otherwise defaults on his agreement. The 2006 Act additionally requires a lender to give the debtor or hirer a notice of sums in arrears when the arrears reach a specified amount, depending on the frequency of the payments due to be made under the agreement. There are separate requirements for fixed-sum credit agreements and running-account credit agreements. In addition, for a fixed-sum credit agreement there is requirement to send further notices at intervals of not more than six months. These have to continue until the debtor or hirer ceases to be in arrears, or a judgment has been obtained in respect of the debt. An OFT information leaflet has to be included with each notice. The requirement to send notices commenced on 1 October 2008 and full details of their content and format can be found on the OFT website. Failure to give the notices means that the creditor cannot enforce the agreement during the period of non-compliance and the debtor or hirer has no liability to pay interest during this period. An impact of this is that creditors must continue to send the notices (and statements) to customers who have 'gone away' (moved without notifying the lender) or deceased customers in order to be able to enforce the agreement. At the time of writing BIS are discussing this issue in more detail with the industry.

The first measure of protection afforded the debtor or hirer is the requirement that before the creditor or owner can terminate an agreement, demand early payment, repossess goods or enforce a security, he must first serve a default notice on the debtor or hirer and allow him 14 days from then in which to put right the default. As stated above, from 1 October 2008, a copy of the current OFT default information leaflet must be sent with the default notice. Only then can the creditor take the specified action against the debtor. Similar rules also apply to terminating an agreement or enforcing the creditors rights where the contract allows this if no default has occurred. In any of these situations it is, however, permitted to prevent a debtor from obtaining further credit with immediate effect, for example, by putting a credit card on a 'stop list'.

Reference was made earlier in this chapter to the 'one-half rule' in the Hire Purchase Acts limiting the liability of a hirer under a hire purchase agreement that he has terminated and returned the goods. This is re-enacted in the Consumer Credit Act, as is the 'one-third rule' forbidding repossession of goods on hire purchase or conditional sale where one-third has been paid, without a Court Order or the hirer's express permission given at the time. The Act also provides that a creditor or owner must not enter premises to effect repossession of goods or land without obtaining the debtor's permission or a Court Order.

Section 93 of the Act provides that where interest is charged on overdue payments, the rate of charge shall be no higher than the APR under the agreement. This has awkward implications for those companies that offer 'interest-free' credit.

Section 101 gives a hirer under a consumer hire agreement an absolute right to terminate the agreement once it has run for 18 months. No 'minimum payment clause' requiring payment of more than 18 months' rental would be given effect by the courts. Few problems exist with genuine consumer transactions where the most usual minimum hire period is 12 months but this Section could have made it commercially impossible to offer leasing facilities for goods to sole traders or partnerships. The '18-month rule' does not therefore apply in the following situations:

- where the rentals in any year exceed £900; or

- where the goods are hired for use in a business and are acquired by the owner from the supplier at the hirer's request, the supplier not being an 'associate' of the owner; or

- where the goods are hired for the purpose of sub-hire.

Note: The 2006 Act has inserted a new section into the 1974 Act that requires the creditor to give notice where default sums (a sum payable by a debtor or hirer in connection with a breach of a regulated agreement) become payable. Interest can only be charged 28 days after the notice has been given and can only be simple interest.

EARLY SETTLEMENT

The 1974 Act allows a debtor under a regulated consumer credit agreement to pay off his indebtedness at any time before the end of the agreement. Regulations provide for the debtor to be given a rebate of the charges where he exercises this right. This rebate must be given not only for a voluntary early settlement but also if a balance is carried over to a new agreement and where a debtor has to pay off the whole or part of a balance owing ahead of time. In no case, however, will a right to rebate arise until payment is made, although of course the debtor can be informed in advance of the rebate to which he will be entitled if he settles on a particular day and he has the right to demand this information.

The rebate rules (known as 'the rule of 78') do not affect hire purchase agreements or running accounts or other transactions where no charges are to be made in respect of any period after the 'settlement date'.

The Consumer Credit (Early Settlement) Regulations 2004 provide for the calculation of the rebate due to the borrower when an agreement is settled early or otherwise ended. The Regulations came into force on 31 May 2005, but with transitional provisions for existing agreements until 2007 or 2010.

An extended version of the formula must currently be used where the payments provided for under the agreement are unequal or are to be made at irregular intervals. Interpolation is not needed where settlement occurs between instalment dates except where the interval between instalments exceeds one month. Where settlement of transactions payable by weekly or monthly instalments is made between instalment dates the next instalment date becomes the 'settlement date'.

To allow the creditor to recover his 'setting up costs' the rebate may be calculated by reference to a date two months after the settlement date. For agreements running for more than five years, only one month's deferment is allowed.

Failure to comply with the Regulations can lead to the OFT or Trading Standards taking enforcement action against the lender. In addition, if the lender fails to provide a correct settlement statement he is not entitled to enforce the agreement, and if the breach continues for a month, this is a criminal offence.

SECURITY

The 1974 Act controls all forms of taking security in respect of regulated agreements, whether given by the debtor, for example a charge, mortgage or pledge, or by a third party as in the case of a guarantor or indemnity. It only applies to a security given by a third party where it is given at the request of the debtor. It does not therefore affect 'recourse agreements' or other forms of indemnity given by the supplier of goods financed. However, since 31 October 2004, as previously stated above, the FSA have regulated those mortgages where at least 40 per cent of the total of the land given as security for a mortgage is used as a dwelling. Variations made on or after that date to contracts entered into before that date are not subject to FSA regulation but may be subject to the Consumer Credit Act 1974.

The Act, and Regulations made under it, impose requirements as to the form and content of guarantees and indemnities which are generally similar to those governing agreement forms (and the statutory statement of the guarantor's rights is one of the longest required in any document under the Act). The guarantor must receive a copy of the guarantee when he signs and a copy of the credit or hire agreement to which it refers within seven days of it taking effect. If these requirements are not met, the guarantee will be ineffective except where creditor can obtain a Court Order to enforce it.

The Act gives guarantors similar rights to information as are possessed by debtors and provides that a guarantor must receive a copy of any default notice served on the debtor or hirer.

Section 113 prevents the Act from being evaded by the use of security. A security may not be enforced to provide a benefit greater than could be recovered direct from the debtor or hirer. There is, however, a specific exception so that a guarantee or indemnity given in respect of a contract by a minor can be enforced as though the minor were of full age and capacity to contract.

The Act forbids the use of negotiable instruments (bills of exchange, cheques and promissory notes) as ways of taking security for a regulated agreement but allows cheques to be used as a means of payment only.

JUDICIAL CONTROL

For all practical purposes, it is the County Court, or in Scotland the Sheriff Court, that has jurisdiction in respect of contracts regulated by the Consumer Credit Act 1974.

The Act specifies various types of order, which the court can make. The first listed is the Enforcement Order which a creditor will have to obtain if he wishes to enforce a contract despite some breach of the strict requirements of the Act. Some more serious breaches of the Act's requirements cannot, however, be remedied by an enforcement order, particularly where a right of cancellation exists as it was mentioned earlier. However, the 2006 Act repealed specific sections of the 1974 Act which means that a court now has the power to determine at its discretion whether agreements are enforceable regardless of the breach in question.

The 2006 Act also requires a creditor to give notice where interest is payable on judgment debts and continue to give further notices at intervals of not more than six months.

A debtor or hirer can ask the court for a Time Order allowing him time to bring his payments up to date or remedy any breaches of an agreement. In the case of a hire purchase or conditional sale agreement the order can deal with sums not due. For other transactions it can only deal with arrears, or where the creditor has called up the entire balance owing on a loan or has sought a possession order in respect of a loan secured on land. Additionally, the 2006 Act has amended the 1974 Act to allow a debtor to apply for a time order after they have received a notice of sums in arrears.

In relation to hire purchase or hire agreements the court can make a Protection Order in respect of the goods pending the actual hearing of the case. The court can also grant financial relief to a hirer under a consumer hire agreement relieving him from financial liability where the owner recovers the goods.

The court has the power to make orders in respect of hire purchase agreements for return of the goods or (more rarely) for the hirer to keep some goods and return the rest.

The court can suspend any of these orders or make any terms of the order conditional on the doing of specified acts by one or other party.

In addition, the court has a general power to deal with any personal credit agreement (even in excess of any upper financial limit in force under the Act at the time), which it holds to be 'extortionate'. For a credit bargain to be extortionate, the charges must be grossly exorbitant or it must otherwise grossly contravene ordinary principles of fair dealing. The Act sets out guidelines for determining whether a bargain is extortionate and gives the court very wide powers to amend or strike down the extortionate transaction.

The court's powers to reopen extortionate credit bargains has been available since 1977 but there have so far been few cases which have come to court and fewer still that have ended in victory for the debtor. The Government have undertaken a consultation and review of this area of the Act.

Note: Sections 19 to 22 of the 2006 Act have repealed and replaced sections 137 to 140 of the 1974 Act which dealt with the court's powers to reopen extortionate credit bargains. The new sections introduce the concept of 'unfair relationships'. The court can consider whether the terms of the agreement are unfair to the debtor or if the way the creditor has enforced his rights under the agreement are unfair to the debtor.

CREDIT REFERENCE AGENCIES

The Act provides a procedure whereby an individual (but not a limited company) can find out what information a credit reference agency holds about him. This procedure comprises two parts.

First, where there have been negotiations for credit (and whether or not these have resulted in credit being advanced) the customer can, within 28 days, make a written demand for the name and address of any credit reference agency used during those negotiations. The creditor must provide this information in writing in response to the request but is not obliged to give other information. In view of advances in technology and in order to meet customer expectations, an individual can now request a copy of their file by making application via most credit reference agency's websites and not just be limited to making a request in writing. The creditor does not have to give reasons for refusing credit or disclose any information about trade or bank references taken up since the sources of such references do not come within the Act's definition of a credit reference agency. Where a creditor takes business through a credit broker and he turns down a request for credit, he must inform the credit broker of the name and address of any credit reference consulted so that the latter can give this information if the customer enquires of him, as the law requires him to do. Again, in order to meet customer expectations and to anticipate the request, most creditors will advise the customer of the name and address of the credit reference agency consulted (if any) and the procedure to follow in order to obtain a copy of their file, should they require it.

The second part of the procedure provided by the Act is embodied in Section 158 to 160 which gives any individual the right to obtain a copy of the information held about him in full (subject to some limitation if a sole trader or partnership seeks this information).

The Regulations also set out a procedure for the correction of wrong information held on file and provide that if the individual and the credit reference agency cannot agree on a correction, either of them can approach the Office of Fair Trading for a final ruling on the matter.

ENFORCEMENT

Under the Consumer Credit Act both the Director General of Fair Trading and local Trading Standards Officers have responsibility for enforcement of the Act, the main day-to-day burden falling on Trading Standards Officers although the Director General may sometimes originate prosecutions, for example, Stop Now Orders; or threaten to revoke the licence of a trader who does not abide by the Act's requirements.

The Act gives powers to Trading Standards Officers generally similar to those under other legislation such as the Trades Descriptions Acts. They can inspect and, if necessary, seize goods, books or records, enter premises, make test purchases and take copies of books and records. In some cases a warrant may be needed to enter premises. As far as consumer credit is concerned, Trading Standards Officers are mostly concerned with traders making misrepresentations or other false claims (Section 56 of the 1974 Act) so that the customer is unable to make an accurate or informed choice and the harassment of debtors under Section 40 of the Administration of Justice Act 1970.

The 2006 Act has given additional powers to the OFT to require information, require access to premises, entry to premises under warrant and deals with the failure to give information.

The criminal offences specified in the 1974 Act do not require the prosecution to prove intent to commit them, but the Act does provide that it is a valid defence that what took place was an accident or the fault of another person and that the defendant took all reasonable steps to prevent the breach of the law.

The Data Protection Act 1998

INTRODUCTION

The Data Protection Act applies to 'personal data'. Personal data is defined as data about a living individual that can be identified from that data. It includes facts and opinions about the individual and it also includes information about the intentions of the data controller towards the individual. Every business processes some kind of personal data, be it information about customers, suppliers, business contacts or employees and thus has major implications for the credit industry.

The Data Protection Act 1998 finally came into force on 1 March 2000. This Act, whilst it mirrored the original 1984 Act, superseded it and introduced a number of key changes. The 1998 Act lays down rules for processing personal information in today's advanced technological environment and applies to some manual (paper) records as well as those held on computers.

Those who decide how and why personal data is processed are referred to as data controllers and it is they who carry the responsibility and must ensure compliance with the rules of good information handling, known as the Data Protection Principles. Data controllers can be the directors, trustees, partners or even a sole trader, in fact anyone that decides how data is to be processed.

Raising public and corporate awareness and enforcement of the Act's requirements is the responsibility of the Information Commissioner. Based in Wilmslow, Cheshire, the Information Commissioner's Office (ICO) handles all aspects of the Act, for example, register entries, complaints, guidance, enforcement and so on.

THE DATA PROTECTION PRINCIPLES

Anyone processing personal data must comply with the eight enforceable principles of good practice:

They say that all data must be:

1.   fairly and lawfully processed;

2.   processed for limited purposes and not in any manner incompatible with those purposes;

3.   adequate, relevant and not excessive;

4.   accurate;

5.   not kept for longer than is necessary;

6.   processed in line with the rights of the Data Subject;

7.   secure;

8.   not transferred to countries without adequate protection.

Detailed guidance is available from the ICO on how the Eight Principles should be interpreted and applied in day-to-day situations.

NOTIFICATION

In the 1984 Act, this was referred to as Registration. Most data controllers (there are some exemptions) are required to notify the ICO of the purposes of their processing, what personal data is processed, to whom the data is disclosed and the overseas locations (if any) that the data is transferred. This information is made publicly available in a register, although the form and content is now more general than previously listed. The notification must be renewed annually.

In the 1998 Act, even if a data controller is exempt from the notification requirements, they must still comply with the eight data protection principles.

PROCESSING PERSONAL DATA

The Act requires that personal data be processed 'fairly and lawfully'. This can only happen when all the requirements of the Act are in place and its conditions met. A Data Subject (the living individual that is the subject of the data) must be informed, prior to providing the information, of the identity of the data controller, that is, the name of the company that will be using the data, why the information is required, to whom the information is to be disclosed (if different) and any other not immediately obvious purposes for which the data might be used, for example, marketing.

Credit Agreements must contain 'notification clauses' informing the borrower of the above together with a statement that the lender will search a credit reference bureau (if this is the intention) and may file information on the performance of the account. This notification clause requirement seeks to ensure that transparency exists in respect of who is processing the data and why.

Processing may only be carried out where one of the following conditions has been met:

- the individual has given his or her consent to their data being processed;

- the processing is necessary for the performance of a contract with them;

- the processing is required under a legal obligation;

- the processing is necessary to protect their vital interests;

- the processing is necessary to carry out public functions;

- the processing is necessary in order to pursue the legitimate interests of the data controller or third parties (unless it could prejudice the interests of the individual).

PROCESSING SENSITIVE DATA

The Data Protection Act makes specific provision and sets out how Sensitive Data must be handled. Sensitive Data is data that includes racial or ethnic origin, religious or other beliefs, political opinions, trade union membership, sex life, health, criminal convictions or proceedings. Such data can only be processed under strict conditions, which include:

- the individual having given their 'explicit' consent;

- being required by law to process the data for employment purposes;

- needing to process the information in order to protect the vital interests of the Data Subject or another;

- dealing with the administration of justice or with legal proceedings.

MANUAL DATA

The Act also covers personal data within paper files that are processed 'manually' and are held in 'relevant filing systems', that is, files that are structured in such a way as to allow access to the data alphabetically, by date, by account number and so on.

SECURITY

Data controllers are responsible for ensuring that the personal data they hold and process is kept secure. They must take appropriate technical or organisational measures to prevent the unauthorised or unlawful processing, access or disclosure of data within their control. Where the data controller uses the services of a 'data processor', the security arrangements in place to safeguard the data must be a part of a written agreement between the two.

TRANSFER OF PERSONAL DATA OVERSEAS

The transfer of personal data outside of the European Economic Area (EEA) (which includes Norway, Iceland and Liechtenstein as well as the EU member states) is restricted. Personal data may only be transferred to third countries if those countries ensure an 'adequate level of protection for the rights and freedoms of data subjects'.

THE RIGHTS OF INDIVIDUALS

The Act confers certain rights on individuals; these are briefly outlined thus:

Subject Access – This right allows individuals to find out what information is held about them on computer and some manual records.

Rectification, Blocking, Erasure and Destruction – This allows individuals to apply to a court to order a data controller to rectify, block, erase or destroy data held about them that is inaccurate or is based on inaccurate data.

Prevention of Processing – Where processing causes or is likely to cause unwarranted damage or substantial distress, a data subject can request that a data controller stop their data from being processed. This right is not available in all cases and data controllers do not always have to comply with the request.

Direct Marketing – An absolute right under the Act, however, is an individual's right to request that a data controller stop processing their data for direct marketing purposes.

Compensation – Whilst compensation cannot be claimed for distress alone in many circumstances, it can be claimed from a data controller who has breached the Act and caused an individual damage or damage and distress.

Automated Processing – An individual can request a data controller to ensure that no decision that significantly affects them is based only on information about them that has been processed automatically.

Telecommunications – Unsolicited marketing via public telecommunication systems must comply with strict rules that apply to faxes, telephones and automated calling systems:

- Unsolicited marketing faxes cannot be sent without a subscriber's consent.

- A subscriber has a statutory right to opt out of unsolicited telephone marketing by registering with a central stop list, for example, the telephone preference service.

- Automated calling systems must have the consent of both the corporate and individual subscribers.

- Corporate subscribers can opt out of unsolicited marketing faxes but not telephone sales.

CRIMINAL OFFENCES

Notification – Failure to notify is a strict liability offence. This occurs when a data controller (not being exempt) fails to notify the ICO of processing that is taking place or of changes to the processing previously notified.

Procuring and/or Selling – An offence is being committed if anyone attempts to obtain personal data, bring about its disclosure or sell it without the data controller's consent. It is also an offence to access personal data or disclose it without authorisation.

Enforced Subject Access – It is an offence (subject to limited exceptions) to ask another person to make a 'subject access' request in order to obtain personal data about them, for example, as a precondition to employment.

ICO Notices – Failure to respond to an 'information' or 'enforcement' notice from the Commissioner is also an offence.

Other Laws

Although most of the law's requirements affecting consumer credit are contained within the Consumer Credit Act, there are a number of other Acts that are relevant and impact directly on some (but not all) consumer credit transactions; they must therefore be mentioned if this chapter is to be complete.

The Banking Act 1987. If the lender is a 'bank' regulated by the Bank of England, the seven principal objectives of this Act will also apply to their business, for example, the advertising and acceptance of deposits. The contents of the European Banking Directive will also be applicable.

The Proceeds of Crime Act 2002 consolidates, updates and expands all earlier anti-money laundering legislation. The principal provisions are:

- It is an offence for any person to acquire or possess criminal property or to provide any assistance to any other person to launder the proceeds of any criminal conduct.

- A mandatory reporting requirement is now in place for regulated sectors (these tend to be those sectors regulated by the FSA) in respect of the knowledge or suspicion of money laundering arising out of any criminal conduct. This requirement also extends to situations where an individual *should have known*, that is, an objective test of suspicion.

The Money Laundering Regulations 2007 and the Financial Services and Markets Act 2000 are the primary pieces of legislation (there are others) that affect those organisations who carry out 'relevant financial business' in

a 'business relationship' or that conduct 'one-off financial transactions' with
an 'applicant for business'. In general, these Regulations apply to credit and
financial institutions and businesses carrying on financial business which is
mostly susceptible to money laundering, for example, revolving credit facilities
that include deposit taking and money transmission facilities.

The key elements of these pieces of legislation place very strict requirements
on organisations to have robust processes in place to ensure that their staff are
aware of their responsibilities, that they identify and 'know their customers',
they have a reporting mechanism in place for suspicious transactions and that
they are able to monitor transactions going through their customers accounts.
These organisations are regulated by the FSA and will be working under the
Guidelines issued periodically by the Joint Money Laundering Steering Group
'JMLSG'. The JMLSG is made up of the leading trade associations in the UK
that are active in the Financial Services industry. Their website can be accessed
through the British Bankers Association.

The Bills of Sale Act 1878–83 regulate the taking of security on personal
property and provide strict rules for the documentation and regulation of such
security. If not observed, such security will be void. It was the very existence of
these Acts that led to hire purchase developing in its present form.

The one remaining part of the Hire Purchase Acts in force is **Part III of the
Hire Purchase Act 1964**. The general rule, where a person buys goods from the
hirer under a hire purchase agreement before the agreement is completed, is
that such a buyer does not obtain good title to the goods until the agreement
is complete and the owner under the hire purchase agreement can recover the
goods or sue for sums still owing under the agreement (or the value of the goods,
whichever is less). The 1964 Act makes an exception to this rule by providing that
a 'private purchaser' who buys a motor vehicle in good faith and without notice
of the existence of the agreement will obtain good title to the vehicle. The owner
under the agreement cannot take action against him or against any person who
buys the vehicle from him. 'Private Purchaser' is defined to mean any person
other than a motor trader or a finance house active in the motor field.

The Administration of Justice Act 1970. As previously mentioned, Section
40 of this Act makes it an offence for a person if, with the object of coercing
another person to pay money claimed from the other as a debt due under a
contract, he harasses the other with demands for payment which, in respect
of their frequency or the manner or occasion of making any such demand, are
calculated to subject him, or his family, to alarm, distress or humiliation.

The OFT has issued Guidance Notes in respect of Debt Collection that clearly state that creditors or their collection agents, must not:

- bring unreasonable pressure to bear;

- falsely claim that criminal proceedings can be brought for non-payment;

- falsely imply that they may legally seize property without going to court;

- compel the signature of documents that allow the repossession of goods;

- impersonate a court or any other official;

- contact the debtor, or their employer, at work with the intent to create embarrassment or fear of dismissal;

- wait outside work on payday;

- call on neighbours pretending to believe that they are the customer;

- send insufficiently addressed postcards or other mail that may then be opened by a neighbour;

- take books or documents that are illegal to assign as security.

The Sex Discrimination Act applies to the granting of credit as to the supply of other forms of services. It prohibits two kinds of discrimination – direct and indirect. Direct discrimination is where credit is not made available to a woman in circumstances where it would be made available to a man or where additional requirements are imposed on a woman which would not be required of a man in similar financial circumstances, for example, if the customer was a woman who earned her own living and a male guarantor was required. Indirect discrimination is where the creditor sets his requirements in such a way that substantially fewer women can obtain credit and where there is no valid reason for setting the requirements that way. A breach of the Act can lead to a claim for damages while the Equal Opportunities Commission has considerable powers to deal with any creditor whose company procedures offend against the Act's requirements.

The Race Relations Act sets out similar rules in respect to discrimination on the grounds of race.

There is a very considerable body of case law affecting hire purchase agreements, which are not regulated by the Consumer Credit Act, particularly concerning the rights of the parties following breach of an agreement.

Hire purchase agreements, both regulated or otherwise, are also affected by the law governing such matters as distress for rent and repairer's lien. **The Unfair Contract Terms Act 1977** and the **Consumer Transactions (Restrictions on Statements) Order 1976** apply in respect of clauses excluding (or attempting to exclude) liability where goods are defective and in many cases prevent the use of such clauses. An 'unfair term' means any term which, contrary to the requirement of good faith, causes a significant imbalance to the parties' rights and obligations under the contract, to the detriment of the consumer.

The VAT legislation affects credit transactions since although credit is an 'exempt supply', the supply of goods on hire purchase or credit sale is normally a taxable supply, so that such an agreement represents two supplies, a taxable supply of the goods and an exempt supply of the credit. Much complication arises out of this.

Codes of Practice

There are various Codes of Practice in existence, some of which (but not all) have been granted stage 1 approval by the Office of Fair Trading. The purpose of such Codes is to lay down accepted 'Industry Good Practice' and to advise the customers of the relevant industry sector to which a particular Code relates as to what standards of service they can and should expect, how and where complaints should be addressed, and so on.

Most credit providers will subscribe to one or more of the following Codes:

- The Banking Code;

- Finance & Leasing Association;

- Consumer Credit Trade Association;

- Guide to Credit Scoring;

- Advertising Code;

- Sales Promotion Code;

- Direct Marketing Association.

Conclusion

This chapter contains no more than a brief outline of the laws affecting consumer credit. Anyone regularly involved in this kind of business will need to study it in greater detail and should refer to more detailed works, a variety of which are available.

Regularly updated, the websites of the OFT and BIS are also an excellent source of information.

PART IX
Commercial Credit Law

22

Legal Action for Debt Recovery in the County Court

Gerard P Barron MBA DMS FICM

• Understanding the four stages of legal debt collection • The cost of legal proceedings – getting things into context • Pre-action checklist • The four stages • Using insolvency and insolvency petitions as an alternative means of obtaining payment •

Understanding the Four Stages of Legal Debt Collection

Most, if not all, debt collection in England and Wales is conducted through the County Courts, it is rare that any debt collection matters end up in the High Court (except for Insolvency Proceedings) and so this chapter limits itself to the realities of County Court debt recovery actions, of which about 2 million are issued per annum.

THE FOUR DISTINCT STAGES

Put simply, there are four distinct stages in collecting debt through the legal system in England and Wales (it is not dissimilar in Scotland).

These stages are:

1.   the letter before action stage (LBA);

2.   the issue of legal process stage;

3.   the 'Journey to Judgment' – the debtors response and entering or obtaining judgment;

4.   enforcing the judgment stage (where payment has not been made).

As an alternative, and in certain circumstances, (see the last part of this chapter) you can also use insolvency as a sanction to get paid. This is very effective but should only be used by expert lawyers.

The simple rule of thumb is that where a debtor has defaulted on the debt, the sooner the intervention, the earlier in the four stage process the debt can be collected

It is also a matter of fact that most debt is collected on the LBA, where the debtor has (a) the willingness (character) to pay and (b) the ability to pay (capacity).

- If the debtor is able and willing – you get paid on the LBA.

- If the debtor is unable but willing – you get paid but possibly later (you may take some security).

- If the debtor is able and unwilling – you should get paid using the Courts.

- If the debtor is unable and unwilling – it is unlikely that using the recovery process after stage one or two will result in any payment.

The Cost of Legal Proceedings – Getting Things into Context

LETTER BEFORE ACTION – OR COMMISSION-BASED COLLECTIONS?

It is important that you recognise that all forms of legal collection involve cost; the cost of sending out an LBA for example is just a few pounds, charged by most of the specialist solicitors.

This means that you can collect a small debt for a very small investment and an even larger debt for an even smaller investment:

- Debt £500 paid on a letter that cost £5 – cost 1 per cent of the debt.

- Debt £5000 paid on a letter that cost £5 – cost 0.1 per cent of the debt.

DEBT COLLECT AGENCIES – AGENCY COMMISSION

Some debt collection agencies and solicitors also charge commission based on the value collected. This can represent a high cost, which may result in deciding to delay placing the debt for collection. That delay may result in the debtor not being able to pay the debt, having paid other creditors that have chased for payment before you.

You should decide to act both decisively and at the correct cost for the value of the debt you are collecting. This could mean finding alternative effective low-cost legal providers.

LEGAL COSTS – AFTER THE LETTER BEFORE ACTION STAGE

Where you have to sue at stage two onwards, it is usual to pay the solicitors the fees paid to Court (normally called disbursements) and the solicitor's recoverable costs – these are added to the debt and are recoverable from the debtor. When the debtor pays the debt after legal proceedings, they are also demanded to pay these fixed costs and fees added to the debt. In the event of payment therefore, the debtor is paying for the majority of the collection process at this stage (except the LBA cost).

If payment is not obtained, that is, where the process is unsuccessful or where a debt is disputed, and you have to actually litigate rather than simply put the debt through a process, the costs of doing so could be high. It is therefore important that some simple rules for preparation are recognised after the LBA stage *but before* you start issuing Court process and incurring additional cost that may not be recovered.

Remember: The further down the legal route you go – the costlier it becomes; the further down the legal route you go – the less likely you are to get payment.

The key is to get paid early in the process, in stage one or two if at all possible. Life is not that simple, some debts will be collected only after pursuing the debtor all the way down the process – remember the debtors 'willingness and ability' to pay (see Figure 22.1).

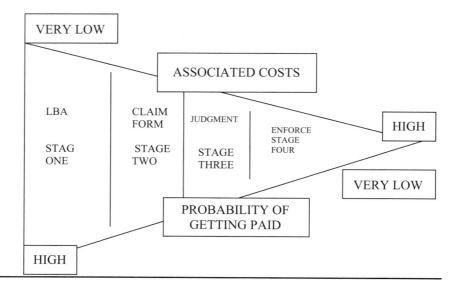

Figure 22.1   Payment probability

Pre-action Checklist

Who or what is the debtor? You should be aware of the legal entity (or personality) of the debtor. Are they:

- a limited company;

- an individual or sole trader;

- a partnership;

- a public limited company;

- a limited liability partnership;

- an unincorporated body (a members club and so on);

- a government department?

The debtor is the 'person or entity' that made the contract (usually the party that placed the order).

LIMITED COMPANIES

It is important that the exact name of the limited company is known and that this name corresponds with the name registered at Companies House. Always check the registered number of the company. The name of a company can change but its number remains the same. If there is a different number it is a different company.

INDIVIDUALS AND SOLE TRADERS

In the case of individuals, you must know their gender; if it is not clear from the name whether the person is male or female this should be established.

From 6 April 2009, a pre-action debt collection protocol for debt collection from individuals has been established. The protocol makes no distinction between consumer debtors and business debtors and dictates that the LBA to the debtor must contain certain help and information for the debtor to seek assistance and debt advice. It also requires the creditor to allow 14 days for a response rather than the previous generally recognised seven days.

The Courts website at www.hmCourts-service.gov.uk can be viewed for further information and assistance and is discussed below in the stage one – LBA section.

PARTNERSHIPS

A partnership or 'firm' may be sued in the name of the firm – for example, Nobrass and Skint (a firm) – or in the names of the individual partners – for example, Chrissie Jones and Johnnie Meller trading as Nobrass and Skint, a Partnership.

Joint and several liability It is always useful to remember that individual partners in a partnership are 'liable – jointly and severally' – this means that not only the entity of the partnership is liable as a trading body, but each and every partner is liable to the extent of their personal wealth – they can be thus sued as individuals. It follows therefore that where you know the identity of the individuals concerned in a partnership you should sue them as individuals trading as 'XXXX' – a firm.

IS THE DEBTOR WORTH SUING?

No matter how much is owed to your company it is pointless issuing proceedings against a debtor who does not have the means to pay. For example, if an individual is unemployed and in rented accommodation, has no assets, and no immediate prospect of further employment, legal proceedings are of no value at this time.

If the debtor's circumstances improve at some time in the future you can still issue proceedings up to six years after the breach of contract. (non-payment). At the time of writing there is consultation in process regarding the reduction of the six year 'Statute of Limitations' rule to three years – a move seen as detrimental by all involved in the credit management and debt collection professions.

Similarly, if a limited company has ceased trading without assets, any judgment against the company is likely to remain unsatisfied. As is often said, 'There is no point throwing good money after bad.'

IS THERE A GENUINE DISPUTE?

If there is a genuine problem with the goods or services provided then every endeavour should be made to reach an amicable solution with the debtor. This may avoid a costly defended action. It must be remembered that the vast majority of disputed cases are settled prior to the trial, frequently only hours or days before the case is to be heard. There is little point in settling an action after incurring substantial legal costs when it could have been settled at the outset.

The Four Stages

STAGE ONE – THE LETTER BEFORE ACTION

A LBA must be sent prior to the issue of proceedings. This can be sent by a solicitor or debt collection agency but can also be sent by the creditor themselves. A reasonable time (usually seven days) for the defendant to respond, should be given, except where the debtor is an individual, when 14 days must be given for a response.

You should set out in the letter:

- a date for responding – a deadline;

- the amount owing;

- what the debt is for where and how payment should be made;

- that the debtor can contact the claimant creditor to discuss repayment.

And for individual debtors: where they can seek independent advice and assistance from certain organizations, including National Debtline, Consumer Credit Counselling Service (CCCS), Citizens Advice or Community Legal.

The letter should make it clear that, if payment is not made, Court proceedings will be issued without further notice and the consequences of such action. It is a useful reminder, for example, to tell debtors that a County Court Judgment (CCJ) registered against them may affect their credit rating for many years to come.

Can I charge interest and charges on the letter before action?

You should also, where possible, use the late payment legislation, that is, the Late Payment of Commercial Debts (Interest) Act 1998. It provides that where contracting parties (which can include individuals that 'engage in contracts' for the supply of goods and services) are engaged in commerce from 7[s] August 2002 (as opposed to consumers) and late payment occurs, the creditor party can claim punitive interest at the rate of 8 per cent above Bank of England base rate from the date the debt became due, plus charges for invoking the reminder for payment.

Where a debt is due under contract you should always include the late payment interest, calculated to the date of the LBA (and set out the daily rate being incurred on an ongoing basis) plus the charges that are claimable. These are set out below:

Size of unpaid debt	Late payment charge
Up to £999.99	£40
£1000 to £9999.99	£70
over £10,000	£100

Dealing with disputes before issue

If a dispute is raised either prior to or in answer to the LBA then you should try to deal with the points raised. If you do not act reasonably you may be penalised by the Court in costs at trial. This may mean that even if you are successful, you do not obtain all your costs from the losing party. For example, if you are asked to give copies of documents these should be given even if they have previously been sent. Where there is a dispute you should consider whether one of the alternative dispute resolution methods would assist in reaching a solution.

Alternative Dispute Resolution

There are two main forms of Alternative Dispute Resolution (ADR): Mediation and Arbitration.

Mediation is a non-binding process where the role of the mediator is not to decide the issues but to try to facilitate an agreement between the parties. It is useful in all types of dispute, especially where the costs of litigation are likely to be significant. Both parties are encouraged to consider a middle ground to avoid the pain and cost of litigation.

Arbitrations are usually binding on the parties. An arbitrator is appointed to decide the case instead of the Court, and arbitrations are useful if there is a single technical dispute between the parties. Rather than obtain a joint report, it is often cheaper and quicker to allow the expert to decide the issue. It is not particularly appropriate where there are many issues or the issues have a legal basis.

The Overriding Objective – The principles of all Court action

This could also be called the 'scaffolding' of all Court action as it supports the shape and direction of all Court cases from simple debt matters to the more complex legal issues to be decided by the Courts.

The Objective is defined:

> *The Court Rules are a procedural code with the overriding objective of enabling the Court to deal with cases justly. Dealing with a case justly includes, so far as is practicable – ensuring that the parties are on an equal footing; saving expense; dealing with the case in ways which are*

proportionate to the amount of money involved; to the importance of the case; to the complexity of the issues; and to the financial position of each party; ensuring that it is dealt with expeditiously and fairly; and allotting to it an appropriate share of the Court's resources, while taking into account the need to allot resources to other cases.

It will be easily seen that even debt cases should be settled by the parties wherever possible without recourse to Court action. This is an ideal that is not that often achieved, but the architecture of the Court system and processes is designed around this objective, and should be borne in mind as we venture further into the system in this chapter.

STAGE TWO – THE COMMENCEMENT OF LEGAL PROCEEDINGS

Assuming that the LBA has not resulted in payment you can now consider issuing legal proceedings. It is, however, the case that a timely, well-written LBA will result in payment in most cases.

You should consider before embarking on proceedings a number of things:

- the value of the debt;

- the known circumstances of the debtor;

- if the debtor already has unsatisfied CCJs;

- where the debtor is an individual – do they own their own home?;

- the costs of taking proceedings – this could seem prohibitive in small-value debt cases;

- the 'attitude' of the debtor to you as a creditor in the past;

- the degree of 'engagement' that you have had with the debtor thus far.

If you calculate that it is worth proceeding then the ensuing guidelines will help. If you are unsure, get advice from an expert before you embark upon the legal route, as they will be able to quickly put the debt and its collectability into context and may suggest another more advantageous route to achieve your aims.

Issuing Proceedings

Proceedings are issued in any local County Court or using 'Money Claim Online' if you chose to issue the proceedings yourself; the latter will enable you to complete the appropriate details to progress a debt claim via the Internet.

You can pay your Court fees by credit card online and the web address for this service is www.Courtservice.gov.uk/mcol/.

In any event you (or your advisers) will be asked to complete a form N1. Copies of all the specimen forms can be found on the Court Service website.

See http://www.hmCourts-service.gov.uk/Courtfinder/forms/n1_0102.pdf

See http://www.hmCourts-service.gov.uk/cms/6303.htm for bulk users.

The front of the form

You will be asked to complete the details of the creditor – now called the claimant, and the details of the debtor – now called the defendant. In both cases you must identify your full name, legal entity and address; any trading styles must also be shown. The gender of the claimant and the defendant must also be shown where known (defendant).

Where 'brief details of the claim' are required underneath the defendant's details – simply use a one line brief description such as: 'Goods sold and delivered. Services rendered. Returned Cheque payment.'

At the bottom left-hand corner you are asked to repeat the defendant's name and address again – this is for the Court to send the claim form in window envelopes. At the bottom right-hand corner of the form frontage you are asked to summarise the amount you are suing for in three boxes with a summary in a fourth box. This includes – *the amount claimed* – do not complete this until you have calculated your debt including interest and late payment charges if claimed.

The Court fee based on the value of the claim

Court fees are shown on: http://www.hmCourts-service.gov.uk/Courtfinder/forms/ex50_web_0709.pdf.

The next box – *solicitor's costs* – is for use when you are using a solicitor to issue proceedings for you. They will add these costs to the debt; they are fully recoverable from the defendant. Many bulk-issuing solicitors only charge these fixed costs as their fees – this means that where a debt is undefended and collected on the issue of a claim form there is no cost to the claimant, all the costs are recovered from the defendant.

In that instance you will also recover your interest and late payment charges in addition to the debt, and there should be no charge to you.

Rear of the form

On the second page of the claim form you are asked to confirm whether or not your claims include any issues under the Human Rights Act 1988. For most debt cases it will usually be appropriate to tick 'no' but, if in doubt, advice should be sought.

The particulars of the Claim

You can either attach them on a separate sheet or use the second page of the claim form. In any event the particulars included here are in much more detail than the front page. You must set out concise details of the claim, specifying what the claim relates to, when and how the debt arose.

In a normal debt matter a short description (goods sold and delivered), together with a list of the outstanding invoices, should be sufficient. Include in the list the date of the outstanding invoice(s), the amount outstanding and the date payment was due. It might also assist to include invoice numbers and any other references that will help the defendant identify the claim.

If you refer to a document in your particulars of claim, a copy of it should be annexed to the claim form.

Interest

As part of completing the particulars of claim you have the right to claim interest.

You can claim interest in one of three ways:

- *Contractual interest* – if your terms and conditions allow a reasonable rate of interest for late payment, then this can be claimed in accordance with your conditions of sale.

- *Late payment interest* – where you have contracted commercially with the debtor and used the late payment charges in your dealings, you can use the late-payment legislation. This is set at 8 per cent above current Bank of England base rate, and is set twice a year. It has been 8 per cent above Bank of England rate since inception. You may also include the late payment charges set out above.

- *Statutory interest* – if the contract did not specify an interest rate, and you have not been able to use the late-payment legislation, statutory interest can be claimed. This is claimed under Section 69 of the County Court Act 1984, where a Claimant is entitled to seek 8 per cent per annum on overdue sums from the defendant. Interest starts to run from the date the payment was overdue and runs until judgment unless the judgment debt is for more than £5000, in which case interest continues to accrue until payment is made.

In all cases the interest claimed must be clearly set out and calculated in the particulars of claim and to claim further interest from the date of the claim, a daily rate should be calculated, shown and included.

Once you have calculated the total claimed, being: **Debt value + interest if claimed + late payment charges if claimed,** you can now add this up to your total claim, calculate the fees payable and complete the boxes at the right-hand bottom corner of the front of the form N1.

The Statement of Truth

You are now asked to complete a statement truth verifying that you believe the facts in the particulars of claim are true and that you are duly authorised to sign this statement on behalf of the claimant.

If a claimant or their advisers make a false statement in a document that is verified by a statement of truth without honestly believing it to be true then they may find themselves subject to proceedings for contempt of Court.

Address for service

On the bottom of the second page you will be asked to complete the name and address of the claimants (or if using solicitors – their name and address) to which documents should be sent by the Court and payments and documents from the defendant.

Your form is now ready for sending, or taking to the chosen County Court, with the appropriate fee for issue. See the Court Service website for the current fee scales.

Service of the claim form

The Court staff will check the procedural accuracy of your completed form, ensure they have the correct fee for the value of the claim and issue the case with a number. Note: this number must be quoted in all future contact with the court – if you do not they can not trace the case.

The numbered claim form is sent to the defendant with a 'Response Pack' by prepaid first class post. You will be notified of the deemed date that the defendant has been served – usually a few working days after it has been posted. This is known as the deemed date of service, and now the clock starts ticking – the defendant has *14 days* from the deemed date to respond, using the response pack sent by the Court with your completed claim form.

At this stage the Court will send you a Notice of Issue. This will include the number assigned to the case. If the claim form is returned undelivered by the Post Office, the Court will notify you and you will be required to attempt to serve it yourself. If you have an alternative address you can amend the claim form and give the Court a new address.

If you serve the claim form yourself, you can send it by first-class post, insert it through the letterbox of the defendant's last or usual place of residence/ business or serve it personally if the defendant is an individual. In that event, you will be expected to complete a certificate of service and lodge it at Court.

STAGE THREE – THE JOURNEY TO JUDGMENT (INCLUDING THE DEBTOR'S RESPONSE)

The defendant has a number of obvious options to respond to the claim for within the 14 days allowed.

Option 1: Pay the debt in full

This will include the principal debt, the Court fee that has been paid, the solicitor's costs if charged, the interest, including the accumulated daily rate from issue of the claim form to payment, and the late payment charges if these have been invoked. You do not have to advise the Court that payment in full has been received.

Option 2: Pay part of the debt

It is not uncommon for defendants simply to pay the principal debt or part of it. There is, therefore, a residue of debt which will include your Court fee, the solicitor's costs and maybe the interest and charges. In that event you are entitled to enter judgment after the elapse of the 14 days for the balance outstanding using the request for judgment that will be sent to you by the Court.

In the view of the author, if the defendant has demonstrated the ability to pay the debt, and indeed the willingness, then it should follow that the residue would be paid. You can enter judgment for the residue, and then simply write to the debtor telling them that you will enforce the judgment for the residue in, say, 10 days unless they pay that over to you in full.

Option 3: The defendant admits the claim but makes no offer of payment

In the defendant's response pack is an admission form which can be used by the defendant to admit the debt. They should provide details of income and expenditure and make an offer of payment.

If the defendant has filed an admission but does not make an offer of payment the claimant can ask the Court for judgment by submitting the request and, as with a judgment in default, the claimant can specify how they would like the judgment to be paid.

Option 4: The defendant does not respond

Where the defendant fails to respond to the claim form within the time required then judgment in default may be entered by submitting the request at the bottom of the Notice of Issue. You can specify further interest from the date of the claim form up to the request for judgment and can also specify how payment is to be made. It is usual to enter judgment to paid forthwith, and immediately and simultaneously start the enforcement process.

Option 5: The defendant files an admission and offers acceptable instalments

If you accept any form of payment by instalments from the defendant, you must ask the Court to enter judgment in those terms so that if the payment is not made you can enforce your judgment. You can do so using the request for judgment form sent to you by the Court.

The first payment will usually be due one month *after* the date when the Court enters the judgment.

Technically a limited company that admits that it can not pay the debt in full, offering instalments, is insolvent. Unless you are able to get director's personal guarantees you should seriously consider rejecting the offer. You should seek advice if you are in this position.

Option 6: The defendant files an admission and offers unacceptable instalments

If you do not accept the instalments being offered by the defendant you can object by completing the form, stating by what instalments you would like the judgment to be paid, if at all by instalments.

You will also be asked to give your grounds for objecting to the instalments. When you submit your response, a senior Court officer (not a Judge) will review (1) what financial information has been given by the defendant (remember nobody is going to ask for all details to be resubmitted if the debtor gives incomplete information), and (2) your objections and set a rate of instalment.

If, on receipt of these terms, you think they are unreasonable, you have to raise your objection in 14 days and ask for the decision to be reconsidered by the Court. You should send a letter to Court setting out why you think the defendant should pay more than has been ordered and give any other grounds for objection.

Option 7: The defendant admits part of the debt

If the defendant admits only part of the amount being claimed, the Court will send you a copy of the admission with a form inviting you to indicate whether you accept the amount that has been admitted in full settlement of your claim. If you do, you will be entitled to judgment for that amount. If you do not accept the amount that has been admitted the case will proceed as a full defended action.

Common sense perhaps dictates that you should be allowed to enter judgment for the admitted sum and fight over the balance; however this is not the case. You will not be given judgment automatically, you will have to make an application to

Court for judgment for the admitted sum (Part 24 Application – see below), and then fight it out for the balance. It is structured this way to ensure that continuing focus is on you as creditor claimant to settle where possible.

Option 8: The defendant files an 'acknowledgment of service'

This is to be used where the defendant is saying *'I have a defence, but I can't put it together in the 14 days allowed – I need more time.'* The effect is that the 14 days allowed to respond is extended by a further 14 days, that is, 28 days from the deemed date of service.

It is possible that the debtors do not have a defence, and are just 'buying extra time' by filing the acknowledgement, or it may be a precursor to a more complex defended case. The debtors may after the extra 14 days take no further action, in that case the claimant has been delayed an additional 14 days, they can now enter judgment as if the claim form had been ignored in the first place as in option 4 above.

Option 9: The defendant files a defence or a defence and counterclaim

The defendant may choose to defend the claim. They may also make a counterclaim against you. You cannot now proceed by default but must follow the procedures for defended actions set out below.

If a counterclaim is lodged (a claim by the defendant against you) you must file at Court and serve on the defendant a *'defence to counterclaim'* within 14 days after receipt.

The counterclaim has the same effect as if the debtor had sued you in the first place, and unless you deal with it seriously and urgently the debtor could be in a position that they could enter judgment against you on the counterclaim and attempt to enforce that judgment. Not only would this be costly, but embarrassing, and the momentum that you sought to gain in the first place would be lost.

What if the defence filed is not a sustainable defence to the claim?

The role of a Part 24 application – Summary judgment

Assume that a sham defence is filed to slow down the debt recovery process – maybe the debtor has had goods, and claims that they never received them, and you have proof of delivery, notes of contacts made chasing the debt and broken promises. Alternatively the debtor has admitted part of the debt and you do not accept their arguments as to the balance (option 7 above), but see no reason why you should not be paid what is admitted.

You do not want the matter dragging on for possibly months, and you require a decision from the Court as quickly as possible. The way to get the process expedited and apply increasing pressure on the defendant is by making an application for *summary judgment*. This is known as a Part 24 Application.

Application is made to the Court supported by written evidence, a fee is payable and a hearing date is set as soon as practicable. The defendant is then served with the application and the evidence, and has the opportunity, in written form, to rebut by written evidence in reply and probe the claimants' evidence.

The process is available to claimants who think they can prove that there is no *reasonable prospect of success* in the defence, and that they can persuade the Court that is the case. If so, the Court at the hearing may dismiss the defence, or dismiss part of the defence, allowing the claimant judgment for that sum.

It may also put the defendant *on terms* whereby they are ordered to prove they can eventually pay by producing the debt claimed or part thereof, to be held in abeyance to 'abide the event' that at least, on payment, proves the debtors have the capacity to pay the debt. If they do not pay, the claimant will be able to enter judgment and proceed to enforcement.

If the application of the claimant is not successful, the Court will usually give directions as to how the matter is to be dealt with going forward, and probably order the costs of the failed application against the claimant.

Similarly if a defendant considers that a claimants' claim has *'no reasonable prospects of success'* the defendant can issue Part 24 proceedings in an attempt to dismiss the claim. Part 24 usually requires expert legal guidance.

Putting defended debt cases into context

The vast majority of simple debt cases never reach the actual Court door; they are dealt with by the Court staff using a series of processes stimulated by the claimant *reacting to* the defendant exercising one of the *options* following the service of the claim form.

It is always the case that the most common route to judgment follows the debtor doing absolutely nothing at all, and the judgment simply being entered in default.

Defended matters are an *inordinate absorber of time* for a creditor in relation to the outcomes and can also be costly. Debtors know this and may use the system to weaken the resolve of the claimant. If the *attitudes* of both the claimant and the defendant allow then settle defended debt cases whenever you can, and only litigate if you have to – in proportion to the probable outcome or benefit.

However for sake of completeness we should consider what happens to defended matters in Court.

Dealing with defended action in the County Court

On the receipt of any defence from the defendant, notwithstanding its content, merit or otherwise, the Court automatically transfers the action to the nearest Court to the defendant's address.

If your solicitors are using the Northampton Bulk Issuing Centre and the debtor is a limited company, the case may be transferred to your solicitor's local Court for convenience as an alternative. The action will keep the same claim number.

The Court sends a copy of the Defence to the claimant or the claimant's solicitors together with an Allocation Questionnaire.

The Allocation Questionnaire

The purpose of the Allocation Questionnaire is to enable the Court to allocate the case to one of three different tracks and give directions as to how the action is to be handled. The *appropriate track* depends mainly on the value of the claim; although the Court may choose to take into account other matters (for example, the complexity of the known facts or evidence or the value of any counterclaim).

The three tracks are:

- **Small Claims Track:** for claims of less than £5000 (this was formally known as the small claims Court);

- *Fast Claims Track:* for claims between £5000 and £15,000;

- *Multi Claims Track:* for claims over £15,000 or complex claims.

The Allocation Questionnaire probes both parties for additional information, for example, asking what steps have been made in an attempt to settle the matter between the parties. As soon as a defence is received, this may be the first time that a dispute has been raised. It is important at this stage to gather together all the relevant evidence and consider who and what is to be presented as evidence to support your claim.

The Allocation Questionnaire asks for a list of witnesses together with any dates when they are not available – however, you are not prevented from calling a witness who is not listed. The Court will use the information you have given on witness availability to give a trial date or a trial 'window' (a period, usually of three weeks, in which the trial will take place). Once the trial date or window has been allocated, the Court will only alter that date in very exceptional circumstances and not, for example, because one of the witnesses is on holiday.

Fees are payable on the filing of the questionnaire by the claimant for debts over £1500. Under that sum there is no fee, above that sum there is a sliding scale of fees payable. As these fees vary and are changed from time to time, please consult the Court Service website for the current fees.

Directions from the Court – The 'way' points of the journey to judgment

Like all journeys the *length, speed and direction* has to be mapped out, the directions from the Court are set to ensure that the overriding objective is observed and that valuable Court resources are not wasted. In all cases (apart from some small claims) the Court will give a 'directions timetable' setting out the steps that should be taken before the trial by both parties.

Disclosure of documents

The initial direction is usually for each party to prepare a list of all documents relevant to the case, those that you intend to rely upon, and serve a copy of that list on the opposing party. This is known as Disclosure.

Open disclosure must be made by both parties of any document on which (1) you wish to rely and must include not only those documents that support your case or the other party's case but also (2) those documents which may seem to you to adversely affect your own case. Copies on request are to be sent by each party to each side.

If a document is 'left out' by either party they may be prevented from referring to it at the final hearing.

Witness statements

Each party will then be asked to send their opponent their witness statements. Witnesses 'of fact' cannot be allowed to give evidence unless a written statement has been given to the other side setting out the evidence of that witness. These statements are extremely important, if relevant facts are omitted that information may never come before the judge.

The witness statement ends with a 'statement of truth'. Any document that contains a statement of truth is evidence before the Court. To knowingly give false information is a criminal offence. You will recall that the claim form contains a statement of truth.

Defended cases – Three Tracks – three different speeds – three different dimensions – same outcomes

Each of the three tracks has their own main points:

The Small Claims Track – Main points

The claim is usually up to £5,000. Once allocated to the Small Claims Track the Court will not usually order any additional costs apart from the fixed costs of issuing and any Court fee. Rarely a Court may hold that a party has behaved unreasonably and order additional costs. The winner can claim their witness expenses that are limited. The hearing is informal and is held in the Judge's rooms. This procedure is designed to enable litigants to conduct actions themselves. Strict rules of evidence do not apply. Solicitors are not encouraged to attend as they can not claim any additional costs against the losing party, if they do attend they are paid by their clients The Court can be asked to deal with a hearing 'on paper' without the attendance of witnesses.

The Fast Track – Main points

This is used for defended actions where the claim is between £5000 and £15,000. The journey timetable should last no more than 30 weeks. A trial should last no longer than one day. The judge will not allow experts to give oral evidence at trial. Expert evidence is usually limited to the written report of a jointly instructed expert. Main evidence is given by written witness statements. Witnesses must now attend to give the other side the opportunity to ask questions. The trial is formal and takes place in open Court before a District or Circuit Judge. Costs awarded may not reflect the costs incurred

The Multi Track – Main points

Claims of more than £15,000 or of greater complexity are dealt with on Multi Track. Multi Track gives a greater flexibility to the Court to manage the case. Often, case management conferences takes place at the key stages. No set time limit for the length of the timetable. The length of the trial may vary according to circumstances and the rules regarding experts are more flexible. Each party may be allowed to call their own expert witnesses. The trial is formal and takes place in open Court before a District or Circuit Judge. There are higher associated costs.

It must also be remembered that if the claimant wins at any trial on each of the tracks, they end up with a judgment – an order to pay – this judgment has no greater authority than the judgment that could have been obtained in default had the defendant ignored the claim form.

It may still be the case that after all this time and expense the debtor has still not got the capacity to pay. For that reason, where there is a positive attitude to settle it should be explored at all costs. Getting paid at the earliest stages is always the best outcome.

STAGE FOUR – ENFORCING THE JUDGMENT

A County Court Judgment (CCJ) guarantees nothing – it does not 'force' the defendant to make payment. Therefore, on most occasions, once you have obtained judgment, you will need to enforce the judgment in order to get paid.

To enable enforcement to work the debtor must have something to lose – if not, there are no remedies available to you. Think about it – if you have no job, no property of value, in rented accommodation, no assets and no prospects of achieving any what can the system take away from you? It is not related just to individuals. Businesses of all shapes and sizes sometimes find themselves in dire circumstances. It is a probable indicator of impending failure of a business if it starts accumulating unsatisfied CCJs.

These debtors either should not have been granted credit in the first instance, or more likely, their circumstances have been catastrophically altered through illness or perhaps redundancy (for individuals), or in respect of businesses, cash flow problems, lack of capital and a 'credit crunch' effect or restructuring, and collapsing order books.

Ironically most businesses that fail have not been able to collect their own debts, either through neglect and non-diligence in credit control or unresolved disputes being left, choking the cash flow needed to survive.

Enforcement – The Reality

Each of the following procedures involves the completion of a request to the Court and paying yet another 'appropriate fee', that is, more cost.

What can be subject to enforcement?	*Method*
Moveable property of value owned by the debtor	Execution
Immovable property – real estate	Charging orders
Incoming wages and salaries	Attachment of Earnings
Debts due to the debtor	Third-party Debt order
Financial savings and assets charges	Third-party Debt orders

What do we know about our debtor?

The answer most of the time is not a great deal. If you have the ability, you should at least enquire if an individual owns their home (you should have done this at the start in fact, before granting credit in the first place!) – in other words, do they have something to lose? Larger businesses can not allow 'reputational damage' to occur by CCJs being registered, as this will affect their own credit rating.

Method 1: Execution against goods

A bailiff in the County Court or a sheriff in the High Court is authorised to attend the defendant's address to either obtain payment or seize goods to the value of the outstanding debt including costs and interest, plus their fees.

For judgment debts below £600 you must instruct a County Court Bailiff.

For judgment debts over £600 you *can* instruct a sheriff's officer.

For judgment debts over £5000 you *must* instruct a sheriff's officer.

What is the difference between a bailiff and a sheriff's officer?

County Court Bailiffs are Crown employees attached to a County Court. Sheriff's officers are employed usually by large independent enforcement companies driven by profit, working within a regulated environment.

The goods to be seized must be:

- of sufficient value to cover the total debt including fees and other costs;

- moveable (although auctions can be held on the premises);

- accessible;

- auctionable (demand must exist);

- owned outright by the debtor.

Execution – The process in a nutshell:

- The debtor is contacted they are asked to pay outright? – Yes I can pay!

- The debtor pays debt and pays all costs – execution has worked!

- The debtor can't pay – the debtor's goods are examined for saleability[1]

---

1   In the event that during the period of walking possession where an installment is not made, or on first contact is made after a levy has taken place the sheriff decides that the goods are of such

are they worth seizing? If so the goods are listed and *levied* upon, if they are not of value the sheriff asks himself – does the debtor appear both able and willing to make reasonable installments? If so, the goods levied upon will be subject to 'walking possession' – this may last some weeks until the debt and costs are paid by reasonable installments.

If the goods are not auctionable in the opinion of the sheriff a 'nulla bona' is reported back to the creditor – 'the debtor's goods are not worth seizure and sale' the process is at an end – execution has failed.

Limits of execution

Both bailiffs and sheriffs have governed and limited rights of entry, although legislation allowing the forced entry onto debtor's premises is under discussion at the time of writing.

Certain goods are protected from seizure by the sheriff, such as tools of the trade, a means of cooking, clothing and beds and linen. In certain circumstances a TV receiver is also not removable. This list is not comprehensive and is likely to be extended at any time.

In addition, goods belonging to a third party may not be seized by the sheriff; the third party must submit a claim to the sheriff as to their ownership of the goods in writing. The claim to ownership can be challenged – if so the goods will then be subject to a procedure known as 'inter pleader proceedings'. These proceedings are both costly and uncertain

Method 2: Third-party Debt Order

Formerly known as a *garnishee* order. Simply put, where a third party owes money to the debtor an application can be made to Court for an order that the third party pay that money directly to the claimant. Such an application is most often used when the debtor has a non-joint bank account and the account is in credit.

---

value and cannot be safely left on the debtor's premises, they may decide to remove goods to the salerooms for auction.

But how do you know?

More often an application is not able to succeed because you don't have the information needed to make an application, or the information you have is not accurate or current. The debt to the debtor *must be due and owing* at the time of the application, if not the application will fail.

The claimant must complete an application for third-party Debt Order (Form N349) and pay the appropriate fee. Details required are:

- name and address of the judgment debtor;

- the amount and details of the judgment being enforced;

- the address of the third party;

- the source of the evidence for the existence of the third-party debt;

- the evidence the claimant seeks to rely upon.

The papers go before a Judge and, if satisfied that the application is appropriate, the Court will make an *Interim Order*, and set a hearing date, which is then served upon the third party first and then defendant (for obvious reasons). The defendant, the third party, or any other person laying claim to the money can challenge the application.

In the meantime the third party must tell the Court in seven days, if there is a debt due or not, how much it is, and not make any payment to the debtor. The debtor can make application to the Court before the hearing for 'relief' against the order, if they can prove that the making of the order and the effective 'freeze' of the payment will cause them undue hardship.

The Court at the hearing can make the following orders:

- Make the Interim Order final and order the third party to pay the claimant the debt or part thereof.

- Dismiss the Interim Order and order costs against the claimant (these may also include the costs of the third party).

- Decide the issues between the parties if there is a dispute over the third-party debt.

- Make an order as to costs.

- Any other appropriate order it thinks fit.

If a third-party Debt Order is made and the third party fails to make payment, the claimant can enforce the order as if they had sued the third party in the first place and obtained a judgment against them.

Method 3: Charging order

Where a debtor owns property, or has an interest in one (jointly owned) the claimant can make an application to impose a charge on the property to the value of the debt. A charge is similar to a mortgage. It is secured over the property in the event of a sale or disposal of the property.

The application for Charging Order on land or property is made on form N379, with the appropriate fee to Court. The application must be supported by evidence that the debtor has an interest in the property, usually be in the form of a search obtained from the Land Registry. The Court will consider the application.

Like a third-party Debt Order, the application is made in two stages.

On examining the Claimant's application the Court, and if successful, the Court makes an *Interim Order*. The Court also sets a hearing date. The Interim Order is then served on the debtor and any other creditors that the Claimant may be aware of.

To secure the claimants' position the Interim Order should be registered at the Land Registry to register the order over the property. It is the claimants' responsibility to register the charge. At the hearing date the Interim Order is made final unless substantive objections are raised by the debtor. Once a final Charging Order is made, it is cautious to re-register the final order at the Land Registry.

The claimant now has become a secured creditor, then, as with a building society or bank mortgage that is in arrears, it is possible to apply to Court for a forced sale of the property. Enforcement of a Charging Order is a separate set of proceedings and is at the discretion of the Court. For it to be successful there must be available equity in the property, otherwise what is the point?

Method 4: Attachment of earnings order

This is an order whereby the debtor's employer is ordered to deduct a specific monthly or weekly sum from the debtor's salary. That sum is then paid to the claimant. The debtor must be employed by a third party, it therefore is not appropriate to self-employed debtors.

It is mainly used for the collection of consumer low-value debt where the debtors may be in regular employment, it is not appropriate for commercial debt. It a long-term 'drip drip' method of getting paid, assuming it is successful.

Application is made by completing a form N337 and (of course) paying the appropriate fee. The Court send details of the order sought to the debtor, asking by questionnaire details of his/her income and expenditure and to also forward details of the debtor's employment. If the debtor fails to complete the questionnaire the Court 'ups the ante' and treats the debtor in contempt – eventually – compelling them to complete the form.

If the debtor is unemployed – it stops there, and no order is made.

Assuming the debtor completes the questionnaire, returns it and is employed, the Court will take into account a figure to allow the debtor to meet essential and existing monthly outgoings and will then make an order that a proportion of any balance left be deducted from the debtor's salary and paid to the claimant. If the debtor is on low pay with large family or social commitments it is possible that the ordered is so low that it is not worth collecting and banking the payments!

Method 5: Order to obtain information from judgment debtors

Not strictly an enforcement method, this was formerly known as an *oral examination*. The procedure allows the Court and the creditor (claimant) to examine the debtor, or a director of a limited company debtor under oath as to details of assets, income, outgoings and means. The purpose of the examination is designed to assist in determining which method of enforcement is most appropriate. Debtors do not usually cooperate either willingly or fully.

One may ask, why should they? Many debtors do not 'engage' with creditors as many would have us believe, their behaviour is one of avoidance and or confrontation.

A request for an order is by submitting form N316 and paying the appropriate fee. The Court sets up an appointment and an order to attend is drawn up. This order must be personally served upon the debtor because it carries a penal notice. Failure to cooperate with the Court may constitute a contempt of Court, with the threat of imprisonment.

If the debtor does not attend, a suspended committal warrant will be issued against him. Needless to say, this usually persuades the debtor to attend.

Claimants, their advisers, and credit managers have usually better access to data about the defendant/debtor from The Land Registry, credit reference agencies and, in the final instance, from enquiry agents, to get enough information to decide the most appropriate method of enforcement, without recourse to this type of enquiry.

Using Insolvency and Insolvency Petitions as an Alternative Means of Obtaining Payment

What has been discussed so far in this chapter represents by far the vast majority of legal debt collection effort and action in England and Wales. However, many creditors may feel the system is cumbersome and possibly costly (particularly for smaller debts), with the majority of cases being dealt with by a simple paper 'form filling exercise'.

To many debtors the threat of *yet another* CCJ means little. The fact is they have no means of paying, no will to pay and an existing damaged credit rating. Many seasoned debtors know the system and can delay or avoid payment – *the unwilling and unable*. Others fearing the prospect of their credit rating being adversely affected will pay – *the unwilling and able*.

IS THERE AN ALTERNATIVE?

Yes there is currently – insolvency. Insolvency for debt collection is not officially encouraged by the Courts, but it is widely used to maximise the pressure on both individuals and limited companies alike to pay their debts as and when they become due. It is not usual to use insolvency for consumer debt collection, however.

Insolvency can be used as an alternative method of enforcement (the sixth method?) but it is not necessary to await the outcome of claim form actions and judgments before considering insolvency for debt matters that are 'clean debts'.

There are strict criteria to be observed:

- the debt must be over £750;

- the debt must not be disputed (a bona fide and or substantial dispute).

You also have to consider if the debtor has anything to lose if they enter into formal insolvency. It is a catastrophic financial event with far-reaching consequences for all involved including the creditor, as it is unlikely that they will recover the debt if insolvency occurs. If they have enough to lose, and admit the debt, then usually the threat alone results in payment, without the time and expense of further Court action.

Two distinct processes are available:

- for individuals, including partners in firms – bankruptcy;

- for limited companies, public limited companies, (LLPs and partnerships) – winding up.

HOW DOES THE BANKRUPTCY PROCESS WORK?

Individuals – The demand

Individuals are able to be served with a *Statutory Demand in Bankruptcy*. This is a form of demand (Form 6.1). The demand is usually prepared by the creditors solicitors, not a Court). Information on the form includes the standard names and addresses of the creditor and the debtor, the creditor's solicitors details and a statement of what the debt is, and how it was incurred. The detail is not dissimilar to the particulars of claim on the claim form in the County Court. You can claim contractual interest, or late interest.

The total amount of the debt as at the date of the demand is 'crystallised' and claimed in the demand, so that there in no confusion as to what amount is being demanded.

The front of the form has a *serious consequences and warning* section to the debtor – telling them that if they fail to deal with the demand in **21 days** from service they may be subject to bankruptcy and they may lose their home.

Because the creditor is making such a draconian threat, the debtor must have the opportunity of attempting to stop or delay the process if they cannot either make full payment in the 21 days, come to an arrangement to pay, or indeed if they dispute the debt. So the creditor must tell the debtor in the demand, how and at which Court they can make that kind of application. It is a prescribed form.

Service of the demand

The demand should wherever possible be served personally. It cannot be served by normal posting. An enquiry agent or similar attempts to meet the debtor and serve the demand. If successful, a report is sent to the creditor certifying the date of service. If unsuccessful, the agent will ascertain if the debtor is resident at the address given, and make an appointment with a *letter of appointment* in a few days. They will then return on the appointed date and time, and if the debtor is present serve the demand on them personally. If the debtor fails to meet the agent the demand will be posted by the agent through the debtor's letterbox – *this is known as substituted service.*

Once served, the debtor has a number of options to take in the 21 days allowed. Either:

- pay up in full;

- offer to pay by instalments (the demand only has a life of four months);

- dispute the debt;

- offer security for the debt (usually a voluntary charge on property);

- compound for the debt (give something other than money or security – maybe goods).

It is incumbent on the creditor to *react to the debtors options* as quickly as possible as the clock is ticking away.

If the creditor does not accept any instalment offered, and cannot negotiate a better settlement, they must say so, and why, in writing by replying to the debtor within 24 hours, to allow the debtor to make his application to *set aside the demand.*

If the debt is substantially disputed and the creditor accepts so, the demand should be withdrawn. If the creditor does not accept that the debt is disputed, they must tell the debtor so again in writing, so that an application can be made to set aside the demand. (Applications to set aside should usually be made within 18 days of service.) If such an application is to be made, it is the debtor's responsibility, and it has to be supported by evidence. The Court will decide on the issues between the parties.

What if the debtor ignores the demand?

They have committed an 'act of bankruptcy' upon which the creditor can *petition* for the debtor's bankruptcy. Issuing a petition is expensive, due to the Court fees involved and a refundable upfront Official Receivers deposit (so that in the event of the debtor actually going bankrupt, at least the trustees' initial costs are covered). The debt must be of sufficient value to risk, say, £1000 in costs on worst possible case scenario.

Where the debtor is made bankrupt the fees and deposit are lost and may not be recovered.

A substantial number of debtors will only be forced into payment at this late, desperate stage. Many petitions are paid off before any Bankruptcy Order is made, this usually includes the creditor's full costs, and the deposit is refunded. The debtor bears the full cost of the proceedings in that event.

The petition

The petition is prepared by the solicitors, citing the debtor's failure to deal with the statutory demand as the act of insolvency/bankruptcy, the fees are paid and the deposit lodged. The Court then fixes a hearing date, and returns the petition to the creditor;s solicitors for service by their agent. *The service of the petition must now be affected personally by the enquiry agent.*

If the agent cannot serve personally and is of the view that the debtor is avoiding him he will report back to the creditor's solicitor, who can then make an application for the Court to decide the method of service, this is known as *substituted service.* The Court will direct what will be deemed to be 'good service' and the agent will be given additional directions as to how the petition can be served. If good service can not be affected, the petition will be withdrawn at the hearing and the deposit refunded to the creditor.

The hearing – Outcomes

If the debtor fails to attend the hearing and the Court is satisfied that the petition and the statutory demand have been dealt with in accordance with the complex rules – the debtor is made bankrupt.

If the debtor attends and is not able to satisfy the Judge that an order should not be made, the debtor is made bankrupt. If the debtor persuades the Judge that they can pay or come to an arrangement with the creditor, the Court may adjourn the hearing to another date. The threat of bankruptcy hangs over the debtor until the next hearing.

If a debtor persuades the Judge that the debt is disputed (notwithstanding the fact that they should have made an application to set aside the statutory demand many weeks earlier), the Court may dismiss the petition, and order costs to be paid.

If the debtor has paid the debt (and agreed costs) or come to an arrangement to settle the debt, where (1) the Court endorses the settlement and (2) there are no supporting creditors – the Court may dismiss the petition.

Post-bankruptcy –What happens next?

If a Bankruptcy Order is made – the likelihood of getting paid is remote. A trustee will be appointed, all of the debtor's assets 'vesting' in that trustee. If the debtor has a property with equity, the property will eventually be sold.

The proceeds of the trustee's efforts to realise the assets will be distributed to creditors after the costs of doing so are paid and any secured and preferential creditors have been paid. If there no assets there is no distribution.

COMPANY OWES A DEBT OVER £750? – WINDING UP – THE PROCESS

A company that can not pay its debts as and when they fall due for payment is technically insolvent. Again, as in bankruptcy, we will have to prove to the Court at the petition stage that the debtor has 'committed an act of insolvency'.

Stage 1 – The demand

Creditors can, if they choose, issue a 21-day statutory demand against a company. It has to be served personally. Alternatively creditors using specialist solicitors can choose to get the lawyers to make demand against the company in writing by letter *giving them a few days* to make payment, or be deemed to admit they can not pay their debts on demand, and face the sanction of a petition being presented to the Court for their liquidation.

Most companies faced with this threat, naturally pay almost immediately.

If the debt is disputed this process must not be used.

If, in the unlikely event the demand letter does not stimulate payment, the creditor then has the option of issuing a petition for winding up or liquidation of the debtor company.

If embarking on this route the creditor should be prepared to see the process through to the bitter end. Experience suggests, however, that a substantial number of petitions are paid at some stage in the process before (and even at) the hearing.

Petition – The process

A Petition based on the debtor's failure to pay the demand in whatever form is presented usually to the High Court. A fee is payable for its issue, and a refundable Official Receivers deposit is paid (slightly more than a bankruptcy). The Court also checks that no other creditor has issued a petition anywhere else in the UK; there should never be more than one petition in existence at any one time. If one exists already you will not be allowed to issue the petition. (In that event you should support the prior petition.)

A hearing date is set about six weeks ahead and the petition is returned to the creditor's solicitors for service. It is served at the registered address, and should be brought to the attention of a responsible person. It is not uncommon for a copy of the petition to be sent to the directors at home if there is some doubt that it may not have got to their attention.

The debtor company is now heading towards oblivion, unless it deals with the debt and the petition; the company must deal with it – urgently.

Supporting Creditors – Note

If another creditor applies for the issue of a petition and is refused because one has already been issued, they have the right to support the prior petition. They do so by writing to the petitioning creditor's solicitors at any time up to the date before the hearing. In that event, the company has to now find not only the petition debt, but also that of the supporting creditors before a petition can be removed.

Payment and dismissal

It is not uncommon that companies served with a petition immediately deal with it by payment. In that event, it is usual to dismiss the petition and obtain the costs of the issue and the solicitor's costs from the debtor company – this assumes that no supporting creditors have emerged. The Official Receivers deposit is eventually returned in about a month.

No payment – What now? The advertisement stage

The next stage in the process is the most dangerous for the creditor. Seven days after service, and not less than seven days before the hearing (7/7 day rule) of the petition, if it has not been paid and dismissed, it (the petition) must be advertised in the daily *London Gazette*. This will advertise to other creditors, including the company's bank, that the petition exists and that there is the possibility of liquidation.

The effects of the advert can be ruinous for the debtor, and could signal the loss of the debt for the petitioning creditor. The bank will freeze the debtor's bank account, so even if they wanted to pay they can't. Other creditors may be alerted and support the petition. Insolvency Practitioners will contact the company to 'assist' them into insolvency. The advert may stimulate another form of insolvency process such as Administration.

The company may not survive the advert, so usually it is placed at the last possible date after service so as to allow the petitioning creditor the best possible opportunity to get paid. As soon as the petition is advertised it can not be withdrawn, other creditors must have the right to support it at the hearing in Court.

The hearing – Likely outcomes

It is not unheard of for companies to turn up to Court at the hearing and pay in cash, or with third-party funds.

The most common outcomes are:

- The petition is adjourned to allow the company to find the payment.

- The petition is dismissed as it has been paid after the advert – no supporting creditors.

- The petition is taken over by another creditor, *and adjourned*, after the petitioning creditor has been paid.

- The petition is dismissed to allow another form of insolvency procedure to take place.

- The petition is dismissed because the debt is disputed.

- The company is wound up.

If the company is wound up at a subsequent hearing by a substituted creditor who may not have been paid, the original creditor may have to repay the debt to the appointed insolvency practitioner.

Specialist solicitors should always be consulted when dealing with any form of insolvency-based debt recovery.

23

Insolvency Procedures

Dean Watson
Begbies Traynor, Manchester[1]

• Introduction • Procedures • What is the purpose of insolvency? • Personal insolvency • Bankruptcy, individual voluntary arrangements • Corporate insolvency • Company voluntary arrangement • Debt relief orders • Corporate insolvency • Company voluntary arrangements • Administration • Pre-packs • Receivership • Law of property/fixed charge receivers • Liquidations • Costs and distribution of funds • Creditors' voluntary liquidation • Procedure for creditors' voluntary liquidation •

Introduction

Insolvency is generally defined as follows: A company is insolvent if it either has more liabilities than assets on its balance sheet or if it is unable to pay its debts as and when they fall due. An individual is insolvent if he or she is unable to discharge his or her debts as they fall due.

Once a company or individual is insolvent, several courses of action are possible, sometimes resulting in a return to solvency. These are different for individuals and companies.

Usually, in an insolvency procedure, a licensed insolvency practitioner (IP) or the Official Receiver (OR) takes control of the assets belonging to the insolvent party and ensures that all creditors are treated fairly and equally, in proportion to their claims and subject to their status or rank in the priority of distribution.

There are many reasons why a company might become insolvent. R3 is the leading professional association for insolvency, business recovery and

---

1   Dean Watson is a Fellow of the Association of Chartered Certified Accountants (FCCA) and a Licensed Insolvency Practitioner authorised by the ACCA. He is an appointment taking Director in the Manchester office of Begbies Traynor and can be contacted on 0161 837 1700.

turnaround specialists in the UK. R3's research shows that the most common reasons for corporate insolvency are:

- Loss of market: where companies have not recognised the need to change in a shrinking or changing market place, because their margins have been eroded or because their service has been overtaken technically.

- Management failure to acquire adequate skills, either through training or buying them in, over-optimism in planning, imprudent accounting, lack of management information.

- Fraud.

- Loss of long-term finance, over-gearing, lack of working capital/cashflow.

- Other reasons include excessive overheads, new venture/expansion/acquisition.

Procedures

The main legislation covering insolvency procedures are The Insolvency Act 1986 (following the first major review of insolvency in the UK for many years), The Insolvency Act 2000 (which introduced the concept of Individual and Company Voluntary Arrangements), and The Enterprise Act 2002 (covering both individual and company insolvency).

An insolvent company goes into administration, administrative receivership or liquidation and an individual becomes bankrupt. Insolvent individuals and companies can also enter into voluntary arrangements. Insolvency procedures and terminology are similar in England, Wales and Northern Ireland, but differ in Scotland.

In general terms, many insolvencies could be avoided if professional advice is sought early enough, that is, the longer that the directors of a company wait before seeking advice then the more likely it is that the company or its business will not be rescued. Similarly, the longer an individual waits before seeking advice, the greater that individual's debts are likely to be.

In addition, in most company insolvency procedures, the IP must report to the Department for Business Innovation & Skills (BIS) about the conduct of directors.

What is the Purpose of Insolvency?

The main purpose of any insolvency procedure is to realise the value of the insolvent's estate and to provide returns to creditors whilst benefitting from the protection of the company's/individual's estate from legal or other proceedings. The amount of the return will depend on circumstances of each case and the availability of assets.

In a company scenario it is generally accepted that greater values for assets and better returns to creditors can be achieved when selling the business and assets as a going concern as opposed to a forced sale 'shut down' situation. This often affords continuity of the business which protects assets such as debtors and work in progress and ensures the continued employment of some or all staff. Where contacted early enough and if achievable an IP would attempt to rescue the business as a primary objective but if this is not realistically achievable, the IP would look to realise the assets of the company for the best price.

Once it is apparent or recognised that a company or individual is insolvent, or considers that it may become insolvent, there are a number of alternatives available. The options available range from informal arrangements with the insolvent party's creditors to formal voluntary arrangements for both individuals and companies and to heavily structured and restrictive procedures such as liquidation, administration and administrative receivership for companies and bankruptcy for individuals.

Personal Insolvency

Personal Insolvency deals with the insolvency procedures available for individuals.

There are three types of insolvency procedure available to an individual depending upon the circumstances being:

- Bankruptcy

- Individual Voluntary Arrangement (IVA)

- Debt Relief Orders

Bankruptcy

Bankruptcy is the administration of the affairs of an insolvent individual by a trustee in the interests of his creditors generally.

BANKRUPTCY PROCEDURE

The procedure for bankruptcy is as follows:

Petition

A petition for a Bankruptcy Order may be issued by any creditor owed more than £750, or by the individual himself on the grounds of insolvency.

Bankruptcy Order

A Bankruptcy Order may be made by the Court following a hearing.

Official Receiver

Immediately on the making of the Order, the OR becomes the Receiver and manager of the estate of the bankrupt individual. This is a temporary role pending the appointment of a trustee who will be either the OR or an independent IP.

The OR is an officer of the Court and an employee of the Insolvency Service, an executive agency within BIS.

Where there are significant assets, an IP will usually be appointed to act as trustee, either by a meeting of creditors called by the OR or by the Secretary of State for BIS.

The OR has a duty to investigate the affairs of the bankrupt and to send a report to the creditors. The investigations are started by the OR issuing a questionnaire to the bankrupt and meeting with him/her to take a statement.

Where no IP is appointed, or where there is a vacancy in the office of trustee, the OR acts as trustee.

Creditors Meeting

Within three months of the Bankruptcy Order being made a meeting of creditors may be convened by the OR to appoint a trustee. A trustee is appointed based on the wishes of the creditors and a vote of the creditors is taken at the meeting to determine the appointment of the trustee.

Duties and functions of the trustee

The general duties of a trustee are to:

- Get in and realise the bankrupt's estate. Some assets may not fall into the bankrupt's estate at the outset.

- Distribute funds to the creditors by way of dividend (also to agree the claims of creditors) in a prescribed order of priority.

- Call a final meeting of creditors to account and report to the creditors on the administration of the estate.

RESTRICTIONS ON BANKRUPTCY

There are various restrictions which apply to a bankrupt and which last until the bankrupt is discharged. The main restrictions on the bankrupt are as follows:

- During the period of bankruptcy the bankrupt must not obtain credit of more than £500 from anyone without disclosing that he is an undischarged bankrupt.

- The bankrupt must not act as a company director without the Court's consent.

- The bankrupt will usually be discharged from bankruptcy automatically after one year, or even sooner if the OR decides to close his file early.

- On discharge, the bankrupt is released from his bankruptcy debts. Certain debts survive bankruptcy and the bankrupt is not released from such liabilities. These include Court fines, matrimonial debts and certain student loans.

Following discharge, the trustee will remain in office for as long as is necessary to realise the bankrupt's estate (which remains under the control of the IP) and distribute the proceeds to the creditors. Should there be any misconduct or should the bankrupt not assist the OR in his enquiries then the restrictions may remain if the OR applies to Court to impose a Bankruptcy Restrictions Order, the bankrupt agrees to sign a bankruptcy restrictions undertaking or the OR applies to court to suspend the bankrupt's discharge from bankruptcy. A Bankruptcy Restrictions Order can last up to 15 years dependent upon the severity of the misconduct of the bankrupt.

Following discharge the credit rating of the bankrupt will be affected. It is usual that individuals belonging to professional bodies (doctors, accountants, solicitors and so on) would be unable to continue their profession once made bankrupt.

ASSETS OF THE BANKRUPT

The estate of the bankrupt vests in the trustee and therefore the bankrupt loses any rights to his property. Items that would not normally fall into the bankruptcy estate include any 'tools of the trade' needed by the bankrupt for use in his business, basic domestic equipment such as clothes, bedding and furniture and certain pension rights.

The bankrupt's (matrimonial) home is a complex area but generally speaking, if the bankrupt has equity in a house where he and/or his spouse and/or former spouse live, it will need to be realised by the trustee. However, the rights of occupants (for example, husband, wife and children) need to be considered and take precedence during the first 12 months of the bankruptcy. The trustee has three years from the date of the Bankruptcy Order to realise or deal with the bankrupt's interest in the house or the interest will revert to the bankrupt. If the value of the equity is less than £1000, the trustee will not be able to obtain an Order for possession and sale of the house.

There are certain clawbacks that the trustee can make. If the bankrupt has surplus income above his needs he may be required to make contributions to the trustee for up to three years under an Income Payments Agreement or an Income Payments Order. Until his discharge, the trustee may also claim any property acquired by the bankrupt after the Bankruptcy Order, such as assets left to him in a will, lottery win and so on (After Acquired Property). Should the bankrupt have any 'tools of the trade' or basic domestic equipment that appears excessive (for example, an antique dining table, Rolex watch and so on) then the trustee has the power to realise the asset and replace it with a more reasonable alternative.

A Bankruptcy Order does not prevent a secured creditor dealing with the charged asset(s).

CREDITOR CLAIMS

There is a set order of priority of creditors' claims in a bankruptcy. This means that some creditors are paid from the funds available for distribution in priority to other creditors. The order of payment which the IP must follow is set out in the Insolvency Act 1986. It provides for payment of creditors claims in the following order:

Preferential creditors

Preferential creditors include employees' claims for:

- wages and salaries of any employee earned in the four months preceding the Bankruptcy Order, subject to a maximum of £800 per person;

- all accrued holiday pay;

- advances by banks (or others) which have been used to pay wages, salaries or holiday pay and have served to reduce claims which employees might otherwise have been able to make defined in 1 or 2 above.

Employees' claims are paid out (in whole or in part) by the Government (Redundancy Payments Office) and the RPO takes the employees standing as a preferential creditor for the amounts that it has paid to the employee. If there are sums over and above the payment that the employee receives from the RPO he/she can claim for them by submitting a proof of debt in the bankruptcy.

Unsecured creditors

Creditors must submit their claims by way of proof of debt. The trustee examines the proofs by comparison with the statement of affairs and the debtor's books and records. He may demand further evidence of the debt if in doubt. The admitted proofs are lodged with the court.

Unsecured creditors share *pari passu* (on an equal footing) in the funds available for distribution after providing for the costs of the bankruptcy and preferential claims.

DISTRIBUTION OF FUNDS

Costs – The trustee should pay the costs of bankruptcy. These would include the costs of the petitioning creditor, OR's charges and so on and should be paid as soon as possible. The basis of the trustee's remuneration is fixed by the bankruptcy creditors' committee. In the absence of a committee, the trustee must call a meeting of creditors to fix the remuneration. If this fails either because the creditors fail to agree the basis of the trustee's remuneration or there are insufficient creditors present to decide, he is paid on the OR's scale, or he may apply to the court to fix his remuneration.

Preferential creditors – If there are insufficient funds to pay all preferential creditors in full, their claims rank equally. If there are sufficient funds, the trustee should pay preferential claims at the earliest opportunity.

Unsecured creditors – Distributions to unsecured creditors are made by way of a dividend dependent on (and usually proportionate to) the amount of the admitted claim of the creditor. If circumstances permit, interim dividends may be paid, with a final dividend on the closing of the bankruptcy.

TRUSTEE'S INVESTIGATORY POWERS

Preferences and transactions at an undervalue can be unravelled by the trustee.

A preference is a payment made, or a security given, to a creditor within six months prior to the petition and which places that person in a better position than they would have been had the payment not been made.

Payments to creditors who are associates of the bankrupt are vulnerable to a preference claim for a period of two years prior to the petition. For example, if the bankrupt owed his wife the sum of £10,000 and he paid this to her before making himself bankrupt a month later the trustee is likely to be able to claim the payment back from the bankrupt's wife.

A transaction at an undervalue (TUV) is able to be set aside by the court if it occurred within the five years prior to the date of the bankruptcy petition. A TUV is a transaction whereby the bankrupt gives a gift, receives no money or monies worth or substantially less by way of money or monies worth than the value of the transaction. An example of this would be the bankrupt selling a valuable antique worth £20,000 to a friend for £500 only three months before he was declared bankrupt.

A trustee can also bring a claim under section 423 of the Insolvency Act 1986 to claim that the bankrupt entered into a transaction with the intention of putting an asset beyond the reach of his creditors. A classic example is the husband that transfers his interest in his property to his wife by way of a gift. The trustee must prove that there was a TUV (which is the case in this example because the wife does not pay any money for the bankrupt's interest in the property) and then that the bankrupt intended to put the property beyond the reach of his creditors.

The trustee may recover any assets seized by the sheriff if they have not been sold before the Bankruptcy Order.

The trustee may disclaim any onerous assets such as unprofitable contracts or unsaleable property.

Individual Voluntary Arrangements

An IVA is a less formal procedure available to insolvent individuals which allows the debtor to avoid all of the restrictions and 'stigma' of bankruptcy. An IVA is effectively a 'deal' or agreement between the insolvent individual and his creditors. It is an alternative to bankruptcy and so for creditors to agree to a proposal for an IVA a debtor would need to offer a greater return to creditors than in a bankruptcy. The process generally costs less than bankruptcy and therefore offers a greater return to creditors.

The contents of the proposal are flexible and depend upon the circumstances of the individual (assets, income, liabilities and so on). More than 75 per cent by value of the creditors (voting at the meeting of creditors) are required to agree to the terms of the proposal. Creditors may propose modifications to the proposal and the debtor may accept the modifications proposed in order for the IVA to be agreed. The IVA is overseen by a 'supervisor' and once agreed is binding on all creditors whether or not they voted. The rights of secured and preferential creditors are not affected by an IVA.

This course is also available to an individual that has been made bankrupt.

IVA PROCEDURE

The debtor instructs an IP or the OR if the debtor has already been declared bankrupt, as the 'nominee'. The individual will put together a proposal, with the assistance of the IP, which should be comprehensive and cover such matters as:

- the reasons for the arrangement particulars of the debtor's assets, and how they are to be dealt with;

- how the liabilities are to be dealt with, particularly preferential creditors, secured creditors and debts due to associates of the debtor;

- the duration of the arrangement;

- the name, address and qualifications of the proposed supervisor;

- the remuneration of the supervisor whether the business (if self-employed) is to continue, and if so, on what terms.

Should protection be required from creditors the individual may make an application to Court for an Interim Order. Once an application has been made no bankruptcy petition may be heard nor any other legal action be pursued against the debtor or his property.

The nominee must report to the Court (nominees report) within 14 days of the Interim Order and if satisfactory, the nominee endorses the proposals and recommends that a meeting of creditors is convened.

If the Court orders, the nominee convenes a meeting of the creditors. The meeting must be held between 14 and 28 days of the nominees report. The meeting may approve the proposal, with or without modifications. The majority required is 75 per cent in value of those voting. The nominee reports the results of the meeting to the Court. If the meeting approves the scheme the nominee becomes the 'supervisor' and proceeds to manage the arrangement.

If the individual does not comply with the arrangement then the supervisor must refer to the terms of the arrangement to deal with such matter. It is likely in this instance that the arrangement will be varied with creditor approval or the supervisor may petition for the debtor's bankruptcy dependent upon the seriousness of the departure from the arrangement.

Debt Relief Orders

Debt Relief Orders (DRO) are an alternative option to bankruptcy for people with very little by way of assets, a low level of liabilities and little or no disposable income. They are granted by the OR and operate so that creditors named in the DRO will not be able to enforce their debts which will be discharged in normal circumstances after the period of one year. As the debtor has no assets and no disposable income there will not be any distribution of assets or payment to creditors under a DRO. Secured debts are not included in a DRO and a secured creditor can enforce its security despite a DRO.

A debtor can apply for a DRO through an approved intermediary/debt advisor only. Application is made to the OR. The debtor needs to provide full disclosure of his/her income and expenditure in the application. An approved intermediary/debt advisor is not permitted to charge the debtor for assisting in the preparation of the application.

The OR will grant or deny the application. If granted the DRO will include a list of the debts which the OR considers are 'qualifying debts' and will state the creditor's name and amount of the debt at the time.

There is a one year moratorium in respect of those debts set out in the DRO so that the creditors included under it cannot commence proceedings in respect of their debt. At the end of the moratorium the debtor is discharged from the debts stated in the DRO. If a DRO is made the debtor will be subject to very similar restrictions to bankruptcy although there is no vesting of the debtor's estate in the OR. If the debtor's financial circumstances improve he/she is to make arrangements to repay creditors. The OR has the power to amend or revoke a DRO. In addition the OR can apply for a Debt Relief Restriction Order which operates in a similar way to a Bankruptcy Restriction Order to extend the period of the DRO for up to 15 years. In line with bankruptcy a Debt Relief Restrictions Undertaking can be given instead of an Order being made. Action can be taken for any transaction at an undervalue or preference but the period in relation to both is two years prior to the date of the application for the DRO.

The Court may suggest to a debtor presenting his/her own petition for bankruptcy that a DRO would be more appropriate than bankruptcy. If that is the case the Court would refer the debtor to an approved intermediary/debt advisor and stay the petition. If a DRO is made the Court must dismiss the debtor's bankruptcy petition.

Corporate Insolvency

There are five types of insolvency procedures available for Companies in England, Wales and Northern Ireland being:

1.   Company Voluntary Arrangement (CVA);

2.   Administration;

3.   Administrative Receivership;

4.   Creditors' Voluntary Liquidation (CVL);

5.   Compulsory Liquidation.

By contrast, a Members' Voluntary Liquidation (MVL) is a solvent wind down of a company and the company should be in a position to pay its creditors in full. Fixed Charge Receivers (also referred to as LPA Receivers) can also be appointed by Fixed Charge Holders to realise the specific assets that they hold a charge over.

Generally speaking, CVA, Administration and Administrative Receivership are used as a method of rescuing the business. Liquidation is normally suited to circumstances where the business has ceased. It is a terminal procedure to formally deal with the winding up of a company's affairs.

Company Voluntary Arrangement

This is a very similar procedure to an IVA but is applicable to companies as opposed to individuals.

The procedure allows the company to reach a formal agreement with its creditors with a view to preserving the business. The procedure is flexible and practically must offer a better alternative to creditors than in a liquidation (or creditors would decide to wind up the company).

More than 75 per cent of the creditors in value are required to approve the arrangement and once approved it is binding on the company and its creditors. Once approved, an IP acts as supervisor to ensure that the arrangement is complied with by the company.

COMPANY VOLUNTARY ARRANGEMENT PROCEDURE

Proposal

The directors of the company submit their proposal to an IP (the nominee). In reality it is likely that the IP will have assisted the directors in preparing the proposal.

The IP reviews the proposal to ensure that it is achievable and fair to both the company and its creditors.

Nominees report

The nominee, if satisfied with the proposal, endorses the proposal and notifies the Court that, in his opinion, a meeting of creditors should be called to consider the proposals.

Creditors' meeting

The shareholders and creditors are then given notice of the meetings together with a copy of the proposals and a statement of affairs. The creditors must achieve more than 75 per cent in value of those voting. If these majorities are obtained, the rest of the creditors, including those that would have been entitled to vote if they had had notice of the proposal and meeting, are bound by the arrangement. If the meetings approve the proposals, the nominee becomes supervisor and the scheme proceeds. The scheme cannot affect the rights of secured creditors to enforce their security, who are free to exercise their rights.

Supervisor

Once the proposal has been approved, the nominee becomes the supervisor and ensures that the arrangement is complied with.

It is not only the directors that may propose a CVA. If the company is in liquidation, the Liquidator may propose a voluntary arrangement and so may an Administrator of the company.

Disadvantages of a company voluntary arrangement are that:

- As there is no Interim Order, the company's assets are vulnerable to actions by creditors in the critical period leading up to the Meetings of Creditors and Shareholders (please see below in respect of small companies and note that at the time of writing the Government is consulting on the possibility of extending the moratorium procedure to all companies).

- The supervisor does not have control of the company's affairs.

- It binds creditors who did not have notice of the meeting, for example, those who may have been overlooked.

There is a CVA procedure available for smaller companies which provides a moratorium but in practice this procedure is hardly used. The use of this procedure means that in the period before the scheme is approved:

- no insolvency proceedings can be commenced;

- no security can be enforced, for example, a Receiver cannot be appointed;

- no assets held in hire purchase agreements can be repossessed;

- no other legal proceedings may be commenced or continued against the company;

- no creditors may enforce their Retention of Title claim.

Administration

INTRODUCTION

Administration is a process that is generally used in situations where there is a benefit over placing a company into liquidation (for example, if a sale of business and assets as a going concern would achieve greater realisations than in a liquidation). Various parties can place a company into Administration. The most common parties are directors and financial institutions (banks, asset-based lenders and so on) that hold Qualifying Floating Charges. These are known as Qualifying Floating Charge Holders (QFCH).

An Administrator must decide which of the three statutory objectives applies to the administration. The objectives are:

- to rescue the company as a going concern;

- to achieve better result for creditors as a whole than a winding up; or

- to realise property to distribute to secured/preferential creditors.

The period of administration is limited to 12 months. However, this is extendable, once by agreement of creditors by a maximum of six months, then by Court depending on the circumstances. The administration may also come to an end if the Administrator thinks the purpose of administration has been achieved or cannot be achieved.

The procedure places the company under the control of an IP and the company obtains the protection of a moratorium; creditors are prevented from taking any actions against the company except with the permission of the Court.

An Administrator may be appointed:

- by an order of the Court. This is by an application to Court by the company, its directors or one or more creditors;

- without a Court Order. This can be made by direct appointment by the company, its directors or a creditor who holds a qualifying floating charge.

A QFCH who is able to make an appointment may also intervene where the company or directors have commenced steps to place the company into administration or if an application has been made to the Court. The QFCH's choice of Administrator will be the one appointed. Should there be a number of QFCHs who have a difference of opinion on the choice of Administrator then the first ranking chargeholder will have the ultimate choice.

On conclusion of an administration:

- the company may be returned to the control of its directors and management (if the company is rescued);

- the company may go into liquidation (if there are funds for distribution to unsecured creditors);

- the company may be dissolved (if there are no funds for distribution to unsecured creditors).

ADMINISTRATION PROCEDURE

A. Out of court appointment by company or directors

- Company must be, or is likely to become, insolvent.

- Notice of intention to appoint Administrators filed in Court. Five working days notice has to be given to a QFCH who is able to appoint an Administrator.

- Notice of Appointment is filed in Court together with statement by Administrator that the purpose of administration is reasonably likely to be achieved.

B. Out of court appointment by qualifying floating chargeholder

- Company does not need to be insolvent.

- Floating Charge must contain provisions enabling the appointment of Administrator.

- Notice of intention to appoint Administrators filed in Court. Two working days notice has to be given to any prior ranking QFCH who is able to appoint an Administrator.

- Notice of Appointment is filed in Court together with statement by Administrator that the purpose of administration is reasonably likely to be achieved.

C. Application to court

- Company must be, or is likely to become, insolvent.

- Application to the Court is presented by company, directors, creditors or Liquidator.

- Supporting statement and report is to be prepared by proposed Administrator that the purpose of administration is reasonably likely to be achieved.

- Notice of Court hearing is to be given to QFCH who is able to appoint an alternative Administrator

STATUS AND DUTIES OF AN ADMINISTRATOR

The Administrator acts as an officer of the Court and must be a qualified IP. The Administrator has a duty to all creditors regardless of who appointed him, must perform his functions with one of the three statutory objectives in mind and must perform his functions as quickly and efficiently as possible.

The Administrator takes custody and control of all property of which company is entitled and manages the affairs, business and property of the company in accordance with the proposals. The Administrator's powers are very broad and include the powers to trade on the company's business and realise its assets.

The Administrator has a duty to submit a report on the conduct of the directors.

The Administrator must advertise and publicise his appointment.

He must set out his proposals and call a meeting of creditors to consider proposals unless it is unlikely that unsecured creditors will receive a dividend. The proposals of the Administrators must be sent out within eight weeks of appointment and a meeting of creditors must be held within 10 weeks of appointment to approve such proposals.

Pre-packs

WHAT IS A PRE-PACK?

A pre-pack is an agreement for the sale of an insolvent company's business and assets which has been agreed prior to a company being placed into a formal insolvency process, usually administration, and completed immediately on appointment of the IP.

They are often used to sell insolvent businesses where commercial pressures require urgent action (for example, wages require to be paid, pending winding up petition that could cease the trading of the business and so on).

R3 commissioned detailed research into pre-packs, and preliminary investigations found the following:

BENEFITS OF A PRE-PACK

- Preservation of jobs.

- Better returns to secured creditors.

- Retention in value in the company.

CRITICISMS OF A PRE-PACK

- Failure to put the business on the open market.

- Insufficient transparency in the procedure.

- Sale of the business back to connected parties.

In January 2009, SIP 16 was implemented which is essentially a 'code of conduct' that IP's must apply when involved in pre-pack insolvencies. SIP 16 is aimed at dealing with the criticisms of a pre-pack.

Receivership

ADMINISTRATIVE RECEIVERSHIP

Receivership can arise only where there is a floating charge (usually termed a debenture) on the company's assets. Under the provisions of the Enterprise Act 2002, holders of debentures and floating charges created after 15 September 2003 are not permitted to appoint an Administrative Receiver.

A debenture holder would appoint an Administrative Receiver if there has been a breach of the terms of the charge or loan agreement.

The Administrative Receiver's primary duty of care is to the debenture holder. The primary task is to take control of the assets, assess the state of the business, and pursue the optimum method of disposal.

The Administrative Receiver has the power to continue the business, and will usually do so, at least in the short term, with a view to selling the business as a going concern.

An Administrative Receiver must prepare a report to be presented to the unsecured creditors of the company at a meeting within three months of his appointment. A typical report would include information such as:

- the strategy for the disposal of the assets/business;

- the amount due to the debenture holder; and

- the amount (if any) likely to be available to other creditors.

If there are surplus funds available after satisfying the preferential creditors and the debenture holder, the Administrative Receiver passes them to the company, or if the company is in liquidation, to the Liquidator. The Receiver cannot agree the claims of unsecured creditors or pay a dividend directly to them and this must be done by a Liquidator.

On completion of the receivership, the Administrative Receiver files a notice of ceasing to act with the Registrar of Companies, and the company, or if it is in liquidation, the Liquidator.

Law Of Property Act/Fixed Charge Receivers

A Receiver may be appointed under a fixed charge, such as a charge on a property. Such Receivers are usually known as Law of Property Act (LPA) Receivers, and their powers are normally limited to the collection of rents, the management of the charged property, and its sale. Such a Receiver is not obliged to notify creditors of his appointment, nor to pay the preferential creditors.

Liquidations

There are a number of reasons that can lead to a company being placed into liquidation. In many situations there is no prospect of selling a business as a going concern, for example, if the business has ceased prior to an IP being approached or is not seen as viable under current economic conditions.

Once in liquidation, the role of the Liquidator is to realise the assets of the company and to distribute the realisations to the creditors, in a defined order of priority. Liquidation is normally a terminal process for a company and it will ultimately be dissolved and removed from the companies register.

An insolvent liquidation will be either a compulsory liquidation which is instituted by petition to the Court, or a CVL, which is initiated by the directors of a company at a board meeting.

COMPULSORY LIQUIDATION

A compulsory liquidation (also known as a compulsory winding up) is a liquidation which is dealt with by the Court. Various parties can petition for a winding up but it is usually on the petition of a creditor, the company or a shareholder. There are a various reasons for making a Winding up Order but the most common is because the company has been proven to be insolvent.

Insolvency is usually determined in two ways being:

- failure to comply with a statutory demand requiring payment within 21 days; or

- by an execution against the company's goods which remains unsatisfied (for example, where a creditor obtains judgement against the company which is not paid).

If it is considered by any interested party that the assets of the company are in jeopardy, an urgent application can be made to the Court to appoint a provisional Liquidator pending the hearing of the petition. The duty of the provisional Liquidator is restricted to that of the Court Order which appoints him. If the provisional Liquidator requires any expertise to perform his role the Court may also appoint a special manager.

Once a Winding Up Order has been made and the company is in liquidation, the matter is referred by the Court to the OR.

The process is similar to that of bankruptcy and, should there be assets in the matter that are likely to cover the costs of liquidation, the OR will usually call a creditors' meeting to appoint a Liquidator. Alternatively, the OR may, using powers delegated to him by the Secretary of State for BIS, appoint a professional Liquidator without calling a meeting. If he does not call a meeting or if there is no Secretary of State appointment the OR will remain in office and deal with the liquidation himself although this is fairly unusual.

The OR retains responsibility for investigating the conduct of directors and performs any other investigation work required. He examines the directors privately, and calls upon them to submit a statement of affairs. The OR reports to BIS as to whether any of the directors should be disqualified from acting in the management of companies.

A Winding Up Order does not prevent a secured creditor dealing with the charged asset(s). In particular, it would not prevent the holder of a debenture appointing an Administrative Receiver.

The Liquidator may disclaim any onerous assets (for example, unprofitable contracts or leases).

The Liquidator can investigate and reverse certain transaction. These include preference transactions and TUV which are referred to above in the bankruptcy section.

There are provisions in the Insolvency Act 1986 under which the Liquidator can void a floating charge created within 12 months of the commencement of winding up. The charge will be void unless the company was solvent at the time the charge was created or if the consideration for the charge was cash, goods or services supplied to the company at the time of or after the creation of the charge.

There are also provisions in the Insolvency Act 1986 which allow the Liquidator to pursue the directors of a company if they have continued to trade when they ought not to have done. Wrongful trading exists where a director knew, or ought to have concluded, that there was no reasonable prospect of the company avoiding insolvent liquidation, and failed to take the necessary steps to minimise the potential loss to creditors. If proved, the director will be ordered to make a contribution to the company's assets.

Fraudulent trading exists where the business of the company was carried on with the intent of defrauding creditors or any other person. Finally, a Liquidator can pursue a director for misfeasance. He must be able to show that the director misapplied, retained or has become accountable for any money or property of the company or has breached his duties to the company. If the Liquidator is successful in such an action the director is likely to be ordered to return the money or property or make a contribution to the company's assets.

PROCEDURE FOR COMPULSORY LIQUIDATION

The Petition is presented by a creditor on grounds of insolvency. It may also be presented by the company itself or the shareholders.

The Petition is required to be advertised in the *London Gazette*.

A Winding Up Order is made by the Court.

The OR becomes Liquidator by virtue of the Winding Up Order. The OR has a duty to investigate the company's affairs and send a report to the creditors. The OR advertises the Winding Up Order in the *London Gazette*.

A Creditors' meeting is convened by the OR within four months of the Winding Up Order being made. A Liquidator is appointed by a simple majority, in value, of the creditors. A creditors committee may also be formed at the meeting.

DUTIES OF LIQUIDATOR

The duties of the Liquidator are:

- to realise assets;

- to agree creditors' claims and distribute funds by way of dividend;

- to call a final meeting of creditors to account to the creditors and report of the liquidation.

Costs and Distribution of Funds

Preferential creditors include employees' claims for:

1. wages and salaries earned in the four months preceding the Winding Up Order, subject to a maximum of £800 per person;

2. all accrued holiday pay;

3. advances by banks (or others) which have been used to pay wages, salaries or holiday pay and have served to reduce claims which employees might otherwise have been able to make defined in 1 or 2 above.

Employees' claims are paid out (in whole or in part) by the Government RPO and the RPO takes the employees standing as a preferential creditor for the amounts that it has paid to the employee. If there are sums over and above the payment that the employee receives from the RPO he/she can claim for them by submitting a proof of debt in the liquidation.

UNSECURED CREDITORS

Creditors must submit their claims by way of proof of debt. The Liquidator examines the proofs by comparison with the statement of affairs and the company's books. He may demand further evidence of the debt if in doubt. The admitted proofs are lodged with the Court.

Unsecured creditors share *pari passu* in the surplus after providing for the costs of winding up and preferential claims.

DISTRIBUTION OF FUNDS

Costs – The Liquidator should pay the costs of winding up. These would include the costs of the petition, OR's charges and so on and should be paid as soon as possible. The Liquidator's remuneration is fixed by the liquidation committee (also known as the creditors committee). In the absence of a committee, the Liquidator must call a meeting of creditors to fix the remuneration. If this fails, he is paid on the OR's scale, or he may apply to the Court to fix his remuneration.

Preferential creditors – If there are insufficient funds to pay all preferential creditors in full, their claims rank equally. If there are sufficient funds, the Liquidator should pay preferential claims at the earliest opportunity

Unsecured creditors – Distributions to unsecured creditors are made by way of a dividend on the amount of the admitted claims. If circumstances permit, interim dividends may be paid, with a final dividend on the closing of the liquidation.

Contributories – If a surplus remains after paying all the creditors in full with statutory interest, it is distributed to the contributories in accordance with their shareholdings and their rights.

Creditors' Voluntary Liquidation

CVL is a liquidation initiated by a resolution of the shareholders, but is under the control of the creditors, who can appoint a Liquidator of their choice.

CVL is the most common way for directors and shareholders to deal voluntarily with the company's insolvency. It is in the interests of the directors to take action at an early stage, in order to minimise the risk of personal liability for wrongful trading.

In addition, unlike a compulsory liquidation, a CVL does not bring the directors' conduct under the scrutiny of the OR, although the Liquidator is required to report to BIS on the conduct of the directors.

Once the liquidation is complete the Liquidator calls a final meeting of creditors to account to the creditors and provide a report of the liquidation

Procedure for Creditors' Voluntary Liquidation

DIRECTORS CONSULT A LICENSED IP BOARD MEETING

The initiative for a CVL comes from the directors of the insolvent company. Once it has become apparent to them that the company must go into CVL, a board meeting should be held at which the decision is made to issue notices of meetings of shareholders and creditors necessary to place the company into liquidation.

The creditors' meeting is normally held immediately after the shareholders' meeting but it can be held up to 14 days after. A notice must be sent to each creditor of a meeting to be held under Section 98 of the Insolvency Act 1986. The notice should state that the purpose of the meeting is to consider the appointment of a Liquidator and liquidation committee. Forms of proxy must be attached to the notice for the creditors to complete. The notice to creditors must state the name and address of the IP intended to be appointed as Liquidator who must give creditors such information concerning the company as they may reasonably require prior to the meeting. Alternatively, the notice must state a place in the relevant locality where, on the two business days immediately preceding the creditors' meeting, a list of the names and addresses of the creditors will be available for inspection free of charge. Notice of the meeting of creditors must be advertised in the *London Gazette* and the company may give notice in such other manner as the directors think fit.

SHAREHOLDERS' MEETING

At the meeting of shareholders a special resolution is passed which places the company into CVL, and appoints a Liquidator. To pass a special resolution, 14 days notice of the shareholders is to be provided to the members. However, 90 per cent of the shareholders can agree to short notice if required. Five days' notice of the shareholders meeting is required to be given to any QFCH who is able to appoint an Administrator.

STATEMENT OF AFFAIRS

Section 99 of the Insolvency Act 1986 requires the directors to present to the creditors' meeting a statement of the company's affairs and a list of the creditors. The statement of affairs is a sworn document and must be available for inspection at the meeting, but it is usual to issue a summary of it within the report which is distributed at the creditors' meeting. The statement of affairs would normally be prepared on the directors' behalf by an IP or advising accountant, who would also draft the report to be presented to the creditors on the history of the company and the causes of failure. However, the report and the information contained in it remains the responsibility of the directors.

CREDITORS' MEETING

A Statement of Affairs and report on the history of the business and causes of its failure is presented to the meeting. One of the directors acts as chairman of the meeting, but the advising IP usually reads the report to creditors and comments on the statement of affairs. The chairman should invite creditors' questions before proceeding to the formal business of the meeting. Such questions often elicit information regarding the assets and the affairs of the company which is useful to the Liquidator.

Creditors are invited to vote on the appointment of a Liquidator. They may replace the shareholders' nominee. Creditors must achieve a majority in value on the resolution. If the creditors fail to pass any resolution, the shareholders' nominee stands. The creditors can also appoint a liquidation committee, comprising not less than three and not more than five members. Creditors wishing to vote at the meeting must lodge a proxy unless the creditor is an individual or a partner in a partnership. Creditors should also submit a statement of claim prior to the meeting.

DUTIES OF LIQUIDATOR

The Liquidator (who must be an IP) must file notice of the appointment with the Registrar of Companies. The appointment must also be advertised in the *London Gazette* and the Liquidator may publicise his appointment in such other manner as he sees fit. In addition, the Liquidator reports the appointment in writing to all creditors, inviting them to submit their claims and enclosing a summary of the statement of affairs; the report also goes to contributories. The Liquidator should also publish an advertisement for creditors to make their claims in the liquidation in the *London Gazette*.

If the Liquidator discovers evidence of fraud or any other offences having been committed, a report must be sent to the Director of Public Prosecutions. The Liquidator must also send a report in every case to BIS under the Company Directors Disqualification Act 1986 and provide any evidence of a director's misconduct.

The Liquidator should investigate whether any of the directors has been guilty of wrongful or fraudulent trading (see above), and if so, should take the appropriate action.

On the completion of the Liquidator's administration, final meetings of the creditors and shareholders are convened at which a summary of the Liquidator's acts and dealings is presented. The Liquidator makes a final return to the Registrar of Companies, who in due course strikes the company off the register.

REALISATION OF ASSETS

The Liquidator realises the assets in very much the same way as a Liquidator in a compulsory liquidation, except that generally he has more flexibility.

The Liquidator must examine the validity of any charges on assets and will investigate any preferences or transactions at an undervalue. The Liquidator consults the committee as in a compulsory liquidation, but does not need the committee's authority to carry on the business or take legal proceedings in the name of and on behalf of the company. It should be noted, however, that in respect of certain claims he does require the committee's authority to bring proceedings as Liquidator of the company.

CREDITORS' CLAIMS

The Liquidator examines the creditors' claims and decides on their admissibility. The rules relating to the ranking/priority of various claims is the same as in compulsory liquidation.

DISTRIBUTION OF FUNDS

Preferential creditors should be paid as soon as sufficient funds are available, providing that enough money is retained to cover the costs of the liquidation. Unsecured creditors are paid by way of dividend on the amounts of the admitted claims. Interim dividends may be paid where circumstances permit. Should there be a surplus after paying the creditors in full, statutory interest is payable on the creditors' claims; any money then left over is distributed to the shareholders.

FINAL MEETING

Once the liquidation is complete and the Liquidator has fulfilled all of his duties, the Liquidator calls a final meeting of creditors to account to the creditors and provide a report of the liquidation.

PART X
Credit Services

24

Invoice Financing

T Glyndwr Powell[1]

• What's the difference between factoring and invoice discounting? • How does invoice financing work? • How does factoring work? • How does invoice discounting vary from factoring? • When to use factoring • Points to be aware of when considering invoice financing • Choosing a factor • Sources of information •

Many businesses are turning to factoring as a method of improving cash flow problems or to outsource the task of credit control from start-up to maturity. Factoring, and its sister method, invoice discounting (known together as invoice financing), are ways of borrowing money against a Sales Ledger, and as more businesses realise the value of this service, so the industry is growing. At the end of 2007, the market in the UK was over £192 billion (Source: ABLA).

What's the Difference Between Factoring and Invoice Discounting?

The main difference is who collects the money from the Sales Ledger. With a factoring arrangement, the factor collects it, and so customers know that their supplier is using a factor. With invoice discounting, the supplier collects the money, and so customers are unaware that money has been borrowed against the Sales Ledger. Therefore, invoice discounting is often referred to as a 'confidential' service. Factoring costs a little more than invoice discounting, reflecting the more intensive service provided, but will almost certainly be more cost-effective than employing Sales Ledger and credit control staff. It may also be an effective way of counteracting the bullying tactics of big businesses over timely payment! Another difference is in the size of turnover required. Some factors will accept a turnover of as little as £50,000 a year, but for invoice discounting it needs to be at least £250,000.

---

1   With acknowledgement to Ted Ettershank for original work in 5th edition.

How does Invoice Financing Work?

In simple terms, the factor and the client enter into an agreement which will usually be for a minimum specified length of time, typically 12 months, but sometimes as short as three. The factor will charge a fee for handling the facility, and interest on the money lent on the security of the invoices.

The deal may be 'without recourse', where the factor accepts the credit risk, or 'with recourse', where the seller retains the credit risk. In certain situations, such as exceptionally large value invoices, the factor may require credit insurance, which will provide funds to reimburse them if they are unable to collect. Factors providing finance on a 'non-recourse' basis are usually quite selective about the type of clients they will accept. If the business comes into one of their high-risk categories they may offer a smaller initial advance against invoices.

Factors will accept export Sales Ledgers as well as domestic ones, and this can help where the culture of payment can be very different from that of the UK. Although most foreign customers have someone who can speak good English, it is quite likely that their accounting staff may not. Factors specialising in export finance have their own multilingual staff and many actually have an associate with an office in the debtors' countries to help collect troublesome accounts.

Generally, invoice financiers prefer a business to have a big spread of customers, but there are some that will fund single debtor Sales Ledgers at a lower advance percentage. If a big order is expected which will put a high proportion of a sales Ledger with one customer, a factor will expect advance warning to ensure the customer is creditworthy and provide guidance on the level of funding to expect on that invoice.

How does Factoring Work?

The seller sends its customer an invoice for sales or completed work. The factor has a legal assignment of the Sales Ledger debt; and this fact must be stated on the invoices, normally by attaching a sticker.

Copy invoices are sent to the factor (usually in batches of an agreed size or value, or at regular intervals such as one week) electronically or by post.

The factor pays a percentage of the total value of the invoices. This will be up to 90 per cent, and is paid either as soon as the invoices are received or at a date agreed with the seller.

The factor can help run the Sales Ledger, issuing statements, collecting payments and chasing slow payers if necessary, using methods agreed at the outset.

The factor pays the balance of the invoice totals, less the agreed charges, when customers pay. The charges consist of a service fee and an interest charge on the funds advanced. The fees are negotiated for each seller. Where there are existing unpaid invoices when factoring starts, the factor will take over the Sales Ledger and advance an agreed percentage on 'qualifying' debts, that is, those which are not in the 'problem' category.

How does Invoice Discounting Vary from Factoring?

The procedure is very similar to factoring, except that:

- The business sends a sales listing to the discounter, instead of copy invoices.

- The discounter pays a percentage of the invoice value to the seller.

- The seller runs its own Sales Ledger, issuing statements, collecting payments and chasing slow payers if necessary.

The seller may have to demonstrate its ability to run the Sales Ledger in a way that satisfies the discounter. Some invoice discounters only accept limited companies as clients, and insist on securing the debt by taking a debenture. This may restrict the seller's level of borrowing from its bank. A debenture will also give the discounter the right to appoint an Administrator, if necessary.

The client pays the money it collects into an agreed special bank account, a 'trust account', and notifies the discounter. The discounter then pays the balance of the invoice totals, less the agreed charges. These consist of a service fee; a percentage of annual turnover and an interest charge on the funds advanced.

In both factoring and invoice discounting, customer disputes or returned goods are dealt with in the normal way: the seller sorts out the problems and issues credit notes which are then notified to the factoring company or invoice discounter.

When to Use Factoring

The main benefit of factoring is the speeding up of cash flow available to help businesses bring their business plans to fruition.

In addition, the fewer management people a seller has, the more important it is for them to concentrate on other aspects of the business than collecting funds from customers. If the business is very small it may be preferable to have the Sales Ledger task carried out by a factor, taking advantage of their professional expertise, rather than employing more staff in the business.

Points to be Aware of When Considering Invoice Financing

Before making the decision on whether to go down the invoice financing route, a seller should:

- ensure it gives them extra flexibility;

- decide if it provides a greater finance facility compared to an overdraft;

- decide if the peaks and troughs of sales provide enough cash to pay suppliers and overheads;

- consider the cost of the annual minimum fee;

- consider the length of the commitment period;

- study the small print on the agreement.

Care should be taken when comparing contract lengths and notice periods, as these can vary dramatically and will have an impact on when the facility can be terminated.

Some small businesses worry that using a factor might lead to a loss of contact with their customers. In this case, they should choose a factor with a flexible approach to customer handling, which allows a seller to set the terms on which they deal with each customer.

Choosing a Factor

The governing body is the Asset Based Finance Association (ABFA) formerly known as the Factors and Discounters Association (FDA). A full listing of members can be found at www.factors.org.uk. Not all factors or discounters are members of the ABFA. As the Association has a rigorous code of practice for members, it ensures a potentially more equitable deal for customers. That is not to say organisations who are not members do not have products of similar standing, but the usual rule of caveat emptor applies.

The decision as to which organisation to use will be determined by the level of flexibility required, the size of the facility and the charges. Many smaller, independent discounters are more flexible albeit they may be more costly. Similarly they may have more generous terms regards concentration (the percentage any one debtor represents) and advance rates.

Sources of Information

Finance and Leasing Association 2nd Floor, Imperial House, 15–19 Kingsway, London, WC2B 6UN. Tel: 020 7836 6511, Fax: 020 7420 9600, Email: info@fl a.org.uk, Website: www.fla.org.uk

Asset Based Finance Association (ABFA) Boston House, The Little Green, Richmond, Surrey, TW9 1QE. Tel: 020 8332 9955, Fax: 020 8332 2585, Website: www.abfa.org.uk

25

Credit Cards

Peter C Coupe FICM
Proprietor, PCC Management Consultants[1]

• Introduction • What are credit cards? • Early development in the USA • UK market development • Credit card spending and borrowing • The cost of credit • The cost of payments • The cost of promoting cards • Fraud and bad debt • Chips and electronic purse •

Introduction

Plastic cards, which provide a payment system and access to credit facilities, now dominate UK consumer spending. They were developed in the USA and, in today's fast-moving, highly technological, 'instant' society, have contributed substantially to a major change to our payment and purchasing habits. Many banks, financial organisations, large retail groups, national institutions and so on, insist on providing their customers and members with their own 'branded' cards for purchasing goods or services, whether it be for settlement immediately or sometime in the future.

The public, the customer, the consumer, the buyer, the borrower all appear to view them, in whatever form, as an accepted and convenient method of settlement for purchases. Their development continues, as does the increase in their usage.

From a relatively straightforward beginning over 40 years ago and a steady expansion of business, dominated by two main bank groups, the humble

---

1   With acknowledgement to previous contributions by AF Cook and to data from the UK Cards Association – the successor body to the APACS Card Payments Group, and CIFAS – the UK fraud prevention service.

'plastic' has grown substantially. In the last five to ten years, there has been an explosion of issuers, of changes in use, changes in operating systems, with changes in costs. The market is now very competitive and it is difficult to foresee its shape in, say, five years' time. Some features such as ever-increasing electronic processing rather than paper transfer, wide variations in interest charges, subscriptions and discounts, will certainly be seen, but who will be providing the cards is much less certain.

In order to understand this volatility with its underlying systems of suppliers and customers, it will be useful to examine what exactly is a credit card, how operations started in the UK, what the traditional framework and organisation has been, as regards the suppliers, their methods of working and funding and to consider the more predictable trends of the future.

What are Credit Cards?

A credit card, or more particularly a credit token, is defined in the Consumer Credit Act 1974 as: 'A card, check, voucher, coupon, stamp, form, booklet or other document or thing.'

This merely defines the object itself – it does not describe how it is used or the variety of uses to which it can now be put. The plastic card is an object which provides first, a means of verification, second, a means of transferring value from a seller to a buyer, and third, use of a credit facility which has already been agreed by, more often than not, a third-party financial institution. The dominant features of these cards concern these primary functions of money transmission and short-term credit. The money transmission can be paper based or electronic through data capture transmission; the credit may be either short term with full settlement at the end of, say, monthly accounting periods (charge cards) or it can extend over longer periods (credit cards).

Essentially, credit cards are personal customer instruments but some organisations allow the use of cards by individual company employees to facilitate necessary payment, for example, travel, petrol and so on. The Visa, MasterCard, American Express and Diners' Club cards have traditionally dominated the market. With cards issued by these organisations, money transmission has always played a very important part. Many bank cardholders do pay their balances in full at the end of the month, effectively using their credit card as a convenient means of payment as opposed to a means of credit.

Credit and payment cards are offered to a very wide, but by no means homogeneous, consumer market by a very wide range of institutions. There are also a wide variety of cards on the market:

- *Credit cards.* Credit cards offer revolving credit: cardholders can repay outstanding balances and incur new borrowing every month without the need to arrange a fresh agreement with their issuers, provided they stay within the specified credit limit and at least meet the regular contracted minimum monthly payments.

- *Charge cards.* Holders of charge cards are sent a monthly statement in the same way as those with a credit card. The difference is that charge card accounts must be cleared in full each month, although some cards entitle the holder to a separate overdraft facility. Charge cards generally have higher fees than most credit cards but no preset spending limit. They may offer additional benefits such as priority bookings on tickets, free travel insurance and so on. Some banks issue charge cards, as do Diners' Club and American Express.

- *Affinity cards.* These are branded credit cards, which allow cardholders to donate money to the organisation or charity specified on the card (and to which the cardholder has an affinity). Issuers make a donation, typically £5, to the organisation or charity when the account is opened. Each time goods or services are purchased with an affinity card, money is donated by the issuer to the cause to which it is linked, normally 20p or 25p per £100 spent. Other than this link with organisations, affinity cards work in the same way as a normal credit card.

- *Co-branded cards.* These are a type of credit card issued jointly by an issuer and a non-financial institution, which has a well-known name. The non-financial institution offers certain benefits to cardholders, normally using a point system. Once cardholders have collected the required number of points on their co-branded card, they are entitled to the benefits on offer.

- *Company cards.* Company cards (sometimes called business cards) are credit or charge cards which are issued to companies for use by chosen members of staff to eliminate the need for large amounts of petty cash. These cards are accepted everywhere standard credit cards are accepted. As well as individual statements being sent to cardholders, a statement is sent to the company detailing all transactions made. Company cards offer the facility to control and analyse business expenditure.

- *Gold or Platinum cards.* These 'prestigious' cards can be either credit or charge cards and are usually issued to wealthier customers. They often have a higher credit limit than normal credit cards. This type of card may also have a higher annual fee than credit cards and are usually linked to an automatic overdraft at preferential rates. They often have a wide range of benefits such as priority bookings with airlines, travel insurance and so on.

- *Store cards.* Store cards are normally issued by a third-party financial institution on behalf of an individual retailer and branded with that retailer's logo. They are normally only accepted by that company, for example, the department store, retail chain and so on, on whose behalf they are branded and issued. Occasionally, the card can be issued on behalf of a group of retailers, that is, a trade association, and accepted by all its members. All transactions are between the issuer and the cardholder, with the retailer acting as broker and merchant. There are three types of store cards: budget cards, charge cards and standard 'option' credit cards. Store cards can be used to make payments and to obtain credit.

- *Others.* In addition to the above 'credit tokens', there are a number of other forms of plastic card that perform various functions and are in common use today. These focus on 'convenience, automation and ease of use' but most do not provide credit or any form of delayed payment option.

The most common of these is the ATM 'cashpoint' card that facilitates access via a 'hole in the wall' machine to funds held in the holder's account. At the issuer's discretion, a limited 'agreed' overdrawn limit might be available, but in other circumstances, any attempt to withdraw monies from an account with insufficient funds to cover the transaction, will result in the card being withheld by the machine.

Another popular card in use is the multi-function card that will combine ATM access, the 'cheque guarantee' function up to £50 or £100 (or occasionally more for prestigious accounts) and the debit card facility. This latter development has rapidly gained popularity with its users as a means of immediate automated cash transmission payment at the point of sale without the risk of having to carry cash. They also avoid the inconvenience of having to write out a cheque and resist the temptation of building up a 'buy now pay later' credit card balance.

Chip cards are now also in every day use. The initial popularity of these cards was brought about by the proliferation of the 'pay as you go' mobile phone and enabled the younger consumer (without normal access to automated cash transmission facilities) to pay for an amount to be credited to their phone. Again, this substantially reduced the administration normally associated with this type of transaction by automating the transmission. These types of cards can facilitate any transaction that might require 'prepayment'.

Early Development in the USA

The true credit card was developed in the USA after the Second World War and many organisations contributed to individual developments. The most important individual component was the development of the sales draft – a voucher created at the point of purchase, which would later be honoured by a credit organisation, reimbursing the shop and charging the purchaser, requiring him to repay at the regular contracted intervals. Such a system could be used by banks as a means of providing short-term credit for their customers and by the travel and entertainment card organisations such as Diners' Club and later American Express and Carte Blanche whose facilities usually required full monthly settlement.

The travel and entertainment cards in particular provided an essential money transmission service in the USA where the unit banking system could make non-cash purchases outside the immediate locality difficult. Obviously the main users initially were those who required travel facilities and hotels and meals, particularly the more affluent traveller needing control of business expenses. This market is still dominated by the American travel and entertainment cards, both in North America and throughout the world.

The American banks recognised the need to satisfy private credit purchasing particularly for consumer durables. Many banks entered the field in the late 1950s and early 1960s but there was no coordination for widespread acceptance, too many individual issuers, over-generous individual credit and no clear understanding of interest rates being charged.

Though many banks had ceased to issue cards, by the early 1960s the elements for success were present in a system created by the Bank of America in California. They identified success based on economies of scale, a proper monthly interest charge to the cardholder, and a discount on the value of the transaction paid in by the shopkeeper or merchant. This system was licensed to other banks in the USA and in 1966 to Barclays Bank in the UK. This licensing has progressively developed into the international bank card system now known as Visa International and a very wide range of financial and non-financial institutions are members. At the same time as the Bank of America technique became popular, competitor banks formed a rather looser organisation first called Mastercharge (under the Access logo) and now MasterCard.

Other retail organisations, especially department stores, have always offered credit; they have accepted the travel and entertainment and bank credit cards from the earliest times but they have invariably remodelled their in-house systems on the lines of the main cards. Nearly all department store credit accounts are operated by plastic cards; either creating paper sales vouchers or electronic data capture in-store with monthly billings to customers, both for charge account settlement and for extended credit.

An increasing number of organisations with many members, such as motoring clubs, national institutions, associations, sporting organisations and political parties, now offer credit card facilities to their large mailing lists. They are usually based on the main card systems and are normally styled affinity cards.

Plastic cards are popular for identification of preferred customer purposes rather than specifically for credit. Airlines, railways, hotel groups and hire car firms are examples of these courtesy cards where credit is available but the greater emphasis is on obtaining customer loyalty, repeat business and preferred bookings.

The boundaries between these types of cards are becoming blurred. In recent years there have been further developments of plastic cards allowing debits to ordinary bank current accounts, banks and others issuing budget account cards in which monthly repayment is a fixed amount and the credit limit a multiplier of this, stores offering cash withdrawal facilities as well as specific purchasing and all are funded and administered by the widest range of institutions. Supermarkets lead the way as they clearly recognise the vast financial savings that can be made with automated transaction processing and the major importance of customer 'loyalty'. Rewarding spending volume by issuing 'points' via cards has become another process where automation and marketing work well together. In addition, technology has allowed the introduction of enhancements for the 'convenience' minded consumer, for example, staff-free checkouts, automated payment at petrol stations and so on.

UK Market Development

Credit cards were introduced into the UK in the mid-1960s, by the Bank of America (BankAmericard). Diners' Club and American Express introduced charge cards. The first British bank to launch credit cards in the UK was Barclays Bank, which began issuing Barclaycard, linked to BankAmericard (now Visa), in 1966.

The other credit card scheme that emerged in the UK alongside Visa was Access. These days all Access cards carry the MasterCard symbol, allowing them to be used throughout the world.

Later, MasterCard and the owners of the Access brand – known then as Midland, Lloyds Bank, NatWest and the Royal Bank of Scotland – agreed to phase out the Access logo.

The card issuing and merchant network, however, is no longer the prerogative of the main clearing banks. Financial institutions, such as building societies (many of whom are now banks themselves) who service the personal consumer market, or the general retail sector via third-party processors, offer their customers credit cards and in many cases a modern money transmission and payment method based on electronic data capture and processing through magnetic stripes on the back of the cards themselves.

The UK credit card market is a mature market, which is still expanding at a considerable pace. There are a substantial number of individual financial institutions issuing cards although the UK credit card market is dominated by five major high street banks – Barclays, Royal Bank of Scotland, LloydsTSB, HBoS and MBNA who together issue two-thirds of the cards in the UK, although their cumulative share is shrinking as a result of competition in the market. This has been brought about in part by incentives to consumers to consolidate card balances and to attract customers from competitors. The UK market for credit cards, while mature, represents an attractive opportunity for new entrants, due in part to the high level of card literacy of British consumers.

Greater competition resulted in the expansion of the market with turnover showing double-digit growth in recent years despite the overall slowing down of the global economy.

Distinguishing between travel and entertainment (T&E cards), bank cards and retail cards provides a way to analyse the markets that they service and customers they attract. T&E cards and corporate cards generally service executive travel and accommodation needs.

Standard bank cards are intended for more universal consumption to be used in the widest range of retail and service purchasing, characterised originally by high street shops as well as hotels, restaurants and petrol stations. However, their range is now much greater and includes subscriptions, public utility bills, Internet, mail order, travel, professional and personal services.

Store cards have a more sharply focused market. The provision of credit is an important part of all retail stores to encourage consumer purchases and loyalty. A substantial part of store turnover is now paid for by credit, which is usually dominated by in-house cards and in-house credit arrangements, as well as international credit cards.

Banks' current account customers and building societies' active account customers are the main basis for bank and financial house credit cards. Each card has an assumed domestic base from which to market its operation with fairly easy mailing sources but it has to rely on more general marketing and advertising to attract other customers. These customers are mainly ABC1s and with assured salaries or income.

Credit Card Spending and Borrowing

Spending on credit cards rose from just over £10bn in 1985, to £41bn in 1995, then up to £81bn in 2002 and then to £102bn in 2007 (the latest figures available prior to publication). This growth is even more impressive if we consider that the number of credit cards in issue stabilised since 1990 and only in 1995 grew back to the levels of 1990. Spending in 2007 using all types of cards, currently stands at £339bn (see Figure 25.1 below).

	All		Credit card		Charge card		Debit card	
	£ billion	% change	£ billion	% change	£ billion	% change	£ billion	% change
1997	96,5		45,6		5,8		45,1	
1998	111,4	15.4%	51,1	11.9%	6,7	13.8%	53,7	19.2%
1999	132,4	18.8%	59,8	17.1%	8,0	19.8%	64,7	20.3%
2000	151,6	14.5%	66,1	10.6%	9,5	18.7%	76,0	17.5%
2001	177,9	17.4%	71,6	8.3%	11,3	20.0%	94,9	24.9%
2002	200,5	12.7%	81,1	13.2%	11,5	1.5%	107,8	13.6%
2003	234,0	16.7%	91,4	12.7%	12,2	5.8%	130,5	21.0%
2004	263,1	12.4%	99,4	8.8%	13,5	10.9%	150,2	15.1%
2005	284,9	8.3%	99,6	0.1%	14,7	8.6%	170,7	13.7%
2006	308,5	8.3%	97,9	-1.6%	15,7	7.3%	194,9	14.2%
2007	339,0	9.9%	102,1	4.2%	16,2	3.0%	220,8	13.3%

Figure 25.1   Purchases value (£ billion) and percentage annual change
Source: The UK Cards Association

Charge cards are currently within a static market of around 5–6 per cent of the total spend on all cards (see Figure 25.2) and credit cards, once the most popular method of payment, have seen a decline proportionally (-17 per cent). Debit cards are now the most popular method of payment, growing from 47 per cent (1997) to 65 per cent (2007).

Spending on credit cards has remained stable at around £100 billion over the last four years. Charge card spending is low proportionally, though debit card spending continues to grow (by at least 13 per cent annually), and currently stands at £221 billion of purchases (2007).

Spending with credit cards is consistently spread across the 11 sectors. Whereas, with debit cards, the largest proportion of expenditure by far in 2007 was food and drink, representing 21.7 per cent. The lowest proportion for debit cards was hotel bookings 1.0 per cent (see Figures 25.5 and 25.6).

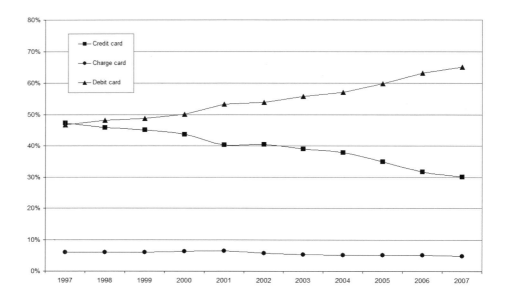

Figure 25.2　Proportion of UK expenditure, by payment method

Source: The UK Cards Association

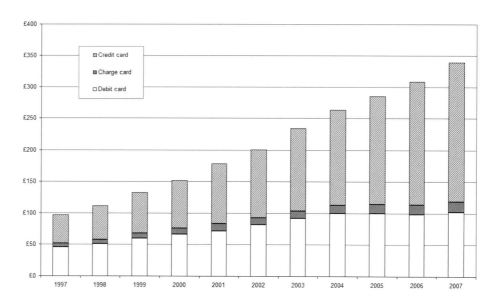

Figure 25.3　Value of purchases, by card type (£ billion)

Source: The UK Cards Association

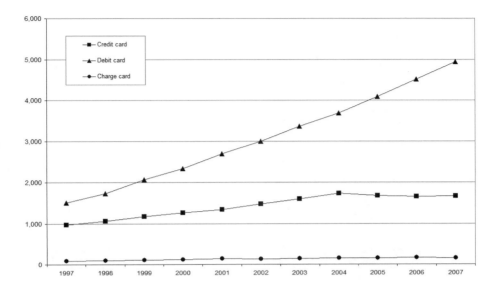

Figure 25.4   Purchases in the UK (volume in millions)

*Sour*ce: The UK Cards Association

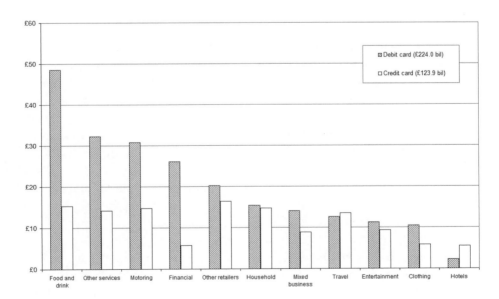

Figure 25.5   Debit and credit card expenditure by merchant sector (2007) – £billion

Source: The UK Cards Association

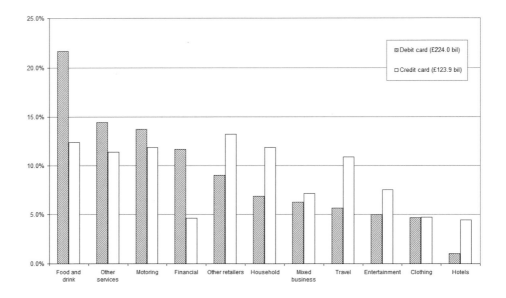

**Figure 25.6   Debit and credit card expenditure by merchant sector (2007)
– %**

Source: The UK Cards Association

Debit cards represented £224 billion worth of expenditure in 2007, whilst credit cards represented £123.9 billion. Credit cards appear to be used more for leisure goods/services, when compared to debit cards, for example, hotels, travel and entertainment.

Other retailers and household merchant groups attract credit card users (these are likely to be for larger purchases, for example, TV's and so on).

Whilst volumes continue to increase for debit cards, sale volumes using credit cards have levelled off in the last four years. Sales volumes paid for via charge cards have remained low throughout the series.

Although credit cards have been around for over four decades in the UK, the market does not appear to show signs of saturation. In the late 1980s the introduction of debit cards led some commentators to predict the end of the credit card industry. Over 20 years after the introduction of debit cards, credit cards still show growth figures, suggesting that credit cards and debit cards have so far been complementary products. Although credit cards are used often as a means of payment equivalent to a debit card (many credit card holders pay their balances in full at the end of the interest-free period), they are used for higher-value purchases and for durable goods and services. The Card Expenditure Statistics, published by The UK Cards Association, analyse spending according to 11 different sectors including high street retailers and services (see Figure 25.6).

Debit cards are widely used in the food and drink and motoring sectors. This combined with rapid debit card growth in the service sectors indicates that debit cards are replacing cheques and cash in routine purchases.

Credit cards, however, are also used as a means to obtain credit or to defer payment until the month end and consolidate usage on to a single payment vehicle. Much of the intense competition in the credit card market is focused on cardholders who borrow. In recent times, a spate of lower-rate cards and balance transfer offers have been launched. Borrowing on credit cards has appeared to grow in recent years, but the headline borrowing figures for credit cards are complicated by the use of cards as a means of payment as well as a source of credit. If the use of cards as a means of payment is growing rapidly, the use of cards as a source of credit may also appear to be growing rapidly. Alternatively, of course, this may just indicate changes in payment methods. Much research has been undertaken in order to better understand the data and as to whether, or not, there is an underlying issue of overindebtedness.

However, data needs to be treated with some caution as the benchmarks used to calculate take-up, usage, borrowing and repayment, have all changed over time, for example, nearly all issuers now charge interest from the date of the transaction, rather than the statement date, cash advances have grown as a proportion of turnover during recent years (in part driven by credit card cheques that issuers treat as cash advances), and discounted and reduced APR offers have substantially increased the number of consumers tactically switching cards and transferring balances.

The principal UK payment clearing systems are through the three separate clearing companies – BACS, CHAPS and Cheque and Credit. Other payment schemes operating in the UK are Visa, MasterCard, LINK and SWITCH Maestro.

The Cost of Credit

The most significant cost is the one concerned with credit. If consumer credit is created then funds have to be provided to service the lending. Bank cards reimburse merchants within a few days of sales transactions being paid electronically into the issuer's bank, but cardholders are allowed substantial repayment periods. Issuers of credit cards advise cardholders monthly of their outstanding balances and call for some level of repayment (at least a minimum percentage of the outstanding balance) within an agreed period. Charge cards require full repayment at the end of such a period.

Card issuers need to fund the payments made to merchants, pending repayments from the cardholders. The number of accounts that earn no interest for issuers has increased steadily throughout the last decade. It was in order to curtail cross-subsidisation between cardholders who pay interest and those who do not, that annual fees were introduced by most major issuers in the early 1990s. Some issuers rebate this in the event that a minimum spending level has been achieved.

Bank cardholders who take extended credit do so over a period that extends from, say, three months to something over two years when only the minimum monthly repayment of the outstanding balance is repaid.

The lending operation is controlled successfully by maintaining a proper margin between the cost of money employed and the income received from cardholders and the fees charged to merchants, but unlike some bank card systems in the rest of the world there is only limited use in the UK of raising money directly from the cardholder population. Bank systems normally obtain their funds through their parent banks from the wholesale market. Other financial institutions providing retail card services do the same although a number of the building societies and savings institutions may well have surplus funds to be used. Retail systems funding their own facilities may borrow advantageously or use accumulated funds. In the charge card market, American Express has substantial financial resources from its other financial operations.

The Cost of Payments

The operational costs of money transfers are significant. They include: crediting the seller, debiting the purchaser and advising him/her of amounts outstanding and then obtaining repayments; the costs of opening the account and servicing it, the cost of processing payments, running sophisticated systems and printing.

The operations are highly automated but the customer care side requires substantial human resources that, with the capital costs of modern equipment, put the optimum requirements on operational efficiency. There are special pressures of increased postal charges because most of the business is handled centrally and serviced through postal networks; the telecommunications costs, where increased charges can represent very substantial extra costs, are often difficult to recover direct from cardholders except through increased operational efficiency and profitable expansion. Some bank cards, as well as T&E cards and charge cards, cover some of the processing costs with annual fees. In order to offset this, and reduce the call volume demands made on staff within the operational support teams, most issuers now facilitate online banking via the Internet. This enables customers to view their statements, carry out payment transactions, money transfers and so on, all in their own time, without adding substantially to the issuer's administration costs.

A significant part of the operational cost is also met by the merchant service charge, a fee paid by the merchant for the facilities provided when accepting cards. These service charges or discounts vary from 1 per cent to 5 per cent of each transaction, dependent on the merchant's volume of transactions, and are mainly controlled by the average transaction value, the volume of business and the potential risk of fraud. The rates are constantly being reviewed because of competition for the business at such rates (although debit cards are often discounted much less) since there are many advantages in the credit card business. Cardholders frequently look for card acceptance when making certain purchases, so casual trade will increase and there is a strong tendency to trade up and buy more expensive items when credit is involved. Merchants no longer need to provide local credit, which is expensive to administer and has a security risk and bad debt.

The cost of providing customers with credit is rationalised as the agreed merchant service charge and it is unlikely that small traders could possibly provide an in-house system at such a price. Larger organisations which have always provided their own credit find that adopting the main card systems or outsourcing their own in-house card system leads to improved profitability, particularly when they can eliminate some of the administration and the funding required.

The merchant service charge is shared between the organisation accepting and processing the merchant transaction and the card-issuing bank, which guarantees payment and debits it to a customer's account. For a small percentage of the sale price, the merchant is able to take payments from cards issued around the world, reduce the handling costs of payments and is largely protected from fraudulent usage of cards and the threat of bad debts.

The Cost of Promoting Cards

The costs of promotion and marketing, and certainly of entry into the national credit card market, are substantial. New entrants have to pay large advertising costs to gain entry into the field. However, this can be offset to some extent, by the increased revenue that can be derived from utilising the mailing and marketing databases that are developed as a part of the operation. The size of operations, the need for sophisticated automated systems, central administration, substantial telecommunications links for the big players and the huge volume of entries, whether electronic or paper based, all require a great deal of expenditure for development and improvement. Smaller card issuers may use a central processing bureau, but historically most issuers have set up their own processing centres.

Fraud and Bad Debt

There are additional special costs involved in credit card work – those associated with fraud and bad debt. Issuers of plastic cards rather than individual cardholders bear the initial cost of fraud. Cardholders' liability ceases the moment they notify the issuer of the loss of the cards. Cardholders' maximum liability on credit and bank-issued charge cards is £50 (less in the case of some issuers) for fraudulent transactions made before the issuer is notified, although issuers can choose to waive this liability. Cardholders' liability is not limited if they have been grossly negligent (for example, writing the PIN on the card) or are involved in the fraud.

Fraudulent activity within the UK continues to increase. Frauds identified were up overall by 8 per cent in 2007 (the latest figures available prior to publication). Although identity fraud decreased by 3 per cent during 2007, the total number of false identity/impersonation cases was still high, at over 77,500. Moreover, the number of application fraud cases increased by 20 per cent in 2007 and facility takeover fraud cases increased by 34 per cent. Source: CIFAS – the UK fraud prevention service.

CIFAS members reported that they prevented fraud with a value of almost £1 billion in 2007, up 25 per cent on the £788 million 2006 figure. This is a major achievement that demonstrates how fraud prevention measures are having an impact and are helping to protect both companies and consumers from the costs of fraud.

2007 card fraud figures released by the UK Cards Association showed that total card fraud losses rose by 25 per cent in 2007 to £535.2m. A key driver behind that was the 77 per cent increase (up £90.5m) in fraud committed overseas by criminals using stolen UK card details – which typically occurs in those countries yet to upgrade to chip and PIN. Fraud abroad now accounts for over one-third (39 per cent) of total card fraud losses.

Chip and PIN continues to have a hugely positive effect on card fraud committed in the UK. Over the past three years losses on face-to-face transactions on the UK high street have fallen by two-thirds from £218.8m in 2004, to £73.0m in 2007. Thanks to chip and PIN the 2007 figures also showed that fraud on lost and stolen cards (£56.2m), and mail non-receipt fraud (£10.2m), were at their lowest levels for 10 years.

Counterfeit fraud losses increased by 46 per cent but the vast majority of this fraud was due to criminals stealing card details in the UK to make counterfeit magnetic stripe cards for use in countries yet to upgrade to chip and PIN. The UK banking industry continues to encourage other countries around the world to upgrade to chip and PIN. This type of fraud will also become more difficult when the European banking industry meets its target to complete its chip card roll-out by 2010.

Point-of-sale authorisation, more secure card delivery methods, card validation and improved monitoring techniques have all contributed to ensure that card fraud does not spiral out of control. Cardholder verification plays an important role in fighting fraud. The current method is the use of chip and PINs at the point of sale. Other methods being considered are 'biometric' techniques such as finger scanning, voice recognition and using a computer to check signatures. Technological and logistical concerns mean that these solutions are some way off, although the advent of chip cards has enabled enhanced card authentication methods.

When a card is swiped through a retailer's electronic point of sale equipment, it can be validated, checked whether it's lost or stolen, the transaction authorised or the processing centre may be contacted. Transactions are processed electronically and have replaced the old method whereby retailers obtained authorisation by a telephone call to the issuer. Referral, where a card transaction required additional authentication, was handled manually to ensure 'logical' input.

Spending patterns are used by some issuers to watch for stolen cards. By monitoring spending behaviour with the aid of neural network computers, issuers have the potential to spot a stolen credit card before its owner notices it is missing. For example, if several high-value transactions are made with a card that is used infrequently, the issuer may 'refer' the transaction and instruct the retailer to check the identity of the person presenting the card.

Bad debt is a constant problem with all forms of credit cards. Lending policies of credit card organisations are very varied; travel and entertainment cards technically have no upper limit to the amount of monthly credit but they monitor very carefully the ability to repay each month's purchases satisfactorily. Bank cards that deal mostly with existing bank customers, usually have good knowledge of credit repayment abilities, while retail cards and cards where there's little known history, must be cautious in balancing increased turnover and profitable sales with irrecoverable profitless debt. The general approach adopted by card issuers is to start a new cardholder with a relatively low credit limit, which can be carefully managed upwards over time. Issuers have a duty to lend responsibility and gone are the days were credit limits are raised at will. Most bank cards have sophisticated credit scoring systems, which identify the poorer risks among applicants. Credit scoring weighs up many factors, which issuers' experience has proved, is relevant in determining whether someone is a good credit risk. Applicants are given a score derived from factors such as age, marital status and employment record. The marks are statistically derived from lenders' past experience and are not arbitrarily chosen. When added up, an applicant's score gives a measure of probable ability to handle a loan. Credit scoring is an objective way to assess risk and is based on lenders' past experience. The use of credit scoring reduces the number of borrowers likely to default and protects the interests of applicants and customers. Credit reference agencies may be used to see how a credit card applicant has handled credit in the past and to validate the name and address.

Recovery policies of outstanding debts are common across all card organisations. Initially firm messages are printed on monthly statements followed by demands for the return of the cards, service of a 'default notice' and collection of the account balance when the problem continues. Successful control is mostly dependent on early identification of delays in repayment, continued contact with cardholders to understand the reasons for failure to repay and, in many cases, establishing a modified repayment programme acceptable to both parties that will ultimately be successful.

In the early days of credit cards, courts were unsympathetic to the legal recovery of debts. However, there is now a clear acceptance that this is a commercial and contractual obligation that requires the same level of support for recovery by the creditor. Both creditor and debtor have responsibilities to each other.

Chips and Electronic Purse

Chip cards are the new generation of plastic payment cards. The success and popularity of credit and debit cards to pay for purchases has demonstrated over the years the gradual trend towards a cashless society and the increase in convenience of safe and secure payment/purchasing methods.

UK banks and building societies have issued more than 100 million credit, debit, ATM and cheque guarantee cards. Many of these cards have more than one function. Most of all credit and debit cards in the UK have a chip in them. This means that the information held by the cards will be contained in a small microchip (no bigger than the nail on a little finger) imbedded in the plastic. The chip is in addition to the magnetic stripe on the back of cards. Because it is a computer chip, it can hold much more information than the magnetic stripe and the information stored in the chip will be more secure. The chip can be as simple as a basic memory device or as advanced as a complex microprocessor.

The UK industry initiative to bring in chip cards was coordinated by APACS supported by the major card schemes. The UK Cards Association was formed in April 2009 as the successor body to the APACS Card Payments Group. It took time and a huge commitment of cost for all cash machines and retailers' terminals to be converted to be able to read the chip. Also, British-issued cards will need to retain the magnetic stripe so that they can continue to be used in those countries where chip cards have not yet been introduced.

The major card scheme organisers are liaising to establish worldwide standards for smart cards so that all chip cards will be accepted overseas in future. The attraction of chip cards is that the chip's enlarged memory enables cards to have more uses and to carry more sophisticated fraud prevention facilities than the magnetic stripe.

The expandable memory and processing ability of the chip means that it can adapt to the enhanced needs of the consumer. For example, it may be possible to transfer money from one card to another and to use chip cards in a wider variety of outlets.

The improved security features are one of the chip card's attractions. The chip is a more secure means of incorporating additional details in order to check that the cards are genuine and that the cards belong to those people presenting them. At present the signature on the card is the means of verifying the cardholders when purchases are made. A chip card will, for example, allow biometrics, such as verification by fingerprint, hand geometry or retina scanning as well as computerised signature checking when they are sufficiently reliable.

The introduction of chip cards has needed substantial investment by financial institutions, but has provided a wider range of uses for them and services for their customers. They can access home banking and home shopping, store points for loyalty schemes or act as 'electronic purses', for example, pre-paid cards. Many functions will be available on one card with new types of cards emerging as chips in payment cards become commonplace.

A chip also enables cards to be electronically loaded with money, used to pay for purchases, for example, mobile phone 'top up' cards, school/college use and so on, and then be reloaded with money – the electronic purse. These cards are aimed at the type of purchases where cash is normally used at the moment – such as in vending machines, to pay for bus and train fares, to buy newspapers, pay car parking fees or to make telephone calls. As their usage and acceptance proliferates, children will be able to have their pocket money on electronic purse cards.

Consumers no longer rely so much on cash, as developments occur they will be able to load chip cards with money by telephone, by personal computer or in a wide range of outlets as well as cash machines. Banks, building societies and retailers will be able to save on the cost of distributing and handling cash.

26

Sales Finance and Leasing

T Glyndwr Powell

• Introduction to sales finance • Benefits of sales finance to buyer and seller • Types of sales finance • Funding the credit advanced • Which product is best for what? • Summary • Sources of information • Further reading •

This chapter gives a concise review of the different kinds of facilities available to finance the credit which is essential to facilitate the sales volumes required these days. Much fuller treatment of each facility can be found in its appropriate context in the earlier chapters, such as the historical development of trade credit in Chapter 1, the vast array of credit cards and their like in Chapter 25, the ways to manage retail credit in Chapter 20, and the various forms of finance for international business shown in Chapters 18 and 24.

Thus, by reference to the contents list at the front of the book and to the index, the reader can select the long or short forms of description, or the collective comparisons of most of them in this chapter.

Introduction to Sales Finance

It is clear that access to credit is a factor in the buying decision, whether that credit is available from the vendor or through independent funding alternatives which the purchaser could find for themselves. Selling for cash is simpler, cheaper and far less risky and the only reason organisations grant credit at all is that, without it, the purchaser may not buy. A clever vendor will research what options are available to enable it to offer extended credit which meets the purchaser's need for finance without adversely affecting profitability.

Leasing, for example, has been around for a very long time. Although the exact date of the first lease transaction is unknown, the earliest known records of leases are of transactions occurring around 2000 BC in the Sumerian city of Ur. These records, written on clay tablets, show various different transactions including hire of agricultural tools, land and water rights, and farm animals. These indicate that access to credit, enabling a user of equipment to pay for it whilst using it, rather than having to buy it and own it, was of value to merchants that long ago.

More recently, in the medieval period, with the rise of cross-border trade, instruments arose such as letters of credit and bills of exchange, which enabled merchant traders to buy and sell goods without having to cart around wagonloads of cash in the very heavy forms of gold and silver. Such instruments not only allowed the payment of commercial obligations in far-off towns, but soon became a method of allowing a further credit period. Either the vendor allowed a greater credit period before receiving its money, or the banker financed it by charging interest. Again, this helped the growth of trade by enabling the vendor to receive cash on or around shipment but giving the purchaser time to pay, either on receipt some months later or even after they had sold the goods and been paid themselves.

With the rise of the Industrial Age, manufacturers were interested in obtaining the best return on their investments, and that meant keeping the factories producing goods, often before their customers were ready or able to buy. One example of this was in the railways, where wagon leasing companies sprang up to finance the purchase of railway trucks by railway companies who had insufficient capital to meet demand. The wagon leasing companies offered long-term hire contracts to the users or railway operators in exchange for a series of rental payments. This enabled the operators to concentrate their capital resources on developing and running the railways, whilst enabling the users, often coal and steel producers, access to transportation to meet the delivery needs of their customers. The end result was a developed transport infrastructure and a greatly increased market for all parties. Not bad for a little extra credit!

The UK Government established ECGD in 1919 to help British exporters re-establish their trading positions following the disruption caused by the First World War. This assistance largely took the form of providing insurance against the commercial and political risks of not being paid by overseas buyers after goods were exported. This assisted the rise in the export of capital goods from the UK to the rest of the world. Such insurance guarantees worked well for UK exporters and enabled the manufacturer to permit the foreign buyer to pay for the goods over their economic life, typically three to five years. Considerably longer periods are now possible for such long-term assets such as aircraft.

Sales finance for consumers was also being developed at the same time and took the form of extended credit offered by shops. Goods were delivered and accounts were typically settled on the net monthly account basis. Some limited hire purchase and bank loans were becoming available but the drive for market-driven sales finance was yet to come.

Following the First World War, there was a rise in consumer demand for credit, which the facilities available in stores could not handle. Waiting up to 24 months for the full price to be paid was greater than their limited financial resources could sustain, so they looked for an extra source of money to pay them on behalf of their customers. This demand gave rise to the birth of the 'finance company'. The finance companies were able to offer payment to the stores at the point of sale and credit to the buyers over a number of instalments. These finance companies were not necessarily banks or discount houses, but included industrialists and others with money to spare, who formed companies offering a new 'device' for money lending, which today we still call 'hire purchase'. Hire purchase companies did not all enjoy good reputations at the time and often their operating methods were not everything that we expect in these days of highly ethical standards and transparency.

In 1938 this gave rise to the first Act to regulate hire purchase, and to protect credit customers from the sharp practices of the less reputable companies, including 'snatch back' whereby goods were repossessed on the flimsiest of default criteria towards the end of the hire period, when the finance company could sell the goods and make a profit out of the hirer's misfortune.

After the Second World War, there was further growth in demand for goods and thus the need to finance the ensuing credit. This time, the demand differed from the hire purchase growth following the First World War, inasmuch as the earlier growth was consumer driven, whereas this demand was business driven. The buyers were now industrial companies who, instead of needing one car or sewing machine, needed a fleet of cars or 50 machines to equip a factory. Industry thus required better-organised finance providers with greater access to financial capacity. This caused the evolution from hire purchase companies to finance companies, which took the original hire purchase agreements and found new ways of lending money to bigger borrowers. These finance houses were, and still are, able to offer finance to borrowers under a structure which was unattractive or inappropriate for the banks to use themselves. Not surprisingly, the banks also started their own hire purchase and finance subsidiaries to exploit the same lending opportunity.

The 1960s saw a new Hire Purchase Act including the need for a minimum deposit. This piece of legislation was introduced by the then Labour Government to regulate the business further and to address the spectre of over-indebtedness by consumers. Such a need for a minimum deposit adversely affected the market, since many consumers simply did not have the cash required. Many in the industry came to the view that this Act directly led to the demise of the UK television industry, and the rise of the Japanese one, since the Japanese manufacturers found ways of financing 100 per cent of the contract price, where the UK manufacturers and UK stores could not.

The late 1960s and the early 1970s saw the introduction of the credit card, initially by Visa in the UK, but soon followed by Access, later to become part of MasterCard. This was a major leap in sales-aid finance as the card issuer made the funds available to the user/buyer at the point of sale. The vendor obtained almost immediate guaranteed payment and the card company received fees from both buyer and seller. Initially this was a domestic market facility, but quickly the benefit of offering cross-border credit for travellers was seen, and joint authorisation agreements were established to enable tourists and business travellers to use their cards abroad.

Whilst charge cards had been available through American Express and Diners' Club for many years, the high salary-level requirement and lack of access to credit made their application and mass acceptance limited.

Those early credit cards have since given rise to the plethora of cards available, through banks, mortgage companies, loyalty schemes where shops issue their own cards, balance transfers and other products where the ease and simplicity of guaranteed time to pay encourage the user to buy.

Benefits of Sales Finance to Buyer and Seller

As with any good commercial relationship there must be benefits to both buyer and seller, and the solution proposed must meet the needs of each. Typically the seller wants payment on delivery and the buyer wants to pay for the goods or services as they use them, or later if possible.

The benefits to the buyer or seller may differ, depending on the position of the individual involved, for example, the user or the management.

BENEFITS TO THE SELLER

Competitive advantage: Giving credit is equivalent to a discount, even if that is only a small interest saving to the buyer. Flexible payment terms, using financing, give the seller a product advantage over its competitor, especially where that competitor cannot offer similar terms. In markets where access to hard currency is a problem, extended terms may give the buyer access to hard currency or an import licence they otherwise could not obtain.

Profitability: Offering extended or flexible payment terms may be more attractive to the buyer than a higher cash discount. It is also possible to mask lower discount levels within a lease rate. Both offer the seller a method of protecting margin and enjoying higher profit. A faster cash flow also improves profitability by reducing bad debt and overdraft interest caused by late customer payments. Furthermore, those companies offering an in-house scheme or having a tied financing partner are able to participate in the financing profit (interest) and thus have an additional source of revenue.

Market share: By providing an effective financing service, the sales force productivity should increase, enabling business to be secured which may otherwise have been lost. Moreover, a sales aid leasing strategy encourages customer loyalty and lends itself to the maintenance and increase of market share.

Customer satisfaction: Sales-aid financing exists to provide customers with alternative options to suit their particular needs and provides a high level of service, making dealing with the seller's bid a problem-free experience. In the event of a problem, the seller or its finance company will often be the first to know, and can trigger remedial action immediately.

Account management and control: Signing up customers with a tied or in-house finance option has the effect of cementing the customer relationship. The seller will be at all times in a position to monitor accounts and be best placed to respond to customer needs, including replacement and/or additional business.

Account protection: Should the customer contact the seller or its finance company for information to terminate a contract, the salesperson will be told fairly quickly and this may allow competitive activity to be thwarted. Also, since the equipment has not been fully paid for, it can be very expensive for competitors to try and buy out the lease, and replace the equipment.

Replacement business: Customers tend to be unwilling to buy new equipment when they are still paying for the old. A well-established finance scheme helps in 'churning' equipment whilst other equipment is still in situ, as the customer is used to paying a monthly or quarterly rental, and is often willing to continue paying a similar amount. Any buyout costs can be included in the new lease. The replacement option is also easier, as the customer does not own the equipment, so can only choose to extend the contract and keep paying, or buy a new machine.

Asset control: As many lease agreements have no purchase option, the seller has control of the equipment at the end of the lease period. This enables the seller to control the market for second-hand equipment, thus maintaining the price of new equipment, equivalent second-hand machines not being available. It also acts as a source of machines to the seller for refurbishment or short-term rental, giving it options to increase market share in the future with specific sales programmes.

Flexibility and speed: The different options offered by sales finance give more room for manoeuvre and provide greater opportunity for alternative deals. More importantly, sales finance permits the salesperson to offer an alternative method of acquisition, which does not require, for example, a further discount being granted. The availability of finance also tends to reduce the buying timescale, as the buyer does not have to arrange credit elsewhere.

The total package: The salesperson armed with a sales finance facility is usually in a position to close the deal on the spot. There is no need to delay the process by arranging external finance and therefore allowing the customer time to reconsider. The customer will also perceive the salesperson to be more influential and helpful, as they appear to be able to manage the whole process.

BENEFITS TO BUYER

The buyer's management or ownership have a distinct set of needs which the seller's schemes are designed to address. Not all will apply to every buyer, but they are useful considerations in particular cases. They are especially useful in major purchases or concept selling, and in marketing sales finance in new situations.

No capital outlay: The buyer can retain cash for use in core business activities such as purchase of stock or raw materials, which is particularly attractive to finance departments. It also may move the budget from capital to overhead, with greater room for manoeuvre.

Budgetary control: Payment is spread over the life of the product, thus aiding cash flow. Additionally, payments can be structured to match the time when the buyer can best afford to pay for the goods or services.

Fixed price: Most contracts are fixed in price for a number of years, thus protecting the buyer against increases in interest rates, devaluation and inflation, and so assisting budget planning for future years. The price can only be varied if a price variation clause or floating rate interest calculation is included in the contract.

Accounting advantages: In lease and long-term rental contracts, costs are incurred as the equipment is used. There is no need to capitalise and depreciate equipment (unless the lease qualifies as a finance lease), which may facilitate acquisition as it could be treated as overhead not capital. Many organisations have adequate overhead budgets, but very tight capital budgets. For commercial organisations, it may provide a source of off-balance sheet finance. This is particularly important to banks and insurance companies, where use of balance sheet funds is especially expensive, and therefore tightly controlled.

Internal approval: Often, more junior managers can sign rental agreements as they can be deemed revenue or overhead items, not capital acquisitions. Lengthy approval processes may be avoided or reduced when rental contracts avoid capital approval procedures.

Tax: Some types of rental or lease may have better tax treatment, for instance, when treated as an overhead budget and written off against tax as incurred, rather than as capital tax allowances permit.

One-stop shopping: In many cases all costs associated with the buyer's needs are handled through the finance bid. This completely avoids the need to deal with third parties such as banks and finance houses. The customer can satisfy all his needs at one time and with one organisation.

Confidence: The fact that the seller is prepared to support the customer fully on all business aspects including providing finance may provide a strong comfort factor to the buyer, and builds a stronger 'relationship-based' account.

Simplicity: Where the vendor has its own finance available, be it in-house or a tied bank, the financial offer and the seller's sales staff are the single point of contact and will be equipped with all the necessary paperwork to close the deal. The customer need do nothing more than sign the contract and the seller will have won the order.

Types of Sales Finance

CONSUMER AND COMMERCIAL FINANCE

The sales finance industry normally splits into two main sectors: consumer finance and commercial finance. Similar products are available with slight differences for each sector. Governments tend to take a protective stance with consumer lending and try to ensure that the terms remain fair to the consumer, who is in a weaker bargaining position. With commercial finance, governments tend to take the view that organisations are free to negotiate the terms, and thus apply less regulation.

The needs of consumers and commercial organisations are often different, as are their risk profiles, which lead to different products for each. For example, cash flow for consumers is driven by the wage packet and disposable income, whereas for business, cash flow is driven by sales generation, with tax treatment and return on capital calculations being greater considerations in the type of finance arranged.

APPLICATION TO CONSUMER OR COMMERCIAL USERS

Figure 26.1 (at the end of this chapter) shows the various types of sales finance and their application. There are four generic forms:

1.   supplier credit-based – including short-term export credit;

2.   bank-related loans or facilities;

3.   asset and rental-based finance;

4.   export finance – medium term.

SUPPLIER CREDIT-BASED – INCLUDING SHORT-TERM EXPORT CREDIT

These are schemes which are put in place simply by the seller, usually by extending credit on terms longer than normally given in the market, and financed by the seller through its own resources. Additional security may be sought for giving longer credit and some examples are noted below.

Extended credit

This is the simplest form of sales financing. The seller gives a longer credit period than its normal credit terms as an inducement to win the order. The seller usually funds this through its normal facilities with its bank, although this is one area where factoring can be of great advantage.

Example of extended credit profitability calculation

If a seller normally gives 30 days credit; and is getting paid at the end of the month following the date of the invoice, the seller is funding 45 days sales (1.5 months).

If interest rates are 9 per cent per annum, this period costs the seller an average of 1.125 per cent of its sales value (45 days divided by 360 days × 9%).

If, to win extra sales, the sales management proposes a special credit period of 90 days, the cost of this will be 2.625 per cent (105 days divided by 360 days × 9% p.a.).

Therefore, for the extended credit to be profitable the seller must obtain increased sales to give a profit greater than the 1.5 per cent additional cost given up (2.625% minus 1.125%)

If one were top look at the additional cost of credit alone, at 10 per cent margin, a 15 per cent increase in additional sales revenue would needed to cover the extra cost of 90 days credit.

Extended credit – bills of exchange. As a way of limiting a possible delay in payment at the end of an extended credit period and to minimise any contract dispute, many companies seek more secure payment, by way of a bill of exchange accepted by the buyer. A bill of exchange is similar to a post-dated cheque, but different in that it is legally valid if given for maturity at a future date. Furthermore, the legal remedies available to sue on a dishonoured bill are very good, greatly improving the overall security.

In some cases, the accepted bills can be discounted with a bank for a better rate than normally paid on the overdraft.

Stock finance. Stock finance is usually made available through a bank where the stock is pledged to the financier who provides the cash for its purchase. It is often used in the agricultural industry to enable wholesalers to purchase goods from farmers at harvest time and fund their stocks until sold on to other bulk buyers.

Floor planning or consignment account. Floor planning (or consignment account) is a form of stock finance provided by manufacturers to their distributors. The manufacturer grants an extended credit period, normally between 90 and 180 days, against a pledge or Retention of Title over the goods. The distributor has to pay the manufacturer either as the goods are sold or at the expiry of the credit period if they haven't been sold by then. The interest rate charged is often attractive. The scheme ensures there is adequate stock available for sale, which is of benefit to both the manufacturer and distributor, helps smooth manufacturing planning and enables purchase and shipment in more economic quantities. Where service and maintenance are also provided by the distributor, adequate stocks of spare parts are also made available. The term 'floor planning' originated in the USA. The term 'consignment account' has been used in Europe for many years.

BANK-RELATED LOANS OR FACILITIES

These are schemes which make use of banks to provide the finance but which may offer the buyer a new additional source of finance, or one which is cheaper or less onerous than their existing facilities.

Avalised bills of exchange

This is a refinement of the bill of exchange whereby the buyer arranges for his bank to add its guarantee, known as an 'aval', to the bill. This makes the bill highly liquid, assuming the guarantor is of sufficient standing, and the vendor can easily sell the 'avalised' instrument in the bank market, or hold it until maturity (see 'Forfaiting or bill discounting' below). Because the bank does not add its aval until after shipment, it is potentially cheaper than a LC, as, in the latter case, both buyer and seller pay bank charges from the day it is opened.

Forfaiting or bill discounting

This comes from the French 'a forfait' which means to give up or forfeit something. It is an arrangement where a bank or specialised forfaiting house buys a bill of exchange, usually avalised, or a LC and gives the supplier cash less a discount equivalent to the interest and the risk premium for the guaranteeing bank or country risk. It is a simple method of generating cash inexpensively for the seller, as banks tend to understand the credit risk of other banks, where they are not so keen on the commercial customer. The interest rate applicable for a first-class Western bank is often considerably lower than the seller is paying on its own overdraft so may represent a better return on the finance. In some cases, banks will buy a bill from a very strong commercial customer without the need to have another bank guarantee it.

Credit lines and loans

This is where a bank makes available a loan for a specific purchase or series of purchases, often with further security in the form of charges over assets or some additional guarantees. It may be arranged by the seller where they have a partnership agreement with a finance house to offer such loans to their customers to assist the sale of their goods, or by the buyer directly with its own bank. The finance house may be more willing to fund these purchases as the loan advanced is being used for a specific purpose and cannot be used indiscriminately or unwisely, which is always possible with an overdraft. Also, if the bank is working with the seller on a long-term basis, it may have a better understanding of the product and the second-hand market, which will mitigate its loss in the event of a business failure or default.

Credit sale agreement

This is a particular form of the credit line or loan where the vendor has arranged a tied finance house to provide loans to its customers to finance the purchase price at the point of sale, being repaid by the buyer over a number of instalments.

Unlike hire purchase or leasing, the buyer usually obtains title to the goods immediately, the bank taking a credit risk on the buyer. It is a popular form of sales financing in retail stores, particularly the electronics industry, where the buyer can be easily credit checked.

An example of this is where building companies arrange with a 'friendly' mortgage company to offer finance on their newly-built houses to qualifying buyers who are interested. The mortgage company gets the business, and often pays the builder a commission for the introduction. The builder gets to sell its houses more quickly and the buyer has a simpler purchase process, without the need to negotiate a mortgage itself separately.

Deferred payment letters of credit

A LC is a guarantee from a bank promising to pay a certain sum of money to the seller within a certain time period against the submission of specified documents. The simplest form of these is called a 'sight credit' because the bank is obliged to pay when it has sight of the documents. This is usually on or just after delivery. Like most bank obligations, the banks have discovered they can help the transaction further by allowing a deferred payment period after delivery, similar to open credit, typically between 30 and 180 days. The seller is still guaranteed payment but the buyer does not have to pay its bank, nor its bank to the seller, until the deferred payment period has expired. This gives the seller the guarantee it needs and the buyer the cash flow advantage it was seeking. Where goods may take a long time to arrive, the buyer rarely wishes to pay for the goods until arrival so this offers the seller the certainty of payment it requires. The seller can seek to discount the LC, before maturity, with its bank or a forfaiting house should it wish to accelerate its own cash flow.

Refinanced letters of credit

Refinanced letters of credit differ from deferred payment letters of credit in that there is no deferred payment period. The seller is normally paid on delivery, and the refinancing bank, usually the advising or confirming bank, gives the opening bank a loan which it repays at the end of the period plus interest. As the opening bank is getting finance, it is usually willing to pass this on to the buyer.

It is sometimes of particular benefit where the country of the buyer has foreign exchange shortages and its central bank requires the commercial banks to obtain extended credit before making foreign exchange available. The buyer may not actually want or need any extended credit but the additional delayed hard currency remittance might be the key to getting the deal approved by the authorities and thus the order signed.

ASSET- AND RENTAL-BASED FINANCE

Asset-based finance is where the lender is using an asset as security in part for the loan. That asset is usually the subject of the sale although, sometimes, additional security might be required.

One of the most important concepts in asset-based finance is that the user does not need to have ownership of the asset to use it. They want the beneficial use of it but not necessarily the beneficial ownership. For example, when a car is damaged and off the road, awaiting repair, the driver often arranges for a hire car. The need is to be mobile, not to own the car. The same can apply to photocopiers; what the user wants is to get copies when they want them, not own photocopiers. In these circumstances, rental and lease contracts are useful methods of acquiring something to be used. If ownership is more important or the item has a long life or high value at the end, loans or hire purchase may be more appropriate.

Hire purchase

Hire purchase allows the customer to acquire the goods and use them, and provides payment to the vendor at point of sale. The customer then pays the hire purchase company periodic rental payments, usually monthly or quarterly, to repay the purchase price and associated interest, usually called the charge for credit. At the end the customer has the option to make a further, normally token, payment to take title (ownership of the goods), sometimes called exercising the option to purchase. There is often a deposit required, although the legal obligation to charge a minimum deposit was removed in 1982. The terms of hire purchase agreements have become highly regulated in the UK due to sharp practice in the last century, so the hire purchase company cannot repossess the goods without a Court Order after a certain percentage of the original price has been paid.

Whilst paying the period payments, the customer is hiring the goods from the finance company and cannot dispose of them without first settling the outstanding rental payments and exercising its option to purchase. Hire purchase is a good method of acquisition where the customer wishes to take eventual ownership of the goods, but has the disadvantage for commercial organisations that it is on the balance sheet as a long-term obligation. It may have less advantageous tax treatment than lease or rental in the UK, as tax is payable on a depreciating balance basis, whereas leasing is 100 per cent of the payments made.

Conditional sale agreement

A conditional sale agreement is similar to a hire purchase agreement in that the finance company has arranged payment at the point of sale to the supplier, but differs in that the customer has purchased the goods on a reservation of title. On payment of all the instalments, ownership passes to the buyer, and it gets good title. Unlike hire purchase, the buyer must take the goods at the end. This is a good example of an effective reservation of title contract condition. Should the buyer not maintain payments or dispose of the goods before having paid in full, the finance company is able to repossess the goods.

RENTAL AND LEASING

The Oxford English Dictionary defines these as:

- *rent:* the sum paid for the use of machinery and so on for a certain time;

- *leasing:* a contract between two parties by which one conveys property to another for a number of years usually in consideration of rent.

Therefore, there is no real difference. The two do the same thing – allow the use of something by another for a consideration. Nothing about ownership and nothing about what percentage of the asset value is paid. Just a fee for using a particular thing, including these days, non-physical rights such as software.

Modern business usage has come to imply that rental is a short-term cancellable contract, whereas leasing has come to mean a long-term non-cancellable arrangement, although the above definitions show that this is not strictly correct.

However, in other countries the English word 'leasing' has come to mean a contract more akin to hire purchase or conditional sale agreements. Under UK and US tax regulations, the user is not normally permitted to take ownership of the goods at the end of the lease without affecting its taxation treatment. In French and other European jurisdictions, this does not apply and the user can acquire the goods at the end for payment of a further, often token, fee. This confusing 'Franglais' helps explain why there is such misunderstanding between what is rental and what is leasing.

The key aspect of rental is that the user obtains the benefits of usage without the advantages and disadvantages of ownership for an agreed price.

Tax treatment of rental and leasing

This retained ownership in a rental is important from a taxation point of view because, as the user does not own the item being rented, it cannot claim capital allowances against tax, but instead gets a full credit for the cost of each rental paid, as it is paid. The finance company on the other hand does own the equipment, so receives full capital allowances on its equipment. This can give rise to a tax and cash flow advantage for the finance house which enables it to give a better implicit interest rate for the deal or make a better margin.

Another aspect of tax treatment of leases and rental is that they are treated as supply of taxable services for VAT purposes. Therefore the VAT liability is spread over the life of the contract, improving cash flow. Normally, in commercial hire purchase contracts, the VAT is not financed and the hirer pays it directly, as most business hirers can reclaim it in their next VAT return.

This is again an advantage for the banks as it creates a VAT output tax-generating revenue stream, and thus enables the bank to reclaim VAT on that part of its business. Banking and finance normally falls outside the scope of VAT. This amounts to hard cash profit contribution to most banks, where otherwise there would be a further considerable irreclaimable VAT cost. In the real world, the customer pays, not the seller, so any irrecoverable cost to the bank would be recovered in the interest rate.

SHORT-TERM RENTAL

Short-term rental can be of particular benefit to the user where the user does not need the item for a long time period and is willing to pay a higher pro rata rate for using the goods, with the ease of returning them incurring no further cost, when it wants. This could be due to an emergency or the breakdown of their usual equipment, a special short-duration project or event or a peak high demand which did not warrant the purchase of new long-term capacity. It can be highly profitable for the hire company. Plant-hire companies in the building sector are a good example. The users do not need the expense of buying every possible specialist tool required for any job, nor in most cases do they have the capital resources. The hire company needs to ensure that the rentals it receives, plus any payment it receives for selling the goods later, is greater than the cost of the item plus the cost of financing it.

In many manufacturing companies, old second-hand equipment, often obtained as a trade-in for new, is used for such short-term rental contracts. This can be particularly lucrative for the rental company, as the equipment is acquired at very low cost but still functions adequately. The potential hirer is interested in the output of the goods rented, so will be pleased to have use of it at a price less expensive than new. It the goods were sold second-hand, the potential user would expect a low price compared to new, but when renting, providing it does the job, the expectation is not so high.

For example, we expect a good discount on a second-hand car compared to the price of a new one, but we do not complain when we get a hire car that has 10,000 miles on the clock. The car hire companies exemplify the advantages and disadvantages of rental to both parties. We expect to pay a daily rate of around £20 or a weekly rate of £100 for a small car. However, when compared to the cost of running a car over a year, it is around 50 per cent of the capital cost of the vehicle. Taken over three years, this is 150 per cent plus around 40 per cent for the resale value of the car, totaling 190 per cent. Very profitable for the hire company, provided it rents the car out for most of the time. If it does it for 60 per cent of the time, its total return would be around 130 per cent, a reasonable profit for the risk. Below one-third usage, it starts to make losses. Hence short-term rentals are pro rata more expensive. With car hire, it is fairly easy to predict usage rates, based on historic data, but the more specialised the equipment, the higher the risk of it not being rehired, so the higher potential short-term hire charge.

LEASING

There are two main forms of lease:

1.   finance or full pay-out leases;

2.   operating or residual value leases.

A finance lease is a rental structure which effectively pays the full purchase price plus interest over the life of the lease; the operating lease pays a percentage of the equipment value over the lease life, leaving a residue to be paid at the end, thereby reducing the rental over the initial period.

There are options which allow for even lower rental cost at the early stages increasing over the life (step leases) or 'balloon' payments, where there is a large single payment at the end. The client can initially buy the equipment and then sell it to the finance house who then leases it back to the user (sale and lease back).

Types of lessor

There are two main kinds of leasing companies: independent third-party lessors and sales-aid leasing companies. The third-party lessors are the likes of the banks and finance houses, who offer their products directly to the lessee. A sales-aid leasing company is an organisation established to provide direct support to the manufacturer or distributor to help its customers purchase the product. These can be a separate division or subsidiary within the vendor corporation or a joint venture with a finance house or bank. In the latter case, the bank will 'badge' or 'white label' the product as the manufacturing company's.

The difference between finance and operating leases

The basis of Anglo-Saxon (UK and US) accounting principles is a concept called substance over form. This says that in properly valuing a business and its assets and liabilities, the accounts should reflect the substance (the reality) of a transaction rather than the letter of the contract. This helps avoid hidden off-balance sheet liabilities, which could overvalue the business to a potential lender or granter of credit.

Leases are a good example of potential off-balance sheet funding, inasmuch as they are long-term liabilities to pay for the use of something, normally treated in the accounts as an expense or overhead, whereas it could be argued that the substance of the transaction is the user acquiring capital equipment fixed assets through another route. For this reason the US and UK accounting standards bodies issued guidelines, namely SSAP21 for the UK and FASB13 for the US, which define leases between finance leases and operating leases.

In principle, a finance lease is one where the vast majority of the capital value of the asset is repaid over the life of the lease. The US rules use a guideline of 90 per cent. The UK is not so specific, but working out the difference between the capital and interest repayments is moot, as the user cannot always work out what the implicit interest really is, especially where additional services are bundled into the offer.

The best description of a finance lease is its alternative name, the full pay-out lease. This effectively describes what's really happening. The user is paying the full or almost the full cost of the capital over the lease life. At the lease end, the user must return the equipment or renew, normally at a token rate.

Similarly, a good description of the operating lease is its alternative name, the residual value lease. The residual value of a lease is the value of the capital still outstanding at the end of the lease. In an operating lease this is a high number, almost certainly well over 10 per cent. In addition, operating leases may have other services included in the offering, including service, maintenance, software licences fees and consumables. At the end the lease can be renewed, but as there is a residual value and other services included, the rental charge on the new contract is often the same as previously. Operating leases are cheaper in the early years than a finance lease as the lessor does not have to pay the whole capital value over the life; the effect of the residual value is that interest only is paid on that portion.

With operating leases the greater the residual value included in the lease, the lower the repayments during the lease, but the higher the capital value the finance house has to be sure of recovering at the end. With cars, where there is a well-established second-hand market, specialist car leasing companies can make high residual valuations and on a portfolio basis recover them, thus making repayments lower.

The example opposite shows the relative cost of an operating lease and a finance lease. It shows the lessor has the option to pay less over three years and return the equipment at the end, maybe then getting the new latest technology, or pay more at the beginning but save money over the long haul.

Sale and lease back

In sale and lease back contracts, the finance company (lessor) does not pay the supplier for the equipment, the user buys the equipment from the supplier, pays for it and then resells it to the lessor. The lessor then leases it back to the user (lessee) for the agreed period in the normal way. This is done where the user wishes to

Example
A customer needs a new printing press and is deciding on the benefit of buying on an operating lease or finance lease basis. • Press costs £10,000. • Interest rate is 10% per annum. • Lease period is 3 years. • There is no deposit. • The press is worth 30% or £3000 after 36 months.

Finance lease	Operating lease
• 100% is repaid over life • Residual value is £1 • Renewed lease payments are £10 per annum after 36 months • Cost per month = £322.70 • Total over 36 months = £11,617.05 • Total for 5 years = £ 11,637.05	• 70% is repaid over life • Residual value is £3000 • Renewed lease payments remain the same • Cost per month = £250.87 • Total over 36 months = £9031.33 • Total for 5 years = £15,052.22

obtain the best price from the supplier and may not want the supplier knowing it is leasing the equipment. It can also be used where the user has a book of purchased fixed assets such as vehicles, plant and machinery and property, which it currently owns, but needs to refinance the business. One option to generate cash is to sell those assets to a bank and then lease them back. This may be a cheaper option to obtain long-term funding or cash release than taking an overdraft or other loan, as the security of those assets back the cash released over the repayment period without necessarily granting further, more onerous security.

Step leases

Step leases are leases whose payments go up or down in steps over the lease life. For example, a customer may have a big budget this year but a small one next year and in year three. Therefore for planning, it is better for the lessee to pay more in year one than in years two and three. The step lease can accommodate that. Similarly, a business which has a small budget for the rest of this year, six months, needs to make minimum payments now, but when the new operation gets up and running it can afford the increased payments. Therefore, a low payment for months one to six is arranged, with increased payments from month seven onwards.

Balloon payments

A balloon payment lease is almost a form of the step lease, just having a very big step at the end. The rental payments are kept at a lower level than would be required to fully repay the capital element of the lease, leaving a high residual value at the end. The lessee then pays a single payment at the end to pay the outstanding capital balance. This single balance is called the 'balloon' payment.

Contract rental or contract hire

These are operating leases but usually include additional services such as maintenance. The car leasing business makes great use of this type of contract where the capital cost is well understood, as is the residual value of the vehicle at the end. In addition, the motor manufacturers have good historic data on the service and maintenance costs of their vehicles, so quoting a total price for both the rental of the vehicle and the associated maintenance costs becomes a simple exercise. This has great benefits to companies with vehicle fleets. It provides a fixed operating cost for running the vehicles, and takes away any risk on disposal of the vehicle at the end. A similar contract is the 'cost per copy' contract used in the office equipment market.

Such contracts almost invariably include a minimum monthly payment, which covers the depreciation of the asset and capital repayment, together with a variable charge based on the amount of usage of the asset. In the case of a vehicle that would be based on mileage and copy contracts on the number of copies produced.

This concept has been further developed into the outsourcing product of 'facilities management' whereby the outsourcing company provides the service, the equipment and the labour for a known cost, usually with a minimum fee to cover the labour and equipment and a variable cost to cover volume or activity-related items.

EXPORT FINANCE – MEDIUM- AND LONG-TERM

Many of the techniques discussed above have application in cross-border transactions. However, over the last century, many governments saw promotion of their nation's exports as being crucial to their economic success and prosperity.

Hence, a new form of state-assisted export credit grew up, with both short-term aspects, mainly dealt with by way of credit insurance, and for capital goods, longer-term credit guarantees or insurance. The UK's organisation providing this service is the Export Credits Guarantee Corporation or ECGD as it is normally known. Generically, these agencies are called export credit agencies and include Eximbank in the USA, Coface in France, Hermes in Germany and EDC in Canada.

These government schemes have continued, but with the reduction in state subsidies for commercial organisations. In many countries, the UK in particular, such schemes have become much more limited both in scope, markets covered and capacity. Being government schemes, they are designed to support goods from their own countries, and historically forbad the finance of contracts with more than a small foreign content. This national content element has now been reduced in the UK case to permit up to 80 per cent foreign content to be financed, in recognition of the multi-national manufacturing base of many UK companies.

Generally, the seller obtains a guarantee or avalised bills of exchange from the buyer or its bank, or if a state entity, the Ministry of Finance. With these the seller can obtain a facility from its own bankers, who will make available funds at various stages of the contract, without recourse to the seller. Normally a 15 per cent deposit is required from the buyer in advance, with 85 per cent being financed plus interest. The general terms and levels of government support permitted are governed by a multilateral agreement to which the main exporting countries are party, known as the OECD Consensus. This limits the amount of subsidies allowed, the maximum amount of finance permitted and the periods of credit appropriate for transactions. These are further regulated by EU competition law which regulates the maximum subsidy a government may grant to its exports.

There are various kinds of schemes available, but the four main forms are discussed below.

Supplier credit

A supplier credit is the simplest form of ECGD-supported facility. It is available for exports with a minimum value of £25,000 and theoretically has no maximum limit. In practice, transactions above £5 million are better handled using other forms which the bank or ECGD will advise on. A supplier credit must be arranged between the ECGD and the seller's bank. Credit periods of between two and five years are available depending on the value of the contract and the types of goods.

The loan is repaid in six-monthly instalments plus interest.

Buyer credit

A buyer credit is where the buyer arranges the loan directly with the exporter's bank and is appropriate for larger contracts. The minimum value permitted is £1 million, but the recommended minimum is £5 million. In this, the buyer arranges a loan agreement directly with the UK bank, which is guaranteed by ECGD. The contract between buyer and seller must make provisions for this loan arrangement.

As with the supplier credit, if the bank is not paid by the buyer, it receives payment from ECGD 90 days after that default.

Line of credit

A line of credit is a loan facility established between a bank in the UK and a bank abroad to finance a series of contracts for various buyers and sellers. As the arrangements have already been made between the two banks, it is simpler to conclude than either a buyer or supplier credit. Minimum value can be as low as £25,000, so smaller contracts can be financed than in a supplier credit. Details of which lines of credit are in place and for which countries is available from ECGD.

Project finance

Project finance is a specialised form of buyer credit where the source of repayment comes from the revenues generated by the project. These are highly specialised transactions and other methods of finance are simpler if the buyer or its sponsor is creditworthy.

Funding the Credit Advanced

Where the seller is allowing credit to the buyer itself, the seller has to arrange appropriate funding to cover the credit advanced. Overdraft arrangements may not be the most effective, as these can be expensive and are generally repayable on demand. The finance arm of the seller needs to know that the credit advanced is matched by the funding available. There are a number of methods available to the finance company to fund itself.

FACTORING AND INVOICE DISCOUNTING

One of the simplest forms of funding the debt is to sell the debt to a third party for a discount. The factoring houses have been doing this for many years. The amount advanced is around 80 per cent. The advance can be 'with recourse' or 'without recourse'. Where the transaction is with recourse, the financial institution advancing the funds can ask for repayment from the seller if the debtor does not pay in the agreed time. On a without recourse basis, the funder takes the risk of ultimate non-payment.

These ways of funding can be on a disclosed or undisclosed (confidential) basis – that is to say, the debtor does not know that its supplier has sold the debt to a third party. Factoring normally involves the finance company administering and collecting the debt, whereas in invoice discounting, the supplier continues to collect its debts itself, using the facility as a source of funding. It is invoice discounting which is more likely to be on a confidential or undisclosed basis. (See Chapter 24 for more on invoice financing.)

BLOCK DISCOUNTING

Block discounting is a form of factoring where the supplier discounts chunks of its debts as it requires funds. It is sometimes used in rental contracts where the rental company discounts a series of future rental payments with a finance house to provide it with cash. It was developed to help stores and larger groups of shops who had their own direct arrangements with their customers but found that they were financing too much debt themselves. The store thus found a source of liquid funds, repaying the finance house as it received the instalments from the customers.

Which Product is Best for What?

Figure 26.1 overleaf shows the factors affecting the choice of the most appropriate method of sales finance.

Summary

We have seen that there are many ways of financing a company's sales. Offering additional credit is a potential source of additional business and at better

Consideration	Aspect	Product
Period of credit	Short term up to 6 months	• Extended credit • Bill of exchange • Deferred payment or refinanced LC
	Short term 6 months to 2 years	• Bills of exchange • Letters of credit • Conditional sales agreement or HP
	Medium term 2–5 years	• Conditional sales agreement or HP • Bills of exchange • Leases • Credit lines or loans • Export credits
	Long term 5–20 years	• Mortgages • Specialist leases • Bank loans
Security	Low risk	• Extended credit • Bills of exchange
	Medium risk	• Leases • HP and conditional sale agreements • Stock finance and floor planning
	Medium to high risk	• Letters of credit • Avalised bills of exchange • Export credits • Bank guarantees
Ownership	Ownership required	• HP • Conditional sale agreements • Bills of exchange with or without aval
	Use required not ownership	• Lease • Contract rental
Tax treatment	Usually determined by ownership	• Lease or purchase
Bank support available	Buyer has support of his bank	• Letter of credit • Avalised bills of exchange • Export credit • Loan

Figure 26.1   Factors affecting choice of finance

achieved margins. It gives a prudent company competitive advantage over its market competitors and access to buyers it may not otherwise have.

Knowing what might be available and which schemes address which buyer needs can certainly help in the drive for increased market share and profitability.

Sources of Information

Finance and Leasing Association 2nd Floor, Imperial House, 15–19 Kingsway, London WC2B 6UN. Tel: 020 7836 6511, Fax: 020 7420 9600, Email: info@fl a.org. uk, Website: www.fla.org.uk

Asset Based Finance Association (ABFA) Boston House, The Little Green, Richmond, Surrey, TW9 1QE. Tel: 020 8332 9955, Fax: 020 8332 2585, Website: www.factors.org.uk

Export Credits Guarantee Department PO Box 2200, 2 Exchange Tower, Harbour Exchange Square, London, E14 9GS. Phone: 020 7512 7000, Fax: 020 7512 7649, Email: help@ecgd.gov.uk

Further Reading

The Finance of International Trade, BPP Ltd Elements of Finance & Leasing, A. Day Credit Risk Management Series (2000): Leasing, B Coyle World Leasing Yearbook, Euromoney.

Product	Description	Commercial use	Consumer use
Extended credit	Vendor agrees credit directly to buyer in a period greater than normal terms.	Extended credit	Not normally available
Extended credit – bills of exchange	Extended credit is supported by the issuance of bills of exchange accepted by buyer,repayable at agreed future dates with interest.	Bills	Not normally available
Consignment account	Loans or credit sales made by manufacturers to distributors to finance warehouse stock, typically repaid on sale to the end-user or at expiry of fixed period, usually between 90–180 days.	Stock finance	Not applicable
Stock finance	Finance arranged to enable purchase of stock for resale secured against the value of the goods or sales to the future buyer.	Stock finance	Not applicable
Avalised bills of exchange	Extended credit is supported by the issuance of bills of exchange accepted by buyer, repayable at agreed future dates with interest, and guaranteed by the buyer's bank. More usual in export sales.	Forfaiting	Not applicable
Forfaiting or bill discounting	The support of extended credit by way of accepted (and/or avalised) bills of exchange which the vendor then sells to a bank for a discount (equivalent to the interest and risk), normally without recourse to the seller. Normally used in export sales.	Forfaiting	Not applicable
Deferred payment or usance letter of credit	A letter of credit usually confirmed by seller's bank, allowing the buyer extended credit after shipment typically between 30 and 180 days, but exceptionally up to 720 days. Seller often then discounts proceeds of letter of credit with confirming bank for immediate cash.	Deferred payment letter of credit	Not applicable
Refinanced letter of credit	Confirmed letter of credit usually payable at sight where confirming bank pays seller and charges opening bank/buyer interest until payment at later date.	Refinanced letter of credit	Not applicable
Credit sale agreement	Loan to pay vendor by finance company, repaid by buyer over agreed period. Ownership transfers on delivery.	Credit sale	Credit sale
Credit lines and loans	Finance company or bank makes available a loan for a specific purchase or series of purchases. Similar to credit sale agreement but finance provider may take extra security.	Credit line	Not applicable

Figure 26.2   **Types of sales finance product and their application to consumer or commercial users**

Product	Description	Commercial use	Consumer use
Rental	A simple rental contract makes the use of goods available to the hirer for payment of rent for an agreed period. Sometimes called short-term rental.	Rental	Rental
Hire purchase	A contract with finance company who pays the vendor of goods in full at purchase and who takes ownership of the goods and then rents the goods to the hirer during the life of the agreement, with ownership passing on payment of final instalment or optional final payment to the hirer/user.	Hire purchase	Hire purchase
Conditional sale agreement	Like a hire purchase agreement except the conditions of the final payment passing title may differ from strict hire purchase. Ownership may pass to buyer immediately.	Conditional sale agreement	Conditional sale agreement
Contract rental or contract hire	A fixed extended period rental particularly used in vehicle or office equipment business, whereby the user pays rental for the agreed period, which normally cannot be cancelled. Maintenance and service charges are often included. Goods being hired must be returned to finance company at end or contract extended. Sometimes called 'operating leasing'.	Contract hire	Contract hire consumers may have option to purchase
Leasing	To all intents and purposes this is long-term rental for the use of equipment.	Leasing	Leasing
Finance leasing	Where the leased equipment appears on the user's balance sheet. If the value of lease payments less interest are for the majority of the equipment's inherent value, typically greater than 90%, the equipment appears as an asset on the user's balance sheet. This is similar to HP treatment but without the ownership option. For VAT purposes, it is treated as rental but may have a different treatment for tax (capital allowances and depreciation.)	Finance lease	Not applicable
Operating lease	This is similar to contract hire, but the user is paying typically less than 90% of the economic value of the equipment over the life of the lease, or where other services such as service and maintenance are included.	Operating lease	Operating lease
Project finance	Long-term finance made available to build a large infrastructure project often involving government guarantees and investment banks.	Project finance	Not applicable

Figure 26.2 *Continued*

Product	Description	Commercial use	Consumer use
Supplier credit	Typically small value loan arranged by seller, made by bank to foreign buyer or bank to pay for capital goods and guaranteed by ECGD.	Supplier credit	Not applicable
Buyer credit	Typically large value loan arranged by foreign buyer, and made by bank to foreign buyer to pay for capital goods and guaranteed by ECGD to a number of different suppliers.	Buyer credit	Not applicable

Figure 26.2   *Concluded*

Appendix

Glen Bullivant

• Membership organisations for credit management personnel • training and consultancy services for credit management • sources of credit information • collections • useful credit publications • query management systems • credit policy and procedures • suggested contents for a credit manual •

Membership Organisations for Credit Management Personnel

The official body promoting the interests of credit professionals in the UK is the Institute of Credit Management (ICM), which is in turn a member the Federation of European Credit Management Associations (FECMA), comprising the national credit organisations of a number of European countries. The National Association of Credit Management (NACM), the USA-based body, has a European arm, Finance & Credit in International Business (FCIB), which runs export-related meetings in most European centres, serving principally, but not exclusively, large multi-nationals.

The consumer credit industry is served by the Consumer Credit Trade Association, and debt collection and credit reference interests are represented by the Credit Services Association (CSA).

The Institute of Credit Management (ICM) The Water Mill, Station Road, South Luffenham, Oakham, Leics. LE15 8NB. Tel: Reception 01780 722900, Email: info@icm.org.uk, Website: www.icm.org.uk

The ICM is the largest professional credit management organisation in Europe. Its 9000 members hold important appointments in trade, export and consumer credit, as well as in related activities such as collection agencies, credit reporting, factoring and invoice discounting, credit insurance, insolvency practice and computer software peripherals (as associated with credit management processes). The ICM is the centre of expertise for all matters relating to credit management. Tel: Membership 01780 722903, Email: membership@icm.org.uk

The ICM's monthly magazine, *Credit Management*, free to members, offers up-to-date coverage of trade and consumer credit developments, export news, financial matters and job vacancies. Tel: Editorial 01780 722910, Email: editorial@icm.org.uk

The ICM offers education, training, seminars and courses (see below), and also operates a successful recruitment service, helping credit professionals to advance their careers and assisting employers to find talented and experienced credit personnel. Tel: Training and seminars 01780 722907, Email: training@icm.org.uk, Tel: Education 01780 722909, Email: education@icm.org.uk, Tel: Recruitment 01780 722906, Email: jobs@icm.org.uk

The ICM operates a technical advisory service, which provides expert advice on both general and specific questions relating to credit management. Through an online, password-protected bulletin board, members have access to the wealth of experience and knowledge of the members throughout the disciplines of trade, consumer, export and related credit matters. Those studying for ICM examinations, in particular, find that the bulletin board is an ideal way of both seeking help and airing ideas, and they are also assisted by an online support service to provide help in home studying. The ICM's Technical Advisory Service responds to Government consultation papers on a variety of issues, and both the consultation papers and the ICM's response are also posted to the website as an adjunct to the bulletin board. Increasingly, consultation includes matters arising from the European Commission, as well as other professional organisations. Tel: Learning support 01780 727271, Email: learning support@icm.org.uk, Tel: Technical Advisory 01780 722900, Email: info@icm.org.uk

Through the bookshop, the ICM offers a wide range of titles covering credit management and related disciplines, many at special rates for ICM student members, with a same-day dispatch service available. Tel: Bookshop 01780 722901, Email: books@icm.org.uk

In 2009, ICM introduced QiCM – Quality in Credit Management – a programme designed to help drive and recognise good practice. Prospective companies can apply for assessment by ICM of their credit policies and procedures and seek both recognition and accreditation. Tel: 01780 722912, Email: qicm@icm.org.uk

The ICM has 26 regional branches throughout the UK, with each branch running a programme of professional and social events, open to members and non-members. Branch meetings offer an opportunity for credit managers and staff to meet and exchange views. Details of branch locations and contacts can be found on the ICM website.

For all credit professionals, membership is strongly recommended:

- It is *the* professional body for credit specialists, setting high standards in business, education and ethics.

- Membership demonstrates an individual's professional standing to employers and colleagues.

- Members are kept up to date with job-related developments.

- Members join a wide network of credit professionals, providing opportunities to exchange views and become part of, and contribute to, an influential body.

- Members have access to all ICM services, usually at preferential rates.

Federation of European Credit Management Associations (FECMA) PO Box 279, 1400 AG BUSSUM, The Netherlands, Tel: +31 35 69 54 103, Fax: +31 35 69 45 045, Email: fecma@sbb.nl, Website: www.fecma.eu

FECMA was formed in 1986 to bring together representatives of professional credit management associations in Europe to discuss problems common to all and to discuss ways in which they might cooperate. FECMA's aims are:

- To promote best practice in credit management by enabling the members of all the FECMA associations to share their knowledge and experience.

- To promote the development of the professional credit manager.

- To encourage and promote research, study, knowledge, and the publication of that knowledge, relating to all aspect of credit management.

- To encourage the highest possible ethical standards in credit management.

- To encourage the formation of national credit management associations in countries where none exists at present.

- To promote good relations and understanding between the various national credit management associations.

FECMA now includes the following credit management associations:

Austria: Verein fur Credit Management Osterreich, Email: office@credit-manager.at, Website: www.credit-manager.at

Belgium: Instituut voor Kredietmanagement, Email: info@ivkm.be, Website: www.ivkm.be Denmark: Dansk Kredit Rad (DKR), Email: sekretariatet@dk-r.dk, Website: www.dk-r.dk

Finland: Luottpmiehet Kreditmannen ry, Website: www.luottomiehet.fi

France: Association Francaise des Credit Managers et Corseils (AFDCC), Email: contact@afdcc.com, Website: www.afdcc.com

Germany: Verein fur Credit Management e.v (VfCM), Email: secretariat@credit-manager.de, Website: www.credit-manager.de

Ireland: Irish Institute of Credit Management (IICM), Email: info@iicm.ie, Website: www.iicm.ie

Italy: Associazione Credit Managers Italia (ACMI), Email: segreteria@acmi.it, Website: www.acmi.it

Malta: Malta Association of Credit Management, Website: www.macm.org.mt

Netherlands: Nederlandse Vereniging voor Credit Management (VVCM), Email: secretariaat@vvcm.nl, Website: www.vvcm.nl

Sweden: Svenska Kreditforeningen, Email: info@kreditforeningen.se, Website: www.kreditforeningen.se

United Kingdom: Institute of Credit Management (ICM), All contact details as above.

The FECMA council meets twice a year and regular conferences and meetings are held in European capitals covering suitable pan-European topics. In addition there is active cooperation between national associations at various levels on topics ranging from matters arising out of EU Directives, cross-border issues and so on through to commonality in education and training programmes.

Finance, Credit and International Business (FCIB) FCIB Europe, 16 Red Lion Street, Alvechurch, Worcestershire, B48 7LF, United Kingdom. Tel: 0121 445 2982, Website: www.fcibglobal.com Specifically for international credit management matters, FCIB is a global association established in the US in 1919, and incorporated in 1972 as the international affiliate of NACM, the US membership association for credit people.

Since 1967, FCIB has represented its European membership through FCIBEurope, holding international round-table conferences on credit, collections, finance and exchange issues in various European financial centres. This is a valuable opportunity for members to discuss topical experience on customers, countries and government actions. Conferences include intensive industry group meetings and workshops, as well as topically specific issues current at the time, such as changes in laws, rules and regulations appertaining to particular export countries and customers.

FCIB issues country and market reports on a regular basis, and has an active bulletin board and magazine.

Consumer Credit Trade Association (CCTA) Suite 4 ,The Wave, 1 View Croft Road, Shipley, West Yorkshire, BD17 7DU. Tel: 01274 714959, Fax: 0845 257 1199, Website: www.ccta.co.uk, Email: info@ccta.co.uk

The CCTA has been established for over 100 years, representing the interests of UK consumer credit, hire and debt collection, motor finance, brokers, insurance, as well as various support services in the industry such as software suppliers, solicitors and credit reference agencies. The CCTA lobbies on behalf of its members in the UK and in Europe, providing a wide range of practical services aimed at enabling finance companies to run efficiently and effectively in today's ever more complex environment of consumer credit laws and regulations.

Credit Services Association (CSA) Wingrove House, 2nd Floor, East Ponteland Road, Newcastle upon Tyne, NE5 3AJ. Tel: 0191 286 5656, Fax: 0191 286 0900, Website: www.csa-uk.com, Email: mail@csa-uk.com

The CSA was formed in March 1988 when the Association of Trade Protection and Debt Recovery Agents, established in 1902, merged with the Collection Agencies Association. The CSA is the only national association in the UK for debt recovery agencies, tracing agencies and allied credit services. It also incorporates the Debt Buyers & Sellers Group (DBSG), and runs educational and training courses to establish and enhance the professionalism of members.

Members of CSA operate to an ethical code of conduct (see Chapter 13).

Training and Consultancy Services for Credit Management

There are many companies which operate public and in-company training, with more that offer advice and consultancy on credit management procedures and organisational problems. Often consultancies are one-man concerns, operated by former credit managers with a wealth of experience in trade, consumer and export, usually with large multi-nationals as well as with small and medium-sized enterprises.

Many organisations benefit from a 'fresh look' from the outside, using a consultant not immersed in company politics, or the frequently encountered syndrome of 'empire' building or protection.

CONSULTANCY

It is unfortunate that in some respects consultants have something of a bad name. Quite often, the departure of consultants after a day, week or month on company premises is followed by 'downsizing' or other cost cutting exercises, the consultants being used as a smoke screen for decisions the client company had in fact already made. The truth is that use of consultants can be highly effective when properly organised. The client should choose the consultant with care, and be sure to select one who demonstrates empathy – the art of putting him or herself in the client's position, genuinely understanding the client's difficulties.

It is important that the client chooses a firm of credit management consultants that has people with many years' *practical* experience in the subject, at the senior end of credit management. It should not necessarily be a firm of general management consultants or, worse, accountancy experts who believe that 'credit control' is within the ambit of any competent accountant. When studying to qualify, accountancy students are taught very little about *real* credit management, and qualified accountants, often in charge of credit managers, rarely view credit management in the context of sales promotion and profitable marketing. It is unlikely that general consultants will have had the personal and practical experience of the credit scene that has evolved in recent years – the need for risk analysis, PC-based data, personal contact on collection problems and all the useful measurements and targeting of credit and collection results. It is also true to say, however, that there are also some failed credit managers trying to earn a living from offering advice to others.

There are thus good reasons to choose a credit management consultant carefully; obtain references and act on personal recommendations. There is usually a basic hindrance to using a consultant, in that the client knows there are problems that they have been unable to solve themselves, but is embarrassed to admit to an outsider that they do not have the skills to manage their way through. It is well known that any consultant, at the outset, is selling himself rather than the solutions – in other words, the client firm must feel that they can work with and respect the opinions of this person.

The key steps in a good credit management consultancy are:

- An initial 'no-cost' discussion, which may be no more than one hour, between the consultant and the potential client senior manager or director, to explore the problem in total confidence. It is at this stage that both parties have the private agenda of deciding if they can work together.

- Following the initial meeting, and ideally within 48 hours, the consultant submits a draft proposal of activity, with timescale and cost. One problem encountered frequently by consultants, of course, is that initial assessments of timescales prove optimistic as on-the-job investigations reveal problems in other areas, not initially mentioned by the client firm, and therefore not covered in the preliminary discussions or estimates. The consultant should identify the people, documents and procedures to be seen, saving a lot of expensive time later.

- During the work that follows, the consultant should keep the client updated on progress. It is far better to give frequent interim feedback, rather than waiting to issue a lengthy report at the end, and in practice, a good consultant can give the advice along the way and oversee its successful implementation.

A good consultant, by working closely with the client along the way, ensures that a 'final report' is often unnecessary, or at the most very short, unless the client dictates otherwise.

A successful consultancy saves the client from reinventing the wheel, by drawing on the experience of an expert with a quick grasp and perception, who has successfully implemented solutions elsewhere. Equally, the good consultant is one who can carry the working staff along the way, making them feel that they are contributing positively to resolving their difficulties and feelings of unhappiness, and that the consultant is there to support them. There can be no worse impression to give than that of a 'here today and gone tomorrow', remote person in an expensive suit, who talks only to the boss. Indeed, it is not infrequent that the staff themselves are very aware of what needs to be done, have raised issues with management and have been ignored. It is a sad indictment of much of today's senior management that they do not listen to their own people, and that only take notice of consultants because they are charging a fee! The better consultancies view clients in the light of offering support by way of solutions or solutions by way of support. The client may well be looking for more, or less, but the good consultant will be able to tailor the work according to requirements.

Just one example of an experienced credit management consultancy firm is Credit Professionals Limited, who offer expertise in all credit disciplines through a network of both in-house and associated consultants, all with years of successful experience in whatever area of need is specified by the client. Many of their consultants are senior members of the ICM and well-known personalities from the industry.

They can offer days or months of support, in-house or off-site, and tailor services provided according to the needs of the client. As a one-stop shop, Credit Professionals Limited enhance consultancy support with debt recovery, credit reporting, credit risk management, query management, computer software, contract dispute advice and litigation.

Credit Professionals Ltd PO Box 83, Crowborough, East Sussex, TN6 1WH. Tel: 0844 736 2634, (International callers use 0800 242 5160), Fax: 0844 736 6194 (International callers use 0800 242 5160), Website: www.credit-manager.co.uk

TRAINING

By any measure, training of staff at any level has to be regarded not just as beneficial for both the individual and the company in a specific area, but also as an investment in the future. Cutting training budgets in a time of 'efficiency measures' or 'cost savings' is both short sighted and potentially very damaging for the future prosperity of the company. The level of seniority is immaterial – the one constant in credit management is that nothing stands still, and there will always be new ideas to grasp and regulations to digest, so senior management should never consider itself any more immune from the need to learn than anyone else. It may even be argued that the better trained the senior management, the better they manage!

Benefits only accrue from training, however, if:

- the trainer has been recommended by a respected source;

- care has been taken to match the needs of the trainee;

- the delegate and his or her boss adopt useful points to put into action;

- after three months, the delegate and his/her boss review the benefits of the earlier training.

It would be entirely *wrong* to:

- send somebody off to any old course just to use up the training budget;

- send a person to a course at the wrong level;

- let the course go cold afterwards without putting any learning into practice;

- neglect training needs identified in staff appraisals.

Always adopt a positive approach to training by contacting the leading training companies and discussing with them the needs of the proposed delegate(s) in order to choose the *correct* training course. Whatever the level or extent of any staff training, the course provided should be regarded as a catalyst for continuing improvement, not as a complete cure, or relegated to a one-off special event. There is always much debate about whether better results are achieved when courses and training events are held off-site or in-house. There is no right or wrong answer, because there are merits in both.

External training

The general benefit of external training – for example, a course or seminar run in an hotel or conference centre – is that delegates from different companies provide all sorts of new ideas and innovations. The delegates who thought that they were the only ones with peculiar customers, difficult sales colleagues or unhelpful computer systems soon realise that others have the same experiences. It is often the case that others have *had* the same problems, tackled and solved them in a particular way and are more than willing to share with new-found soul mates! The uninterested or 'loner' delegate will be influenced by the application and enthusiasm of some of the others, especially in group workshop or syndicate activities. All delegates can quietly measure themselves against the others and remedy the gaps in their knowledge, often without revealing them. Excellent contacts can be made for the future, and many a professional relationship has blossomed from being thrown together on a tough but enjoyable training course. Possibly the only real disadvantage of external courses is their relevance to every single participating delegate – the more generalised course may be of interest to some, but not to others, and boredom can be a great turn-off. The risk of this emphasises the need to speak carefully to the potential providers before signing up, and choosing courses which meet specific needs.

In-company training

This has the distinct advantage of being cheaper (per delegate), provided there are five or more delegates, and it can be more readily tailored to meet the client company's actual needs. Trainers can use the client's own procedures and paperwork in illustrating methods and processes. The staff also get the benefit of the trainer's experience being specifically applied to their own familiar ways of working, and they can feel comfortable in their own surroundings and with people they work with every day. On the other hand, that very familiarity with both surroundings and people can have a negative effect – no one likes to look silly in front of colleagues or bosses, and staff could feel less inclined to ask questions or expose what they perceive to be their own ignorance in front of everyone else. In-company training can also suffer from the demands of the employer, or the pull of the desk or telephone – it is all too easy to be called away by others simply because you are still on-site and therefore 'available'.

THE INSTITUTE OF CREDIT MANAGEMENT

As the professional body for credit specialists, the ICM runs an extensive programme of training and education.

Over 100 one-day and two-day seminars and conferences are run by the ICM every year, covering all aspects of credit management, from risk assessment to litigation. The courses and seminars are designed to cater for trade, consumer and export, and are structured to meet the needs of credit professionals at all levels, from junior credit staff to senior management. The Annual Conference is an event of some prestige, with keynote speakers from industry, commerce, politics and national interest, and incorporates a high-profile Awards Dinner, where the high flyers, personalities and innovative leaders in the industry are publicly recognised for their efforts. In addition, the ICM is widely experienced in designing and delivering in-company training for individual companies and organisations.

Great emphasis is naturally placed on education, and the ICM's own education scheme provides students with a thorough grounding in credit management principles and practice. The examination syllabus meets the requirements of the QCA (Qualifications and Curriculum Authority) who have also granted the ICM awarding body status. Students working for the MICM(Grad) qualification can choose to study through evening classes at colleges in various UK centres, from home by distance learning or through a combination of the two. Those choosing to study from home have the help of the ICM's Learning Support Service, offering online assistance and support throughout.

Dun & Bradstreet Ltd Marlow International Parkway, Marlow, SL7 1AJ. Tel: 01628 492000, Website: www.dnb.co.uk

Dun & Bradstreet offer, through their Learning Centre operation, a range of workshops, seminars and in-house training on a full range of credit control and risk assessment topics.

Sources of Credit Information

There are a great many organisations now offering credit reports and financial information, and the following list is by no means exhaustive. The information market is highly competitive, with new providers and new products constantly appearing, and inclusion in this list is not indicative of any favourite. Equally, exclusion is not indicative of anything detrimental. The reader should always be aware that service providers are many and varied, and neither recommendation nor non-recommendation is intended here.

The greatest change in recent years in respect of credit information has been online availability. Requests for company reports by telephone or by fax have long been well overshadowed by clients' direct online access to service providers' databases, and more rapid credit decisions are a direct consequence. Clients can select by cost as well as by content, so instant access is now the major selling tool for all providers.

Experian Ltd Landmark House, Experian Way, NG2 Business Park, Nottingham, NG80 1ZZ. Tel: 0115 941 0888 (For credit reports 0844 481 8000), Website: www. experian.co.uk

Experian has been providing business information for 175 years, and their credit database includes details of every limited company in the UK, as well as one of the largest databases of non-limited businesses in the UK. Every country is covered to the greatest extent possible, and by combining officially filed documentation (such as Companies House in the UK) with its own intensive research, knowledge and experience, they are able to provide comprehensive information to suit the needs of all clients. On a daily basis, Experian will issue

30,000 credit reports, over 250,000 will be connected and 90 million online transactions will be completed

Companies House Crown Way, Maindy, Cardiff, CF14 3UZ. Tel: 0303 1234 500, Fax: 01222 380323, Website: www.companieshouse.gov.uk, Email: enquiries@ companies-house.gov.uk

Companies House is an executive agency of the Department of Business Innovation and Skills (BIS) and is the company registration office for Great Britain. It holds the public records of all companies incorporated in England and Wales and its two main statutory functions are:

- the incorporation, re-registration and striking off of companies and the registration of documents required to be delivered under companies, insolvency and related legislation;

- the provision of company information to the public, for which purpose it enforces compliance with statutory requirements.

Though part of Companies House, a separate register is appointed for Scotland to undertake the parallel functions under Scottish jurisdiction. Companies House, Scotland is located at 4th Floor, Edinburgh Quay 2, 139 Fountainbridge, Edinburgh, EH3 9FF.

Companies House has its headquarters in Cardiff, with an additional office in London. Electronic filing and public access via the web has overtaken 'walking in off the street' and company records, previously stored as paper, and later transferred to fiche, are now stored electronically. Most requests for files are now online, and the majority of records can now be delivered to the enquirer online. The documents most commonly requested are Annual Returns, Accounts, Mortgage and General.

Dun & Bradstreet Ltd (see above for contact details). Most D&B products are available through subscription, and cover a variety of reports, publications, classifications and services.

D&B also publish *International Risk and Payment Review*, a valuable monthly digest of data on over 100 countries. The data covers payment terms, local payment and hard currency delays, if any, other risks or information relevant to exporters, and the availability of credit insurance cover from the major credit insurers. (In the opinion of this editor, this is a most useful publication, and should be on the shelves of all export credit managers.)

Equifax PLC, Website: www.equifax.co.uk. Equifax is a leading provider of information and decision support services. Their database incorporates:

- consumer credit profiles in the UK and 400 million worldwide;

- companies, and owners, worldwide;

- marketing databases;

- online authentication, verifying user identity;

- analytical and consultancy experience.

Graydon UK Limited Hygeia Building, 66 College Road, Harrow, Middlesex, HA1 1BE. Website: www.graydon.co.uk, Email: mail@graydon.co.uk, Tel: 020 8515 1400.

Established by three of Europe's largest credit insurance companies (Atradius, Coface and Euler Hermes) and issues credit reports throughout the world

Callcredit Limited One Park Lane, Leeds, West Yorkshire, LS3 1EP. Tel: 0113 244 1555, Fax: 0113 234 0050, Website: www.callcredit.co.uk

ICC Information Limited Field House, Oldfield Road, Hampton, Middlesex. TW12 2HQ. Tel: 020 8481 8435, Fax: 020 8941 6014, Website: www.icc.co.uk, Email: info@iicc.co.uk

ICC have been providing business research services for over 40 years and are part of the Bisnode group, operating in 18 countries with some 23,000 employees. The database is extensive:

- Over 400 million original document images;

- Over 7 million UK and Irish companies;

- 1.8 million unincorporated businesses;

- 10 million directors and shareholders;

- Data on over 30 million European companies.

SkyMinder.com, Website: www.skyminder.com. An online source for credit and business information on 50 million public and private companies in 230 countries. The service is provided through the web by offering users the choice of report and source.

OTHER SOURCES

There are numerous other sources of information available to the credit manager (and some useful addresses follow), but the customer itself should not be overlooked. Company secretaries of plcs (Public Limited Companies) are quite used to being telephoned for the latest company 'glossy', the brochure it uses to impress the City, its bank and its investors. Most corporate brochures amplify the mandatory set of accounts with stories and photographs of company activities. Many credit managers obtain their financial data on major customers from this source. It is always possible, as a potential supplier, to request internal accounts from the prospective customer, and many companies are willing to supply such data. They realise that if they needed further funds from their bank, they would have to supply them latest financial information, and in many ways the position of the trade supplier is little different. After all, some credit managers have to allow credit lines greater than a customer's bank overdraft! Company reports are also available free of charge from the FT Annual Reports Service.

Trade directories, the daily press and financial press should be part of the credit manager's resource and many public libraries have extensive commercial reference sections with a great deal of company information.

Useful Addresses

Business in the Community 147 Shepherdess Walk, London, N1 7RQ. Tel: 020 7566 8650, Website: www.bitc.org.uk, Email: information@bitc.org.uk

British Chambers of Commerce 65 Petty France, London, SW1H 9EU. Tel: 020 7654 5800, Fax: 020 7654 5819, Website: www.britishchambers.org.uk, Email: info@ britishchambers.org.uk

British Bankers' Association Pinners Hall, 105–108 Old Broad Street, London, EC2N 1EX. Tel: 020 7216 8800, Fax: 020 7216 8811, Website: www.bba.org.uk

The Chartered Institute of Arbitrators 12 Bloomsbury Square, London, WC1A 2LP. Tel: 020 7421 7444, Fax: 020 7404 4023, Website: www.ciarb.org.uk

The Chartered Institute of Purchasing and Supply Easton House, Easton on the Hill, Stamford, Lincs. PE9 3NZ. Tel: 01780 756777, Website: www.cips.org.uk

CBI (formerly Confederation of British Industry) Centre Point, 103 New Oxford Street, London, WC1A 1DU. Tel: 020 7379 7400, Website: www.cbi.org.uk

Asset Based Finance Association (ABFA) (formerly known as Factors and Discounters Association Ltd) Boston House, The Little Green, Richmond, TW9 1QE. Tel: 020 8332 9955, Fax: 020 8332 2585, Website: www.abfa.org.uk

Federation of Small Businesses (The National Federation of Self Employed and Small Businesses Ltd) Sir Frank Whittle Way, Blackpool Business Park, Blackpool, FY4 2FE. Tel: 01253 336000, Fax: 01253 348046, Website: www.fsb.org.uk

The Forum of Private Business Ruskin Chambers, Drury Lan,e Knutsford, Cheshire, WA16 6HA. Tel: 01565 634467, Website: www.fpb.org.uk, Email: info@fpb.org.uk

Institute of Directors 116 Pall Mall, London, SW1Y 5ED. Tel: 020 7839 1233, Fax: 020 7930 1949, Website: www.iod.com

The Institute of Export Export House, Minerva Business Park, Lynch Wood, Peterborough, Cambridgeshire, PE2 6FT. Tel: 01733 404400, Fax: 01733 404444, Website: www.export.org.uk

SITPRO (Sitpro Ltd) Kingsgate House, 66-74 Victoria Street, London, SW1E 6SW. Tel: 020 7215 8150, Fax: 020 7215 4242, Website: www.sitpro.org.uk, Email: wnfo@sitpro.org.uk

Note: SITPRO (founded in 1970 as Simpler Trade Procedures Board) is a Government-funded organisation providing help for UK exporters. Its mission is to assist UK traders in improving their competitive position by using the most effective practices and information systems and to improve the efficiency of the overall trading process. The service includes simplified export documentation, checklists for letters of credit, management guidelines, fact sheets, advisory services and a day-to-day helpdesk.

The Insolvency Service 21 Bloomsbury Street, London, WC1B. Tel: 0845 602 9848, Website: www.insolvency.gov.uk

Collections

Readers should refer to Chapter 13 on the matter of choosing a collection agency and to Chapter 22 for legal action on debt recovery. Both collection agencies and firms of solicitors come in all shapes and sizes throughout the UK, and it is not the editor's intention here to make any specific recommendation in respect of which agency or which solicitor. Credit managers should choose on the basis of fit for purpose and meeting their need. Quite often the smaller collection agency is more focused, hungry even, and can therefore be in a better position to tailor collection activity accordingly. Equally, with solicitors, it is important to remember that only those solicitors with dedicated debt collection departments and staffed by experienced debt litigation personnel should be considered – you would not go to a specialised matrimonial lawyer with a debt to collect, any more than you would go to a specialist debt litigation lawyer with your matrimonial troubles!

The following are intended merely as examples:

Commercial Credit Management Moorgate Point, Moorgate Road, Knowsley Industrial Park, Liverpool, L33 7XW. Tel: 0151 545 1500, Fax: 0151 546 1400, Website: www.creditmanagementpays.co.uk

Coltman Warner Cranston LLP Unit 3, Coventry Innovation Village, Coventry University Technology Park, Cheetah Road, Coventry, CV1 2TL. Tel: 02476 627262, Fax: 02476 227691, Website: www.coltmanco.com, Email: info@ coltmanco.com

Gerard Barron MBA DMS FICM, Director of Commercial Debt, Drydens Ltd. Mobile: 07764 228617,

Useful Credit Publications

There are now many hundreds of books available covering all of those areas it is generally accepted fall within the expected knowledge range of the competent credit manger. Equally, in turbulent times, articles are printed daily in trade magazines, the business press and the national press on how best to manage credit risk, collect overdues, streamline cash flow and all the rest.

For those studying for the ICM qualification, the best source is the ICM Bookshop (books@icm.org.ik) who publish every year a list of recommended titles, all available from the bookshop itself. Surfing the Net is perhaps an equally good way of finding just what you are looking for, if wanting to specialise or explore any particular aspect in greater depth.

Query Management Systems

Customer queries and disputes are a fact of everyday business life. All companies should naturally strive to 'get it right first time', which of itself should help to minimise the level of customer queries. However, mistakes will occur, and in even the most efficient customer care environment, the old adage of not being able to please all the people all the time will still apply.

In credit management terms, it is important to act on customer queries without delay – the sooner any dispute is resolved, the sooner the account can be paid and cleared from the ledger. What is needed is a process which can identify and categorise queries. Analysis leads to identification of root causes, and enables companies to put right practices which they are doing wrong.

The complexity of most organisations and decision-making processes, together with the wide variety of Sales Ledger systems, means that to be effective, a query management system has to be customised to each seller's needs and interface with their own individual Sales Ledger process. Many credit managers have developed their own, using off-the-shelf database software to build programs and practices which they can operate from their own PCs.

In recent years, many companies in the debt collection software business have developed query processes as an addition to their collection packages, designing them to feed into, and draw from, the various Sales Ledger packages in common use.

Typical providers are:

Credica Ltd 32 START Electron, Fermi Avenue, Harwell Science and Innovation Campus, Harwell, Oxfordshire, OX11 0QR. Tel: 01235 438449, Fax: 01235 438451, Website: www.credica.co.uk, Email: info@credica.co.uk

I-many International Ltd Suite 2.2, Three Tuns House, 109 Borough High Street, London, SE1 1NL. Tel: 020 7832 2936, Website: www.imany.com, Email: info@imany.com

The Prompt Payment Code

Throughout the late 1980s and into the mid-1990s the debate on late payment in trade took on heated proportions, and many initiatives were launched to try to resolve what appeared to be a particularly 'British' disease. It was commonly held that big business was holding small business to ransom with payment beyond terms and that the only remedy would be to legislate.

Successive UK governments initially resisted these calls, preferring instead to attempt to influence the payment culture with a number of exercises and initiatives. These involved a CBI Prompt Payment Code, launched following a CBI survey in 1996. There was a British Standard (BS5750) on prompt payment, and numerous handouts and publicity exercises to raise awareness. Success was limited, and the incoming Government in 1997 pledged to legislate, leading to the Late Payment of Commercial Debts (Interest) Act 1998, later fully in force and in line with European Directives on the same issue.

The government always recognised, however, that legislation was not enough on its own, because the legislation allowed choice – companies were not *obliged* to charge interest, or enforce interest under the Act, but simply *enabled* to do so if they chose. It was recognised that changing a culture would take a longer period of time and would require education and publicity. Through the then Department of Trade and Industry, the Better Payment Practice Group (BPPG) was launched, with the objectives:

- to promote good payment practice amongst all UK businesses;

- to monitor the effects of the Late Payment Legislation and produce guidance on its use;

- to ensure the programme of measures to promote a better payment culture is meeting the needs of and is supported by the business community.

Through its website (www.payontime.co.uk) access was available to free guides on the Late Payment legislation, together with tables to calculate interest, and the opportunity to sign up to the BPPG Prompt Payment Code. There was also a helpdesk feature, free letters and forms and a guide to better payment practice. The BPPG provided answers to technical questions and also published private sector performance tables.

The BPPG also offered an excellent wall chart, prepared originally by Burt Edwards, FICM, FIEx (editor of the first five editions of the *Credit Management Handbook*), as well as the then DTI publication, *Make The Cash Flow*, to help companies to follow the correct sequence of actions for collecting their funds faster.

A good many companies and organisations made up the core group, meeting regularly to discuss progress, initiatives and general relevant topics. For some reason, in the fullness of time, the UK Government appeared to lose interest, perhaps linked to Government department reorganisation and the replacement of the Department of Trade and Industry (DTI) by the Department for Business Enterprise and Regulatory Reform (BERR), now BIS. Government funding and support gradually dried up, and in spite of strenuous efforts by solid supporters such as ICM, the end of the BPPG appeared inevitable

In 2008, as everybody knows, the world tottered on the brink of financial meltdown. As bank lending took on all the proportions and scarcity of rocking horse droppings, the topic of slow or late payment came back to the fore of Government thinking. The ICM was consulted, asked to produce helpful leaflets and publications on the subject of sensible credit management and to co-operate on initiatives to improve the payment culture.

To cut a long story short, the ICM now sponsors, hosts and administers, on behalf of BIS, the Prompt Payment Code (www.promptpaymentcode.org. uk). Companies and organisations are encouraged to sign up for the Code, and approved signatories undertake to:

- pay suppliers on time:

    - within the terms agreed at the outset of the contract;

   – without attempting to change payment terms retrospectively;

   – without changing practice on length of payment for smaller companies on unreasonable grounds.

- give clear guidance to suppliers:

   – providing suppliers with clear and accessible guidance on payment procedures;

   – ensuring there is a system for dealing with complaints and disputes which is communicated to suppliers;

   – advising them promptly if there is any reason why an invoice will not be paid to the agreed terms;

- encourage good practice by

   – requesting that lead suppliers encourage adoption of the Code throughout their own supply chains

Although this initiative is in many ways no more than a re-run of the BPPG, the prospects are perhaps better for continuation due to the dynamic support of the ICM.

Credit Policy and Procedures

Finally, in this section of practical help and sources of advice to the credit manager, what follows is a list of recommended written-down credit procedures.

A manual of credit procedures is not 'bureaucratic nonsense', as claimed by those managers content to operate by instinct or by the seat of their pants. The existence of a written and agreed policy indicates a planned approach by a profit-conscious company to its investments in a major asset, its debtors. Even the preparation of the policy is a more than useful exercise, awakening realisations as it does in the responsibilities and expected actions of individuals and their recognition by others in the company.

All Sales Ledger, credit risk and collection procedures should be reviewed regularly and a checklist maintained of key features. The checklist can then be used for producing the operating credit manual as well as for management information purposes. In preparing and reviewing both the procedures and the manual, gaps can be detected and rectified.

A credit manual is useful for:

- day-to-day reference to resolve problems;

- training new starters and integrating them more quickly;

- giving to auditors, to reduce staff time wasted in explanations reviews of procedures at intervals by senior management.

Suggested Contents for a Credit Manual

1. Credit objectives and policy:

    - a clear statement by top management;

    - responsibilities of departments – for example, sales and production – for their relevance to credit policy;

    - industry standards and competitors' practices.

2. Credit organisation:

    - organisation chart, showing reporting lines;

    - job descriptions of credit personnel;

    - qualifications/background for each job;

    - training systems, in-company and external;

    - performance appraisals and salary reviews.

3.   Budgets and plans for debtors:

- process and timetables for longer-term plans, annual budgets and monthly or quarterly forecasts;

- information required from sales and others.

4.   Monthly reporting:

- forms and instructions for debtors;

- forms and instructions for credit department expense.

5.   Credit checking procedures, including:

- credit information sources to be used;

- calculating and using credit limits and risk categories;

- range of possible payment terms;

- securities and guarantees for risky accounts;

- credit insurance procedures;

- procedures for handling problem orders;

- stop-shipment policy and procedures.

6.   Invoicing procedure.

7.   Collection procedure, including:

- responsibilities for classes of accounts;

- timetable for standard procedures;

- treatment of special accounts, for example, government;

- rules for using third parties, collection agents and solicitors;

- insolvency and write-off procedures;

- handling of disputes and debit notes.

8.   Appendix of forms and reports, including samples of:

- application for credit facilities;

- letter sent to new accounts;

- order confirmation;

- invoices and credit notes;

- conditions of sale;

- statement of account;

- collection letters/alternative wordings;

- Aged Debt Analysis;

- all computer analyses, reports and copy screen displays;

- departmental logs, reports and forms;

- corporate forms with clear instructions;

- budget forecast forms;

- email templates/guidance, where applicable.

All documents should have simple explanations and examples, and the credit manager should ensure that the manual is kept updated with changes as they happen. The best way to make sure that this is done is to have the manual in daily use.

Index